Dunsmuir
CALIFORNIA

Centennial Book

1886 - 1986

**ITS FIRST
HUNDRED YEARS . . .**

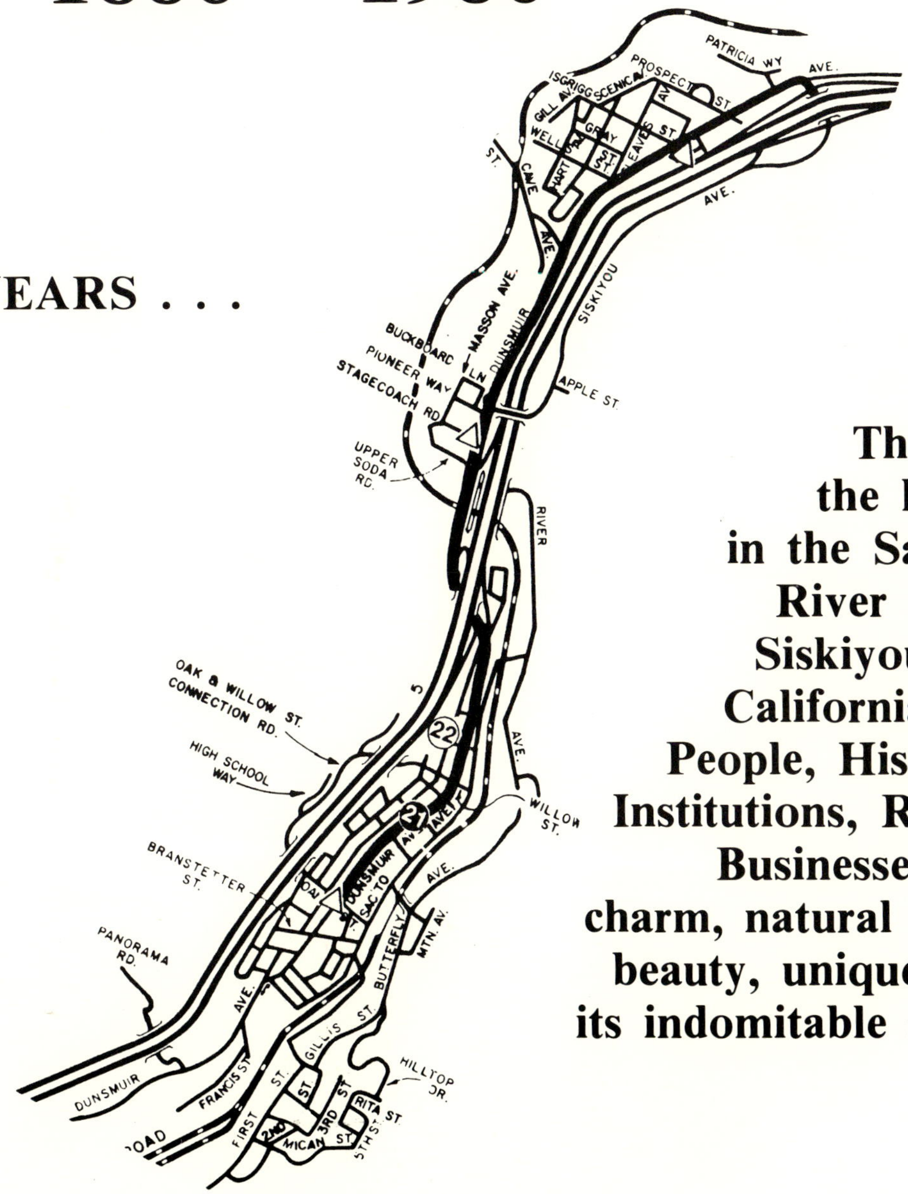

**The story of
the little town
in the Sacramento
River canyon in
Siskiyou County,
California . . . the
People, History, Arts
Institutions, Recreation,
Businesses . . . the
charm, natural resources,
beauty, uniqueness, and
its indomitable spirit . . .**

*The Dunsmuir Centennial Committee
is proud to dedicate this book
to
REVA PATRICK COON
our inspiration, our leader in all
Centennial efforts . . . our guiding spirit.*

*Reva Coon (R.), Editor-in-Chief, and Grace M. Harris (L.), Editor,
ask Santa for a sell-out of the book.*

Library of Congress Catalog Card Number: 85-50084

ISBN No. 0-9614838-0-6

Printed by
Walker Lithograph, Inc.
P.O. Box 205, Red Bluff, CA 96080

TABLE OF CONTENTS

Craigdarroch Castle, Victoria, B.C., built by Robert Dunsmuir

FOREWARD

The citizens of Dunsmuir, California, past and present, who have made our town the charming home it is, have made this book possible. It is the desire of the writers of this book to put on paper for the edification and enjoyment of present and future generations some of the stories of those whose lives have made history over the past one hundred years. Many pioneers, unfortunately, have passed on without leaving a written record of their lives, their work, their entertainment, their achievements. This book is a tribute to them, a grateful expression of our deepest appreciation for the heritage we enjoy today.

By no stretch of the imagination can the contents of this book be considered an exact, accurate history. It is, rather, a folk history, told by many. We cannot verify the truth of these stories, but we believe they are for the most part accurate. This is a folk history about the folk by the folk. The sources of the stories were interviews, newspaper and magazine articles.

This book is a work of love. We hope you enjoy it.

Grace Harris, Editor
Reva P. Coon, Editor-in-Chief

DUNSMUIR GREETS YOU

Dunsmuir is a village lying in the shadow of majestic Mount Shasta. The mountain dominates the landscape and looms above the tiny hamlets at its foot like a broody hen with wayward chicks.

Situated on Shasta's southern slope, Dunsmuir clings precariously to its lava shelf and is indeed built upon a rock, a volcanic rock.

The wild white infant Sacramento River and Southern Pacific's strong steel rails bisect this deep canyon. Quaint aged houses clamber up and down its steep slopes, as do its inhabitants.

Mighty forests abound. Crystal streams, waterfalls and the rarest of flowers are there to appreciate.

We are pleased and proud to say, "Yes, Dunsmuir, in the land of four seasons, is our home!"

SPRING

A blue, blue sky after winter's last storm . . .
Sunshine and rain and rainbows . . .
Manzanita, redbud, dogwood, violets and daffodils . . .
Shiny roads, warming earth, forest paths that lead into summer . . .

SUMMER

Wildflowers, infinitely varied, seeking sanctuary as springtime
      retreats up canyon walls . . .
Giant oaks, welcome shade . . .
Birds' nests, gray squirrels, flying squirrels . . .
Cottontail, shy deer and wiley raccoon . . .
White river, inner tube and kayak . . .
Picnics in the park . . .
Shasta lily, towering pine and fir . . .
Mossbrae, Hedge Creek and Pacific Crest Trail . . .

AUTUMN

Long shadows stretching across the canyon . . .
Crisp nights . . .
Chrysanthemums and Blackeyed Susans . . .
Oak leaves and pine needles . . .
Flaming maple and scarlet dogwood making small safe bonfires
      on mountain sides . . .
Leaves to press and pods to pick . . .
First snow and shovels to wax for winter . . .

WINTER

Great trees sparkling under their glistening burdens . . .
White silence — then: friendly chatter of a train, a locomotive
      rhythmically telling itself that it can make it over the lip of
      the canyon . . .

This is Dunsmuir, our home from which we greet you!

—June Wright

(PHOTOS BY SCOTT HARRIS)

PART I
A CENTURY OF LIVING

CHAPTER I
THE INDIANS AND THEIR LEGENDS

The First Inhabitants

(Excerpts from *The First Inhabitants*
by Audrey Herrera)

"The *"Contributions to North American Ethnology, 1876,* described the Indians as, 'a peaceful, effeminate and sensuous race devoted to joyous rituals, ceremonial dances and merry making'. The term 'Pomo' denoting 'earth people' describes their belief that their first ancestors were created directly from the soil of their respective dwelling places. 'They were one with the earth' and never considered the land as belonging to them. They were not always peaceful, many tribal conflicts arose, such as the slave dealing at the Dalles on the Columbia River and the battle of Castle Crags in 1855 when the Shasta Indians joined with the miners and settlers in attacking the Modocs.

"All of the tribes were basketmakers and used the willows, hazel, pine, alden, red bud, maiden hair fern, squaw grass, porcupine quills and tules to form the beautiful handwork. Even though tribes had the same basic beliefs their characteristics and languages were quite different. The three main nations inhabiting Siskiyou County were the Karok, meaning 'upstream' located on the upper portion of the Klamath River; the Shasta, the origin of the name is vague — different appellations such as Sasti and Shastika are found throughout historical accounts, were prominent in

Scott Valley and Shasta Valley; and the Modoc, probably the most tribal nation, situated in the Lost River, Tulelake area. Sub-families such as the Achomawi, Atsugewi, and Okwanucho resided throughout the county, but accounts of their existence are sparse. The Wintu nation located mainly in Trinity County did extend up to the McCloud River area and the general ethnic designation has been referred to as Shasta.

"Their legends and customs are delightful and intriguing. One example is the protectiveness of kinsman names. When a person passes into the other world, his name is not spoken and anyone with the same name changes to another, so the deceased would not be thought of by his name. For the same reason, children were not named for several years until it was determined their chances of surviving in the world were very good. The Karoks practiced religious ceremonies such as Isivsanen Pikiavish. This renewal of the world for another round of seasons was held in April, August, early and late September at different places along the river to ask the ancient spirit for good harvest, plentiful acorn crop, a healthy run of salmon as well as other religious blessings.

"A beautiful Shasta fable recorded in

1876 represents their faith and knowledge, 'When it rains there is some Indian sick in heaven weeping. Long, long ago there was a good young Indian on earth, and when he died all the Indians wept so much that a flood came on earth and rose up to heaven and drowned all the people, except one couple!

"The Wintu Indians believed the Wicked Indian Ghost was the grizzly bear, and they would not eat the flesh of a grizzly lest they absorb some wicked soul. Yet the black bear was lucky and a sacred beast."

\# \# \#

"The tales of majestic Mt. Shasta are as popular as the Coyote and Grizzly legends, ranging from the creation of the mountain as a teepee for the Old Man Above to the Chief, who while waiting for the return of his daughter on top of Mt. Shasta, called the clouds to cover him for warmth. The clouds covered him with a white mantle of snow."

\# \# \#

"The descendants of this vanishing race are proud of their heritage and dedicated to the preservation of their Indian ancestry."

Sketch by Charles Masson

Old Johnny and his spear pole.

Drawing by Charles Masson

INDIANS FISHING

"In those days," adds Rosborough, "it was a wild country, full of game. I have seen runs of salmon so numerous in the big holes along that part of the upper Sacramento River, that you couldn't see the bottom of the stream. There were lots of Indians around and when the run of salmon was at its height they would come from far and near and congregate at some convenient gravel bar on the river to spear and dry these fish for Winter's food supply. Bucks, squaws and children came to participate in the fishing which seemed to be a time of happy gathering, coupled with the more serious item of securing food. Their mode of taking these salmon was most interesting to watch. The bucks perched on rocks, or standing in water at the lower end of a long pool, where it was shallow, had long straight spears made of wood some 15 feet in length terminating at the business end in two prongs. Onto each of these prongs fitted a short tip, sharp at the point. Midway on these tips a long, strong string connected the end of which was tied with plenty of slack to the spear pole. When the spear prongs went through the fish the tips came loose and crossed the spear pole as the prong was withdrawn, thus leaving the salmon hanging to the spear pole by the string. With the bucks ready at the end of the pool, the squaws and children would proceed around to the head of the pool and with armfuls of large wild rhubarb leaves, which grow along the water's edge and hands filled with stones they would commence a fish drive down the pool by throwing in the big leaves and pelting the water with the stones, thus sending the salmon scooting downstream to the waiting spears below. They made a happy time of it, laughing and hollering as they drove the fish before them and soon the splashing of fighting fish and the yell of the bucks as they waded to shore to leave their salmon and rush back to spear again, made a wild picture of action and joy. As the big squirming salmon were brought to the river bank they were taken in hand by the squaws who cleaned and cut the fish to spread out flat when they were laid out on willow racks in the sun to dry. I have gone through a food-making Indian camp where rack after rack were loaded with drying, loud smelling salmon. On one occasion, while passing one of these camps, we saw an Indian whose thumb had been mangled and one side of his head formed one big scar. He and another Indian had tracked and shot a big bear, which apparently was dead. He laid down his gun, drew his hunting knife and was just about to 'stick' him (cut his throat) when the bear quickly rose and rushed at him with a mad roar. So close was he that when the Indian threw out his hand it went right into the bear's mouth. The bear closed his teeth on it and with his paw raked the side of the Indian's head. The other Indian ran in close and shot the enraged animal in a vital spot killing the bear and then released his wounded companion, who recovered."

THE LEGEND OF TWO FACES

Blue smoke curled lazily up from the Indian encampment. The tribe was at peace but every warrior was alert, for nearby their despised enemies, the Modocs, were entrenched deep in Castle Diablo whither they had been driven by the Klamaths.

Chief Wampum was contentedly puffing his pipe as he related stories of heroism and bravery and of their most recent skirmish with their enemy. The squaws were busy with evening tasks before the fires. Young braves were fishing for the abundant salmon and trout that abounded in the nearby river. It was a peaceful scene; yet at the sound of the name "Chickaweea" all eyes turned toward their chief, for Chickaweea was a traitor. During their last conflict Chickaweea with deceitful cunning had deserted his chief in battle, had betrayed his tribe's secrets and now lived with the Modocs in the Crags.

Lakadowa, Wampum's only son, was a tall, strong brave. He sat beside his father fitting sharp, black arrowheads onto strong, straight arrows. He listened to the old warrior, who thought proudly that one day his son would lead the tribe. Lakadowa's mind was not entirely on his arrows or the words of his chief. His eyes often strayed to the beautiful Indian maiden, Rippling Water, as she completed her evening chores. Her tepee was nearest the river, and his heart skipped a beat as he glimpsed her raven-black hair shining in the last rays of the sun. He had once feared that she loved the sly, cunning Chickaweea, but she had scorned him and had given her true love to Lakadowa.

Now it was nearly nightfall. Chief Wampum had finished his tales of war and of the wild and of Mount Shasta, the white home of the Great Spirit who watched over the Klamaths. The sun had set and a golden glow filled the sky. From the mountain's icy peak a chill breeze sent its frigid fingers through the camp. One by one the fires were banked for the night, and the Indians slipped into their tepees for a peaceful sleep.

Only Lakadowa could not sleep. He said goodnight to his beloved Rippling Water and then lay on the fragrant pine needles and looked up the shaft of a magnificent tree until its dark branches seemed lost in the starlit sky. Deep shadows stretched across this silent scene, dying campfires flickered and a spell lay over the peaceful village.

Now the moon arose with its wonderful inquisitive light. It shone on the river in a ribbon of silver and Shasta's luminous, shimmering sides sent back a reflection that made one tremble.

From behind a giant pine tree piercing dark eyes scanned this scene. Furtively and unseen someone moved, intent on revenge. It was Chickaweea, the traitor. His plan would incite to fury the slumbering hate of the Klamaths. He wore only a loin-skin, but was armed with a bow and a quiver filled with arrows. An obsidian knife hung at his side. Around his neck was a string of rattlesnake rattles. From it he deftly removed three rattles, took an arrow from his quiver and swiftly cut three notches into it. To these he fastened the rattles — a declaration of war!

With a quick pull and a death-dealing "pang" the arrow sped from the shadows through the tent of the sleeping Rippling Water. A heart-rending cry broke the stillness as this missile of death with its sharp point and ugly message found lodging in the heart of Lakadowa's beloved Rippling Water.

With a blood-curdling yell Lakadowa leaped from the ground. In seconds he was beside the dying girl, who was feebly tugging at the fatal dart. She gasped, "Kill him! Kill him before you die." With a mighty oath Lakadowa swore to avenge her death. As he laid her gently back on her couch, a chill crept over her and she lay still.

With a whispered word to the chief and a call to the tribe's braves, Lakadowa plunged into the depths of the forest. Like a bitter wind he sped in pursuit of his sworn enemy.

The next day a battle raged from the foot of Mount Shasta to where the Modoc and Klamath trails met. Never had the great mountain looked down upon a fiercer struggle.

At last Lakadowa was able to single out Chickaweea for his vengeance alone. With clenched teeth he sprang upon his quarry. Over and over they rolled in a fight to the death while their kinsmen battled among the boulders and through the forest. Both warriors were nearly exhausted. A sharp sudden jerk and Lakadowa seized his enemy. With one violent motion he twisted Chickaweea's head until the traitor fell to the ground. Placing his foot on the breast of the fallen brave, Lakadowa turned his eyes to the home of the Great Spirit with the fervent wish that he could once more see his beloved and show her that the revenge was complete. There high among the eternal snows he saw her at peace.

With a sigh he sank wearily to earth and as the light faded from his eyes, he prayed that he would ever see her thus, and that he could guard her from her enemies throughout eternity. The Great Spirit heard and granted his request.

Today you may see them both: Lakadowa a great warrior face on the dome of Castle Crags; and Rippling Water sleeping peacefully and safely among the snows of mighty Mount Shasta.

—Adapted from the legend recorded by Leaton Foster in the 1923 edition of the Dunsmuir High School yearbook

Elinore Van Fossen Harrison was a student in Dunsmuir High School when she wrote this hauntingly beautiful legend.

Many moons have passed but the tales of gold hidden in Castle Crags persist. This, then, is such a story:

TIMILU AND FALLING FEATHER
(A Love Story)

One summer while staying at a nearby resort I heard a curious story concerning buried treasure on the Crags. After some inquiring, I found that an old squaw was the only one who knew the facts.

One day while on a walk, I came to an old tumble down hut at the foot of Castle Crags, and knocked at the door. Slowly it opened and there stood an ancient squaw.

I had never seen such a creature. One could hardly call her a person. Her body was stooped and twisted and her face a network of wrinkles. With her matted white hair falling in her eyes, she was a fearsome sight to behold.

I inquired for baskets, and mumbling, she motioned for me to enter the hut. The interior resembled its inhabitant, dark, gloomy and dirty.

After looking at baskets and selecting a few, I was loath to leave such interesting surroundings. Finally I asked her why she stayed in such a place, and after some persuasion, she told the following story:

Many moons ago, Timilu, the only daughter of the wise Chief White Crow, was young and very lovely. She was happy, too. The great warrior, Falling Feather, loved her. The flowers nodded it; the brooks sang it, and the great tall trees whispered it.

One day as she was sitting in her favorite place high in the Crags, Falling Feather came to her. How handsome he was. Her heart trembled with love. Taking her hand in his, he pointed down the canyon where a trail wound along the river. Miles and miles away she could see a slowly moving speck on the trail. She looked inquiringly at Falling Feather knowing that when he was ready, he would explain it all to her. In the meantime she was content merely to be standing there beside him.

"Those white men," Falling Feather began. "They take big box of gold to fort on Klamath River; pay soldiers. Soldiers then kill Indians. No good. Shastes kill men. Take gold and hide it in Crags. I, Falling Feather, will lead them." (The Shastes did not like the white men who gave them firewater and then took their squaws from them.)

Timilu looked startled and shook her head. "No! Falling Feather, no lead them, please." Her heart beat like that of a captured rabbit. "Timilu is afraid. White men have guns. Maybe kill Falling Feather. Timilu would die of sorrow."

Falling Feather took her in his arms and quieted her. "Have no fear, Falling Feather will come back to you." So saying, he left her and bounded down the mountain side to the camp at the foot of the Crags. After awhile, Timilu slowly made her way down but the small band of Indians had already gone.

Falling Feather stationed his warriors on each side of the trail, and he, himself, kept watch on the most prominent point from which he could see up and down the canyon.

Soon the squad of soldiers came into sight. When they were opposite the Indians, they gave a great war whoop and charged. The soldiers fought valiantly, and the spirits of many Indians went to the Happy Hunting Ground in the sky.

Falling Feather became reckless, and the last soldier shot him.

After it was over, the Indians took the gold and their dead back to camp. Falling Feather was still alive but soon his spirit joined his fathers in the Happy Hunting Ground.

Timilu wanted to go there with him, but he made her promise that she would live to guard the gold. He asked that he might be buried near the treasure.

That night the rising moon looked down on a dark line slowly winding its way up the Crags. All of the warriors were buried near the gold.

Every moon, Timilu would climb to the secret burial ground to see that nothing had been disturbed. One time she went in the spring and found the little dell was covered with golden flowers, each shaped like a falling feather.

As time went on the white men became friendly with the Shastes who, however, never told about the gold buried within the granite spires of Castle Crags. Now Timilu is the only one still alive, and she is too old to go to the secret hiding place. It is certain that when she dies, the knowledge of the location of the treasure dies too.

Many white men have tried to find this treasure, but no one has yet seen a golden flower shaped like a fallen feather.

Hedgecreek Falls — Photo by AuraLee Floria

FOLK HISTORY
By Dick Murdock

Introduction

Dunsmuir's charm is her natural beauty, the rugged all-around splendor. Foremost, world-renowned Castle Crags stands as the town's southern sentinel while guardian to the north is majestic, inspiring, snow-crowned Mt. Shasta.

Other distinctive features embrace clear water, pure air, pronounced seasons and friendly people. But I'm particularly fond of Dunsmuir because she accepted me as a writer and Southern Pacific engineman from 1951 through 1955 which contributed to the moulding of my future.

The centennial year — 1986 — indeed marks a milestone. Despite many threatening situations, economic and otherwise, the town has survived, special charm intact, due primarily to the remarkable spirit of her residents. I've seen these people pitted against paralyzing blizzards, coping with recession, adjusting to railroad cutbacks and layoffs, and through times of revolutionary change (often labeled "progress") such as the great transition from steam to diesel power and the bypassing of downtown Dunsmuir by I-5.

Dates and events described here may not include the more common ones, yet each has historical significance concerning the town and railroad. As flavoring I've sprinkled in a few personal experiences. But first let's return to days long gone. The names Cedar Flat, Upper and Lower Soda Springs, Nutglade and Pusher crop up prominently in early writings, and Pusher was the location the town settled upon. Pioneer families mentioned most often include McCloud, Masson, Scott, Weed,

Lockhart, Silva, Bailey, Brown, Boylan, White, Van Fossen, Branstetter and, of course, many others.

Alexander Dunsmuir, on a rail trip through the territory in 1886, suggested naming the town after his family. Alex was the second son of the Honorable Robert Dunsmuir of British Columbia coal interests. When the proposal was adopted, in appreciation, Robert presented the famed fountain that stood so many years between the depot and old SP hospital. In bygone summers it was filled with large trout from Mt. Shasta hatchery much to the delight of train travelers pausing at Dunsmuir, often to sample "The Best Water on Earth" from another nearby fountain.

In 1968 I returned to research an article for *Railroad Magazine* entitled *Old Days at Dunsmuir Depot* which was published in the January 1969 issue.

I had the pleasure of talking with the late Annie Fussler who was nearly ninety at that time. "Do you remember the first depot?" I asked.

"Indeed," she replied, her faded eyes alight. "It was a boxcar standing in a wooded area. Also, it served as a telegraph and express office — and the new town's first city hall!"

Mrs. Fussler then recalled that the second station was there at the time of the Pullman Strike in June, 1894. "I remember the militia guarding it," she said.

Annie was reminiscing then. How fascinating to listen to her tales! She was nine when the family moved to Mott a few miles north. One day when she was 17, Annie and her younger sister, looking out their bedroom window, caught sight of a fire on the railroad trestle that crossed a deep ravine.

"Mother sent us running through the brush to notify Mr. Houston, the station agent," she said. "My sister was too chubby to keep up so I arrived first and blurted out the news."

Mr. Houston got on the wire just in time to have a westbound train flagged down. And a good thing, for among the passengers was Mrs. Leland Stanford, wife of one of the Big Four who had founded the Central Pacific. The fire, however, did little damage. Mrs. Fussler recalled Chinese laborers building that trestle. "They were friendly and sometimes had little gifts for us girls," she said.

By the time Annie graduated from high school in 1897, one problem the railroad had was keeping firemen. Tossing cordwood into hungry fireboxes wasn't easy. Perhaps pay had something to do with so many quitting. An old timebook of Henry T. Long's notes that $3.73 was the standard rate for a 12-hour day, with overtime after that *if* you worked more than 14 hours! But only $1.78 for 17 hours overtime between

Red Bluff and Dunsmuir!

In 1916, the Shasta Division was created, encompassing the area from Gerber, California, to Ashland, Oregon, and later to Klamath Falls and Alturas. A large switching yard was built on the flat bordering the river a mile south of Dunsmuir to help cope with the surge of World War I rail traffic.

During this period it's interesting to note that the elevation of Mt. Shasta was diminishing! A postcard, circa 1910, shows a train with the mountain behind and states: "Mt. Shasta, California, Altitude 14,444."

Then in a 1916 release, S.P. printed, "Ahead rises Mt. Shasta's snow-covered crest, 14,380 feet above sea level."

Only in comparatively recent times has the mountain's elevation settled down to a steady 14,161 feet.

The railroad liked to publicize scenic spots along the route, and did so regularly in the *S.P. Bulletin* and other publications. Here are a few samples:

SHASTA SPRINGS, Cal. — Alt. 2,564. To Portland 446 miles. To San Francisco 325 miles. Shasta Springs is noted for its natural sparkling mineral water and its charming location. Trains stop for ten minutes giving passengers ample time to drink at the rustic spring in the station grounds. The hotel and cottages, with a fine swimming tank, are on the pine-timbered plateau above and east of the station A cable incline car takes visitors from the station, carrying them up the pine-covered side of the canyon past cataracts and cascades.

From the top a magnificent view is had of the canyon below. The plateau is also reached by a delightful mountain path that zigzags the canyon's sides, with steps at intervals, rustic seats, and bridges across the little torrent that tumbles to the river . . .

SHASTA SPRINGS HOTEL — Rates, $4.50 and up per day. American Plan. Trout fishing, swimming pool, tennis court, Mineral water. Open May 26th, Wm. Watson & Sons, lessees, P.O. Shasta Springs, Cal.

NEY'S SPRINGS — Two miles from Cantara Station, reached by daily stage. Hotel and tents. Rates, $4.00 per day, $25 per week, American Plan. Fishing and hunting. Open June 1st to October 15th. Telephone, telegraph service through Sisson. Mr. R. C. Ney, manager, P.O. Cantara or Sisson, Cal.

SHASTA RETREAT — Hotel and cottage system. Rates in hotel without bath, $4.00 per week; with meals, $25 per week. Cottages, $8.00 and up per week. Fishing, swimming and hunting. Mineral springs on grounds. Near Shasta Springs and Dunsmuir. Open April 1st. G. A. DeWitt, Manager, P.O. Retreat, Siskiyou County, Cal.

DUNSMUIR MINERAL SPRINGS — One mile south of Dunsmuir, Siskiyou County, between Mt. Shasta and Castle Rocks on the bank of the Sacramento River. Rates per day in tents, 75¢ to $1.50; $3.50 to $7.00 per week. No meals. Bath house, medicinal waters, fishing and hunting. Tent houses. Open May 1st to October 1st. Henry McGuiness, Manager, Dunsmuir, Cal.

CASTLE CRAG — At Castle Crag Station. Hotel, cottages and log cabins. Hot and cold shower baths with each room. Rates with meals, $4.00 per day; $28.00 per week; $4.50 for one day only. Hunting, fishing in Sacramento River and Soda Creek . . . Hotel opens May 1st. D. C. Brown, Manager, P.O. Castle Crag, Cal.

CRAG VIEW HOTEL — At Castella station. Rooms, cottages and tents. Rates, $4.25 and up per day; $26.50 and up per week. American Plan. Hunting, fishing and swimming; tennis and dancing. Near Castle Crags and other points of interest. Season April 1st to November 1st, H. O. Wicks, Manager, P.O. Castella, Cal.

On September 16, 1919, President Woodrow Wilson's westbound special stopped at Shasta Springs for 40 minutes while the chief executive inspected the grounds including Moss Brae Falls, pronouncing the area beautiful and fascinating. At Dunsmuir he was presented with 100 choice mountain trout caught in the Sacramento River that morning.

Through the years other presidents and dignitaries paused to speak of Dunsmuir's charm from observation car platforms. During my short sojourn, Harry Truman, Richard Nixon, and Ethiopian Emperor Haile Sellaise came through . . .

Numbing tragedy, as oldtimers remember, struck Dunsmuir about 12:40 p.m. October 11, 1923, near the Oregon border. Three DeAutremont brothers — Ray and Roy, 23-year-old twins, and Hugh, 19 — staged a bizarre holdup, stopping at gunpoint, Train No. 13 at the west portal of Tunnel 13, a 3108-foot bore at Siskiyou Summit.

Occupying the cab of S.P. locomotive 3629, a 2-10-2, was engineer Sidney L. Bates and fireman Marvin Seng, both of Dunsmuir. Once the train was stopped with the engine out of the tunnel, the bandits dynamited the mail car with such force the explosion instantly killed clerk E. E. Dougherty inside.

Brakeman C. O. Johnson walked rapidly through the tunnel with a lighted fusee to find out what happened. Ray deliberately shot and killed him. The brothers ordered the engine detached but the coupler had been damaged in the blast. The DeAutremonts then, in desperation and cold blood, shot and killed Sidney Bates and Marvin Seng!

With four murders on their hands and no loot, they lost nerve and fled, somehow escaping a great network of lawmen, railroaders and private sleuths that quickly formed to comb the rugged terrain.

Not until years later, February 11, 1927, did patient detective work track down Hugh, by then in the U.S. Army, Philippines, under a phony name. On the following June 9th, the twins were picked up at Steubenville, Ohio.

The trio was given life imprisonment for agreeing to "tell all."

In 1973, Ray DeAutremont was twice returned to Tunnel 13 after 50 years for the filming of a TV documentary and newspaper stories. The year before he had been pardoned by Governor Tom McCall, and at this writing, Ray is the only surviving brother, his twin having died in a State Hospital. Hugh was paroled in 1950 with cancer and lived but a short time.

Prohibition affected the Dunsmuir locality to a greater extent than many other regions of the nation because a spirited bootlegging business erupted from stills hidden in rugged mountain gullies. It was easy to get a drink lots of places but particularly at bordellos in and around Dunsmuir that had been catering to the needs of lumberjacks, miners, and railroaders for years. At one time the town boasted about 3,000 population, half of them S.P. workers pumping railroad money into a wild, booming economy.

Many still alive recall the late Mike Padula. I knew the little fellow well. He ran a barn-like bar in Castella called Mike's Place. It flourished back when the fabulously rich William Randolph Hearst sought escape on the McCloud River at his famed Wyntoon Estate. Hearst, with his girl friend, film star Marion Davies, and a select group of executives from companies he either controlled or owned, threw parties of a nature that would have been the envy of the Great Gatsby! This was accomplished when baby-blue-eyed Marion would "buy" Mike's Place by the simple expedient of locking the door until the bash was over.

"Next morning," Padula said, "there would be $20 bills under all the ashtrays."

Another significant date in Dunsmuir's history is April 27, 1927. That marked the day the 279-mile Cascade Line called the Natron Cutoff, between Black Butte, California, and Natron, Oregon, was opened to through rail traffic. This new, more direct route to Portland via Grass Lake and Klamath Falls, was faster, less curvy with easier gradients which spelled doom for scores of helper jobs at Hornbrook and Weed as rail service over the Ashland line was substantially reduced.

A few years later found Dunsmuir in the middle of the Great Depression. Hundreds of railroaders, loggers, sawmill workers, and miners were laid off as the economy ground to a near halt.

In the midst of it all came the winter of 1937 with its record snowfalls. Not even heroic efforts could keep highways and rail lines continuously open. Great drifts gathered almost everywhere. Many stores had snow tunnel entrances. Winter had the town in a paralyzing grip. Snow was even shoveled by hand onto flatcars which were hauled below town and the dirty white stuff disposed of in the river. One hundred eighty carloads were unloaded in this manner.

Depression and the weather had teamed up to deal Dunsmuir a crippling blow. The town's spirit may have faltered but it never failed. Before long the economy's pendulum began a swing when the new government-financed high-speed rail line around and over Shasta Lake went into full operation May 24th, 1942, barely in time for the great surge of business created by World War II. In the realignment process, Centralized Traffic Control was installed from Redding to Black Butte, the first in the area.

But 1937 didn't end heavy winters. I'll never forget Dunsmuir in January, 1952. I was daylight hostler on the turntable job across from the watchful eyes of the superintendent's office in the depot. Shasta Division was in the process of becoming dieselized.

The storm was heavy enough to keep two laborers at the business end of a steam hose around the clock, washing snow from the turntable area.

Just before quitting time one afternoon, two four-unit F-7 diesel consists came in coupled together. The first set was already called. My helper, Freddie Brieno, walked to get the lead consist for servicing. By the time I climbed to the cab, he had released handbrakes and was at the cutting lever between the two sets of units, giving me signs to pull ahead.

I notched open the throttle, making the separation, then moved slowly to give Freddie time to line the derail behind, a device for protecting the turntable should something get loose from the top end receiving tracks. Once across the table, I spotted the first unit for sand. While my helper was filling the receptacle, engineer Rex McMillan climbed to the cab. "Are you responsible for those other units, too?" he asked.

"Yes," I said.

"Well, they're on the ground."

It developed that the incoming engine crew had set handbrakes only on the first consist, notifying Earl Nino, the top end hostler. But before Earl could tell us, we had snatched away the called units, leaving the others free to roll quietly down the incline and off the derail, the lead engine's pilot gathering a great mound of snow before it and coming to rest just a few feet short of an open turntable pit!

Fortunately, only the lead trucks had derailed, the accident blocking but one of the two receiving tracks leading from the top end or the railroad would have really been tied up. Even so, a week passed before the cripple was rerailed. Meanwhile, the rear three units, still on the track, had been cut away and pressed into blizzard service.

The following December 6th, another paralyzing storm struck. Again the division was welded into a common cause — keeping the line open. Giant steam rotaries chewed away while snow filled the cuts almost as fast as they were cleared.

I was due out of Dunsmuir at 5 p.m., fireman on the *Shasta Daylight*. But when the phone rang, crew dispatcher Tony

Barber said, "Relax, Dick. They're holding No. 9 at Klamath Falls and don't know when they'll turn her loose. Line's tied up from Grass Lake to Black Butte."

So I stayed comfortably at home watching great white flakes add silently to the strangulation. At that time I, along with about 25 other firemen who had already passed their engineers' exams, officially became a hoghead. It happened because Bill Hughes was used as an engineer in an emergency at Weed, which gave all promoted men above him an engineer's date of December 6th, 1952, in accordance with provisions of a "Home Rule" then in effect.

On the last day of October, 1967, the mile-long 15-track yard south of town was closed permanently. The Shasta Division had been eliminated, absorbed into the Sacramento and newly-created Oregon Division, seniority districts expanded accordingly.

So gone are those fascinating and colorful days when passengers waiting for trains tossed coins in the fountain donated by Honorable Alexander Dunsmuir, or drank from the one labeled, "Best Water on Earth." Sounds from the busy complex across the tracks have faded into the past — the *ping* of a machinist's hammer on a main rod, a giant lathe grinding away, riveters and boilermakers playing their steel calliopes.

Also gone forever is the sight of huge cab-first mallets easing onto the turntable, airpumps stroking gently, and the smell of steam and hot oil mingling with the pine-scented sweetness from the woods beyond the roundhouse. Only the sound of a happily chuckling river remains . . .

The golden era of steam usually returns briefly to Dunsmuir each summer during the annual Railroad Days celebration. Engine 25 — a spiffy little Prairie with a 2-6-2 wheel configuration — comes down from McCloud bringing with her a trunkful of nostalgic memories.

In 1982, writer, photographer, artist, radio personality and rail enthusiast Larry Green and I — using No. 25 — instituted a steam whistle blowing contest which has become quite popular, an event we hope is already a Railroad Days tradition.

The morning sun blazed into the room with warm brightness, and I woke up suddenly . . . I rubbed my eyes and felt little beads of perspiration beginning to stand out on my forehead. I lay there a few minutes more and just listened to a switch engine at work in the yards.

The switchmen were making up trains, and the switch engine was kicking cars down different tracks. The whining sounds of the big diesel would alternately rise and fall. I would hear the squeaking of steel slowly turning on steel, and then after a long moment would come the great loud thud of a freight car banging in to couple up with a string of cars.

—Excerpt from STREAM RUNNER
by David Seed

All was blackness and the sound of the river roared past me . . . I decided to cross the Shasta Retreat Bridge to the other side of the river where I could walk down stream along the railroad tracks until it was light enough to fish . . . I shivered and the hair on the back of my neck stood up as I inched my way across the bridge in the cold blackness with the river roaring under me . . . The shiny steel rails glistened dully in the darkness.

—Excerpt from STREAM RUNNER
by David Seed

After Father got me started fishing that summer, I went day after a day without catching a trout. I fished behind every rock I could reach and gradually worked my way up stream and through town. I tried Blackberry Hole and behind the Roundhouse and spent several days trying a couple of pools above the Roundhouse. I followed the river up as far as the Bend which was a deep hole just down stream from where the cement highway bridge arched high across the river north of town.

—Excerpt from STREAM RUNNER
by David Seed

DUNSMUIR AND THE SHASTA ROUTE

By Frank H. Wintering

One of the famous Daylight engines assigned to the Shasta Division. It was built in 1943.

Photo - Reineking

—*Photo courtesy Guy L. Dunscomb*

Dunsmuir was a train watcher's delight from the earliest beginning. All service facilities for steam locomotives were directly in view of the passenger station. Sand house, fuel storage tanks, water columns, back shops, roundhouse, and turntable were available twenty-four hours a day every day of the year — a continuous performance witnessed by traveler and employee alike.

The Depot, quite rambling for a small town, was not only the ticket and baggage office, but, also, the headquarters for the Superintendent of the Shasta Division. His chief clerk and office crew were housed in the north wing which, at an earlier day, had been the freight warehouse. Beyond them was the very nerve center of train movement, the Chief Dispatcher and his force. Once telegraph, but now telephone, connected the trick dispatchers with each agent or operator on his subdivision. A good dispatcher usually knew his train and engine crews, anticipated their movements, and transmitted orders to them so that trains moved with the slightest possible delay.

Company houses for local officials were in a park-like area just north of the offices. Japanese and Mexican gardners kept things neatly trimmed and well watered during the years that these homes were all occupied.

South of the station was the famous fountain donated by Alexander Dunsmuir, who, also, donated his name to the town. In summer months the pool was filled with mountain trout brought from the Mount Shasta Hatchery. Having plenty of food both from regular feedings and from insects attracted by the bright lights around the station, the fish grew several inches during the season.

Next to the fountain was the Southern Pacific telephone exchange which, also, housed the trainmaster's and the road foreman's offices. Beyond the green, well-groomed lawn and the "Best Water on Earth" drinking fountain, was the old club house building now housing the crew dispatchers' office and the engineering department. When they were in town, "Going down to the Crew" was a daily ritual for most of the conductors, brakemen, engineers, and firemen. There they all could get together to talk over their problems, last trip, hunting, fishing, or, a favorite topic: railroading. Do you suppose that they ever mention their girl friends?

The Southern Pacific Office Crew, 1913
Pictured is J. W. Metcalf, Superintendent, eighth from left; and Kate Masters Berry, the first woman employed in the Dunsmuir office. A picture taken ten years later, which is in the Collection of Mrs. Alzade Gash, shows that by 1923 half of the office crew were women.

—*Photo courtesy of Lloyd Carter*

9

Beyond "the crew" was the Railway Express office and then the freight station and its warehouse. The last building was the ice house. Much ice was used during the summer months for air-conditioning the passenger trains in the early days.

Neatly fitted between the main line tracks and the Sacramento River, directly across from the passenger station, was the round-house and all of its dark mysteries. A lightly used, high footbridge over the tracks gave safety in crossing, especially when trains were at the depot.

Located between the great brick back-shop and the twenty-four-stall engine house was the powerhouse and its high smoke-stack. During the pleasant weather the doors would usually be open, and the two-story-high boilers with their roaring fires could be seen. At all times at least one boiler would be supplying steam to pump fuel and water, to compress air, to dry sand, to heat buildings (including the elementary school) and to fire up locomotives. Much the same as with old-time fire engines, the steam derrick of the "relief outfit" was kept warm constantly by steam from these boilers. Crews to man the "wrecker" reported promptly in case of emergency, so no time was to be lost waiting to raise steam pressure.

The "stationary engineer" along with tending the boilers, also sounded the whistle at the beginning and the end of work shifts, summoned the "wrecker crews," and even the local fire department depended upon his "special" whistle. This fire whistle, installed in 1925, could be heard for miles up and down the canyon much as a ship's whistle can be heard in the fog.

Except for most of the through passenger trains, all locomotives came to the roundhouse for servicing. "Helpers" returning down hill had a specific whistle signal, a kind of reverse grade-crossing sound, indicating that they were to go to the sand house. Coming down the inbound lead they were usually met by the hostler and spotted for fuel, water, and sand. A locomotive inspector, complete with his dainty little, long-handled, brass hammer, checked moving parts for loose nuts or bolts, picked up the engineer's work report, and recorded his findings.

All engines soon found their way to the turntable and were put into an empty stall in the roundhouse. Here, on a great black-board, each locomotive's number was recorded next to its pit or stall number. The blackboard, also, was used to call engines as well as to assign work to all the different machinists, boilermakers, "rod cups," and lubricator people. The underside of each engine was fully inspected, and, as work was completed, it was so marked on the blackboard, the last being the time of completion under the heading, "ready for fire." If the engine was called for duty, the "fire lighter" soon took over. With a flash of flame from the firebox door, a thunderous roar, a cloud of smoke, the engine was brought to life again. Soon the hostler

Southern Pacific's Back Shop and Powerhouse, Dunsmuir, 1965
—Photo: F. H. Wintering

Turntable and Roundhouse at Dunsmuir after 1942.
The last four stalls of the Roundhouse collapsed in January, 1966.
—Photo: Eastman Studio

came, his helper lined the table, air pumps were started, and the engine, in a noisy bath of steam, was put on the "ready track" to await its crew. Heavy trains needing several engines, as most did eastward bound, required that this process be repeated until all the necessary power was ready on the outbound lead.

The passenger helpers, after being serviced, were left near the sand house so that these engines could be promptly attached to the front of the road locomotives as they were being serviced on the main line. It was important not to delay these trains!

Engines requiring classified repairs due them because of mileage or of time found their way to the back shop just north of the roundhouse. The huge brick building was originally laid out in 1887 and measured 83 by 214 feet. Remodeled, enlarged and re-equipped by the 1940's, it could easily accommodate all but the very largest engines. Flues could be renewed, fireboxes repaired, and even the entire engine lifted free of its wheels by the Whiting Hoist which was first installed in the 1920's. Steel driving wheel tires, soon worn by sharp curves and heavy grades, were turned by a machinist at the wheel lathe. At a vertical boring machine, re-babbited bearings were bored to fit their axles. Water pumps and air compressors were renewed at the pump shop, while the "air man" disassembled, cleaned, repaired, and graphite lubricated the many, many tiny parts of the locomotive's air brake systems. Gauges were also tested, set, and made ready for service, as were safety valves, injectors, water glasses, and all the dozens of valves on the engine. Eventually, all parts, as if by some feat of legerdemain, would find their way to a specific place and the entire engine would be lowered back on its wheels by candlelight. No wine was served at this party! Soon the refurbished drive rods were attached to the proper wheels and all the machinery made as new. After pipe fitters, sheet metal workers, painters, and other mechanical personnel finished, the boiler washed free of oil, steam tested, and safety valves set at working pressure, the engine was again ready for thousands of miles of battling grades on the Shasta Division.

Crowded east of the shop and north of the roundhouse was the store department. All supplies necessary for the operation of a railroad were handled here. Everything from a pair of safety shoes to a tire for an engine, from a car load of oil to the oil can for the engineer, from a lantern to a brake club, from a typewriter to a train order form, from a tie or a rail to a spike were available from this store. At least twice a year a supply train would be operated over the division to deliver necessary stores to division points and to remote sections. Usually the superintendent and his private car, named *Shasta*, would accompany the train so the line could be fully inspected at the same time. Everyone in train or engine service called for duty on this train looked forward to being invited to the private car for lunch at which none of the niceties was

spared. White tablecloth, linen napkins, fine china, crystal ware, and polished silver were all used. The meal might consist of a delightful roast served with salad, mashed potatoes, vegetables; hot, freshly baked rolls; plenty of hot coffee; and lastly, delicious apple pie, or was it homemade lemon pie? The "Old Man" then might offer a fine cigar to all who smoked! This was one of those times about which cartoonist J. R. Williams frequently said, "When you would like to live forever!"

At least on one occasion, the lunch was two hours late. The story goes like this: After the brakeman and engine crew started walking back to the car *Shasta*, one of the

working foremen needed a "re-spot" for the job they were doing. A local trainmaster, suffering from a not uncommon fireman's disease called Throttle Fever, decided he could do the job. His "start" of the "short movement" was fine, but the "stop"? Applying only the engine brakes caused all the slack and the heavy private car to run in with a crash. Everything stopped! That is everything but the food, dishes, chairs, and tablecloth. They went to the front of the car in a pile! "Please, come back for lunch in a couple of hours." Several years later, at meal time, the chef on the official car was heard to nervously ask, "The trainmaster ain't goin' to move the engine, is he?"

Southern Pacific installation uptown, Dunsmuir

—*Photo: Eastman Studio*

Engine #4269 with Sidney Fischer, engineer, on Dunsmuir turntable in 1954

—*Photo: F. H. Wintering*

There were other offices and departments on the railroad property at Dunsmuir that come to mind. The Maintenance of Way Department included the offices of the Roadmaster, Bridge and Building, Water and Fuel, and the Signal Department. The Motive Power Department included the Master Mechanic, Master Car Repairer, and the various foremen at the roundhouse. The railroad company even had its own police officers who went under the title of Special Agent. Truly, a cross-section of many diverse occupations was required to run an important railroad division.

Track maintenance was under the supervision of the Roadmaster and his many section foremen. The "Sections" were about ten miles long and it would seem that the crew assigned to a section would do everything necessary to keep the track in good physical shape as well as nice in appearance. Many miles of grade had cobble-size stones evenly placed along the dividing line between the ballast and the surrounding earth. A great number of Mexican Nationals came to work on the track during the Second World War. A friendly, happy lot of men they were! Stepping back to wave as a train roared by, the concussion would blow their straw hats straight up in the air, much as corks pop from bottles. Everyone enjoyed a good laugh over this!

For many years, all switchyard activities were carried on uptown as were all car repairs. As engines got larger, the roundhouse and turntable expanded, and trains grew longer. Room for expansion was not available, so, slowly extra yard tracks were added at Nutglade about two miles south of Dunsmuir and near the original site of that station. Finally, on June 30, 1926, the Yardmaster's office was, also, transferred there. A "rip track" for light car repairs was put in, but heavy jobs still came uptown for awhile longer.

Dunsmuir by the 1940's was considered to have tracks numbers 1 to 4 uptown and number 5 to 18 in the yard, although two

were never installed. The grade was about 1%, and all cars or trains left standing had to have the hand brakes set, or they soon rolled away.

Much of the time two heavy switch engines were kept busy making "up trains," cutting in helpers, setting out cars for repairs, or changing cabooses, as each regular assigned conductor had his "own" caboose. In fact, some were almost homes away from homes.

Keeping a busy yard working smoothly was a handful for any yardmaster under the best of conditions. When the snow began to fall, all bets were off. After a few cold hours, snow piled in between and on top of the cars. Switches couldn't be thrown, hand or lantern signals became impossible to see, and the storm-caused silence made it extremely dangerous for every man working on creek ground. Switchmen, trainmen, car inspectors, and checkers were exposed to the real danger of falling and being run over by steel wheels silently moving in the snow. For awhile, simply cleaning switches sufficed; but, eventually, plows had to be summoned, and the work of removing the snow, one track at a time, began. Under the worst conditions, all movement ceased until the essential tracks and switches could be cleared.

Three engines snowed in on the Weed Line. Among the crew members were V. G. Barnthouse and George Gash.
—Photo: Courtesy of Mrs. George Gash

A diesel engine out of Dunsmuir at Gazelle, California, after having plowed through a snowdrift at Park's Creek in February, 1959. Please report, "The windshield wipers are not working."
—Photo: F. H. Wintering

Myrtle Kohlbaker at Nutglade, the original site of the Station of Dunsmuir
Photo: Courtesy of F. F. "Buzz" Kohlbaker

Usually, wing snowplows, flangers, to undercut between the rails, and the heavy spreader to widen cuts were sufficient to keep the line open. However, they were no match for the drifts made at Black Butte by eighty-mile-an-hour drafts. As a last resort, the big guns of snow removal were rolled out, the great rotary plows, and Dunsmuir had two. Awesome to watch at work, their immense steam-driven fan wheels cut the snow and pitched it several hundred feet to the side! Staccato exhaust and smoke filled the sky with sounds and smells we will never again experience. They were fascinating to watch and difficult to operate. Visibility was less than zero! Signals to the pusher engines and the plow engineers were given by whistle from the pilot who was located just behind the wheel. Everyone in the vicinity was covered with snow or soaked by melting snow. Like many things — they did the job!

World War II, following a long depression and a reduction in forces caused by the opening of the Natron Cutoff in 1927, found the railroad extremely shorthanded. Every qualified fireman was promoted to engineer, and brakeman to conductor. New men were hired and trained as rapidly as possible. Many young men were drafted into the military, leaving the remaining men to do the work! Freight trains were sandwiched in between five passenger trains scheduled daily for each direction. On occasions as many as thirty sections of passenger trains were operated. In 1942 the opening of the new line between Redding and Delta, around the Shasta Dam, and the installation of Centralized Traffic Control on to Black Butte eased the problem considerably. However, those of us who finally returned from the military found many of our friends to be tired, old men!

All too soon the Diesel engines began to crowd out the steamers. Less frequent maintenance, lower fuel costs, no water stops, and the ability of one man to operate several engines were strong factors in their favor. No need for the roundhouse or the back shops could be found, so employees were dismissed, transferred, or retired, and the facilities permanently closed. An inspection, fueling and sand facility was constructed at the yard, and the engines were no longer brought uptown except if they should require turning on the table. For several years, even the crew dispatchers were moved to the Yard.

Effective April 26, 1964 at 12:01 a.m. the issuance of Portland-Shasta Division Timetable #1 abolished the Shasta Division forever. Tracks from Dunsmuir to Gerber were made a part of the new Sacramento-Salt Lake Division, and the remainder was absorbed into the Portland-Shasta Division. Then on October 25, 1964, a new Oregon Division was formed eliminating even the name "Shasta" from the Timetable. During the fall months of 1965, the train dispatchers' offices were closed in Dunsmuir, and in 1968 the Yard eliminated. The crew dispatchers were returned uptown and now occupy the train dispatchers former offices.

Few of the old buildings remain, but Dunsmuir is still a railroad town. Train and engine crews still are changed here, helper engines are maintained here, and other departments, including freight, communications, Assistant Division Engineer, Roadmaster, Trainmaster, Roadforeman of Engines, and police are in evidence. Oh, you can still watch trains, but with your permission I'll remember Dunsmuir in the glory that is gone! It was only yesterday!

Dunsmuir Yard About 1901
Originally numbered 229, this engine #2800 was designed and built in 1882 in the Central Pacific Shops at Sacramento by J. R. Stevens, Master Mechanic. It was Southern Pacific's first and Central Pacific's only 4-8-0 and was the first of 84 locomotives of this type to eventually be put into service.

—Photo: Courtesy of Mrs. Lester Gilzean

Diesel and Steam at Dunsmuir, 1955
—Photo: F. H. Wintering

The conductor's view of it all!
—Photo: F. H. Wintering

California had been admitted as a state in 1850 and by 1852 both Shasta and Siskiyou Counties had been created, but no direct wagon road connected those two counties until Willard P. Stone opened his Pit River and Soda Springs Turnpike in 1865. At last there was a short stage route from the south between Red Bluff, Shasta, and Yreka. For many years the Federal Government had tried to settle people in this area of Northern California. As late as the 1870's and the 1880's, the population was hardly 5,000 people in Shasta County and barely 7,000 in Siskiyou County. Little land had been sold for homes, ranches, or agriculture. A railroad was an absolute necessity for military reasons as well as for commerce.

As early as 1863, a railroad survey had been made by the California and Oregon Company. Generally, it followed the Sacramento River to Siskiyou County, crossing into Shasta Valley via Wagon Creek. Then it more or less paralleled the stage road in use at that time which passed through Yreka and continued down to the Shasta River Canyon and up the Klamath River and, then following Cottonwood Creek, entered Oregon at Cole's Station. Later surveys left Yreka several miles west of the proposed route. But despite all the activity, actual construction was extremely slow in getting started.

The officials at Washington correctly figured that, if a land grant line was authorized, the builders of the railroad would do everything within their scope to sell the sections of land that they would be given by the Government; and then, of course, the Government land of the adjoining sections could be sold easily. Land grants were not just a "big giveaway"! The railroad would have to construct the track and operate the road in order to receive the land. They did not get the mineral rights to the property, but they could use or dispose of the timber. Close to tracks much of it was used in construction or as fuel for the steam boilers and locomotives. Also, from then on the railroads were required to handle, at half the posted freight rates, all Government shipments.

During the 1870's railroad companies were formed and disappeared with equal speed. Several small companies were organized together in 1868 to form the California and Oregon Railroad which in turn consolidated with the Yuba Railroad to make up the California and Oregon Company of 1869. This group completed the first portion of the line toward Oregon into the new town of Redding during 1872. Meantime, the Oregon-California Railroad, building south from Portland, was stalled at Roseburg, Oregon. Since a railroad north to the California State Line had very little value and even less chance of survival, the California and Oregon Company would do nothing further in construction up the Sacramento River until the Oregon line showed progress. In 1870 the California and Oregon Company was absorbed by the

Central Pacific Railroad Company.

For ten long years, Redding was the northern terminal of the California and Oregon Railroad. All freight and passengers bound for north of Redding had to change to wagons, stages, horses, or walk the rest of the way. All were unhappy about the situation, all except the freight "forwarders" who had plenty of work. The shippers were not pleased, and the passengers didn't like to transfer. The politicians, both State and Federal, wanted the railroad to continue with the construction. Rumors began to circulate, and by the spring of 1882, it seemed that at last the construction along the Sacramento River was to continue. Wonderful, exciting times were starting in far Northern California and Southern Oregon. A new kind of horse was about to be introduced — the smoking, steaming, roaring horse! The Iron Horse was coming! Newspapers from Jacksonville, Ashland, Yreka, Redding, and Red Bluff carried articles reporting the immediate resumption of construction. Surveyors were working as far as the River Bridge some twenty-six miles north of Redding. This report indicated that the line would be primarily on the west side of the river. No roads or bridges existed in the area; therefore, construction supplies would be difficult to move to the front.

A great deal of speculation continued throughout the year 1882, and early in 1883 work began with determination. Freight trains coming north were busy hauling wagons, carts, horses, and men to Redding. First of all, trees and brush were cleared and a road was constructed. As quickly as a final grade could be established, Colonel James Scobie and his masonry gang began building culverts and bridge abutments. All of the construction was of cut stone. Absolutely no river rock was used. Col. Scobie saw to it that the work was done in a first-class manner. One hundred years later much of this careful work is still visible and still serving its original purpose. The masonry crews usually were several miles ahead of the other crews.

In 1882 Samuel S. Montague was the Chief Engineer of the construction. Montague, a clever, imaginative innovator, had little to do with the actual construction of this mountain division as he fell ill at Strawberry Valley (Mount Shasta) and died there in September of 1883. Many old-timers speculated that the design of the actual railroad would have been considerably different had he survived a few more years. It was felt that the line from Snowdon to Henley (Hornbrook) would have stayed higher up in the foothills away from Willow Creek and would have crossed the Klamath River at a greater elevation, easing the grade somewhat. Also, the steep grades at Bailey Hill would have been less, and the drop back down to Cole's Station would have been eliminated.

By December of 1881, propositions for railroad ties were asked to be immediately submitted. The ties had to be a red fir cut while the sap in the trees was down. They had to be eight feet long and eight inches by six inches in shape. Anything undersized was a "second," and the Central Pacific didn't ask for "seconds" for their track. Mr. James Dobkins of Butteville sent a proposal for 30,000 ties, and Mr. Sullaway of Berrydale (Mount Shasta), a proposition for 100,000 ties to be delivered in a year. Prices were from twenty-three cents to sixty-five cents for each tie. In comparison, redwood ties, delivered on the beach, could be purchased for 17 cents, and for twenty-cents they would be delivered to Benicia.

Soon camps for workers were established along the proposed route. It was reported in April of 1883 that within a week there would be some 5000 Chinese and 2000 white men working on the right-of-way north of Redding. By the fall months of 1883, the Sacramento River Canyon was scattered for miles with lumber camps, graders (workers) and stone masons. In many cases the masons were forced to work waist deep in the river. Col. Scobie's masonry foreman moved their headquarters on up the Canyon. The crews intended to work during the winter getting all footings in while the river was low and then finish before high water in the spring. They, also, had to locate sites for quarries which were close to the right-of-way. Since roads were non-existent, it was extremely difficult to transport the required quantities of cut stone for any distances.

The bridge at Backbone Creek was not completed by December of 1883 even though the false work for the structure had been up for some time. For this reason this point was the terminal of work for the winter. It was felt that if the weather permitted, track would be laid up the Canyon as far as the Sacramento River Bridge by July of 1884. Mr. Charles Crocker, one of the owners of the Central Pacific, believed that the line could be open to Strawberry Valley (Mount Shasta) by the winter of that same year. He was, of course, wrong about this.

What were the wages being paid by the Central Pacific? The locomotive engineers were getting $125.00 a month; conductors, $85.00 to $115.00; firemen, $85.00; brakemen, $65.00; baggage men, $75.00. The wipers were getting $2.00 a day, while the Chinese laborers were paid 95¢ a day to $30.00 a month. Eventually, the patient Orientals struck for $1.15 per day. Most spoke no English and had no money. They were not successful, so they finally returned to work at the original rate. In comparison, Mr. Strowbridge, the Chief of Construction under Mr. Crocker, was paid a healthy $50.00 a day.

All this early railroad work was dangerous, so hazardous that the Rule Book stated, "Employees, in accepting employment, assume the risks." The link and pin coupler caused many injuries. It was said that you could always spot a new brakeman — he had all of his fingers. The unbelievable amounts of Judson powder used in blasting frequently caused injuries from flying rock and concussion. Carpenters occasionally fell from bridges or were injured by huge timbers in tunnels. In fact, John Hayward, P. Noble, J. Stewart, and B. F. Barnes were injured by a fourteen-foot fall while putting up timbering in Tunnel #10, a bore near Sim Southern's place.

Redding was reported to be a busy place during the construction years. There were several locomotives there as well as fifty-five ballast cars and Chinese laborers to load and unload them. Regular train and engine crews were kept for the engines located in Redding, because it was felt that personnel familiar with the new construction should handle this work.

In early February 1884, the work on the Oregon-California Railroad was suspended. It was reported that a cheaper route was thought to be possible, but in all probability financial problems were again plaguing the company. Henry Villard, the brilliant, young, financial wizard sent over from Germany by the bond holders of the Oregon-California Company was now finding himself in troubled waters. Although Villard had little finances of his own, as a strong representative of moneyed men, he was soon in control of the Oregon-California Railroad, president of the Northern Pacific Railroad, and organizer of the Oregon-Washington Railroad and Navigation Company. Villard, his associates, and stock and bond holders wanted to lease the Oregon-California Company to the Central Pacific, but Collis P. Huntington of the Central Pacific could see that by delaying action a ripe plum would soon fall by its own weight into the hands of Central Pacific.

By May of 1884, the Oregon and California Railroad had reached Ashland, Oregon. Alas, revenue was slow to develop for the uncompleted line. Oregon politicians were once again planning to withdraw the land grants. Expenses of operation, unpaid bills, wages, and interest were bringing financial ruin to Villard. To help matters along, the Central Pacific brought men (Messers. Brown, Pratt, Curtis, and Wright) up to a spot some thirty-six miles above Redding for the purpose of selecting a site for a station. This station was Delta, and work above this point would not proceed for some time. The waiting game began!

To muddy the water a bit, the Central Pacific had leased their road to the Southern Pacific Railroad Company on February 17, 1884. This was an acknowledgement that both companies were actually under the same management, as on one day, Leland Stanford signed the lease agreement as president of the Central Pacific, and the following day, he was elected president of the Southern Pacific. Such an arrangement assured the three remaining "old men" of the Central Pacific, Huntington, Stanford, and Crocker, that their lines in California and over the Sierras

would have an outlet to the East even though the Union Pacific might become uncooperative at some time in the future. This merger of the Central Pacific and the Southern Pacific instigated an investigation by the Federal Government as both were land grant operations. Litigation was to continue for years before final approval was granted by the Government.

Early in January of 1885, the Oregon State Senate rescinded the land grants of the Oregon Central, and all lands adjacent to the uncompleted railroad were to be forfeited. Only a few days later, the Oregon and California Company of Henry Villard passed into the hands of a receiver — bankrupt. High construction costs, light business, and delays in completion of a through connection were cited as the causes. It was hoped that if the Central Pacific were to lose their land grants, the company would continue working, as they had already spent in excess of two and a half million dollars on their road, and the land that had been given them, if sold, would not bring $250,000.00.

On April 4, 1885, the State of California passed a resolution giving the Central Pacific only two years to finish its track to the Oregon boundary line and to complete a connection with the Oregon and California Railroad. If not done in the allotted time, all unearned lands of either road, and lands opposite unfinished portions of the road, would be forfeited. (It was noted that our own senator from this district, E. W. Taylor, conveniently neglected to vote on this resolution.)

During most of the summer of 1885, rumors of an impending renewal of construction were frequently circulated but never verified. William Hood was now the Chief Engineer of the construction. In his letters to Dr. Louis Autenrieth of Yreka, who now owned the toll road originally constructed by Mr. Stone, he gave no indication of the renewal of work. But on the 9th of September, Mrs. Autenrieth announced that no further tolls would be collected, and no more maintenance of the road would be done. The Central Pacific had taken possession of the road and would use it.

At last the notice came — work to start on the road north! Engineer Marsh would be at Slate Creek. Superintendent Strowbridge would arrive the next day, and Engineer Hood would set up camp at Upper Soda Springs in a very few days. Surveyors were also working in the Siskiyous near the State Line at Cole's place as well as in the Sacramento River Canyon.

Yreka newspapers continued their speculations on the Oregon and California Company, but little new developed until October of 1885. It was then announced that the entire line of about 451 miles would be sold for $10,500,000 in bonds to the Central Pacific, who had agreed to complete the road between Ashland and Delta within three years. This was quite a project as there were 133 miles and thirteen more

crossings of the Sacramento River to be completed.

Although the railroad had been completed to Delta in 1884, and trains had been coming as far as that point, nothing further had been done up until the sale was made to the Central Pacific. Despite the late date and onslaught of bad weather, as many Chinese and white workmen as possible were promptly returned to the construction work. Early in November, it could be reported that work had progressed as far as Portuguese Flat and grading finished near Slate Creek two miles above Sim Southern's. At least 1500 men were on the job in Shasta County. Rain hampered train movements often causing slides, washouts, and soft track.

By the first months in 1886 railroad construction was under way in the grand style. Over 2000 men were working above Delta. Tunnels numbers nine, ten, and eleven were being crowded along as rapidly as possible. The iron bridge at the sixth crossing of the Sacramento had been finished, and Mr. Flanders, the Superintendent, and his crew were moving to the seventh crossing. During May the track was laid as far as Gibson's. To add to the excitement of it all, four loaded box cars left on the siding at Slate Creek ran away passing Delta at an estimated forty miles per hour. Fortunately, as they slowed on the flat near Smithson's, track walker John Roch was able to board the last car and set the brake. An engine finally managed to catch the wild little train.

June found the track gangs as far as Sim Southern's at Hazel Creek, and the word was that they should be to Bailey's and Lower Soda Springs by August. The Siskiyou County line was getting closer! Some forty surveyors were in the Canyon below Sisson's searching for a grade and looking for bridge and tunnel sites. Here the Sacramento River Box Canyon almost stumped the engineers. Retired locomotive engineer Harry A. Stone, grandson of the toll road builder, Willard P. Stone, likes to tell a tale of this search. While the survey crew was standing on a flat about a mile below Stink Creek pondering their problems, a lone sheepherder wandered up to pass the time of day. After listening to the engineers' problems, the herder remarked, "There is nothing you can do but to make a big turn across the river, go up the other side, and get out of this canyon." This was what was done, and we know this feat of engineering as Cantara Loop.

The Delta terminal was finally closed as a transfer point, and all business was forwarded to Sim Southern's, where a temporary box car, telegraph office was opened. It was expected that Delta would soon wither and die, as, hereafter, all stage connections would be at Sim Southern's.

The Central Pacific bridge gangs under Flanders no doubt became exceptionally proficient as, during the autumn of 1886, they managed to install nine iron truss bridges over the Sacramento River from north of Delta to the Siskiyou County line. This brought the total to fifteen crossings with at least three more to come. Two bridges were avoided at Fish Rock by changing the course of the river.

Toward the end of July, 1886, practically all construction work was being done in Siskiyou County. The grade of the track increased from near one and two tenths percent to two and a quarter percent as the Canyon became more difficult. Near Upper Soda Springs, an extremely solid rock point had to be removed. Holes were drilled and packed with fourteen tons of explosive, and a new type of detonator was employed which used electricity instead of a fuse. Everything seemed ready. The holes were filled and tamped, the caps inserted, wires connected, and the warning signal given. The magneto handle was forcefully pushed down, and — nothing! The blast was a failure. Some of the powder did not explode but only burned.

By the end of August of 1886, the railroad had reached to what is Central Dunsmuir today and was heading north to present-day Mount Shasta, Weed, Montague, Hornbrook, and Ashland. It is interesting to note that R. Beers Loos reported in his newspaper, the *Yreka Union* dated August 26, 1886, that a new shipping point had been moved from "Hazel Creek to Cedar Flat or DUNSMUIRE" and advised his readers to use "your own pronouncement." Spelling DUNSMUIR correctly, the *Yreka Journal*, on August 28th, announced that a new station had opened the previous Monday on the California and Oregon road called DUNS-MUIR. "This is ten and a half miles above Hazel Creek and twenty-three miles above Delta." By December, however, "DUNS-MIEUR was nearly snowed in!" Wrong spelling again in Mr. Loos's paper! Also, early in September of 1886, the Yreka papers reported that a very heavy train arrived in Dunsmuir, the present terminal, consisting of two engines and twenty-four cars of rail. More carts and other equipment were arriving daily. So the Iron Horse and all that was needed to keep it running had come to Dunsmuir.

In April of 1887, the Government commissioners Stoneman, Cook, and Pound were appointed by the president to inspect the new line from Delta to a point sixty miles north, or near Park's Creek in Siskiyou County. Tracks, bridges, tunnels, buildings, and telegraph lines were all given approval and recommended for governmental acceptance. Stoneman, Cook, and Pound traveled in one of the new style Pullman sleeper cars as they inspected the line. John Signor, in researching for his book, *Rails in the Shadow of Mt. Shasta*, uncovered actual copies of the commissioners' reports from which the following information is gleaned:

Southern Pacific Depot, Dunsmuir, 1964
Built of redwood, assembled using ten sizes of square-cut nails (1¼" to 6"), and, through the years, painted seven different colors: very light beige, Depot Buff, Union Pacific mustard yellow, very light Pewter grey, Southern Pacific letter grey, sea green, and, lastly, light seafoam green. All the colors had been instilled with over eighty-five years of wood, coal, and oil smoke when the building was demolished in 1973.
—*Photo: F. H. Wintering*

The newly constructed clubhouse, later the Crew Dispatcher's Office, served as a backdrop for this picture of the Southern Pacific Band. Mrs. E. H. Harriman had donated the building for the use of the employees.
—*Photo: Courtesy Siskiyou County Museum*

DUNSMUIR

Main line - 60 lbs. rail steel
2 side tracks — 1655 ft. & 1311 ft. and 1 spur 695 ft. all 56 lbs. rail iron
1 water tank, 50,000 gal., redwood standing on iron columns with concrete foundation
1 sand house of pine, 24′ x 30′ and 3 tool houses 12′ x 16′
1 wood 56 ft. turntable
1 stock corral 52′ x 117′ divided into 2 pens
1 section house for white men 16′ x 24′ plus a 12′ x 14′ addition
1 section house for Chinese men 18′ x 20′ plus a 12′ x 14′ kitchen
1 roadmaster's dwelling and office 21′ x 38′ plus 10′6″ x 11′ addition
Buildings were of pine for white men and redwood for Chinese
A wood house for fuel was not deemed necessary

No other buildings were listed. However, a depot of redwood and a quarter circle, eighteen-stall engine house, which required one and a half million bricks to build, were soon constructed. The "unnecessary" wood house, 385 feet long by 24 feet wide by 16 feet high and holding 1152 cords of wood, was finished before another winter. Also, during the summer of 1887, a huge back shop and a car shop were laid out. Newspaper reporters felt that at least 300 men would be employed.

The struggle up the canyon and the final exit was nearly over. The first crossing of the Sacramento River at Tehama consisted of four stationary spans of over 150 feet each plus a single swing span of 173 feet to allow shallow draft river boats to pass. The total of the Howe truss sections and the approach trestle was 4,177 feet — a nice pile of cedar, redwood, and Puget Sound pine timbers. Now iron bridges numbers sixteen, seventeen, and the temporary deck bridge number eighteen, at the great fourteen degree loop above Uncle Dick Mannon's Soda Springs were coming along nicely. Also, Stewart and his mill crew were turning out timbers eighty feet long for use in the four-span, 110-foot-high strain beam structure over Big Canyon high above the river canyon.

By the fall of 1886, a new town near Berryvale, named Sisson in honor of J. H. Sisson who donated the land to the "poor" Central Pacific Company, had been surveyed. Excursion trains brought in prospective buyers, and corner lots, it is said, quickly sold for as much as $250.00. A water tank and a turntable were being constructed there.

To avoid more tunneling, the original plan of following Wagon Creek through the divide near the old stage road into Shasta Valley was abandoned. A new route using several long, sweeping curves brought the grade to a gap near Muir's Peak (Black Butte) into Boles Creek drainage. Though quick and easy to construct, the grade down to Butteville (Edgewood Post Office) and the flat Shasta Valley was steep.

Indications are that the passage through the Deitz ranch near Sisson was purchased with a stipulation that passenger trains would stop at the ranch to pick up members of the family, a prerogative that Mrs. Deitz, on occasion, exercised.

Winter came late in 1886. Progress was rapid during the early part of the winter, and Superintendent J. A. Filmore announced that, as of Saturday, January 1, 1887, the California-Oregon extension, the Shasta Division, would be open for traffic to Edgewood. At that time trains ran from Red Bluff to Dunsmuir, and a "swing" train operated from Dunsmuir to Edgewood and returned. The conductor on the "swing" train was Flunk Warner, the brakeman, Jack Maghar, and the baggage was handled by Alex Riddel. Engineers Mel Church and George McReynolds, on alternate days, came through on the Red Bluff end.

Selecting a route through Shasta Valley was simple as Hood had chosen the best spot years earlier. Getting from Edgewood to Edson's (Gazelle Post Office) seems to have been the problem. Two wooden bridges were necessary at both Shasta River and Park's Creek; and from then on, putting as much track as possible on nearly flat ground seemed the idea. Little excavating was required and so little was done that critics claimed that the line in the valley seemed not to be permanent.

Late in January, track layers were scurrying toward the new town that L. D. Norton was laying out at mile post #6 of the Little Shasta road on land that had been donated by C. C. Webb and the Prather brothers. Named in honor of the late Chief Engineer S. S. Montague, this place was to be the stopping-off place for Yreka. Track would be brought into Montague on completion of a 481-foot bridge over the Shasta River.

The end of January, C. P. Huntington announced that the Southern Pacific Company would take over the Oregon and California Company and finish the line to a final connection at Ashland, Oregon. The work force was to be increased to 5000 men as soon as possible, full steam ahead!

During the beautiful January weather of 1887, Oliver Richardson and his crew managed to find time to replace the temporary wooden bridge at the eighteenth and final Sacramento River crossing. In February the weather changed and snow began to fall. More and more snow covered the countryside, until it was reported that snow was two feet deep at Yreka with four to six feet in the mountains. The *Yreka Union* of February 26, 1887, told that a plow and four engines finally opened the line through to Edgewood after Sisson had been snowed in for ten days. There were more delays between Montague and the Klamath River which were caused by rain, melting snow and mud, "dobie" mud. The rain ceased and the Shasta zephyrs soon dried the land allowing the Central Pacific

to continue its efforts. Four bridges completed on Willow Creek brought track to the Klamath River. Delay waiting for iron bridge parts to arrive allowed the engineering department sufficient opportunity to run a line over Bailey Hill to Cole's Station and Oregon. Unfortunately, late in March, Oliver Richardson, the able head bridge carpenter, fell fifteen feet from the second Willow Creek bridge and was killed. The Company lost a man with at least thirty-five years experience in bridge construction.

David Horn sold his ranch along Cottonwood Creek near Henley to the railroad and saw it promptly converted to a new station named in his honor, Hornbrook. Here ample room for a turntable, depot, water tank, and a huge wood house was available for a permanent helper engine terminal. It was announced that effective May 1, 1887, the new terminal was to be Hornbrook. Almost immediately, a daily train, the "Oregon Express," started operating. The schedule left San Francisco at 4:00 p.m. on Sunday and was to arrive at Hornbrook Tuesday at 9:30 a.m., some forty-one and a half hours later.

Following the announcement that the Central Pacific would take over and complete the Oregon and California line, and, again as the Southern Pacific took charge, rumors indicated the Southern Pacific would re-survey the line over the Siskiyous. A new, longer tunnel from one mile to seven miles long with less grade was sought. Even switch-backs were considered — just anything to get the track open and to get the revenue started in order to prevent the loss of California land grants. A tunnel on Bailey Hill was deemed absolutely certain!

Villard apparently had a word to say about his former Oregon and California Company, as he wanted compensation for the work done on the unfinished Summit tunnel. The Southern Pacific, now under

Engine #50 was regularly used in the construction of the railroad in Siskiyou County. The train and its crew posed at Hornbrook, California, for this picture.

—*Photo: W. E. Sanford collection*

17

Count 'em! Six engines struggling up Bailey Hill with only 2400 tons.
—Photo: Courtesy George White

Huntington, at first refused, but finally, in the end agreed to reimburse him. Henry Villard out-maneuvered earlier by Huntington, in the long term, regained his losses and returned as the head of the Northern Pacific. A few years later, in 1890, he acquired the Edison Lamp Company and Edison Machine Company and combined them into the Edison General Electric Company, known now as General Electric.

By April, 1887, William Hood was supervising all work in the mountains and with thousands of Chinese and white men and hundreds of horses laboring, progress was being rapidly made. Fogarty's crew, including William Tonkins and J. O'Brien acting as foremen, was on the flat near the Klamath River while Sullivan's graders and Managan's white crew were tackling Bailey Hill. Potholers (blasters) were drilling holes twenty-five feet deep to be packed with Judson powder to open the deeper cuts. Explosions filled the air with flying rock, dirt and smoke.

Scobie's masonry crews were busily engaged in bridge footings and culverts. One huge arched culvert across Heudon Creek to have been 175 feet long, 105 feet wide and 45 feet high seems to have never been built, as the Commissioner's report of 1889 shows a sixty-six-foot bridge. The header of the rock wall is still visible, although the bridge was filled in years ago. Without a doubt the spectacular point on Bailey Hill was the high trestle over a gulch near the top consisting of forty-nine spans. From there, six miles of new construction could be seen stretching back nearly to the Klamath River.

Yreka Journal Editor Nixon announced in April of 1887 that tunnel contractor, E. J. Jeffry, had twelve men opening up the north end of Tunnel 13, the Siskiyou Tunnel, which had been closed since February of 1884. About 1200 feet of unfinished work at the summit bore had been left to flood as fires were pulled from the boilers and pumps were withdrawn from the north end when construction was stopped by the Oregon and California Company.

Despite the brawling, drinking, and wild whiskey emporiums at "Hell Town" on Bailey Hill, the railroad progressed at an amazing rate. It started to look as if the track to Ashland could be finished by the fall of 1887. A cut thirty-five feet deep on Bailey Hill obviated a tunnel, but the grade zoomed to 3.3% or 175 feet to the mile. To illustrate, a fifty-foot-long boxcar is about twenty inches higher on one end than on the other when traveling up the grade.

Abandonment of the longer Hurlburt seven-tunnel survey on the Oregon side sent, for the final time, surveyors searching for a new route. One might suppose that after the time spent by the Oregon and California Railroad finding a suitable grade, all choices had been tried. However, Mr. Graham and his men found one grade that was shorter, steeper, and with less tunneling necessary which avoided Buck Rock. Actually, this new line, which still used the Siskiyou Summit Tuinnel was indeed an engineering marvel.

The new survey allowed the railroad to be promptly finished, and it also equalized the grades between Hornbrook and Ashland to about three and three-tenths percent to three and six-tenths on both sides of the mountain. That it was a difficult road may

The Southern Pacific Railroad's Upper and Lower Wall Creek (Oregon) trestles before 1897.
—*Photo: Waters, courtesy of Siskiyou County Museum*

of the four bridges — two on the middle grade, a trestle and a bridge, were almost directly below the two on the upper line, separated only by a few hundred feet in elevation and a couple of miles of uncompleted railroad. Of the four, absolutely the most spectacular when finished was the 544-foot-long upper bridge across the North Fork of Wall Creek. It consisted of three eighty-foot Howe truss spans twenty feet thick resting on wooden towers at a total height approaching 180 feet. No walkways, no guard rails, and the track was on the top of the Howe truss! One safety precaution was barrels of water spaced at intervals along the crossbeams, handy if anyone had nerve enough to walk out to use them! No doubt the vibration of passing trains sloshed most of the water from the barrels.

When finally completed, some iron-nerved crew would operate the first test engine and train over the creaking timbers of the high bridge! Ten years it served the purpose well until it was finally replaced in 1897 by the present 183-foot-high steel version. (Water continues to splash from the present fire barrels.) Late in September, Tunnel #13 was at last finished, and supplies could be forwarded through to the north side. Number 14, the 14° spiral tunnel, was expected to be finished in only four weeks, or about November 1st. Reports dated October 20, 1887, show that the first passenger train had arrived at Siskiyou via the new tunnel where, for a time, oil lamps were kept burning constantly so that track walkers could keep everything well inspected.

A new turntable was installed at Siskiyou so that engines could be conveniently turned, as three engines were needed for the climb from the south.

The sharply curved Tunnel 14 was holed through according to the Yreka paper of October 27th. To celebrate as usual a few barrels of beer were opened for the enjoyment and refreshment of the crews. Rumors had it that a fight started when it was finally discovered that the actual bore was off a few inches where the two facings merged. Nothing serious, but just enough for each crew to blame the other. Between tunnels 14 and 15 for many, many years, a visable surveyed trail took off down the mountain toward the short opening at Tunnel 16. This was used to transport pumps, a boiler, and other supplies from the lower to the upper level.

Back in Dunsmuir the engine house and shops were going along rapidly. Included was to be a large hydraulic drop table to remove engine wheels without raising the entire locomotive. Much of this and other shop machinery was being built by the railroad in its own general shop at Sacramento. The new powerhouse and boiler room was to be about thirty feet square.

Most of the heavy work was grinding toward a halt after these many long years! As the various brush crews, pot holers, graders, and the like completed their

be seen by the fact that in the twenty-five miles from the Oregon line to Ashland there are only 188 feet of level track. As at Cantara Loop, fourteen degree curves were required to reverse direction at three additional places: Gregory, north of Cole's Station; Tunnel 14, mentioned below; and Dollarhide, about eleven miles south of Ashland. For years after completion, the "loop" in the Siskiyou mountains of the Shasta Route was publicized as being "so grand, so daring, that it throws all other experiences of trestles, bridges, and loops in the shade." It was clever! Descending, the track enters 1200-foot-long Tunnel 14 on a sharp fourteen degree curve, only to emerge and pass through a very short tunnel that has no purpose but to strengthen the upper level. Here the lower grade lacks only

eleven inches from passing under the upper. Be encouraged to travel this old route should the opportunity arise during the Centennial.

What a delightful place this must have been from which to watch construction during the summer of 1887. Walking down hill from Siskiyou and the tunnel, following the new grade, one would have soon come to a pleasant little stream gushing down the mountain, Wall Creek. A bit farther on, the great steep canyon of the North Fork of the same creek would be reached, its clear water racing to the valley far below. By following the trail to the left around the hillside, one could eventually reach the north side without climbing to the canyon floor. Here, finding a spot free of the workers, one could see the construction

*Believed to be Engine #211 on a construction train near Siskiyou,
Oregon, in 1887. Notice the Telegraph Operator with Key
at center-front.*
—Photo: W. E. Sanford Collection

portion of the job they were dismissed. On October 29, 1887, it was announced that the new 212-mile Shasta Division would soon be completed from Red Bluff to Ashland, and that J. A. Filmore would be the Superintendent with headquarters at Dunsmuir.

Torrent Creek, now called Slide Creek, Neil Creek, and Clayton Creek were promptly crossed leaving the grade ready for the track gangs. Of the thousands of workers previously employed by the company, the first of December, 1887, saw only about one hundred men left laying rail on the mountain. The work was nearly finished!

The white men believed that the "Chinamen no savvy," and the Chinese thought that the "Amelican man no muchee no sabie." Despite all their differences, the two diverse cultures managed to work together well enough to build 170 miles of difficult mountain railroad in five years.

Only eleven days before the final Gold Spike ceremony, a meeting was held in Ashland to determine the location of a roundhouse, repair shops, various sheds, and an eating house for the passengers. Representing the Southern Pacific at the meeting were: General Manager A. Towne, General Superintendent J. A. Filmore, Superintendent Wright, Master Mechanic Stevens, and Master Car Builder Walsh. From the Oregon and California end, which was now under the Southern Pacific, were General Manager Roehler and Superintendent Brandt. As a result of this meeting, Chief Engineer Grondahle of the Oregon and California was given the job of laying out the tracks, buildings, and other facilities according to the newly adopted plan.

To quote a few lines from the *Sutter County Farmer* as printed by E. Beers Loos in the *Yreka Union*, "The completion of the California-Oregon Railroad marks an epoch in the history of California second only to that grand overland — the Central Pacific. Other overland roads were but followers and additions while the Central was by many years the pioneer. So with this Oregon road, it is the long looked for pioneer that will throw light, enterprise, and population into a hitherto neglected region — neglected for want of transportation facilities, and the distance from the busy hive of people and the markets of the world."

Long-time locomotive engineer Donald S. Whitney of Ashland, now deceased, was a well-known and well-liked employee of the railroad for fifty-two years. His personal mail from the president of the railroad frequently was headed "Dear Don." As a young lad, Mr. Whitney witnessed the driving of the Gold Spike at Ashland on December 17, 1887 at 5:10 in the evening. In relating the events of that long ago day, he would indicate that several of the passengers and guests on the Special Train coming from Dunsmuir for the celebration had left the train on the north side of Tunnel 13 after witnessing the grades on Bailey Hill and the Siskiyous. They absolutely refused to continue down the mountain and left the train to finish the trip by stagecoach. (Had they seen the spectacular, high bridge at Wall Creek, no doubt, other timid travelers would have deserted the train at Siskiyou, also.)

The winter day in Ashland was cold and blustery. Delayed several times, the train was late and getting later. Many of the waiting spectators gave up the vigil and wandered off as the sky darkened into evening. At last a whistle echoed from the hills and the oil headlight of an engine approached, but it was only the Helper running ahead of the Special Train. In a few moments, however, the long awaited official train, carrying the dignitaries, followed around the curve at East Main Street and pulled to a stop at Ashland!

The site for the ceremony was a few

20

hundred feet south of the present station. Bonfires were lighted, the band played a tune or two, and then Charles Crocker held up the Gold Spike for all to see, spoke a few words and, with a silver maul, tapped the final spike into place. In only a few, brief moments a monumental construction job was officially completed, and for one cold little boy it was a story he could remember all of his life. Speeches were made by W. H. Mills, Governor Pennoyer of Oregon, the Honorable Horace Davis, Colonel John P. Irish, and others, but to Young Whitney, Crocker had said IT ALL!

A locomotive of some long-forgotten special train at the Dunsmuir Roundhouse, shortly after 1891.
—Photo: Courtesy of Siskiyou County Museum

A new engine for the new railroad — S.P. Engine #237, built by Stevens at the Sacramento shops in 1888, was shortly after posed with her crew at Hornbrook, California, for the camera of Yreka dentist, C. A. Larison

—Photo: J. Leach Collection

A BOY'S RECOLLECTION OF
STEAM RAILROADING IN DUNSMUIR

By Larry Green

To a young boy barely 11 years old, whose father had served as a locomotive fireman for the Southern Pacific Railroad during the busy war years, few things in life were more awe inspiring or impressive than a million pounds of locomotive, puffing and grunting with a full head of steam as it pushed or pulled heavy tonnage over steep, winding rail beds. If you were looking for steam in the height of its glory, Dunsmuir was certainly the place to be prior to 1955, when dieselization of all railroads finally sent these great iron horses to the cutting torch and scrap piles.

Not all kids were fascinated by steam, but to those of us that were, Dunsmuir had much to offer. In 1948, the year I first came to Dunsmuir, I was 11 years old and totally infatuated with steam locomotives, not just any steam locomotive mind you, but only the biggest and most powerful, like the massive 4100 and 4200 classes' articulated consolidation locomotives called Cab Forwards, or Malleys for short. Designed to run backwards with the cab in front and the tender behind, so as to place the engine crews ahead of the exhaust fumes, these back peddling Cab Forwards represented the ultimate of steam power used exclusively to tackle the steep grades of the mountainous terrain of California.

Dunsmuir was home to dozens of Cab Forwards that were on 24-hour call to assist in getting tonnage over the Siskiyou Mountains. The first place my dad would take and drop me was to the train station in Dunsmuir, where for hours on end I would watch with boyhood enthusiasm the very essence of steam's finest hours in action. The smell of hot steam and burning bunker Type C fuel oil was sweet and familiar to my nostrils, and the sound of steam whirling through a steam-pyle generator, the pulsing drone of a Worthington feed water pump and especially those sharp, whistling exhausts of a pair of Westinghouse compound air pumps unique only to Cab Forwards was sheer music to my ears.

Dunsmuir's roundhouse and turntable was a busy place in 1948, as hostlers wrestled engines to and from the roundhouse across the turntable and onto the fueling, water, and sand stations. The massive Cab Forwards, Decapods, Mountains, Mikados, and Mogals alike were kept hot 24 hours a day, ready for the call of duty. The extra engines that were needed to help eastbound freights north over the grade were added on here in Dunsmuir, and it was during this brief pause that a young boy like myself could have his eyes filled with the motions of steam.

Engines that had sat for a period had to be relieved of the water that would accumulate in their massive cylinders, of which the Cab Forwards had twice as many as other non-articulated engines. Engineers and hostlers alike would open all the pet-cock valves so that when the locomotive would first begin to move great clouds of steam would rush from the bottoms of the cylinders and climb up around the engine. Soon that white face unique to Cab Forwards would emerge like black ghosts from clouds of steam as the engine moved to take its position on the head end of a long freight.

Once coupled on, usually in front of the depot where I'd so often sat, I'd watch skilled engineers and responsive firemen start the tonnage rolling, a task a lot easier said than done. Fine sand, white and hot from sitting in large domes atop the Cab Forward's massive boiler, would flow through pipes just ahead of the driving wheels and rain down upon the track to help the wheels bite into the rails and keep them from slipping. With the safety valves ready to pop off under a full 250 pounds of steam, the engineer would just whistle three blasts, which means reverse, and then a hogger (I thought too small to run such a massive machine) would often stand up, face the rear, place the reverse lever or Johnson bar into reverse and then widen on the throttle until the great locomotive would ease back to take up the slack in the stretched out train of a hundred cars. Just as quickly, the hogger would then, from a still standing position, pull the Johnson bar into the forward position and open the throttle even wider, bringing all 16 main drivers first to a stop and then forward again. Two blasts of the engine's Nathan six-chime whistle would signal forward and always send an eerie chill up my spine.

Steam leaking from every loose packing gland, the engine would roar with an exhaust unique only to articulated consolidations, for if the engine's two sets of drivers on separate frames were not perfectly synchronized, you'd hear not one but two exhaust reports from the engine's twin stacks. The earth would tremble, the engine would shake and strain under the load, and often one of the sets of drivers would break free, slip and run wild until the engineer could shut the throttle off to stop the drivers and then just as quickly as they stopped, open the throttle again with just enough proficiency to grab the rails again before loosening what little bite on the rails it had gained. Between exhausts, which quickened ever so slowly as one by one the gained slack would be stretched out of the train. One agonizing mile per hour would become two miles per hour and so on until the full train was finally moving on its ascent up the hill.

Great skill was needed by both the fireman and engineer to properly start some 8,000 or more tons of train rolling; but if anything could do it, it was these great Cab Forwards. The later, heavier, rectangular tendered 4100 and 4200 class Malleys could develop about 6,000 horsepower at a good lope. In between the ear deafening exhaust blasts you could hear those sweet sounding, whistling exhausts of the air pumps as they shot bursts of white steam skyward to mix with the black, oil-fed exhausts as the fireman would widen on the firing valve. Finally, the entire train would roar out of town at a 10 m.p.h. romp, often with three or more locomotives coupled in at varying distances between cars of the train. It was just as much fun watching the last engine shove the train out of town as it was watching the first engine pull away from the depot.

None of this seemed to have any profound effect on the large rainbow trout that swam in the big circular, aerated fountain at the depot. This was the same trout pond that now sits by the ballpark at the entrance to Dunsmuir's City Park. But the locomotives did have a profound effect on the Dunsmuir housewives, who would hang their clothing on clotheslines to dry. For once clearing the Sacramento street crossing, the fireman would toss a half-dozen scoops of sand into the heart of the locomotive's firebox, where the enormous draft would then wisk the sand through the boiler's flues to clean the scale off and make the engine steam more efficiently. Much of this soot would eventually end up on the damp clothes hanging on clotheslines throughout Dunsmuir. Housewives did not feel the same about steam as I did.

Train after train would come and go, stopping for crew changes and additional engines in Dunsmuir, where at full peak nearly 2,500 men labored at work either running, fixing, or moving steam locomotives for duty in Dunsmuir. These were earth-shattering monsters of the rails, which you either loved or hated, but for a railroad-born boy of 11, the memories were nothing short of sheer fascination and love of a machine.

Quietude came to Dunsmuir only after the diesels replaced steam in 1956. But what the diesels gained in favor with housewives and some crew men, they could not replace the same enchantment and fascination as did the great iron horses that served Dunsmuir for so long and created many a love affair with steam enthusiastic enginemen. Railroading would never be the same again. You can still go to the Dunsmuir depot and watch much of the same train movements, but there is little excitement for a boy born and raised in the days when big steam power ruled the rails. Gone are the greasy overalls, armbands, and eerie steam sounds that so brought the canyons of Dunsmuir alive with sound.

Today I often still sit at the depot by the very spot I sat nearly 40 years ago to watch the trains, but the romance that once dominated these rails is no more. Gone, too, are the big trout in the old Dunsmuir fountain, the black smoke in the canyons and all the spine-tingling sights, sounds, and smells of steam in its fullest glory. Only when I drench myself in nostalgia and when I'm free of present thought, can I sit here now, close my eyes and sometimes envision those white-faced Cab Forwards pushing ahead of white clouds of steam and oil-fed smoke. Only occasionally can I visualize the sounds of air pumps, feed water pumps, and pyle generators, and rarer yet is the visualization of steam whistles that echo off canyon walls as they did some 40 years ago.

You can read about steam railroading in Dunsmuir in some fine books, and see some nostalgic pictures, but to really understand what steam railroading was in Dunsmuir, you would have had to have been here in and around the locomotives that so many old, retired Dunsmuir railroad men from Dunsmuir still remember. Not all felt the same about steam as I did, but there were many like myself whose souls were grabbed by the likes of steam and who still remember Dunsmuir as it was prior to 1956. For those of us left, Dunsmuir with its old turn-table, Malley house, and fragments of its once busy roundhouse, now long removed from here, will always be home to the memory of

the Cab Forwards reduced from a fleet of 195 such locomotives system-wide to merely one remaining monarch of its time.

Cab Forward #4294 still remains in the California State Railroad Museum in Sacramento, California. Yet without fire in its belly, smoke from its stack or movement of any kind, children around the age of 11 still gasp at its size and image of power when they gauk with disbelief at the massive locomotive now sitting in the museum, a locomotive that at one time called the City of Dunsmuir home.

ABOUT THE AUTHOR

Larry Green is an author, writer, photographer, artist, radio broadcaster, teacher, lecturer, conversationist, naturalist, cartoonist, fisherman and hunter. He is 47 years old, married for 25 years to his wife, Mary; has a daughter, Karen, and a son, Scott; and is a native-born Californian.

For the past 11 years Larry has served as host, writer and producer broadcasting the popular "FISHERMAN'S FORECAST" radio shows (12 per week) over KCBS/CBS in San Francisco, a 50,000-watt station.

As an active member of the Outdoors Writers' Association of America (OWAA) since 1962, Larry has had more than 1,300 feature articles published in more than 36 leading outdoor magazines. Served 8 years as Field Editor for FIELD & STREAM Magazine and now holds the current titles as Conservation Editor and Regional Editor for WESTERN SALTWATER FISHERMAN; Contributing Editor for ANGLER Magazine; Western Regional Editor for SALTWATER SPORTSMAN Magazine.

Larry has co-authored a number of outdoor books on fishing and hunting subjects and has contributed to the WORLD BOOK ENCYCLOPEDIA's Fishing Sections. He has authored his own book "TEN SECRETS TO MORE PRODUCTIVE FISHING," by BMC, Inc.

Larry is currently serving as outdoor editor columnist for the following newspapers: San Francisco Progress, San Jose Mercury, Oakland Post, Dunsmuir News, and the Mt. Shasta Review. His syndicated columns "Outdoors with Larry Green" now appears in more than 22 newspapers statewide.

Larry is currently retained on a paying basis by a number of large corporations that serve fishermen and hunters and general outdoors people with products that relate to the out-of-doors. The position is one of planning, designing, testing and evaluating consumer products for sportsmen.

Larry spends approximately 4 to 5 days out of every week traveling the north and

central state exclusively covering the outdoors scene in California. He has hiked, fished and hunted his way across practically every foot of Central and Northern California since age 10.

He currently serves as Column Editor with weekly columns in two major outdoor Tabloids which are: FISHING & HUNTING NEWS, Seattle, and the FISH SNIFFER NEWS, which is published in Elk Grove, California.

Larry holds Life or yearly memberships (active) in the following organizations: Cal Trout, Federation of Fly Fishermen, Siskiyou Fly Fishers, Isaak Walton League of Anglers, National Rifle Association, Audubon Society, California Academy of Science, Monterey Bay Aquarium, and many more.

He can be seen on television on Wednesdays, NIGHT REPORT ON FISHING at 10:15 P.M., KICU-TV, Channel 36, San Jose, CA.

Cab Forward entering Dunsmuir railyard in 1949

Cab Forward 4277 leaving Dunsmuir at City Park in 1949

Cab Forward downgrade at agriculture stop, 1948

Cora A. Remaly - S.P. Telegrapher

Built by Bob Pedroncelli - fine masonry contractor

Telephone Company, Pine Street

* * * * *

M. Steen
E. Schiesz
A. Fahs
V. Tait
T. Roberts
M. Roney
Joe Floyd
M. Rossi
F. Grassman

* * * * *

Circa 1947

GRAND OPENING

Of Beaty Bros.

Moving Picture
SHOW

At Skating Rink, which will be
known in the future as the

Novelty Theater

Friday, April 2

Two performances each evening. First performance 8 p. m., second 9 p. m.

THIS PROGRAM
2 NIGHTS ONLY

PROGRAM

A Beautiful Story of the Devil.
By a Woman's Wit—Very Sensational.
The New Maid—Extremely fine.
The Messmerizer—Absolutely great.
The Arrest—Wouldn't it jar you.

Beautiful Colored Pictures. Far better than
The Passion Play.

Beautiful Solos by Little Winnie Whelchan.

FINE MUSIC.

At SKATING RINK, in the future to be known
as the NOVELTY THEATER.

A Complete change of Program Sunday, April 4

Admission 10c

*Flyer for Sacramento Avenue
Showplace - very early*

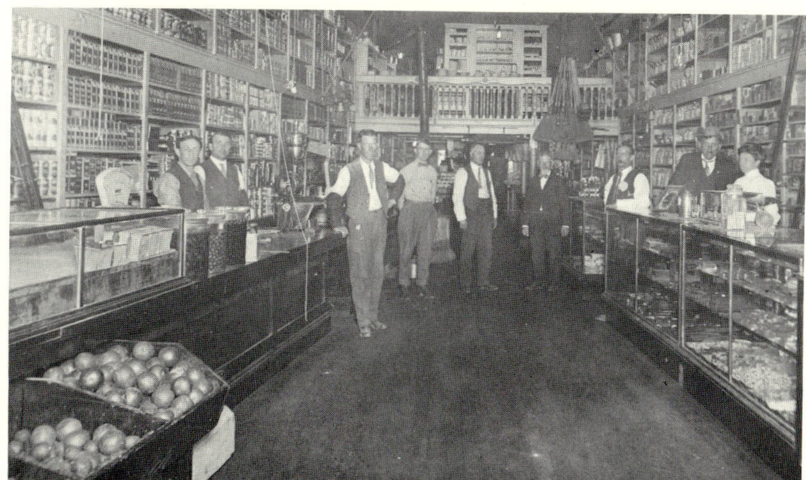
Mercantile Co. of Eherenman & Teatreau - Sacramento Ave.

DUNSMUIR BUSINESS PAST AND PRESENT

By

MARJORIE YOUNG

Marjorie Young   *Photo — Reineking*

Business houses in Dunsmuir have a history of constant change — fires and economy were the main causes.

In the early days of the community, business was related to the activity of the railroad. Businesses were constructed along Sacramento Avenue.

The fire of 1903 destroyed all the buildings in the main business block, but they were rebuilt.

From 1924, the business gradually begins moving to Florence Avenue as automobile on the highway was becoming an important factor to business. Florence Avenue then became the main business section of the town.

The fire of 1924 destroyed all the buildings north of the Rostel building on Sacramento Avenue. Those places were never rebuilt. It also destroyed all the buildings in that block on Florence Avenue. There business buildings replaced all the homes.

Because of the topography of the town, the only way for expansion was along the highway through the canyon. Just beyond the main business section was Gib's Service Station. In the 5500 block is Thriftway Foods and the Post Office. Further on in the next block is a residence now, but formerly was a grocery, an Italia restaurant, a hospital, Brewer's Plumbing (Kohlbakers), the Dunsmuir Garage, Dr. Townsend's office, the Travelodge, and the Ford Garage (Rodley's, Thom's Chevrolet), Mr. Selby's blacksmith shop was behind the Travelodge.

Continuing north beyond the bridge on the east side were the Buick Garage, Martin's Cleaners and Corwin's Grocery. These places were closed out when I-5 was constructed. On the west side was Talmage's Joyland and camp ground. The Hitching Post and Don's Frostie are presently in this area. Brown's Auto Court, bought by Bob Dewey, was divided to create the Chevron Station, a trailer court, Wiley's (formerly Mac's Market) and Cave Spring Motel. Ma Green's restaurant remained by Cave Spring Motel until her death.

Farther north are the motels — Bavarian Lodge, Whistle Stop, Garden Motel (Oaklo), Cedar Lodge and House of Glass. There are also Marjid's and Meyer's Plumbing Shop.

On the south end of town are several service stations, McLaughlin's Grocery, the former location of Diamond National, Manfredi's Grocery, El Rancho Motel, Al Rossi's Garage (Gene's), and Bill and Delberta Murphy's Railroad Park (a restaurant and campground).

At the top of Oak Street is Shasta Daisy Lockers and Ice Company, operated now by Vince and Shirley Congi (formerly by Chris Christenson, before that - George and Elinore Harrison).

Some of the earliest business houses have disappeared and without street addresses, which were never given in their advertisements, it is difficult to pinpoint their exact locations. Perhaps some of the names remembered are Lanning (Contractor), Callish (electrical service), Sam Isaac Wells (real estate), C. O. Clark (insurance), Sam Cortese (shoe repair), Charles Williams (fuel and beer distribution), Byrd (the barber), and Thelma Thoresen (photographer).

An early day automobile stage and bus line was purchased by Leonard Morrison from Vern Norris in 1924. Mr. Norris had operated the line since about 1920. The stage left from the Weed Hotel in Dunsmuir, traveled north through Mott and Azalea on to Mt. Shasta, stopped at the Park Hotel, then on to Weed, stopping at the Weed Hotel. In 1926, Morrison leased the stage line to Myrtie Davis of Mt. Shasta; he sold the franchise in 1928, or '29, to Pacific Motor Transport.

Presently there is a stage line operating between Dunsmuir and Mt. Shasta. It is a quaintly decorated auto stage.

There were also some individuals who conducted their business away from the main business sections. Some of these were Frank Van Fossen (lumber, building materials and insurance); Wilkins Bros., lumber mill; Huff and Craven's Steam Laundry; also, a Chinese laundry, and men who distributed milk to the community — Martin, Masson, Noyer, and Brown.

The following charts indicate the location of past and present businesses:

PINE ST. EAST OF DUNSMUIR AVE.

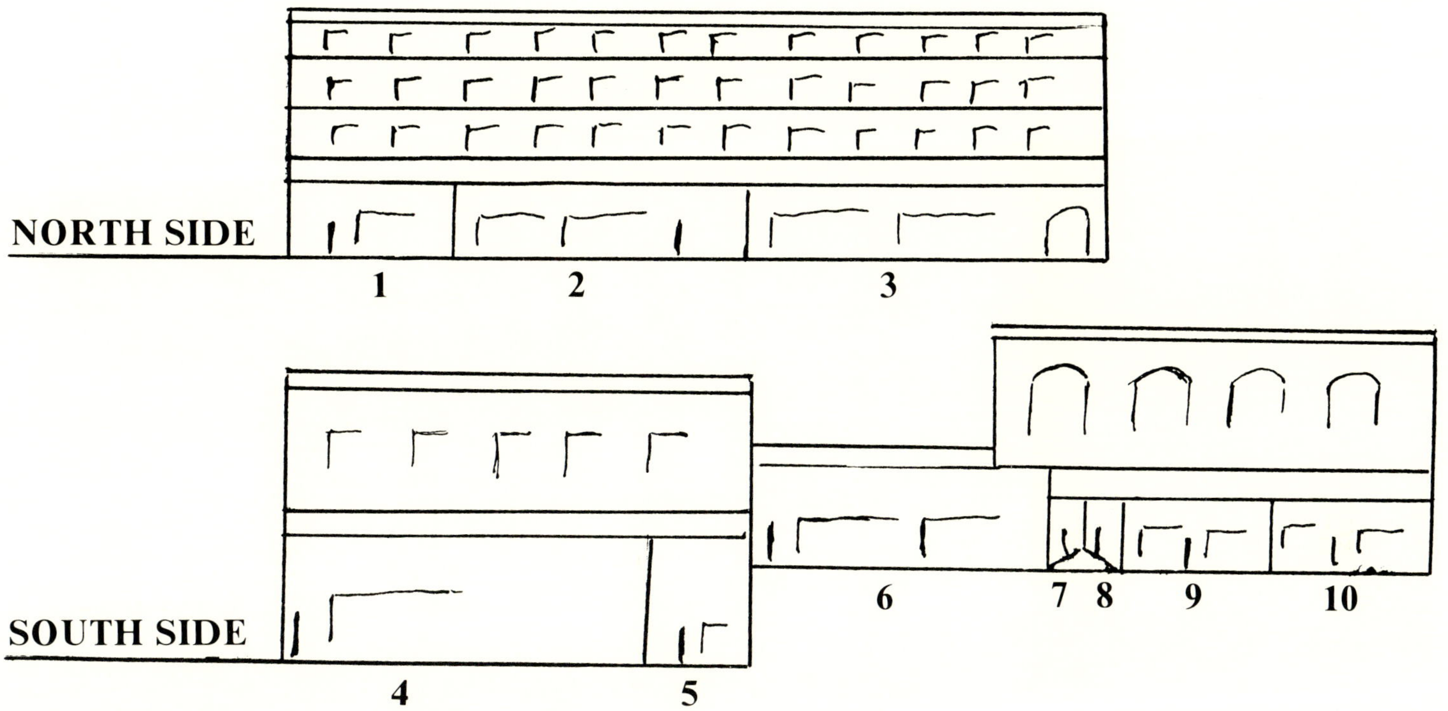

(Current businesses are listed first, moving from west to east)

NORTH SIDE:

1. Dunsmuir's Museum: Andreatta's Insurance Office, Weed and Jeffry's Men's Clothing

2. Part of the defunct Pizza Parlor: Furniture Store, Burnt Wood Sweets, Ice Cream Parlor.

3. Depot Pizza Parlor: Rubidoux Greyhound Bus Depot, Baccilieri's Travel Agency, Weed Hotel Lobby

SOUTH SIDE

4. Palm Cafe and Bar (Tom Loftus)

5. City Market Meats (Laughlin & Morrison) } At present no buildings stand in these locations.

6. Woodmon Construction, Fun Center, Dunsmuir News Office (editors: Orlo Mohr, Elmer Jenks), State Bank of Dunsmuir (G. A. Hufaff)

7. Barber Shop ("Curly" Lutrell's), Carlson's

8. Union Office

9. Hamilton and Hayward Bookkeeping, Jewelry Store, Beauty Parlor (owned by Jenny Eagle, Leta Taylor, Clara Clausnitzer), Warner's Grocery

10. C. O. Porter Insurance, Shasta Electric (Seavy)

PINE ST. WEST OF DUNSMUIR AVE.

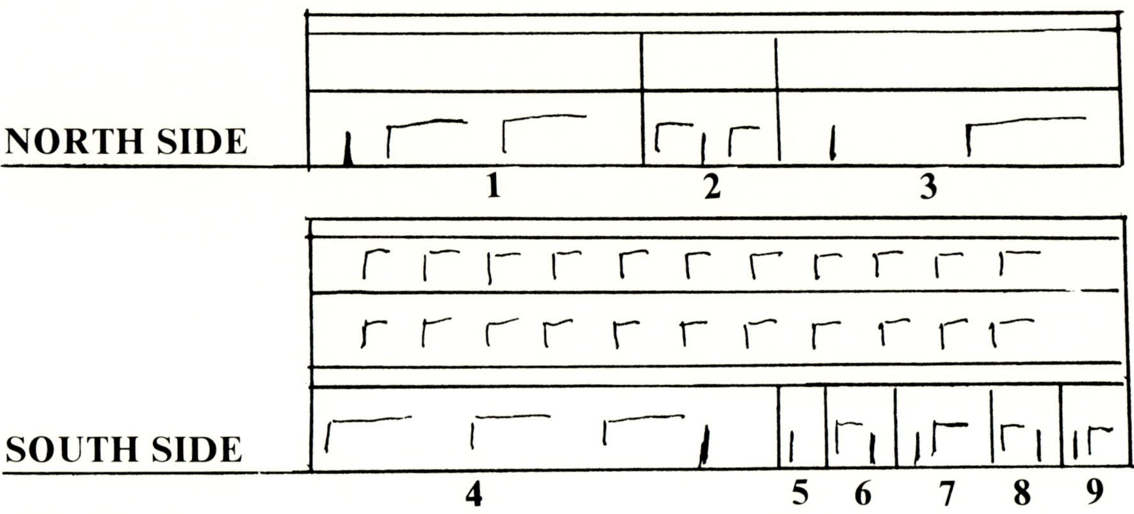

(Current businesses are listed first, moving from west to east)

NORTH SIDE

1. Laundromat: Belland's Shoes, U.S. Post Office

2. Dunsmuir NEWS: Storage room for Sprouse-Reitz, Man-fredi's Bakery

3. Garden Court back entrance

SOUTH SIDE

4. Sports 'N More back entrance

5. Old Entrance to Travelers Hotel used before the present lobby was built.

6. Lloyd's Barber Shop: Glover's Barber Shop

7. Ceci's Hair Unlimited: Beauty Shops owned by the following: Toni, Bonderson, Carol's, Marie Glover's Dress Shop, and the Telephone Office.

8. Video Shop: Golf Club Repairs, Water Company office

9. Sharing

8 & 9 previously were doctors' offices: John Steele, Paul Wright, E. Cornish, Malone

5700 BLOCK EAST SIDE DUNSMUIR (FLORENCE) AVE.

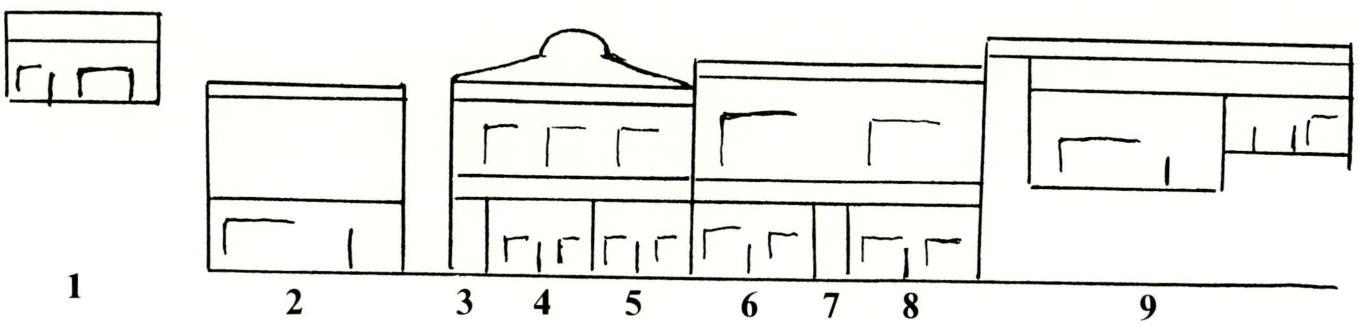

(Current businesses are named first, moving from north to south)

1. Texaco Service Station, owned presently by Ish Valenzuela; previously by Jim Lambert

2. Library: Offices of Dr. Anderson and Dr. Kleaver, Safeway Grocery, L. & L. Hardware

3. Corwin Building: Entrance to upstairs apartments, formerly doctors' offices; Hotel California

4. Sims Realty: Rainbow Club Bar; Restaurant

5. Humane Society Thrift Shop

6. 7. 8. Erickson's: formerly Cethil Jones Building

6. Used Appliances: Ralston's Grocery, Purity Grocery, Morrison's Grocery

7. Entrance to upstairs apartments: Ada Armstrong's Dress Shop; Ruby Scharff's Dress Shop

8. Sears: Mannee's Drug Store; Cethil Jones Pharmacy; Morrison & Laughlin Meat Market

9. Dunsmuir Apartments: Dunsmuir Hotel restaurant and entrance to hotel; formerly, the back of the Weed Hotel.

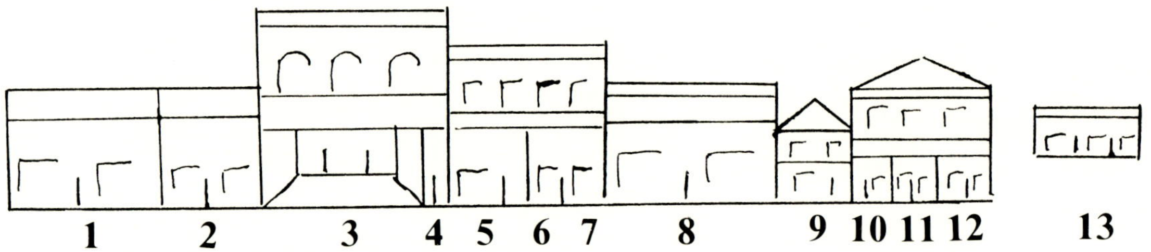

(Current businesses named first, moving south to north)

1. Garden Court Florist and Gifts: L & L Hardware; Porter's Jewelry Store; Cethil Jones Pharmacy and Fountain; Canyon Bakery

2. Print Shop: Sprouse-Reitz; Connor's Plumbing

3. California Theater

4. Entrance to Masonic Temple: also, doctors' and lawyers' offices

   (5, 6, & 7. Billie Lee Building)

5. Dunsmuir Auto Parts: Littrell Auto Parts; Western Auto; U.S. Post Office

6. Entrance to upstairs apartments

7. Siskiyou Vacuum Repair and Sales: The Spinning Wheel (Alice's Yardage); Copco Office; Cethil Jones Drug Store

8. Cornets:

   (In the spaces 3 through 8 stood Beem's Stable and Feed Store and Cleanatorium)

9. Residence

10., 11., 12. Unoccupied at present

10. Sam Verdi's Shoe Repair, in the past

11. Barber Shop: Dor-Lee Beauty Shop

12. Nick Aguilera's Sandwich Shop; Hal's Sandwich Shop

13. R and S Repairs and Greyhound Bus Stop (Ray and Sandy Brown): Shatzy's Shop and Greyhound Bus Stop; Cleaners; Bob Hall's Service Station

5800 BLOCK EAST SIDE DUNSMUIR
(FLORENCE) AVE.

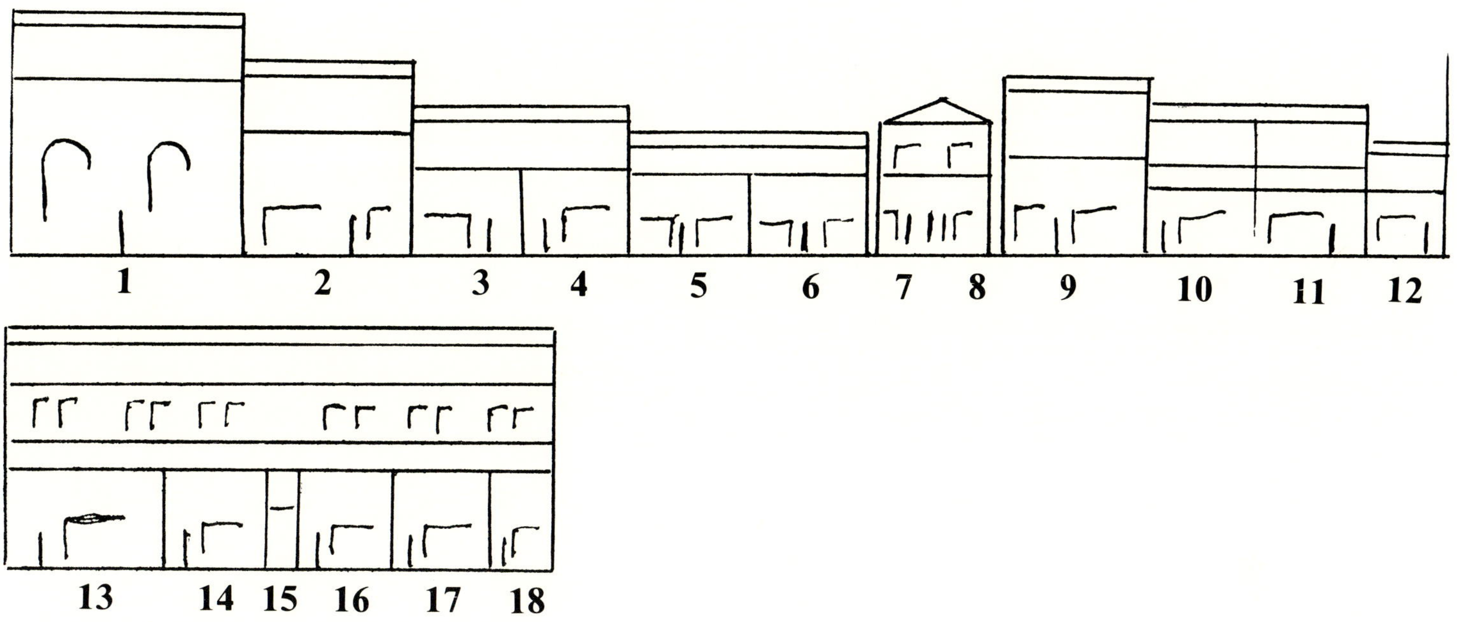

(Current businesses named first, moving north to south)

1. Old U.S. Post Office before 1925

1. Bank of America: originally the space on the south side of B of A was occupied by a series of dress shops; Helen from Mt. Shasta; Myhre; Porter and French; and DeWitt

2. Mr. G's: Sturgess; Lachenmeyers; Scearse and Frank; The Levis

3. Canyon Bakery

4. House of Sandwich: Paddy's Place Bar

5. Gift Shop of Dunsmuir Pharmacy: Steppin' Out Shoe Store; Gas Company Office; Dunsmuir Meat Company (Metzger and Mackle)

6. Dunsmuir Pharmacy (Jim Alspach); Petrovic's Pharmacy; variety store; Shannon; Army Surplus; Groceries; Mc-Enerney; Bascom

7. Stromsness and Jones Law Office; dress shops; Dorothy Tallerico and Mabel Naves; Ada Armstrong

8. Dunsmuir Centennial Office; law office for Jones; Gerald Shannon; Earl Weaver; and Postal Telegraph Office

(7 & 8 Levi Van Fossen Home, built in 1903 after the devastating fire of that year)

(9, 10, 11, & 12 spaces were the location of the Brick Garage, owned first by Montgomery and Swartout, later by Strand. Upstairs - Dougherty alterations; Bertie Lee Keene Dresses and Beauty Salon)

9. Dunsmuir Hardware: L and L Hardware; Young's Furniture Store; Collett's Department Store; Heath's Department Store. Upstairs - Carol's Beauty Shop.

10. Trading Post: Employment Office; Mac's Market

11. Health Food Store: Tommy Stott's Restaurant; Montgomery Ward Store

12. Clark's Insurance Office: Bauer's Insurance; Appliance Store (Huddle, J. Smith, Potter; Office for Brick Garage

13. Late Bloomers (sewing and lingerie): A series of dress shops; Crowes's, Evelyn Stevens, Sturgess, and Helen's; Red and White Grocery Store

14. Sally's Beauty Shop: "Pat" Patton's office

15. Entrance to the Mossbrae Apartments

16. Dr. Burr's Chiropractic Office: Part of Barnett's; Mrs. Voorhies, optometrist; photographers; Red Cross Workshop, Western Union Telegraph Office

17. Stereo Equipment and Toys: Part of Barnett's; Flower Shops, owned by the following: Fred and Betty Hale, Marian Briggs, Jo Welsh, George Signor, Hazel Peterson, and Minnie Armstrong

18. At present, vacant. In the past, Norman's Barber Shop; Dress Shop; Tallerico Shoe Repair; Cameron's Shoe Repair.

(16, 17, and 18 comprised Barnett's Floor Covering and Furniture.)

5800 BLOCK WEST SIDE DUNSMUIR (FLORENCE) AVE.

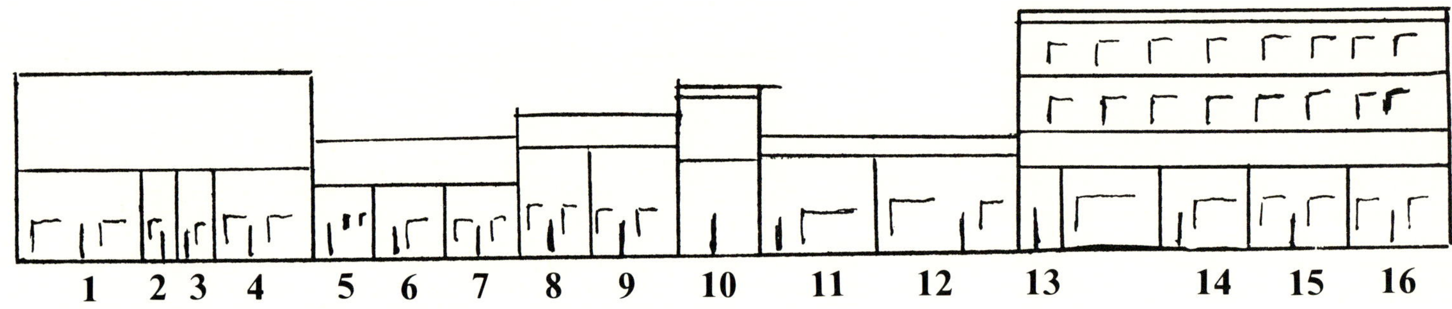

(Currently owned businesses listed first, moving south to north)

1. Blanca Rosa Restaurant: Donna and Patty's Restaurant; Garden Court Florists (Grace Renoud and Marjorie Young); Liquor and Sporting Goods (owned at first by Wheeler; later by Patterson); Meek's Grocery Store

2. Kitchen for the restaurant; Bauer's Insurance; Girdler's Insurance; Carlquist Lunch Counter and Sporting Goods.

3. Barber Shop (Chet Carlson and John Kish); Flower Shop (Laura Dodson, Erminia Marianni, Betty Hale); Beauty Parlor (Ina Macauley and Mrs. Kleaver).

4. Part of the Flamingo: Restaurant (first by Tommy Stott, then by Bogarts); Dom Sirianni's Insurance; Girimonte's Men's Clothes; George Beer's California Cafe.

5. Flamingo (owned by Tom Loftus; then Slimmer); Bunch's Barber Shop

6. Shoe Repairs: Sweet Shop (owned first by Joe Bianchi; later by Don Bottega).

7. Heilman's CPA Office: Huddle's Jewelry Store; also owned by Griffin, Muma's, Voorhies, and Evans.

8. Vacant now (1984): Nu-2-U; Jack's Shoes; Huddle's Jewelry; Mossbrae Pharmacy ("Beanie" and Nellie King).

9. Playpen Ceramics: Stars and Stripes Children's Clothes; Pon's Grocery; Fred Lloyd's Variety Store; Heath and Collett's Variety Store; IXL Men's Clothing (owned by Bill Welsh).

10. Fred and Shirl's Bar: Carquist's Smoke Shop; Cowley's People's Cash Grocery Store.

    (11, 12, 13, and 14 was the location of Talmadge's Auditorium, destroyed by fire in 1921.)

11. Kids' Caboose (children's clothing); Siskiyou Appliance (Jack & Evelyn Stevens and Bill Murphy); Ben Slimmer's Furniture Store; Restaurants owned by Ch. Carlquist, Byron Long, Gus Econome, and S. Buzzalero.

12. Leather Shop: Golden Rule Department Store (Harry Harper, Sr. and Jr., and Mr. Brown).

13. Entrance to the Travelers Hotel and Lobby

14. Travelers Coffee Shop

15. Amber Lounge: Drug Store operated by the following: Petrovics, Cone, Gooch.

16. Sports N' More: Big Liquor and Sporting Goods; Eherenman's Hardware; The White House Department Store.

5900 BLOCK DUNSMUIR
(FLORENCE) AVE.

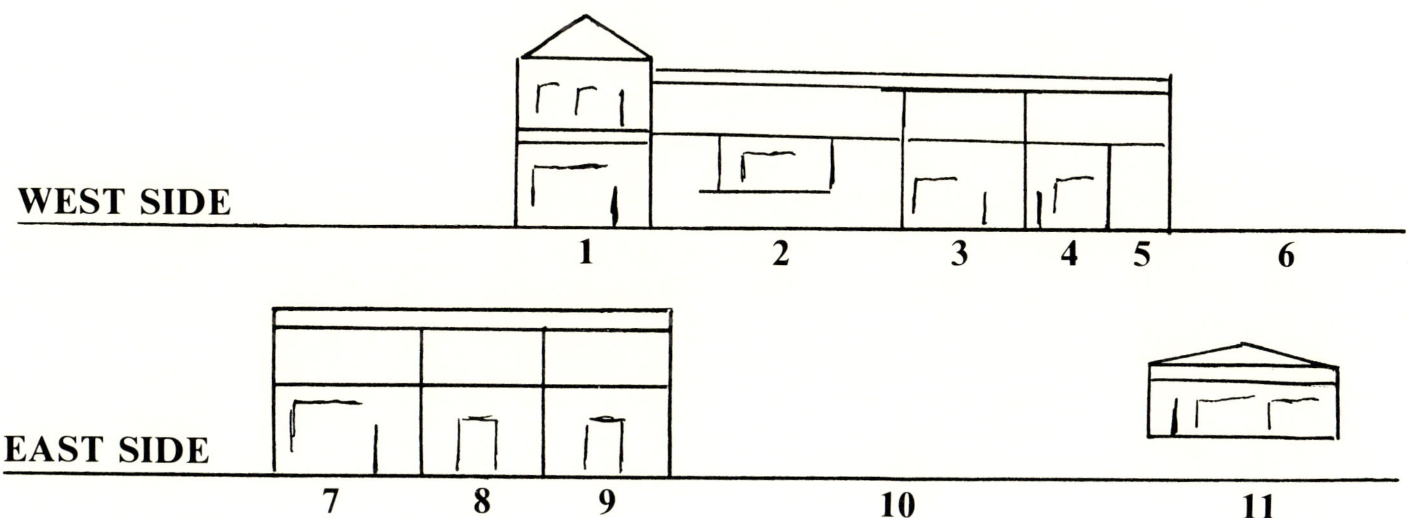

(Currently owned businesses listed first, moving south to north)

WEST SIDE

1. Mrs. Ogburn's Lunch Counter (at present, a residence)

2. Parking lot: Commercial Garage; proprietors, first Jack Wyatt; then, Roscoe Kimble.

3. City Office: Herb Gordon Bar; Sprouse-Reitz

4. City Office

5. Dunsmuir Printing: present owner, Joe Seely; formerly, Bill Hatfield

    (3, 4, and 5 spaces originally housed the Dunsmuir *NEWS*: owners in this location, first, Chap Wentworth; then Carl Clements)

    (4 and 5 housed Young's Furniture Store)

6. Parking Lot: Associated Service Station; owners, Ray Kick, "Pat" Patton, La Lawrence Stewart.

EAST SIDE

7. City Hall, Justice Court, Council Chamber

8. Fire Trucks

9. Fire Trucks: formerly, moving back in time, apartment occupied by the Harry Bender Family; The Dugout (DHS Recreation Center); Yount's Appliances; Belnap's Restaurant; Fisher's Restaurant; Mrs. Chapman's Millinery Shop.

10. On this space, formerly, the residence of "Fine Day" Decker

11. Burger Barn: formerly, Standard Service Station

5700 BLOCK SACRAMENTO AVE.

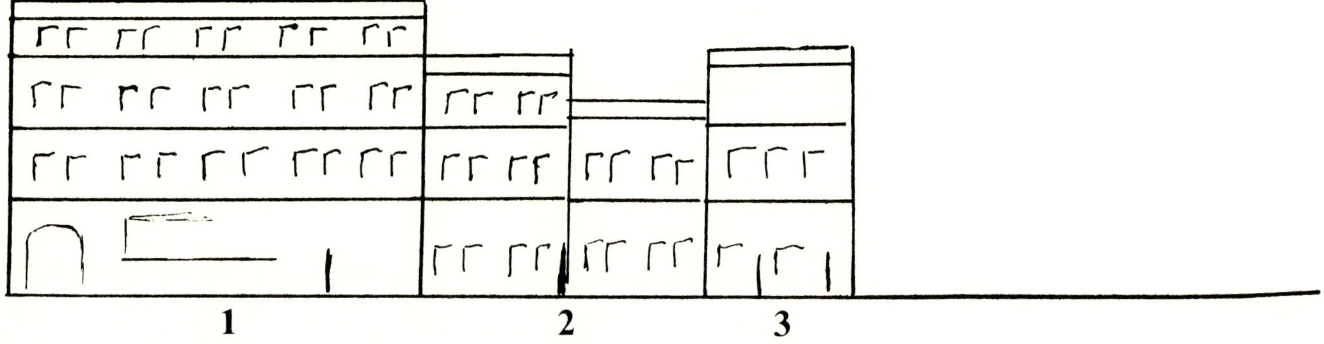

(Current businesses listed first, moving south to north)

1. The Depot Pizza Parlor: Rubidoux — Pete Baccilieri's Travel Agency; Hotel Weed Lobby and Restaurant

2. Bradley Apartments: formerly the Weed Annex

3. The Rostel Building, perhaps Dunsmuir's oldest building: Art Gallery; Dance Studio; Chinese Store.

All buildings north of the Rostel Building were destroyed by the 1924 fire, a full account of which appears in Part Three, the Chapter entitled, DUNSMUIR: A SURVIVOR.

5800 BLOCK SACRAMENTO AVE.

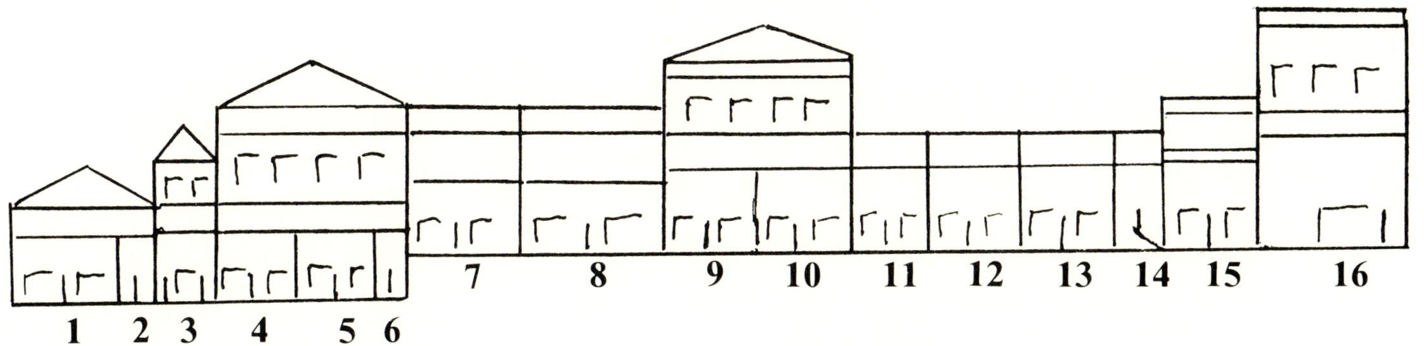

(Present day occupants listed first, moving south to north)

1. S and J Parking Lot: Ralston's Grocery; Chinese Restaurant

2. Barber Shop: Roy Huffman

3. Interior Decorating Shop (Tiffy Burr): Castro's Barber Shop; the Smoke House (Talmadge and Wyatt)

4., 5., and 6. Tillotson's Garage: formerly, Branstetter Building; Lodge Rooms upstairs.

4. Young's Furniture; Wards Furniture

5. Dunsmuir Meat Company: Mezger-Mackle; Kirkendahl

6. Wheeler's Exclusive Ready-to-Wear

7. Monday's: formerly, Finney's Fix-It Shop; Eherenman's Groceries and Hardware.

8. Woodmon's Contractors; Joe Ailes Contractor; Levi's Department Store; McCarvell's Shoe Department.

9. Motto's Bar

10. Restaurant: Lancasters; Pon's

(9 and 10 location at one time of the Strand Theater)

11. Chain Saw Shop: Chinese Restaurant; Drug Store (Ben Gooch; H. L. Huntington)

12. Restaurant: Ice Cream Parlor (Hunt's, Kilbourne and Batchelor's.

13. Factory Outlet: Girimonte Men's Clothes; Scarce & Frank; Burgess Men's Clothing.

(14, 15, 16 structures were destroyed by fire. Presently, Better Homes Realty is located on the corner where The Palm Cafe once stood.)

14. Jewelry: Nunamaker & Carlquist; Hufaff & Carlquist

15. Reception Billiard Parlor (Hollis, Chamber, Wheeler)

16. Palm Bar (Tom Loftus) and Palm Cafe; C. E. Wickes; Rooms upstairs.

5900 BLOCK SACRAMENTO AVE.

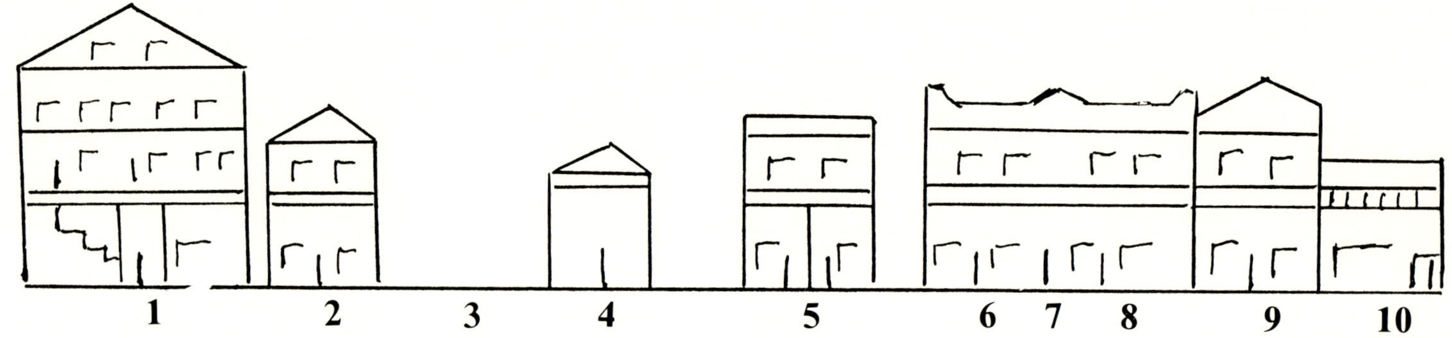

(Moving from south to north)

1. Young's Funeral Parlor on the ground floor; the Young home above.

2. Sellaro's Shoe Repair Shop (destroyed by fire).

3. Eagles' Parking Lot: formerly Mrs. Williams home and rooms, destroyed by fire.

4. Eagles' Hall: Andreatta's Grocery; Ammirati's Grocery.

5. Apartments

6. Army Surplus Store: Girimonte's Clothing; F. and P. Clothing Store.

7. Entrance to Riverside Hotel.

8. Pontier's Grocery, restaurant.

9. & 10. Ruben and Darlene's Market (also known as S & J Market. Formerly, Joe Bado & Sam Mazzie's Market; Andreatta's Market.

10. Del Youtsey's Storage; Bowling Alley; Bitonti's Tailor Shop.

DUNSMUIR FIRE DEPARTMENT

By
REVA P. COON

Research by
NICK MELO

This chapter will touch upon highlights only of the history of the Dunsmuir Fire Department. It is this writer's hope that someone will take the foregoing statement as a challenge and write a book, *The Gallant Ones.*

What you are about to read is the story of almost 500 valiant men willing and ready to help others in desperate need. Hats off to the D.F.D. men who risked life and limb

for the people of Dunsmuir!!

The first group of firemen was organized in August, 1897, under the name of the Dunsmuir Volunteer Fire Company. The company was to function under the auspices of the Dunsmuir Improvement Club and under the direction of Fire Chief Abe L. Huff. The men who signed and agreed "to answer all fire alarms and obey all orders" are listed below:

Studying the names above, one notes that several names are found today as names of streets.

It was not until January 18th, 1963, that the Dunsmuir Fire Protection District was established, and that after a long, hard struggle. Six or seven times, the voters defeated the proposal to form a fire district. Voters finally saw the dire need but only after the county had stated that county fire trucks would no longer be dispatched to do what Dunsmuir fire trucks should do. Below appears the charter granted by the State of California.

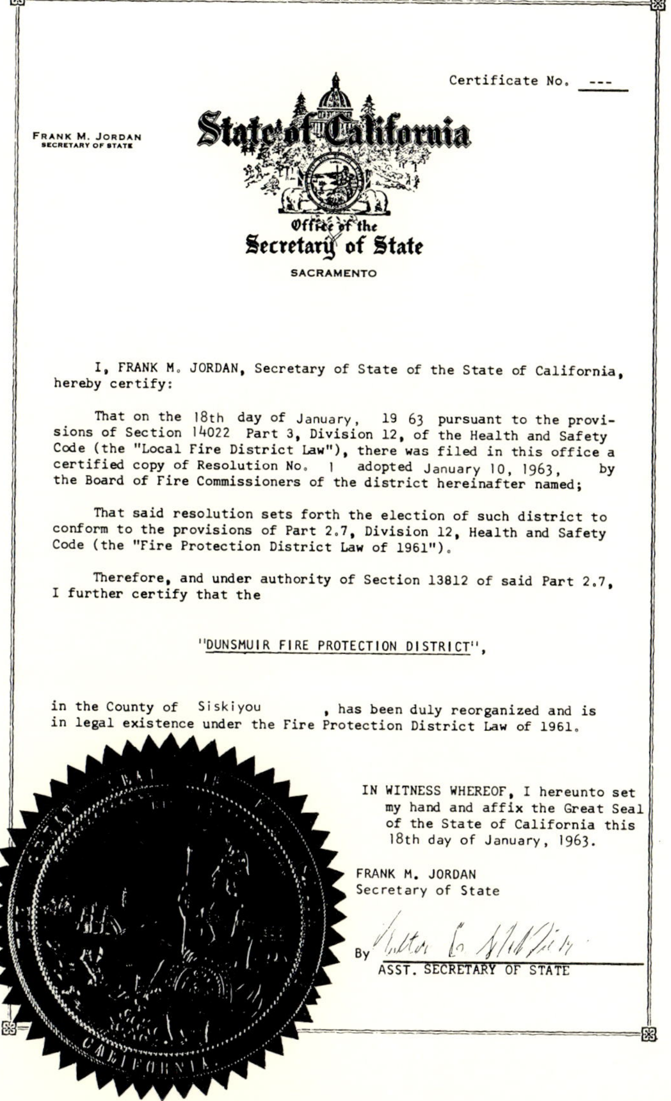

Certificate No. ----

State of California

FRANK M. JORDAN
SECRETARY OF STATE

Office of the
Secretary of State

SACRAMENTO

I, FRANK M. JORDAN, Secretary of State of the State of California, hereby certify:

That on the 18th day of January, 19 63 pursuant to the provisions of Section 14022 Part 3, Division 12, of the Health and Safety Code (the "Local Fire District Law"), there was filed in this office a certified copy of Resolution No. 1 adopted January 10, 1963, by the Board of Fire Commissioners of the district hereinafter named;

That said resolution sets forth the election of such district to conform to the provisions of Part 2.7, Division 12, Health and Safety Code (the "Fire Protection District Law of 1961").

Therefore, and under authority of Section 13812 of said Part 2.7, I further certify that the

"DUNSMUIR FIRE PROTECTION DISTRICT",

in the County of Siskiyou , has been duly reorganized and is in legal existence under the Fire Protection District Law of 1961.

IN WITNESS WHEREOF, I hereunto set my hand and affix the Great Seal of the State of California this 18th day of January, 1963.

FRANK M. JORDAN
Secretary of State

By
ASST. SECRETARY OF STATE

Not only do firemen fight fires, they do many things for the community as well. In the early years, the firemen took over the city band which had won for itself quite a reputation. The department had badges made especially for the band members: the fireman's badge with a harp thereon. On another occasion, when the City Hall flagpole rope needed to be replaced, it was installed by the firemen. Somewhat later, the firemen, answering the cry of the town baseball team for a sponsor, assumed the support and thereby gained some good firemen in the bargain. The firemen have also been enthusiastic participants in Dunsmuir parades highlighting town celebrations. These examples simply serve to indicate the variety of service to the community by the Fire Department.

Life in the fire department is not always serious. At one time the Royal Order of Billy Goats was organized, sheer fun its only purpose. Application for membership posed fifteen wild questions like the following: What do you use water for? Are you 100% American? Who is your favorite bootlegger? Do you play pinochle? There were ten charter members.

Fire alarm! Two engines dash to River Avenue; a brush fire. The fire was extinguished, thereby preventing it from spreading up the hillside. Trucks back in fifteen minutes. A routine run for the firemen.

Siren! Dash to the fire station! The engines roll to a flue fire. Back in twenty minutes. Just another call.

Siren! There goes the volunteers' hope for a quiet evening. Race to the station, man the trucks and go to the blaze in the liquor store at the head of Jail Hill. In this fire a fireman lost his life. He was the fire-police officer; he was in the street directing traffic down Dunsmuir Avenue (Florence, then). The firemen inside were wearing protections against the burning liquor, and so they were safe. However, Belnap, the fire-police officer, being outdoors, was thought to be safe and wore no protective gear. The clouds of smoke rolling from the burning liquor was toxic, and so Belnap was overcome by smoke inhalation from which he never recovered. The fountain downtown right near the spot where the fireman was stricken was erected by friends in his memory. Just another night for a volunteer fireman?

In 1941, Mrs. Steele, widow of Dr. John Steele (tragically drowned in a hunting accident), presented the Fire Department with a resuscitator. She expressed the wish that the equipment be made available to the people of Dunsmuir and vicinity.

Siren! Not for a fire this time. A child has fallen into the river. The firemen dash to aid in the search. Five-year-old Eugene Hurley had fallen into the high water of the Sacramento — unusually high, for it was mid-May. When the child was found, the firemen worked tirelessly for hours to revive him. The child's body was taken from the river at about 3:45 p.m. Heart action was discernable. Several firemen led by Fireman Jesse Blackburn, assisted Dr. E. A. Opacity in administering resuscitation. They worked patiently and unrelentingly for three hours on the bank of the river; then removed the child to the hospital, all the while continuing efforts to revive him. Their efforts were in vain! Even so, the parents, one week later, publicly expressed their gratitude to the firemen. Another day for a dedicated fireman!

On the night of September 25, 1944, the Weed Hotel was completely gutted by a conflagration. Firemen, in a dramatic action, saved two people from death in the fire. Austin Badger, an S.P. brakeman, having gone to his room on the fourth floor of the hotel to get personal belongings, was trapped there. Responding to his call for help, the firemen ran up the department's longest ladder, but it was not long enough to reach Badger. Fireman Jim Murdock cautiously mounting the large ladder, carried a short ladder with hooks on one end. Murdock, reaching the top of the ladder, handed the smaller ladder up to Badger. It was long enough, but the hooks turned the wrong way. The smaller ladder was sent to the ground to have the hooks reversed. In the meantime, the fire was growing in intensity; and, as the flames drew threateningly near, Badger hooked one leg over the ledge and leaned as far out as possible. Soon the ladder with the hooks turned the right way was brought up and hooked over the window ledge. For a few tense moments a cloud of dense smoke hid the man; but, when he was again visible, he was safely on his way down. Jim Murdock and Harold Kramer had placed themselves in a window on the third floor below the trapped man and had steadied the ladder as he climbed down to safety. No time for cheering, for the firemen were rushing to rescue a woman trapped on the fourth floor of the Sacramento Avenue side of the hotel. Miss Blanche Fowler was rescued in the same manner as Badger; however, this time, Jim Murdock was assisted by Clyde Jordan. Together they went up the long ladder, climbed in a third story window, and steadied the shorter ladder so that Miss Fowler could escape, all the while being reassured and urged on by Murdock. The three firemen, Murdock, Kramer, and Jordan, received the highest praise from witnesses to the daring rescue. Just another day in the life of a volunteer fireman!

In more recent years, the expert care of the personnel on the Dunsmuir Fire Department Rescue Squad has brought prompt life and death aid on many occasions to victims in need of medical treatment. Many people have benefited from and are appreciative of the comfort and physical aid the Rescue Squad has rendered.

On Engine: Clyde Jordan

Back Row:
  Jesse James
  Jim Murdock
  Nick Melo
  Jack La Barre

1st Row:
  Steve Abgaroff
  Kenny Griffith
  Elmo Trafton
  Bill Cravens
  Herbie Willman
  Delbert Stafford

2nd Row:
  John Petty
  Stan Burlingame
  Loran Dietrick
  Chief Jim Lambert
  Dick Murdock
  Jesse Blackburn
  Wilbur Jordan
  Larry (?) Martin
  Don Banks
  Don Fauber
  Boyd Cravens
  Harold Kramer
  Harley Stoffel

Pictured are:

Front, left to right:
  Willie Osborne, Driver
  R. L. Kenoyer, Chief
  S. A. Nystrom, Asst. Chief
  Ralph Dorst, Lieutenant
  Ron LaRue, Lieutenant/Master Mechanic
  David A. Van Heest, Secretary/Fire Marshal
  Ish Valenzuela, Captain
  Pat Whitten, Fireman
  L. E. Thunborg, U.S.F.S.
  Ray Rivera, Fireman

Top, left to right:
  R. K. Bigard, Fireman
  Gary C. Newman, Sr. Captain/EMS Officer
  A. D. Nelson, Firefighter
  Jim Evans, Fireman

Not shown are:
  D. C. Fauber, Driver
  S. K. DeClusin, Lieutenant
  Francis Seitz, Driver
  Mark Valenzuela, Lieutenant
  Scott Robinson, Fireman
  John Stafford, Fireman
  R. T. Thompson, Fireman
  J. D. Robinson, Fireman
  T. L. DeBrueler, Fireman
  A. M. McGuire, Fireman

Left to right:
  David A. Van Heese, EMT-IA
  S. A. Nystrom, Asst. Chief
  Ron LaRue, EMT-IA
  Gary C. Newman, EMT-IA/EMS Officer
  Ralph D. Dorst
  Willie Osborne, EMT-IA

Not shown are:
  D. C. Fauber
  Mark Valenzuela
  John Stafford, EMT-IA
  Scott Robinson

FIRE DEPARTMENT IN THE '40's

DUNSMUIR FIRE DEPARTMENT 1984

DUNSMUIR FIRE RESCUE SQUAD

39

Dunsmuir's fire chiefs have been the following men:

Abe Huff, first chief starting in 1897
Schnebele
J. F. McDill, served for eight years
Al Wilkins, held the position for 7 years
Art Pickthorn, 1931 to 1937
Harold La Due, 1937 to 1946
Jim Lambert, 1946 to 1965
Nick Melo, 1965 to 1977
Bob Kenoyer, 1977 to ....

Keeping abreast of the times, the fire department welcomed the first female to the force on July 5, 1983. A. D. Nelson, known as Dianne, expressed great enthusiasm in serving the community as a volunteer firefighter. She is the regular day shift dispatcher for the Fire Department and the Dunsmuir Police Department. She began dispatching for Dunsmuir on 01/26/81. When asked why she wanted to join the Fire Department, she read the following:

"What is a fireman?

He's the guy next door.

He's a man's man with the sharp memory of a little boy who never got over the excitement of engineers, sirens, smoke, and danger.

He's a guy like you and me with hopes, worries, and unfulfilled dreams.

Yet he stands taller than most of us . . . he's a fireman.

He puts it all on the line when the bell rings.

A fireman is at once the most fortunate and least fortunate of men.

He's a man who savors life because he has seen too much of death.

He's a gentle man because he has seen too much of the awesome power of violent forces out of control.

He's a man responsive to a child's laughter because his arms have held too many small bodies that will never laugh again.

He's a man who appreciates the simple pleasures of life . . . hot coffee held in numb unbending fingers . . . the flush of fresh air pumping through smoke and fire convulsed lungs . . . a warm bed for bone and muscle compelled beyond feeling . . . the comraderie of brave men . . . the divine peace of selfless service and a job well done in the name of all men.

He doesn't wear buttons, wave flags, or shout obscenities; and when he marches, it is to honor a fallen comrade.

He doesn't preach the brotherhood of man . . . he lives it . . ."

—Author Unknown

***

For the members of the Fire Department, this piece expresses their feelings about why they are volunteer firemen.

The City of Dunsmuir salutes its Fire Department!

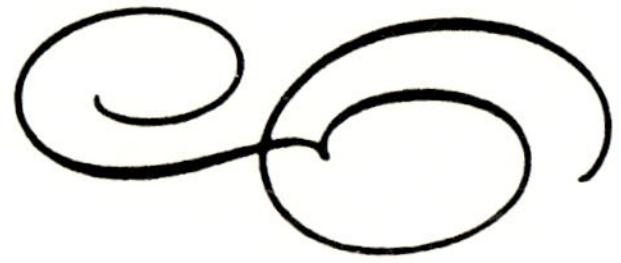

DUNSMUIR POLICE DEPARTMENT

Dunsmuir has been fortunate to have had a relatively crime-free existence although there have been occasions when murder, fighting, robbery, and arson have occurred. However, the town still enjoys a quite lawful existence compared to other areas, and life for its citizens has been relatively safe and pleasant. This situation is partly due to the efficiency and dedication of the Dunsmuir Police Department through the years. The force has always been small, but there have been many brave and dedicated men, and women, who have served the city.

Some of the police chiefs are Frank Daw (see chapter on "Disasters"); Allen B. Cottar (later became Siskiyou County Sheriff), Leland Clark, Collins, Phillip Summers, Eliseo Roy Zanni, John Arnold Richardson, Edmond Jack Gillespie, John R. Rowland, and Vernon Wederbrook.

The chiefs have been assisted by good men and women who chose to take less pay in a small city police force in order to live in this area, rather than join a police force in a more metropolitan area.

The people of Dunsmuir salute these fine people.

Photo — Grace Harris

"HOME OF DUNSMUIR'S FINEST"

DUNSMUIR RECREATION DISTRICT

A Recreation Committee first met on February 16, 1944; it was funded by donations from the Dunsmuir High School, the Dunsmuir Elementary School, and the Roseburg Foundation. After summer activities, in 1945, the first priority of business was repairing the swimming pool and making plans to purchase it from Joyland. The Dunsmuir Recreation District (DRD) was formed by the election of June 4, 1946 under the Public Resources Code of the State of California.

In April, 1953, at the request of the City Council, the DRD signed a five-year lease with a five-year option on the Ball Park and the City Park. There was one condition: the District was to erect four more light poles and furnish lights for night football by August 1. The DRD was to pay out all moneys and receive all financial returns for the use of the park.

Nineteen fifty-six saw the installation of light guards and a cedar fence around the Ball Park. In February, 1960, the DRD signed a 25-year lease to the Ball Park. There was a sub-lease to the Lions to build a community center building on the parking lot. The DHS shop class, in 1962, built a new dugout for the Ball Park. In the same year, the Dunsmuir Machine Shop built eight metal bleacher sections. In 1963, the Lions gave the DRD the community building. The city crew furnished the labor to effect a new parking lot.

After the community building roof collapsed in 1966, the city turned over $25,000 to DRD to rebuild the structure. In 1968, the district partly leveled the football field and reseeded for a new sod. The same thing was done seven years later.

Over the years, grants have provided the moneys, willing hands the labor for expanding, beautifying, and improving the City Park. As part of this work was the installation, to the west of the community building, of the Dunsmuir Fountain, a gift to the city in 1886.

The community building has been the center for social, cultural, educational, civic, and sports activities. There have been wedding receptions, art shows, many different classes, voting precincts, dances, and the annual Doll Show, Craft Fair, and Toy Fair — all the latter presented by the Dunsmuir Recreation District.

Photos by Grace Harris

FRIENDS AND NEIGHBORS

This old photo from the Dunsmuir Recreation District shows the Dunsmuir pool in its original incarnation as an attraction at Joyland. The wooden diving towers and old cars are gone, but the pool remains a big part of summer for Dunsmuir kids — and their parents.

Almost 50 Years of Keeping Cool

What's blue and white and contains 400,000 gallons of chlorinated water — plus a few dozen screaming and happy kids?

Obviously, it's the Dunsmuir Memorial Pool, which since 1928 has helped cool off parents and children alike on the blazing-hot summer days typical of Dunsmuir.

The Dunsmuir pool, one of the largest outdoor pools in the north state, has become an institution. It's more or less replaced the old swimming holes on the Sacramento River which are now left to fishermen and only a few adventurous souls.

Up until the time the pool became public property in the mid-1940s, Dunsmuir had two major swimming holes in the river — one at Shasta Retreat, one under the highway bridge. The Shasta Retreat hole, at the end curve of Hart Avenue, was popular as late as 1944, when floats roped off sections of the river and sand was trucked in to improve the "beach."

The Dunsmuir pool, which is 25 yards wide and 50 yards long, was originally constructed in 1928 by Frank Talmadge,

owner of Joyland, the entertainment complex located near the city park.

The Dunsmuir City Council leased the entire park, except for the ballgrounds, to Talmadge in September 1928 for five years. He was to improve the park grounds with picnic tables and a playground, and install the pool on his Joyland property.

Pictures from the Joyland ear show the pool much as it is today, except for the lack of a fence. The old wooden diving towers and the antique cars parked in front give away the age.

When Joyland shut over ten years later, the pool sat unused, but the idea of a swimming pool was still on Dunsmuir's collective mind.

One 1943 suggestion was to install a new pool near the railroad yard, to take advantage of "a constant supply of steam" for heating.

Through the work of the Dunsmuir Elementary School PTA and the Dunsmuir Lions Club, the pool was purchased from O. F. Crenshaw and "Slim" Davis with a combination of donations and public

funds. One old newspaper says the money came from fees paid by residents of the Dunsmuir Elementary School District.

A committee painted and cleaned the town's new pool, and a contest was held for the best name. "Dunsmuir Memorial Pool" was chosen in 1945, "in memory of those who gave their lives and kept the Bill of Rights intact."

The new pool was dedicated at a Fourth of July ceremony with many contests, the *Dunsmuir News* reported.

The pool was also the beginning of the Dunsmuir Recreation District, which was approved in 1946 election.

Operation of the pool was still not in the black, however. A canvassing drive was begun by the Lions Club in September of 1946 to help pay off the purchase price and operation fees.

By October of 1946, the Lions had helped raise half of the $4,500 goal; and the pool happily opened in June 1947 — and has stayed open every summer since.

(Thanks to Mildred Lockart for the research.)

Sketch by John Signor

DEDICATION STATE HIGHWAY BRIDGE DUNSMUIR
COPYRIGHT 1916 BY LAWLESS PHOTO SISSON CAL

Dedication of Highway Bridge - 1916
North Dunsmuir

45

DUNSMUIR LIBRARY

By
Sharon Hall and Joyce Reigel

In an 1890 *San Francisco Chronicle*, a news item refers to a "reading room and library maintained by railroad men."

In December of 1917, the library became a branch of the Siskiyou County Library system.

Records show that in 1920, the Dunsmuir Library was in the Candy Store and was looked after by DuBose and Kilborn. The librarian at the S.P. Club Room was Mr. Scott.

In 1922, Mrs. Hope T. Winkley was the librarian. The library was in the Methodist Church, located where the Texaco station is now. The church burned in April, 1924. In September, 1924, a room was rented from F. B. Van Fossen for $15.00 per month "until a new City Hall is built." The library moved into upstairs of the City Hall on December 1, 1925, and later moved to the lower level.

Mrs. Bertha Woolley was Librarian from 1922-1928. The P.T.A. held a "Library Book Shower" in April 1928.

Mrs. Clara Hanna was appointed Librarian on May 1, 1928, serving until her death in 1953.

Mrs. Leta Taylor Bectel was appointed Librarian in 1953 and resigned April 14, 1962.

Librarian Ada Wilson was appointed on April 16, 1962, and resigned October 31, 1973.

Mrs. Reta Matthias was appointed on November 1, 1973 and retired in October, 1981. At that time Joyce Reigel was appointed and is currently the Librarian.

In 1972 the Chamber of Commerce started a library fund with one of its members making the first donation. In 1975 an accumulated $2,500.00 was given to the City as a down payment on the building at 5714 Dunsmuir Ave. The dedication was held on May 22, 1977. This new building was made possible by the citizens, former citizens, the City, the Chamber of Commerce, and Siskiyou County working together.

In January, 1984, Friends of the Dunsmuir Library was formed as a support group to help in the planned expansion of the library into the unfinished half of the building at 5714 Dunsmuir Avenue.

Sources of information: Siskiyou County, Dunsmuir Library, Library Committee of 1972.

DUNSMUIR CITY GOVERNMENT
Incorporated 1906

CUMULATIVE LIST OF MAYORS
(Unofficial)

TERM	TITLE	CLERK
1909	Levy, A., Trustee	Parker, A. E.
1910	Albaugh, F. M.	"
1911	Connolly, Trustee	Albaugh, F. M.
1912		"
1914	Walker, F. M., Trustee	
1915	Malone, G. E. Trustee	Allen, Elmer E.
1916	Walker, F. M., Trustee	"
1920	Wilkins, S. J., Trustee	Schnebelle, G. H.
1925	Cornish, Trustee	Hawkins, E. H.

1927 reference to trustees & board of directors became mayor & councilman.

Records from 1927 to 1941 missing.

TERM	TITLE	CLERK
1941	Renoud, Harry, Mayor	Hawkins, E. H.
1942	Kintgen, Mayor	"
1946	Colthart, Robert, Mayor	Huff, Chas. S.
1947	"	"
1948	Taylor, "Babe", Mayor	"
1950	Ailes, J. H., Mayor	"
1952	Lloyd, Fred O., Mayor	Beaughan, N. E.
	"	"
1956	Petrovic, Vic, Mayor	"
1957	Jones, Morgan, Mayor	"
1959	"	Cavin, Elizabeth
1960	McClintock, D., Mayor	"
1962	Anderson, D. R., Mayor	"
1964	Slade, J. C., Mayor	"
1966	Dewey, Robert, Mayor	"
1968	Jones, Morgan, Mayor	Lindt, P. W.
1969	Cosentino, John, Mayor	"
1970	Larson, Elmer, Mayor	"
1971	Morlock, Ray, Mayor	"
1971	DeBoer, Wayne, Mayor	"
1972	Maben, Claude, Mayor	"
1973	Rogers, Robert, Mayor	"
1974	Lovelle, E., Mayor	"
1975	Young, Ivan, Mayor	"

TERM	TITLE	CLERK
1976	Maben, Claude, Mayor	Wopschall, Ardith
1976 (June)	Renoud, Harry, Mayor	"
1978	Young, Ivan, Mayor	"
1979	Torgerson, Dora, Mayor	"
1980	Osborne, V. L., Mayor	"
1981	Blank, B. J., Mayor	"
1982	Thunborg, Margaret, Mayor	
1983	Seely, W. J., Mayor	Ritchie, Elizabeth
1984 (Apr)	Hill, Emmett, Mayor	"
1984 (Nov)	Dolf, Ron, Mayor	"

Photos by Grace Harris

MEMORIES OF DUNSMUIR

The little town of Dunsmuir
Lies nestled in the hills,
With a river running through
Beside railroad tracks laid there;

Mother Nature did her best
For Dunsmuir planted there;
She left Mt. Shasta standing by
To guard her day and night,
Like a parent guarding child.
She even let the sun and moon
Shine on the mountain fair
To paint her different colors,
Beautiful beyond compare,
For all to marvel at and thrill,
And to love her, remote and still.

She gave four seasons, too,
And in the quiet of the night
Drops snow on cedar, fir, and pine,
And makes each branch
A lovely, lovely sight;
Children race on sleds,
And their laughter fills the air.
In spring the hills are fragrant
With wild lilacs everywhere.

White dogwood blossoms splash the hills
Amidst the green of leaves.
The summers are a joy for tourists, children, all;
There's camping out and picnics,
Fishing, hiking, playing ball;
And Shasta lilies nod and call
To the tiger lilies tall.
In autumn time the hills around
Are cloaked in brilliant hues
When maple, oak, and dogwood trees
Each one out view the other.

So many memories run through this mind o' mine;
Tis a heavenly place with pleasant folk so fine.
Happy Birthday, Dunsmuir Town, Happy time.

— *By Mina Kimble (Mrs. Roscoe)*

R.R. Days Parade — Parade Marshal, R. P. Coon

The Shastones
(L. to R.) Brian Hembling, Del Poe, Bob Cervelli, Mike Christ

R.R. Days Parade — Centennial Caboose, built by Herm Kostiz

CHAPTER V

THE SERVICE CLUBS

James and Mildred Lockart

DUNSMUIR SERVICE ORGANIZATIONS

By
James and Mildred Lockart

The railroad came, bringing with it the many people necessary to support its project. A city was born — a dynamic, vibrant city — that soon attracted businessmen, merchants and entrepreneurs. Organizations dedicated to the improvement of business and living conditions appeared. Almost from its beginning, Dunsmuir was helped and guided by its service organizations.

THE WOMEN'S IMPROVEMENT CLUB

Many of the most effective early service organizations were women's clubs. One of these was called "The Women's Improvement Club." This group of dedicated ladies exerted all of the wiles inherent in their femininity to improve the cultural and physical aspects of their community. They quickly adopted the cause of a high school for Dunsmuir, and in 1911 two ladies, Mrs. Frank Van Fossen, Mrs. Herman Woodward, carried a petition to the County Superintendent of Schools at Yreka requesting a high school in Dunsmuir. Shortly thereafter, this group of inspired females celebrated by hosting a reception for the new High School Principal, Professor Briggs.

One treasurer's report of the Women's Improvement Club published in the *Dunsmuir News* of April 26, 1912, recounts some of their activities: painting school room, curtains for it; street signs, refreshments for high school reception, fixing school yard, buying reference books for high school. Their income was derived from May Day Dinner, Strawberry Social, Hard Times Ball, Art Exhibit, Amateur Night Picture Show, Teas, and Mock Trial.

No further records appear concerning the activities of this most fruitful club; however, the exercise of very little imagination projects its members into the "High School Mother's Club" whose formation was announced in the *Dunsmuir News* of March 7, 1919. Their stated purpose was: "To advance the welfare of the child in all directions." If success can be measured in terms of participation, this was indeed an instant one. By March 24, 1919 — only 17 days after its organization — this group had outgrown its meeting place.

The many meetings hosted by these ladies and the constant pressure on the citizens of the city undoubtedly hastened, if not caused, the building of the new high school. By August of their first year as a club, this group of determined mothers had become so powerful that they assumed responsibility for the construction of the new school auditorium.

The new high school building was on its way. The Mothers Club, having placed one of its members, Mrs. Sue Cornish, on the High School Board of Trustees, turned to other needs. They volunteered to clean up the elementary school — because there was no janitor; they hosted social events for children from ages 12 to 19, because there was nothing for the kids to do. Finally, the Mother's Club organized into the Parent-Teachers Ass'n., which still serves the city's schools; and though it may have a different name, the stated purpose of the organization remains the same.

The character and humanity of the early citizens of the City are clearly displayed in their willingness to form into groups to offer aid and assistance to their less fortunate fellows. Through the years, references are found to organizations formed for the purpose of alleviating suffering of other communities which have suffered disasters. The *Dunsmuir News* issue of April 28, 1906, carried the announcement of an organized group of citizens to "collect food, money, and clothing for San Francisco earthquake unfortunates."

During the years of the First World War, *Dunsmuir News* articles told of compassion demonstrated by our ladies:

5-25-1917. *"A branch of the Yreka Chapter of Red Cross was formed. G. A. Hutaff, Chairman; Mesdames C. O. Clarke and George Dickson, Vice-Chairmen; Alice Campbell, Secretary; Mason Bailey, Treasurer."*

4-5-18. *"Mrs. J. R. Eherenman, who has charge of the Red Cross surgical department, reports that 3503 of the 10,000 special #17 surgical dressings have been completed and will be finished in another month."*

5-24-18. *"Dunsmuir Branch of Red Cross has doubled its relief fund."*

8-2-18. *"Red Cross establishes a canteen to serve soldier boys and draftees while passing through Dunsmuir. There are only 20 stations in four western states. Donations gratefully received. The Mrses. Hutaff, Gardner, and Van Fossen in charge."*

The January 26, 1923 issue of the *Dunsmuir News* carries short articles announcing the birth of two organizations that have been a vital part of the City for over sixty years. The Dunsmuir Lions Club and the Dunsmuir Chamber of Commerce stand shoulder to shoulder through the years — forces for improvement of the business climate and the welfare of the citizens of the town.

THE LIONS CLUB

The Dunsmuir Lions Club organized around the principles of "full and hearty cooperation with all other civic clubs; to participate in all movements in the community which seek to promote any betterment — civic, industrial or educational, and any plans looking toward the elimination of class distinction." Officers selected for the first year:

F. B. Van Fossen

Dr. E. J. Cornish

G. B. Chambers

J. R. Eherenman

Officers not shown were Cethil Jones, Vice President; A. L. Shoupe, Secretary/Treasurer; C. E. Wicks, Lion Tamer; N. T. Crawford, Tail Twister; A. Leach and Dr. F. W. Evans, Board of Directors.

On November 11, 1923, the Club, presided over by the above officers, received its charter. The Dunsmuir Club — the only club north of Chico — was sponsored by the Oakland Lions Club.

Accomplishments during the first year include the following:

3-28-24: Will head clean-up/paint-up campaign. School children to be offered prizes for best front yard gardens. Mayor Wilkins addressed the club. He pointed out the need for a city scavenger and some method of compelling the citizenry to pay for collecting and disposing of trash and garbage. "People are still throwing debris under houses and into the street," he said.

4-18-24: Lions Club purchased a flag pole for the elementary school. At the same meeting it was suggested that merchants close from 12 noon to 3 P.M. on Good Friday.

The Chamber of Commerce and Lions Club played baseball game. The receipts were donated to the Boy Scouts.

5-2-24: A full-page ad was tekan in the *Dunsmuir News* to commend the Dunsmuir Fire Department in controlling a conflagration that destroyed the block of buildings on the north end of business district. Among those burned out was the *Dunsmuir News* which, notwithstanding, was still operating. "Congratulations to our paper" said the ad.

8-26-24: Lions Club collects $500 for Salvation Army.

9-26-24: Secretary appointed to draft resolutions and send them to metropolitan newspapers condemning untruthful news items carried recently about slides on Mt. Shasta and playing up the horrors of the mud flow on the McCloud side of the mountain. "Relatives," the article said, "are imploring residents to leave before disaster strikes."

On October 24, 1924 the Lions Club was responsible for the start of the 4-year "Love Affair" between Babe Ruth and the City of Dunsmuir.

At their meeting of that date, two baseball players from Weed — Elbert Felts and C. D. Painter — were visiting. They knew that Babe Ruth and his teammate, Bob Meusel, were in Portland for exhibition games and would be leaving for San Francisco shortly. On the spur of the moment, the idea was born to invite Babe and Bob to stop in Dunsmuir. At the urging of the Lions they telephoned Christy Walsh, Babe's Publicity Manager, with the proposition. He agreed to stop for a fee of $1,000. The Lions could only guarantee $300 and it looked as if the "King of Swat" would not be coming until Frank Talmadge offered to guarantee $750.

On the day of the Exhibition Game a half-day holiday was proclaimed — schools and businesses closed — and 800-900 people poured into the Ballpark. After Babe and Bob gave an exhibition of "long distance" hitting (some even going into the surrounding trees), two teams, composed mostly of Weed and Dunsmuir ballplayers, played a 7-inning game — Babe on the Dunsmuir team and Bob on the Weed team. A great time was had by all!

After the game the Lions Club treated Babe, Bob and Christy to a duck dinner and presented them with Life Certificates in Lionism. Then they attended a dance at Joyland and stayed until their train left. In a letter from them afterwards, they said what a wonderful time they had had and they would be back! Much publicity was given Dunsmuir as the only town to have the "pep" to invite them for exhibitions on their way to San Francisco.

While in Dunsmuir, Christy had told the Lions that Babe had a distinct horror of wearing anything but his "birthday suit" when he retired. A month later in Los Angeles, the trio attended their first Lions Club meeting as "Baby Lions," and there Babe was presented with a package from the Dunsmuir Lions — a beautiful red flannel nightgown. The *L. A. Times and Herald* had pictures of him with the nightgown and an article that said: "Not to be outdone by Mary Garden's open-air methods for reducing the waistline, Babe Ruth — in interests of better snoring — has launched a campaign against such useless encumbrances as nightgowns and pajamas. All along the exhibition trail, Christy and Bob have tried to convince Babe he should wear nightclothes. When the 'Roaring Lions' of Dunsmuir heard this, they pledged assistance, thus the nightgown presentation yesterday under the auspices of the L. A. Lions. Babe says an unexpected blizzard in L.A. might force him to wear it but he was against it!"

Six months later Babe spent a month in a New York hospital; and at his first press conference from the hospital, he said, "None of his surprises and cheering messages was more beautiful than a big box of roses that came all the way from California. Last winter he had played an exhibition game with Bob Meusel in Dunsmuir, a little mining and railroad town near Mt. Shasta. We happened to sock a few home runs up into the nearby pine trees and to give the folks a good show. Their population is less than 4,000 but their pep and hospitality is as big as all New York."

The next year Babe arrived in Dunsmuir for a 24-hour stay. He was met at the station by a large crowd of citizens and welcomed by the Mayor, then taken on a fishing trip. In the evening he appeared at the California Theatre and, among other things, presented the Championship Cup to the 1926 Dunsmuir High School football team.

In January of 1928, the Lions Club received a humidor from Christy Walsh. It was covered with pigskin and shaped like a football, and was inscribed with the names of "Tad Jones," Yale Football Coach, "Pop Warner," and "Knute Rockne." The base was inscribed with the name of the Club and the donor, Christy Walsh.

For the next sixty years the Dunsmuir Lions Club continued to support — or originate — ideas that would benefit the community; just as the appearance of Babe Ruth was the highlight of 1924, so other events highlighted nearly every subsequent year.

The summit performance for 1925 came in November. At a meeting of the San Francisco "Den," which met for the purpose of pledging support in entertaining delegates to the Lions International Convention to be held in San Francisco, each club was asked to bring a box containing samples of products from its community. Dunsmuir brought down the "house" when John H. Young, Secretary of Dunsmuir Lions, storde into the room garbed in fisherman's clothes — hip boots, hook-trimmed hat and all. He nearly broke up the meeting when he presented a nice catch of rainbow trout from the Sacramento River and two steelhead from the Klamath, plus a bottle of "The Best Water On Earth." At each plate was a bottle of mineral water from Soda Springs together with a glass containing orange juice. The bottles were uncapped at the table and poured into the orange juice — a most delectable drink.

During the balance of the decade this extremely active club (1) entertained International Governor Ben Jones of New Jersey; (2) participated with Siskiyou County and Southern Oregon Clubs in a unique display at International Convention. It contained revolving pictures of the north and south sides of Mt. Shasta. In addition were two cages, one housing mountain lions and the other, live quail; also, there were trout frozen in ice. The whole display was housed in a log cabin at the back of which was a projector showing points of interest from Crater Lake to Castle Lake. (3) Suggested the merchants of the City have a Christmas Opening. (4) At the request of Mt. Shasta Chamber of Commerce, agreed to support and work for a district college at Mt. Shasta. (5) Acting in conjunction with Chamber of Commerce, they managed to persuade the Highway Commission to complete construction of the highway from Shotgun Creek to the County line in one project rather than stretching work over a 2-year period.

Through the early years of the depressed "thirties," the Club continued to originate or support civic activities and for a time acted as a Chamber of Commerce. The return of better times in the late "thirties" and through the war years offered the Lions many challenging opportunities for service to the community. The Club did not forget the Lions Motto "We Serve." Nor did they lose their sense of humor.

In 1943, Dr. W. B. Mason won the Annual Liars Contest by telling of a rattlesnake that had become real friendly with him and had assisted in the capture of an intruder in his bedroom by wrapping its middle around the ankles of the intruder, its neck around the bedpost, and holding tight while extending its tail out a window and buzzing frantically for a police officer!!

Some of the club projects consumed several years in their completion, and some of them are still a part of the club activities. About 1956, the club acquired a small piece of land on Soda Creek. The place had been used as a campground or picnic spot by many, but had fallen into disuse. It was called "September Morn." The name was bestowed by a group of local matrons who camped by the creek for several nights. The picture "September Morn," at the time, was prominent in cultural circles. On the last morning before leaving for home, the four ladies bathed in the creek. One of them pointed to a flat rock that rose above the water level in the middle of the stream. "That might have been the place where the model posed for 'September Morn.' Why don't you demonstrate?" The challenged matron replied, "Oh, what the heck — there's just us girls." She climbed onto the rock and posed in the manner of the famous painting. (This is said to be the true story of the naming of a place.)

The campground has been improved and is used by civic groups for outdoor meetings. It is available to any organized Youth Group.

One of the projects during the "Fifties and "Sixties" was the building of a scout hut (for Boy and Girl Scout meetings). It was first erected at the north end of Castle Avenue but the State Highway Commission purchased the property for a right-of-way for the new highway. Using the money thus obtained, plus public donations and fund raising activities by the Lions and other civic organizations, the club rebuilt in North Dunsmuir just north of the swimming pool. In June of 1962, the Dedication Ceremony was held. Lion President, Gary Girdler, dedicated the building "To the Youth of the Community" but pointed out it was for use of all the people of the Dunsmuir area.

After operating the new building for several years, the Lions presented it to the City of Dunsmuir. It collapsed during a heavy snowfall in 1967 and was rebuilt with insurance money (and there it stands to this day). It is interesting to note that as the original building neared completion, funds ran out. Dave Anderson (then President) asked each Lion to donate the sum of $60. "It is," he said, "a chance to put your money where your roar is."

During the late "1960's" Lion President, Jimmie Murdoch, proposed the adoption of a Flag Program. It called for the Club to purchase flags and provide a means of flying them in front of businesses on specified holidays. The program was adopted, and it is an activity that is still at the forefront of the Lion year.

A call for used glasses was heard by the Club and action followed. In 1961, in cooperation with Lions of District 4 C1, one hundred thousand pairs of glasses were collected and sent to the eye clinic in Calcutta, India. This is still a project of the Dunsmuir Lions Club.

Every club needs a headquarters — a place to gather. Lion Pace Paletta had a dream. He said, "Let's take that old garage building behind the Chamber of Commerce office (we might lease it from the City) and remodel it into a club house." He repeated his argument for this project until he attracted the attention of a bunch of "live wires." The club house is now completed — a miraculous conversion of an old sheet metal garage — and the grounds around it have been cleaned up. A barbeque pit has been built and picnic tables installed, and this area now serves as the location for the Annual Railroad Days Barbeque, which is cooked and served by the members of the Club.

Cast of a Christmas Holiday play, sponsored by Dunsmuir Lions Club as a fund raiser, in approximately 1949 or 1950. It was staged at the Dunsmuir High School Gymnasium. Top row, left to right: 1-Delbert Luttrell, 2-Dorothy Luttrell, 3-Henry Schroeder, 4-?, 5-Robert Coon, 6-Paul McCune, 7-Buddy Lucero, 8-Don Donlap, 9-Paul Reginato, 10-"Red" Crowe, 11-Cliff Schwergel, 12-?, 13-?, 14-?, 15-?. Bottom row, left to right: 1-William Welsh, 2-?, 3-William I. Humphreys, 4-?, 5-Mrs. Bill Paul, 6-?, 7-Dorothy Kimsey, 8-Louise Estep, 9-?, 10-Diony Estep, 11-Mrs. "Bunny" Frye, 12-?, 13-Bunny Frye, 14-(Boy) David Estep, 15-Alan Cottar, 16-?, 17-?, 18-?, 19-Dick Bottega, 20-Dan Decker, 21-?.

—Photo courtesy of Louise Estep Phelps

CHAMBER OF COMMERCE

The Dunsmuir Chamber of Commerce — organized in 1923 with Chester O. Porter as its first president — immediately went to work. Their first attempt at the booster action that is a Chamber of Commerce characteristic was to suggest that dust or mud streets were not proper for a live, growing, young city. "The streets should be paved," they cried, "and cement sidewalks should be poured on the sides."

But these boosters were not satisfied with only one project. They adopted the cause of saving the large trees that bordered the highway coming into the City, and suggested that five miles of this timber be protected by law from the woodsman's axe. "It should be established as a memorial to veterans of the world war (WW I)," they maintained, "and an archway should be built across the entrance on each end."

They asked that the office of the California State Auto Ass'n. be located in Dunsmuir, but failed. The office was established in Yreka; however, at a later date a branch office was located in the city.

Feeling that the town had progressed to a point that made free delivery of mail a necessity, the Chamber of Commerce circulated a petition requesting the service and forwarded it to the U.S. Postal Department.

Never quite satisfied with the stastus quo, this body of Dunsmuir Boosters did the following:

1. Endorsed the idea of Community Chest for Dunsmuir.
2. Entered into an organization whose object was the promotion of the Pacific Highway (99 or now, I-5). Other cities were Sacramento, Placerville, Dixon, and Willows.
3. Instructed Secretary, Ted Hawkins, to write to Chamber of Commerce at Redding, Red Bluff, Weaverville, Mt. Shasta, Weed, and Yreka, asking them to participate in erecting and maintaining signs on the Redwood Highway (Highway 101) directing tourists to the Pacific Highway (now I-5).
4. Asked City Council to require that power poles be removed from Florence Ave. before streets are improved.

It is interesting to note that during the next several years a great deal of their talk and efforts were directed towards a special election — the issue being the establishing of a junior college in this area.

A report prepared by Secretary, Ted Hawkins, listed many accomplishments for the year of 1929, some of which were these: wrote answers to inquiries from 1127 people interested in the area; assisted the Southern Siskiyou County Good Roads Committee; in cooperation with Lions Club, installed a cabin for Boy Scouts at their Camp Na-Wa-Kwa in the Sierras east of Chico; promoted interest in creating a State Park at Castle Crags; hosted Governor Patterson of Oregon.

Knowing that the building and care of an airport rightly belonged to the Federal Government, the Chamber of Commerce actively promoted support in Dunsmuir and all surrounding cities in asking the government to take over the airport.

The close of 1932 also saw the demise of the Chamber of Commerce. Perhaps the pressure of keeping their own businesses afloat during the depressed years was all the responsibility merchants needed — and wanted.

The booster group (C of C) was reorganized in 1935 and functioned well during the presidency of Arthur Cravens. The latter was a hard-driving man blessed with a positive attitude — like a bulldog. He wouldn't let go of a project until it was successfully completed. But, the group again disappeared near the end of 1936 and was not heard from again until 1949. It was then reactivated by an organization known as "The Booster Club" who, believing that they could better serve the community under the name of "Chamber of Commerce," voted to change their name (but not their ideals) to the Dunsmuir Chamber of Commerce.

This civic organization assumed the promotion of "Railroad Days" and sponsored the Retail Merchants Ass'n. and other satellite organizations. Also, their big lighted Christmas tree in the center of town was a pretty sight for many years.

The new Chamber of Commerce quickly espoused any viable plan to improve the business and cultural aspects of the City. They voted to support the Southern Pacific Co. in its efforts to purchase the Pacific Fast Freight lines; through the Retail Merchants Ass'n. they established a Better Business Bureau and elected Dom Sirianni as its executive officer; they voted to support a chair lift for skiers on Mt. Shasta and appointed Chap Wentworth, owner/editor of the *Dunsmuir News*, to head a Steering Committee to coordinate surveys of the project and put them in final form to be presented to the public. The presidents of the Chambers of Commerce of Weed, Yreka, Mt. Shasta, Redding, and Dunsmuir, and McCloud Services District, plus John Reginato, Secretary of Shasta Cascade Wonderland Ass'n. were also on the committee. They were instrumental in getting an out-of-service steam engine, "Old 1727," which is now located by the ballpark.

The interests and activities of this very effective organization stretched far and wide. It was concerned about proper signing and caused signs advertising the City to be erected; an Industrial Development Committee was formed whose task was to gather information that could be used to attract light industry; because unemployment had begun to be an issue, this committee conferred with the Manager of the State Employment Office.

During this era of change, this booster group tackled every problem that was brought before it. Parking in the business district had long been a growing problem. These boosters voted for a feasibility study and an architect's drawing of an elevated platform to be built over Pine Street between the Bank of America building and the Dunsmuir Hotel.

Progress and Improvement have always been the motto of this group. Dunsmuir has been fortunate to have so many dedicated citizens.

JR. CHAMBER OF COMMERCE

Another club that shone brightly in local affairs for a time was the Junior Chamber of Commerce. First organized in 1940, the Club selected Al Marske as President; "Red" Adams as First Vice President; Nick Girimonte as Second Vice President; Lionel Stone, Treasurer; John Reginato, Secretary; Alva Nelson, Sergeant-At-Arms. With this slate of officers, the Jr. C of C embarked on a nearly continuous course of action.

(1) They held a dance — both as a fund raiser and for the solidifying effect on their membership.
(2) They voted to aid with Christmas entertainment for children, to sponsor a Town Basketball Team, and to sponsor a home talent show in order to raise funds for basketball team uniforms.
(3) In December of 1940 they produced a benefit show. The money obtained was distributed among needy families.

Thus, they completed their first year of existence. In 1941 they:
(1) Met with the Lions Club for the purpose of making plans for promoting the State Ski Jumping Championship Tournament to be held at Snowman's Hill.
(2) Were instrumental in conducting a successful scrap metal drive. Funds from this sale was to be used to buy equipment for the playground at the City Park.

With the coming of 1942, the club voted to undertake a defense and bond sale. They asked the businessmen to close from 12 noon to 12:15 to devote their time to the sale.

The membership was composed of younger men. Consequently, the manpower shortage that occurred during World War II depleted their membership to such an extent that the Jr. Chamber of Commerce ceased to exist for about 14 years. It was re-organized in 1956.

The service body initiated programs to help the ailing Junior Rifle Club and to purchase an electric scoreboard to be installed at the ballpark for the high school.

In 1956, at the request of the Railroad Days Committee, they accepted responsibility for organizing and conducting a Queen contest for the celebration. This is believed to be the first Queen contest for this event. Harold Fawcett was appointed chairman of the Queen Contest Committee.

From the Jr. C of C came a concordant organization — the wives of the Jaycees — called the "Jaycee-ettes." This ladies group saw a need for youth employment. Their President, Nancy Fawcett, instigated a program to help young people obtain summer and after-school jobs. A committee called Jaycee-ettes Organized Youth got and took requests for employment for youths that did not compete with adult labor. It was noted that the Jaycees had launched a Clean-Up, Fix-Up, Paint-Up campaign to beautify Dunsmuir, and it was felt that this project would provide some employment for the youngsters.

The measure of success of this project can be found in Mrs. Fawcett's report: "One hundred applications for work were received, and eighty-five placements made."

Again, the problem of younger men — working and raising a family, etc. — cut into the membership of this useful and active body. No further reference can be found of the Jaycees. It was a progressive body that the City could ill afford to lose.

DUNSMUIR
ROTARY CLUB

On September 30, 1950, the Dunsmuir Rotary Club was chartered at a formal dinner ceremony at Shasta Springs as the 7600th Charter Club into Rotary International.

Rotary began in a chicago office in 1905 when a group of young businessmen convened to become better acquainted and to help each other with their respective vocational problems. It soon spread through Chicago and soon became an International lunch hour organization of businessmen. Their main functions are: (1) Club Service; (2) Community Service; (3) Vocational Service; (4) International Understanding — brought about by exchange of experiences and ideas of businessmen all over the world (except Russia).

The spirit and membership of the Club in Dunsmuir developed to the point that in 1958 it took on the responsibility of hosting the First District Conference of Rotary International District 516. Over 550 members and their wives arrived by means of train, private automobiles, and planes.

In 1966 Dunsmuir again hosted District 516's annual conference — a remarkable tribute to the community of Dunsmuir to host such an event twice in less than 10 years. The theme chosen was a take-off on a then popular song, "Getting to Know You." However, this theme soon faded in preference to a more expressive idea, "Back To The Sticks In '66." It is still referred to as such and recalled with pleasant memories to this day, by old-time Rotarians.

Major projects in the life and experience of the Dunsmuir Rotary Club include the annual Pancake Breakfast held for fishermen and the community on the opening day of each trout season. The 29th annual breakfast is scheduled for the last Saturday in April, 1986. The breakfast has been the major fund-raising project for the Club and has enabled it to carry on its programs for scholarships, the building of shelters to provide protection for students while waiting to be picked up by school buses, international projects, and City Park playground equipment. In recent years the Club has helped sponsor a new Rotary Club in Weed and a South-Siskiyou Chapter of the Inner Wheel women's organization. Other civic contributions have been:

In 1952 Rotary gave 150 redwood street signs to the City which they had varnished and the names had been carved by Herman Kostiz. They also voted that year to present a Jr. Citizen's Award each year and send a boy to Boys' State.

In the years that the high school students have taken over the City Government for a day, the Rotarians have been their host for lunch. In 1951 they gave a police radio to the City and helped buy an incubator for the hospital.

Many years they have chosen a Rotary "Man of the Year" and have assumed the responsibility of the "March of Dimes" campaign.

Dunsmuir has been very active in international service. In 1974, Knut Egeland, a young Norwegian, spent a month in Dunsmuir as part of a District 516 "Christmas in California" project. In 1981-82 Erich Veit, a Swiss student, came to Dunsmuir while Dunsmuir students Julie Arno and Jeff Andresen spent the year in New Zealand and Finland, respectively. In 1983-84, Jeff's family returned the favor, hosting Antti Paavilainen, from Finland.

In 1957, the Dunsmuir Rotarians had the novel idea of offering two trout to members of every Rotary Club in the District that had 100% attendance in October. Seven clubs — including Dunsmuir — qualified, bringing up the District's average to 93.76%. Dunsmuir happily furnished and delivered 710 fish!

THE KEY CLUB

A stranger in Dunsmuir at the beginning of the sixth decade of the Twentieth Century might have seen a small man — a smiling man — who carried a cane and spoke with sincerity. He might be seen on the streets or in one of the town coffee shops talking to people. Sometimes he invited friends to his office to discuss civic needs in the city. The man was Alfred A. "Shorty" Smith, Justice of the Peace, and what he was doing was organizing the Key Club of Dunsmuir.

At the completion of this recruitment the Key Club was formed, "To focus the entire energy of the community on the most important civic projects." The method of operation of the new civic body was to help existing civic groups and service clubs in getting their important projects completed.

The meeting of July 7, 1960 was used to elect a corps of officers: A. A. "Shorty" Smith, President; George "Red" Adams, First Vice President; Chuck Williams, Second Vice President; Peggy Walsh, Third Vice President; Ed Benson, Treasurer; Cleo Lambert, Secretary. These officers led a discussion that pinpointed many objectives of immediate importance. Two of these which they deemed most important were a "Freeway Day" celebration and assisting the Lions Club to complete the Community Building.

It was apparent that many of the local merchants were apprehensive about the effects of moving the highway out of the city. The Club, acting on the premise that a "good offense is the best defense" prevailed on the business people to sponsor a "Freeway Day" celebration marking the time when Florence Avenue was no longer "The Highway." "It has been returned to the city," they proclaimed, "perhaps it is the best thing that could happen!"

Though members of the Key Club did most of the work, the effect of enlisting those, who might suffer the most adverse consequences of the highway move, established a new attitude among these merchants. "Dunsmuir was still on the move!" The celebration was called a smash hit!

A "Win A Trip to Hawaii" contest was held to finance the Celebration. Although this contest was a part of the Freeway Day observance, it generated such great interest and caused so much activity that it deserves to be treated as a separate activity.

Books of ten tickets were printed and distributed to contestants. Each ticket entitled the seller to 100 points. The contestant who got the most points won a Hawaiian vacation for two consisting of an eight-day stay at the Waikiki Hotel and a trip around the island.

The contest was won by Sally Nealon who remembers her prize: "I don't remember all that I did," she says, "but I sure had a good time!" "Bill (her husband) didn't want to go so I asked Anita Mei to go with me."

"I presented the Governor of Hawaii with a jug of Dunsmuir's 'Best Water On Earth'," she remembers, "and he took us on a tour of the Island. Then he took us down into the artesian wells where Hawaii gets its water and that was kind of scary."

Several Dunsmuir people, led by Cleo Lambert, Secretary of the Key Club, accompanied the winner. They were entertained by four Rotary Clubs; they attended a radio show (not much TV in 1960) luncheon. All praised Sally as a most gracious "Ambassador to Hawaii" and stated that she had indeed left a favorable impression of Dunsmuir with Hawaii.

With the projects completed the booster body began making plans for an ever larger event — a Sports Jamboree with events peculiar to the area. At their meeting of December 8, 1960 they talked of special money-making booths and refreshment counters. All organizations were to be invited to participate.

At a later meeting plans were finalized: a trout fishing pond; a log sawing contest; a gold panning contest; a carnival; a parachute jump; a fire demonstration; a fly-casting competition. All of these events to be preceded by a Pancake Breakfast cooked and served by the Dunsmuir Rotary Club.

Nearly everyone agreed with a column called "Strolling Down The Canyon" in the *Dunsmuir News*: "Without a doubt the zeal and efforts sparked by Judge Smith in realization of the Sports Jamboree is worthy of high praise."

One resident of Castella may not have agreed that the Jamboree was an unqualified success. This man brought his grandson to the Dunsmuir Memorial swimming pool, which served as the trout fishing pond. The charge for fishing was determined by the total number of inches of all fish caught by a person. Rumor has it that before the gentleman could stop the boy from fishing he had run up a bill of $20.00!

Money accumulated from the Jamboree was distributed for the aid of several deserving community projects. A good example was the sum of one thousand and fifty dollars to the Community Youth Building Fund. Today, one can find a plaque on the fireplace in that building stating it was built with funds donated by the Key Club. Thus was accomplished the second of their original objectives.

Among many other projects, the Key Club sponsored, built and equipped a T.V. Translator located on Mt. Bradley. This structure supplies off-the-air T.V. signals to residents of Dunsmuir, Mt. Shasta, and Castella. It is still in use and serves all people not using cable facilities.

The Key Club of Dunsmuir exists today — still continuing its policy of assistance to worthy projects for the betterment of the City.

DUNSMUIR BUSINESS AND PROFESSIONAL WOMEN'S CLUB

The NATIONAL organization was established in 1917 and the same objectives stand today.

> To elevate the standards for women in business and the professions.
>
> To promote the interest of Business and Professional women.
>
> To bring about a spirit of cooperation among the Business and Professional Women of the United States.
>
> To extend opportunities to Business and Professional Women through education along lines of industrial, scientific and vocational activities.

The local organization was chartered January 28, 1938. The charter officers were: Dorothy Leporini, President; Cleo Lambert, Vice President; Helen Hostetter, Secretary; Blanche Voorhies, Treasurer.

The local organization has followed the National and State programs for the betterment of all women.

In 1955, the local organization instituted a special program for graduating senior high school girls. At the present time a scholarship grant of $100.00 is awarded at the yearly breakfast when the girls are guests of the club.

Also to be of service to the high school seniors, an exploratory career seminar is held at the high school yearly.

In 1955, a program was inaugurated to honor a woman for her outstanding contribution of service to the local community.

The local club also helps to finance a girl for the Girls' State program.

Fourteen years ago the club took over the Community Calendar sales to raise money for the above-mentioned projects.

Following National and State programs in Legislation, Individual Development and Career Advancement, the local organization holds a monthly meeting to which interested persons in business or the professions are welcome. All members are encouraged to take an active part in community affairs.

The organization is non-partisan and membership is open to any woman or man interested in the objectives and who are engaged in a business or profession.

(Thanks to Grace Renoud)

DUNSMUIR FEDERATED WOMEN'S CLUB

The Dunsmuir Women's Club was formed in April of 1952 for the purpose of projecting plans for the highest and broadest culture and to promote educational, moral, civic, and charitable measures for the betterment of the community.

In the years following its organization, musicians and artists have brought their talents to the meetings; doctors, lawyers, business persons, and politicians have shared their knowledge with them; and representatives of the school, law enforcement agencies, fire departments and environmental groups have made known their concerns to the Club. From these guests and from the interests within the group have come the projects and goals of the Club.

Varied have been the Club's undertakings: contributions for both elementary and high school equipment and a sewing contest for the DHS Home Ec class; sponsoring of garden and art shows and Girl Scout Troops; donations to Tony Welch Fund, Boy Scout Camp vacation, piano at DES and many charities; installation of 2 benches and building of a fence around the neighborhood playground on Oak St. where the Methodist Church now stands; have supported educational opportunities available to young people of Dunsmuir such as Christian Youth Exchange and the Presidential Classroom; and helped furnish the Community Building with silverware and folding tables.

In 1956, Dorothy Warner was chairman of an interesting project — to collect recipes for those women who had lost theirs during the terrible floods in the valley. Twenty-four complete sets were sent to the Yuba City Women's Club for distribution. In a later year they were presented with an award from the State President for 100% activity in sending packages to Viet Nam and Hong Kong.

In 1957 their project for the year was the renovation of the Dunsmuir Public Library and in subsequent years to help finance its relocation to its present site.

In 1957, too, the Club won a District Award for spearheading the project to bring foreign exchange students to Dunsmuir under the American Field Service and welcomed Ulla Berntson from Sweden as the first one.

When Dunsmuir needed a dog pound, the Club raised over $1,000 to be used by the Dunsmuir Public Works Department in building a four-run structure.

Other projects and institutions that have received support are: Penny Pines, a reforestation project; State and District scholarships for nurses and teachers; Juvenile Hall; Ventura School for Girls; Veteran Hospitals and DeWitt Mental Hospital. Contributions have been made towards the sidewalk in front of the Ballpark, band and athletic uniforms, and city beautification. One year, a celebrity — Queen For A Day — was brought to Dunsmuir to ride in the Railroad Days Parade.

Still in existence today, the Dunsmuir Women's Club has been given many awards for its efforts from both the State and District Federation.

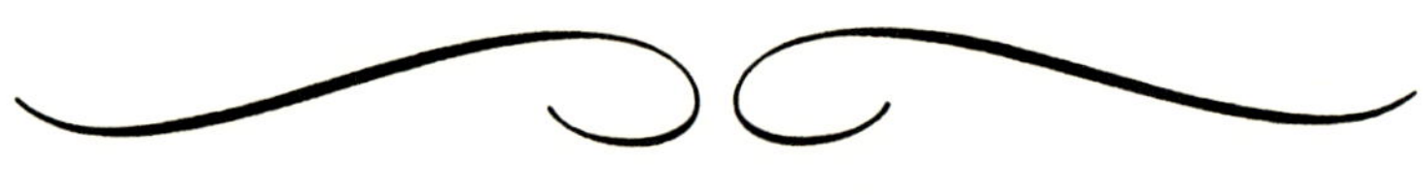

20-30 CLUB

The life of some service organization is sometimes limited by its requirements for membership. Two such clubs in Dunsmuir were the Twenty-Thirty Club and the Junior Chamber of Commerce. Both of these excellent service bodies required an unending well of young men and limited their term of membership according to age. Thus, through attrition and lack of an adequate supply of replacements, these very useful and active clubs flourished for a short while and then disappeared.

The 20-30 Club was formed either in late 1929 or early 1930. By 1932 the club had reached a high level of activity. In June, 1932 they voted to assist in obtaining members for the Castle Crag Park Association and entered into a contest with the Lions Club: which club could sign up the most new members for the Association? In September of the same year the triumphant Twenty-Thirtians attended a dinner, paid for by the Lions, who had lost the contest.

At this meeting, O. G. Steele of Yreka Lions Club asked the club's support to influence the Highway Commission to finish the Klamath River Highway.

Alden Dickson was chairman at a meeting which featured a C.I.F. athletic director, who explained changes in football rules. The club, at this time, voted to actively support high school football games.

During the November meeting, club members voted to sponsor a town basketball team. They planned a large league and invited any local residents who could play basketball to try out for the team.

In 1934, the 20-30 Club district convention was held at Shasta Springs (sponsored, of source, by the Dunsmuir Club). Wives were entertained at a Sunday morning breakfast hosted by the Dunsmuir 20-30 wives and the Dunsmuir Gamma Club. The local convention committee was: Ed Roberts, Cap Wessong, Ed Morrison, Floyd Fox, Eldon Waite, and George Signor. (Many of these names appeared on the Lions Club roster a few years later.)

At some time during the year this club developed a plan to put lights on the ballpark in order that night games might be held. While no documentation can be found, it is remembered by several local citizens that lights were installed at the ballpark, and a softball league was formed. To begin the season, a parade of participating ball teams marched from downtown Dunsmuir to the ballpark and though the lighting was not excellent, it did permit the playing of several games.

The remembered experience of one of the players is interesting: "If the ball was hit too high, it was lost in the dark upper sky," he said. "If it came down in left field, it was hit beyond the effect of the light. I know — I caught one in the eye!"

In 1935 the Dunsmuir 20-30 Club became the largest club in District 8. Stewart Waite became District Governor and took a delegation of Dunsmuir members to Redding to establish a club in that city.

During 1936 the club: participated in a "Talent Show" at the high school which must have been a lot of fun because it featured By Chambers in a hula skirt, Dr. G. E. Malone as a bride, Jack Wyatt as the groom, E. R. Deering in knee pants and Harry Harper in rompers; purchased a traffic sign for the elementary school highway crossing; arranged and managed a "Christmas opening" (window displays and prizes for the best one). During many of these years, drawing for Christmas turkeys was an important feature.

And then this valuable, active body of younger citizens slowly faded away — at least no further references to them were found. In retrospect, it was the City who lost.

BOOSTER CLUBS

The young City had scarcely reached the age of twenty-five when a plethora of "Booster Clubs" appeared. Each was organized to promote the city, or the area, or the business climate.

The first of these, instituted in February 1910, was called the South Siskiyou Promotion Association. Its stated purpose was to advance the political, social, and commercial interests of the people of South Siskiyou County. Officers were F. J. Tetreau, President; A. Levy, 1st Vice President; B. F. Dunn, 2nd Vice President; Gus Hutaff, Secretary; Fred Gerkey, Treasurer. More than 200 people are said to have attended the organizing meeting. Their slogan: "A long pull and a strong pull for Southern Siskiyou during 1910."

Scarcely a month later, the "Dunsmuir Booster Association" was formed. Motto: "Get together and Boost." Purpose: Inoculating into people the necessity of getting together and boosting the natural advantages and attractions that lie between Edgewood and Sims.

Neither of these clubs seem to have gotten very far off the ground. However, about ten years later "The Dunsmuir Promotion Club" was formed. It is interesting that this club had a membership fee of 50¢.

This "Booster Club" wasted no time in getting into action. They immediately attacked the problem of a playground for Dunsmuir and recommended the block between Florence (Dunsmuir) Ave. and Sacramento Ave. between Oak St. and Branstetter St. as a temporary playground for youngsters.

They considered the possibility of a campground (in the area of the present ballpark). The need for such a park was stressed: tourists have no place to park for a stay in the area and consequently do not stop in Dunsmuir. The U.S. Forest Service offered to help in maintaining such a campground. An option was taken on the property and two men — Jack Gill and W. W. Walker — offered to guarantee a loan for half of the three thousand dollar price, provided that the remaining fifteen hundred dollars was raised by the Club. They must have obtained the property because the *Dunsmuir News* of March 4, 1921 contains an article saying that a ball diamond will be built on ground that was given to the City by the Booster Club.

The May 19, 1922 issue of the *Dunsmuir News* notes the demise of these fine clubs by complimenting the City Trustees for keeping alive "the progressive spirit in Dunsmuir" in the absence of a promotion club or Chamber of Commerce.

During 1938 a new Booster Club was formed. Forty-four members strong, this boost-body elected Dr. J. R. W. Campbell as President and chose Babe Taylor as Secretary/Treasurer. Being a booster club, they decided to boost. They caused two signs, advertising the City, to be erected near Redding and raised $140 to sponsor a series of radio broadcasts advertising the area. They sponsored a contest among school children for drawing the best emblem for the Club, and another for writing the best Community slogans.

Secretary Babe Taylor said of this Club, "one of the reasons for the Booster Club growth is due to the participation of every member, and to the fact that each of them makes a personal effort to push Dunsmuir forward." And push they did. They asked the City Council to install street signs at intersections on main street so that "lost tourists" could locate "hard to find streets," and they didn't quit until the signs were up. They requested that the Bank stay open on Saturday afternoon for the convenience of Christmas shoppers; and, early in the year 1940 listened to a proposal for a celebration "unique to Dunsmuir" — a celebration to be called Railroad Days. This Club, composed mostly of business people, joined with Southern Pacific employees to create the greatest celebration the City has ever held and is still being held every year. An example of the cooperation obtained through the members of the Club was the composition of the Board of Directors for R.R. Days appointed in 1949. It consisted of three railroad men — Henry Schroeder, Norman Green (called the father of R.R. Days) and James Hanratty. To these were added three businessmen and one retired businessman — Frank Bascom, Pat Patton, Dom Sirianni, and R. E. Frye.

In December of 1949, the Club, continuing to boost Dunsmuir, changed its name to Chamber of Commerce. It is still with us!

Many booster-type promotional clubs have been formed during the first century of Dunsmuir's existence. Most of these organizations were, or are, single interest clubs — organized to accomplish a single objective. Other clubs that can be included in this category are those which, after succeeding in the promotion of a single project, faded into oblivion.

THE COMMERCIAL CLUB

The Commercial Club was probably founded in 1910 or 1912. The first record of the activity of this club was an announcement that it was still alive. Then in 1913 a rally was held in the Opera House with sixty members present. Amid cheers from the members and interspersed with music from the Town Band, these 60 faithful proclaimed the purpose: "To boost for a better and more prosperous Dunsmuir."

A project of immediate importance, in their perception, was the location of the "Great Highway." Through their efforts, the Great Highway (later Highway 99 and finally I-5) was routed up the Sacramento River and through Dunsmuir.

The success of routing the highway through the city reminded them that there should be a place for travelers to stop (the first rest stop?) so this civic body obtained a piece of land that was located between Florence Avenue and the Blacksmith Hill road and built a park.

No further reference to this club can be found.

DUNSMUIR RELIEF ASS'N. and DUNSMUIR EMPLOYMENT COMMITTEE

Depression! People were out of work! People were hungry! Perhaps adversity stimulates certain persons to successful action. At any rate two organizations were formed to combat and correct adverse conditions, and out of them came leaders.

The Dunsmuir Relief Ass'n. and the Dunsmuir Employment Committee were instituted. Which was first or whether these two committees merged cannot be determined; however, they operated in the same areas.

In 1931 Mayor Wilkins was chairman. Some of the committee's accomplishments were: (1) a local citizen offered to slaughter one or more of his hogs and distribute the meat among the needy; (2) thirteen unemployed men obtain work on the highway construction; (3) the City government was able to offer employment to several unemployed persons.

At a 1933 meeting of the Siskiyou-Shasta Relief Ass'n., they determined that one of their efforts would be to request the Highway Commission to have the Big Canyon Curve elimination work done by day labor instead of contract in order for local labor to be used. At that meeting, Mayor Sellman assured them that the Dunsmuir Relief Ass'n. would cooperate with the larger organization and would provide food for those who were hungry.

NATIONAL RE-EMPLOYMENT SERVICE

With the year 1934 the National Re-employment Service came to Dunsmuir. Three citizens of the City demonstrated the caliber of men who had built and maintained Dunsmuir. They were F. B. Van Fossen, William Welch, and C. F. Pendleton, County Supervisor.

These men knew the officers and the authorities of the N.R.S. They also knew how to get to them and what to say to get what they wanted. This they did and when they came back home, they came with a political plum for the city — the N.R.S. district office for the largest district in the State of California, with jurisdiction over the largest part of three counties.

U.S.O.

When in 1941 Dunsmuir was found to be lagging in its U.S.O. quota, some of the city's women, under the leadership of Elinore Van Fossen (Harrison), made a house-to-house campaign and Dunsmuir went over the top of its goal. In 1944, a canteen was established in the city. It was the only active canteen in Northern California and during the first month 950 servicemen and women passed through its doors. What took place there is best described by Mrs. Grace Harris in the following:

"During WW II, Dunsmuir Ladies operated the U.S.O. in the Rostel Building on Sacramento Avenue (just north of the now Dunsmuir Hotel). To this warm, hospitable spot came soldiers from the troop trains that stopped in Dunsmuir for servicing and changing of crews. Here, for a few precious moments the boys could enjoy home-cooked food and talk with mother and girl friend figures. The call of 'all aboard' brought the soldiers running back to the train, often with a piece of cake in hand and waving goodbye to the girls they were leaving.

"The U.S.O. also provided a place for evening sociability in the basement of the Episcopal Church (now the Baptist Church) where the boys, who were stationed near Dunsmuir to guard the railroad bridges and tunnels, could play pool, have refreshments, dance, and find 'a home away from home'."

CANYONEERS

In the Dunsmuir Elementary School year of 1953-54 a new teacher, Chester Conley, arrived. He soon found that there were no activities for the girls of the school so he started a drill team and a softball team. The members of the drill team named themselves "The Canyoneers." That fall, Mr. Conley produced a variety show using the proceeds to buy black and white capes for the Elementary School Band.

About this time, several happenings were taking place in Dunsmuir that were to result in one of the most helpful organizations that Dunsmuir has ever known — the "Weldonians" (a Bay Area youth marching band) were participating in our Railroad Day parades; Donna Gritton had organized her "Tiny Twirlers"; and, Mr. and Mrs. Wayne Turner had arrived — Mrs. Turner as the chorus teacher at DES and Mr. Turner as the band teacher for both the elementary and high schools. From then on the bands were not only playing bands but marching bands because he felt marching bands gave students prestige and a sense of pride.

In the *Dunsmuir News* of February 10, 1955 was an article which said: "Youth program to be launched at meeting tonight. The words 'do nothing' have been thrown out of Dunsmuir's vocabulary in a new movement to build the town's youth activities. The purpose of the meeting is to organize a large number of young persons interested in school bands, choruses, drill teams and individual talent." And so was born "The Canyoneers."

The officers for the new organization were Counselors Wayne Turner, Chester Conley, Reva Coon, and Donna Gritton; Reva Coon, Chairman; Mrs. Dale Hutton, V. Chairman; Mrs. Moe McGregor, Secretary; Mrs. Buz Kohlbacker, Treasurer. Other officers were chaperons for the elementary and high school performers; finance, advertising, transportation, uniform care, and Ways and Means Committees. From this list one can see a great many people were needed and, in fact, all parents of band and choral students were automatically considered Canyoneer members.

The Ways and Means Committee immediately went into action by planning a refreshment booth at R.R. Days and to have a candy sale at the Canyoneers' very first variety show the next month, which was part of a 3-day entertainment event. The proceeds from it were used to buy new high school band and drill team uniforms. The program included chorus numbers, a faculty play, twirling act and a Can-Can dance act by the Dunsmuir Rockettes **pictured at right:**

The Canyoneer units made their first Railroad Day appearance that year of 1955. They were 250 strong, which included the DHS marching band and drill team, the DES band and Jr. High drill team and the Tiny Twirlers.

In September of 1955, Chester Conley, who had led the Canyoneer units for the first 6 months, resigned because of new duties as Principal of Castle Rock Elementary School. Mr. and Mrs. Turner took over active leadership.

In January, 1957, the Canyoneers voted to sponsor ten $25 scholarships to send Dunsmuir students to music camp, and to take on the awesome project of purchasing a grand piano for the elementary school. The next month the new Steinway grand piano was unveiled at a program at the auditorium during which Duane Hampton, teacher-composer of Redding, performed. Admission was Family Membership pledges or purchase of a $10 piano key.

With such ambitious plans as the purchase of elementary school band uniforms, instruments, music, new lockers for Jr. High at DES, and the grand piano, the parent group began an annual fund raising program of selling Texas Fruit Cakes. Also instrumental in the raising of funds were almost annual variety shows that in later years featured local talent from many organizations.

The last variety show (March, 1963) that this writer can remember, played to standing room only and was a lot of fun! It was called "Clown Capers" and was sponsored jointly by the High School PTA and the Canyoneers. The proceeds were used to purchase 2 banks of footlights for the high school auditorium. The program started and ended with numbers by the Community Band, led by Robert Shipley, and featured the Clown Chorus — a group of 22 — dressed in clown outfits. (We still remember how much fun we had putting on make-up for clown faces at Claudia Mather's home.) Also on the program were dances, solos, German Band, Barbershop double quartet and instrumental solos. The finale was a shower of balloons by the Clowns.

When Mike Wright, Dunsmuir Elementary School band teacher, knocks on your door and asks, "How many Texas Fruit Cakes do you want to order for this Christmas?", you know that the Spirit of the "Canyoneers" still lives.

"DUNSMUIR ROCKETTES"
Patty McEnerney, Sandra Holmes, Katherine Nelson,
Mary Lockart, Judy Penman, Betty Bisagno

DUNSMUIR
SCHOLARSHIP FUND

In early 1980 a group of concerned Dunsmuir citizens met at the high school. Their concern — Dunsmuir's own scholarship fund, one that would be supported by Dunsmuir citizens and benefit Dunsmuir students.

Through the efforts of many of those present at that meeting and the publicity generated in the *Dunsmuir News* by its Editor, George Rentschler, the Dunsmuir Scholarship Fund was incorporated in time for a graduate of that year (Mark Zanotto) to be its first recipient.

Those receiving scholarships since that first year are: 1981 — Monica Heisel and Nancy Orrell; 1982 — Angela Green, Jeff Andresen, and Art Sandoval; 1983 — Scott Nystrom, Laura Hopkins (returned as unused), Jeff DeBoer, Jim Imhoff, Brad Davis and Anna McGuire; 1984 — Stacy Dragmire, Tammy Wilson, Jesus Villapando, Jeff DeBoer (renewal), Brenda Barnes and Nick Mitchell.

To be eligible to receive a scholarship, the applicant must be a graduate of Dunsmuir High School, either in the current year or a previous year. Up to this date, the scholarships have been in the amounts of $250 or $500. A pen and pencil set is also given each year to those graduates who are scholastically in the top 10% of their class. The Dunsmuir Scholastic Fund is supported by memberships, contributions and memorials. For the small sum of $11.00 a year one can be a member of this very worthwhile Dunsmuir service organization. Membership also allows one to vote on the scholarship applications.

Current officers are: Rose Ellis, President; Billie Jean Blank, Vice-President; Jim Arata, Treasurer; Joan Dragmire, Secretary.

What better way could there be to show love for a departed family member or friend than to establish a memorial in the Dunsmuir Scholastic Fund!

CHUMP'S CLUB

Another single purpose — and *extremely* self-centered — service organization was formed by L. D. "Babe" Taylor. The *Dunsmuir News* of July 3, 1936 contains the following announcement:

"New Organization Offers Solace For Lovelorn Males." Does your girl-friend run around with one of the perennial vacationists while you are busy at your daily occupation? Does she pull any of those little tricks commonly known as "chiseling" so as to make a "chump" out of you? Does she get in a little cheek-to-cheek dancing when she thinks you are too engrossed in your glass of beer to notice? If so, you are eligible to become a member of the "Chump's Club," a recently organized group of local young people whose purpose is mutual sympathy for woeful males.

As of this date, the list of members furnished by the "Kingfish" of the organization, Babe Taylor, includes: Earl Woods, Guy Bunch, Averett Weedon, John Donovan, Bill Smith, Maurice Beck, Joe Baldo, Harry Carrick, Joe Champion, Kenneth Turnbow, Lester White, Leon Estes, Clinton Morey, Jim Lovelle, Lawrence Roman, Jim Powers, Don Wallace, Jim Moore, Elmer Manning, Penn Mesner, Vic Pereira, and Bob Dickson. New members are rapidly joining the ranks.

While the constitution and by-laws of the new organization have not been made public, the assumption is that the Ass'n. will be a society for passing out mutual sympathy among members. It has been suggested that members equip themselves with copies of Liddia Spinkham's "Advice To The Lovelorn" for literary refreshment and as a guide to restore their charms upon the damsels of their dreams.

CHAPTER VI
THE PROFESSIONS
DUNSMUIR'S PROFESSIONAL PEOPLE

By
Reva Coon

Over the past one hundred years, many professional people have served Dunsmuir and contributed to its business, social, and cultural activities. The research of Phyllis Coon Gilzean has produced the names of these doctors, lawyers, dentists, and pharmacists.

THE DOCTORS

From its beginning, Dunsmuir has been cared for by a long line of doctors. The first physician to come to Dunsmuir was Dr. Benjamin M. Gill. He arrived in the lively, little town in March, 1891. He delivered the first child born in Dunsmuir, a boy named Dunsmuir S. Neher. Dr. Gill built a swimming pool on the east side of the Sacramento River at Shasta Retreat. The pool, a dammed up part of the river, was open to the public. Of considerable interest to the townspeople was the fact that the doctor owned a four-wheel bicycle that could run on the railroad tracks. In his spare time, he could be seen pedaling up the tracks, his long coattails flapping in the breeze behind him, going to see how his philanthropic project was doing. The old Gill home, one of the fanciest residences in town, stood at 513 Sacramento Avenue. Dr. Gill sold his practice to Dr. Charles E. Thompson.

Dr. Thompson owned a black, motor buggy, probably Dunsmuir's first automobile. The doctor endeared himself to many of his young patients by taking them riding in his new machine. Dr. Thompson handed over his practice to Dr. D. H. Horner, who was not only a family doctor but also one who examined eyes and fit glasses. Dr. Howard Parker bought the Horner practice. In the 20's, Dr. Cordes Ankele took Dr. Parker's place. Dr. Ankele converted a home on the corner of Willow Street and Florence Avenue (now Dunsmuir Avenue) into a small hospital. The *News* of 2/25/10 carried the story of Dr. E. J. Cornish buying the practice from a Dr. Cross. Dr. Cornish then built a sanitarium on the hill east of the Sacramento River overlooking the main S.P. railroad yard. Ten years later, he enlarged his hospital to forty-bed capacity. Dr. Cornish was very active in community affairs and served the city as its mayor for several years. In 1924, when "Babe" Ruth gave an exhibition in Dunsmuir, Mayor Cornish declared a half-day holiday.

Two other doctors who came to Dunsmuir were Dr. A. H. Tucker and Dr. Paul Wright. The latter built a swimming pool on the west side of the river at Shasta Retreat and opened it to the public. Dr.

Photos by Claire B. Sheehan

The swimming pool in the river. Looking east

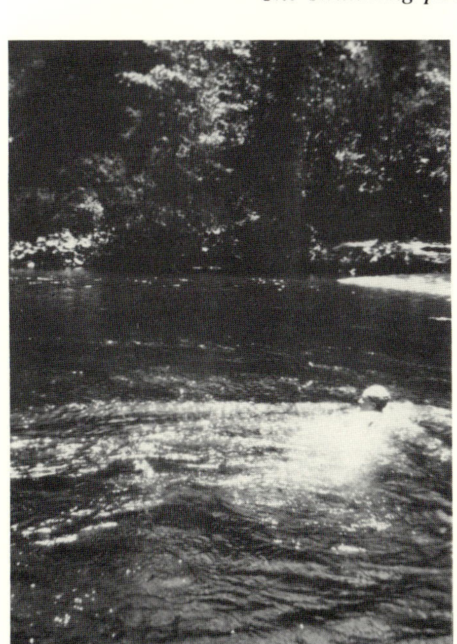

Looking west

Wright had come first to Mount Shasta in 1909, where he built a large, general practice. He was also the physician and surgeon for the Southern Pacific for seventeen years. In 1935, he moved his practice to Dunsmuir, where he was an associate of Dr. Cornish. He died in 1953 and is interred in the Dunsmuir cemetery.

Just after the 1929 Crash, a young doctor came to Dunsmuir. He was Dr. Albert H. Newton. He purchased a home on the northeast corner of Willow and Shasta Avenue and transformed it into a small hospital. Later he moved his home and practice to Yreka. Over the following years these doctors served Dunsmuir: J. R. Campbell; John H. Steele, who was drowned in a tragic hunting accident; Russell Merritt, who went from here to San Francisco; E. A. Opacity; D. D. Todorovic, who came here in 1947; Eugene Anderson, who after years of participation in civic activities went to the Bay Area, where he worked for Permanente; H. C. Chappell, whose life was cut short by an automobile accident; H. H. Lord; J. W. Reynolds, hometown boy, who built the Medical Center in North Dunsmuir and served the medical needs of the city single-handedly for more than two years, while an effort was being made to attract another physician to Dunsmuir; William Baker, who moved here to share the load that Dr. Reynolds had carried alone; T. B. Srivastiva, who bought Reynolds' practice upon the retirement of the latter. Over the years Dunsmuir's many doctors have added richly to the town's heritage.

THE PHARMACISTS

Keeping Dunsmuir healthy by filling the doctors' prescriptions were several pharmacists. Many of their pharmacies were popular social gathering places; the teenagers after school enjoying their favorite "goodie" and, at night after the movie, grownups feasting on chocolate jerseys or a piece of Nellie's delicious cake. Gus Hutaff established, according to report, the first pharmacy in Dunsmuir. The following men filled prescriptions in the Dunsmuir Pharmacy: H. L. Huntington; Ben Gooch; C. J. Cone; Vic Petrovics (the full story of his business to be found in the Dedication section of this book); and Jim Alspach, who bought the pharmacy upon the retirement of Petrovics. The Mossbrae Pharmacy began with Hubert Marsh and F. T. "Beanie" King. Later King hired Alden Dickson, who, with his wife, moved to Yreka. From then on, King operated the drug store alone. One hastens to add that the excellent fountain was presided over by his wife, Nellie. Cethil Jones established the Jones Pharmacy, where he and Orvil Graham filled orders. Many years later he sold the store to George Mannee. Floyd Glica bought out Mannee and moved the business to North Dunsmuir across the street from the doctors' offices. At the time of this writing, Dunsmuir's two drug stores are the Dunsmuir Pharmacy and Glica's Pharmacy. These professional men have contributed richly and freely to the city's development.

THE DENTISTS

Nine dentists have kept Dunsmuir's teeth clean and sparkling: Dr. W. B. Mason, who married Vera Van Fossen, daughter of Levi Van Fossen, one of the city's founding fathers; Dr. George Malone, a civic leader and a town trustee; Dr. M. L. Kleaver, who had many friends even among his patients; Dr. O. Dimick; Dr. Hamilton; Dr. Litzsinger; Dr. William Townsend; and Dr. Russell Elgin. Each in his own way contributed notably to the community.

THE CHIROPRACTORS

Seven chiropractors have had practices in Dunsmuir: Dr. A. I. Jones; Dr. Hines; Dr. Barton ("Doc") Clay, who was very active in the city and was president of the Rotary Club; Dr. W. H. Spry; Dr. Margene Brookmiller; Dr. V. L. Palmer; and recently Dr. R. A. Burr.

THE LAWYERS

Throughout the years, six attorneys have, through their legal advice, kept Dunsmuir well directed. Henry McGuinness was not only a lawyer but also became a California Senator. His colorful personality sparked many an otherwise dull event in town. Roy Weaver followed McGuinness, as did Gerald Shannon, Paul J. Aiello and Arnold Breyer. Howard Jones was, and is, very active in many phases of town life. Chris Stromsness, at this writing, is a member of the high school Board of Trustees, belongs to the Audubon Society, is a valued member of the Dunsmuir Centennial Committee, and is the City Attorney.

The teachers' story has been fully told in the chapter on schools.

Dunsmuir's professional people have been a very real part of the city and in many different ways have enriched the life of our historic, little railroad town. Each has left an unmistakable footprint in the records of Dunsmuir.

S. P. Co. Shasta Division Heads, left to right: J. C. Slade, L. P. Oberkamp, R. B. Baymiller, and A. W. Kilborn (seated).

CHAPTER VII
THE SCHOOLS

Dunsmuir's First Schoolhouse — 1891

DUNSMUIR ELEMENTARY SCHOOL

By
Dorothy Delgado

Dorothy Delgado

The Dunsmuir Elementary School District was established on July 8, 1887. The boundary was corrected in 1896, 1902, and 1957.

School was first held in a house at 319 Florence (Dunsmuir) Avenue, known as the Isgrigg House. Here J. B. Atchison taught seventy-nine pupils in 1890-91 and received a salary of $90.00 a month. There was a class, also, at 615 Florence Avenue in a house across the street from the first school house.

The first school house was built in 1891 on land between Florence and Sacramento Avenue (510 Florence Avenue). The yard was fenced with a high board fence on the north and south side. On the east and west facing Florence and Sacramento Avenue there was a picket fence with stiles for entrance. The school building was a two-story frame building facing north. The upper floor was used for social activities and there were two classrooms on the lower floor. J. S. Osborne, as principal, taught from fifty to sixty-five pupils in the four upper grades or Grammar Grades as they were then called. Lou Hellmuth taught from forty-six to sixty-eight children in the first four or Primary Grades. Mr. Osborne received a salary of $95.00 a month, and Miss Hellmuth was paid $75.00 a month.

Before the opening of school in September, 1891, a dedication ball was held. A Mr. Anderson, who was then State Superintendent of Public Instruction, was a guest of honor.

In 1895 Mrs. J. J. Shaefor started a kindergarten. She held classes for six-and-a-half months and was paid by private subscription. She continued to teach in the primary grades until May of 1916.

Mr. N. T. J. Beaughan was principal from 1900-1920. A complete story of his educational services in Siskiyou County is told in an article in the 1964 *Siskiyou Pioneer*.

From 1920-22 a Mr. Birch was principal and during this time a 1921 news article reported the Dunsmuir Grammar School was the largest in the county with 13 teachers and an Average Daily Attendance of 395.

The Board minutes of July 1, 1923 report the following staff members: W. L. Kleaver, District Superintendent; Betty Steele, K; Ruby Dixon, 1B; Muriel McLaughlin, 1A; Lillian Aberson, 2; Elva Willett, 3B; Merle Stevenson, 3A; Yvette Baker (Stone), 4B; Delia Parker, 4A; Laura Evans, 5B; Alice Aldridge, 5A & 6; Lora Dixon, 6; Wilda-rene Cole, 7; Frank Johnson, 8. The Board members were F. L. Weamer, G. Schnebele, and Jennie Ward.

In 1924 the graduation was held in the Methodist church. Mildred Grant was on the teaching staff. She later became County Superintendent of Schools.

In 1925 the original building was destroyed by fire. A new two-story building was accepted October 20, 1925. "Whereas, Geo. D. Hudnutt Inc. constructed an eight-room reinforced concrete unit of the Dunsmuir Grammar School — rushed the work so that school could commence within two weeks of the usual starting time." (Board minutes.) There was a small wooden building on the school lot. It was used for Manual Training and Kindergarten. In 1926 it was moved to the west side of the lot and continued to serve through many alterations as cafeteria, music room, nurse's office, and classroom, in addition to the original uses. At this time there was also a one-room, one-teacher school in the Champion Park area. It opened in 1924 and Mrs. Edith Ralston taught first through fifth grades there until 1932.

The new school was inadequate for the enrollment so a new building of six classrooms was added south of the original building, bringing the total to fourteen. The 1926-27 list of teachers added three long-term teachers: Abigail M. Hanavan, Ollie Hendricks, and Sidonia E. Beaughan — all taught here for about 30 years. Others were: Audrey J. McDowell, Pearl A. Thomas, Mary P. Hickey, Bernice L. Tunison, Kathleen M. Logue, Ida Browning, Ruby D. Williams, and Margaret Rasmussen. In 1928 a special tax was passed to build a north wing of two additional rooms. Elizabeth Parker Wendell came to teach in 1927, followed by her sister, Barbara Parker Stewart, in 1929.

Mr. E. R. Deering served as superintendent from 1929 to 1939 when he advanced to the State Department of Education. For many years there was a high and low of each grade as some students entered at mid-term. This practice was discontinued in the thirties and all students entered in the fall. By 1935 some new names were added to the staff: Nellie Masson, Ann Garner, Geraldine Stevens, Melba Shearin, Fred Fox, and Harriet Countryman. Albert W. Marske came in the fall. He taught eighth grade for 33 years and was "Coach" to many winning basketball teams.

Through the years the school has been fortunate to have an outstanding music department. Melvin D. Stanley taught band and orchestra for 16 years starting in 1934. He was followed by Wayne and Margaret Turner. Then came David E. and Esther Leighton. They were followed by Robert Shipley. All of the men taught at both the high and elementary schools, dividing the day in half. The ladies taught vocal music at the elementary school. When Oren Sapp came in the sixties he taught only at the elementary school. Mike Wright came in 1968 and taught band at both schools. During his time in military service he was replaced by Peter Reinheimer. When Mike returned, he took over at the elementary school and Peter continued at the high school. Mike has done a wonderful job with 4 concerts a year. This includes a fall, Christmas, mid-winter, and spring program, plus several Gilbert and Sullivan operettas, tours, reviews, and marching in several parades. The excellence of his program is confirmed by many trophies on display in the school library.

In 1939 Mr. Hartsel Gray came as principal and stayed until 1955 when he joined the County Administrator's Office. During the mid-forties the school was so over-crowded it was necessary to hold a kindergarten class in a building at "the Project" south of Dunsmuir. With the increased enrollment there was also an increase in traffic so it was deemed necessary to form a Boys' Traffic Patrol to ensure the safety of the younger students as they crossed the main highway. These boys were out in all kinds of weather several times a day. They were rewarded at the end of the year by a trip to San Francisco with Glen Minuth. They usually attended a baseball game.

In 1948 an addition was built south of the school. It housed a new school library, 4 classes, and an auditorium with a fine stage. Huldah Seed took on the task of forming the new library. She later became secretary for a few years, then left to become the librarian at the College of the Siskiyous. Teachers added under Mr. Gray included: Celeste Wyatt, Anne Erhart, Lulu Thornton, Veronica Kelby, Adelaide Lee, Ethel Kern, June Wright, Chet Conley, Glen Minuth, June Cravens, Nina Barr, Eleanor Vaughn, Helen Bell Markse, June Hale, Dorothy Delgado, Lois Bectel, Harriet Spatafora (Alto), and Bernadine Nelson. During this time the number of staff members rose to thirty.

Mr. Roger Ellis was superintendent from 1955 to 1962 when he joined the faculty at the College of the Siskiyous at Weed. The school was still crowded so the library and stage were used as classrooms. The enrollment was very close to 700. Some new staff members were: Alpha Tolbert, Fred Rasmussen, Walter Butcher, Paul Lewis, Grace Harris, and Mr. Beglinger.

Albert Kempton followed as superintendent from 1962-1968 when he, too, joined the State Department of Education. A bond election passed and a new school was planned. At this time a new program was instituted — aides in the classroom. Among the first hired was Jimmie LeMere. She has been joined by many more so that now there is an aide for every classroom.

A new site was selected north of town on Siskiyou Avenue and a facility composed of four one-story units was dedicated September 14, 1968, with a new superintendent, Mr. Eugene Evans. With the completion of the freeway and changes at the S.P., the enrollment dropped to about 450. Some new teachers added during this time included: Sharon Stromsness, Fred Vogel, Lucy DePoli, Ray Kermode, Bruce Batchelder, and Linda Wallace. Mr. Evans served until 1982 with a new auditorium-cafeteria building being added in 1981.

From 1982-1984 Superintendent Paul Chaffin introduced us to the new world of computers.

The fall 1984 staff list is as follows: Superintendent Robert Wilson, Sharon Stromsness, Pat O'Connor, Harriet Alto, Jerry Skinner, Paula Damico, Pat Rhinesmith, Barbara Ulbrich, Linda Lutz, Tom Heiser, June Vogel, Susan Keeler, Susan Grabek, Cindy Rinne, Karen Ely, Penny Heilman, Fred Vogel, Mike Wright, Stephane Possen-RST, and Carol Simpson-Science/Gates. James Koch is teaching for the county in the little kindergarten building. It is a special program for the severely handicapped.

A last look into the past reveals an interesting list of teachers who attended the local schools, then returned to teach here: Mableclaire Ralston, Ernest Kelby, Beverly Mason, Louise Adams Dick, Eddie Roberts, Lois Dalla Lasta, Molinos Hill Wickes, Ruth Holcomb Shelton, Edith Holland Elliott, Robert Eachus, Alice Jane Coon Eachus, Lois Roberts Bectel, Dorothy McGee Delgado, Vickie Petrovics Lucio, and Mike Wright. There are many students who attended D.E.S. and went on to become teachers in other places, but that is a list for the future.

First Graduating Class, D.E.S.

Top row, right to left:
Melbourne Dunn
Harry Kilbourne
Frank Regan
George Scholes
George Wells

Front row, right to left:
Mr. J. S. Osborne, teacher
Mertis Neher
Annie Scott
Rose Miller
Jennie Patrick
Myrtle Dunn

New School Building, 1925-1968

New gym under construction, 1948

New School Building, 1968-

April, 1909, Mrs. Shafor, teacher. Primary grades.

Late '20's, Mr. Will Kleaver, principal; Alice Aldridge, teacher.

Hartsel Gray

D.E.S. SUPERINTENDENTS

Roger Ellis

Gene Evans

Albert Kempton

And some
Faculty
Through the
Years

A. Marske

H. Aito

A. Lee

G. Minuth

B. Stewart

R. Ellis

B. Nelson

Y. Stone

J. Wright

E. Vaughn

V. Keiby

N. Barr

H. Seed

L. Thornton

H. Marske

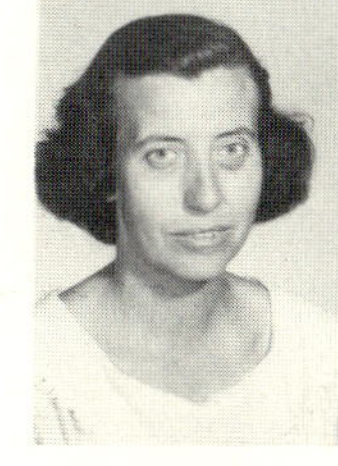

G. Harris

D. Delgado

L. Bectel

D.E.S. Sports   Al Markse, Coach

D.E.S. Traffic Patrol

66

Mr. Melvin Stanley
and the D.E.S. Band

Mr. Michael Wright
His 1985 Band which performed in Disneyland

DUNSMUIR HIGH SCHOOL

By
Grace M. Harris

A high school for Dunsmuir was first proposed by citizens in June, 1909. Students wishing to complete high school at that time had to attend high school in Yreka or other areas. By 1911 an election was held on August 17, and the measure to have a high school passed. The school was to have one teacher the first year with the salary not to exceed $1800. A vacant room in the elementary school was to be used.

By the summer of 1912 the first year report made by principal, Professor Briggs, stated there had been 26 pupils with the average daily attendance of 18, and it was recommended that two teachers be hired for the next year. On June 18, 1915, the first graduation exercises were held.

By 1919 there was much discussion in town about the need for a high school building. Some suggested a high school be built as a memorial "to the boys who went to France." A Mothers Club was formed and discussion was held about a site for the school. By June, 1919, Dunsmuir had voted decisively for the new school, and the Mothers Club accepted the responsibility for the building and equipment of the auditorium of the new high school. By February 20, 1920, the high school bonds carried for $24,000 and this was considered sufficient to build the school.

20's AND 30's

On May 16, 1920, the high school cornerstone was laid. Mrs. E. J. Cornish, secretary of the Board of Trustees, was in charge of the affair. The Hon. J. C. Luttrell of Yreka was the principal speaker and Master of Ceremonies.

Nevertheless, in September, 1920, the high school had to open still using the old rented quarters on Florence Avenue, for the new building was not ready. Mr. J. W. Palmer was principal and there were 27 students enrolled. That same month the Mothers Club organized into the local P.-T.A. Officers elected were A. Makle, President; H. Burch, First Vice Pres.; Mrs. Wallace, Second Vice Pres.; Martha Stauffer, Third Vice Pres.; B. Ward, Secretary; and Mrs. Moran, Treasurer.

By October, 1920, the students had moved into the new building and in November, 1920, bids were called for completion of the high school building. By January, 1921, however, there was a mass meeting about the understanding of the people concerning the high school site selection, and by August 19, 1921, the rear wall had to be repaired, and a drain and retaining wall was to be installed to protect the school from earth slides. (The hillside continues to be a problem to this day!)

By September, 1921, there were 70 students enrolled at the high school and Mr. Leslie A. Phillips was principal. The following article, written by Andrew Leach, Class of 1917, is found in the second *Crag Echoes*, 1921:

"Our Dunsmuir High School is now completing the tenth year of its existence. And what a change from the one room, in the old grammar school, which was used for the first year. We graduates are surely envious of those attending in the new building. But, nevertheless, we had much for which to be thankful and our high school days are all fond memories.

"While the graduates are but eight in number, we must call to mind those who completed their fourth year in other schools which were accredited. The first graduating class was in 1915 and consisted of Bessie Sutherland and Violet Brown. The former is residing in Portland, where she has a responsible position with the Southern Pacific Company. The latter, now Mrs. George Shintaffer, is still living in Dunsmuir.

"The 1916 class was composed of Mildred Van Horn, Olive McCarville, and Laura Reid. This was the largest class of all to graduate and the commencement exercises were quite an event and were well attended. Each one had prepared an original composition and these readings displayed the excellent teachings of the Dunsmuir High School. Each one of the three is now married and are known as Mrs. Earl McAllister of Alameda, Mrs. B. W. Park of Dunsmuir, and Mrs. Louie Evans of Bray, California, respectively.

"Ileen Girard, now Mrs. J. E. Hanratty, and Andrew Leach of the class of 1917 are both in Dunsmuir. This class was tendered an elaborate banquet and party at Crag View by the Student Body and each was presented with the D.H.S. pin, a very attractive little emblem and something one is proud to own.

"Edmund Mahon of Castella was the only graduate in 1918 and the last one until the class of 1921. He intends to enter the University of California this next fall.

"In addition to the above, who graduated from the four-year course, there must be included those who completed the two-year commercial course: Edwin Carter, Eva Reid, and Margaret McEnerney. As mentioned before, there are quite a few that attended Dunsmuir High School but graduated elsewhere. Among the most prominent of these are Lucille Beaughan, Ethel FitzGerald, Edna Carlson, Bryan Ahl, June Summers, Germaine LaFleur, Alfred Mahon, and Grace Bass.

"To complete this article and not mention Miss Hudson would be an injustice that all the alumni would greatly resent. Miss Minnie N. Hudson was principal for four years and the difficult years of all when our high school was new and the Dunsmuir people did not appear to appreciate and support a school. Miss Hudson is remembered, by each of the eight graduates, as the best teacher that they could possibly have had, and liked as one of their best friends. How we would all love to see her again! And we know that she would be pleased to see the recent progress in the Dunsmuir High School.

"Undoubtedly the next ten years will witness single graduating classes that will number several times the total graduates of the first ten years. But no one graduate will have the interests of the Dunsmuir High School at heart any more than any one of the first eight. May the alumni of the Dunsmuir High School greatly increase in number."

—Andrew Leach, '17

By December 8, 1922, the auditorium was completed and dedicated. Students had donated war savings to finish it. A basketball game with Sisson on November 17, 1922, was its first use. By March 23, 1923, an observance of Public Schools Week was held there. Weed, Sisson, McCloud, and Dunsmuir participated, and Charles Adams, Past Grand Master of Masons in California, was the speaker.

A sidewalk and then a road to the high school was urged. In June, 1922, five graduated; and in June, 1923, seven graduated. On June 13, 1924, there were nine graduates. One, Elinore Van Fossen (later Harrison), graduated with the best record ever made at D.H.S. Beverley Mason was also one of the nine. (Today, Beverley Way and Elinore Avenue are reminders of these two graduates.) By August, 1924, 67 students registered at the high school. In June, 1925, there were 17 graduates. The *Dunsmuir News* in August 1925 reported in an article entitled "New Life Apparent at High School" that there was new class equipment, dressing rooms had been built on the auditorium stage, a restroom had been built for the girls, and fifty steel lockers had been added.

During January, 1926, Principal L. R. Switzer told the Lions Club that there was a need for a new high school site or enlargement of the present quarters to take care of the probable enrollment in coming years. He suggested a site north of the bridge, for it was expensive to keep the hill from sliding into the present school, and this probably would continue to be a problem as long as the school was in its present location!

By April, 1926, the possibility of a new site was given up and an engineer was hired to see if an addition could be built on the present building. However, in February, 1927, Castella and Sweetbriar high school districts voted to join the Dunsmuir High School District, making it Dunsmuir Joint Union High School District. This action added $700,000 in taxable property to the district and made possible the needed improvements. The high school expansion bonds carried 4 to 1 in August, 1927, and in March, 1928, an editorial in the *Dunsmuir News* suggested a change in the location of the high school to one on a city park site near the ball park. The state architect had refused permission to add on to the present building, so a separate unit of four rooms south of the present building was needed. It was felt that a change of location should be made before any more money was spent on the present building. However, nothing came of this.

By April, 1928, a contract was awarded to build a six-room separate addition to the present high school building, with the two buildings to be connected by a corridor.

That June, thirty graduated; and in October, 1928, the new addition opened. Names on the faculty list at this time included Ralph T. Wattenburger and Reva Patrick (later Coon).

During 1931 and 1932, H. T. Ashford was principal, and Lois Dalla Lasta was named Honor Student for the year 1931-32. Reno Cesaratto had held that honor for the two preceding years. Among the seniors could be found the names of Joe Kelby, Horace Porter, Richard Patrick, George Taylor, Vern Leahy, Jack Fahs, and Richard Lamb.

Beginning in 1935, Ralph T. Wattenburger was principal and he continued in that position until the end of the school year, June 1946.

During the 30's Dunsmuir High School students did not let the Depression dampen their enthusiasm. This period was outstanding in the production of musical comedies, including several Gilbert and Sullivan operettas. The music department boasted of an orchestra as well as a band. In athletics, the D.H.S. athletes won many championships. The years were hard on both the town and the school, but the Tiger Spirit never dimmed. The following names can be found on the faculty list during this time: Floyd Stone, Viola Weamer, Sarah Woodyard, Melvin Stanley, Irvine Carner, June Ames, Beverley Mason, John Glaese, Katherine Titus, George Bican.

At the close of the 30's a new gymnasium was built south of the additional classroom wing. This building included a stage, dressing rooms, and room for a shop below the gym. Tennis courts, constructed by the WPA were southwest of it. On a rainy Memorial Day weekend in 1940 the Junior Prom was held in the new facility. The class of 1940 had 74 graduates . . . a record.

40's — THE WAR YEARS

As Ralph Wattenburger continued on as principal, the following names appeared on the faculty list: Grace Maddern (later Harris), Etta Chandler, Elizabeth Trueb, Ernest Dobson, Margaret Menig (later Hendricks), and Clair Tatton.

D.H.S. students came to school on Monday morning, December 8, 1941, with the knowledge that the United States was at war with Japan. Senior boys began talking of enlisting in the services. Principal Wattenburger urged teachers who had had first aid to take an emergency advanced first aid course which was to be held that week in Weed, nightly. By the following weekend when the school play was in progress on the stage of the new gym, an air alert occurred and a blackout was ordered by the civil defense authorities. The audience was required to sit in complete darkness for approximately two hours. To while away the time, the group sang. It is said that every song was sung that could possibly be remembered by anyone there. Later, black-out curtains were put on the windows to avoid a repeat of that memorable evening.

By 1942 the high school had lost two faculty members to the armed services — John Glaese to the army, and Irvine Carner to the navy. Later, Dorothy Dean joined the SPARS. By 1943 the high school had adopted a half-day school schedule — running from 8-12 with shortened periods, thus allowing students to work in the round house and shops of the railroad and at other jobs. Some worked on Victory gardens, and all helped the war effort by collecting fats, rubber, and cans. More and more students and alumni joined the armed services, and, which was inevitable under the circumstances, some gave their lives for their country. They are not listed here for fear that some names might unintentionally be left out. The Maekawa family, which contained notable D.H.S. scholars, Dunsmuir's only Japanese-American family at that time, had to leave Dunsmuir and was interned.

During the 1944 school year a Cadet Corps was formed under R. T. Wattenburger, and Elsie Ellington's name appears on the list of faculty members. The 1945 *Crag Echoes* is dedicated to the boys in the service, and Mr. Wattenburger wrote,

"You students of Dunsmuir High School are to be congratulated for your stability during the past school year. Standards of scholarship, morality, and extra-curricular activities are comparable to the normal pre-war trend. You are taking the war in stride. In your own way you have been helping the boys at the front. It is you they are fighting for and you that they want to see unchanged when they return."

The 1946 yearbook was dedicated to "world peace and the security of mankind," and was also dedicated to David Erickson, the language teacher. In 1947 John Glaese, back from his war service, became principal when Ralph Wattenburger accepted a position as principal of Livermore High School. During 1949 California celebrated its 100 years as a state, and the '49 *Crag Echoes* used the Centennial theme. Noted new names on the faculty at this time were Paul Reginato and Herm Kostiz.

50's

John Glaese served as principal of Dunsmuir High through 1952 and the names of Bob Wright and Al Neasham appear on the staff. Al Neasham was custodian until 1965.

By now the State of California was planning Interstate 5 through this area. Much controversy was felt in Dunsmuir over the proposed route through town. Many citizens hoped that the freeway — as long as it was taking so many good houses and other property — would go through the high school property, thus giving the community a chance to pick a new high school site and get rid of the sliding hillside for good. But the State Division of Highways decided to cut below the school (they argued that the grade through the school property would be too steep). This meant that the new highway cut between the school and the town.

In 1953 Delwin Poe became principal when John Glaese accepted a position at Sonoma High School. Mr. Poe served Dunsmuir High School through 1972 — a twenty-year dedication to the school and town. He and his wife, Mayme, still reside here.

During the '50's Charlotte Samuelson taught at D.H.S., Melvin Stanley retired, and the American Field Service program was started. This exchange with students from other countries continued for about ten years, and in later years students in the Rotary Club program and other exchange programs have attended D.H.S. (See special article on exchange students.)

It was during this decade that there was a movement urging the consolidation of the school districts in southern Siskiyou County. It was proposed that a high school be built near the intersection of highways 89 and I-5 in the Mott area, to serve the communities of Weed, Mt. Shasta, McCloud, and Dunsmuir. A large high school complex would offer larger vocational, scientific, and athletic facilities and more academic opportunities, although the personal "give and take" of a small school would be lost. This idea, it was agreed, would necessitate a large fleet of buses, but it was agreed that savings would be realized in supplies and maintenance.

However, in 1958 McCloud built and occupied its new high school building, and soon afterward Weed, Mt. Shasta, and then Dunsmuir followed with new buildings also. After all — whoever heard of Loggers, Cougars, Bears, and Tigers living in harmony?

'60's — THE TURBULENT YEARS

Dunsmuir High School survived the '60's under the guidance of Del Poe and his faculty. Other faculty names appear: Ramey Drake, Coach Elliott, Wally Trapnell, Charles Bispala, Coach Jim Bujol, Dave Blount, Bob Shipley, Leo Smith, Louise Thompson, and Marian Nichols.

In 1963 on November 22, President John F. Kennedy was shot, and the student body was in such a state of shock, that the Senior play, "The Plaster Bandit," was postponed until a week later.

The agony of Viet Nam marked this period and again many of the youth of Dunsmuir High School and its alumni served their country in this difficult conflict.

Toward the end of the '60's the high school building was showing its age and state earthquake laws were getting more stringent. The high school board began plans for a new school building. It was decided to build on the same site and keep the gym building, but to put the new two-story building south of the gym. Much discussion ensued as to the plans, and in the end the "open classroom" idea was adopted.

70's

The 1970's began with the new school becoming a reality, and it also marked the end of Delwin Poe's tenure as principal. Mr. Eugene Douglas took over the helm of Dunsmuir High School — a new principal, with a new job, a new community, and a new school building — not an easy task. In the spring of 1974 the student body had a Moving Day. Everyone came to school and helped move. Students and teachers trotted back and forth from the old building to the new, carrying desks, chairs, typewriters, boxes of books, equipment, etc. Heavy furniture and other large items were moved by dollies and a truck, until Dunsmuir High School had actually been moved from the old building into the sparkling new one. The slogan of "many hands make light work" proved to be true. Then students and faculty watched spellbound as bulldozers actually "mowed down" the old building that had been such a source of pride in 1920.

The new building boasted of an elevator for its two stories, a beautiful central library, carpeted in gold and with a ceiling of wooden beams, a lecture room, and 8 class rooms. At first the classrooms on the upper floor were open to the library area; but, through use, these rooms have been closed off and the library itself restricted by walls to the eastern end of the original area. It was found that the "open classroom" concept had its drawbacks. The lower floor of the new school building contained three classrooms, a multipurpose room with stage, offices, kitchen for a hot lunch program, and a large shop for a work experience program was in operation during this period as well as a vocational foods class.

Some faculty names appearing through the '70's were: Bill Birch, Robert Dietrick, Bob Knapp, Ron Dolf, Jim Rinne, Mark Reiner, Anita Knapp (nee McFall), Charlotte Olson, Mary Day, Don Brannon, Grace Harris, Leo Smith, Doug Simpson, Jody Manley, with Boyd Cravens and Archer Van Heest involved with school maintenance.

Dr. R. Halbert Christensen took over as principal in 1979 when Mr. Douglas moved to Redding. The enrollment of Dunsmuir High School was falling toward 200 students as Dunsmuir felt the economic crunch of the Recession, as the concentration of railroad jobs moved to Roseville, and as the slump in the lumber and building industries hurt the area.

The 1979 football varsity boasted only twelve players. They called themselves the dirty dozen. Robert Hubbard, one of the dozen, wrote:

"Although we did not win a game all season, we really did win in our hearts. We put forth more effort than a championship team and that is what counts."

Truly that was the Tiger Spirit in essence.

Another team that persevered during this time was the Ski Club which braved the snow on the mountain under the direction of Bill Birch. The closing down of the Ski Bowl brought an end to skiing as a sport. The new tennis courts finally were finished after difficulties had been resolved with the contractors. The courts were placed on the area once occupied by the old school building. Dunsmuir High School tennis players distinguished themselves in county and area competition. The end of the '70's saw many of the long-time faculty members retiring: Leo Smith, Herm Kostiz, Louise Thompson, Mary Day, Grace Harris, and Mildred Lockart, who had served as school secretary.

Dr. Christensen stressed "Dunsmuir High School — Home of Scholars and Champions." He inaugurated the Tiger Award program which each year honored students in all categories of achievement — academic, athletic, and service and vocational. Community leaders were invited to present the awards.

THE PRESENT

By 1984 the enrollment hovered around 150 students. The "Spirit Stick" was still held high, and the faculty and students added computer science to their accomplishments. Inflation had taken its toll as far as school moneys were concerned, but Dunsmuir High continues to offer opportunities to learn for those students who wish to learn.

As Dunsmuir reaches its Centennial Year of 1986, many classes are planning reunions — keeping the flame of the Tiger spirit alive. One thing all the alumni have in common and that is a great love for the little high school in the Sacramento River Canyon at the foot of Mt. Shasta.

DUNSMUIR HIGH SCHOOL
STUDENT EXCHANGE PROGRAM

AMERICAN FIELD SERVICE

During the years that this program was in operation in Dunsmuir, D.H.S. students could apply for a summer abroad when they lived in the home of a family in a foreign country. Foreign students coming here spent one year attending Dunsmuir High School, as part of the senior class, and they lived with Dunsmuir families.

Class of 1958:
Ulla Berntson, Goteborg, Sweden — Jim Lockart family. Ulla has stayed in touch with the Lockarts and has visited here, and so have her parents. Ulla and her husband and two daughters were here in 1982 and Ulla came in June, 1984, to her class reunion. Mildred and Jim Lockart traveled to Sweden in 1979.

Class of 1959:
Dieter Heinrich, Frankfurt, Germany — Durward Gass family. Dieter is now an M.D. in Essen, Germany, and still keeps in touch.

Summer of 1958:
Susan Thom went to Germany.

Class of 1960:
Inger Saedder, Denmark — L. D. Asher family.

Summer of 1959:
Tom Seed went to England.

Class of 1961:
Walter Kuenzler, Switzerland — Sam Burton family. Walter became ill before the school year was over and had to return home.

Summer of 1960:
Terri Fawcett went to Denmark.

Class of 1962:
Gisela Ludecke, Patterborn, Germany — Jack Samuelson family. Gisela returned to California, married an American and is presently living in Fresno, CA, with her husband and two children.

Summer of 1961:
Paul Burton went to Germany.

Class of 1963:
Carlos Leiva, Chile — Roger Ellis family. Carlos has returned to Dunsmuir once to visit. However, he returned to the U.S., got his Ph.D. in electronics in N.Y., worked for NASA, and now works for Electronics Assoc. in N.J. He married in the U.S. and has two children.

Summer of 1962:
Michael Wright went to Austria.

Class of 1964:

Jose Saldeno, Venezuela — Bill Anderson family. Jose went on to become an engineer. Last heard he was married and living in Caracas, Venezuela.

Summer of 1963:

Kathleen Harris went to Bjornskinn, Vesteralen, Norway — Torleiv Hansson family. In the summer of 1965, Borgny Hansson came to visit the Harris family. Then in 1969 Mike Harris went to the Hansson farm in Norway after he returned from Viet Nam. In 1977 Grace Harris visited Borgny, her husband Martin Nikolaisen, and two children at their home in southern Norway. In 1981 the Nikolaisens came to New Orleans to live for two years while Martin studied oil procedures from American oil companies. Christmas, 1982, found the Nikolaisens celebrating with the Harrises in Dunsmuir. They returned to Norway in 1983.

Class of 1965:

Roger Soliva, Iloilo City, Philippines — Kenneth Griffith family.

Summer of 1964:

Louis Dewey was chosen as the Summers Abroad student, but no home was available.

Class of 1966:

Gianna Guardasoni, Reggio Emilia, Italy — Parsons family.

Class of 1967:

Sally Webster, Australia — Howard Jones family. Sally is now married, has two children, and still lives on the same sheep station where she was raised. Writes and exchanges pictures with the Jones family once or twice a year. "Has two lab pups, too."

Class of 1968:

Hanne Anderson, Allborg, Denmark — Bill Nealon family. Hanne keeps in touch. She is married to a chiropractor and lives in England. She came back to Dunsmuir to visit in 1978, and has hopes to come back in 1985 or '86 to help Dunsmuir celebrate its Centennial.

INTERNATIONAL CHRISTIAN YOUTH EXCHANGE

Class of 1968:

Jutta Lippke, Essen, Germany — Bob Bectel family and Bob Dewey family. Married Dunsmuirite, Albert Pon. They are now living in Germany, where Albert is an M.D. and specialist, and Jutta has several degrees and is a teacher. They keep in touch with the Deweys.

Per Lundburg of Sweden spent an exchange week in Dunsmuir under this program.

JAPANESE INTERNATIONAL CULTURAL EXCHANGE

Class of 1979:

Aoi (Holly) Jo, Hiroshima, Japan — Roger Ellis family. Holly came back to attend C.O.S. where she got her A.A. degree in three semesters. She now works for the Ford Motor Co. in Hiroshima. Keeps in close touch with the Ellises. Roger and Rose Ellis traveled to Japan for a two-week vacation in 1982.

ROTARY CLUB EXCHANGE STUDENTS

Class of 1982:

Erich Veit, Switzerland — Stromsness and Wopschall families. He kept in touch with both families.

Jeff Andresen of Dunsmuir went to Finland for a year's study in 1981-82.

Julie Arno went to New Zealand for a year's study, 1981-82.

Class of 1984:

Antti Paavilainen, Finland — Andresen family. Jeff plans to travel to Finland in 1985 and take his Mother with him. They will visit Antti.

Class of 1922

A TEACHER'S PLEA

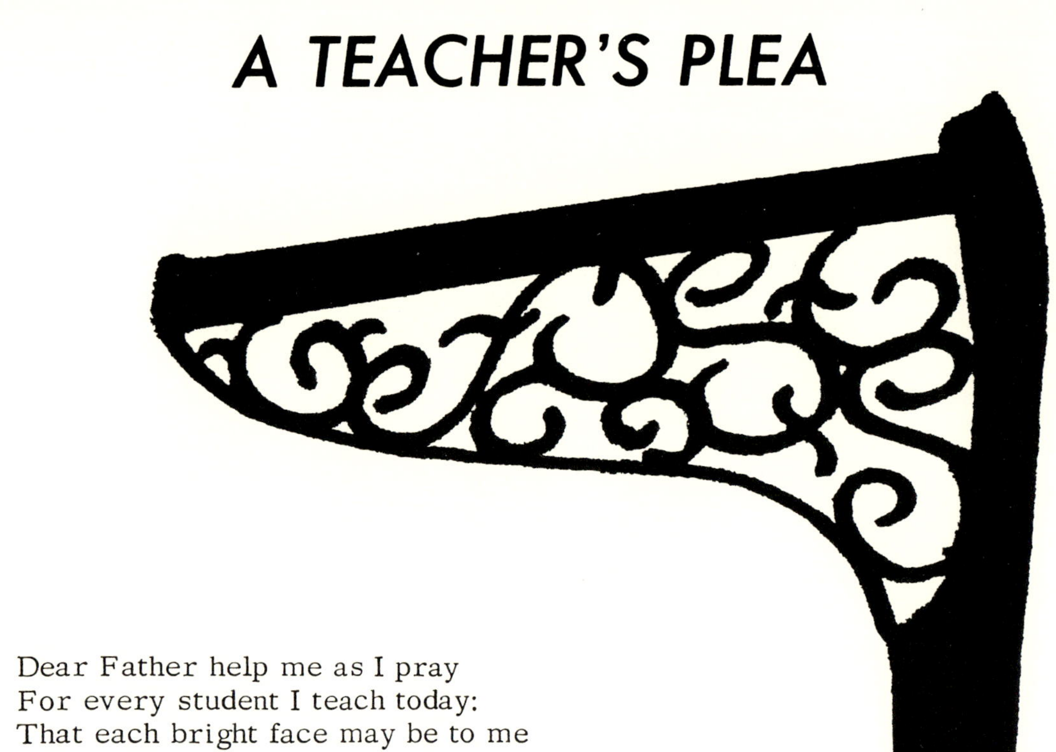

Dear Father help me as I pray
For every student I teach today:
That each bright face may be to me
A cherished photograph of Thee;

THE MYSTERY IS SOLVED . . .

Many have wondered why there was no *Crag Echoes* of 1922. Here is the answer. The costuming for the dramatic production put on by D.H.S. that year cost so much, that there was no money left for the annual. The pictures above show some of the costumes. The name of the production has been forgotten, but it had something to do with Columbus discovering America — hence Queen Isabella and the Indian brave. The queen is Elinore Van Fossen Harrison and the Indian chief was Beverley Mason.

Office force—1st row: Jean Crahane, Mr. Wattenburger, Eva Rossetto, Edith Comstock, Violet Durante, Louisa Consentino; 2nd row: Gerry Smith, Margaret Stanley, Helen Martin, Anita Pedroncelli, Constance Jones.

Top: Ralph T. Wattenburger
Right: John Glaese
Left: Delwin H. Poe
Center: C. Eugene Douglas
Lower right: R. Halbert Christensen

THE HILL!!

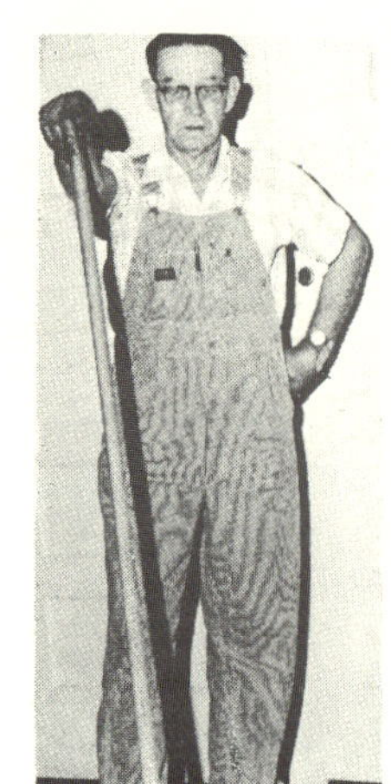

FOOTBALL
1942

1st row, left to right: Robert Wheeler, Julio Rossetto, Bill Bostwick, Wayne Olsen (captain), Cordes Smith, Ben Kivett. 2nd row: George Maekawa, Vincent Padilla, John Lund, Vincent Holbrook, John Jones, Vance Biddle. 3rd row: Wesley Gurr, Ramon Martin, Joe Barajas, Willis Cleaver, Ivan Young, Bill Wheeler. 4th row: Frank Wheeler, Leslie Jones, Harold Olsen, Jim Holland, Marion Hull, Duane Rupp. 5th row: Gale Pachuca, Junior Martin (Asst. mgr.), Alfred Barnum, Paul Livingston (Mgr.), Coach Bican, Lavelle Davis.

BAND
1st row, left to right, Avanelle French, Gene Stanton, Charles Masson. 2nd row: Lewis Masson, Bob Corwin, Pat Sherwood, Treva Jo Hatchett, Delores Brown, Harry Harper, Winnifred Humphreys, Bob Daw, Wesley Barnum. 3rd row: Virginia Bissell, Eugene Lamb, Jim Jaeckle. Willis Cleaver and Albert Benkosky are not in the picture.

NOW

AND

THEN

Photo: Reineking

CHAPTER VIII

THE HISTORIES OF THE CHURCHES OF DUNSMUIR, CALIFORNIA
By
Flora Stokoe Wintering

Wherever there are two,
 They are not without God;
And wherever there is one
 alone, I say I am with Him.
Raise the stone, and there
 thou shalt find me;
Cleave the wood, and there am I.

—Fifth Logion of
Oxyrhynchus Logio

In the middle of the 1880's, as the railroad construction crews of the Central Pacific Company worked their way north through the pristine beauty of the Sacramento River Canyon and on toward a juncture with the line at Ashland, Oregon, the elements of an organized society were venturing close behind. By the time the decade had come to an end, there would be the families and homes, the schools and libraries, the services and governments that, when meshed, would produce villages of varying attributes, and one such village would be the community of Dunsmuir.

As it was in all other young towns, the people who came to make up the community of Dunsmuir brought with them their diverse religious faiths. Which of the Christian faiths first held services in Dunsmuir, and on what date they held them only can be wondered about.

However, in June of 1890, an article concerning Dunsmuir appeared in a Sunday issue of the *San Francisco Chronicle*, and it mentioned that the town had two churches. One of the two churches would have been the one erected by the Methodist Episcopal society the year before. Possibly the other church referred to was the one just being completed that month by the Presbyterian congregation. The Roman Catholics and the Episcopalians were holding services in homes and halls whenever one of their missionary priests visited the area, but within a few years each of these congregations would have its own edifice for the worship of God. If by 1890 public worship by other faiths had begun in Dunsmuir, this researcher failed to find out about them.

So it was that by 1890 at least four denominations had planted roots in Dunsmuir. Others would come and, before one hundred years had passed, some would have succeeded while others failed. Organizing a group of people into a religious society and building a home for it took money, hard work, and persistence. The dedicated among the members set to work at once contributing their time, soliciting pledges, securing loans, and sponsoring projects in order to accumulate the necessary funds for the building programs. It was in Dunsmuir as it was in most places, after the buildings were in place came the struggles to survive. Enthusiasms waned. Ministers and priests were difficult to secure. There was a succession of them in the churches. As one Episcopal bishop remarked, "We need men with 'staying' qualities." In spite of all the difficulties encountered in the past century, God and religion stayed on in Dunsmuir.

THE FIRST BAPTIST CHURCH

At least one other attempt was made to establish a Baptist church in Dunsmuir before the present congregation was started as a mission of the Mt. Shasta Church in August of 1962. Services at one time were held in the basement of the Dunsmuir Hotel. At the time that the Reverend Fred Pace, his wife, and sons Jimmy and Billie were ministering to the congregation in 1954, the membership moved to a house on the corner of Prospect and North Highway. This information was reported in the *Dunsmuir News.* The venture appears to have failed shortly after the move.

In 1962, the Mt. Shasta Baptist Church became interested in sponsoring a mission for the Dunsmuir Baptist community. Meetings were held in 1962, and the Dunsmuir Southern Baptist congregation was organized on November 3, 1963, with twenty-four charter members. The building housing Shannon's Gift Shop and Nursery was purchased and remodeled to be used as a church. The structure had been built in 1928 to be a checking station to register out-of-state cars coming into California.

Later it became Mac's Grocery before being purchased by the Shannons.

Following is a list of the pastors who have served the Dunsmuir church and the year in which each came:

Thomas Burkes, 1962
Henry Asbury, 1963
John Park, 1963
Robert Ainsworth, 1966
Gene Willeford, 1967
V. E. Boyd, 1971
Grady Estes, 1977
Stephen Rogers, 1978

At about the time that the St. Barnabas Episcopal congregation had come to realize that its church building was too large and too expensive for its dwindling membership to maintain, the Southern Baptist congregation found that it was outgrowing its home. In 1969 negotiations began to purchase the "Rock Church" from the St. Barnabas' members. The Episcopal Bishop in Sacramento agreed to the sale, with the St. Barnabas' congregation receiving, as a down payment, the little frame building belonging to the Baptist membership. The

Baptist would pay the remainder off on time, which they have done.

On December 3, 1969, the First Baptist congregation met in its new home for the first time. Since then, the church has been refurbished and remodeled to fit the needs of the present membership. A baptistry has been added at the back of the sanctuary. Classrooms have been built in the large parish room in the basement. In 1981, the house on the south side of the church was purchased to provide office and more classroom space. Recently this addition was dedicated and named "Faith House."

The rock church, with its three stained-glass windows and small, rooftop, shell cross, is an attractive edifice in downtown Dunsmuir. In 1982, speaking about the church to a reporter from Redding's *Record Searchlight,* the present pastor, Stephen Rogers, said, "We enjoy it. It is very different than normal Baptist architecture."

Much of the information about the First Baptist Church was contributed by a member, Claudia Thompson of Dunsmuir.

DUNSMUIR'S FIRST CHURCH
OF CHRIST, SCIENTIST

It was not until 1912 that the students of Christian Science held their first meeting in Dunsmuir, but an interest in having a Church of Christ, Scientist had been shown many years before that date. Perhaps the editor of the *Dunsmuir News,* and others no doubt, were anxious to have the group organize, for it was he whose comment in the February 22, 1902, edition of the paper expressed this interest. The *News* had received an invitation to attend a Christian Science lecture the previous evening in Ashland, Oregon. The lecturer was the Honorable W. H. Ewing of Chicago. The editor asked, "Why not come down to Dunsmuir?" If the Honorable Ewing ever did get to Dunsmuir, it was not at that time.

The brief history of Dunsmuir's Christian Science Church provided for this chapter by Bernice Scribner of Weed, California, tells that the Christian Science Society first met in Dunsmuir in 1912 at the Weed Hotel, and in 1914 the Society was organized and recognized by the Mother Church in Boston. The group met in the homes of members, and according to notices in the local newspaper, by 1921 members were meeting in Branstetter Hall every Sunday

morning and every Wednesday evening for the midweek testimonial services. In June of that year the Society was re-organized and on July 15, 1923, was incorporated under the laws of the State of California and became the First Church of Christ, Scientist of Dunsmuir. At that time services were being held in the Odd Fellows' Hall.

On September 29, 1920, the Society had purchased property on Florence Avenue (now Dunsmuir Avenue) for the purpose of erecting a church building. It was not until the winter of 1923-1924 that the very attractive edifice with its decorative columns, pictured in the Dedication section of this book, was built. Sunday, July 10, 1932, was the dedication day for the building. The July 15th issue of the *News* reported that a morning and an afternoon service had been held, and that good size congregations were present at both meetings with many attending from neighboring communities.

The First Church of Christ, Scientist just had been completed in 1924 when, in April, fire destroyed the buildings belonging to the Methodist and Episcopal congregations. Immediately, the Christian Scientists offered the use of their building to the

Episcopalians for their Sunday evening services. This offer was accepted gladly, and when the Episcopalians completed and dedicated their new St. Barnabas Church in 1925, they publicly expressed their appreciation for the assistance they had been given by the congregation of the Church of Christ, Scientist.

In 1969 some remodeling was done at the church. To make the front portico more easily accessible from the street, double run staircases were added leading up to the top landing. A planter was built at the sidewalk level between the beginning of the two stairways.

Believing that . . . "all Thy children shall be taught of the Lord; . . ." (Isaiah 53:13), the church holds classes each Sunday for pupils up to the age of twenty. They are taught the Scriptures, and they use the textbook, *Science and Health With Key to the Scriptures,* by Mary Baker Eddy, the Founder of Christian Science. As stated in the brochure provided by the local church, the pupil "finds that the age-old lessons are filled with treasures of spiritual understanding and healing which he can apply to his own daily activities."

DUNSMUIR'S PENTECOSTAL CHURCH

According to Vicki Pierce, who prepared the following information about the history of the Christian Life Center Church, the first Pentecostal message was brought to Dunsmuir in the fall of 1914 by a Brother Kresley. After a few meetings in the homes of interested members, a room was secured in the old Knights of Pythias Hall by Frank O'Brien, where believers met for worship and fellowship. The church was then called the Pentecostal Mission.

Kresley was followed by Frank Lindbland, who was then succeeded by Brother M. F. Draper in 1917, but about that time all meetings were closed on account of a flu epidemic that swept the town. At the same time the lease on the room at the hall was lost, but Brother Draper was able to get permission to hold meetings in the Methodist Church on Sunday afternoons. Other meetings were held in the members' homes. Sunday School, which was started under Brother Lindbland's ministry, was taken up again immediately when the quarantine was lifted. It was conducted in a home.

In 1918, the small congregation, numbering between twelve to fourteen people, secured a lot on Shasta Avenue and purchased lumber to build a church structure. The congregation was holding services before there was a roof on the building. When completed, the building became known as the Dunsmuir Pentecostal Church.

Soon thereafter, the Dunsmuir Pentecostal Church affiliated with the General Council of the Assemblies of God and changed its name to Dunsmuir Assembly of God. A roll-call of the early pastors of Dunsmuir's Assembly of God after Brother Draper, who oversaw the building of the church, is as follows: Clarence Radley, Sister Ludwig, and Oscar Arenison from the Glad Tidings Church in San Francisco, which is the oldest established Assemblies of God Church in California. (Dunsmuir's church is the second oldest church of the denomination in California.) Following Brothers Wernicay and Ellison, who stayed less than a month, was a Brother Hendrichison, W. C. Anderson, J. S. Farrer, Lloyd C. Pershing, Martin Brunswick, C. C. Catledge, Wm. C. Ross and Vernon Winters.

The church records are scanty from 1950 on to the early 70's. On June 7, 1974, the Dunsmuir Assembly of God purchased the Church of the Nazarene at 4304 Stagecoach Road, the present location of the congregation. The name of the church was changed again from Dunsmuir Assembly of God to Christian Life Center, but it is still affiliated with the General Council of the Assemblies of God. The pastor at the time of this purchase was Andrew L. Fliflet, who was in the Dunsmuir ministry for eight years. During the time Brother Fliflet was here, the congregation purchased property on Buckboard Lane and built a residence for their pastors. Currently serving in the Pastorate is the Reverend Wayne A. Edwards and his wife, Deborah, who prior to this church ministered at the Assembly of God in Crescent City, California.

Dunsmuir's present-day Christian Life Center operates a State-licensed Pre-School, has a thriving Sunday School ministry, and an active women's group.

ASSEMBLY OF GOD CHURCH
(1918-1974)

The building still stands on Shasta Avenue, but is no longer used as a church.

THE CHURCH OF JESUS CHRIST
OF LATTER-DAY SAINTS

The following material has been quoted almost word-for-word from the historical information provided by Ann Ball of Dunsmuir, and I appreciate her getting this information together for me.

The earliest account of a Church of Jesus Christ of Latter-Day Saints organization in the Mount Shasta area was the work instigated in the summer of 1925 by Clara Connelly and her mother, Gertrude Wood, in Dunsmuir with the aid of two lady missionaries from Redding. This small group got started by holding meetings in the small apartment of the Connellys on North Dunsmuir Avenue. Clara, a young bride at the time, tells of how she had to roll the large, upright piano into a big closet between meetings in order to get around her small apartment. At that time, Joe Cole was called to the branch presidency, and the branch was officially known as the Mt. Shasta Branch, Shasta District, Northern California Mission, and its area was Dunsmuir, Sweetbrier, Mt. Shasta, Kinyon Camp, McCloud, Weed, and Edgewood. Some of the active member families were the Bounds, Benkes, Neilsens, Woods, and the Connellys. The branch disbanded after only two years because all the members, except Clara and her mother, had moved away.

Then, in 1930, a few saints who reorganized under the leadership of Tom Gibson, were holding meetings at homes of different members in Mount Shasta. A similar group was meeting in Dunsmuir. Maud Daley, Clara Connelly, and a few others, whose names we do not have, were holding meetings in the Blue Room of the Masonic Hall with Joe Knowe as a leader. In 1932, these two groups got together and were meeting in a small home near the Brown Shasta Ranch. A beautiful, antique organ was donated by a non-member whose name is not known. Song books, lesson manuals, and any other items belonging to the church were stored in a large chest. This unification increased in numbers and strength and some activity started. All went well for a year or so until disaster struck. A fire at the home in which the meetings were held burned the house, and the congregation lost its organ and chest with all its belongings in it. This disaster must have been a shattering experience.

About 1937 or 1938, during the Mission presidency of Elder Aird McDonald, a small group, which had been meeting intermittently in a room over the Mount Shasta movie theater, started meeting regularly in Howe Hall. Clarence Parker was called to the branch presidency, and the organization has been continuously growing to this day.

In 1938, President Parker called Maud Daley to organize the sisters into the first official Relief Society, and she became its first president. Under her dedicated leadership, the group became well recognized for its spiritual and compassionate service. This active Relief Society consisted of eight charter members: Maud B. Daley, Marie Knowe, Mabel Neilson, Lola Bounds, Ida Extell, Clarecie Bounds, Stella Burdock, and Clara Connelly. Membership soon grew to include the following ladies: Helen Smith, a much needed and talented organist, Iris Peterson, Ethel Paul, Celeste Wyatt, Julia Anderson, Ethel Bean, June Frost, Elsie Jensen, Eva Lay, Vivian Weston, Thelma Raymond, Elenor Lark, Marie Hutchens, and Veatrice Porteous.

The present church in Mount Shasta was begun in 1959, and it was dedicated in October of 1960, and it is the only Church of Jesus Christ of Latter-Day Saints to serve the Mormon community of South Siskiyou County. Except for the following paid employees, the members of the church did the building: Ross Miller, the construction superintendent; Dean Johnson, his helper; Mr. Zanni, who constructed the pulpit; and Mr. Scarbella, a famous local rock mason, who, with the direct assistance of lay members, did the beautiful rock work on the exterior of the building. Ross and Dean worked during the day with what help they could get. Those who had other jobs during the day came to the project later and worked with the other men far into the night. Driving the big, long spikes through the eight-inch timbers that made the beautiful vaulted ceiling, made the strongest workers go home with stiff and aching muscles.

Recently, there has been extensive remodeling of the building to make improvements and to bring it up to earthquake safety standards. During this period of work, the congregation held meetings at the Community Building in Dunsmuir and at Sisson Elementary School in Mount Shasta. The renovated chapel was rededicated in December, 1984.

THE CONGREGATION OF
JEHOVAH'S WITNESSES

In Pittsburgh, Pennsylvania, in the fall of 1884, a former clothier, Charles Taze Russell, incorporated the Christian, religious society based on God's Word that he had founded in 1872. Today, the organization is known as the Watch Tower Bible and Tract Society, and its members are referred to as Jehovah's Witnesses. Members have been witnessing in Dunsmuir since about 1940. For a time, they met for services with the group in Mt. Shasta. Later on, meetings were held in the Dunsmuir homes of the members; and, in 1974, the group purchased the old Dunsmuir Laundry on Butterfly Avenue and remodeled it to be the Kingdom Hall for the local congregation. The membership, having outgrown its present home, has bought the property on Florence Loop that was once the Ford Garage's used car lot. The congregation is hoping to construct a new Kingdom Hall at that location in 1985.

A Body of Elders deals with the spirituality of the congregation, keeping it encouraged and fed on the proper food of God's Word. Children and adults alike attend the services held three times each week. At noon Sundays the group gathers for two hours for the Public Talk service at which the Elders and others speak. Tuesday evening is Book Study Night, when the books of the Watch Tower are studied for an hour. The Theocratic Ministry School meets on Thursday evening to study the Bible for two hours. The public is invited to attend the meetings.

The above information was prepared from material given to the writer by the Congregation of Jehovah's Witnesses of Dunsmuir.

When first did Episcopalians worship together in Dunsmuir? This question is difficult to answer. There may have been a society of this faith organized about the same time as Episcopalians living in the once busy town of Mott organized themselves. According to information in the 1976 Centennial Book published by St. Mark's Episcopal Church in Yreka, their rector, the Reverend T. H. Gilbert, D.D., who served them from 1886 to 1890, made regular trips to Mott, Sisson, and Dunsmuir. He held the first ever Episcopal service in Mott in July, 1889, and arrangements were made at that time for him to come there every two weeks. The hall in the upper floor of the new Mott school building was to be used for divine services. This would lead one to believe that during Father Gilbert's term at St. Mark's Church, there were at least informal gatherings in the halls and homes of Dunsmuir for the purpose of holding Episcopal services. If so, 1889 was no doubt the year that such gatherings began in Dunsmuir.

The July 19, 1890 issue of the *Dunsmuir News* stated that Mott would soon have an Episcopal Church erected in that village, and in the August 9th edition, the Editor was reporting that the Church would have the "seats in and be ready for services next Sunday night." Commenting on the new church, the *Yreka Journal* reported that, when finished, the church at Mott would be one of the neatest little churches in the county.

Consecrated to the "Glory of God and St. Andrew," the church in Mott may not have had a resident priest, as there is no mention of one in a September newspaper item which reported that Dr. Gleaves, Lu (J. U.) Donmeyer, and a "consort of ladies" were presiding over the Sunday School. For the first few years of its existence, no doubt, St. Andrew's depended upon the rectors of St. Mark's, Yreka, and on an occasional visit from the Right Reverend J. H. D. Wingfield, Bishop of the Diocese.

At this time, St. Andrew's Church evidently was the only church edifice in Mott, as the *Dunsmuir News* reported that the congregation welcomed and encouraged other congregations to share their building. But St. Andrew's was destined not to grow. As a community, Mott faded away and so did its Episcopal congregation. St. Andrew's Church was mentioned in this chapter about the churches of Dunsmuir, because some of the Episcopalians living in Dunsmuir attended the services in the Mott Church, and after St. Andrew's held its last service, many of its parishioners came to live in Dunsmuir and to worship with the existing St. Barnabas' congregation.

Following the Reverend T. H. Gilbert's Episcopal ministry in Siskiyou County, the Reverend Charles Fitchett was in Yreka in 1891 and 1892, and he traveled a circuit serving the Episcopal communities of Southern Siskiyou County.

To digress, early in 1890, the Presbyterians had built a pretty little church in Dunsmuir on Spruce Street between Florence (Dunsmuir) Avenue and Sacramento Avenue. The property had been deeded to them by the Pacific Improvement Company of San Francisco. After several years of attempting to put together a sustaining congregation, the Presbyterian Board decided not to replace the pastor and to allow the Episcopalians to use the church, and, reluctantly, sold them the building finally. It may be that the Reverend J. H. Cornwall, who left for Oregon in 1892, was the last Presbyterian minister at the church. Evidently, the congregation was not contributing enough to pay him a salary. So it may have been as early as 1892 that the Episcopalians began to use the church. Still, it would not have been before March of that year, as a letter to the Editor of the *Dunsmuir News* that month had been written by the Reverend Charles L. Fitchett in which he explained why he had not held Episcopal services the previous Monday evening in the Methodist Episcopal Church. There had been a misunderstanding between him and the Reverend Miller of that church, who was holding a revival service when Fitchett arrived for Episcopal services. Piqued, he ended his letter announcing, "I will be very glad to visit your town for services at any time, providing a public hall can be secured."

Father Fitchett appears to have been a bit thin-skinned, but the St. Mark's Centennial Book refers to him as an eloquent and interesting speaker. However, neither he nor his successor, the Reverend Lewis DeLew, who came to the county in November, 1892, kept good church records, which may be the reason there is little information about the work done to establish a church in Dunsmuir. "Doctor" DeLew, as he was called, was a kind, gentle, and learned man. He, too, spent just one year as a missionary priest in Siskiyou County, and he died about three years after leaving the area.

The priest who put forth a great deal of effort to promote St. Barnabas Mission in Dunsmuir was the Reverend Alfred George, who came to St. Mark's Church in 1893. Like others before and after him, Father George was a dedicated man with a large territory to cover as he traveled by horseback, stage, or railroad from one end of his mission district to the other in bad weather as well as in good. Regularly, he came to Dunsmuir, Mott, and Sisson for divine services.

By the first year of 1896, the *Dunsmuir News* began reporting the events being held by the Episcopalians, especially the money-making schemes of the ladies of the congregation. On February 7th the ladies held a social in the Presbyterian Church for the benefit of the church, and a first-rate time was had by a large crowd. The February 15th edition of the newspaper mentioned that the ladies were communicating with the Presbyterian Board in regards to buying the building. The Editor remarked that if the purchase were made, the Episcopal Church would be a credit to the town as the building would be improved and beautified. He went on to say, "Let everyone who can, lend a helping hand to the ladies, for they all realize that church work is very uphill at its best." New sidewalks were already being put in. Later that month the church was referred to as St. Barnabas' Mission. Two services were being held on the Sundays that the Reverend George came to Dunsmuir, and Confirmation classes were in progress. The Right Reverend Wingfield would be in Siskiyou County in early spring for Confirmation. In April the ladies of St. Barnabas gave a successful musical and literary entertainment. Strawberries and ice cream were served and the admissions were twenty-five and ten cents.

By June of 1896 the Reverend George had received $200.00 from the East to help toward raising the purchase price of the church. When one evening of entertainment and dance held at the Knights of Pythias' Hall in September realized thirty-five dollars, the ladies now had made $300.00 in Dunsmuir. As a result of the December fair and doll show, the ladies and Father George accumulated enough to pay for the church building.

Bishop Wingfield suffered a stroke some time during 1896. The Bishop-in-Charge of the Diocese was the Right Reverend Anson Rogers Graves, Bishop of the Platte, Nebraska. It was he who visited in February, 1897, and confirmed the following people at St. Barnabas' Church: Mae and Sue Dickey, Al. Schadt, Mrs. S. A. Gordon, Mrs. Lucy Neher, Mrs. J. Hubsch, Miss Tammy Law, and Mr. Frank Jenkens.

In the meantime, one of the largest Sunday Schools in the county had been established at the church. The *Yreka Journal* in April reported that the St. Barnabas scholars held a festival service of song and the church was simply packed, and a large number of people were not able to get in.

The Reverend George continued to serve his congregations regularly and with enthusiasm. For an example, one week in April he held services for large congregations at Dunsmuir, Keswick, Delta, Anderson, Mott, and he was back to Yreka for services there on Sunday. So that supplies could be purchased for the church, the ladies continued their money-making efforts. "Necktie and Apron Parties" seem to have been the vogue of the day, and they held several of them.

ST. BARNABAS' CHURCH (EPISCOPAL)
as it appeared perhaps in 1905 after extensive
repairs had been completed.

Though not clearly stated in the *Dunsmuir News*, one would suspect that the consecration of St. Barnabas' Church took place on October 29, 1897, when the Right Reverend Graves held services there. The newspaper had had an item in its May 28, 1897 issue which read as follows: "Services were held at the Presbyterian Church in this place last Sunday by the Rev. A. George. That date closed the second year's work of the church. During that time nearly $2,000 in cash has been raised. . . The legal obstructions which have prevented the purchase of the church property now used have been removed, and within a couple of weeks the Episcopalians will become the owners of the property." And then the August 13 issue says, "On Monday last the legal transfer of the church in this place heretofore owned by the Presbyterians to the Episcopalians was formally effected."

In October of 1897, the Reverend George announced that he would soon leave Siskiyou County to accept the charge at the church in Redding, and would be missionary priest to the area from Castella to Chico. The Reverend Bernard Duncan Sinclair came in November to replace him. Fr. Sinclair scheduled himself to be in Dunsmuir on the fourth Sunday of every month. He immediately interested the young people of the congregation in organizing a society which would meet in the rectory Sunday before Evening Prayer. The twenty-five charter members appointed Miss Ida Mathewson, Mr. Bickford Whiting, Miss Frankie Kilborn, Mrs. Beemer, and Mr. George Malone to be officers. Miss McCaskey, Maud Fellnagle, and Elizabeth Whiting were asked to be committee

chairmen. This group was very active for awhile.

The ladies of the church continued to busy themselves providing entertainment and money. Before Christmas they held a parlor bazaar and high tea at the home of Mrs. H. L. Walthar which ran for three consecutive afternoons. On Christmas Eve that year, they sponsored a ball which was a grand success. The newspaper reported that a "large and fashionable crowd was present."

Fr. Sinclair stayed in Siskiyou County until April, 1899, at which time he was replaced by the Reverend Octavious Parker who left the county in October, 1900. The St. Mark's Centennial Book suggests that perhaps "neither Fr. Sinclair nor Fr. Parker could face another winter traveling horseback in the ice and snow throughout the county." However, much can be said for Father Parker. According to the Dunsmuir paper, it was he who insisted that improvements be made to St. Barnabas Church. It said, "He was a rustler and deserves great credit — a clerical gentleman who is not afraid of manual labor. At 100 degrees he was clearing the yard of rubbage, etc." Mr. Chase of Mott had been the contractor on the job, and he was assisted by Frank Bragg and Waldo Charles.

Sometime in 1899 William Hall Moreland became the Bishop at Sacramento. In April, 1900, he was in Dunsmuir to confirm a class presented to him by Father Parker. The members of the class were: the Mesdames F. N. Fuller, Knight, Sulloway, Forcetti, Cross, Calkenona, Ladlow, and the Misses Perry and Calkenona, Mr. George Geisendorfer, and Master Calken-

ona. A "jolly wagon load of teachers and pupils of the Episcopal Sunday School were picnicking at the Cave and Hedge Creek Falls in June," and both Dr. Brewer, headmaster at the military school at San Mateo, and the Reverend James O. Lincoln of Castle Crags assisted Father Parker at services. But by September of 1900 Father Parker had tendered his resignation, and he left in October.

All appeared to be doing well when Father Parker left, but the Dunsmuir church seems to have been in a decline after the Reverend W. E. Couper came to minister to Yreka's St. Mark's and the South County churches. About 1903, Bishop Moreland, writing in the *Missionary District of Sacramento*, mentioned Dunsmuir and its unstable population. He said that St. Barnabas' Church had had twenty-two communicants one day and two the next when the Southern Pacific Company had moved many of its employees to Ashland, Oregon. He wrote, "In recognition of this fact, the Bishop of Oregon presented the mission with a bell as a gift from the Sunday School children of his diocese." (It is interesting to note that after several attempts at strengthening the steeple of St. Barnabas' Church, the Reverend A. W. Bell of St. Mark's Church, Yreka, recorded this memo: December 1, 1915 — There was an exchange of bells with St. Barnabas', Dunsmuir. Their bell was too heavy for St. Barnabas' tower and had a richer tone than St. Mark's bell, which weighed less.) "The church at Dunsmuir, with its new belfry and bell, its fresh paint and neat appointments, is the prettiest place of worship in town, and has now to gather a new congregation." The Company shifting men from Dunsmuir to other communities along its lines was not limited to this one time. It happened many times and each time resulted in diminished congregations in local churches.

Sometime in 1901, South Siskiyou County received its first resident priest, the Reverend Upton Gibbs, who was to be located in Sisson and was to serve St. Barnabas' Church, also. Sunday School, that had been suspended at the Dunsmuir church in the spring, was resumed in October, and religious services were conducted by Father Gibbs one evening a week. The Episcopalians joined the Methodists in giving their children a fine Christmas Tree that year. Not a child was forgotten when Santa Claus distributed the gifts. A Shrove Tuesday pancake and Valentine social was held in February, 1902. The ladies held a pink tea at the home of Mrs. C. O. Clarke, and a nice sum was realized to be used in purchasing Sunday School supplies and to make improvements on the church building.

Father Gibbs' ministry in South Siskiyou County was not long. By June of 1903, the Reverend Charles H. deGarmo was located at McCloud and was attempting to build a congregation in that community as well as serving Dunsmuir and Sisson. He reported to Bishop Moreland, "At Dunsmuir and Sisson . . . which have been put under the care of the missionary at Mc-Cloud, the outlook is encouraging. I say 'outlook' — for at present it is only the aspect of the future that gives hope. Yet there is a nucleus of faithful people at both of these places . . . with an earnest, courageous man of God to minister . . . to them, I see no reason to doubt the ultimate growth of these little bands of Christians . ." "Little bands" they surely were, because it was about this time that St. Barnabas Church was down to two or three communicants. But Father deGarmo chose not to be the "Man of God" to build up the congregations, and he left the area in October. Extracts from Bishop Moreland's Diary for October, 1903, noted that he was in Siskiyou County seeing to the construction of a church in McCloud, and it mentioned that the South County missions were without a pastor.

In February of 1904, the Reverend Sidney H. Morgan came from Hawaii to be resident priest at McCloud, and on Sunday, February 7, St. John's Church there was consecrated by Bishop Moreland. The following day, the Bishop, the Reverends Couper and Morgan, and Archdeacon Swan tramped through snow from Upton to Sisson, and then came by train to Dunsmuir for services. Dunsmuir was "awakening to new life," and the Bishop made arrangements for services to be held there "one whole Sunday a month, besides week days." Father Couper had been coming from Yreka to visit the South County churches and to secure subscriptions for the rector's salary. At Dunsmuir he had reorganized the mission which, owing to removals, had become almost dormant. It now gave promise of a "bright and vigorous future."

That year Easter services were held at St. Barnabas on Monday evening. "The southbound train being five hours late, the priest-in-charge had to drive from Upton." The church was decorated beautifully; the choir was augmented by friends from other churches and included a violin accompanist. The church was crowded, and the Masons and Eastern Stars attended.

Father Morgan was enticed away from McCloud, and again by September the first, the Bishop was advertising for a priest to fill the pulpit there, in Dunsmuir and in Sisson. The Reverend C. S. Linsley came in November. The salary was $900.00 and no rectory, although the congregation at Dunsmuir had built a room on the church and furnished it for the use of the priest. The Guild's November rummage sale cleared enough to pay off the $40.00 indebtedness on the room, insure the church for three years, and put a new roof on the building. Father Linsley reported that the church membership had suffered from a fire in the town the past summer and

from the removal of some of its best workers so that it was difficult to "inspire the remaining ones with enough courage to take the work up again."

Father Linsley had fallen in love with one of the young ladies of the choir at the Placerville Church. She was the eldest daughter of the late Reverend Summers of San Luis Obispo. She and Father Linsley were married in January, 1905, at the Chapel of the Holy Innocents, Corte Madera. In the fall of 1905, Father Linsley left the ministry of South Siskiyou County. Father Webster Clark conducted Christmas Services in 1905.

By March of 1906, the Reverend Henry T. Adams of Newkirk, Oklahoma, began appearing in reports as a missionary to Dunsmuir, Sisson, and McCloud. Easter that year was the first Easter Sunday service that the Dunsmuir congregation had had the privilege to enjoy in years. Father Adams did much to "revive the languishing work" at Dunsmuir. The St. Barnabas Guild began meeting weekly. The Vestry began improving the living conditions for the priest. They added a kitchen to the church and enlarged the vestry's room and furnished it as a living room and bedroom for the priest. They refurbished the church and added electric lights to replace the coal oil lamps. Father Adams moved from McCloud to Dunsmuir, although he continued to be in charge of both churches. He was busy and energetic. Christmas Eve, 1906, found him attending a tree for the Sunday School at St. Barnabas. He then took a train to Sisson where he conducted midnight service. At 5 a.m. he was on southbound train from Sisson to arrive back in Dunsmuir for 11 a.m. Christmas Day service.

St. Barnabas Church was in greatly improved condition by Easter Sunday, 1907. Matting had been placed in the aisles, and window sashes and frames stained dark and varnished. Friends in Sacramento and Berkeley had sent calla lilies which, with the white hangings, looked beautiful. An overflowing, reverent crowd gathered to hear the music and Father Adams' sermon. The choir of St. Barnabas' was growing quite large and proficient.

The ladies Guild continued to be very active. In July they gave a fancy lawn party at the A. J. Knight home at which, it was reported, the Junior Guild sold many kinds of homemade candies. During 1907 and 1908 St. Barnabas seemed to thrive and to meet its obligations to the Diocese. But sometime in 1909, the Reverend Adams left to be priest at the church in Arcata. Bishop Moreland's reports mentioned that on July 27, 1909, Henry Robinson Powell, the infant son of the missionary at Dunsmuir, had died. Mr. and Mrs. Powell had been the recipients of extraordinary kindness by the people of Dunsmuir. This is the only reference found to a Father Powell having been assigned to St. Barnabas. Perhaps, because of the death of the baby, his tenure

was not long.

The South County Episcopal Churches seemed to enter a period of little activity about this time. St. Barnabas failed to contribute to the Diocese, although C. O. Clarke and Al Knight's names did appear as contributors to the Endowment Fund of the Diocese. Then in 1910, The Reverend James W. Wright came to St. Mark's Church in Yreka, and he was to take care of Ft. Jones and the South County missions and set up a congregation at Kennett. Although he was in Yreka for three years, perhaps the circumstances of his private life prevented him from giving the time that he should have given to St. Barnabas' Church. In June of 1911 he was granted a leave to go home to Brooklyn, New York, for his wedding. Mrs. Wright returned to occupy the Yreka rectory with him. Sadly, in November of 1912, again he was given leave to return to Brooklyn to bury his wife, whose death was attributed to a complicated pregnancy. He left the county in 1913.

For several years St. Barnabas and the other South County churches seemed not to have had a priest nor much spiritual guidance. In reading excerpts from Bishop Moreland's appointment calendar, one realizes that often on his visits to Yreka he passed through Sisson and Dunsmuir without getting off the train to greet those few church people who might have appreciated his encouragement.

The Reverend John J. Cowan came to Yreka in 1913 and by April, 1914, had reported to the Bishop that "Dunsmuir is stirring just enough to be hopeful that, with patience and skillful nursing, our small flock will again be the influence it is reported to have been in years gone by." However, when Father Cowan left in November of 1915, St. Barnabas still did not have an active congregation. Arthur William Bell replaced him as rector of St. Mark's and missionary priest of South Siskiyou County. It is evident that sometime during his ministry Dunsmuir's Episcopal congregation came to life again.

In 1922 the Reverend Arthur J. Childs was assigned to St. Barnabas' Church, and he seems to have had quite a strong, active church group. Following World War I, church membership in the United States was as high as it had ever been, and Dunsmuir churches experienced the same growth as the rest of the nation. By 1924 the rectory had been added to, and the church itself enlarged to accommodate the growing choir. When the Reverend Stanley Theodore Boggess and his family arrived from Sparks, Nevada, to assume the ministry of the Episcopal congregation, he had held two services before tragedy struck. Those services were Palm Sunday, April 13, 1924, and Easter.

To go back in time, on Saturday afternoon, August 17, 1892, the Knights of Pythias' Hall on Sacramento Avenue had been dedicated. It had been financed, not by the fraternal organization of that name,

St. Barnabas' Church dressed for Easter, 1924.
In less than a week it had burned to the ground.

but by public subscription. It was long considered a fire-trap, having been the scene of several small fires during the years leading up to 1924. At 12:20 the morning of April 25 of that year, a fire that started in the Knights of Pythias' Hall extended up Sacramento Avenue and on to Florence Avenue, consuming buildings as it traveled north and westward. Among the structures destroyed were the impressive new Methodist Episcopal Church, its parsonage, the newly renovated St. Barnabas' Church, and its rectory. The Episcopalians loss, said to be $7,000.00 was covered by $4,000.00 in insurance.

Immediately, Bishop Moreland came from Sacramento to meet with the Episcopal Vestry to guide it in making decisions about rebuilding. It was decided to buy two pieces of property on Florence (Dunsmuir) Avenue belonging to J. W. Hawkins of San Diego. One house was occupied by Mrs. Louise Shoupe, her son Eugene, and his wife. The other house would be moved back on the lot and used for a rectory. In the meantime, church services were held at the Strand Theatre, the rectory, and the Christian Science Church, located across the street from the newly purchased property. The Church School classes were held at the Dunsmuir grammar school.

Father Boggess and the Episcopalians began the job of creating a second home for the St. Barnabas congregation. By Saturday, May 7th, the ladies of the Guild were giving a benefit dance for the young people of Dunsmuir at the Sciot's Hall, and the newspaper guaranteed good music and the

usual good time for all who came to "trip the light fantastic." The proceeds would be used to equip the rectory and the church when it was built. The Guild sponsored a party to organize the young people of the congregation. Twenty-four men of the church organized a men's group at a meeting at the home of Mr. and Mrs. Cowley. The women served a delicious meal and provided entertainment. Mr. Cowley was elected president and Mr. J. A. Martine, secretary-treasurer.

By August, 1924, work had begun on the new church. Vestry members, C. O. Porter, E. J. "Ted" Hawkins, William Cowley, and Henry Riley, awarded the contract for the stone work to Robert Pedroncelli. Native Black Butte rock was to be used. On September 15, 1924, the mayor of Dunsmuir, Dr. E. J. Cornish, laid the cornerstone of the foundation. Over thirty people contributed $100.00 or more to the building fund, and many hours of volunteer labor went into the construction. The congregation's determination paid off. The very pretty little church was completed, and at Palm Sunday services on April 5, 1925, the new St. Barnabas Church was dedicated by Father Boggess, whose first service in Dunsmuir had been the previous Palm Sunday. The twenty-member choir that sang at the services was the first vested choir to have been seen in Dunsmuir. Mr. Henry Riley played the organ prelude, Mrs. A. Nelson sang "The Palms," and Mr. George Farnum was the tenor soloist. The Lions Club attended in body the morning service, and the Odd Fellows were present

that evening. Father Boggess expressed his and the congregation's appreciation to all who had helped them during the year, and special thanks were given to the Christian Scientists. Bishop Moreland came to Dunsmuir on April 26 to see the new building and, no doubt, to consecrate it to the "Glory of God and St. Barnabas." The church prospered for a few years. The Sunday School grew, and the church choir was large and impressive. The congregation was enthusiastic.

About the time in 1927 that Father Boggess left Dunsmuir, the Southern Pacific Company had opened its Natron Cutoff between Kirk and Oakridge, Oregon, which abolished many of the "helper jobs" at Dunsmuir. The population of town and churches went down.

The Reverend John J. Cowan came to St. Barnabas, but left within a year. A Father Barr G. Lee signed the church records several times in 1928 and 1929, but he seems not to have been a resident priest. Arthur William Bell, who had served in Yreka from 1916 to 1922 appears to have returned to minister in South Siskiyou County from 1929 to 1931. The Reverend Edward A. McGowan replaced him and was at St. Barnabas until 1934.

Times became difficult for St. Barnabas with the onslaught of the Depression, and the resulting economy measures taken by the Southern Pacific Company in 1933. This was the year that the Reverend Noel Porter replaced the Right Reverend Moreland as Bishop of the Sacramento Diocese. Bishop Porter's first visitation at St.

Barnabas' Church was June 16, 1933.

When Father McGowan left Dunsmuir in 1934, the Reverend Richard R. Houssell came in 1935, and the Reverend Crompton Sowerbutts in 1936. The Reverend Cyril Leitch then came for four years. By this time Dunsmuir was once more a very busy railroad town. The economy had improved and then World War II had started. Evidently, there was no resident priest in Dunsmuir after Father Leitch left in November, 1940, to be rector at Yreka. The Reverend A. G. Clarke may have been the priest-in-charge between 1942 and 1945, as he signed the records of the confirmation classes during that time. Many congregations were without pastors for awhile, because, along with "Johnny," the ministers had "gone off to war." St. Barnabas was making a war-time contribution in another way, also. The parish hall in the basement of the church was the local USO Center for the soldiers who were here to guard the railroad tunnels and bridges. Toward the end of the war, the Reverend John H. Rayner served the parish from 1944 to 1946.

During World War II the Southern Pacific Company began replacing the oil burning steam engines with diesel locomotives, and within eight years all the steam engines were gone from this Division. The switch to diesel power drastically reduced the personnel needed in Dunsmuir. When finally the local shops and yard were closed and the switchmen left, St. Barnabas congregation was down to a handful of families and a small Sunday School. In the meantime, about ninety homes were taken out when Interstate 5 Freeway was cut through Dunsmuir. This further diminished the population.

St. Barnabas Church had a Canadian priest in 1947, Father Thomas W. Jones. It was said that he was exceptionally good with the children and the young people of the congregation. From 1948 to 1953, the Reverend Robert R. Reed ministered to the congregation. He was a hard worker for the church, and to augment his salary he worked in a lumber mill. Because of his dedication and hard work, he was featured in an article in *Time Magazine* during his years in Dunsmuir. After Father Reed left, the church was served for a time by the Reverend Thomas B. Tumbull of Redding. Then Stanley Macgirvin became vicar of the church, and it was while he was in Dunsmuir that some of the church records were stored in a garage that was destroyed by fire, and the oldest records of St. Barnabas' Church were lost. Succeeding Father Macgirvin in 1956 was the Reverend Barton M. Kendrick. In 1957, Clarence Haden was consecrated Bishop Coadjutor of the Diocese, and he became Bishop in January, 1958, replacing Bishop Noel Porter. About this time, Father Bordman Read was at St. Barnabas' Church. He left in 1961.

For a time the Church was without a priest, and for many months Dunsmuir's City Manager, William Hansen, was the lay reader; and he, with the faithful few and the vestry members, C. O. Porter, Chester Grenvik, Ferdinand Brown, and Selma Porter, the treasurer, were able to hold the Church together during the time the membership was decreasing rapidly. Ila Brown headed the Altar Guild, and Rhoda Diridon was the church organist. Jean Geyman, Betty Kelby, and Flora Wintering conducted Sunday School for about fifteen children. The Women's Guild continued to be active, and mention should be made of faithful worker, Stella McIntyre, and Edna Park, who for many, many years was the treasurer of the guild. Finally, Bishop Haden assigned the Reverend John Metzler to the Church. He, his wife, and their little daughter were in Dunsmuir for just a short time.

Father Metzler was replaced by Father Thomas Cartwright, who came in January of 1966. By October of that year, John W. Crowther, rector of St. Mark's in Yreka, had left Siskiyou County, and Bishop Haden had appointed Father Cartwright to serve the Yreka church, also. Two years later the Bishop moved Father Cartwright to Yreka. This left St. Barnabas' Church without a resident priest once more. For five and a half years, Father Cartwright served as missionary priest to St. Barnabas' and St. John's, holding services once a month in each place. Father Cartwright had been a bachelor when he came to Dunsmuir, but in April, 1970, in an impressive service at St. Mark's, Yreka, he married Jocelyn Stewart, a counselor at the high school there.

St. Barnabas' members struggled along for several years. They wanted to keep the "Rock Church" as their home, but besides the problem of declining membership, there was the building itself which needed much, much work done on it. It was deteriorating. Finally, economically it was no longer feasible for the congregation to keep the Church. In 1969, a plan was worked out with the First Baptist congregation, who owned a small chapel at the corner of Dunsmuir and Wells Avenues. This building would be accepted as the down payment on the "Rock Church," and the Baptist congregation would make payments to the St. Barnabas' Fund until the difference was paid off. This they have done. So, in 1969, the St. Barnabas' congregation moved into the third home the Episcopalians have had in Dunsmuir. The little chapel was furnished with the altar, pews, font, organ, and other equipment brought from the "Rock Church," and some improvements have been made in the building itself.

The Reverend Iver J. "Bud" Torgerson and his wife, Dora, were called to the church. They arrived in January of 1974. Their two children, Dorene and Donald, both adults at the time, are married and have given the Torgersons five grandchildren. Because of health problems, Father Torgerson retired in February of 1982, but he and Mrs. Torgerson continue to make Dunsmuir their home. While Father Torgerson ministered at St. Barnabas', he served St. John's in McCloud until its closure in 1979. Under Father Torgerson, St. Barnabas' membership began to increase again, responding to the schedule of regular services and enthusiastic leadership.

The Episcopal Churchwomen of the Diocese held its 1976 convention in Dunsmuir. Betty Kelby was chairperson of the very successful event. Throughout its long history, the St. Barnabas' Women's Guild, though at times small in number, has been an active organization, serving the church and the community.

While Father Torgerson was ill, and before a new priest was called to St. Barnabas', several supply priests came for services. One who came most frequently and brought his music ministry with him, was the Reverend William A. McClain of Big Springs, Siskiyou County. Father Howard Mitchell Park was assigned as deacon in December, 1982. He was born in Minnesota and had had a long career as a construction engineer in Alaska. He felt the call to the ministry. He graduated from the Divinity School of the Pacific and is a member of the Order of St. Luke, a healing ministry. Because Father Park came to St. Barnabas' as a deacon, it was a special event for the Episcopal congregation and Dunsmuir when, on April 25, 1983, in a service full of pageantry, he was ordained a priest. The service was held at St. John's Roman Catholic Church with the Right Reverend John L. Thompson in attendance. The year 1983 was a happy, busy one for Father Park. On July 4th, he and Dorothy Lundquist, a member of the congregation, were married. They now live in Mount Shasta.

St. Barnabas' Church, no doubt, will not "live" to celebrate its 100th birthday anniversary in Dunsmuir. The Diocese and the congregation realize that if there is to be just one Episcopal Church in the south county, because of its central location, Mt. Shasta is the logical place for it to be. The first steps are being taken toward relocating the church in that city. Quoting from the May, 1984 Diocesan *Missionary* publication, the Right Reverend John L. Thompson, Bishop, wrote: "Most exciting is the purchase of a lovely ten-acre lot in Mt. Shasta as the future site of our ministry to Dunsmuir, McCloud, Mount Shasta, and Weed." This property is located on Lassen Lane. It will be a sad day when the Episcopal congregation which, in the 1890's, was organized with such hope for the future, must give up its church in Dunsmuir. But as one member wrote about the congregation, ". . . it is full of love for God . . . and for one another." It will survive.

I appreciate having had the use of historical material prepared by Grace Harris, Ila Brown, Rhoda Diridon, Chris Stromsness, Jack Morgan, and Isobel Jones.

ST. BARNABAS' . . .
ITS FUTURE

Pictured in the prize-winning float entered in Dunsmuir's Bicentennial Railroad Days parade in 1976 are members of the St. Barnabas' Sunday School: Jim Powell (crucifer), Holly Charles (Miss Liberty), and a load of Patriots. Visible are Matthew and John Waters and Rune Stromsness.

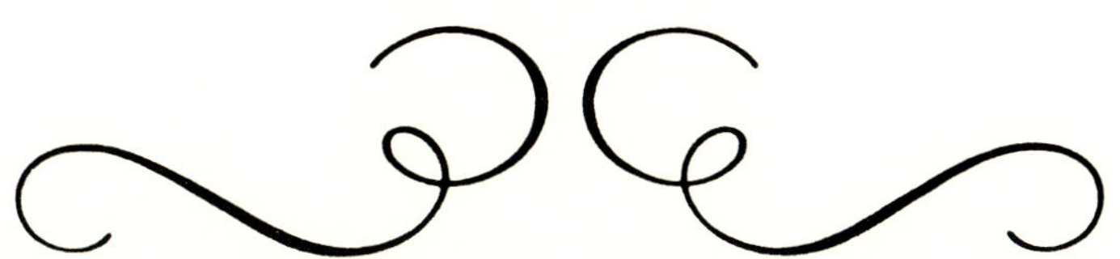

THE CHURCH OF THE NAZARENE

In 1950 the Church of the Nazarene began holding meetings in Dunsmuir at the Veterans' Hall with the Reverend Gellar, who had been sent to help those who were interested in organizing a church of that faith. His stay was brief for, once it became obvious that a church was needed, the Reverend James Dole was called to be the organizing pastor. The church was organized in 1953. The meeting place for worship was moved to a section of the Government Housing Project which was located across the Sacramento River and south of Champion Park. However, by 1955, the church had moved to Stagecoach Road in North Dunsmuir. At the time the freeway was being constructed through Dunsmuir, an old house had been purchased, moved and placed over a basement that had been

prepared for it. The basement was used for a worship area and for Sunday School rooms. For a time, the main part of the house was used as the Pastor's home. As the church membership grew, it became necessary to use the house proper for worship services. This part was remodeled and an addition made to it which is the sanctuary of the present church building. Now needing a home for the pastors, the congregation purchased property on Masson Avenue and built a house on it. This building has since been sold.

About 1974, wishing to move the church congregation to Mount Shasta, the Nazarenes sold the church building to the Assembly of God congregation of Dunsmuir. The Church of the Nazarene then purchased four acres of land on Lassen

Lane in Mount Shasta and constructed a building with a Sanctuary, Fellowship Hall, and Educational units.

Following the Reverend Dole as pastors of the Dunsmuir church were the ministries of Richard Rothel, Gordon Gibson, Willard Turner, Dwight Delp, and Leo Borbie. Then, in 1984, the Reverend Robert Wilden, after serving pastorates for forty-one years, decided to retire from the full-time ministry. Replacing him and Mrs. Wilden were the Reverend and Mrs. Bruce Maier and their three children.

I would like to thank Margie Pence and Lenoir Smith for the information concerning the Nazarene Church that they provided for this chapter.

An interior view of the Rustic Chapel about 1955

THE FIRST LUTHERAN CHURCH:
THE RUSTIC CHAPEL

For writing the first thirty-five years of the history of the Lutheran Church in Dunsmuir, I have had the use of the scrapbook kept by Marie (Wehrheim) Reid. At the times of the twentieth and the twenty-fifth anniversaries of the church, brief histories were compiled, the work of the Reverend Martin Schabaker, Sr., and members of the congregation, with help from former pastors, Henry and John Rische.

Beginning as far back as 1928, services were being held occasionally in the southern communities of Siskiyou County by Pastor Harry Young of the Lutheran Church in Medford, Oregon, and the Reverend August Hansen, Secretary of the California and Nevada District Missions. These visiting pastors would meet the flock gathered in Dunsmuir Elementary School, the Episcopal Church, the Masonic Lodge, the California Theatre, as well as in various buildings in Weed and Mt. Shasta.

By 1930, recognizing a need for a resident pastor in the area, the newly ordained Reverend Henry Rische was sent by the Mission District to gather together the members of the Lutheran community. He met with them for the first time on November 2nd in the Kindergarten Room of the Dunsmuir school. When only five

people showed up for Christmas Eve services, church services were given up for a time. But Pastor Rische was a man with great creative and artistic ability. If one of his plans did not work well, he quickly went on to something else.

On January 11, 1931, Pastor Rische began a series of lyceums of musicales and lectures which were held on Sunday afternoons in the Blue Room of the Masonic Temple. These became known as "Twilight Hours" and were well received. Attendance at them went from sixty people at the first meeting to four hundred at the end of the second year. Henry Rische worked hard as a pastor. It was evident that "defeat" was a condition he did not accept. He organized the "Twilight Hours" well, got local talented people to participate, brought in good speakers, and presented refined, profound programs.

The "Twilight Hours" were aimed at an adult audience, but there was something to teach and to entertain the children, too. Shortly after his arrival, Pastor Rische organized the "Saturday Morning Club" which, for almost two years, met at the Episcopal Church before moving to its new clubhouse at the site of the present Rustic Chapel in November, 1932. These meetings were popular with the young folk. In

February, 1931, the club published "Volume 1, Number 1" of "The Littlest Magazine in Siskiyou County," a monthly collection of clever bits of this and that written or drawn by the children and Pastor Rische.

In 1932 Pastor Rische began holding Easter services at the California Theatre, which within three years were drawing crowds of up to seven hundred people from around the county. Marie Reid noted in the scrapbook, "The altar was always very beautifully decorated. The arrangements with colored flowers, scenes, and lighting made the scenes very realistic and breathtaking."

People will come to be entertained, but Pastor Rische had hoped to build in people a need to attend church. However, this desire manifests itself very, very slowly in some; and, of course, there must be a church to attend. In 1933 the Lutherans began holding services in a corner of the old McGill plumbing shop on Shasta Avenue, which they rented. Little by little, the room took on the appearance of a church. Eventually, the congregation purchased the lot and the building from the owner, Dr. Malone, for two thousand dollars. The job of remodeling began in earnest. Pastor Rische and members of the congregation brought in logs to be used in the renovation work. A pastor's study was added to the front of the old structure. Strips of bark were used for exterior siding. Many hours of paid and volunteer labor went into making the old building into the charming Rustic Lutheran Chapel.

"Behold, I build an house to the name of the Lord my God, to dedicate it to him."
—*II Chronicles, 2:4*

At morning service, May 22, 1938, with two hundred and fifty people gathered, the Chapel was dedicated in services conducted by Pastor Rische, the Reverend Harry Young of Medford, Oregon, and the Reverend August Hansen, Mission Director. An afternoon service was held, also, at which time the speaker was the Reverend Victor Halboth of Yuba City, California. Rische, Young and Hansen had truly committed themselves to gather together the pioneer Lutherans of the area. Working from a nucleus consisting of the Schock, Simon, and Reichman families of Montague, the L. Paulsons of Weed, the Heldsteads of McCloud, and the Copitzkeys, Wehingers, Kings, Moelks, and Wehrheims of Dunsmuir, a substantial congregation was put together.

Pastor Henry Rische was from Milwaukee, Wisconsin. In the Minnesota Building at the 1933 Chicago World's Fair, he had met a Minneapolis girl, Lois Borne, whom he married in 1935 and brought back to Dunsmuir. Knowing the congregation could not afford to buy a parsonage, using the household allowance granted him by the District Missions, he purchased a house on Cedar Street across from the Rustic Chapel, where he and Mrs. Rische began raising a family of three sons and one daughter: Henry, twins Robert and David, and Catherine.

When the Rische family left the Dunsmuir ministry, the congregation was able to buy the house from them. It was used as a parsonage until after the Reverend John Cramer came as pastor, at which time another, larger house on Patricia Way was purchased from the Larry Newtons. At this writing (1984), the retired Pastor Erhard Rupp and his wife, Leona, occupy the house. The present Pastor William Woollen makes his home in Mt. Shasta.

Ever eager to provide clean amusement for the young people of his parish and of Dunsmuir, Pastor Rische set up an entertainment center in the basement of the church. A bowling alley was put in, dart boards were hung, and games were available. The Pastor was also cubmaster of Pack 48.

A replica of the Rustic Chapel was constructed to be exhibited at the San Francisco 1939 World's Fair on Treasure Island. A choir from Dunsmuir went to sing at the exhibit. People who had enjoyed the Rustic Chapel at the fair stopped in Dunsmuir to visit the real church.

The Lutheran congregation had something special to offer the people of Dunsmuir on VE Day, 1945. An old abbey bell from Exeter, England, rang out the news that war was over in Europe. Bill Kamrath of Orange County, California, who was a commander of an LCT boat during the invasion of the Normandy coast, had sent the bell to Dunsmuir hoping that it could be rung at the time of his marriage to Gladys Detlefsen of Dunsmuir. However, the bell arrived a week too late, so it was decided to ring the bell for the first time on VE Day. With the help of a Mt. Shasta blacksmith, Harry Lassen, and church member, George Schrader, Pastor Rische was able to ready the bell for the memorable occasion.

Gradually, the Chapel was becoming a very attractive church. Pillars of cedar logs help support the roof structure. Around the sanctuary above the knotty pine wainscoting is scenery wallpaper. A Black Butte rock fireplace is the point of interest on the south wall. A smaller one in the basement sits in the north wall. An antique chandelier was hung many years ago. At the end of the chancel, stained glass windows were placed on each side of the altar.

In 1942 the church was incorporated and became the First Lutheran Church of Siskiyou. The congregation had hoped to be self-sustaining within ten years, and in 1956 this dream was realized. The depression and pre-war years had been difficult for this church as well as all others in Dunsmuir, but the church membership and Sunday School attendance went down slightly only, and by war's end had risen again.

After seventeen years of dedication to the Lutheran Church in Dunsmuir, Henry Rische was offered the position as Editor of a new Lutheran family magazine called *This Day*, and he accepted. The congregation sadly said their farewells to the Rische family as they left for their new home in St. Louis, Missouri, where Pastor Rische would work at the Concordia Publishing House. Lutherans and people of Dunsmuir who knew him still speak fondly of him and his family. They knew him as a man of imagination, persistence, and hard work, who must be given a chance to broaden his influence in the Lutheran community. They knew that he was an excellent man for the position in St. Louis. He later published the sermons that he had delivered in Dunsmuir. The book was titled, *"When the Lights Are Low."* Henry Rische later was minister at the church in Estes Park, Colorado, and is now retired.

The congregation was without a resident pastor until November, 1948. The vacancy was served by District Supervisor, Pastor Hansen, and assisted by the missionary pastors, the brothers Menzels from San

THE RUSTIC CHAPEL: Before and After Views

Francisco. The congregation went into debt once more to purchase the Rische home for $5,000. With a vacant pulpit and parsonage, they hoped for a pastor soon. In November, Pastor John Rische, brother of Henry, accepted the call. He was installed by Pastors Hansen and F. H. Menzel at an impressive service. The choir was under the direction of Mrs. R. E. Shelton, and Mr. and Mrs. R. B. Manley sang a duet.

Pastor John Rische, his wife, Doris (Mehrhoff), and their children, Lydia, John, Paul, and Ruth, occupied the newly purchased parsonage. While the Rische family served in Dunsmuir, a son, Stephen was born to them. Philip, Rhoda, and Mary Ellen joined the family later.

By the time John Rische came to the Dunsmuir ministry, the main floor of the church had become crowded, and it became necessary to use the basement for Sunday School rooms and social area. For about $1200 and volunteer help the remodeling was accomplished.

In the spring of 1953, John Rische was called to serve a new mission in the Bayview area of South San Francisco, and the Rustic Chapel was without a shephard once again. Until such time as a new resident pastor was called, Pastor John Naas of Trinity Lutheran in Redding came for services in Dunsmuir on Tuesday night. While the parsonage was empty, the congregation took the opportunity to raise $2000 to spend improving it.

In October of 1953, a call went out to Pastor Martin Schabacker, Sr., of Minden, Nebraska, who accepted and came with his wife, Otilia. The couple had adult children who had homes of their own; Martin, Jr., Ruth, Paul, and William. In 1941, Pastor Schabacker, Sr., had had the privilege of ordaining his son, Martin, and installing him as pastor of the Lutheran Church in McCook, Nebraska. On October 11, the son, Martin, Jr., pastor of the Redeemer Lutheran Church of Chico, California, took part in the services of installation for his father. He was assisted by the Reverends Martin Paul of Yuba City, E. Paul Riedel of Ashland, Oregon; Richard Graef of Klamath Falls, John Maas of Redding, and C. Nahnsen of Red Bluff.

During the years of Pastor Schabacker's ministry at the "Rustic Chapel," the church work moved along quietly and without interruption, reflecting the prosperous and peaceful post-war years the country was experiencing. Both Pastor and Mrs. Schabacker were active in the community. Otilia Schabacker gave piano lessons. Pastor Schabacker was a past-president of the Rotary Club and served as its secretary for many years.

The members of the congregation were busy. The church sponsored a successful Boy Scout Troop and conducted Vacation Bible Schools. The Walther League, the Lutheran Women's Missionary League, and the Ladies Aid all were active.

The buildings were steadily being improved and furnishings added. In 1955, pews replaced the folding chairs in the sanctuary. By 1959 the Memorial Fund was sufficient to purchase a lovely communion service. In 1960, Pastor Schabacker reported that money had been spent improving the parsonage.

Under the leadership of two faithful members, Don Stevens and John Knack, a major building program was undertaken to improve the foundation of the church and to modernize the basement. The work was completed and dedication ceremonies were held in October, 1964.

The twentieth anniversary of the "Rustic Chapel" was celebrated in 1956, and on October 15, 1961, both Pastors Henry and John Rische returned to Dunsmuir to assist in the elaborate celebration of twenty-five years of the First Lutheran Church. The church will celebrate its first half-century the year of Dunsmuir's Centennial.

Pastor and Mrs. Schabacker dedicated twelve years to the "Rustic Chapel" and to the Lutheran communities in Siskiyou and Shasta counties. Besides serving the Dunsmuir congregation, Pastor Schabacker went once or twice a month for services at Happy Camp and once a month at Glenburn. Also, they took their turn conducting summer services in Lassen Park. During those years, the membership at the "Rustic Chapel" almost doubled; although, as with other church congregations, Pastor Schabacker reported when he left Dunsmuir that the Sunday School attendance was at a new and alarming low.

After completing over forty-nine years in the pulpit, Pastor Schabacker conducted his last service September 26, 1965, and he and Mrs. Schabacker left for Southern California to become semi-retired near Bakersfield. Beth Jones, a member of the congregation, wrote in a farewell poem when they left, "We felt your responsible, diligent care."

At this point I wish to express appreciation to Pastor Woollen, Nellie King, Ellen Kafer, and Leona Rupp for the help given me in writing the following material.

Next to occupy the pulpit of the Lutheran Church was the Reverend John Cramer who came with his wife, Elsie, in 1966. They had no children until several years later when they welcomed Jimmy into their home and hearts and adopted him.

It was while the Cramers were living in the parsonage across the street from the "Rustic Chapel" that the congregation decided to sell the house and to purchase the home at 4233 Patricia Way in North Dunsmuir. It was a larger and more modern house.

Pastor Cramer was born on Easter Sunday in Portland, Oregon, and was raised there. He attended Concordia Theological Seminary in St. Louis. After graduating, his first pastorage was at Moab, Utah. He then returned to Missouri before coming to Dunsmuir. In 1971, he left Dunsmuir to accept a call to the church in Eureka, California. Seeking more training, he attended college in San Francisco where he earned his doctorate in philosophy. He is now in marital and family counseling for the Lutheran Social Services in San Diego.

In October of 1971, an experimental ministry was begun at the church, when the Reverend Erhard C. Rupp, who was retiring as pastor of the church in Healdsburg, California, accepted the call to come to Dunsmuir under a new type of contract. It was the first attempt of such a contract by this District of the Synod and was made necessary because of the semi-retired agreement the congregation was to make with Pastor Rupp, who already was sixty-five years old. The contract was reviewed yearly as the congregation and the Pastor discussed growth and success.

Pastor Rupp and his wife, Leona, had moved their family to California from Michigan in 1962. They are the parents of three daughters, Noreen, Doris, and Eileen, all married; and the grandparents of four children.

In the course of time, the ministry began to experience blessings. The attendance within eight years grew from about thirty-five to one hundred and twenty-five, in a chapel which seats eighty-five comfortably. The Sunday School advanced from about five to fifty-five children in 1979. New hymnals and Bibles were donated for the pews. Kneelers were installed, and a piano was added to edify the music program for worship purposes.

There was an active ministry in many phases supporting the membership of the church and reaching out into the community and the mission field. The Monday morning "prayer-and-share" group met regularly. The ladies of the church carried on money-making projects. There were classes and a young people's group. Leona Rupp, an accomplished musician, directed the music ministry of the church. The "Joyful Singers" group was organized.

In 1979, Pastor Rupp, having completed forty-nine years of serving pastorates, made the decision to enter full retirement, which he did except for periods of ministering to the Lutheran community of the Burney, California, area until 1983.

The present pastor of the "Rustic Chapel" is the Reverend William Woollen, who was called to the pastorage at Dunsmuir in 1979. He, his wife Leona, and their young son Mark came here from ministering to a congregation in San Francisco. Pastor and Mrs. Woollen's two other children, daughters Louise and Diane, are married and live in Milwaukee, Wisconsin, and Washington, D.C., respectively and have given the Woollens six grandchildren. In the summer of 1983, Leona Woollen, who had been ill for a number of months, died. Pastor Woollen and Mark, a high school student, continue to live in the family home in Mount Shasta. Pastor Woollen was born in Minnesota, but came to the Bay Area when a small child. He served in the Army during World War II. Later, he was a mechanical designer at the Lawrence Livermore Laboratory. When he was about forty years old, he felt the call to the ministry and so went on to receive further education at the Missouri Synod's seminary in Springfield.

After graduating, he served churches in Washington and Oregon before he went to San Francisco and then came to Dunsmuir. Besides holding services at the "Rustic Chapel," he meets with the Burney congregation on Sunday afternoons, unless weather does not permit it.

Pastor Woollen sees his congregation as a cross-section of the communities of South Siskiyou County, where a large percentage of the population is retired. Taking an overall look at the area served by the Lutheran Church, he and his congregation are asking themselves, "In what manner can we be of use to the people? What service can we provide for our church members — for the whole community?" Pastor Woollen envisions that someday the congregations of the various denominations in the large geographic but sparsely populated areas such as ours will unite their efforts into one support group to serve all the people in the area, and still they would continue to worship in their own churches and in their own way.

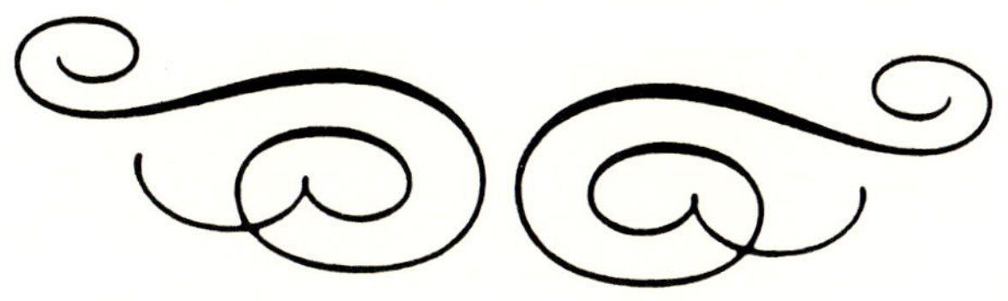

DUNSMUIR CHURCH OF CHRIST

The ministers who have been called to serve the Church of Christ in Dunsmuir are the following men:

V. K. Allison, 1943

Clarence Boulton, Jan. 1944 to May 1944

Woodrow Phillips, 1944-1945

Don Jessup, 1945-1951

Marshall Coller, 1951-1953

James Caulley, 1954-1957

James Weldon, 1957-1970

Richard Scott, 1970-1979

Carl Melhorn, 1979-1981

Bud Corless, 1981-1982

Dale Farnsworth, 1982-

As did several other religious groups of Dunsmuir, the members of the Church of Christ, also, held their first meetings in Branstetter Hall on Sacramento Avenue. Seven interested adults met there with the Reverend V. K. Allison in July of 1943. The Dunsmuir church was organized, and the first members were George and Jennie Dickson, Dan and Iris Decker, Elmer and Ivy Sanford, Elmer and Margaret Runkle, Charles and Tillie Lamb, Ralph and Helen Yoder, and Joe and Audrey Crahan. In spite of the decrease in the population of Dunsmuir during the intervening years, from this small group of charter members has grown a fairly large, active congregation.

After serving as minister a few months, Mr. Allison left Dunsmuir. His ministry was succeeded for a short time by that of Mr. Boulton. Mr. and Mrs. Boulton left in May of 1944, and in June of that year, Mr. Phillips and his family came to stay a year. It was not until Mr. Jessup came in June, 1945, and stayed for six years that the church had a minister in residence long enough for him and his congregation to see the plans they made materialize.

In August, following Mr. Jessup's arrival, the congregation purchased the Brown house on Sacramento Avenue. It stood on property leased from the Southern Pacific Company for the sum of twenty-five dollars a year. This building was used as the church until fire destroyed it Sunday afternoon, January 1, 1949. While the membership was without a place to worship, the Episcopalians offered the use of St. Barnabus' Church to them. It was there that the Church of Christ held their services on Sunday afternoons during 1949 while the new church was being constructed. The first service in the completed building was held on January 1, 1950. One of the special features of the new building was the picture of Mount Shasta painted back of the Baptistry by Mrs. Ada Anderson of Gold Hill, Oregon.

The church had purchased a parsonage at 4425 Needham Street and this became clear of mortgage in January of 1953. There was a fire at the parsonage three days after the Reverend Caulley, his wife Zena, and their children moved into the home in January, 1954. The house was repaired and continued to be used as a parsonage for some time.

Those who have come to minister to the congregation of the Church of Christ and have stayed the longest was the Weldon family. Mr. Weldon was here for thirteen years. Both the Weldon children, Janet and David, graduated from Dunsmuir High School. Janet Weldon married a young Dunsmuir man, Larry Sword. Mr. Weldon drove a school bus for a number of years, and Charlotte, his wife, worked as an aide at the elementary school.

When the Weldons left in 1970, Richard and Doris Scott came to minister. Their children are Steve, Sonya, Shirley, Susan, Sharon, and Shadrack, who was born after the family had come to Dunsmuir. Mr. Scott started the School of Missions and the Annual Snow Ralley for the young people. He was interested in local government and served on the Dunsmuir City Council.

During the time that Mr. Scott served as minister, the congregation, wanting to expand, realized their dream of having a new location for their church, a location that would be their own property. Land above the House of Glass Motel and Restaurant was obtained from Mr. Morgan Jones. A street was cut into the property from Siskiyou Avenue and was fittingly named Hope Lane. After a basement had been dug and a new entry made, the old building was moved from Sacramento Avenue to the new site. Mrs. Doris Scott, who provided information for this article, remarked, "It was quite a job getting the building under the freeway overpasses and up the steep hill."

The Church of Christ now has a beautiful location! Looking, as one does, across the canyon and up toward Mount Shasta, one cannot but think of the words of the familiar old hymn, "Nearer My God To Thee."

Mr. Scott retired from the ministry in 1979. At the time, Carl and Linda Melhorn came to serve the church. Their son, Jeremy, was an infant when the family arrived in Dunsmuir, and their daughter, Charisa, was born in 1980. While Mr. Melhorn was here the church sponsored a Vietnamese family and helped the family get started in the United States. The church provided a furnished home for them and helped them get schooling. After a few months the family was able to move to the San Jose area where better opportunities awaited them.

Following Mr. Melhorn's departure from the church in November of 1981, Bud and Ruth Corless came to stay for a year. At this time (1984) the ministry of the church is in the hands of Dale and Sidney Farnsworth.

The women of the church are organized into the Ladies Bible Study group. It meets twice a month on Tuesdays for study and fellowship.

THE METHODIST CHURCH

As it was mentioned at the beginning of this chapter, the Methodist Episcopal building was evidently the firt church in Dunsmuir. But before it was built there was a group of Methodists who would gather whenever a visiting minister came to the village. According to the Mott *North Star*, as early as October 1887, the Reverend C. H. Darling of the Methodist Episcopal Church in Yreka was sent by Presiding Elder W. R. Gober to see about conducting alternating Sunday services in Sisson, Mott, and Dunsmuir. From early news items, it appears that Mr. Darling came monthly to hold services in South Siskiyou County. He met with the Dunsmuir congregation in either the Railroad Reading Room or in the Dunsmuir School House. These visitations continued through 1887 and 1888 and may have continued into 1889; but by April, 1889, the Reverend Darling seems to have been in Sisson each Sunday, perhaps as resident pastor there.

The Pacific Improvement Company of San Francisco deeded three lots on the corner of Spruce and Florence Streets to trustees of the Methodist Episcopal community of Dunsmuir in May, 1889. With a gift of $250.00 from the Board of Missions and a loan from it of $500.00, a miniscule congregation set to work constructing a church building. In September of that year, the *North Star* wrote that Mr. J. E. Williams was building the Dunsmuir church, and that it would be completed soon.

Writing in 1974, Ed Stanley, who had come to Dunsmuir in 1904, described the Methodist Episcopal Church as he saw it at that early date. He remembered being told that Mr. and Mrs. Charlie (?) Kirkpatrick had been very active in building the church. Mr. Stanley wrote as follows:

"The church was, of course, a crude wooden structure with homemade pews, and the windows painted over with white frosting. The sanctuary was not large, and the pulpit was across the end of the room towards the tracks. There was a small room towards the street for Sunday School and other purposes. The church was heated by a large, sheet iron stove . . . The pulpit extended almost across the east end of the church . . . and on the side toward town was an organ and seats for the choir. The church had an old locomotive bell in the belfry. (The March 25, 1893 issue of the local newspaper reported that Mr. Oscar Bissell had donated to the church a very nice pulpit made by John McClurg.)

When in May, 1890, the *Dunsmuir News* started publication, the Reverend W. C. Robins was mentioned as being the pastor at the church. Since he is not included on the list of ministers in the present records of the church, it may be that at that time the church was part of a circuit that he served. However, he was mentioned as having held services each Sunday evening until October 18, 1890.

In addition to the church services being held, fun events and entertainments were happening. The ladies of the church worked to raise money in order to help the men meet the expense of running the church. Dinners and fairs and shows brought in amounts of money which seem very little to us in our day of inflated dollars; but in the value of yesteryear's dollars, those amounts often kept the church solvent.

In the middle of October, 1890, the Reverend G. W. Richardson and his wife arrived from Texas to assume the pastorage of the church. The November 29th issue of the *Dunsmuir News* first printed a "Church Directory," and for some time the Methodist Episcopal Church was the only listing. The Reverend Richardson left the Dunsmuir church for one in Salem, Oregon, in August of 1891; and the Methodist Episcopal Conference meeting at Pacific Grove appointed the Reverend W. E. Miller to preside in Dunsmuir. Thus, was the beginning of a ministerial turn-over pattern that was to continue for years. With few exceptions, the ministers stayed in Dunsmuir only a year. From time to time, it was necessary for the Dunsmuir church to share its pastors with the congregations in Sisson, Shasta Retreat, and Castella. Following is a list of the ministers and the years in which they served in Dunsmuir:

G. W. Richardson, 1890
W. E. Miller, 1891
T. E. Sisson, 1892
W. H. Northup, 1893
W. C. Gray, 1894
E. H. MacKay, 1895
H. C. Langley, 1896
W. H. Johnstone, 1897-1898
W. G. Trudgeon, 1899-1901
Henry Pearce, 1902
W. G. Trudgeon, 1903-1904
C. O. Oxnam, 1905
Thomas Leak, 1906-1907
A. D. Wagner, 1908-1909
C. B. Allen, 1910
N. F. Hoffpauir, 1911-1912
A. F. Lacy, 1913
Arnold Nelson, 1914-1915
C. F. Withrow, 1916
F. Graham, 1917
Alfred Kummer, 1918
U. L. Walker, 1918-1919
J. W. Winkley, 1920-1921
F. D. Conway, 1922
Adam Bird, 1923
H. E. Wells, 1924-1927
A. H. Clark, 1927-1929
A. P. Beal, 1930-1931
B. F. Donovan, 1932-1933
A. J. Clements, 1934-1936
Thomas J. Cuddy, 1937-1942
Francis R. Johnston, 1943-1944
Kenneth M. Goode, 1945-1947
T. Elmer Smith, 1948-1950
R. M. De Wolf, 1950-1957
Olan Terrell, 1957-1961
Wayne H. Long, 1961-1965
R. Ned Smith, 1965-1966
Philip L. Hall, 1966-1970
John E. Smith, 1970-1973
Seth A. Wood, 1973-1978
Natalie Scholl, 1978-1979
Leanord Brown, 1979-

During his term in Dunsmuir, Mr. Miller had a parsonage built and tastefully "fitted up." When he was replaced, he left a comfortable home for his successor. He worked hard for the congregation and increased the membership of the church. While he was pastor, the church notices in the newspaper read, "Come and see us, and we will do you good." A surprise party was given in honor of Mr. and Mrs. Miller in August, and they were given a handsome souvenir in appreciation of the work they had done in building up the congregation. In a short time they had transferred.

The Reverend T. E. Sisson accepted the charge at Dunsmuir and arrived in October, 1892. He immediately began a series of "Town Talks" on Sunday evenings. The title of the first one was "Jay Gould and His Shekels, or the Proper Disposition of Wealth." A later subject was "The Evils of Cigarette Smoking."

Christmas Eve that year the church sponsored a Christmas Tree Party. The name of every child in town was given to Santa Claus, 'twas said, and all presents were to be turned in ahead of time to be ready for Santa to distribute. This event was a BIG success and was repeated over the years.

In the early years of the church's history, in the years before movie theaters, radio, and television, various ministers, missionaries, travelers, and "professionals" came to Dunsmuir to present programs at the local churches. Presiding Elder A. T. Needham and Professor D. L. Isgrigg were among those who often spoke on subjects of an educational nature to large audiences gathered at the Methodist Episcopal Church.

In 1893, Mr. Sisson was replaced as pastor by the Reverend W. H. Northup, and in 1984, W. C. Gray was sent to be pastor in place of Mr. Northup. Evidently, little of note happened during the time Mr. Northup served the church, but it was while Mr. Gray was in Dunsmuir that plans were made for a camp association to be formed and a retreat built.

In the fall of 1895, the Reverend E. H. MacKay was sent to minister to the Dunsmuir and Sisson congregations. He was a well liked, energetic man. He supervised erecting a fence around the church property which greatly improved the looks of the church, according to the editor of the *Dunsmuir News*, who also commented that the trustees of the church should either move the parsonage or put one up by the church as a convenience for the pastors. In May of 1896, Mr. MacKay moved up to Shasta Retreat to manage affairs at the camp to keep it on a paying basis. He was to attend to the church in Dunsmuir, also. It was written that the grounds at The Retreat began to look better almost immediately.

In September of 1896, the Reverend MacKay left Dunsmuir to attend the Conference at Pacific Grove. The local congregation was hoping that he would be returned to serve another term at the Dunsmuir church. The newspaper reported that he had done a fine job. When he came, the church at Sisson was a "total wreck and is now a fine church and free of debt." The previous year the affairs at Shasta Retreat were in a "hopeless condition, but the new directors are delighted with the financial status of the Retreat." There was a great improvement in the Dunsmuir property, also. It was with sadness that the people learned that Mr. MacKay was to be replaced in Dunsmuir, but he would be manager at Shasta Retreat. He left in September of 1897 to spend the winter studying in Edinburgh, Scotland, and would return in the spring to the Retreat.

On April 1, 1895, a meeting had been held at the Yreka Methodist Episcopal Church for the purpose of organizing a mountain camp association as a complement to the seaside camp at Pacific Grove, which was run by a group of Methodist ministers. The company formed at that time was named the Shasta Vicino Camp Association, and the property, when it was developed, would be referred to as Shasta Retreat.

The company had acquired 240 acres of land lying on either side of the Sacramento River about a mile north of Dunsmuir. (Later, additional land was purchased to the south as far as Cave Springs.) The capital stock was $10,000, divided into 2,000 shares. The stock would be interchangeable for lots on the property at par value. Within six days, Yreka and Dunsmuir residents had purchased $2,000 worth of stock in the company. The Reverend W. C. Gray, of Dunsmuir, was appointed secretary of the Shasta Vicino Camp Association, and the Reverend J. A. VanAnda, the Honorable J. S. Beard, and G. D. Butler were appointed as the committee to receive the subscriptions for the stock.

The Association went to work immediately to build cottages, bridges, a hotel, a tabernacle, a store, and a swimming pool, all to be ready for the 1895 season. Streets were laid out and named for the ministers, Gray, Wells, Hart, Needham, etc. The Tabernacle was said to be the largest hall for public meetings in the county. By July, guests were arriving daily.

A summer at the Retreat was a busy time. Mr. MacKay surveyed a hiking trail from the Retreat to Castle Lake. There were camp meetings, Chautauqua assemblies, grand concerts, train excursions between Dunsmuir and Sisson, and fishing expedi-

tions to the McCloud River. Soon it seemed that Shasta Retreat was the most popular "watering place" north of Pacific Grove and Monterey. The Southern Pacific set excursion prices to the Retreat. Day after day, during the summer season, twenty or more passengers would disembark. The Reverend MacKay, as the people of Dunsmuir knew, was a very good manager to have put in charge. For several years the camp flourished, and then things began to change. The Reverend MacKay was replaced, and the mode of vacationing became different. Rapidly, automobiles began altering the patterns of travel. They took the vacationers in any direction to look, to see, and then to move on. Resorts along the railroads were no longer important. In time, along with others, Shasta Retreat failed. By 1902, "neat cottages," which were already no longer the property of Shasta Vicino Camp Association, were being advertised for re-sale. Finally, the Retreat closed down, and that property is now a residential district of Dunsmuir.

When the Reverend E. H. MacKay left the Dunsmuir church, he was replaced as pastor by the Reverend H. C. Langley. It was during the latter's stay that the *Dunsmuir News* reported, "Railroad Week in Dunsmuir, and the Christian Endeavor was their freight!" In July of 1897, the Christian Endeavor held a convention in San Francisco, and the Southern Pacific Company moved some 24,000 young people into that city from all parts of the United States and Canada. As the trains passed through Dunsmuir heading south, it was hoped that many of the young people and their chaperons would stop to enjoy Shasta Retreat on their return trip. A few did, and several of the ministers preached in the Methodist church. The Convention provided a heyday for the Dunsmuir boys. As the trains went through, they were at the Depot selling trinkets. Rocks containing fool's gold were sold as being California gold quartz, and pots made of lava by Henry Wells were marketed. When the Christian Endeavor trains headed home, and the bevies of young ladies got off the trains at Shasta Retreat, there was so much traipsing up to the camp by the young men and boys of Dunsmuir that the editor of the local paper suspected that there might be at least a few marriages come from the trips. If there were any, he did not make mention of it in his paper.

The Methodist Episcopal congregation was still small and struggling when in 1897 the Reverend Langley filed his yearly report. There were 16 members, 66 in the Sunday School, the church was valued at $1500, the parsonage at $600, and the pastor was being paid $500. (This information was provided to the Dunsmuir church in 1954 by Dr. B. J. Morris, President of the California-Nevada Methodist Historical Society.)

In 1897, shortly after W. H. Johnstone's arrival to replace Mr. Langley as pastor, the Reverend L. C. Renfro, General Secretary

of the Methodist Episcopal Church, was "up the road" looking for property to start a summer school resort which he hoped would equal Shasta Retreat in popularity. Perhaps the resort was developed, but it may have been discussed and then the idea dropped.

The pastors of the church came and left, but the Ladies Aid Society continued to be busy. The women were innovative and clever in their choice of social and money-making projects. If forty or fifty dollars were cleared when an event was held, they had done extremely well. The society of Methodist women went under the name of Ladies Aid until 1940 when the group became the Women's Society for Christian Service. This name was used for the organization until recently when the group became the United Methodist Women.

W. G. Trudgeon came to Dunsmuir as pastor in 1899, served for three years, left, and then returned a year later to spend another year. He may have been willing to spend more time in Dunsmuir because his father lived in the area. According to the 1974 report of Mr. Ed Stanley, Mr. Trudgeon was a dedicated man who "built the church up tremendously under his leadership." Mr. Trudgeon's annual report in 1900 gave seventeen church members with seventy Sunday School students. The ministers salary had been raised to $1100. By 1910, there were eighty-eight members and a Sunday School of one hundred sixty-five. The Reverend A. D. Wagner was receiving a stipend of $1250.

Between the Reverend Trudgeon's two terms of service Henry Pearce came as pastor in 1902, and following Trudgeon's fourth year was C. O. Oxnam.

Much of the following information about the ministers and the Methodist Church history is from material written by Mr. Ed Stanley, who was eighty-six years old when he recorded his memories.

Thomas Leak, his wife and daughters, Florence and Edith, and son Leslie, came to the Dunsmuir ministry. A good speaker, Mr. Leak was a sober man and a stickler for form. He wore a Prince Albert coat when in the pulpit. He may have been from England. His daughter, Edith, married a local young man, Arthur Shoupe, who later was Road Foreman of Engines at Klamath Falls, Oregon.

Pastor A. D. Wagner was young and athletic. He organized an athletic club for the young folks which met in the Knights of Pythias Hall and was well attended. The church prospered under his ministry. He and his wife had a daughter, Martha. Mr. Wagner was ninety-five years old when Mr. Stanley last saw him and Mrs. Wagner.

The Reverend Arnold Nelson followed C. B. Allen, N. F. Hoffpauir, and A. F. Lacy to the Dunsmuir pulpit. He was a pleasant young man and was highly respected. He, too, was athletic and kept himself in good physical chape. His wife was an accomplished musician. Together they ministered well. Mr. Nelson's great ambition was to climb Mount Shasta; and, finally, he and some of the young boys attempted the climb. He, Andrew Leach and Tom Wheeler were together on the mountain when a large rock rolled down, hitting Mr. Nelson in the groin, and he bled profusely. One of the boys lay down to serve as a sled, and Mr. Nelson was rolled onto him. The other boy pulled them down to a half-way house. In spite of the young boys' heroic efforts, Mr. Nelson was dead by the time they got him there.

Mr. Stanley remembered well his fine Sunday School class of which the two boys mentioned were members. Among the others were Ernie, Austin, and Jack Wheeler, Austin Cromwell, and George and Ellsworth White, all good students who kept Mr. Stanley on his toes.

C. F. Withrow followed Mr. Nelson, and after him came Tom or F. Graham. Mr. Graham served in Dunsmuir just a few months before he died. He is buried in the Dunsmuir Cemetery. The Reverend Alfred Kummer was sent to finish his year.

The Reverend U. L. Walker came in 1918 and stayed for two years. Mr. Stanley described him as a large, ruddy complexioned man who had a great sense of humor. He was a forceful speaker. Pastor Walker found the church building in a very run-down condition. It was declared unsafe by the Methodist architect, Wilson J. Wythe, and the City Inspector condemned it. In February of 1919, a committee was chosen to make plans for a new church building. By May, Architect Wythe of Oakland had prepared and presented the plans for the new church. But the progress of the church in Dunsmuir was slowed down due to World War I and the influenza epidemic. The church was in poor health financially, and money to build a church was slow in coming. It was not until Mr. Wagner was replaced that construction on the building began.

In 1920 the Reverend John W. Winkley was sent to Dunsmuir to minister and to get construction going on the new building. The congregation was asked to raise the pastor's salary from $1200 to $1800 as an incentive to Mr. Winkley. Writing to Robert DeWolf, pastor of the church in 1954, Mr. Winkley said, "I accepted the appointment and in six months had a new church under construction." One suspects that the Reverend Winkley was an enterprising person. (He later became Curator of the Pacific School of Religion.) He came to get a job done, and he did it.

The first step taken was to move the old building onto the rear of the property and to move the parsonage south a few feet. This was accomplished with the help of a professional mover, Rollin Wooley, and Emmett Hale, uncle and father of Marvin Hale. This left room enough to build the large, impressive building pictured below. In August of 1921, the old building had been altered and a new front portion added. By September, services were once again being held in the old church, and the new church was going up rapidly. It was finished in time for Christmas, 1921. Following its completion, Articles of Incorporation were drawn up and signed by the Reverend Winkley and the trustees of the church.

In describing the church, Mr. Stanley wrote that "it had a balcony above the sanctuary framed with a runway and guardrail, and opening from this were a number of Sunday School rooms." Quoting from historical material put together by David E. Erickson, "All branches of the church's work now showed new life and vigor." The old church, now a gymnasium, served both the church congregation and the community for meetings and athletic programs. The Dunsmuir Branch of the Siskiyou County Library was housed in it. Mr. Erickson commented, "The Epworth League grew, the Ladies Aid did splendid

work, and the Boy Scout organization was very successful. The Sunday School attendance rose to two hundred."

Because Mrs. Winkley's health would not permit her to live in Dunsmuir, Mr. Winkley was replaced in 1922 by F. D. Conway, who stayed for a year. The Reverend Adam Bird was assigned to follow Mr. Conway in 1923. Mr. Stanley described him as a very large, forceful man. He preached fine sermons and was a dedicated pastor. However, the church soon found itself in serious financial difficulties. To build the new church, the trustees had borrowed $10,000 from the Bank of Dunsmuir. There was a $10,000 policy on the old building, but Mr. Bird and a few others felt that the premiums were excessive on the $19,800 policy held on the new building by the Church Mutual Insurance. Finally, on April 22, 1924, the trustees voted to reduce the policy to $10,000, but by that time the policy had lapsed. Less than seventy-two hours later, tragedy struck!

At twelve-twenty the morning of April 25, 1924, the nearby three-story Knights of Pythias Hall on Sacramento Avenue, built in 1892 and long considered a menace, started a fire which caused about $100,000 worth of damage to the area. The beautiful Methodist Church and its parsonage were among the buildings destroyed. Still not free of debt, the policy held on the old portion of the building did pay off the note at the bank. The congregation had lost everything except the lots upon which the buildings had stood, and it was several years before there would once again be a Methodist Church building in Dunsmuir.

The next decade, or so, was a difficult time for the congregation. For many months their services were held scattered around the town. The Sciots, Branstetter, Odd Fellows halls were used at first. Then two highway department buildings on Florence Avenue used.

The Reverend H. E. Wells had replaced Mr. Bird in the fall of 1924. It was a disheartening time for all concerned. Church attendance began to go down, and soon there were only seventy Sunday School students, but the faithful stayed on. The Ladies Aid, now meeting in members' homes, worked hard to raise money. Mrs. Emmett Hale was the president for a number of years. In 1927, A. H. Clark came to minister at the church.

It was some time before the members had enough courage to rebuild. First, the decision was made to sell the lots on Florence Avenue. In due time the Texaco Oil Company purchased them. In 1928, the trustees voted to acquire the present church property on Oak Street between Shasta and Castle Avenue for $8000. The house on the property was to be used for a parsonage. (It is now the Fellowship Hall.) Through pledges, donations, and loans, the building fund became sufficient to begin construction. Plans were drawn by Mac and Will Stille and John C. Morss and under the supervision of Mr. Morss and volunteer

Dunsmuir's Methodist Episcopal Church, 1921-1924-

help, the work got under way. A two-story structure was planned which was to be used for a church only until such time as a permanent edifice could be built, and then the building could be used for classes and as a recreation hall. "Only until" became a period of thirty years.

Mr. Stanley described this new church, which was dedicated October 27, 1929.
The building was large with twelve-foot ceilings. The roof was too low pitched for a building without interior support. This proved to be true when on January 4, 1966, the building collapsed under heavy snow. There was a small steeple at the front entrance. The bell was recovered from the ruins of the old church. (Another source of information claims that the bell was originally in the church at Keswick, then the one in Kennett, and in 1929 was brought to Dunsmuir by George Wheeler.) At the pulpit end was a stage shaped like a shell and with provisions made for drapes and spot lights. Below the stage was the pulpit.

Lee McDill paid almost the entire amount necessary to install a lighted cross on top of the building. It became known as the Church with the Electric Cross. The Reverend Clark's 1930 annual report placed the value of the church at $15,000 and that of the parsonage at $7250. He was being paid $1760. The church was in good condition and off to a new start.

The Depression hit the country, and Dunsmuir and the Methodist Church were not spared the hard times ahead. Membership and income dropped. If the church was without a minister, the leadership came from within the congregation. A retired minister occasionally held services. Mrs. Grace Pickthron (Renoud) helped, also. Mrs. Clara Gibson, mother of L. A. Gibson, served as Primary Sunday School Superintendent. Sunday School attendance rose to almost two hundred and fifty. Mrs. Reva Coon was choir director and produced many lovely programs. Through the years, Esther Simington and then Wilma Jean Freysinger were faithful organists. Mr. and Mrs. Harcel C. Gray were enthusiastic workers with the youth groups. The workers succeeded in holding the congregation together.

After Mr. Clark left, A. P. Beal, B. F. Donovan, and A. J. Clements came. Then, in 1937, the Reverend Thomas J. Cuddy was assigned, and he was the first to stay five years. Because of the stability of having a minister stay more than one or two years, progress was made. Much was done to make the inside of the church more attractive. And it was during this time that there was a union of the three Methodist Churches in the United States, and "Episcopal" was dropped from the name.

Following Mr. Cuddy was the Reverend Francis R. Johnston and then Kenneth M. Goode, and it was while he was here that the 1921 $2,000 debt to the Home Missions and Church Extension was paid. On Father's Day, 1945, Mrs. Cora Leach and Mrs. Clara Gibson had the honor of setting torch to the document. Once again the congregation grew.

The movement away from Dunsmuir of shops and men by the Southern Pacific Company following World War II, and the change to diesel engines kept the people of Dunsmuir uncertain as to the future of the town. The Methodists long had wished to build a church at the Shasta Avenue-Oak Street corner of their property. Finally, under the ministry of Robert DeWolf, in March of 1955, a building committee was formed with Lee Huddle, chairman, and Ronald Christison and Harry Harper, Jr., as secretary and treasurer. Plans were drawn for the entire plant — sanctuary, fellowship areas, and class rooms. The drive to raise funds began. Not until Olan A. Terrell had come as pastor did construction begin in June of 1959. The workmen, Mr. Terrell, and many volunteers rushed the job to completion by Christmas of that year. The church was so consecrated by Donald Harvey Tippett, Bishop of the Methodist Church, on December 27th, with District Superintendent William H. Gould in attendance.

The present Methodist Church is a beautiful, modern structure built of concrete blocks with a sanctuary large enough to seat 300. Mr. Erickson described it as a church "with light, airy interior, lofty ceiling, and delicate colored windows." The church includes an office and a small fireside room. Although the original plans called for more extensive construction, attendance has not warranted the additional space being added.

The Reverend Philip L. Hall and his family came to Dunsmuir in 1966, and it was while he served that, at special evening services March 9, 1967, Mr. Lee Huddle presented the mortgage papers to Mr. Edward Stanley, a trustee, who then presented the deed to the church property to Bishop Tippett for dedication. Hallelujah, the church was free of debt!

The ministries of John E. Smith, Seth A. Wood, and Natalie Scholl followed Mr. Hall. At this time (1984) the Reverend Leonard Brown has been faithfully serving in Dunsmuir since 1979. Mrs. Brown is the church organist.

The congregation of the church is still marching forward. In recent months, through the generous donations of money and time by the members, the old parsonage has been remodeled into an attractive Fellowship Hall. In true ecumenical spirit, the United Methodist Women have entertained in the new hall women from all the Dunsmuir churches.

The Methodist choir joins with singers from other Dunsmuir churches to form a united choir to prepare an evening of music to be presented to the community during the Christmas season. Mrs. Reva Coon is the director. This is always well received.

In preparing this material about the First Methodist Church, I appreciate having the use of the collection of papers belonging to Marvin Hale and the help given by Mildred Lockart.

ROMAN CATHOLIC CHURCHES:
SACRED HEART and ST. JOHN THE EVANGELIST'S

The quoted information in these paragraphs is taken from material written for this section by Monsignor James Casey of Red Bluff, formerly at St. John's Church in Dunsmuir. The rest of the information came from researching area newspapers and church records.

"Before the railroad came to Pusher, later named Dunsmuir, there were no towns in Southern Siskiyou. Scattered settlers were in the Sacramento River canyon and in the Sisson area. For obvious reasons, churches did not exist, either on an organized or a parochial basis. Construction of the railroad brought in its wake a pioneering population.

"On June 13, 1888, the Reverend John Quinn came from Red Bluff to celebrate Mass in the home, presumably a section house, of a McCann family. Present for this first Mass in the locality were the families of Joseph Mott, George McInneney, Patrick Furlong, Charles Gill, Tim Ryan, plus single construction workers, and a few friends of other religious affiliations. Over the next three years, newspaper reports indicate, a priest (Father McGrath) came from Yreka perhaps once a month to celebrate Mass in various Southern Siskiyou communities. Catholic parishes had been established in Mother Lode and Northern gold mining camps, including Sawyers Bar and Yreka, soon after the discovery of the precious metal.

"While in Red Bluff, Father Quinn was untiring in caring for isolated members of his flock in an extensive territory, in Old Shasta, in Dunsmuir to the north, and in Fall River Mills to the east. He would give public lectures, attracting virtually the entire population of a town. A man who heard him said that non-Catholics attended out of curiosity, at first suspicious, if not hostile. Father Quinn won their friendship by his genial personality, his powers of oratory, and his appealing presentation of the traditional faith. He was transferred to Yreka in 1894, and then to the Cathedral in Sacramento.

"Father Quinn and the Most Reverend Patrick Manogue, Bishop of Sacramento, were in Dunsmuir in July of 1891, when Mass was celebrated in a local hall (Gonguer's). On the occasion of this visit, reportedly, property was purchased 'above town,' that is, where St. John's Church now stands. At this time also, a newspaper reports, the bishop inspected the 'Catholic Ranch' to the north of Dunsmuir. Some three years previously, the Red Bluff pastor and two associates envisioned a 'Catholic summer resort' on a forty-acre site just south of Hedge Creek. The property, owned by Father Quinn, was to have a large building, modern facilities, mineral baths, landscaped grounds. Apparently, nothing came of the project. Perhaps it was too visionary for the time and place. (At least one building was on the property. In August of 1891, the newspaper mentioned that Miss Irene Scott, who later married Dennis Freel, and two Miss Dawsons were running the hall at the Catholic Ranch.)

"Bishop Manogue was in Dunsmuir again in August of 1891, encouraging local Catholics to open a subscription drive for a new building, to be called Sacred Heart Church." Joseph Mott's name and donation of one hundred dollars headed the list, and, before the evening was over, eight hundred dollars had been pledged for the church building. Evidently, construction began shortly, as the November 12, 1891, issue of the *Yreka Union* stated that Father McGrath had reported to the editor that the foundation of the new Catholic Church in Dunsmuir was completed, and that the contract for the wood work and framing of the church was for $2,000.

Father McGrath showed a great interest in the church, and he was down often to attend to the affairs of the church and to celebrate Mass. It was said that "Reverend Gentleman" worked hard himself at the construction site. In January of 1892, he came to help with the plans for the altar and to build a fence around the lot. Mr. Maurice Harmon, a Southern Pacific section man, was Father McGrath's assistant on the church work. Maurice was to be married soon and would have his ring blessed in the church. Father McGrath spent much of the month of October, 1892, in Dunsmuir, supervising the construction and conducting services, which by this time were announced as being held in the church. By the end of the month, the building was nearly finished on the inside. There was a nice little altar furnished with all the symbols of the church, including very beautiful candlesticks.

No doubt, the rush was on to get the building ready for winter. By December, the public was being invited to attend the Christmas Eve services when High Mass would be celebrated. The newspaper admonished, "Come Christmas Day if no other day of the year. The sermon will be 'Christmas — Myth, Mystery, or Miracle?'."

The congregation and Father McGrath were still working on the building in February of 1893 when the indebtedness was only twenty-six dollars. There was sufficient lumber on hand to complete the sanctuary, but not the seats. Fr. McGrath was down again in March to help in casing the windows and in doing any other work that was necessary. Just how long it took to complete the work on the church is not known. Finally, the happy day came when in September, 1894, Bishop Manogue dedicated the attractive little Church of the Sacred Heart. A large crowd attended the service. Many came from Sisson. The Roman Catholic community of the South Siskiyou area was grateful that at least it had a church to attend.

SACRED HEART CHURCH
Construction began in 1891 - Burned in 1932

Apparently Father McGrath and Father Quinn were the priests who continued to serve Sacred Heart Church until 1899, when a parish was established. "The Reverend Daniel Meager was the first resident priest. He remained until 1903.

"The Reverend Patrick Carr, appointed as pastor in Dunsmuir in 1903, saw the growth of Catholic congregations at the local level as well as in three developing neighboring communities within the parish boundaries, McCloud, Sisson, and Weed. They were termed missions of the Dunsmuir parish. The vigorous priest, a respected civic leader, would travel by stage or train to celebrate Mass and administer the sacraments, often spending several days, even a week, in each community." (It was often said that the time of church services in the Southern Siskiyou area depended upon the arrival time of stage or train.) "Advancing in age, Father Carr became ill and was admitted to a hospital in Oakland, where he died in 1919. He had relatives in the East Bay City." (Mrs. Mary Madden, his cousin and housekeeper, was named in his original will. She died before he did. In the will he wrote in November 1918, he left his property to the Right Reverend Bishop Thomas Grace of Sacramento.)

"During Father Carr's time, his friend, Father Quinn, was granted a leave of absence, as it was termed euphemistically, and retired to his 'ranch' north of Dunsmuir. Conjecture had it that there was a lack of rapport between the urbane, progressive priest and the new Bishop Grace, reputedly a conservative, even a reactionary. Resuming an active role, Father Quinn was named pastor of Winters, California, where he died in 1921. He had sold the Dunsmuir property to a family named Wehrheim, from the Midwest, of Lutheran affiliation. More than thirty years later, Mrs. Wehrheim, who had saved newspaper clippings and pictures, was pleased to supply information on the era for the local priest. She said that Father Quinn and friends would return for vacation interludes, camping in the apple orchard as guests of the family. Much of the Wehrheim place was purchased by the State of California when the freeway was built.

"Succeeding Father Carr were several immigrant priests, whose tenures were brief. . . The Reverend Patrick Cronin remained until May, 1922. The Reverends James Grealy and Michael Myles filled in as visitors until October of that year, when the Reverend Thomas Molyneaux was named pastor. He departed after a few months.

"The Reverend Michael McGoldrick, appointed to Dunsmuir in 1923, became well known in Southern Siskiyou over the ensuing nine years." There was a rectory just behind Sacred Heart Church facing Spruce Street. When it was built is not known. After Father McGoldrick arrived, "the present parish rectory, facing Shasta Avenue, was built in 1926, designed to house two priests who would serve the large parish territory, then extending to the Oregon state line. The vigorous priest was also instrumental in the building of a church in Mt. Shasta, and in addition, the unique Shelvin siding, log-cabin style church in McCloud, dedicated in 1931. Father McGoldrick was restless, impulsive, and self-driven. Like many dedicated, overzealous men, he was not always careful in regard to routine details . . . The onset of the great depression, in 1929, led to a degree of financial chaos in the parish. Revenue dropped . . . The priest was transferred to Sacramento in 1932.

"Soon after the arrival of the Reverend Michael O'Connell, in 1932, fire ravaged the church to such an extent that it had to be demolished. The fire was attributed to carelessness on the part of altar boys who neglected to extinguish lighted charcoal in the incense thurible. Since the unemployment rate was high, little or no trouble was encountered in recruiting men from the congregation to excavate the site for an entirely new structure, erected by Luigi Cosentino and volunteer workers at a cost of $7000, which was completed in 1935, and dedicated to St. John the Evangelist. No explanation can be found as to why the name was changed. (A picture of St. John's Church appears on a page in the Dedication Section of this book.) Despite hardships of the depression decade, the needs of Catholics in McCloud and Weed were met by the establishment of separate parishes in both lumber-mill towns. McCloud had its first resident priest in 1934; Weed, in 1935. Dunsmuir parish, reduced considerably in area, retained Mt. Shasta as a mission." Assisting Father O'Connel in his work was the Reverend Patrick J. Lyons, brother of the present priest, Father Vincent Lyons.

"Father O'Connell, departing in May, 1947, was replaced by the Reverend James Casey . . . He responded to appeals by Mt. Shasta Catholics, whose hopes had been frowned upon, by aiding in founding a new parish for them, in November of that year. Later, noting that property adjacent to the Dunsmuir rectory, on the north side, was for sale, he secured a loan to purchase the house and lot, thus rounding out the parish real estate to include the whole city block.

"During and after World War II, Dunsmuir was a bustling railroad center, headquarters of the Shasta Division of the Southern Pacific. As St. John's congregation increased, the church was getting too small. A special feature was an enthusiastic choir, trained in and dedicated to traditional Gregorian chant. A Baldwin electronic organ was bought. For recurring festive observances, especially for Midnight High Mass at Christmas, the choir attracted non-Catholic friends. A savings account, increasing annually, was opened with long-range hopes for a more impressive edifice, liturgically functional, on higher ground north of the rectory, replacing the smaller building which was described as 'down in a hole.' Under subsequent regimes, these provisional hopes were abandoned." The change to diesel-powered locomotives and the closure of railroad shops in Dunsmuir caused the population of the town to decline. Also, contributing to the drop in population was the construction of Interstate 5 through the residential districts of the town. Many, many houses were taken out and not replaced.

"In 1954, Pope Pius XII named Father Casey as a Monsignor, a title of honor, the first of its kind in Siskiyou County. Aware of a growing concern, Father Casey invited Sisters of the Holy Family to conduct annual cummer school sessions. This Order of teachers was founded in California to provide adequate religious instruction for public school students. After an interval of two or three years, with all four parishes of the area collaborating, the Holy Family Sisters instituted a foundation in Southern Siskiyou. Four of the Holy Name Sisters came to reside in a convent, with chapel, dedicated in Mt. Shasta in 1959. Classes, tied in with the school year, were scheduled on a weekly basis in each parish. Frowned upon was the obsolete concept of 'Sunday School'." In recent years, failing to get the support for the foundation that they felt they must have, the Sisters withdrew all but one of their members from the southern area of Siskiyou County. The one remaining member lives in Weed.

25th Anniversary

"Appointed as Dunsmuir parish priest in September, 1963, was the Reverend William Broderick, who remained until May, 1965, when he enlisted as a chaplain in the armed forces and saw combat service in Vietnam. He was succeeded by the Reverend Patrick Lanigan, during whose term a parish hall was built and who, in 1973, was succeeded by the Reverend James Vaughan. The latter, while in a doctor's office in Weed for a check-up on December 17, 1974, died suddenly of a heart attack. Returning temporarily from Red Bluff, Monsignor Casey arranged for the funeral and was administrator of the parish until the end of February, 1975, when the Reverend Sean O'Leary came as pastor.

"A few months after Father O'Leary's arrival, an arsonist tried to burn down St. John's Church." According to parishioner Pat Girard, only a chance visit to the church by Emma Martinez, now deceased, saved the church from complete destruction. "Though the edifice was saved by the fire department, sanctuary furnishings and altar were destroyed; also, extensive smoke and water damage were incurred. Securing an insurance settlement, the priest had the interior restored." James Cosentino, son of Luigi Cosentino, had built the main altar, two side altars, and two podiums for Sacred Heart Church, and it was he who again built these furnishings after the fire.

"The Reverend Vincent Lyons, succeeding Father O'Leary, was appointed as pastor of St. John's parish in Dunsmuir on August 1, 1981." For more information about Father Lyons, read the page about him in the Dedication Section of this book.

Beginning with the time of construction of Sacred Heart Church and continuing to the present time, the Catholic women have been busy. They have held dinners and dances, fairs and bazaars, raffles and rummage sales, to help build churches and to help furnish and maintain them. They commenced holding the St. Patrick's Day balls and suppers immediately, and they became annual affairs. Father Quinn came to one such event in 1896 when, at midnight, supper was served on shingles. For Christmas, 1892, they raffled two watches that were advertised as real gems. The gentleman's watch was a full-jeweled B. W. Raymond in a gold case; and the lady's, an elegant one in an engraved gold case of the latest style. There was forever some project for which money or time was needed.

Today, St. John's Guild takes an active part in the life of the church. The members work hard and faithfully to raise money for the needs of the congregation and for the outreach programs of the church. The group lends support to the Foreign Missions and makes contributions to various funds, such as the Right to Life movement. For St. John's, it supplies the flowers, candles, and fair linens. It brings solace and comfort to members in time of sorrow and distress. It contributes financially to the church when there is a need to do so.

The Confraternity of Christian Doctrine (CCD) program has its dedicated workers, also, who give willingly of their time to bring instruction in catechism to the youth of the church.

A more recently formed committee is the one which runs the Friday night bingo games. The profits from these games are used to purchase needed equipment for the church and parish hall.

Following is a list of priests who are known to have served the Dunsmuir Catholic churches as visitors and those who have been resident priests. The years in which they served are in parentheses.

SACRED HEART
Father D. Meagher .... (1899-1903)
Father John B. Ruddy .... (1903
Father Patrick F. Carr ...... (1903-1916)
Father Joseph A. Sullivan . (Visitor-1919)
Father Patrick J. Cronin .... (1919-1922)
Father James Grealy ...... (Visitor-1922)
Father Michael Myles ..... (Visitor-1922)
Father Thomas Molyneaux (Visitor-1922)
Father Michael M.
    McGoldrick .... (1923-1932)

ST. JOHN THE EVANGELIST'S
Father Michael J. O'Connell . (1932-1947)
Father Patrick J. Lyons
    (Assistant) .... (1947-1948)
Father James Casey .... (1947-1963)
Father William Broderick ... (1963-1965)
Father Patrick Lanigan ..... (1965-1973)
Father James Vaughn .... (1973-1974)
Monsignor James Casey ..... (1974-1975)
Father Sean O'Leary .... (1975-1981)
Father Vincent Lyons .... (1981-   )

THE SALVATION ARMY

In 1865 the groundwork was being laid in London for a religious philanthropic body which, by June of 1878, was to become known as the Salvation Army. The operations of the army expanded rapidly until in every country its uniformed soldiers were recognized, and its brass bands were heard calling the sinners and needy to its Christian Missions. By 1887, the army was fanning out into the areas north of San Francisco and Sacramento. The Mott, California, *North Star* reported in July of that year, "The Salvation Army flourishes in Petaluma." Finally, the Salvation Army arrived in Dunsmuir.

Grace Renoud, of Dunsmuir, prepared the following information to be used in this chapter, and her material has been quoted in its entirety.

After due consideration, the Salvation Army was to establish a permanent Corps, or Church, in Dunsmuir in June of 1923. What a pleasure this must have been to A. J. Pickthorn, the Southern Pacific Agent, as before coming to the United States, he had observed the workings of the Salvation Army in England and was a great admirer of General William Booth, the Founder.

The installation of the first Corps Officer, Captain L. Wycoff, was conducted by Staff-Captain Robert McClelland, of Sacramento, on June 11, 1923. This ceremony was held in the Sciots Hall on Sacramento Avenue. An item in the *Dunsmuir News* for that date states that thanks was expressed to the Sciots and the Lions Club for their financial support. As the work progressed, Mr. Frank VanFossen donated the use of a hall downstairs on Cedar Street for a meeting place. It was here a Sunday School was started. The work of the officers consisted of holding Open Air services on Sacramento Avenue near the sight of the Reception Hall, of spending many hours in visitation in Dunsmuir, Mt. Shasta, and Weed; and of selling the Salvation Army's publication, the *War Cry.*

Over the years, several different young officers came to Dunsmuir to command the work here.

COMMANDING OFFICER
6-11-23 to 6-1-25 __Capt. L. Wycoff (Watson)
6-2-25 to 7-26-25 _________ Capt. F. Partridge
7-26-25 to 12-14-25 __Capt. B. Boysen (Ward)
12-31-25 to 3-17-26 _____ Pr. Lt. Mary Foster
3-17-26 to 5-23-26 ___ Pr. Lt. Joy Kirkpatrick
5-23-26 to 6-23-27 _________ Capt. F. Partridge
6-23-27 to 11-1-29 ___________ Capt. M. Sims
11-1-29 to 2-?-30 ______Pr. Capt. John Phillips
2-5-30 to ?-30 _____________ Capt. E. Hedquist
8-21-30 to 11-27-30 ______ Pr. Capt. D. Moffitt

ASSISTANT
6-11-23 to 2-20-24 _________ Pr. Lt. Effie Purdy
2-20-24 to 10-29-24 __________ Lt. Fern Estby
6-1-25 to 3-17-26 _____ Pr. Lt. Joy Kirkpatrick
5-26-26 to 6-23-27 _____Pr. Lt. Grace Vrieling
6-20-27 to 6-1-28 __________Lt. Naomi Peugh
9-15-28 to 8-7-29 ___________ Lt. M. Morlan
6-4-29 to 11-1-29 ______Pr. Lt. Violet Roberts

Due to financial difficulties of the depression, the work in Dunsmuir was discontinued in March of 1932. However, later a Salvation Army Extension Service was established with Mr. Frank Bascom being one of the first Committee Chairmen. The work of the Extension Service has continued. It is carried on by volunteers and, at this time (1984), is supervised by Grace A. Renoud, chairman; Marjorie Young, treasurer; and Dunsmuir's Police Chief John Rowland and his staff. The work consists of helping transients and local needy persons. The funds for this work is augmented by contributions from five of the local churches.

GRACE (PICKTHORN) RENOUD
pictured when she was
Pr. Lt. Grace Vrieling

THE PRESBYTERIAN CHURCH

Although the Presbyterian faith had an early start in Dunsmuir, its history here is all too brief. Perhaps the congregation had been meeting in homes and halls before a church was built, because in May of 1890, the *Dunsmuir News* mentioned that the Reverend James McDonald would "preach to the Presbyterians." However, on June 7, 1890, the newspaper reported that work on the new Presbyterian Church was progressing rapidly; and the Saturday, June 28th, issue announced that there would be "preaching" at the church the following day, both morning and evening. The pastor was the Reverend N. P. Teitsworth. For several months the local paper continued to announce church services for the Presbyterians with Mr. Teitsworth as the pastor. Then, on November 30, 1890, the Pacific Improvement Company of San Francisco deeded to A. F. Brown, L. Van Fossen, and M. C. Roberts, trustees of the Presbyterian Church of Dunsmuir, Lots 14, 15, and 16 in Block 13, in the Town of Dunsmuir.

In October of the same year, Mr. Teitsworth went to the Presbyterian Synod meeting held in San Francisco. All the clergy on the "Coast" attended if they were able. He reported that the men had had a grand time of it. By the month following the convention, Mr. Teitsworth had received a call from the church in Gridley, California, which he accepted. He preached his farewell sermon at the Dunsmuir church on the Sabbath following November 1, 1890. The local newspaper wrote that the Reverend Teitsworth had done a great deal to build up the Presbyterian community in Dunsmuir, and all were sorry to see him go. The best wishes of the community went with him.

In May of 1891, an announcement stated that again the Reverend James McDonald would preach in the church at both the morning and evening services, and the public was cordially invited to attend. When a successor of Mr. Teitsworth arrived in Dunsmuir is not clear. There were social activities happening at the church during the months following his departure, and one would suppose that Sunday School was being conducted regularly. Perhaps the visiting pastors were coming more regularly than the newspaper reported.

April, 1892, found something "new" being held one Wednesday evening at the Presbyterian Church. The young ladies would be dressed in fancy costumes and would have refreshment baskets for sale. The gentlemen who bought baskets could invite ladies to share its contents with them. During the evening the Daughters of the Regiment would dispense soda. This event had a large attendance.

The minister to succeed the Reverend Teitsworth must have been Mr. J. H. Cornwall, as it was announced that he would attend the General Assembly of Presbyterian Churches in Portland, Oregon, May 19, 1892. Also, it was he who in June officiated at the wedding of William J. Fleming and Miss Mary C. Hunter; and in July, married John J. Hendrick and Miss Maud S. Hackett. By August of 1892, the *Dunsmuir News* reported that Mr. Corn-well would leave here soon to take a church in Oregon. There were never many Presbyterians in his church and "like every other mortal, he cannot work without a salary."

The church building was still referred to as "Presbyterian" when in February of 1896 a new sidewalk was put in at the church. Just when the Episcopalian congregation began meeting at the Presbyterian church is not known, but the same issue of the *Dunsmuir News* that reported the sidewalk, also reported that, through the kindness of Mr. Masson of Upper Soda Springs, the Episcopalians had been able to communicate with the church board about buying the Presbyterian building. By December of 1896, the Reverend Alfred George of St. Mark's Episcopal Church, Yreka, and the Episcopal ladies of Dunsmuir had raised enough money to make the purchase, and the church was consecrated as St. Barnabas'.

If ever again there was an attempt to have a church in Dunsmuir for the Presbyterian community, it was not successful. From time to time a Presbyterian minister spoke in or held programs in other Dunsmuir churches, but that seems to have been the extent of Presbyterianism here. One such program was held in the Methodist Episcopal Church in August of 1923, when the Reverend J. W. Lundy, pastor of the Presbyterian Church in Marysville, California, presented an "excursion to Ireland" with stereopticon views. Admission was twenty-five cents for adults and for those under twelve, fifteen cents.

UNDENOMINATIONAL RELIGIOUS GROUPS IN DUNSMUIR

Not all religious organizations were affiliated with established churches. Some were strictly undenominational. The King's Daughters and Sons was one such group. According to the 1915 edition of the *New International Encyclopedia*, this was an international order, organized in New York City in 1886, as a "distinctly spiritual force." At first, only women were admitted, but later men and boys were allowed to join. The local groups were referred to as "circles" which were given free choice in choosing what special work they would do, so the social and religious services were varied. The idea was to work "first for the heart, next the home, then the church, and after that the great outside." A silver Maltese cross was the badge of the society. The badge bore the initials I.H.N. (In His Name). The organization published a magazine named the *Silver Cross*.

Dunsmuir had a King's Daughters Circle before the turn of the century. As early as 1891, they were holding meetings in the Methodist Episcopal Church, according to notices in the *Dunsmuir News*. The Daughters held their socials and a variety of entertainments, and an advertisement appeared quite frequently in the newspaper: The King's Daughters will take orders for plain sewing. Mending a specialty. Material furnished, if desired. Address, Mrs. Mann, President, Dunsmuir, California.

How long the Dunsmuir Circle continued to be active, or who were members in Dunsmuir other than Mrs. Mann is not known. Apparently, the King's Daughters and Sons is no longer in existence.

Through the years, Dunsmuir was visited by Evangelists. They came to hold revival services in churches, business buildings, tents, halls, railroad cars, or in the outdoors. Many of these preachers drew large crowds. Some came to conduct Bible Schools for the young people. In July of 1932, Mrs. O. Pennington, of Los Angeles, was in Dunsmuir for the purpose of running an interdenominational morning, summer Vacation Bible School. The classes were to be held in a building on Shasta Avenue that had been Mr. McGill's electric shop and was later to become the "Rustic Chapel."

The "Evangelist Car" was on a siding in the Dunsmuir Yard and was drawing crowds in January of 1896.
tian Temperance Union in Dunsmuir. Mrs. Skelton was in town in February of 1893 and was successful in organizing a local group. The Editor of the *Dunsmuir News* listed the officers and commented about Mrs. Skelton by writing, "The old lady has lots of common sense and told some sublime truths."

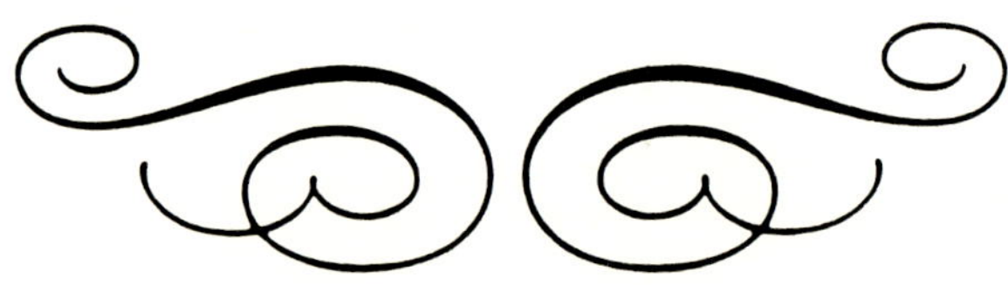

CONCLUSION

In closing this chapter concerning the establishment of Christian worship in Dunsmuir, we would like to explain why the accounts of many of the churches have been brief. This is due to the small amounts of information on record about them and, also, due to the shorter periods of time that they have been organized. On the other hand, the Roman Catholic, Methodist, and Episcopal Churches each have a history almost as long as Dunsmuir's; and, in fairness to those denominations, many more pages were devoted to their stories. Pains have been taken to ensure the accuracy of the material, but we hope that errors and omissions, if they appear, will be forgiven. Mentioned have been just a few of the many people who, with dedication and enthusiasm, helped in organizing congregations and building churches in Dunsmuir.

Perhaps reading church statistics may be dull; but, as the Reverend Martin Schabaker, at one time pastor of the "Rustic Chapel," once wrote in his annual report, "They represent the precious souls redeemed by the blood of the Lamb."

For where two or three are gathered in my name, there am I in the midst of them.
—Matthew 18:20

CHAPTER IX
FRATERNAL ORGANIZATIONS

By
Carolyn Miller

Carolyn Miller

During the 19th century's closing years, with the world poised on the threshold of a new century, Southern Pacific's stop-over south of Mt. Shasta metamorphized. Aptly known as Pusher, this boxcar campsite provided the extra engines needed to push northbound trains up a nine-mile gradient thousand-foot climb out of the Sacramento River canyon.

Re-christened Dunsmuir, the town developed when the world seemed so young, so wonderfully relaxed, so undisturbed. Through the warm air that hung soft and still in summer, the hum of insects would be heard behind the whirr of a lawn mower, the sudden slam of a screen door, and the muffled clip-clop of horses' hoofs on unpaved streets.

Winter brought whizzing sled rides, children's joyful shouts carrying far through the winter's grey, still air; air etched in wood smoke curling above roof tops. Work, school, home, church, fraternal activities soon became regular routines for the residents of Dunsmuir. Combined overall, their teachings constructed our community's firm foundations. Today, far through the 20th century, these lessons remain true; their strength sustaining Dunsmuir's successful first century.

Let us relive these lifestyles through actual articles published in the *Dunsmuir News*. Their phrasing cannot be improved upon; their cadence the pace of Dunsmuir progressing through its first 100 years.

Realize that in those times there were no Social Security programs, nor burial plans. The fraternal orders filled these needs. First the men's lodges, then the ladies' orders, provided these funds. The lodges and orders also provided a place for entertainment, fellowship, and friendship in a world without the silver screen, radios nor motorized mobility. Today, with advanced technology in the forms of T.V.s, V.C.R.s, computers, world-wide instant communications by satellite, fraternal members are still dedicated to their principles. Moneys raised and donated to various charities is still on-going. Their service to their city strong, they face the oncoming century with dedicated will.

7-23-89: Knights of Pythias, Eagle Cliff Lodge 163, instituted at Mott. A large Dunsmuir membership is a very prominant part of the Lodge.

10-10-89: Dunsmuir Lodge No. 297, Free and Accepted Masons, was charted. Charter members were men who were drawn together by the tie of fraternity and who felt that it would be a good thing to organize a Masonic Lodge in this city. They were for the most part railroad men, employed on the Southern Pacific Railway, transplanted to a new town and, in some cases, away from loved ones. They needed the fellowship that comes through mixing together in a fraternal manner. So these thirteen Masons met in a secluded portion of the Southern Pacific Railway round-house in Dunsmuir and held their first communication.

The following are charter members of Dunsmuir Lodge No. 297:

> Andrew Thompson Creelman
> William Baylor Roberts
> George Howard Ingham
> Levi Van Fossen
> Wilber Earnest Snapp
> Fred Bertrand Farmer
> Ambrose F. George
> Alfred Jenks
> William Josiah Leland
> Charles G. Poilicke
> James Robertshaw
> Thomas Bevis
> Charles E. Paunt

Rihard Stephen Culverwell was the first candidate of Dunsmuir Lodge and was made a Mason October 26, 1889.

7-5-90: Knights of Pythias participate in 4th of July activities at Sisson.

7-19-90: Eagle Cliff Lodge 163, Knights of Pythias, Mott, installed their officers for the term Friday evening, July 11th. A large battalion of Knights charted Mr. French's overland, side-hill team, and went up from Dunsmuir to attend Lodge. We have road (as spelled) on everything from a Newfoundland Punt to a Yankee Coaster on the Isle of Scholes, from an accomenation of the Rio Grand, to an Apache pony, but we never had a worse shaking up than on that trip. Otherwise, it was a very pleasant affair.

8-2-90: On Wednesday, a party of about 30 Knights of Pythias took the train from Dunsmuir and Mott for Yreka, to institute Yreka Lodge, Knights of Pythias. Members of (the) new lodge gave all a royal reception (K.P.'s from Sisson, Montague, Ashland, and Medford, over 100 in all, including Yreka) began work at 7:30 p.m., initiated 26 members. At 12 (midnight) a banquet was served at the Franco American Hotel, followed by speeches which lasted an hour or so when all returned to the Lodge room and worked till daylight. Many ladies accompanied their Knights of Pythias.

8-16-90: We would state to all Knights of Pythias here that T. J. Crowley, in a private letter, informs us that he will be up here to attend the big blowout and ball at Mott on (the) 23rd, also visit lodge on 22nd, as will Grand Chancellor J. G. Swinerton.

8-23-90: Remember the Pythian Ball tonight. Take your best girl and go to Mott, for there will be a big time there tonight. The *elite* of the land will assemble in the Pythias' Hall, while music's softest strains will kiss away the clouds of cares, and draw the truant lover to the fair ones' breast in the whirling waltz, go there and see.

8-30-90: (Headlines of the 8-30-90 issue): THE ANNIVERSARY BALL — GIVEN BY EAGLE CLIFF LODGE K.P. THE EVENT OF THE SEASON — A GRAND TURNOUT — ENJOYED BY ALL.

Last Saturday night, Eagle Cliff Lodge, Knights of Pythias, held their anniversary ball at Mott. About 8 o'clock in the evening, carriages began to arrive from Dunsmuir, Sisson, etc. (Earlier in the afternoon, several (couples) had arrived from Yreka and Sisson by train.) 45 from Dunsmuir — 90 couples at the banquet. The Ball commenced in the pavilion about half-past 9 — 80 couples (were) in the grand march. At 12 (midnight) repaired to the Shasta View Hotel for (a) grand banquet. Grand Chancellor Swinerton reviewed history of Knights of Pythias from its formation 27 years ago in Washington, D.C., by three men to its present membership of 300,000 in United States alone. After the banquet — "dancing resumed till the sun began to shine on the brow of Mount Shasta."

9-6-90: On Thursday nite, September 18th, the I.O.O.F. Encampment of Dunsmuir will give a grand ball and banquet. The ball will be held in the new hall, now in course of construction by Sam Gongwer. This will be the event of the season.

9-13-90: Ball date changed to September 20th (Gongwer hall not completed).

9-27-90: (HEADLINE) THE I.O.O.F. BALL. The Encampment Ball given by that degree of the Odd Fellows last Saturday nite in Sam Gongwer's new hall in Dunsmuir was a success in every sense of the word. They had employed Lemay's able band of Yreka, which rendered charming music, which needs no recommendation from us. The Hall was decorated for the occasion, and had a fine smooth floor for dancing on. They had the use of the Odd Fellows Hall to retire to between the dances which made it far more comfortable, and left the entire dance hall free from loungers during the dance. At 12 (midnight) they all repaired to the Mt. Shasta Dining Rooms where Mrs. French had set a delicious supper which was indulged in by about 125 guests.

After supper, dancing was resumed till 5 o'clock in the morning, when everyone retired to their homes wishing for another opportunity to throw themselves in the whirling dance.

The ball was the largest ever gotten up in Dunsmuir and was well managed, the receipts being considerably more than the disbursements.

10-4-90: The members of Knights of Pythias of Mott have changed the night of meeting from Friday to Saturday. There are strong rumors now of moving the Lodge to Dunsmuir.

11-8-90: The locomotive Engineers and Firemen have their posters out for their grand ball to be given at Sisson Thanksgiving night, November 27th. They will run a special train from Dunsmuir. This will be the grandest ball of the season.

11-22-90: The members of Castle Rock Lodge No. 349, I.O.O.F., had a big celebration Wednesday night, November 19th, when they were visited by the Grand Master John Glosson of Grass Valley and M. B. Lynes of San Francisco. After Lodge, they repaired to the California Hotel where a grand banquet was held which lasted until 2 o'clock in the morning. A large number of Odd Fellows were down from Sisson, Mott, and Edgewood.

11-29-90: (HEADLINE) THE BROTHERHOODS BALL — A GRAND SUCCESS. The Thanksgiving Ball given by the Brotherhood of Locomotive Engineers and Brotherhood of Locomotive Firemen in the dining room of the Depot Hotel, Sisson, on the 27th, was the most successful affair gotten up in some time. The Special train leaving Dunsmuir carried 60-odd passengers. The Ball opened in the dining room about 9 o'clock. At midnight repaired to La Grand Hotel where about 100 couples sat down to a sumptuous turkey dinner, there being about 110 couples at the Hall altogether. After supper, dancing was resumed until about 5 a.m.

1-17-91: The Masonic Lodge of this town has bought a new organ for their lodge room, for which they paid $100.00. It is one of those aeolian Organs, which you can play on with your hands, or put a roll of music in and grind out with your feet.

4-18-91: (HEADLINE) MASONIC BUILDING ASSOCIATION. At a recent meeting of the Masonic Stockholders of the Masonic Building Association, permanent directors were elected. The Directors have incorporated the Association and a meeting held the 1st of this week they elected officers. Plans for the building and Lodge rooms are being prepared and the work of the organizing is being pushed right along.

5-1-91: The Directors of the Masonic Hall Association held a meeting last Monday night at which they adopted a new set of By-Laws. They are now negotiating for a suitable lot to erect their building on.

7-18-91: The Brotherhood of Locomotive Firemen have bought the old school house and moved it across the street. They intend to make a fine lodge room out of it.

8-1-91: Officers of Castle Rock Lodge, Dunsmuir, Knights of Pythias, went to Sisson on the 25th to help in the institution of a lodge at that place.

9-26-91: There were a number of visiting Masons in Dunsmuir Thursday nite attending lodge. After the Third Degree, they had a big supper at the California Hotel.

2-13-92: The Knights of Pythias Lodge at Mott is to be moved to Dunsmuir. A Committee of Eagle Cliff Lodge, K. of P., has purchased two lots from the P.I. Co. on Sacramento Avenue, Dunsmuir, and will erect a fine two-story building on them. The upper story will be used for lodge purposes and the lower part for a public hall.

4-16-92: The stockholders of the K. of P. Hall Association met at the California Hotel Tuesday night. A Board of Directors was elected, issuing 3,000 shares of stock, 2,000 of which are already subscribed for. They will erect a 3-story building, the upper story of which will be used for lodge purposes and the 2nd story for a public hall.

7-23-92: The Knights of Pythias Hall now being erected on Sacramento Avenue will be an ornament to the town when completed and a source of income to the stockholders. The building will be three stories high. First floor — stores; 2nd, town hall for public meetings, dances, theatres and other amusements. This hall will be 30′ by 60′ and have a stage in the rear. Third story exclusively for fraternal societies, and when completed will be one of the finest lodge rooms between Sacramento and Portland.

10-28-93: Any of the Engineers' wives who wish to join the G.I.A. to Brotherhood of Locomotive Engineers will please call and leave their names at Mr. A. D. Kilborn's.

5-19-94: U.R. — K. of P.: Fourteen young men from Dunsmuir traveled by train Wednesday morning to Red Bluff, where they were initiated into the New Division of Uniform Rank. The Lodge will be known as Mt. Shasta, Division No. 9. It is composed of Sir Knights from Red Bluff, Dunsmuir, and Sisson — 47 members on Charter Roll. Headquarters of the new Division will be in Red Bluff.

9-1-94: The Masonic Order instituted a Lodge of O.E.S. in Dunsmuir Friday night. The instituting officer was Deputy Grand Patron of the Grand Chapter, R. S. Tapscott, of Yreka.

9-8-94: Fidelity Chapter, No. 131, Order Of The Eastern Star, was instituted August 31, 1894. A telegram was received about 5 p.m. of that day, stating that members of Stella Chapter of Yreka were on their way to Dunsmuir to help those eligible to membership to organize a chapter. This meeting had been talked of some months before, but we had not heard any more about it till the telegram was received. We, of course, had no meeting place. At that time there were the Knights of Pythias Hall, where the Masons held their lodge, and Gongwer's Hall. Some of the Masons hurried about to find a place where we could meet. They were told we could have Gongwer's Hall at the close of a meeting being held there that night. We went to the hall at 10 p.m., selected our officers and took instruction in what was to be our work, and about 11:30 p.m. we went to the K of P. Hall and took the obligation, and the following officers were installed:

Worthy Matron, Mamie Cummings; Worthy Patron, B. M. Gill; Associate Matron, Ada Culver; Secretary, Tillie E. Van Fossen; Treasurer, Alexander Culver; Conductress, Fidelia Fairbanks; Associate Conductress, Myrtle Gill; Star Points were Florence Gill, Mary Ingham, and Charity Walthers; Warder, George Ingham; Sentinel, Harry Walthers; Organist, James Robertshaw.

These, with Will Roberts, Levi Van Fossen, John Cummings, and George Pairbanks, composed the charter members, there being seventeen. After Chapter closed, we went to the California Hotel for a Banquet. At that time the electric lights were turned off at midnight, but arrangements were made to have them on until 1 a.m. Very soon after we sat down to the table, we were in darkness; but candles were brought in and we finished our repast by the light of other days. "Auld Lang Syne" was sung by A. E. Raynes, Siskiyou Pioneer.

11-10-94: The lady members of Fidelity Chapter, 131, O.E.S., will give a Thanksgiving Ball in the K.P. Hall at this place Thursday night, Nov. 29. The ladies intend to make this the grandest affair that has been gotten up in Dunsmuir for a long time. They will prepare the supper themselves and serve it in the rooms under the Hall. The price of admission will only be 75¢, everyone to have a ticket, which entitles them to supper.

12-1-94: (HEADLINE) THE O.E.S. BALL — A NOTEWORTHY EVENT AND A LARGE ATTENDANCE. The members of the Order of The Eastern Star gave their first ball in Dunsmuir Thanksgiving night. It was a notable affair and well attended. The hall was comfortably crowded and everybody was on the floor when the music played. The music was made by the Dunsmuir brass band and they did very well. Dunsmuir's four hundred were all there and some of our rising dudes put on all the frills the occasion and season would stand. The ladies were arrayed in their newest finery and looked attractive enough to jar the pyramids. Some of them would create a warmth in the glacious breast of Mt. Shasta. Supper was served in the dining room of the California Hotel, James Harris very generously giving the O.E.S. the free

FIDELITY CHAPTER #131
FIFTIETH ANNIVERSARY, 1944

Left to right: Mary Ward, member 50 years; Vera Mason, candidate; Erma Cooper, First Patron (Ada); Albert McCann, Vice-President; Josephine Weeks, Third Patron (Esther); Jennie Dickson, Second Patron (Ruth); Grace Bascomb, Fourth Patron (Martha); Arthur McGee, Treasurer; Ethel Beckman, Guard; Harry Brown, Sentinel; Dr. George Malone, Secretary; Norma Kintgen, Conductor; Agnes Weamer, President (Matron); Kate Berry, member; Helen Cochenour, Fifth Patron (Electa). The program was put on as Initiation of 1867 ritual. Josephine and Arthur McGee were Matron and Patron of the chapter in 1944.

FIDELITY CHAPTER #131
SEVENTY-FIFTH ANNIVERSARY, 1969

Left to right: Erma Harrell, First Patron (Ada); Olga Orr, Treasurer; Roberta Belland, Guard; Dorothy Welch, Conductress; Mildred Tillotson, Chaplain; Ruth Asher, Third Patron (Esther); Worthy Grand Matron, Florence Dunn, the candidate; Opal Morgan, Fourth Patron (Martha); Margaret Olsen, Second Patron (Ruth); Kathleen Graves, President (Matron); Laura Billington, Fifth Patron (Electa). Officers in 1867 Initiation ceremony not shown: Paul Collins, Vice-President; Elmer Graves, Secretary; Cecil Welch, Sentinal; Josephine McGee, Promptress. 1867 Ritual presented June 25, 1969.

use of his dining room for that purpose. The ladies did their own cooking and waiting on the table so they were not out much for the supper. They charged every person who entered the hall, lady as well as gentleman, 75¢, including supper. There were in the neighborhood of 250 present, so with their small expenses, they will make money out of the operation. Out-of-town guests came from San Francisco, Mott, Sisson, Yreka, Ferndale, Kennett, Oregon. The ladies were attired in black silk, black cashmere, Henrietta white silk.

1-12-95: The Officers-Elect of Dunsmuir Lodge No. 297, Free and Accepted Masons, will be installed at the regular meeting Thursday, January 17th. After installation, there will be a banquet. J. D. Cummings, Worshipful Master (News editor & publisher).

3-3-95: The Knights of Pythian Ball a success February 22nd, re: their foundation celebration.

5-25-95: O.E.S. SOCIAL: The following will show that the good people of Dunsmuir are still in the land of living and know how to enjoy themselves. The most enjoyable affair your correspondent has witnessed for quite awhile took place at the Knights of Pythias Hall last Tuesday evening, the occasion being the first social given by the "Eastern Star" of Dunsmuir. The beauty and intelligence of our little town was certainly well-represented, together with the many elegant toilettes worn by the ladies, rendered the scene a maze of beauty. The stage settings were most perfect in detail and brought praise from many. The hall was brilliantly lighted and all were merry as a marriage bell. The music furnished by the home band certainly was never better. The program was a mixed and interesting one. First was a Grand March, then solos, recitations, tableaus. When they had concluded, dancing began in earnest and kept up to an early hour.

10-17-96: THE REBEKAHS ORGANIZE A NEW LODGE IN DUNSMUIR: A lodge of Rebekahs was instituted in Dunsmuir last Friday night. After work completed, the new members with guests and members of I.O.O.F. of Dunsmuir, repaired to the Mt. Shasta Hotel where a sumptuous banquet was spread.

11-28-96: THE MACCABEES DANCE: Crystal Tent No. 55, Knights of The Maccabees, gave a grand ball in the K.P. Hall, Dunsmuir, Thanksgiving eve. There was a large crowd present from Dunsmuir and quite a number from Sisson. Supper served at California Hotel and the Ball kept up till near morning.

8-28-97: Uniform Rank, Knights of Pythias, instituted in Dunsmuir, Tuesday night, Division 19 with about 30 members. Only U.R. north of Red Bluff. Wednesday night there was a public installation with dancing and banquet.

10-23-97: First anniversary of Rebekahs celebrated by banquet and entertainment.

11-13-97: Brotherhood of Railroad Trainmen and Brotherhood of Locomotive Firemen Grand Ball about January 15, 1898.

1-1-98: Masons and Eastern Star held a joint installation and banquet in Dunsmuir Thursday night. The installation ceremonies were held in the K.P. Hall and the banquet at the Western Hotel. Several of the members came down from Sisson to attend the affair.

2-5-98: (HEADLINE) JOLLY KINGS OF PURGATORY: Local Pythians are deeply interested in a new organization within their ranks, known as the I.O.K. of P., which means the Infernal Order of Kings of Purgatory. It is learned that a meeting for the institution of this new Auxiliary degree of the Knights of Pythias was recently held in S.F. and was presided over by George W. Montieth, who stated that the idea of such a body had its origin in the Golden City Lodge. The idea was fully explained and discussed and the Organization was effected by the choice of a Committee that will report the names of Officers at the next meeting. A newspaper report says it is proposed that the I.O.K. of P. shall hold a session on the 19th of February each year, the anniversary of the foundation of the Order of Pythians. No one shall be eligible to membership but the members of the Order of Knights of Pythias; but the degrees of the new Order, which will be several in number, may be conferred on any members or non-Pythians who will be permitted to apply for the privilege of becoming inducted into the several mysteries, on the recommendation of members. The ritual that has been prepared with great care is, it is said by those who have pursued it, one of the most interesting of any side degree that has ever been presented. The candidates will be given an insight of the workings of some secret societies, which will make them feel at times somewhat startled, but the lesson they will learn will be most instructive. The paraphernalia necessary for the carrying out of the degrees and the uniforms to be worn by the kings of purgatory, namely the sublime king and his four imps; it is said will be very fine. Another feature will be the selection of a queen for the day of celebration. Each lodge will be permitted to suggest one lady; then a vote will be taken. The one receiving the highest will be the queen, and the four next will be her maids.

2-19-98: New Red Men at Sisson-Shasta Tribe #95.

2-26-98: The Knights of Pythias Ball: The Uniform Rank, K.P., and Rathbone sisters gave a dance in the K.P. Hall Saturday night. About 40 couples were present and they had a very sociable time. The music was made by J. M. La Due and J. Shilling, of Redding. The supper was served by the Rathbone sisters in the rooms under the hall. The dance was kept up to about 4:00 in the morning.

3-5-98: LAST ISSUE J. D. CUMMINGS — left for the far North — Klondyke, leased *Dunsmuir News* to R. H. Whitson.

3-26-98: MASONIC DEGREE CONFERRED: Thursday evening — marks an unusually interesting epoch in the annuals of Dunsmuir Lodge No. 297, F. & A.M. A call meeting was held in K. of P. Hall, the occasion being the conferring of the 3rd or Master Mason Degree upon Dr. C. C. Gleaves by W. M. A. Levy. After the business meeting, which lasted until 12 o'clock, the newly-honored member invited those present to a sumptuous banquet which was served in the brilliantly lighted dining rooms of the Mt. Shasta Hotel. No pains were spared to make this a success, and Landlord Mueke added to the fame of his popular resort. The hour was spent in discussing the elaborate menu enlivened by social conversation and brief addresses by different members. Dr. Gleaves proved himself a most charming host, and the evening will long be remembered by his delightful guests.

4-23-98: Mrs. Clarissa J. Morris, of Oakland, state organizer of the Ladies of the Maccabees, arrived here Thursday morning, and will remain over Saturday. Mrs. Morris addressed an audience of ladies at K. of P. Hall on Thursday afternoon explaining the objects and working of the Order which she represents. Almost all the ladies present signed a petition expressing their desire to become charter members of the local L.O.T.M. and a hive of 24 members was the result. Mrs. Morris is a forceable and pleasant speaker. She gave some interesting statistics regarding this beneficiary Order, it being the *first fraternal society to provide insurance for women*. Since its organization in 1892, the growth has been phenomenal. Friday afternoon, the hive was formally organized and the officers elected.

12-18-97: Eagle Cliff Lodge K.P. visited by Grand Chancellor. The ladies of the Rathbone sisters spread a sumptuous supper — dancing afterwards to a late hour.

4-30-98: SIR KNIGHTS TENDER THE LADY MACCABEES A BANQUET: The members of Crystal Tent, Knights of Maccabees, tended a banquet to their ladies and a few other invited guests at the K.P. Hall. The newly-organized Hive of the Ladies of Maccabees, which has the largest membership of any hive in Northern California, was out in full force, and gave a most interesting drill, their mystic badge L.O.T.M. — "Lean On The Men." Banquet with speeches, dancing till midnight.

4-30-98: The Calico Ball and Maypole Party, given by Mossbrea Lodge #29 of the Rathbone Sisters: Music by Schilling La Due orchestra, Redding; 9 p.m. — winding of Maypole by 16 lil girls — in red, white, blue, yellow — Rathbone Sisters colors. There was a lil queen of the evening with attendants.

6-28-98: G.I.A. entertains B. of L.E. — songs, cards and banquet.

2-22-02: (HEADLINE) I.O.O.F. LODGE REORGANIZED: Elaborate Banquet rendered by the Rebekahs — State Officers were present: It was a great event, that of

Monday night, among the Odd Fellows and Rebekahs of Dunsmuir. For five years, Castle Rock Lodge of Odd Fellows No. 349 has been dormant and the few remaining members concluded to surrender their charter and merge into and associate with the Sisson Lodge, and had been associating therewith until now, when they decided it was time to reorganize and start a home lodge.

Consequently, they applied to the proper officials and appointment was made that the Grand Master and the Grand Secretary should come to Dunsmuir on Feb. 17 and re-establish the lodge here. Wm. Nicholls, Jr., Grand Master, and George Shaw, Grand Secretary of the Grand Lodge of Odd Fellows of California, were on hand and business was begun by obligating some twenty-two members into the Dunsmuir Lodge 120; several of these were formerly of the Castle Rock and many had withdrawn cards from other lodges.

Those who went in as Charter members and were made officers (so far as the latter went) are: N.G., H. B. Basham; V.G., L. R. Huff; P.G., J. J. Wilson; Perm Sec, W. J. Branstetter; Treas., S. R. Gongwer; Chap., G. C. Scholes; Warden, O. Trammel; R.S. to N.G., V. G. A. Levy; L.S. to N.G., E. A. Bissell; R.S. to V.G., Jas. McMann; L.S. to V.G., W. T. Tuckwell; Con'r., J. J. Malone; O.S.G., T. R. Skillington; I.S.G., L. O. Vaughan; R.S.S., J. O. Rhoads; L.S.S., W. J. Cadjew; F. Sec., R. W. Emerson, H. Scherrer, F. B. Gongwer, L. W. Gerdey, H. W. Wilson, F. M. Walker.

A. S. Ward, Postal Clerk, acted as Grand Marshal in all the Ceremonies in the lodge, and he is said to have been "right at home" in that role.

While all of this work was going on above, the good Sisters Rebekah were busy below spreading the collating, and otherwise enjoying themselves playing cards, talking, singing, and passing time until about midnight, when the goat would be stabled and all repair to the feast in the large hall. The Committee of Arrangements for the Banquet were Mrs. G. C. Scholes, Mrs. S. R. Gongwer, Mrs. H. B. Basham, Mrs. E. A. Bissell, Mrs. H. W. Brown, being assisted by Messrs. Emerson and Bissell.

The decorating committee were: Mrs. E. J. Bowen, Mrs. S. Gongwer, Misses Lulu and Fannie Scholes, Miss Jessie Cave. The colors were pink and green and the display was elegant, the walls being dressed with various emblems of the Order of Odd Fellows and Rebekahs, in a most attractive manner. The tables were conspicuous with a profusion of carnations, both red and white (which Miss Scholes had ordered from Oakland), daffodils, Chinese lilies, and other exotic tropical plants and flowers.

One cute design was a fragrant button-hole bouquet of fresh violets bound with silver threads among the gold. There was one under every plate. They were taken away as souvenirs.

The tables had been set and loaded with the good things that tickle the palate only. Mrs. Josephine Lee busied herself doing the carving, which was to the "Queen's taste." One of the most unique dishes seen was that of a whole pig, the contribution of Mr. and Mrs. J. J. Malone. It was the intention to have it roasted in a standing position with decorations; but the Home Baker, where it was cooked, was compelled to rest little "pig-hog" in a reclining attitude, but the roasting was perfect; and the pig, like the one of John O'Pound, the fifer's son, was eat and with a relish at the proper time. The roast chicken, the cold boiled ham, head cheese, bread and butter, salads, relishes, the most beautiful and bountiful display of cakes, of a dozen different kinds, with steaming, delicious coffee, made this one of the most elaborate suppers of the year.

A very pleasant feature of the evening and morning during eating hours was music, both vocal and instrumental, rendered by Misses Lulu and Fannie Scholes and Miss Jessie Cave. It was low and sweet, giving a decided effect to the surroundings.

As the clock struck 12, the lodge took a transfer, and bodily marched to the banquet hall. There, Grand Master Nicholls escorted Mrs. Minnie Neville, N.G., of the Rebekahs, and Grand Secretary Shaw escorted Mrs. Frank Gongwer, V.G., of the Rebekahs, to seats of honor at the table. The local Odd Fellows saw their visiting brethren, some thirty in number, of the Sisson Lodge No. 370, comfortable at the parallel tables and there invited to partake of the feast. The tables seated about eighty-eight and there were fourteen, mostly Rebekahs, who served as waiters and then ate at the second table.

After a glorious and sumptuous repast, which was as a "feast of reason and flow of soul," Grand Master Nicholls was called on to address the audience.

The usual greetings exchanged and the lodge returned to their work, closing about 2:30 in the morning. The Lodge voted an expression of thanks to one and all, individually and collectively the Lady Rebekahs for their earnest and liberal endeavors to entertain their visitors and the local members and their families, which they did to perfection. All honor to the dear sisters and may they have many and often such pleasant feasting-gatherings.

2-22-02: Knights' Pythias Hall was the scene of a merry juvenile gathering on last Saturday afternoon, when the Lady Maccabees gave a Valentine party in honor of their children. There were about forty-five youngsters in the happy group. Short musical and literary exercises came first on the program. A series of living pictures were received with great applause.

After the program, a post office was established when the postmistress dispensed a pretty valentine to each child. Comic valentines were also provided for the grown-ups and created much merriment.

The children were given a generous treat of nuts and fine, juicy oranges and at a late

hour departed, happy in the knowledge that for one afternoon the interests of the parents had been subordinated to their own, and that they had been the guest of honor.

3-29-02: LADIES AUXILIARY TO THE B. OF R. T. LODGE INSTITUTED: On Thursday, March 20th, was instituted at K. P. Hall a lodge of "The Ladies Auxiliary to the Brotherhood of Railroad Trainmen."

Grand Lodge Organizer, Mrs. Kate Talbott, assisted by twelve other members of the Order from Oakland, was in attendance and officiated at the ceremonies.

There were present from Oakland Mesdames Kate Talbott, Mary Ross, Margeret Phelps, Ellen Turnbull, Effie Rieves, Margaret Steece, Lucy Heck, Alice Arterburn, Mattie Cheadle, Francis Thompson, Clara Norcott, Elizabeth Reburn, Mattie Martin, and Mr. Victor Heck, as councilman.

The meeting was held at 2 p.m., the new members being obligated and instructed by Mrs. Talbott, who was assisted by other ladies of her team. The following were elected to fill the offices of the new lodge:

Councilman, A. R. Bomar; Past Mistress, Mrs. Clara Clausnitzer; Mistress, Mrs. Clara Bomar; Vice Mistress, Mrs. Maude Maxey; Secretary, Mrs. Nellie Reid; Treasurer, Mrs. Emma Cotter; Conductress, Miss Annie Kelly; Chaplain, Mrs. Hannah Kelly; Warden, Mrs. Pauline Creason; Inner Guard, Mrs. Mollie Renfro; Outer Guard, Miss Mamie Clausnitzer.

Previous to the meeting held for organization, the delegation of ladies from Oakland were taken in hand by a committee of Trainmen and were conducted to the famous Upper Soda Springs; also, Cave Springs, and other places of interest. Many were the words of praise and bouquets showered over our little town and surroundings by the people from the Bay.

In the evening after the organization, there met at the residence of Mr. and Mrs. A. R. Bomas the members of Castle Crag Lodge No. 458, B. of R.T., with their ladies; and a most enjoyable time was spent with games, music and recitations.

Refreshments were served later in the evening. Each lady from Oakland was presented with a view of Mount Shasta, representing the new lodge organized; and Castle Rocks for the Brotherhood, and one of Dunsmuir Fountain. Also, a piece of lava, tied with white ribbon, for each one. Speeches of thanks and congratulations were given on all sides, and everyone was satisfied with having spent a most enjoyable evening.

7-5-02: WOMEN OF THE WOODCRAFT — While E. G. Weber, District Organizer of the State, was up here last week, he succeeded in perfecting an organization of a "circle" of seventeen charter members, fourteen being initiated.

The number of the order is yet blank; the name selected is Castle Crag Circle. The uninitiated are hereby notified that a Circle of Women of the Woodcraft is a contingent of the Woodmen of the World.

7-26-02: OFFICERS INSTALLED. Saturday evening last was probably one of the grandest occasions ever experienced by the Order of the Odd Fellows at Dunsmuir. The Lodge had been beautifully decorated by Mrs. Hubsch and Miss Lulu Scholes. There were many visitors and a dainty spread is said to have been displayed and dispatched. The following exhibits the joint installation:

The District Deputy Grand Master of District 97, I.O.O.F., Deputy Grand Officer G. C. Scholes, Grand Marshal; Steve Knight, Grand Warden; Brother Philips, Grand Secretary; H. Lassen, Grand Treasurer; H. Winkle, Grand Guardian; installed the officers of Dunsmuir Lodge, No. 120, I.O.O.F.

The joint installation included officers for Rebekah Lodge of Dunsmuir.

11-29-02: EVERYBODY PRAISES IT. The Rebekahs' Ball, which came off promptly Wednesday evening at Pythian Hall, was a success from start to finish. By those who know, it was said to be superior in every respect to any similar function ever got up here before. In fact, it was swell, inasmuch as it presented more originality in the get up of characters, the neatest and daintiest costumes, and the sociability and all-around good time experienced by everyone in attendance. For pleasure and profit, the entertainment was A No. 1. Besides the untiring energy displayed by the Lady Rebekahs, wherein liberal advertising was the principal feature, nothing to conduce to the completion of this annual affair was left undone. La Due's orchestra furnished the music, all of which was especially prepared for the occasion, and made the dancing easy and pleasant to those thus indulging.

Those winning prizes were: Best sustained character, lady representing a Christmas Tree, Mrs. Turner; Best dressed lady, representing Folly, Mrs. George Eugwicht; Best sustained character, gentleman, representing Hod-Carrier, Ed Knapp; Best dressed gentleman, representing a Spanish Cavalier, F. M. Campbell. The presents were respectively: A jewel box, a thermometer, an ink-stand, a pocket toilet set.

There were in all ninety-six maskers. At midnight, at a given signal, all unmasked.

Soon thereafter, supper being announced, the attendants to the number of one hundred four repaired to the Western Hotel, where Mine Host Muehe had prepared the finest and most palatable supper of the season for his guests. Under his management, no one was neglected and each and every one felt it was an agreeable privilege to be at W. F.'s Thanksgiving Eve Supper.

10-4-07: RED MEN ORGANIZE. Last Saturday Night Was Big Time for the Red Skins — Banquet and Other Matters: Teton Tribe, No. 197, was organized last Saturday night with one hundred and seven (107) petitioners, of whom eighty-seven (87) Palefaces were present and twenty Palefaces were absent, who paid a total of One

Hundred and Nine Dollars. The absentees will be obligated at the next meeting, or as soon as they present themselves. A total of seven hundred and eighteen dollars ($718) was turned over to the Tribe. Winema Tribe No. 187, of Weed, conferred the degrees. Owing to the lateness of the hour, the Chief's degree was omitted, but will be conferred some time in the near future. The Great Sachem, G. S. Godeau, assisted by the Great Senior Sagamore, Frank Bell, both of San Francisco and of the Reservation of California, instituted the Tribe.

The following prominent citizens of Dunsmuir were selected as officers of the new Tribe, until January 1, 1908: Prophet, G. C. Spaeth; Sachem, Fr. W. B. Mason; Senior Sagamore, Frank B. Gongwer; Junior Sagamore, Abe Huff; Chief of Records, Judge Chas. O. Clarke; Keeper of Wampum, J. D. Williams. The balance of the officers of the Tribe will be appointed at the next meeting, on Saturday evening at K. of P. Hall. Prof. P. Varney, the Drill Master of the Reservation of California, will meet with the new Tribe on Saturday evening and instruct them in the Ritual and drill work of the Order. The Exemplification of the Adoption and warrior Degrees by the Weed Tribe was certainly highly commendable and praiseworthy. About two hundred Redmen and newly adopted Brothers participated at the Corn and Venison (prepared by Mrs. Baxter), which was excellent. Altogether, the Teton Tribe, No. 197, of the Hunting Grounds of Dunsmuir, starts under very favorable conditions. We predict that the new Tribe will soon rank as one of the leading fraternal orders of the city. The Organizer, G. W. Canning, has been ordered to Redding at once, where a petition has been sent to the Great Council for a Tribe.

7-28-11: POCAHONTAS INSTALLATION: Teton Temple, No. 107, installed officers last Tuesday night, District Deputy, Mrs. Chambers, acting as installing officer. Below is the list of officers installed: Prophetess, Anna Clark; Pocahontas, Emma Cotter; Powhatan, Mr. Miller; Wenonap, Emma Spencer; First Scout, Minnie Miller; Second Scout, Mrs. Swanson; Keeper of Records, Louie Derby; Keeper of Wampum, Marie Huckson; First Warrior, Mr. Becker; Second Warrior, Mr. Grove. Following the installation, a banquet was served and a good time enjoyed by all.

8-11-11: K. of P. HALL BADLY DEMOLISHED BY FIRE: The top story of the K. of P. Hall was destroyed by fire at 8 o'clock Wednesday morning. The prompt response of the S.P. fire department, assisted by numerous volunteers succeeded in the extinguishing a fire that for a time threatened the upper part of this city. The origin of the blaze is unknown at the present time, although many theories have been advanced. The loss will not exceed $3,000. Practically all the property belonging to the various orders that occupied the hall was saved. For fully two hours, six powerful streams of water were

played on the fire by willing hands and to their heroic efforts is due the fact that not a building on either side was even scorched (as spelled). Fire Chief Abe Huff was on the firing line and exemplified his ability to handle a fire of this nature. All hail the fire fighting kids!

8-11-11: THE LOYAL ORDER OF MOOSE ORGANIZES: W. R. Hampton, Deputy Organizer for the Loyal Order of Moose has been in Dunsmuir for several days and has succeeded in enrolling a large number of representative Dunsmuir citizens as charter members. It is expected in the neighborhood of two hundred will form the nucleus of the order in Dunsmuir. The Moose slogan is "Purity, Aid, Progress" and Howdy. Pap? is the jovial style of salutation. It has beneficiary provisions and social attraction which will add much influence to the already large fraternal prosperity of Dunsmuir. The new lodge, Peter Scott, No. 673, Loyal Order of Moose will meet Saturday evening at 9 o'clock at the K. of P. Hall. Those desiring to become members apply to Geo. Hampden at C. O. Clark's office, or J. J. Wilson. On Tuesday evening, the Lodge will be formed. It is safe to say that this fraternity will start in a more flourishing condition than any other organization ever instituted in this town.

10-22-16: KNIGHTS OF COLUMBUS INSTALLED OFFICERS: (from *Mt. Shasta Herald*): At a special meeting in I.O.O.F. Hall last Saturday evening, Mt. Shasta Council No. 2599 initiated a class of eleven candidates into the first degree. On the same evening, John T. Donohue, of Chico, installed the newly-elected officers for the coming year as follows: Grand Knight, J. F. Mackey; Deputy Grand Knight, Chas. McCabe; Financial Secretary, Gerald Bannister; Chancellor, Leo Girimonte; Inner Guard, A. Fontanna; Outer Guard, V. Bruno; Trustee, S. Spatafora; Advocate, Jas. Kiernan. After the ceremonials, a lunch was served in the banquet room of the hall.

1-9-20: LODGE OF PYTHIAN SISTERS IS FORMED: Dunsmuir Temple No. 99, Pythian Sisters, was instituted Tuesday evening at K. of P. Hall by Mrs. Leone Mayer, Grand Manager, assisted by Tilly Vest, both of Chico Temple No. 93. The following officers of the new lodge were installed: P.C., Edith Selby; E.S., Reitha Renoud; E.M., Luch Minter; M., Emma Dias; P., Margaret Price; M. of R. & C., Bertha Huffman; M. of F., Linna Smallwood; O.E., Frances Parr. Initiations were held for twenty Pythian Sisters and Sixteen Knights. Sisters Johnson and Gouette of Shasta Temple 127, led the degree staff of Sisson Temple, ten ladies taking part. The work was made more beautiful by the decorations, which were in the lodge colors, entwined in evergreen. The altars were especially decorated with roses and ferns. The banquet room was decorated with the lodge colors and evergreen, and the tables were adorned with roses and ferns. One hundred persons were seated at the banquet, which was delicious and

A group of Dunsmuir women — 1921 — thought to be a bridge club From left to right: Mrs. John Davidson, ? (Mrs. Parker), Mrs. Clarke (Judge Clarke), Mrs. Arthur Coggins, Mrs. Ted Hawkins, Mrs. Les Hamilton, Mrs. Huff, Mrs. Beverly Ward, Mrs. Malone (Dr. Malone), Mrs. Cornish (Dr. Cornish), ? (Mrs. Cravens), Mrs. James Stanley.

appetizingly served. Toasts and speeches followed. The toastmistress presented the Grand Manager with a bouquet of white chrysanthemums and ferns, eliciting an appreciative response. The District Deputy G.C. of Sisson being ill and unable to attend, was remembered with a similar bouquet. Simmington brothers furnished music for the entertainment. The Dunsmuir temple extended a vote of thanks to the Sisson, Kennett and Chico temples for their support and attendance, which made the occasion a memorable one and to all the others who assisted in making the institution of the new lodge such a success. Wednesday morning, the Pythian Sisters made a trip to the headwaters of the Sacramento River, the fish hatchery and other points of interest in the vicinity of Sisson, returning to Dunsmuir for afternoon practice. The visitors were entertained in the homes of the lodge members during their stay here. They returned to their homes Thursday.

3-18-21: PYRAMID OF SCIOTS TO BE ORGANIZED: (Headline, front page). Plans are being formulated by local Masons for instituting in Dunsmuir on the evening of a Pyramid of Sciots. The wide-awake and progressive spirit of local lodgemen was largely instrumental in obtaining this organization for Dunsmuir, which will be the only one in the country. Organization of the Pyramid of Sciots in Dunsmuir will be a red-letter day in the history of Masonry in this county and arrangements are being made to take care of a big number of visitors who will be here from many parts of the county and outside to help institute the Pyramid and make the affair a success.

4-15-21: MANY NORTHERN MA-SONS JOINED ORDER OF SCIOTS HERE LAST SATURDAY. Masons from nearly all parts of Siskiyou County were in Dunsmuir last Saturday night when the Ancient Egyptian Order of Sciots, Pyramid No. 22, was instituted. A class of 223 was initiated at the Auditorium.

Waldo F. Postel, Pharoah; Carl Eber, Supreme Scribe; and Chas. H. S. Pratt, Supreme Lecturer, of the Supreme Pyramid of San Francisco, were here to institute the local pyramid.

Entertainers from San Francisco were one of the happy features of the enthusiastic celebration.

Masons from Hilt, Ager, Yreka, Sisson, Fort Jones, Redding, Weed, and Castella participated in the inauguration of the local pyramid. Light refreshments closed the evening's festivities.

There were short talks by Geo. A. Tebbe, Chas. Luttrell, G. A. Hutaff, Dr. G. E. Malone, J. W. FitzGerald, Henry McGuinness, and A. Levy.

The following officers were installed: J. H. Biederman, Toparch; R. L. Chamberlain, Mobib; A. J. Lebourveau, Hauspice; F. E. Slater, Pastophori; P. A. Bryan, Scribe; C. O. Porter, Chancellor; G. A. Hutaff, G. E. Malone, J. W. FitzGerald, Trustees; E. M. Babb, Chief of the Me; L. M. Hamilton, Sub Chief; A. Levy, Marshal; G. C. Schandel, Standard Bearer; Henry McGuinness, Proclamator; C. E. Glidden, Neorori; A. M. Ager, Mazari; A. L. Shoupe, Chief Musician; C. E. Wickes, Klasachar; R. L. Butler, Captain of the Guard.

The San Francisco delegation was taken around in automobiles and expressed keen delight with the varied and interesting mountain scenery.

5-20-21: Local Eagles to Observe Memorial Day: The Fraternal Order of Eagles of this city will observe Memorial Day here this year on Sunday, May 29. A program has been arranged by the lodgemen and they are planning on a fitting observance.

5-20-21: Knights Of Pythias Will Give Dance For Benefit Of Memorial Fund May 28: The Dunsmuir Knights of Pythias will give their next dance for the benefit of the Memorial Fund on May 28. The Knights are striving valiantly to raise the price of this monument, which will be in the neighborhood of $3,000, and deserve the support of every patriotic citizen in the county. Excellent music will be furnished for this affair and dancers from all parts of the county are expected to be in attendance, as it is being widely advertised. The purchase of a ticket will entitle you to an evening of wholesome enjoyment and at the same time aid a good cause.

5-20-21: Sciots Are Having Their Hall Remodeled And Have Bought Billiard Tables: The Sciots have had their hall here remodeled and have purchased two billiard tables for use in their club rooms, which they are having fitted up. Petitions are reported to be coming in fast for the big ceremonial that will be held here on July 16.

5-20-21: Sciots Will Take Part In Memorial Day Observance — To Celebrate At Weed 4th: Members of the Dunsmuir Pyramid of Sciots have been notified to assemble at Sciots Hall to participate in the Memorial Day observance here on the 30th. All members are to wear their fez. It is possible a number of the other fraternal and veterans' organizations will take part in the observance. The Sciots are also planning on taking an active part in the Fourth of July celebration to be put on at Weed this year.

7-15-21: (HEADLINE) STOCK WILL SOON BE PLACED ON SALE FOR NEW BUILDING. At a rousing meeting of the Dunsmuir Masonic Temple Association, it was decided unanimously to erect a Masonic Temple in this city on the site just south of the post office. This is the site that has been under contemplation by the Dunsmuir Development Company. Attorney Henry McGuinness was instructed to file articles of incorporation for a new company with a capital of $100,000, divided into 1,000 shares, par value $100 each. It is desired by the association that every citizen of Dunsmuir keep informed of its progress and motive. The building is not intended for the exclusive use of the Masons, as tentative plans call for a theatre, two lodge rooms, banquet room, dance floor, club rooms and other features to be decided by the directors. What is wanted now is the promise to purchase stock just as soon as the association is ready for its sale.

9-16-21: Sciots Will Permit Use Of Their Hall For Dancing-Band Boys First: At the last meeting of the Sciots, they decided to permit the use of their hall for dancing. Inasmuch as there is not now a place of any

105

kind in Dunsmuir where dances can be held, the Sciots thought it would be well to surrender the use of their hall (the old Strand Theatre) for a reasonable consideration to fraternal orders or others wishing to use the hall for that purpose, since there is no other place in town that could be used for that purpose.

The weather is becoming too cold to dance on the outdoor platforms and, with the coming of winter, a dance hall is almost a necessity here. Young people will dance, and the action of the Sciots will make it unnecessary for them to go out of town to do so; which, in fact, would be impossible when the snowy season sets in.

D. C. Baker will have the management of the Sciots' Hall and is exercising every effort to have the floor and hall put in first-class condition for dancing. The club rooms of the Sciots will have to be changed and considerable work done to accommodate the dance crowds, but the work is being pushed rapidly and will be completed by Saturday night, just in time for the band boys to give the first dance in the hall.

Mr. Baker states that fraternal organizations will have the first chance at the hall at all times, and that no one will be allowed to tie it up for an unreasonable number of dances.

12-30-21: SCIOTS MAKE CHILDREN HAPPY AT CHRISTMAS TIME — Dunsmuir's first community Christmas tree was given by the local Pyramid of Sciots Christmas Eve. The affair was a tremendous success, and an immense crowd of children and adults attended. The program rendered was received with enthusiasm by the audience, and consisted of talks by Toparch E. M. Babb, G. A. Hutaff, and Dr. George Malone, and a cantata by the children, after which Santa Claus came down the chimney and delighted the little folks. The distribution of presents followed, which was rather a long task. Each child who registered at the Callisch Electric Station and with members of the Sciots, received a present wrapped in a neat package and bearing his name. Over four hundred presents were distributed to the happy children.

4-14-22: SHRINER'S CEREMONIAL WAS VERY BRILLIANT FUNCTION: The visit and ceremonial of the Nobles of Islam Temple of San Francisco, last Saturday, is considered the most successful and pleasing, if not the most elaborate, of any similar function ever held in Dunsmuir.

The Pullmans, containing the visitors, arrived at 11:35 a.m. and the party was immediately taken in charge by Horace Weed and William R. Lee, official committeemen, assisted by Chas. Bess, C. O. Porter, Frank Callisch, Geo. Wilson, and others. The day was blustery and the weather decidedly different from what most of the visitors were used to; and, while some were taken out in cars after lunch, many

stayed in town for the parade at 3 o'clock. This was a beautiful pageant and comprised more than 100 people, including the band of 24 pieces, the richly uniformed patrol, and the candidates, who were appropriately and extravagantly dressed. The outward show impressed observers as to the worth and stability of Masonry; it was a gorgeous and attractive ceremony. The Islam Nobles said that they enjoyed the unique experience of parading in a snow storm — it was a novelty worthwhile. The local Committee made arrangements for the special mess of weather during the parade, which included: dust, bright sunshine, and a healthy snow storm, all at once. As some of the visitors never had seen snow falling before, they appreciated the arrangement, and pronounced it the best stunt ever pulled off by an entertainment committee. The visitors were entertained at dinner and after the evening's ceremonies, at a banquet at the Weed Hotel, both of which functions were of the usual high character furnished by Landlord Wickes and his able staff. The ceremonial lasted far into the night, thirty-four gentlemen becoming Nobles of the Mystic Shrine.

Sunday was a beautiful day, and was consumed principally with short sight-seeing trips. Local Shriners put their cars at the disposal of the visitors and they were taken out to Shasta, the Hatchery, Castle Crags, and many other points of interest. C. O. Porter, who drove a party up to the snow line on the McCloud road, says his passengers had the time of their lives. Some of them, who had never seen snow before at close range, got out and rolled in it. Everyone had a good time and told about it.

Islam Band gave a concert in the park at about 3 p.m., which is pronounced as good as is ever heard. The music was beyond criticism and highly appreciated by an audience of about 1500 people. The perfect day ended with the departure of the visitors at 4:55, the train slowly pulling as the strains of "Aloha" floated back in the golden notes of the band leader's cornet.

4-21-22: DE MOLAY CHARTERED — Officers Are Installed and New Chapter Is Launched With Pleasant Prospects: The Dunsmuir Chapter of the De Molay for boys was organized last Friday night, and officers installed. The installation ceremony was conducted by Frank Killam, of the Sacramento Consistory No. 7, assisted by Chairman Nourse, C. F. Woodin, Marshal; C. O. Porter, Orator; each of whom contributed important portions of the work.

Nineteen officers were installed, starting the chapter with pleasing prospects, and with a very capable body of young officers. It is hoped that the organization will include every boy in town who is eligible. All desiring to join are invited to consult some one of the officers. The chapter will meet regularly on the second Friday in each month, at Branstetter Hall.

4-28-22: ODD FELLOWS CELE-BRATE 103RD ANNIVERSARY — Dunsmuir Lodge No. 120, I.O.O.F., held a fitting celebration of the 103rd anniversary of Odd Fellowship in America Monday night at their lodge hall and the hall of the Sciots. About two hundred and fifty persons, including members, their families, and invited guests, attended the entertainment which was provided by the lodge, consisting of a minstrel show, musical numbers, dancing, card games and a banquet. It was pronounced by those who attended as being one of the best celebrations ever held by local Odd Fellows.

9-21-23: SCIOTS' INDOOR CIRCUS CLOSES: Monday night was the close of the Sciots' Indoor Circus which ran for five nights and drew a big crowd each night, many of them coming from neighboring towns. The entertainment seemed to please those who attended and a niminal sum was netted to be added to the Sciot charity fund. Of the five most popular ladies, the first four received a diamond ring apiece, the fifth a silver mesh bag. The five most beautiful babies received honorary mention. The Chevrolet automobile was won by Conductor E. T. Joy.

12-28-23: MEMORIAL FOUNTAIN BEING ERECTED TODAY: The memorial drinking fountain, which the local lodge of K. of P. has been promoting for quite awhile, is now being erected in front of the post office (today in front of Masonic Temple). The fountain, which is built of California granite, is a very fine one, and is dedicated to the soldiers of the great war who went from Siskiyou County. It is of the latest type of sanitary drinking fountains, and when it will be completed today, will present an imposing sight. The fountain has cost the lodge a little over $600. The inscription which is cut in a plate of polished granite, is as follows: "Memorial to our Soldier Boys of Siskiyou County who served in the world war. Erected by Eagle Cliff Lodge No. 163, K. of P., A.D. 1923." The fountain is a credit to the town and to those who erected it and is a very fitting memorial to our soldier boys.

7-25-24: FUNDS ROLL IN FOR THE NEW TEMPLE: Architect expected here next week to go over ground: F. S. Weamer, secretary of the Dunsmuir Masonic Temple association advises that payments on purchase of Masonic Temple stock are coming in quite satisfactory, there being few subscribers who are delinquent in their payments. At the close of business July 23rd, there was on hand in the bank the sum of $26,268, leaving a balance of $3732 yet to be raised before active operations can commence.

Carl Werner, San Francisco architect, will arrive in Dunsmuir around the end of this month to look over the property of the association and consult with the directors as to plans of the proposed building. The directors of the association have been endeavoring for the past thirty days to acquire a small strip of property to increase the width of their lot, but they have been unsuccessful in their negotiations with adjoining property owners. This means that the association will now proceed along lines originally proposed and the building will necessarily be confined to property 50 feet by 150 feet.

The names of the subscribers to be framed and placed in the building, will be made up in the early part of September. This will give all subscribers an opportunity to make their payments and be included in the list.

9-26-24: LADIES OF EASTERN STAR TO GIVE DANCE: The Ladies of the Eastern Star will give a dance at Joyland on next Wednesday night, October 1. The ladies are preparing to entertain a big crowd of dancers and it is certain that those who will attend will spend an enjoyable evening. Bulowski's Joyland orchestra will furnish the music.

9-26-24: LODGE DIRECTORY: ORDER EASTERN STAR, FIDELITY CHAPTER NO. 131 will meet second and fourth Fridays of each month in Branstetter Hall at 8 p.m. All visiting members are cordially invited to attend. Rubena Sears, W.M.; Agnes Weamer, Secretary. / K. of P. — Eagle Cliff Lodge No. 163 will meet the first and third Friday nights of each month at 8 o'clock at 421 Florence Avenue, E. M. Commons, C.C.; W. Ladlow, K. of R.S. / DUNSMUIR PYRAMID No. 22, A.E.O.-S. — Meets second Fridays in Branstetter Hall at 8:00 p.m. A. D. Liniger, Toparch; P. A. Bryan, Scribe. / I.O.O.F.-Dunsmuir Lodge No. 120, meets every Monday night in Branstetter Hall. / W.O.W.-Dunsmuir Camp No. 474, Woodmen of the World, meet the first and third Fridays of each month in Branstetter's Lodge rooms. Claud Branstetter, C.C.; F. S. Stanley, Clerk. / W.B.A.O.T.M. (Women's Benefit Association of the Maccabees)-Dunsmuir Review No. 25, meets every second and fourth Saturday evening of each month in Branstetter Hall. Mrs. Mabelle Naves, Commander; Minnie Huff, Collector. Visiting sisters are invited to attend. / REBEKAH-Oriole Lodge No. 217, meets every first and third Saturdays at Branstetter Hall. All visiting members invited to attend. Bertha Wooley, Noble Grand; Mayme McGuinness, Secretary.

11-7-24: The G.I.A. to the B. of L.E. gave an entertainment and whist party for the members and their husbands in Branstetter's Hall Thursday evening, the prizes going to Mrs. Harry Marsh, Mrs. G. J. Marsh, Mr. Clark and J. Wagner. Refreshments were served.

11-7-24: ORIOLE REBEKAH LODGE TO INITIATE AT WEED TONIGHT: Oriole Rebekah Lodge No. 217 of Dunsmuir will initiate at Weed tonight and be the guests of their sister fraternity at that place.

11-14-24: CALIFORNIA SCIOTS CEN-TER ATTENTION AT REDDING THIS WEEK — Many members of the Dunsmuir Pyramid of Sciots are in attendance at the annual convention of Sciots, which is being held in Redding this year. Many more Sciots of Dunsmuir are contemplating attending the closing festivities at Redding today and tomorrow. The convention started yesterday and will close tomorrow night.

12-26-24: MANY ATTEND SCIOTS' TREE MONDAY EVE.: The community Christmas Tree and program given at Joyland Monday evening by the Dunsmuir Sciots was a grand success and was attended by one of the largest crowds of children and grown-ups that ever attended an affair of this kind in Dunsmuir. There was estimated to be eighteen hundred people in the hall, including children and grown-ups. Some eight hundred children were present and each received a present suitable to age and also a stocking full of candy, fruit, and nuts. Seven hundred and eighty-three kiddies were registered to receive presents, and it was indeed a wonderful sight to see so many children together.

Santa Claus had rather a hard time getting to Dunsmuir in time for the festival according to the messages received from time to time. Santa was detained at Weed and then was stuck on Black Butte, due to the negligence of one of our Supervisors in having the snow cleaned off in time. The children greeted Santa Claus with much enthusiasm, and one small tot shouted, "I've got you, Santa."

The local Pyramid of Sciots have the community tree made possible a number of seasons, and in this way Christmas cheer that would otherwise do without. Much credit is due to Dunsmuir Sciots for the spirit shown for the children of the community.

Dunsmuir Pyramid No. 22 wishes to thank the public of Dunsmuir for the generous support given them in the community tree venture, without which, could not have been made possible.

11-13-25: THREE GENERATIONS ARE ODD FELLOWS: Donald Branstetter received his degrees in Odd Fellowship here Monday night. There are now three generations of the Branstetter family living in Dunsmuir who belong to the local order. His grandfather, William Branstetter, has been an Odd Fellow for over 52 years.

1-15-26: OFFICERS INSTALLED BY W.B.A.; BANQUET: New officers for Dunsmuir review, No. 26, Women's Benefit Association (of the Maccabees) were installed Saturday by Past Commander Mabelle Naves, assisted by Rachael Chambers and Helena Wilkins as ladies of ceremonies, and Louisa Ross as Chaplain. A large number of members were present to witness the impressive installation ceremony.

Following installation the members went to the Travelers Hotel, where a sumptuous chicken banquet was served at eleven o'clock. After dinner speeches, songs, and music rounded out a most enjoyable evening.

4-23-26: G.I.A. to B. of L.E. OFFICIAL PAYS VISIT: Mrs. Elizabeth Airey of San Francisco, vice-president of the Grand International Auxiliary to the Brotherhood of Locomotive Engineers, was the guest of Mrs. J. A. Fillmore division here Tuesday on her visit of inspection and instruction.

A luncheon was served at one o'clock in the banquet room of Branstetter Hall Tuesday. Part of the work was exemplified at the morning session and the remainder during the afternoon meeting.

Wednesday afternoon, Mrs. Airey was the guest of honor at a dinner party given by Mrs. George Dickson. She was taken by automobile to points of interest around Dunsmuir following the dinner. She left on train number 13 that evening for her home in San Francisco.

4-23-26: DE MOLAY ACTIVE — The Dunsmuir Chapter of the De Molay for boys has been showing renewed life of late and a large class of boys will be initiated this week or two into the Order. C. O. Porter has been largely instrumental in keeping the organization alive during the past few months.

4-23-26: SCHOOL WEEK OBSERVANCE IS ARRANGED — Public Invited To Attend Program at High School Auditorium: On Wednesday, April 28th, at 8:00 p.m., there will be an entertainment at the auditorium of Dunsmuir High School for the purpose of promoting interest in the public school to which everyone is invited to attend. It will be part of a statewide program for spreading knowledge relative to the needs of the public school system.

The week originally was celebrated in Masonic lodge rooms, but owing to the increased public interest last year, meetings were held in public halls and school auditoriums, with the public in general invited. The same procedure is being carried out this year, Charles Albert Adams, former grand master of Masons of California, being Chairman of the general state committee.

5-14-26: COUNTY ODD FELLOWS TO HOLD BIG PICNIC — Arrangements have been completed for the Reconsecration Day observance by the Odd Fellows of Siskiyou County at Murphy Field, one mile east of Weed, on Sunday, May 23rd.

The general features will be a concert by the Dunsmuir Band at 11:30 a.m. to 1:30 p.m., and a varied program from 1:30 p.m. to 2:30 p.m.

Hon. C. J. Luttrell, Superior Judge of Siskiyou County, and Grand Lodge officer of the Order, will address the gathering and selections will be given by the McCloud Lodge male quartet and the Fort Jones High School Glee Club.

After this part of the program is over, the

Jonathan Club of Dunsmuir will get into action. This boosting organization will have a surprise and an unusual entertainment to offer, among which will be a tug of war between Weed and McCloud.

All are urged to bring a basket lunch and provide for one extra person to serve to those unable to bring lunches. Ice Cream and Coffee will be furnished free by the Committee, but those who attend should take their own cups, spoons, milk, and sugar.

It is expected that at least 2,000 people will attend this picnic if the weather is at all favorable. There are ten Odd Fellows Lodges in the county, and it is expected that all of them will be largely represented.

5-28-26: MASONS HEAR ORATOR AT WEED SATURDAY — A number of Masons from this city went to Weed last Saturday evening to attend the lecture given by Truly Knowles, orator of the Ben Ali Temple of the Mystic Shrine at Sacramento. Mr. Knowles is a member of the National Board of Education and also President of the College of the Pacific. Those attending from this City reported a real good treat. G. A. Huttaff of this city, junior grand warden of the California Grand Lodge, also addressed the Lodge.

6-25-26: (Masonic Temple completed): TEMPLE IS OUTGROWTH OF UNITED PUBLIC EFFORT: Edifice Stands as Monument to Concerted Effort Regardless of Creed, Nationality or Color — Fine Spirit: King Solomon's Temple was not built in a day or in a year, nor without tremendous effort. When it was completed, it was the most beautiful and substantial edifice of its day. The Dunsmuir Masonic Temple was not built in a day, or a year, for there was a great deal of thought, time and effort spent to make it possible for this city to have the beautiful building which will soon be dedicated, and to which this edition of the *Dunsmuir News* is devoted.

The Dunsmuir Masonic Temple is not owned by the Masons of this city, but it was built through the subscriptions for stock from not only Masons, but people who have never belonged to the order. These latter people bought stock in the building, not so much for the dividends it would pay in cash, but for the higher ideal of securing dividends for the City of Dunsmuir. The Masonic Temple stands as a monument to concerted effort, regardless of creed, nationality, or color. It is the dominant note in the march of progress that Dunsmuir is now taking, and which will soon bring it into the front line among the most progressive cities of the state. It is only true that the erection of this magnificent building has had the effort already of convincing the people of this city that Dunsmuir is to be considered seriously and that it is here today and grown. On all sides are evidences of this renewed faith and hope for the future. No matter what some may say, it is only true that all the improvements that are now being made in this city, not only by the city administration, but by private parties as well, are being made a little better and more permanent because the Masonic Temple Association came into being.

Any city to deserve the name of "city" must have certain things to round out the life of the community. There must be good schools, housed in appropriate and modern buildings; there must be churches that attract the worshipper; there must be civic clubs and associations. These should all be going concerns, and not slipshod organizations, in order to bring the greatest good to the greatest number. The fraternal life of the city must not be neglected, for in these fraternal organizations friendships are made that stand the ravages of time, and bring to each member a higher and better idea of the life we are living here on earth. Like the other organizations, the lodges of the city are right in their desire to have attractive and comfortable lodge buildings or lodge rooms. It was this desire on the part of some of the older members of the Masonic fraternity in this city, who had been the pioneers and who had met in ramshackle buildings, and sometimes in out-of-the-way places, that made the new Masonic Temple in this city possible.

Several years ago, the agitation was started by these older members and pioneers for the present beautiful Masonic Temple. Several false starts were made, and several discouraging years were the result, but these men never lost faith in the ultimate results of their efforts, and today the new temple stands as a reminder that no matter how discouraging things may appear at times, everlasting serious thought will win in the end. These men are happy today in the thought of a job well done. They will enjoy to the full completion of this building, and as the years roll by, they will feel that it is worthwhile to have high ideals and work for them.

Two major stock selling drives were necessary to secure the funds for the Masonic Temple, and the men who took part in these drives are entitled to all the praise that should be given them. For without their work, the building would not have been possible. The first drive to sell stock in the Masonic Temple Association was held from April 16th to 30th, 1924, inclusive, and was very successful. The reasons given to prospective stock purchasers were contained in a circular published at that time, and they were as follows:

1st — It should be a profitable investment.

2nd — Masonic Temple will increase Dunsmuir property values.

3rd — It is a community enterprise.

4th — Dunsmuir needs the contemplated moving picture theatre.

5th — Dunsmuir needs the contemplated rooms.

6th — We need $60,000 to erect the building and furnish the lodge rooms.

The circular then went on to say that "The Dunsmuir Temple Association is incorporated for the purpose of selling stock, the proceeds of which will go towards the erection of a building on property owned by the Association, just South of the Post Office.

"In its proposed stock selling drive, $60,000 worth of stock will be offered to the public. This amount of money will enable the Association to erect a two-story reinforced concrete or brick building on lots which are 50 feet wide and 150 feet long."

Then the circular went on to say: "Dunsmuir badly needs what a Masonic Temple will provide, namely:

"1st — A sanitary, safe and modern moving picture theatre.

"2nd — Two nicely furnished, up-to-date lodge rooms, with banquet room, located a sufficient distance from railroad yards so that noise of locomotives will not interfere with the proceedings of organizations meeting there.

"3rd — Store and office space which will help pay dividends on stock." (The plan for storage space in the building was later abandoned.)

The stock was placed at $100 a share, and could either be paid all at once in cash, or extended over ten monthly payments.

Stickers were furnished those who bought stock in this drive, reading "We Own Dunsmuir Masonic Temple Stock."

7-2-26: SOCIAL EVENTS TO SIGNALIZE OPENING: Several brilliant social events will signalize the opening of the new Masonic Temple. Officers of the Temple Association are planning to hold open house to the public on the top floor of the building next Wednesday night.

The officers of the Dunsmuir Pyramid of Sciots expect to celebrate the opening by a big party to which all Masons, members of the Eastern Star, and DeMolay will be invited. An exceptionally interesting program is being arranged by a committee that was appointed several weeks ago to prepare for the entertainment.

The dedication of the building will be a Masonic affair, the ceremony of which will be conducted by Grand Master, Albert E. Boynton. The tentative date fixed for the dedication is July 17th.

7-23-26: MASONIC TAMPLE IS DEDICATED — Grand Lodge Officers Take Active Part in Dedication Ceremonies. Accompanied by all the solemn ceremonies of the Grand Lodge of California, the new Masonic Temple to this city was formally dedicated Saturday evening. Masons from all over the northern part of the state by their presence showed their intense interest in the event, and as a unit extended most hearty congratulations to Dunsmuir Lodge No. 297, F. & A.M., upon the completion of its beautiful new home.

Among the visitors and those who took part in the ceremonies were some of the most prominent men in the business and civil life of this state, who dropped their usual work and came to Dunsmuir to show their friendly, brotherly spirit. Many Grand Lodge officers — at least half of them — came here for the dedicatory exercises and were loud in their praise of the progressive body of men who made the new temple possible. They also came to Dunsmuir to pay their respects to G. A. Hutaff, who is Grand Junior Warden of the Grand Lodge of this state. At the dinner before the ceremonies, all the speakers stressed this point. The visitors all spoke of the progress made by the Dunsmuir Masons, starting as they did in 1889 with thirteen members, and meeting in the round house of the Southern Pacific Company, until now the Lodge has a membership of over 200. At eight o'clock, the gathering adjourned to the Blue Lodge room where the formal dedicatory exercises were held.

While the Masonic Lodge initiated the movement for the new Masonic Temple, the officers of the Order are not forgetting the large part played in the financing of the building by the citizens of Dunsmuir, irrespective of lodge and religious affiliations. To those citizens is due in large measure the magnificent building that will stand for decades as a monument to civic progress. While they may have purchased stock in the new building as a financial investment, yet in their thoughts was the idea that they were taking an active part in the upbuilding of Dunsmuir.

7-23-26: SCIOTS WILL ENTERTAIN MASONS SATURDAY EVE — Invitations have been issued to all Masons and their families, all members of the Eastern Star, and DeMolay to attend the opening entertainment and dance to be given by the officers and members of Dunsmuir Pyramid, No. 22, A.E.O.S., in the new Dunsmuir Masonic Temple, Saturday evening, July 24th.

This will be the first jollification meeting of the Sciots in the new temple to celebrate or mark the date when the Sciots will again be a social factor in the community. No expense is being spared to make the evening a most enjoyable one.

As a special entertainment feature, the five acts of vaudeville that appear at the California Theatre that evening have been engaged to appear during the evening and repeat the show as given on the California stage.

The entertainment will commence at 8 o'clock. Dancing and refreshments will follow at the conclusion of the program.

It is safe to say that all Masons and Eatern Star members will make a special effort to attend the entertainment, as the Sciots have a real reputation as entertainers.

8-2-26: W.B.A. TO MEET IN NEW MASONIC TEMPLE. Among the fraternal organizations that will hereafter meet in the new Masonic Temple is the Women's Benefit Association of the Maccabees. This organization of ladies will meet on the second and fourth Wednesdays of each month in the new building. The first meeting of the lodge will be held in the new quarters next Wednesday evening, August 11.

8-13-26: FORESTERS OF AMERICA TO HAVE CELEBRATION: The Foresters of America, an Italian organization, with a lodge in this city and another at Weed, will hold their annual picnic at the Murphy Ranch at Weed tomorrow and Sunday. The festivities will start tomorrow evening and continue through Sunday, the Weed orchestra furnishing the music. There will be a program of sports for which prizes will be given and there will be games and lunch concessions to interest those attending. It is expected that a very large crowd will attend the event. Leo Girimonte, of Weed, will be president of the day, with Ella Zinotti, of this city, acting as vice president. There will be addresses delivered by several prominent Italians of this part of the state, and it is expected that officials from the state organization from San Francisco and Sacramento will attend the two days' celebration.

8-26-26: MANY ATTEND LAYING OF TEMPLE CORNERSTONE: Grand Master of Masons David J. Reese Conducts Impressive Ceremony Amid Showers of Rain. An event long looked forward to by the Masonic Fraternity and others of Dunsmuir took place last Saturday afternoon with the laying of the cornerstone of the Dunsmuir Masonic Temple.

Grand Master David J. Reese of the Masonic jurisdiction of California, had charge of the beautiful ceremony which was impressively performed. Masons from practically every Masonic Lodge in Siskiyou County and a number from Redding and other points were in attendance. The Knights Templar Commanderies of Yreka and Redding participated in the ceremony and lent a dash of color to the occasion in their plumed headgear and uniforms.

Although the weather was threatening and showers fell at intervals, a good-sized crowd was present to witness the ceremony that meant so much to Dunsmuir.

The offices of the grand lodge of Masons, members of the fraternity, the Yreka and Redding Knights Templar, and the Dunsmuir band assembled at the Episcopal Church, where the line of march was formed. A canvas shelter had been set up in front of the rising walls of the building under which Grand Master Reese and others who filled the roles of grand officers for the occasion took up their positions for the ceremony.

A. R. Wilkins, as Master of the Dunsmuir Lodge of Masons, on behalf of the members of the fraternity and the people of the town in general whose assistance had made the building possible, invited Grand Master Reese to proceed with the ceremony. After the invocation by Grand Chaplain Rev. S. T. Bogges, the Grand Master delivered an eloquent address in which he praised the officers of the Temple Association, the members of the Masonic Lodge and the people of the town who had given time to the planning of the building and subscribing stock to finance the project. Grand Master Reese then took up the actual laying of the cornerstone, assisted by the grand lodge officers, which included G. A. Hutaf, deputy grand master of Dunsmuir. Every Masonic Lodge in Siskiyou County was represented among the grand officers present.

Before the beautifully inscribed stone was lowered into its position, a metal box containing proceedings of the seventy-fifth annual communication of the Grand Lodge of Masons, California jurisdiction, 1924; a roster of the Dunsmuir Lodge, No. 297, F. & A.M.; a 1925 jubilee coin; a list of subscribers and stockholders in the Temple Association, including names of the officers and directors; data concerning the Masonic Temple stock selling campaigns and names of parties taking part in such drives; names of the county officers as of September 19, 1925, and officers of the City of Dunsmuir; names of the grammar and high school trustees; a copy of the *Dunsmuir News* and names of the workmen on construction of the building as of September 19, including the name of the architect, contracting firm, and foreman and inspector of the work.

After the stone had been placed in position, Grand Orator Charles J. Luttrell delivered an interesting address in which he pointed to some of the ideals of Free Masonry and lauded the progressive spirit that had led the people of "Siskiyou County's metropolis," to enter upon this big undertaking.

After the benediction by the grand chaplain, the assemblage was dismissed and the Masonic bodies, headed by the band, marched to the Episcopal Church where they disbanded.

In the evening, a banquet and reception was held at McCloud in honor of Grand Master Reese. It was largely attended by members of the various lodges of the County. G. A. Hutaff, inspector of the fourth Masonic district, was master of ceremonies.

8-27-26: W.B.A. CARD PARTY SUCCESSFUL EVENT: The card party given by the members of the Women's Benefit Association in the Masonic Temple, Wednesday night, was well attended despite the fact the power was off and it was necessary to play by candlelight.

10-8-26: PARTY FOR B. OF L.E. AND AUXILIARY, OCT. 23: An entertainment and social evening will be given by the Brotherhood of Locomotive Engineers and the Ladies Auxiliary on Saturday evening, October 23, at Branstetter's Hall, to which all engineers, including the recently promoted engineers who have a date on the seniority list whether members of the brotherhood or not, and their wives and all members of the auxiliary and their husbands are invited to attend. All are asked to come in costume and prizes will be given for the best costumes. An entertainment will also be given.

10-8-26: ENDOWMENT FUND FOR DE MOLAY IS PLANNED — Chester O. Porter has been appointed a member of the national committee to secure DeMolay endowment fund. A committee will be appointed from the community to participage in a campaign during the month of October.

Altogether, 1500 will conduct the campaign throughout the United States, the goal being one million dollars.

The income from the endowment, according to the announcement, will be used for scholarships, vocational guidance, and to aid members to complete their education.

10-8-26: ODD FELLOWS OF COUNTY FAVOR JUNIOR COLLEGE: When the Odd Fellows of Siskiyou County met in convention in Mount Shasta City last Saturday, they went on record as favoring the proposal of a junior college for this county. The proposition is to be put up to the voters for decision at the general election in November.

11-19-26: CONVENTION OF K. OF P. AT MOUNT SHASTA — The Knights of Pythias will hold their district convention at Mount Shasta Saturday evening. The district is composed of the lodges of Yreka, Weed, Dunsmuir, and Mount Shasta. Dunsmuir will take an active part in the ceremony at Mount Shasta tomorrow night. The rank of Page will be conferred upon a large class.

11-26-26: MEN OF WOODCRAFT ENTERTAIN MEMBERS — Last Tuesday night, Castle Crag Circle of Woodcraft initiated six candidates in the mysteries of the Order, leaving three more applicants to be taken in at a later day.

After the initiation, Ruby Root, captain of the social degree, put on the work which caused a great deal of laughter and fun. Later, Robert Brown, chairman of the local committee, announced that everything was in readiness in the banquet hall and forthwith a delicious hot supper was served by the men of the order.

11-26-26: SPLENDID MUSICALE AT MASONIC TEMPLE — One of the finest musical programs ever heard in Dunsmuir was rendered at the Masonic Temple last Tuesday night. Sherman, Clay and Company presented the musical through arrangements with the officers of the local Masonic Lodge. Members and friends of the Lodge were the invited guests.

12-10-26: I.O.O.F. ANNUAL ROLL CALL MONDAY — In observance of a custom that has prevailed in Dunsmuir Lodge, No. 120, I.O.O.F., for many years, members comprising committees headed by J. C. Naves are completing extensive preparations for the annual Roll Call dinner meeting which is to take place Monday evening, beginning at six-thirty p.m. A turkey dinner will be served, after which the roll will be called, each member present responding with a greeting, and letters and telegrams from those who are at

a distance or unable to attend will be read to those present. Following the roll call, the assemblage will convene in the lodge room where the Dunsmuir team will exemplify the Initiatory Degree to a number of candidates.

A musical program will be presented by members of the Order. All Odd Fellows are urged to attend this meeting.

12-24-26: TEMPLE BALL ROOM IN HANDS OF DECORATORS — On Friday evening, January 7th, the Masonic Temple ballroom will open to the public with the first dance of the season. These dances will continue every Friday night throughout the winter.

The ballroom is now under process of decoration, which will include every necessity that will have a tendency to lend the proper atmosphere intended for these dances. The Masonic Temple Association is striving at this time to place before the people of Dunsmuir a diversion in amusement, and they feel that in the opening of this ballroom this feature will have been achieved.

Special lighting effects are being installed which will greatly add to the splendor of the ballroom. The fact that the best heating system will be enjoyed, as well as the central location, the ballroom will be all that the citizens of Dunsmuir would care to ask for.

The music will be rendered by the Temple Ballroom Orchestra under the direction of Francis LeMere, who is well-known to the people of this city. The decorating is being done under the supervision of C. F. Meeker, who will also manage the dances for the Temple Association, with the assistance of C. H. Weaver. Don't forget the opening date, January 7, at 9 o'clock.

1-21-27: PYTHIANS ON PROGRAM OF EXTENSION — Eagle Cliff Lodge Of This City To Take Part In Enlarged Activities — The international extension program announced recently by officers of the Supreme Lodge Knights of Pythias, will, in a large measure, direct the activities of Eagle Cliff Lodge, according to Chancellor Commander M. J. Maloney, who was recently installed with eight other officers of the lodge to direct the work of the Pythian fraternity in this city during the year.

Commenting on the outline for the new year, Chancellor Commander M. J. Maloney said: "The program is intended to make the lodge a real factor in the life of the community and to aid in the extension of the benefits of fraternal membership by performing its share in the great national movement. The movement is supported by nearly one million members in the United States and Canada. We have over 6,400 lodges and it is the purpose of the program of activity to make every one of those lodges the center of fraternal accomplishments in performing the service for which the fraternity was founded to make better homes and better communities in which to live.

"The Pythian Order" now operates eighteen homes for aged members, their

widows and orphans. Five other states are building homes. Investment in this phase of Pythian endeavor amounts to more than $4,000,000 and over 2,000 men, women, and children are provided with home comforts. Five grand domains have established educational trust funds by which worthy young men and women are given opportunity for advanced college training. Nearly two hundred are now being kept in colleges through loans from these funds.

"The Pythian Sisters," the women's auxiliary to the Order, has a membership of nearly a half-million and distributes annually more than $250,000 for the care of orphaned children and for the comforts of the aged and poverty-stricken.

The military department is very active and is offering to the young membership a military training almost equal to that obtained in barracks maintained by the various states.

The following offices were installed by the Knights of Pythias recently: Chancellor Commander, J. J. Maloney; Vice Chancellor, G. V. Coon; Master of Finance, E. M. Commons; Master at Arms, F. H. Sylvia; Keeper of Records and Seal, W. Ladlaw; Master of Works, F. W. Cole; Prelate, C. R. Price; Outer Guard, W. G. Estes; Inner Guard, G. Edler.

2-25-27: KNIGHTS OF PYTHIAS OBSERVE ANNIVERSARY: Eagle Cliff Lodge, No. 163, Knights of Pythias of this city, and Lily Lodge, No. 184, of Mt. Shasta, jointly celebrated the sixty-third anniversary of the Knights of Pythias order last Friday night in this city. A number of friends of the members of the two lodges also were invited to the observance, there being about one hundred persons in attendance. One of the pleasing numbers on the program was a number of songs rendered by Jack Stone, a member of the Knights of Pythias in New York, who appeared on the California Theatre Vaudeville Saturday. The speakers included I. U. Luttrell of Mt. Shasta, C. M. Commons of Eagle Cliff Lodge, and Mrs. Lulu Shewey of the local Pythian Sisters Lodge.

2-25-27: TEMPLE BALLROOM DANCE SAT. EVENING: As announced in this paper and by posters, the regular Friday evening dances that have been held in the Temple Ballroom for some weeks past, have been changed to Saturday evenings, beginning tomorrow evening. These dances have been found to be very popular among those people who wish to indulge in dancing under the best possible conditions, and it is thought that the change to Saturday evening will accommodate many more people who felt they could not attend on Friday evenings. Tomorrow evening, there will be a surprise program during the hours of dancing that will be greatly enjoyed by those attending.

2-25-27: COLONIAL PARTY MUCH ENJOYED BY WOODCRAFT: Woodcraft Circle No. 502, had a social time following their meeting Tuesday night. As it was Washington's Birthday, colonial costumes showing the styles of past years were much in evidence. Pictures were taken of everyone present as many original and unique clothes were worn. The grand march was led by Dr. D. L. Himes and Mrs. Jennie Murphy, as their costumes were considered as the best. Mrs. Ina Aacaulay tied with Mrs. Murphy for first prize for the best costume. Old-fashioned dances were indulged in, the quadrille being favorite. Music was furnished by Robert Simington, John Beem, and Mrs. Dorothy Simington.

2-25-27: MOOSE LODGE TO BE INSTITUTED SUNDAY: Sunday will be another day in the City of Dunsmuir, by the institution of the Moose Lodge. The first class to be initiated into the new lodge will be in honor of Mayor Cornish. This class will consist of some of the leading businessmen of the city. The ritual work of the lodge and the institution and installing of the first officers will be in charge of the Redding Moose degree team. This work will be under the supervision of the national director of the Loyal Order of Moose, Harry W. Millspaugh, who will be here for the occasion. The Moose Lodge in Dunsmuir will meet every Thursday night in the Maple Room of the Masonic Temple at 8 o'clock and after meetings will hold a dance for the members and their friends. The members of the Weed Lodge will be in attendance and all other brother Moose are cordially invited.

8-12-27: EDITORIAL — VALUE OF MASONIC TEMPLE TO CITY SHOWN: The good judgment and foresight that prompted the sponsors of the Masonic Temple enterprise to push forward and conquer the seemingly insurmountable obstacles that set themselves up in 1924 when the financing of the project was undertaken are manifesting themselves with more than usual force this month. Last week the fire department of Dunsmuir entertained the visiting firemen of the Pacific Coast here at a banquet served in the Masonic Temple. The Masonic Temple made it possible to entertain them, for the simple reason that there is no other place in the city anywhere near large enough to accommodate the 250 persons that sat down to the banquet. Tomorrow there will be one hundred or more visitors in the city to attend the monthly session of the Sacramento Region Citizens Council. This organization represents twenty-one interior counties of Northern California and several representatives from each of the counties are expected to attend. The Masonic Temple offered the only solution to the problem of where to take the visitors for the meeting. On August 30 and 31 and September 1, the school teachers of the county will gather here for their annual institute. There will be some two hundred of them and again the Masonic Temple will be used to house the gathering. None of these gatherings could have been as successfully conducted had the Masonic Temple not been available to hold them in, and it is

possible that none of them would have been brought to Dunsmuir had it not been for the temple. Thus, it will be seen that the foresight of the promoters of the temple and the cooperation of the citizens of the city in buying stock in it have been responsible for bringing these gatherings to Dunsmuir, which will do much to advertise the city as nothing else could.

8-12-27: ODD FELLOWS AND ORIENTS INITIATE: More than a score of Odd Fellows from McCloud, Weed, Mt. Shasta joined with the local members of that order last Monday night to witness the Dunsmuir Lodge confer the first degree on a class of candidates. Following this work, the gathering retired to the Encampment's Room adjoining the Odd Fellows Lodge room and initiated a number of Odd Fellows into the mysteries of the Orients. This is a degree put on for laughing purposes only and everybody got a "kick" out of it.

9-30-27: PIGEONS CARRY BIDS TO SCIOT CONVENTION: An official invitation to attend the seventeenth annual session of the supreme pyramid, Ancient Egyptian Order of Sciots, in Fresno, November 3, 4, and 5, was received by Dunsmuir Pyramid No. 22, via pigeongram, September 17. The invitations tell something of the convention program, which is replete with entertainment. The invitation was received in Dunsmuir by Toparch Cethil Jones and will be read at the next regular meeting. Fresno expects more than 10,000 to attend the convention.

10-14-27: MOOSE WILL RESUME ONCE-A-WEEK DANCES: The Dunsmuir Lodge of Moose have resumed giving dances in the Maple Hall of the Masonic Temple. The Moose gave dances every week last winter, and many disciples of terpsichore derived a great deal of pleasure from them and will be pleased to know the lodge will give dances again this fall every Thursday night.

6-8-28: ODD FELLOWS IMPROVE DUNSMUIR CEMETERY: In line with their program of improvement, the local lodge of Odd Fellows have just completed a new wire fence on the north side of the cemetery and have installed a modern toilet. Lot owners and visitors to the cemetery will appreciate the improvements.

6-8-28: SCIOTS' "STEMWINDER" CEREMONIAL SECTION OF THE *DUNSMUIR NEWS*: Life of Dunsmuir Pyramid filled with achievement: From modest beginning, Siskiyou Lodge of Sciots has grown to be one of the strongest organizations in the county. The history of any worthwhile organization is interesting and when that particular organization is devoted to the uplife of its members and of service to the community, then the chronicle becomes absorbing.

To alleviate some of the suffering in the world, and to cultivate the social life of the animal called man, certain organizations have been brought into being. To make them a little more effective, perhaps,

ceremonials and rites are practiced to impress its members with the usefulness of the organization, and there may be certain secrets entrusted to its members that have for their whole object some great lesson of life.

The Masonic Fraternity is such an organization. From the root of Masonry, there have been branches thrown out to do specific useful things. One of these branches on the West Coast is the Ancient Egyptian Order of Sciots, whose success in Dunsmuir is being celebrated by this newspaper at this time by devoting considerable space to its accomplishments.

On January 17, 1921, A. Powers, Charles O. Porter, and N. R. Graham, then residing in Dunsmuir, went to Chico and became members of Chico Pyramid No. 17. At that time, J. H. Biederman of this city was a member of Sacramento Pyramid No. 3; and Fred Kaizer, also of this city, was a member of Stockton Pyramid No. 5. These latter two gentlemen accompanied the first three gentlemen named to Chico, to see to it that they were properly initiated into the mysteries of Sciotry.

After the ceremony, and while on the train en route to their homes in this city, the five men started to talk about the advisability of starting a Sciots' organization in Dunsmuir. On or about February 15th of the same year, several of these men met again and resumed the talk relative to organizing a pyramid in this city. After some discussion of the matter, they determined to make the attempt. They forthwith succeeded in signing up fifty charter members for the proposed local organization and telegraphed the fact to the Supreme Pyramid officers and asked for a date for the ceremonial. They were informed that they had done splendidly, but that the laws of the supreme pyramid demanded that in order to organize a local pyramid, it would be necessary to have 100 charter members. Within three weeks, Supreme Pharoah Waldo F. Postel was informed that the required number was secured, and again asked for a date for the usual ceremonial of installation of a new pyramid. Whereupon, the date of installation was set for April 9, 1921. Upon the arrival of the supreme pyramid officials on that day, they asked just how many members had actually signed up and were told that 186 had signed the charter roll. But before that evening, this had been increased to 236 charter members.

Dunsmuir pyramid has members scattered from Columbia, South America, to Port Angeles, Washington. At the time of this pyramid being instituted, there were members from every state in the United States except two. Among the candidates that will join are men from Dunsmuir, Mt. Shasta, McCloud, Castella, Weed, and Judge C. J. Luttrell of the superior court of Siskiyou County will have charge of a delegation of candidates from Yreka, the county seat.

During the years of 1921, 1922, and 1923,

111

the Sciots of this city maintained a community Christmas tree for the children of this city. The last year, the Sciots entertained 850 children, between the ages of one and twelve years at Joyland rink in north Dunsmuir, because there was no other building in the city large enough to stage the affair. These community celebrations became such big affairs that no organization of the city could finance them successfully, so none have been held of similar magnitude in recent years.

Ever since Dunsmuir pyramid has been in existence, it has given supplies and money to families that have been reported as being in dire need, and in a number of cases have been successful in securing county aid for them. They have also assisted in staging community Christmas trees in several of the other towns of the county. Last year, funds were made available to the Parent-Teacher Association so that the pupils of the grammar school enjoyed a huge picnic. The Sciots also donated between $200 and $300 toward the purchase of uniforms for the Dunsmuir Union High School Band and a contribution was also given to the musical department of the Weed High School. Not one cent raised by the Sciots has gone into the treasury of the order, but has been spent for useful purposes throughout the county.

6-22-28: SCIOT CEREMONIAL LIVED UP TO ALL EXPECTATIONS — Parade Was Best Ever Put On In County By A Fraternal Organization, Many Grand Officers and Visitors Attend.

Officers and members of Dunsmuir Pyramid, No. 22, Ancient Egyptian Order of Sciots have cause to feel well pleased over the big ceremonial, parade, dance, and other entertainment that was really a part of the evening's festivities, stated in this city last Saturday evening.

There were fifty-six candidates for membership in the Dunsmuir Pyramid, and the Marysville Sciots brought one to be inducted into the order for the pyramid of that city. The initiation ceremony was the event of importance to the members of the Sciots and the candidates and this part of the program was taken care of in splendid manner, but the feature of most interest to the public generally was the parade which preceded the ceremonial itself.

It was undoubtedly the finest parade ever put on by any fraternal organization in the county and probably in this end of the state.

The Nicaraguan Guard of the Dunsmuir pyramid was commended by C. H. Kintgen. They were better than good, and added great quantities of spice to the parade.

Commendation is due the Mt. Shasta Band, the Dunsmuir Fire Department Band, the DeMolay Band, and Epps Post Bugle and Drum Corps for the stirring music that was so much enjoyed by the great crowd of people that thronged the line of march from Branstetter Street to the Sacramento River Bridge.

The Dunsmuir DeMolay boys are to be most heartily congratulated upon their splendid appearance in the parade. There are 36 in the drill team, accompanied by a band of 18 pieces. They received much well-merited applause along the line of march on their appearance and peppy marching.

One of the outstanding features of the parade was the new Lybian Guard of Dunsmuir pyramid. Their costumes gave a splash of color to the parade that was pleasing, while their drill during the ceremony and at the dance brought forth well-merited applause. The members of the guard have worked hard to perfect themselves and their appearance in the parade showed that their hard work was not in vain. All along the line of march they were the chief attraction judging from the applause and remarks of the people.

The 1910 Ford touring car in the parade had it over the one-horse shay, for it really made the trip to Joyland without falling to pieces.

The four-division parade featured eight floats with Sciots on foot from Dunsmuir, Redding, Red Bluff, Marysville, and other points.

The theatre party at the California was composed of 137 ladies, consisting of the wives of the visiting Sciots and ladies reception committee of Dunsmuir pyramid, who acted as hostesses for the occasion.

The dance after the ceremonial was one of the most pleasant features of the event, there being between 500 and 600 people on the floor at one time. All who attended the dance are agreed that it was one of the most pleasant dances ever held in the Shasta Wonderland.

It is hard to imagine how the affair could have been a more complete success and Toparch Weamer, Scribe Liniger, and other officers and members who worked tirelessly to "put it over" may well feel proud of their efforts.

9-7-28: SCIOTS' CIRCUS STARTS THURS. — Ladies' and Babies' Popularity Contest Gets Underway, Many Interesting Features: On next Thursday, September 13, the Sciots Circus will begin and run five days at Sciots Hall. More than the usual county-wide interest is being taken in this affair, which its sponsors declare will eclipse anything of the kind ever attempted in Dunsmuir. There will be a variety of good, clean amusement and present indications are that big crowds will be in attendance each and every night to enjoy it. One of the features of the circus will be the choice of the most popular lady and most popular baby in the county. This contest started last Friday and already there are entrants from several towns in the jurisdiction of the local lodge of Sciots, which comprises the whole county. The votes will be counted each Saturday until the winner is named, valuable prizes to be awarded the winners.

10-12-28: DUNSMUIR BECOMES MASONIC CAPITAL OF STATE TODAY — Installation of G. A. Hutaff as Grand Master in San Francisco Today Will Bring Dunsmuir Into Prominence: With the installation in San Francisco today of G. A. Hutaff, of this city, as Grand Master of the Grand Lodge of Masons in the State of California, Dunsmuir becomes the Masonic capital of this state during the year the local man will head the fraternity, though the fact that Hutaff will continue his residence here during his tenure of office.

Although the grand lodge sessions of the Masonic fraternity are held in San Francisco, Mr. Hutaff, the newly installed grand master, will continue his home in Dunsmuir and it will be here that the policies of the grand lodge will be formed and other business of an executive nature performed.

Mr. Hutaff could have made his headquarters in San Francisco, while he is grand master, had he desired; but he preferred to stick by his old home town and, thus, Dunsmuir will get the credit of the state during the coming year.

The installation ceremony being held in San Francisco today, at which Hutaff will be made state head of the Masonic fraternity, is being attended by representatives from the Dunsmuir pyramid of Sciots, of which Hutaff is a member, as well as by a large number of friends from Dunsmuir and throughout the county; and, in fact, northern California, where he is well known.

Gustav Albert Hutaff was born in Santa Rosa, this state, October 5, 1879, and is a son of John Henry Hutaff. He pursued his early education in the public schools of San Francisco and afterwards entered the University of California from which he was graduated with the class of 1900, winning the Ph.G. degree.

He then engaged in the drug business in Dunsmuir, successfully conducting his store until 1919. Before the completion of his college course, he had rendered military aid to his country by serving in the Spanish-American War with the United States Army in the Philippines as a member of the hospital corps, being one of the youngest pharmacists in the service.

His active association with the banking business began when he became a director of the State Bank of Dunsmuir in 1910. He was elected to the vice presidency in 1913, and in 1916 was chosen president. He remained at the head of the institution covering a period of more than eleven years, until the State Bank of Dunsmuir was made a branch of the United Security Bank and Trust Company in 1927, when he became the chairman of the local board of directors.

Mr. Hutaff has large property holdings in Siskiyou County and he has always interested himself in projects which have had for their goal the betterment of conditions in his home city and elsewhere in the state.

He is president of the Masonic Temple Association of Dunsmuir, which recently completed the erection of a $100,000 Masonic Temple.

Mr. Hutaff has long been active in

fraternal circles. He is a past master of Dunsmuir Lodge No. 297, F. & A.M.; member of the Dunsmuir Pyramid of Sciots, Cyrus and Fidelity Chapters of Eastern Star; a Knight Templar; a member of the Scottish Rite Bodies of Sacramento, K.C.C.H.; and a member of Ben Ali Temple of the Mystic Shrine. He likewise has membership with Benevolent and Protective Order of Elks, Veterans of the Spanish-American War, and the Lions Club.

He was inspector of the Fifth Masonic District for sixteen years; was elected junior grand warden in 1925; senior grand warden in 1926; and deputy grand master in 1927. For many years he worked on important committees of the grand lodge.

10-12-28: HUNDREDS OF ODD FELLOWS HERE THURS. — Caravan of One Hundred and Twenty-Five Autos on Way to Mt. Shasta: Upwards of 600 Odd Fellows, who had been attending the state Odd Fellows convention at Redding, were in Dunsmuir for a short time yesterday noon, being on their way in automobiles to Mt. Shasta city, where they enjoyed a mule deer barbecue at Barnes' automobile camp.

Florence Avenue was gaily decorated with flags when the caravan passed through this city, and every business house had a large sign in one of its windows welcoming the visitors to the Shasta Wonderland. There were approximately one hundred and twenty-five automobiles in the caravan, which was by far the largest that has ever passed through Dunsmuir.

Nearly every city and town in the state was represented in the auto caravan, and the only regret the people of the Shasta Wonderland have is that it happened to be an unusually cold and windy day yesterday, so that the visitors could not enjoy themselves as much as they would have had the weather been on its good behavior.

They were the guests of Mt. Shasta Encampment No. 87, which is composed of Odd Fellows from McCloud, Dunsmuir, Weed, and Mt. Shasta. About an even dozen fine bucks had been provided for the barbecue, with plenty of coffee to go with the feed.

While in the Shasta Wonderland, the visitors called at the state fish hatchery at Mt. Shasta, the Brown-Shasta Ranch, the summer school of the Chico State College north of Mt. Shasta, and other points of interest in that vicinity.

The local committee on entertainment consisted of W. W. Martin, Chairman; L. B. Noble, Leo Wolfe, Lee McDill, J. C. Morss, John Blodgett, and Robert Brown; and from reports received in this city last evening, every one of these committeemen exerted themselves to the utmost in dispensing Shasta Wonderland hospitality.

10-12-28: QUARTET TO FEATURE BIG SCIOT SHOW: The Sciots have been particularly fortunate in securing the Schubert male quartet for their show to be given in the California Theatre, Dunsmuir, October 31st.

One show will be given that everning, commencing at 7:45 p.m., consisting of a good motion picture, news reel, comedy, and concert of the above quartet of one hour and thirty minutes. Tickets will be on sale at several business establishments in Dunsmuir, and also in Weed and Mt. Shasta at a popular price of seventy-five cents for reserved seats, and a limited number of children's tickets at twenty-five cents.

The Schubert quartet was organized some four years ago by George O. Miner, eminent Canadian basso, and since its organization, this sterling singing group has made three transcontinental tours of America, all of which have been remarkably successful.

Toparch Weamer of the Dunsmuir pyramid of Sciots states that the Schubert quartet is one of the very finest singing groups and the highest priced musical talent ever to appear in southern Siskiyou County, and he is hopeful that the music lovers of this locality will seize a rare opportunity to hear artists of the finest magnitude.

7-19-35: EAGLES BALL CLUB HEADS LEAGUE RACE: Local team downs McCloud Knights of Pythias Here, Sunday - 22 to 4. By defeating the McCloud Knights of Pythias on the Dunsmuir diamond Sunday to the tune of 22 to 4. The Dunsmuir Eagles boosted themselves into the top berth of the Siskiyou County baseball league race. Last week the locals were tied for first place with the Weed Sons of Italy, each having won seven games and lost three; but when the Weed Sons of Italy lost to the Weed Redmen Sunday, Dunsmuir was left in the top position.

9-27-35: K. OF P.'S WELCOME GRAND LODGE LEADER: Knights of Pythias lodgemen of Redding, Mt. Shasta, Yreka, McCloud, Weed, and Dunsmuir gathered at Dunsmuir Friday night to receive Grand Chancellor Henry J. Wildgrube, head of the Knights of Pythias lodges in California, on the occasion of his official visit to District 2. Following an interesting lodge session, where Wildgrube delivered an instructive and inspiring address, members of the order repaired to the Travelers Hotel where a delicious banquet was served at tcn-thirty.

10-18-35: CHARTER IS GRANTED NEW O.E.S. LODGE: Word was received here last evening that the Grand Chapter, Order of Eastern Star, now in session at Coronado, California, has issued a permanent charter to the new chapter which was instituted under dispensation by Grand Officers in this city a little over a year ago. The official name is now recorded as Dunsmuir Chapter, No. 536, Order of the Eastern Star.

10-25-35: STATE LODGE HEAD FETED HERE TUESDAY. About sixty representatives of the Pythian Sisters Lodges of McCloud, Mount Shasta, Weed, and Dunsmuir gathered Tuesday afternoon in the Blue Room of the Masonic Temple

for the annual convention of District No. 3 and to greet Grand Chief Rachel Robertson, of Wilmington.

12-13-35: EAGLES PLEA FOR AGED DEPENDENTS. A committee from the Eagles Lodge at Dunsmuir, headed by Harry Young and J. C. Naves, which appeared before the Board of Supervisors to urge that adequate care be taken of Siskiyou's aged under the old-age pension act, were assured by the board that everything in their power was being done along this line. William T. Davidson, chairman of the board, stated that the board had decided upon $20.00 per month for aged pensions, and had budgeted accordingly. Mrs. Susan Jaques, welfare officer, offered to make regular visits to Dunsmuir if a suitable room were provided where she could interview applicants. She declined, however, to discuss individual cases in public, stating she did not feel it fair to the applicants, as she considered it a strictly private matter.

1-3-36: WOMEN'S BENEFIT TO SEAT OFFICERS: Newly-elected officers of the Women's Benefit Association will be installed at a big special meeting to be held in the Masonic Temple next Wednesday night, January 8. Julia Ginn of Los Angeles, state field director for the order, will come to Dunsmuir to serve as installing officer for the occasion. The following members of the local lodge will be officially stationed in their respective positions: Gladys Smith, president; Margaret Dodd, vice-president; Sadie Brown, past president; Ellen Moelk, lady of ceremonies; Ellen Kafer, financial secretary; Maude Lockstone, recording secretary; Anna Wallace, treasurer; Mary DePue, chaplain; Tillie Cirby, inner hostess; Doris Geiger, captain of the guards; Bessie Anderson, sergeant. The public is extended a cordial invitation by the officers of the lodge to attend the installation ceremony.

4-3-36: MANY ATTEND ODD FELLOWS PARTY HERE: One of the largest and most colorful gatherings of Odd Fellows, Rebekahs, and invited guests to be held in Dunsmuir in many years, occurred Saturday night in the Dunsmuir Masonic Temple when a huge party was given in honor of W. W. Martin of Mount Shasta, incoming grand master of the grand lodge of Odd Fellows of California. Nearly six hundred members of the Odd Fellow and Rebekah orders attended the affair, which is said to be the largest ever held in Dunsmuir by the two fraternal bodies. Practically every subordinate body in northern California and southern Oregon was represented at the gathering. Dunsmuir Lodge, No. 120, was host at the function. Martin, who is a member of McCloud Lodge No. 432, I.O.O.F., is the first state grand master ever to be elected from Siskiyou County and also of northeastern California since 1915. Martin expects to take the high position at the grand lodge sessions at San Diego in May. An elaborate program was presented. Following the program, cards and dancing were enjoyed, climaxed by a sumptuous banquet served in the Maple Room under the able direction of A. A. Ranzulo, manager of the Hotel Weed dining room, and his efficient staff. Over four hundred persons were served at the banquet which was buffet style. Dancing continued after the banquet until four o'clock in the morning.

10-30-36: EAGLES WILL AID VICTIMS RECENT ORE. FOREST FIRE: First-hand appeals for help to relieve the suffering and privation in the fire-devastated district at Bandon, Oregon, fell on the sympathetic ears of the Dunsmuir aerie of Eagles and the auxiliary Monday night while conducting their respectively regular meetings at the Masonic Temple. The two bodies voted unanimously to quickly do what they could for the residents of the Bandon area.

Mrs. Ferdinand Brown, Mrs. A. B. Cravens, Mrs. F. H. Kohlbaker, Mrs. George Farnum, and Mrs. Cecil Neasham, representing the auxiliary, and Burress Coon, Bill Orr, and W. O. Mobley, representing the aerie, were appointed to arrange for the gathering of clothing, kitchen utensils, bedding, carpenter tools, and furniture that is serviceable. Money will also be sent, but the need for clothing, household articles, and furniture is most important at this time. All Eagles and other citizens of Dunsmuir are asked to bring contributions to the Hotel Weed service station not later than Thursday noon. A truck, donated and driven by N. C. Jones, will leave at four o'clock Saturday afternoon for Bandon. W. O. Mobley and Harry Young will accompany Jones on the trip. The major oil companies are furnishing the gasoline and oil for the truck. While at Bandon, the three men will survey the situation, take pictures, and report any further needs to Dunsmuir aerie. W. O. Mobley states that although Dunsmuirites are responding loyally to the call, a great many more things are needed.

4-5-40: RAINBOW GIRL LODGE WILL BE STARTED HERE: Local Organization Will Be Instituted Saturday, May 11. Dunsmuir and Fidelity Chapters, Order of the Eastern Star, have completed arrangements for the organization of a lodge of the Order of the Rainbow for Girls, a fraternal order for girls nationwide. Approximately fifty-three girls have signed up for membership. Mount Shasta people have been asked to join with the local group in forming the lodge. All girls of good character, members of whose families have Masonic or Eastern Star affiliations, between the ages of thirteen and eighteen, are eligible for membership. Girls whose families have no Masonic connection may become members if they are sponsored by a Mason or an Eastern Star member.

Mrs. Eugenia Brown will be Mother Advisor of the group; Mrs. Ethel Milner, Chairman; and the advisors will be Harry O. Brown, Ralph Wattenburger, Mesdames Mable Rochford, Grace Bascom, Goldie Wood, Charles L. Miller, and Elaine Halsey. Mrs. Mary Sheldon of Mount Shasta has also been invited to act as an Advisor. Institution of the order will take place Saturday, May 11, in the Masonic Temple. Mrs. Cornelia Cooper, grand worthy advisor, will conduct the ceremony, assisted by Mrs. Zilla Whitford Sampson, of Corning. Officers and members of the Corning and Redding orders will come to Dunsmuir to assist the grand officers. All parents are invited to attend. The membership roster is still open and Mrs. Brown will be glad to interview and assist any girl who would like to join. Meetings will be held twice a month. The organization is especially adapted to girl life and things in which every girl is deeply interested. The objective is advancement of education; training to become useful citizens; to give them proper activities to occupy their minds and time until they reach their majority.

4-19-40: KNIGHTS COLUMBUS TO INITIATE BIG CLASS HERE SUNDAY: One of the largest classes ever to be accepted by the Knights of Columbus will be initiated into the order at a meeting to be held Sunday, March 21, in the Masonic Temple. The group will be known as Father Michael J. O'Connell's class, honoring Father O'Connell of Dunsmuir. The second California district, consisting of Mount Shasta Council, No. 2599; McCloud Council, No. 2714; and Siskiyou Council, No. 2454, are sponsoring the initiation under the direction of District Deputy William Elliot, of Weed. The program planned for the day is: Mass at St. John's Catholic Church in Dunsmuir at 10 a.m.; first degree exemplified by McCloud Council team at 11 a.m.; second degree exemplified by Mount Shasta Council at 1 p.m.; third degree exemplified by the state team with Dave Supple of San Francisco the conferring officer, at 3 p.m.; and the banquet at 6:30 p.m. Dominic Sirianni will be the toastmaster at the banquet. The program for the banquet is as follows: Opening prayer, Father Fitzgerald of Weed. Welcome by Grand Knight Joseph H. Seitz of the Mount Shasta Council. Response by E. J. Cone, president of the Dunsmuir Booster Club. Introductions of visiting grand knights and officers. "My Years With Father O'Connell," Father M. McTague of McCloud. Response by Father O'Connell. "Where the River Shannon Flows," song by Yreka choir. "Early Church History of Siskiyou County," Father O'Connell of Yreka. "Our Duties as Members of the Knights of Columbus," Ernest H. Woodfelt, master of the fourth degree in the Bay area. Closing prayer, Father S. Stack of Fort Jones.

5-22-53: L.A. TO B. OF R.T.: The Ladies Auxiliary to the Railroad Trainment held its regular meeting Monday evening, May 18, in the Blue Room of the Masonic Temple. A pot-luck supper was served at 6 p.m. During the meeting, it was decided to have no entry in the Railroad Days Parade. Following the meeting, cards were played with prizes going to Marge Howerton, Catherine Laas, and Muriel Hutton. Serving on the entertainment committee were Ruth Newman, Olympia Poole, and Rayola Hanlen. The next regular meeting will be held June 15.

5-22-53: WOODCRAFT THIMBLE CLUB: The Woodcraft Thimble Club met Tuesday, May 19, at the home of Pearl Massey, with Julia Cleaver as co-hostess. President Betty Benkosky presided at the meeting, after which refreshments of cake and coffee were served to the members. Those attending were Betty Benkosky and daughter, Susan Irene McElroy; Mable Benkosky, Olivia Arnold, Deloris Lewis, Mimi Luperini, Edith Ferguson and children, Josie Benkosky and son, Donald; Irene Turner, Esther Simington, Bertha Jones, Clara Neibecker, Clara Gibson, Lillian Rowlinson, Jane Lewis, Helen Cannata, Ruth Newman, Marge Weliver, Marion Roberts and children, and Mrs. Caroline Howe was a guest.

5-22-53: ORIOLE REBEKAHS: Oriole Rebekahs Lodge No. 217 met in regular session with Noble Grand Marion Roberts presiding. Sister Amanda Cook of this lodge, newly installed district deputy president of District 69, retired and was escorted into the lodge room by her marshal, Alice Langdon. After receiving the honors of the degree, she was welcomed with a few words from the noble grand and voted that the initiation be held before the business of the evening. Candidates Mildred LaBarre, Lois Bectal, Gladys Erickson, all attired in lovely formals, were then conducted through the beautiful and sacred Rebekah degree before an audience of over half a hundred members and guests. During the good of the Order, the noble grand held a memorial service for deceased sisters. Sisters Ione Radtke, Dorothy Grenvick, and Julia Cleaver placed flowers at the altar while Mildred Lockhart sang the hymn, "In The Garden." Ethel Marsh closed the service with a prayer. Also under good of the order Sister Edith Glover, noble grand of McCloud, announced that they were going to initiate June 11 and invited all who could to attend. After Silent Sisters were thanked for cards and presents, the meeting adjourned. The Odd Fellows joined the Rebekahs for a supper of crab louie, pickles, rolls, and cake. Among those attending from out of town were Mary Frizelle, Mary Montgomery, Edith Glover, Margaret Stoner, Mr. and Mrs. A. L. DeSoza, Alice Miller, Mr. and Mrs. C. T. Kernahan, Fern Woodall, Lucile Boehm, May Arneson, Roberta Kerr, L. Hoffman, and Greta Kottinger.

5-22-53: 106 ATTEND G.I.A. CIRCUIT MEETING: One hundred and six members of the G.I.A. to the B. of L.E. attended the circuit meeting held in the Blue Room of the Masonic Temple last Thursday. The meeting opened at 10 a.m. After the meeting was called to order, Mrs. Myrtle Bothwell, first assistant grand vice president of Ogden, Utah, was escorted to the rostrum and formally introduced. Following the introduction of the visiting grand officer, the meeting opened in regular form, the past grand officers and organizer-inspectors were escorted to the rostrum and formally introduced. Past grand guide, Eleanor Anderson of San Francisco, is also a grand organizer-inspector, as is Ruth Turner of Tracey, and Elizabeth Payne of Roseville. Dunsmuir had one charter member present, Mrs. Julia White, who was given a seat on the rostrum with the grand officers. The presidents of the different sub-divisions were escorted to the rostrum, identifying themselves and their divisions. Dunsmuir division then put on an initiation, having one candidate, Mrs. L. P. Wilmuth, now residing in Ashland, Ore. At 12:30 p.m. a recess was declared and all adjourned to the Travelers Hotel, where a delicious luncheon was served to 99 members. The tables were decorated with May baskets filled with homemade candy, and hawthorne down the center. G.I.A. was seeded out with hawthorne blossoms. The afternoon session resumed at 1:45 p.m., with the Fresno division exemplifying the form of welcome transfer; Stockton balloting; Roseville, the Cassell drill; Oakland, draping the charter; and Tracey, installation. Before closing, Mrs. Bothwell thanked the Dunsmuir division for the courtesies shown her and how happy she was to be able to attend, and for the invitation extended her to be at the meeting. She complimented the different divisions for the nice work they had done. The grand officers spoke about the meeting and the nice attendance. The Blue Room was beautifully decorated with harmony depicting the theme. In back of the president's station, the word "harmony" covered with silver metallic and a musical staff just below, hung on the blue backdrop. On this there was a spotlight. Over the vice-president's station, there was a blue drape on which was hung silver musical notes, at each station were musical silver staffs on stands. Placed about the hall were large bouquets of dogwood, hawthorne, and vases of tulips, iris, and baby breath. At 8 p.m. in the Maple Room, the Past Presidents Club of the G.I.A. entertained all members with a card party and refreshments, which was very well attended. There were prizes for each table, the flowers that were used for the circuit meeting were in the Maple Room.

ODD FELLOWS AND REBEKAHS WILL PICNIC SUNDAY: The annual picnic of District No. 97, I.O.O.F., will be held Sunday, August 9, at Murphy's Grove in Weed. The picnic will start at 12 noon, with all Odd Fellow and Rebekah Lodges in the county participating. A varied entertainment program has been arranged and state lodge officials will be present. James Lockart, noble grand, Dunsmuir Lodge No. 120, I.O.O.F., urges all members and their families to attend. The picnic site is just off Highway 97 at the northeast end of Weed.

NEW OFFICERS OF WOODCRAFT CIRCLE NO. 502: Esther Simington, musician; Ethel Prather, magician; Irene Turner, installing officer; Julia Cleaver, guardian neighbor; Helen Clark, past guardian neighbor; Mimi Luperini, advisor; Betty Benkosky, attendant; Edith Ferguson, captain of guards; Marion Roberts, outer sentinel; Josie Benkosky, manager; Clara Gibson, clerk; Irene McElroy, outer guardian; Chum Gibson, manager; Ruth Newman, banker; Marvel Gaither, inner sentinel; Mabel Benkosky, correspondent.

60TH INSTALLATION CEREMONIES FOR FIDELITY CHAPTER: Edna Reed was installed as worthy matron, and Glenn Hull, as worthy patron, of Fidelity Chapter, No. 131, O.E.S., at the lodge's sixtieth installation on Saturday, November 21. The Blue Room of the Masonic Temple was beautifully decorated for the occasion. On the drop curtain in the East was a large three-tiered silver star, surrounded by smaller stars. Bouquets of chrysanthemums were placed about the room. In the West, on a blue plaque, the worthy matron's theme appeared — "Stars of Lights." Emily Crenshaw, the hostess for the evening, gave the welcoming address. D.G.M. Willie Adams, of Weed, was escorted to the East. Erma Cooper and Olga Orr were marshals; Josephine Weeks, chaplain; Jennie Dickson and Helen Eachus, escorts; Mildred Davis and Cloyd Haney, installing officers; Janice Belau, musician; Wilmajean Freysinger, soloist; Mina Kimble, accompanist. As the worthy matron, Edna Reed, stood at the altar, Pamela Dickson presented her with a white Bible, a gift from the chapter. She was then escorted to the East and given the grand honors. The soloist sang "Whispering Hope" and "Star of the East." The following officers were then installed as follows: Worthy Patron, Glenn Hull; associate matron, Opal Morgan; associate patron, Fred Lloyd; secretary, Margaret Olsen; treasurer, Esther Grey; conductress, Alice Langdon; associate conductress, Gwendolyn Baymiller; chaplain, Nellie Babcock; marshal, Mildred Tillotson; musician, Betty Hale; warder, Laura Carey; sentinel, Kathleen Graves; Adah, Josephine Mcnely; Ruth, Genevieve Tillotson; Esther, Anna McClintock; Martha, Delcia Burleigh; Electa, Laura Billington; Junior past matron, Mildred Davis, and the junior past patron were given their jewels. The new worthy matron received a gavel, a gift from her husband. Refreshments of assorted sandwiches, cake and coffee were served. A harvest scene was the theme of the decor in the Maple Room. In charge of decorations for the Maple Room were Minnie Armstrong and Opal Morgan. Chairman for refreshments was Elinor Belau; and chairman for the decorating of the Blue Room was Emma Ramsey. Dancing was enjoyed by the guests.

7-7-55: MEMBERS OF THE LADY ENGINEERS DRILL TEAM ARE: Carol McMillan, Ethel Cahow, Reta Langhrer, Elizabeth Shoupe, Ruth Bachand, Vera Carlson, Gladys Creason, leader; Alice White, Signe Ahlstrom, Elaine Dews, Celesta Grable, Betty Wendell and Theresa Weedon. Well known here, the ladies are earning a reputation in other parts as well. June 6, they performed a series of drills and routines for the B. of L.E. and G.I.A. International Western convention in San Francisco's St. Francis Hotel. They also performed for Railroad Days.

8-11-55: The Official Drill Team of Shasta Daisy Lodge No. 292, G.I.A. to the B. of L.F. & E. are: Betty Beck, musician; Jean Wagner, captain; Clara Connelly, Jessie Weedon, Esther Daniels, Nelda Durbin, Dolores Olsen, Eola Cool, Thelma Boggs, Helen Flowers, Hazel Wagner, Violet Beck, Eleanor Bradshaw, Winifred Behnke, Ellen Fischer, Helen Rodgers, Beth Silva, and Phyllis Robinson. The ladies drilled the night of the inspection visit of Emma Hoffman of San Francisco. Mrs. Hoffman is grand instructor for the G.I.A.

12-29-55: RAINBOW GIRLS GREET YULETIDE WITH COLORFUL CHRISTMAS PARTY. A group of young people enjoyed the annual Christmas party and dance given by the Rainbow Girls in the Banquet Room of the Hotel Dunsmuir the evening of December 22. The room was festive with a Christmas tree in one corner. Silver stars, metallic paper pine cones and tissue paper balls hung from the ceiling. Tables were arranged cabaret style around the room. Each table held a candle with greenery in keeping with the motive. Dancing was started with a snowball dance. Games of musical chairs, charades, poison towel, and newspaper dress were enjoyed by all. Sandwiches and punch were served.

4-25-63: ORIOLE REBEKAHS TAKE FRIENDSHIP LAMP TO McCLOUD: The members of Oriole Rebekah Lodge No. 217 traveled to McCloud April 18th to present the Friendship Lamp to Shasta Lily Rebekah Lodge No. 345. This was the last trip for the Lamp. The proceeds from each visit to the lodges in the District have gone to the Children's Home in Gilroy. As each lodge visited another, they have presented entertainment. The Dunsmuir members enjoyed putting on an Easter parade of fashions of years gone by from 1880 to 1930. The McCloud lodge put on the skit.

5-16-63: RAINBOW GIRLS VISIT WEAVERVILLE: Dunsmuir Rainbow Girls motored to Weaverville last Friday evening, May 10, for a "Get Together" with Weaverville Rainbow Girls. Arriving about 7:30 p.m., they played basketball and volleyball with the Weaverville assembly, which was the start of two days of fun. Up at 6 a.m. Saturday morning, after a slumber party, the girls breakfasted, then roamed around town until time to report to the elementary school grounds for a softball game with the Weaverville girls. Dunsmuir won 32 to 5. Girls and the advisors who made the trip were Rose Hughes, Linda Dorrigan, Linda Bogart, Kathy McLaughlin, Kathy Harris, Jane Mannee, Sheila Stanley, Carol Parsons, Janet Saunders, and advisors Mrs. Ione Hughes and Mrs. Vera Parsons. With many thanks to their advisors for transportation, the girls reported a wonderful time.

6-20-63: REBEKAHS AND I.O.O.F. INSTALL NEW OFFICERS: The newly elected Rebekah District President Hazelle Strom, of District 69, and District Deputy Grand Master, I.O.O.F., Chet Grenvik of District 97, were installed at an impressive ceremony Friday night, June 14, in the Blue Room of the Masonic Temple. The installing officers were Paul Foster and Berniece Meek, outgoing district grand officers of Yreka. They were assisted by their marshals, Bill Singleton and Floy Johnston, and the District Deputy President's drill team. Presentations of past district deputy pins were made to Mr. Foster by his wife and to Berniece Meek by Mr. Vic Henderson, in behalf of his wife, the district deputy president who had passed away recently. Mrs. Meek had been her marshal for the past year. Members from all lodges of the district attended the ceremony. An enjoyable program followed, consisting of a group of folk songs by Dion Von Hein and a modern dance by Gretta Kottinger. The Blue Room was decorated with white baskets of camellias and roses. Refreshments were served at tables decorated with rose and blue three-link place favors.

6-27-63: EAGLES INSTALL OFFICERS AT JOINT MEETING. A joint installation of Dunsmuir Aerie No. 1149, Sisson Aerie No. 342, and their auxiliaries, was held in Arcade Hall in Mount Shasta on June 18, with the following officers seated: Dunsmuir Aerie had Ralph Freeman as Worthy President; Frank G. Cozine, vice-president; Byron H. Hampel, chaplain; W. I. Humphreys, secretary; B. M. Coon, treasurer; Jack Walling, conductor; and Paul Weaver, trustee. V. L. Palmer is the junior past president. The Dunsmuir Auxiliary seated Winifred Day as junior past madam president; Dorothy Weaver, madam president; Elsie Knoles, vice-president; Hazel Kohlbaker, chaplain; Helen Snead, secretary; Mary Ann Hampel, treasurer; Hannah Humphreys, conductor; Edna Frizell, trustee; Irene Pratt, inside guard; Florence Palmer, outside guard; and Alma Forester, official mother.

10-10-63: KATHY HARRIS IS RAINBOW GIRLS ADVISOR: Kathleen Harris became Worthy Advisor of Assembly 82 Order of Rainbow Girls at the 69th Installation ceremonies held Saturday evening, September 28. She chose the "Guiding Hand of Faith" as her theme; the dove for her emblem; blue and gold for her colors; blue asters and gold chrysanthemums for her flowers; and for her song, "Autumn Leaves." After the ceremonies the entire membership joined in singing "Rainbow Dreams."

11-14-63: MASONS INSTALL JAMES LOCKART: Dunsmuir Lodge No. 297, Free and Accepted Masons, held an open installation of officers Saturday evening, November 9, at Masonic Temple with 125 attending. Robert C. Harris, Past Master of Dunsmuir Lodge, acted as master of ceremonies. Newly-installed Master, Mr. Lockart expressed his appreciation and introduced members of his family with the sly comment he had insisted on their attendance to make sure he had an audience. Bill Schooler, P.M., Redding Lodge No. 254, a member of the Masonic Home Endowment Board, spoke on Masonic Homes in California and presented the Dunsmuir Lodge with a gold star, putting it on the honor roll for contributing an excess of $2 a member to the endowment home fund for the past year. Following the installation ceremonies, refreshments were served in the Maple Room.

4-16-64: CALENDAR OF EVENTS: TUESDAY, B. of L. F. and E., Masonic Temple; WEDNESDAY, Rainbow Girls, 8 p.m., Masonic Temple; THURSDAY, DeMolay, Masonic Temple; 2nd MONDAY, Knights of Columbus, 8 p.m., St. John's Hall; 2nd TUESDAY, Eagles and Auxiliary, 8 p.m., Masonic Temple; 3rd MONDAY, B. of R. T., Masonic Hall, 7:30 p.m., Ladies Auxiliary of B. of R. T., Masonic Hall, 8 p.m.; 3rd TUESDAY, G.I.A. to B.L.E., 8 p.m., Masonic Hall; Rainbow Girls, 8:00 p.m., Masonic Temple; 3rd THURSDAY, DeMolay, Masonic Hall; Masons, 7:30 p.m., Masonic Hall; 4th MONDAY, Eagles and Auxiliary, 8 p.m., Masonic Hall; 4th TUESDAY, Eagles and Auxiliary, 8 p.m., Masonic Hall; 4th WEDNESDAY, W.B.A. (Woman's Benefit Association, formerly Lady Macabees), 8 p.m., Masonic Hall; 4th THURSDAY, Eastern Star, 8 p.m., Masonic Hall; 4th FRIDAY, Odd Fellows, 8 p.m., Masonic Hall; Rebekahs, 8 p.m., Masonic Hall.

6-18-69: G.I.A. MEETS: Tuesday afternoon at 1:30 p.m., the Past Presidents of the G.I.A. were hosted for a dessert luncheon, at the home of Mrs. Betty Wendell. Following the business meeting, there were three tables of Canasta. The winners of prizes were Mrs. Carol Livingston, Katherine Sellman, Bobbie Smith, and Maleta Green. Their next meeting is a picnic meeting at the city park on August 12, which will include the members and their families.

7-2-69: FIDELITY CHAPTER CELEBRATES 75th CELEBRATION: Ione Hughes, Worthy Matron, and Morgan Jones, Worthy Patron, were hosts as the Fidelity Chapter 131, Order of the Eastern Star, celebrated their 75th Anniversary, Wednesday, June 25. The past matrons and past patrons of Fidelity exemplified the ritualistic work as it was done in 1867 in the costumes of that period. There were about 250 persons present. Nellie Poirire and Rubena Sears were presented life memberships and an Eastern Star pin by the Grand Matron. Refreshments were served in the beautifully decorated Maple Room by Associate Matron Dorothy Delgado and her committee.

7-9-69: RAINBOW GIRLS WILL HELP RAISE FUNDS: Marie Glover announced that the Dunsmuir Rainbow Assembly No. 82 will help in the sale of Easter Lilies for the benefit of the Siskiyou Crippled Children's Society fund on Thursday, July 10th.

7-23-69: Eagles Aerie No. 1149 and Auxiliary will hold a pot luck picnic in the Dunsmuir City Park at 6:30 p.m. Those attending are advised to bring their own service. All Eagle members and their guests are invited. It is also requested that all members also bring prospective members. Any member of an out-of-town lodge visiting in this area is cordially invited to be our guest.

2-8-84: CALENDAR: Thursday, Order of the Eastern Star meets at 8 p.m. at the Masonic Hall.

4-4-84: WEEKLY CALENDAR: Masonic Lodge No. 297 meets for a potluck dinner at the Masonic Temple building. Bring only hot vegetable or salad. Monday, Fraternal Order of Eagles meets at 8 p.m. at the Eagle Hall on Sacramento Avenue.

8-1-84: HANNAH HUMPHREYS HONORED BY EAGLES: The Ladies Auxiliary and the Fraternal Order of Eagles Aerie No. 1149 honored the "mother" of the Ladies Auxiliary, Hannah Humphreys, and welcomed her back home with a party. A potluck dinner was served. Tables were decorated in green and white, with black-eyed susans for flowers. A special table was set with red and yellow and a beautiful cake of green and yellow was presented by Madame President Dorothy Steigler and husband, Arthur. A corsage was presented to Mrs. Humphrey by Doris McGee. A welcome card was printed and hung on the wall, stating: "Hannah, we love you - Ladies Auxiliary and Fraternal Order of Eagles Aerie No. 1149." Dancing was enjoyed by all. The Eagles' next meeting will be August 13th at 8 p.m.

Beta Sigma Phi

INTERNATIONAL

Since 1951, over 275 women in Dunsmuir have pledged themselves to the "aims and purposes" of Beta Sigma Phi, and they hope the community is a little better because of their experiences. It was organized in Abilene, Kansas, in 1931. Along with their cultural and social growth (stimulated by the varied and interesting programs at their meetings), the women have given, with open hearts, their time and money to help solve some of the emotional and financial needs locally, nationally, and internationally. There are five degrees of membership and each has chapters:

Nu Phi Mu Degree is for young women between ages of 17 and 22. Dunsmuir does not have a chapter.

Ritual of Jewels Degree. The Kappa Phi Chapter in Dunsmuir was sponsored by Klamath Falls Xi Delta Chapter and initiated by them on August 23, 1951. Their first meeting was held in the home of Jacquie Larsen, President. Helen Herring was Sponsor, and Beth Jones, Director. Kappa Phi Chapter "Friendly Ventured" (sponsored) the first Beta Sigma Phi chapter, Omicron Upsilon, in Mt. Shasta and initiated them November 30, 1954 in the Dunsmuir Hotel. A Rho Omega Chapter was started in 1956, the Silver Anniversary of Beta Sigma Phi, but they lost too many members so affiliated with Kappa Phi.

Exemplar Degree. The Xi Zeta Zeta Chapter received its charter October 29, 1956. After 5 years of membership in the Ritual of Jewels Degree members may progress to this Degree.

Preceptor Degree. The Epsilon Lambda Chapter weas started in Dunsmuir in May, 1973 and thirteen women progressed to that degree after 6 years of service in the Exemplar Degree.

Preceptor Laureate Degree. This Degree was conferred on 7 members of the Epsilon Lambda Chapter on December 8, 1981, those who had been members of it for 8 years. However, because there are not 10 members necessary to form a chapter for this degree, the following women are waiting: Viola Dorst, Rose Ellis, Ellen Fischer, Billie Mathes, Ruth Osborne, Betty Spencer, and Flora Wintering.

Varied have been the money-making projects of the members to finance their many contributions. In late years, most of the financial appeals have been met by all three Chapters. However, originally it was the Kappa Phi Chapter whose members worked hard to be benevolent. At their very first meeting, they decided upon a project which has been one of the main sources of fund-raising for service work ever since. A doll was purchased under the guidance of Forest Gass, a wardrobe made, and some furniture supplied; and it was raffled off at Christmas time of 1951. The first year's profit from the doll was sent to Camp White, Oregon, to be used to buy canteen script books for the soldiers. The following years the raffle proceeds were used to set up a milk fund for needy children at Dunsmuir Elementary School and continued until 1974 when the Federal Government took over that program.

More varied than the manners in which these chapters have made money are the number of causes to which they have made contributions and given their time — Red Cross drives, March of Dimes, Kidney Disease, Early Detection Clinics, Blood Bank, Easter Seals, voter's registration, a yearly contribution to Beta Sigma Phi's Endowment, Loan and Scholarship Funds and to their California Philanthropic Project, supporting research in Cystic Fibrosis. One of their most widely publicized contributions was the one in which they sent several shipments of clothes to the needy children of Viet Nam. Articles about the donation appeared in Saigon newspapers and "The Torch," the Beta Sigma Phi publication.

Locally, the chapters have sponsored Girl and Boy Scout troops, benefit dinners for ill and injured patients, 8th grade dances, kiddie parades, and Miss Dunsmuir pageants. They have given boxes to the needy, sent cookies and candies to local boys overseas, and graduation gifts to American Field Service exchange students; sent gifts to Shriners Hospital, Ranch Hope, Inc., Siskiyou County Juvenile Hall and special schools for troubled boys and girls; given donations to support local groups such as the Swim Team, Tigerettes Basketball Team, Babe Ruth, and Little League teams; contributions have been made to help local people meet major medical expenses, to the Kidney Van and many national organizations devoted to eliminating diseases.

Locally administered organizations have not been forgotten either — such as United Way, Salvation Army, Traveler's Aid, Dunsmuir Scholarship Fund, etc. Contributions have been made to help in furnishing the Recreation Building; maintaining Hedge Creek Falls; restoring the Railroad Coach; Opportunity Center; supporting school bond to build Cafetorium at Dunsmuir Elementary School; to send students on various educational trips, such as the Presidential Classroom; and in the drive to beautify the City.

As said by Karen Christ, Rose Ellis, and Flora Wintering, who provided the information about their organization, perhaps the most important of all their contributions is that the members have given support to sisters in time of sickness, sorrow, and need. They have taken food and comfort where there has been illness, loss, or tragedy. They have brought money where there have been financial troubles. Simply stated: "They have cared and are proud to be Beta Sigma Phis."

CHAPTER X

CELEBRATIONS

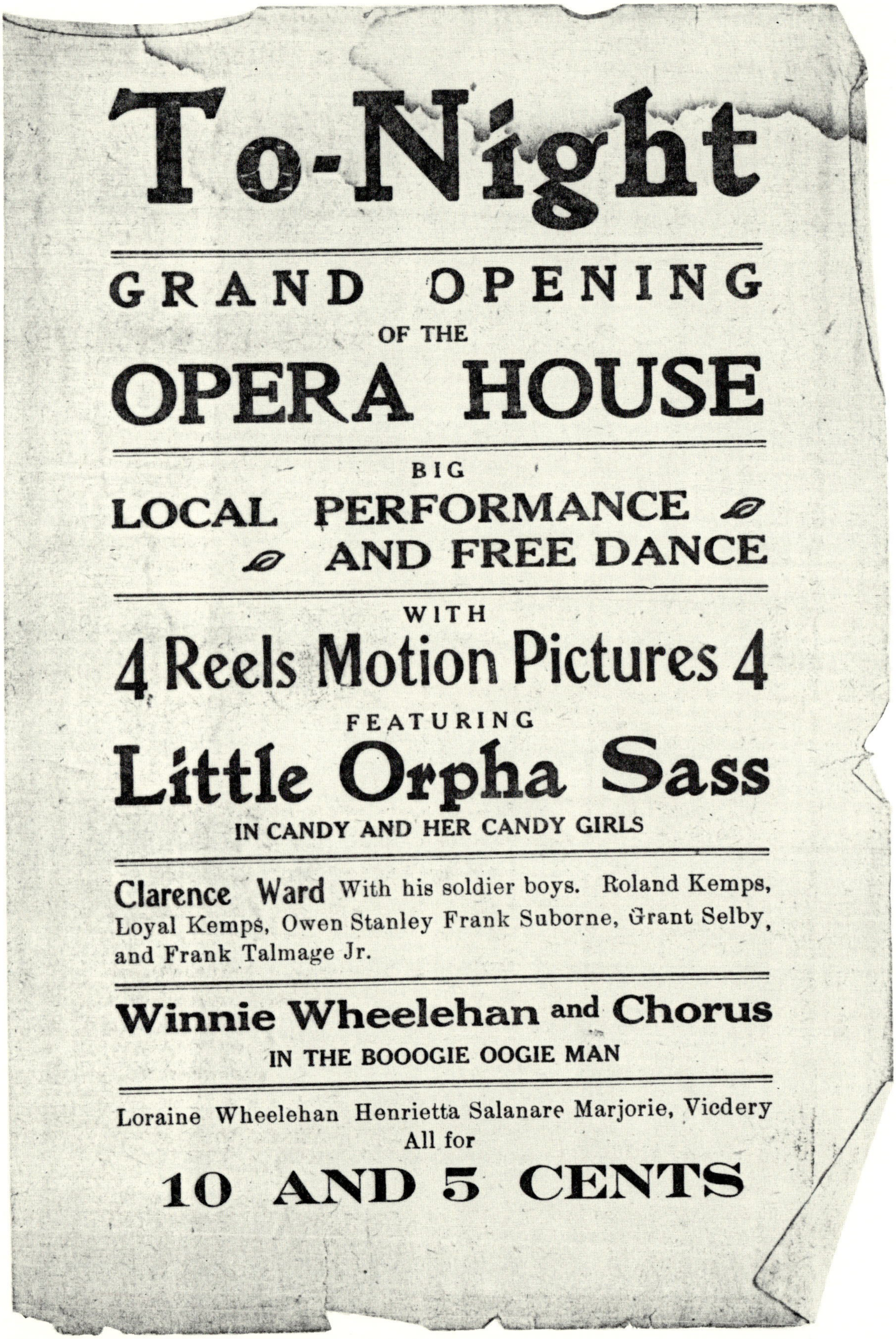

To-Night

GRAND OPENING

OF THE

OPERA HOUSE

BIG

LOCAL PERFORMANCE

AND FREE DANCE

WITH

4 Reels Motion Pictures 4

FEATURING

Little Orpha Sass

IN CANDY AND HER CANDY GIRLS

Clarence Ward With his soldier boys. Roland Kemps, Loyal Kemps, Owen Stanley Frank Suborne, Grant Selby, and Frank Talmage Jr.

Winnie Wheelehan and Chorus

IN THE BOOOGIE OOGIE MAN

Loraine Wheelehan Henrietta Salanare Marjorie, Vicdery

All for

10 AND 5 CENTS

CELEBRATIONS

By

Phyllis B. Hubbard

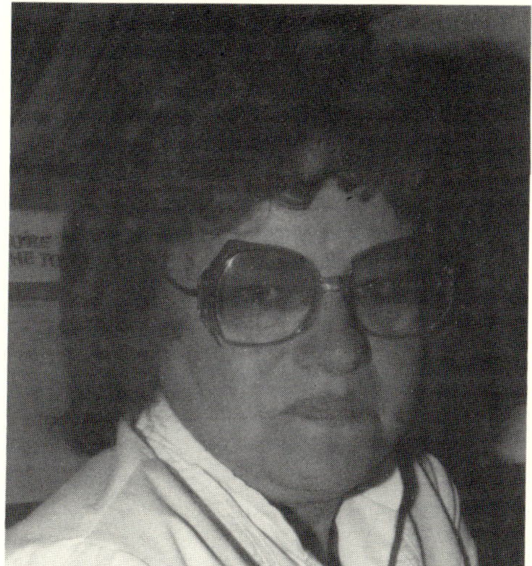

Phyllis B. Hubbard   *Photo - Reineking*

Americans probably have more holidays and reasons for celebrating than any other people in the world; we honor past Presidents, mothers, fathers, grandparents, war dead, veterans, birthdays, Thanksgiving, Christmas, Halloween, St. Patrick's Day, St. Valentine's Day, etc.; but the word celebration itself means to rejoice for some special reason and many of our holidays are really intended to create a pause in our lives to remember something or someone special — memorial services to give honor to those no longer among us. So, not all occasions are technically celebrations, but the 4th of July certainly qualifies as an occasion to be celebrated.

In 1904, Dunsmuir was getting ready to stage such a celebration, for, as one visitor described it, "Dunsmuir is the only town within a radius of 200 miles to celebrate the day befittingly." On this day, Dunsmuir would play host to many visitors from the county and even from the communities of Redding and Red Bluff. People would come by train, wagon, autos, horses, on foot — just to take part in the festivities. There would be parades, dances, baseball games, bands, and it was estimated that as many as 5,000 people came to our small town to help in this celebration of our hard-won independence.

There are certain elements which are necessary for a good celebration; friendly people, pretty girls, children who would run and play, yell, shoot off fireworks, get dirty, cry, and generally have a good time, and of course there were speeches. These were not just "say a few words to the people," but full-blown oratories; flowery, pretentious, bombastic, delivered with much rolling of R's and gesticulations, usually delivered by the mayor or one of the city fathers.

It was the custom in those early years of the century to hold the celebration on the 4th of July in a different city each year, and all the people of the county would attend. It was held in McCloud in 1904 and in 1906. In 1907, it was in Yreka and, in 1908, it was in Dunsmuir again. It was in 1904 that the newspaper accounts first tell of a Goddess of Liberty who reigned over the celebration. In that year, it was Miss Doris Coon and she rode on a float and presided over the festivities in general. In later years, other towns entered candidates and the winner was picked by a panel of judges. They gradually added more and more events to make the occasions more fun; a confetti-throwing contest in 1910, boxing matches in 1920, a baseball tournament in 1922, and a marathon race up Mt. Shasta in 1925! In 1938, they had a swimming and diving exhibition and a bathing beauty contest.

Ever mindful of the need to keep the celebrations refreshing and new in context, in 1927 the committee for the program asked if there was any young couple in Dunsmuir (already planning to be married!) who would like to be married as part of the celebration, with the entire town and visitors as guests. One young couple, Grace Cramer and Horace Selby, agreed and they were placed on a float in all their wedding finery and, after the parade, were joined in holy matrimony, still on the float, on Pine Street while hundreds of people watched. Later, a reception was held at the home of the bride's parents.

That same year, Dunsmuir had both a Goddess of Liberty and a Queen of Shasta Wonderland, both young ladies having coronations and sharing the duties of officiating over the many activities.

In 1918, a made-to-order reason for celebration! The Armistice had been signed and they blew the shop whistles, the shop girls paraded, the band played, impromptu street dances were held, and everyone who could be spared was given a half-day holiday.

Dunsmuir staged its last large 4th of July celebration in 1939 and the first Railroad Days Celebration was held in 1940. The brainchild of Mr. Norman Green, an S.P. conductor, this new celebration was designed to honor the railroad and its employees who were responsible for the existence of the town in the beginning, and certainly for its continued existence. It was also intended as a way of paying tribute to the beautiful area in which our town lies. That first celebration boasted a parade, 3 bands — including the Southern Pacific band from San Francisco, and a multitude of other smaller events. The next year, Railroad Days again took place with a parade and a drum majorette contest, but that was 1941 and later on that year, America was plunged into World War II and the celebrations were put on the shelf . .

. . .

During those war years, Dunsmuir staged bond drives and in 1942 held a program to dedicate the new city park on the 4th of July. In 1946, we again returned to the observance of Railroad Days and the 4th of July celebration was held in Weed.

Nineteen forty-seven through 1950, there were no celebrations held in Dunsmuir, but in 1951 we returned bigger and better than ever.

During the Railroad Days of 1951, it is estimated that 16,000 people attended the events. The Weldonians from Oakland appeared; we had a huge local talent show, marvelous model railroad exhibits, a parade; and we repeated that performance again in 1952 and 1953. In 1954, the biggest crowd arrived for the events; it was followed by a nearly record crowd in 1955.

In 1956, we held the first Railroad Days Queen contest. Ticket sales determined the winner, who received a trophy and $300.00. In 1957, girls from other towns were invited to participate and the finalists in the ticket sales were then presented to a panel of judges for selection of the winner.

During the years of 1959 through 1966, there were very small celebrations held — partly due to the highway construction — and largely due to lack of funds by the local committee. There was no carnival, just local booths, and in 1964 the opening of the Museum at Railroad Park. In 1965 and 1966, the Oldtimers' picnic was the big event and was attended by a fairly large group of people.

In 1967, we held our first Canyon Homecoming Festival: The first Queen contest based on a regular bathing beauty format was staged, Dunsmuir artists held a display, and there was a giant Smorgasbord prepared by the Catholic Church. Canyon Days continued as the theme for 1968, 1969, 1970, and 1971. Nineteen seventy-two consisted of a small celebration staged by a small group of local people, and 1973 consisted largely of a 25th high school reunion held by the Class of 1948.

In 1975, we initiated River Daze and included the first-ever river raft race in any celebration held in this area. This proved to be very popular and was continued as part of the format, along with carnivals, a Queen contest, local talent shows, through 1979. In 1980, we returned to the theme of Railroad Days and began the slow process of building that celebration up to where it would again attract people to our community to see how we live and how we play.

So, we come to this point — perhaps the largest celebration we will ever attempt — our 100th birthday! We were supposed to be living in a ghost town by now, but somehow we held onto our town and most of our traditions and our small town way of life and we still put on parades and bring in a carnival, bring out the pretty girls, the speech-makers, the local talent, and we hold a celebration; not just because it's our birthday, but maybe mostly because this is Dunsmuir, Siskiyou County, California, the United States of America — a good reason to celebrate any time.

119

At right:
Parade, July 4, 1904,
corner of Sacramento
Avenue and Pine Street.

Girls on cannon:
Lucy Scherrer and
Alice Campbell

...nce 8   ...cond 9 p. m.

THIS PROGRAM
2 NIGHTS ONLY

PROGRAM

A Beautiful Story of the Devil.
By a Woman's Wit—Very Sensational.
The New Maid—Extremely fine.
The Messmerizer—Absolutely great.
The Arrest—Wouldn't it jar you.

Beautiful Colored Pictures. Far better than
The Passion Play.

Beautiful Solos by Little Winnie Whelehan.

FINE MUSIC.

At SKATING RINK, in the future to be known
as the NOVELTY THEATER.

A Complete change of Program Sunday, April 4

Admission 10c

CHAPTER XI
SPORTS

TOWN TEAM BASEBALL
by
Charles "Bud" & Eva Carlquist

Charles "Bud" and Eva Carlquist

A baseball team known as the "Baseball 9" was organized in Dunsmuir in 1902. The members were Willie Lee, Stanley Shearer, Jim Hubeck, G. B. Farnsworth, A. G. Selby, F. W. Murphy, F. L. Isgrigg, John Ryan, and G. Woodman.

Baseball was the only sport at this time and was a serious event among the players and spectators. The articles which appeared in the Dunsmuir News were both humorous and explicit in describing the games, and I quote: "The only casualty at the ball ground during the July 4th celebration was a misdirected ball from the hands of Pitcher Rice, which took Earl Fussler below the belt, causing him to go lame for awhile."

The Dunsmuir 9, LaMoine, and Gazelle ball teams were always present in the parades held on July 4th. The games were played in Champion Park, also known as Shady Park. Their opponents at that time (1906) consisted of Sisson, Igerna, Gazelle, LeMoine, and Weed.

The local team held dances at the Brass Band's Pavilion opposite the post office as a means of raising funds for uniforms.

The following appeared in the July 30, 1909 edition of the *Dunsmuir News* and is printed here exactly as it was in the paper.

NOW ISN'T IT AWFUL REDDING?
**Tigers Decisively Beaten &
Up Goes Tremendous Howl**

The much rooted ball game between the Redding Tigers & Dunsmuir occurred last Sunday at Red Bluff & ended in a victory for the home team by a score of 8 to 3. But of course the Redding papers with their customary and antiquated tactics didn't have the decency to come out and give a good and unbiased account of the game, but on the other hand scantly and stingly mentioned the battle & then closed their articles with dirty sarcasm, splean, and mud slinging. Ah, for shame Redding. Wake up. Don't let your mind fall into that somnolent state wherein you imagine that Redding is like the ubiquitous word of God, because fears are entained for a sad and sorrowful awakening. The game was splendidly fought out and as the Free Press styled it, won by the Dunsmuir-Red Bluff combination. Certainly our dear, Reverend Brother. But in the same breath, why didn't you tell the people that the Tigers were considerably strengthened by the appearance of Charley Enright, the Sacramento shortstop, and "Home-run" Kelly of Fresno. More evidence of your desire to show up others defects and conceal your own imperfections. Slush. The poor, vulnerable body of Redding has been sorely assailed and the healing balm seems to be in the escaping of gas, shaken well and applied through the columns of the Free Press and Searchlight. Cheer up, Brothers, the worst is yet to come.

Dedicated to the memory of Redding and sung from the car window at Redding as our boys were leaving for home — Tune "Dolly Gray."

Goodbye Redding, we must leave you,
Tho it breaks our hearts to go.
Something tells us that we beat you
  in that little town below,
'Twas a shame to take the money,
But we won it once before.
Goodbye Redding, we must leave you,
Shall we come back once more?

The second verse was sung at Kennett as the train pulled up and stopped at the depot.

Hello Kennett! Glad to see you
Redding Tigers were too slow,
Poor ordinary little Dunsmuir
Surely had them on the go.
We all knew you were rejoicing,
'Twas a shame to take the dough.
We're going back with flying colors,
To a town that's not so slow.

The curtain drops. A dark cloud must be drawn over the past, and if Charles Braynard puts up that $1000.00 that he talked of at the "BLUFFS" someone will have the sad duty of writing another obituary notice for Redding.

A baseball park association was organized in April, 1921, for the purpose of raising funds to equip the city park with a baseball diamond. They raised $2,642.00 and over $3,000.00 in pledges.

"Babe" Ruth was an honorary member of the Dunsmuir Lions Club and played an exhibition game here, October 22, 1924. Also appearing in Dunsmuir with the famous "Bambino" was Bob Meusel, Ruth's teammate on the N. Y. Yankee Club. They were accompanied by Mgr. Christy Walsh. The "Babe's" appearance here was guaranteed jointly by the late Frank Talmadge and the Lions Club.

Approximately 900 attended the game and Dr. E. J. Cornish, Mayor of Dunsmuir, declared a half-holiday. Seven dozen baseballs were used in the seven inning game as the "Babe" used up one baseball after the other with autographs for children.

Players from Weed and Dunsmuir participated in the game. According to the edition of the *Dunsmuir News* of October 24th, 1924, the players on Meusel's team were Kaer, Valencia, Meusel, Russell, Painter, Coffen, Huse, Ray, and I. Wells. The "Babe's" team consisted of Ruth, Felts, Welsh, "Bones" Coon, Carter, Shoupe, Buckley, L. Wells, McBride, King, and bat boy "Boose" Coon.

The following letter was received from "Babe" Ruth following his appearance in Dunsmuir:

"To everybody (and that means everybody) in Dunsmuir, Calif.

We don't know yet how to tell you what a wonderful time we had in Dunsmuir.

Our long trip is nearly over.

We have been treated royally in little towns and in big cities, but when it comes to beautiful girls, wonderfully-fine fellows, and the real two-fisted genuine spirit of California — little old Dunsmuir gave us more laughs, more hospitality, more thrills, and more things to remember than any place between Broadway & Shasta.

We didn't expect to visit Dunsmuir, but believe us, we will positively be back (in person)!"

Babe Ruth
Bob Meusel

"Babe" Ruth at bat in Dunsmuir ballpark, 1924

"Babe" Ruth, making another trip to the West Coast, stopped in Dunsmuir on December 22, 1926. Members of the Lions Club took him fishing on the Klamath River. The next evening he presented the championship football trophy to the Dunsmuir High School football team. The high school football league at that time consisted of Dunsmuir and Yreka.

Baseball continued to be a favorite sport in Dunsmuir, and many exciting games provided Sunday afternoon entertainment for the avid spectators. During the years the Baseball 9 became known as "The Colts" "The Bears" "The Oaks" "The Eagles" "The Railroaders" and finally "The Dunsmuir Merchants."

During the year of 1923, Dunsmuir players Lyle Wells and Martinelli signed to play with Oakland in the Coast League. "Bones" Coon, in 1924, had a try-out with the Oakland Oaks. Gene Spores in 1927 had the opportunity to try out with Los Angeles.

"Bones" Coon, in 1925, led the Dunsmuir Bears hitting a 417.

August 23, 1929, Dunsmuir Town Team won Siskiyou County Baseball League championship   defeating the Weed Sons of Italy 6-2.

Dunsmuir town team won the county championship defeating Mt. Shasta 10-2 in 1935.

The lineup was as follows: Richmond, CF; E. Spores, 3rdB; Percoacha, SS; Beck, SS; Coon, 2ndB; Reginato, LF; Minasian, CF; Morrison, RF; Tyrer, 1stB; Richart, P; T. Spores, P.

Back Row: L. Carter, W. McBride, D. Gerloch, C. Pine, Martinelli, R. Holden, Miller
Front Row (L to R): E. Spores, T. Spores, L. Wells, G. Murchis, B. Coon, G. Goslin; mascot, "Boose" Coon.

Dunsmuir Ball Team - 1928

Photo courtesy
Phyllis Gilzean

1948 PRESIDENT'S CUP WINNING TEAM
Top, L to R: Cliff Flowers, Bud Carlquist, Ron Behnke, Romo Crispi, Eldred Hanson, Lyle Turpin, Johnsey Robinson, Harold Carrington. Bottom, L to R: Bob Reid, Wayne Olsen, Tony Barber, "Bones" Coon, Maurice Beck; Batboy, Rusty Behnke.

A special train consisting of seven cars and 300 enthusiastic fans aboard rode to Redding on August 12, 1938, to see Redding win a thriller in ten innings against Dunsmuir.

The only time-out in baseball history was called in Hilt, Calif., where the center fielder had to kill a rattlesnake before play could be resumed.

The Dunsmuir baseball town team was again organized by "Bones" Coon in 1945 — after its absence from sports for the duration of World War II.

In 1948, the Dunsmuir Eagles won the President's Cup in the season's best game. Dunsmuir defeated the McCloud Loggers 3-2 on Lyle Turpin's four hit pitching.

*   *   *   *   *

"We remember the enthusiasm and dedication of Miles Richmond, "Beany" King, Roscoe Kimble, Tony Barber, Romo Crispi, Wayne Olsen, Bud Carlquist, Ron Behnke, Bob Reid, Bob Harris, Harold Carrington, Clint Morey, Maurice Beck, Lyle Turbin, Cliff Flowers, Eldred Hanson, Johnsey Robinson, Perk White, Cliff Schwergel, Bill Nealon, and 'Bones' Coon."

"Bud" and Eva Carlquist

TOWN BASKETBALL TEAM

At a meeting of basketball fans held at the Travelers Confectionery on September 10, 1926, Andrew Leach was elected president of the local basketball association; Burton Coon, secretary-treasurer; William Welsh, Beany King, and Dr. M. L. Kleaver, directors.

A basketball league to be known as the Northern California Athletic Association, composed of Dunsmuir, Weed, Redding, Anderson, Cottonwood, Red Bluff, Gerber, El Camino, Los Molinos, Corning, and Chico was formed in Redding, October 22, 1926. The league was divided into two divisions: northern and southern.

The Dunsmuir Cardinals — champions of the Northern California Basketball League won 15 games without a loss, having defeated every team in Northern California and also having won two games from Southern Oregon Normal of Ashland. The players were Clarence Pine, guard; "Chick" Conley, forward; Sky Herr, forward; Reuben Perry, forward; Owen Stanley, forward; Burton Coon, guard; Homer Dickson, center; Ralph Moeller, guard; Dom Sirianni, forward. The Cardinals played the Auburn Cubs the first night; Roseville, the next night. They lost the Auburn game and won the game in Roseville.

Left to right: C. Pine, S. Herr, R. Perry, C. Cawley, D. Sirianni, O. Stanley, B. Coon, R. Moeller, H. Dickson.

February 24, 1928, the Cardinals again won the championship and went to San Francisco to play in elimination contests for the state championship. They lost to the S.F. Athens Club, 55-22.

The team traveled to San Francisco again on February 28, 1930, after winning the county championship. They played against the St. Ignatius frosh college team — losing 26-18.

Coach Chris Bonderson used his first string as starting lineups in the elimination tournament. Burton and "Boose" Coon were in their regular positions as guards; Dick Moore, at center; and Bradshaw and McMahon, at forwards.

The Dunsmuir town team, now known as the Firemen, again won the county cage title in February, 1931, defeating McCloud 24-19. Outstanding players were "Boose" and Burton Coon, Marske, Leahy, Sirianni, Moore, and Jaeckle.

February 16, 1940, the town team basketball, now known as the Boosters, won two titles defeating McCloud 63-24 in unlimited and 44-35 in limited class. Unlimited class team: Bill Padula, Bob Durbin, forwards; Bill Reid, center; John Reginato and Irwing Trafton, guards. Limited class team: Cecil Huse and Bob Reid, guards; Charlie York and Max Estep, forwards; Al Marske, center.

GOLF

The Dunsmuir golf and country club held its first tournament October 2, 1925. The course was located on the McGuinness property south of Dunsmuir. Dues were one dollar a month, paid in advance. In April, 1928, a nine-hole golf course was built at Castle Crags resort.

GIRLS SPORTS

Girls Basketball Team - circa 1914

BASKET BALL
AT THE
AUDITORIUM
Tuesday Even'g, Jan. 27

High School Girls' Team

Constance Brown	} Centers
Germania LeFleur	
Bessie Sutherland	} Guards
Olive McCarville	
Maude Manning	} Forwards
Grace Bess	

Young Ladies' Team

Elda Wentz	} Forwards
Alice Campbell	
Clara Scherrer	} Centers
Mrs. Greenman	
Gertrude Vickery	} Guards
Alta McCarville	

BOYS' LINEUP

"Whites"
Pixley, Gay, Pixley, Duggan, Shoup and Masterson.

"Reds"
Gilzean, Huse, Heaton, Steadman, Greenman, Cordray

Referee For Girls	Ralph Gay
Referee For Boys	W. G. Huff

DANCING AFTER THE GAMES
First Game Called at 8:30 p. m.
ADMISSION Including Dance :— Gents 50c., Ladies 25c., Children 15c

Handbill for games, January 1914

Team of '66 — #30, Bill Carlquist
Extreme left rear - Coach Jim Bujol

Carlquist, #30, carries the ball

(Subtitles and pictures added by Editor-in-Chief)

HIGH SCHOOL SPORTS — 1920-1950

By
Charles "Bud" & Eva Carlquist

Accomplishments in the athletic field were very few during the year of 1920 at Dunsmuir High School. The high school was too small to carry on any athletic program. However, they did manage to secure a building in which to practice basketball. Members of the team were Conrad Klein, Harold McEnerney, Owen Stanley, Hubert Marsh, and Merle Dale. They played three games against McCloud, winning one of the three.

The local paper during this year (1920) did mention five former Dunsmuir High School students who were outstanding in athletics at St. Mary's College: Clarence Ward, Van Horn, and Clyde Kirkendall, all outstanding in football; and Gillis Wells and La Due, in other sports.

The following year (1921) found the school in the same condition. The girls did not have a basketball team as they didn't have a place to practice. A coach could not be found for the boys, so they struggled through the season on their own.

The girls did manage to have a baseball team. Although the team was not a winning one, the girls at least entered competitive athletics. Members of the team were Louise DeWitt, Jennie Hamlin, Elinore Van Fossen, Vera Wilkins, Marcia Hollis, Louise McCarton, Hazel Tucker, Ethel Greene, and Bernice Bennett. They played the local grammar school and lost. A game was scheduled with the Weed girls; but for some unknown reason, the Weed girls failed to show up.

The boys organized their baseball team late in the season; nevertheless, they entered the league winning a number of games. The league was divided into two sub-leagues: League A - including Yreka, Fort Jones, and Etna Mills; League B - including Weed, McCloud, Sisson, and Dunsmuir.

During this year, the Dunsmuir boys won the sub-league championship but lost at the finals for the County Championship. Members of the team were Henry Heggland, Marvin Upton, Owen Stanley, Archie Clausnitzer, Kenneth Kleaver, Raymond Marsh, Camillo Sirianni, Billie Kleaver, Ruben Perry, and John Price.

The first basketball game played in the new auditorium was on November 24, 1922. The girls baseball team of 1923 consisted of the following: Louise DeWitt, Phyllis Coon, Bernice Grubt, Marjorie Young, Erna Heggland, Leona Metzger, Mildred Graham, Mildred Lockstone, Maurine Stille, Louise McCarton, and Reta Brown.

The members of the girls basketball team in 1923 were Bernice Grubt, Erna Heggland, Louise McCarton, Reta Brown, Mildred Lockstone, Joy Dunn, Jean Bell, Leona Metzger, and Clara Clausnitzer.

During the year of 1926, it was decided that Dunsmuir High School would play football. The baseball ground was repaired so that it could be used for both football and baseball.

The first football coach, J. H. Acheson, Stanford graduate, was hired in 1926. Forty turned out for football.

Tiger football team won over Yreka 6-0 to capture county title. In 1926 and 1927, three high schools played football: Weed, Yreka, and Dunsmuir. Members of the Dunsmuir team were as follows: A. Roberts, E. Roberts, F. Salinsky, C. Norman, H. Fischer, G. Lockstone, B. Leahy, A. Makle, J. Ammiratti, J. Malone, E. Kelby, A. Wallace, E. Branstetter, E. Taylor, W. Johnson, J. Pontier, H. Murphy, and R. Taylor.

In 1928, Dunsmuir Tigers played for the Northern Hoop Title. They played Marysville for the Northern California Championship. A & B's both won County Championships, but lost to Marysville, 29-22. The B team won over Red Bluff, 19-13, thus winning Northern California Championship and the right to play Sacramento for the Central and Southern Sections of state. They lost, 23-19.

In 1929, the Dunsmuir High School baseball team played in the Northern California Athletic League Championship, winning against Willows, 9-5. The following week they won the County Championship winning over Yreka 12-10. This gave them the opportunity to play in the NCHSAL at Colusa, but they lost to College City High School, 6-5.

Dunsmuir High School in 1937 set a record in winning basketball championships in three divisions. The A team defeated Tulelake 33-25; the B team defeated Fort Jones 48-21. The C team had already won in the fall. The D team lost in playoff. The A and B teams were coached by Dick Minasian; the C and D teams by Ralph Wattenburger.

1937 BASEBALL TEAM
Top row, L to R: Fred Piperio, Fred Segrette, Harry Carrick, Stub
Weedon, __________ , Loyd Null, Batboy Cecil Huse. Bottom row,
L to R: Coach George Hunter, Eddie Ashford, Jim Periera, Howard
"Bud" Johnson, Primo Martini, Angelo Reginato, Dan Briggs,
Harvey Bishpam. Top of photo: "Hop" Porter.

The Tigers, in 1938, won the A Division championship in basketball for two consecutive years by defeating Yreka 40-33. High scoring honors went to Paul Reginato and Joe Padula, both having 17 points. Paul Reginato played center; Joe and Bill Padula, forwards. Guards were Babe Trafton and "Bud" Carlquist; Lloyd La-Camp and Armand Trafton were the only substitutes. Dunsmuir defeated Tulelake 45-15 for county championship in playoff series.

Football players of the 30's who went on to play college football were Angelo Reginato, University of California; Albert Reginato, Sacramento State; Pace Paletta, Modesto J.C. and Washington State; Ford Sexton, Placer J.C. and Washington State; Rebelle Baldo, Armand Trafton, Bill Reid, John Reginato to Placer J.C.; Paul Reginato, St. Marys; John Reginato, University of Missouri; "Bud" Carlquist, Santa Clara; Joe Reginato, San Jose State.

The Dunsmuir A basketball team traveled to Berkeley to play against the University of California frosh team for the first time in any sport. Dunsmuir was defeated 42-24.

The year of 1939 was the first time in league history that all basketball teams — A, B, C, D — won championships and then went on to win four county championships.

Dunsmuir Tigers defeated Weed 12-0 to win the county football championship. Tigers on the All County first team were Allen Becker, LeRoy Thomas, Ed Thorne, Bud O'Kelley, and Johnny Reginato. Second team — Jim Cosentino, Terry Rossetto, and Gerald Phillips.

The C basketball team won six consecutive county championships and the D team had won three at the end of the 1939 season.

In track, Harry Renoud set a new mark in 880-yard run for the north state in 2 minutes and 15.4 seconds. Alva Nelson won the 220 dash. These scores made it possible to compete in Sacramento C.I.F. meet. Nelson placed second in this meet.

Dunsmuir won the county B championship in track, winning third place in unlimited class, piling up 7 more points than any other school — a total of 73 points in the two divisions.

Dunsmuir Tigers in 1934 won the football title for the third successive season by defeating McCloud 41-13.

Dunsmuir gridders, in 1936, won Class A Championships. The Tigers won the playoff game with the Yreka Miners in a double header played in Mt. Shasta, the score 20-0. They went on to defeat Weed, 7-6, for the lead in the league. The Tigers defeated Yreka 57-0 for the County Championship. Records for the season were as follows:

Dunsmuir		Opponents
6	Grants Pass	7
20	Redding	0
31	Mt. Shasta	0
0	Ashland	0
68	McCloud	0
34	Yreka	0
7	Weed	6
57	Yreka	0
223		13

The Tigers won the county championship four times in a five-year span: 1932, 1933, 1934, and 1936.

Angelo Reginato, former Dunsmuir Tiger, became a regular member of University of California football team in 1936. He was one of thirty squad members to be awarded the Block C letter for that year.

The year 1940 again brought the Dunsmuir High School basketball team four county championships. A great record was established when the A team defeated Tulelake 36-21 in the third and deciding game of the series. The school had claimed a total of 13 championships in two years.

By defeating the Weed Cougars on their home turf, the Dunsmuir Tigers became the champions of the Siskiyou County football league for the season of 1940. This was the second successive year the Tigers had defeated Yreka by a 46-13 score in the Armistice Day "Big Game." Seniors who played were "Bud" O'Kelley, Johnny Reginato, Sam and Frank Tallerico, Cleaver, Olsen, Al Neasham; and Young. Tigers who made All County were O'Kelley, Capovilla, Sam Tallerico, Johnny Reginato, and Frank Tallerico.

Dunsmuir 1940 A basketball team won the county championship for the sixth consecutive year by defeating Tulelake 25-9.

1927 — The Class A basketball team (consisting of Donald Basham, Parker Getchell, Burton Leahy, William Johnson, Joe Pontier, Esmald Branstetter, Eddie Roberts, George Lockstone, Harvey Fischer, Jack Malone, and Joe Ammiratti) looked good at the beginning of the season. On one occasion a six-hour trip to McCloud through three feet of snow proved disastrous. The boys were so fatigued when they finally arrived at 9:00 p.m., they lost to McCloud in all three games.

1932 — Outstanding Athletes: Alva Nelson, Florence Kempsky

1933 — Charles York, Helen Jenks

1935 — Katherine Reginato, William Reid

1936 — Margaret Makawa, Ford Sexton

1937 — Marina Farnea, Pace Paletta

1938 — "Bud" Carlquist, Norma Brun

The name "Reginato" was synonymous with football in Northern California and was becoming known in other sections as well. John F. Reginato of Castella played in the line on the University of Missouri football team. He was a member of the squad that played in the Sugar Bowl in 1941.

Angelo Reginato scored the winning touchdown for U.C. in the Big Game with Stanford in 1938.

Paul Reginato, who was a member of the varsity football team at St. Mary's College, was also elected to students "Who's Who" 1941-42.

Albert Reginato who had been a regular on the D.H.S. football team, played football for Sacramento Junior College. He is the brother of Angelo and Johnny. Yes, we believe that "Reginato" and football were synonymous. Katherine Reginato, sister of Angelo, Albert, and Johnny, was chosen best girl athlete of DHS in 1935.

A study was made to build a football field at the high school, but the board decided $23,500 was too expensive. The DHS team was unable to play any games at home due to a ruling by state authorities that games must be played on turf fields. At this time the players were playing on a dirt field, covered with rocks, a condition which does not make for ideal playing conditions.

The players before each game would walk the field picking up rocks and debris that would hamper or injure the players. The goal line was right at the edge of the fence.

In later years the entire student body would spend one day cleaning the field. In 1939, the school obtained permission to play at the City Park, providing the field was covered with sawdust.

The first home game played on new turf, in September 1942, was played against the Weed Cougars, ending a three-year grid drought. This was the first game that had been played in Dunsmuir since 1939.

The Tiger B Hoopsters won the county championship in 1943 and 1945.

The DHS football team defeated Weed in football 13-12 for its first win in two years. In 1946 the A basketball team won the county championship. From 1936 on Dunsmuir won at least one championship each year except in 1942. Records are as follows:

        1936 — C
        1937 — A & B
        1938 — A
        1939 — A, B, C, & D
        1940 — A, B, C, & D
        1941 — A
        1942 — None
        1943 — B
        1944 — C
        1945 — B
        1946 — A

The year 1940-41 was outstanding as Dunsmuir won football, all four basketball, and baseball county championships.

1931 TEAM

Top row, L to R: Max Estep, Ben Murray, "Hop" Porter, Lloyd Null, John Bryan, Dave Fidler, Silvio Sartor, Coach George Hunter. Middle row: Stanley Kafer, Ray Rains, Bill Hulse, Jim Lockart, Ed Starr, Dick Patrick, Charlie York, Avery Weedon. Bottom row: Bob Malone, Angelo Delgado, Sid Fischer, Alva Nelson, Lyle Hall, Captain George Taylor, Mark Hanna, Angelo Reginato. In front: Assistant Manager Cecil Huse, Manager George "Red" Adams.

Goal line at edge of field

"The dirt field covered with rock"

Note the different uniforms of players & referee

Dunsmuir High School ended the 1949 football season in a tie with Weed and, after much protesting, was picked to represent the league in a game with Shasta High School in Redding, the winner of the Valley League. In a close game, Dunsmuir came from behind to defeat Redding 25-19.

COACHES - DHS — 1927-1939

1927 — Joseph Acheson - football, basketball and baseball

1928 — Ralph Wattenburger — A basketball, baseball, and track

1928 — Ralph Munger — football, B & C basketball

1929 — Ralph Wattenburger — football, A, B, & C basketball, baseball

1930 — V. W. Helma — football, A, B, & C basketball

1931-1932 — George Hunter — football, A, B, & C basketball, track & baseball

1935-1936 — Howard Woodside — football; Ralph Wattenburger — A, B, & C basketball

1937-1938 — Richard Minasian — football, track; Ralph Wattenburger — A, B, & C basketball; Edwin Morrison — D basketball

1939-40, 41, 42 — George Bican — football; John Glease — A, B, & D basketball; Ralph Wattenburger — C basketball

FOOTBALL

1954:
>Dunsmuir 13, Orland
>Dunsmuir 53, Fall River 0
>Dunsmuir 0, Weed 18
>Dunsmuir 6, Yreka 19
>Dunsmuir 6, Trinity 0
>Dunsmuir 7, Corning 38
>>Paul Reginto, Coach

1955:
>Dunsmuir 6, Orland 13
>Dunsmuir 25, Modoc 6
>Dunsmuir 13, Trinity 28
>Dunsmuir 13, Red Bluff 38
>Dunsmuir 13, Weed 28
>Dunsmuir 0, Yreka 35
>Dunsmuir 12, Mt. Shasta
>Dunsmuir 40, Fall River 20
>>Paul Reginto, Coach

1956:
>Dunsmuir 34, Tulelake 0
>Dunsmuir 47, Modoc 21
>Dunsmuir 66, Trinity 0
>Dunsmuir 33, Central Valley 0
>Dunsmuir 21, Fall River 7
>Dunsmuir 33, Mt. Shasta 7
>Dunsmuir 6, Yreka 7
>Dunsmuir 19, Weed 6
>>Paul Reginto, Coach

This was the year that they got the scoreboard.

1957:
>Dunsmuir 34, Tulelake 0
>Dunsmuir 47, Modoc 21
>Dunsmuir 66, Trinity 0
>Dunsmuir 33, Central Valley 0
>Dunsmuir 21, Fall River 6
>Dunsmuir 6, Mt. Shasta 7
>Dunsmuir 19, Yreka 7
>>Lynn Elliott, Coach

This was the year that they were the Co-Champs.

1958:
>Dunsmuir 36, Hayfork 6
>Dunsmuir 47, Tulelake 6
>Dunsmuir 6, Trinity 13
>Dunsmuir 28, Central Valley 0
>Dunsmuir 34, Fall River 7
>Dunsmuir 32, McCloud 0
>Dunsmuir 18, Weed 14
>Dunsmuir 27, Mt. Shasta 7
>Dunsmuir 20, Yreka 7

1959:

This year they were the Shasta-Cascade League Champs.
>Their record was: 8-1
>>Lynn Elliott, Coach

1960:
>Dunsmuir 22, Corning 0
>Dunsmuir 34, Central Valley 7
>Dunsmuir 21, Anderson 0
>Dunsmuir 7, Trinity 0
>Dunsmuir 19, Hayfork 0
>Dunsmuir 13, Yreka 13
>Dunsmuir 0, Weed 0

1961:
>Dunsmuir 14, Central Valley 13
>Dunsmuir 13, Anderson 20
>Dunsmuir 20, Trinity 19
>Dunsmuir 26, Hayfork 6
>Dunsmuir 19, Fall River 12
>Dunsmuir 13, Weed 13
>Dunsmuir 19, Mt. Shasta 0
>Dunsmuir 7, Yreka 21
>>Walt Butcher, Coach

1962:
>Dunsmuir 13, Corning 7
>Dunsmuir 12, Central Valley 7
>Dunsmuir 7, Anderson 19
>Dunsmuir 45, Trinity 0
>Dunsmuir 39, Hayfork 7
>Dunsmuir 19, Fall River 6
>Dunsmuir 6, Yreka 18
>Dunsmuir 7, Weed 47
>Dunsmuir 0, Mt. Shasta 18
>>Jim Bujol, Coach

1963:
>Dunsmuir 13, Trinity 0
>Dunsmuir 19, Modoc 12
>Dunsmuir 20, Central Valley 0
>Dunsmuir 38, McCloud 38
>Dunsmuir 25, Hayfork 0
>Dunsmuir 6, Fall River 6
>Dunsmuir 12, Mt. Shasta 38
>Dunsmuir 15, Yreka 6
>Dunsmuir 6, Weed 45

1964:
>Dunsmuir 46, Central Valley 6
>Dunsmuir 42, Trinity 0
>Dunsmuir 58, Hayfork 12
>Dunsmuir 14, Fall River 0
>Dunsmuir 28, Modoc 7
>Dunsmuir 13, Weed 4
>Dunsmuir 13, Mt. Shasta 0
>Dunsmuir 20, Yreka 7
>>Jim Bujol, Coach

1965:
>Dunsmuir 46, Central Valley 6
>Dunsmuir 42, Trinity 0
>Dunsmuir 58, Hayfork 12
>Dunsmuir 14, Fall River 0
>Dunsmuir 28, Modoc 7
>Dunsmuir 13, Weed 14
>Dunsmuir 13, Mt. Shasta 10
>Dunsmuir 20, Yreka 7

1966:
>Dunsmuir 19, Central Valley 6
>Dunsmuir 6, Trinity 14
>Dunsmuir 52, Hayfork 0
>Dunsmuir 27, Fall River 6
>Dunsmuir 31, Modoc 7
>Dunsmuir 27, Yreka 7
>Dunsmuir 0, Weed 7
>Dunsmuir 25, Mt. Shasta 7

1967:
>Record — 4-4-1
>>Jim Bujol, Coach

1968:
>Record — 3-4-1
>>Jim Bujol, Coach

1969:
>Record — 0-8
>>Jim Harington, Coach

FOOTBALL
1970-1984
By
Students in H. W. Trapnell's Leadership Class

The Tigers didn't kick off the 1970's too well, going 2-7 under Coach Fred Jones. It was Jones's First year of coaching at DHS. Their only wins came against Etna and lowly Trinity. Kim Griffin and Tom Gillespie were the team captains.

The 1971 season was again a disappointing one for the Tigers and Coach Jones. They went 2-6-1, beating Weed and Mt. Shasta and tying the Fall River Bulldogs.

The Tigers and Coach Jones had a great deal of optimism heading into the 1972 season. Ten lettermen were returning. The team's high hopes were shot down by a 2-7 season. The JV's gave the school some hope for the future, going 5-4 and becoming the only school to beat the Weed Cougars that year.

The 1973 season started out with a bang for the Tigers. They beat Etna 20-6 in their opener, but then proceeded to lose six and tie one. The team finished the year 1-7-1. Bill Birch and Ron Dolf shared the coaching duties and Dave Thunborg was the team captain.

In terms of records, the 1974 season at DHS was the school's best since 1967. Coach Jim Rinne guided the Tigers to a 4-4-1 record. They started out the season on a high note, beating Etna 19-2, Happy Camp 25-0, and Tulelake 27-8. In their next five games they could only salvage a tie against Burney until a season ending victory over Trinity. For their efforts, the Tigers placed two players on the all-league team. They were Dave Thunborg and Brian Ballard.

The 1975 Football season at DHS saw the Tigers improve slightly on last year's mark, going 4-3-2 in their first year in the Evergreen League. The Tigers impressed their new league with a 4-1 record, losing only to Big Valley by a single touchdown. As for the JV squad, they won the EL Championship, with an impressive 7-2 record overall and 5-0 in league.

The 1976 season saw the Tigers continue to improve their record year by year. Coach Rinne led the squad to a 5-4 overall mark. They were 2-3 in league play. This was a disappointing year, but nothing like what DHS would encounter in the 1977 season, going 1-8. Their lone win came at the hands of Bonanza. It seemed the Tigers couldn't put together back to back successful seasons.

The 1978 season might have been the low point of the 70's for DHS Football. The team was winless at 0-7. Although this was a down year, there were high hopes for the following season. Eight players were returning and a new coach was in town. The Tigers and their new coach, Rawley Brink, once again had a relatively down year. They finished the short 1979 season at 2-4. Their two wins came at the hands of Bonanza and Butte Valley. This year closed out another decade of Tiger Football. Overall, DHS had a 23-57-5 record over these ten years.

DHS started off the 80's in impressive style, finishing 7-2-1 overall and 3-2-1 in league. The Tigers contributed four players to the all-league team. Co-Captain Meto Linares was selected to the team as a halfback and Guard Tim Gorsuch also made the squad. Defensive back Richie Summers and Lineman Greg Beck were honorable mention choices.

The 1981 season, Coach Brink's third at DHS, proved to be a successful one. The Tigers went 5-1 in league to capture a share of the Evergreen League title. Their only loss came against Butte Valley. It turned out to be Coach Brink's last year at the school, but he went out a winner. His three-year overall record was 15-9-1, quite impressive.

The 1982 season was filled with controversy. The Tigers ended the year at 7-2, and would have made the playoffs except for a poor call by a referee in the Big Valley game. DHS lost.

The 1983 year saw the Tigers put forth, and match any year they've had before. An 8-2 record placed the Tigers in second place in the EL. Runningback Pete Clemens rushed for over 1,800 yards, putting him third on the Superior California rushing list. He also played in the Lions All-Star game.

After three such successful years, 1984 was a downer at DHS. The Tigers finished the year at 2-7. However, considering the lack of interest in the school, this record didn't look too bad. Scott Porter and Burt Barnes, JV coaches of the year before, coached the squad when Coach John Carter resigned. Danny Christensen and Kevin Hampton were selected to the all-league team. Clint McGill was selected Mr. Defense, and Bret Barnes received the most valuable lineman award.

BOYS BASKETBALL

1952-1984

In 1952, the Dunsmuir High School "A" team won the title of Siskiyou County Champions. The team consisted of Bob Fidler, Doug Sorenson, Ken Martin, Ralph Hall, Art VanDrimmelen, Ray Decker, Chad Gilzean, Danny Rodriguez, and Dick Hardy. Their coach was Mr. Wiliford and their season record was 11 wins and 1 loss. Mr. Wiliford also coached the "C" and "D" teams that year. The "B" team was coached by Mr. Reginato.

In 1957, under the supervision of Coach Dave Blount, Dunsmuir's "D" team took the championship of their division. Their season record was 7 wins and 0 losses. Mr. Blount also coached the "A", "B" and "C" teams that year.

Both Dunsmuir's "C" and "D" teams took their division titles in 1958. The coach for both teams was Mr. Blount. Nineteen sixty-three was Mr. Blount's last year as coach at DHS.

The Tigers' first year of Evergreen League Competition was 1976. On November 30, 1976, the Kevin Young Memorial Scoreboard/Clock was dedicated in honor of Senior Kevin Young, who was killed in a car accident in the spring of '76. The clock still hangs in the gym.

GIRLS BASKETBALL

1960-1962:

There was never a girls basketball team, although there was a girls' block "D". Girls could get the "D" by being in the Pep Club and other things.

1963:

In this year they had two teams. The first team was:
  M. Girard
  C. Poe
  J. Bisagno
  D. Logan
  K. Harris
  B. Carvens
The second team was:
  J. Lowe
  H. Pon
  P. Anderson
  L. Jones
  D. DuBose
  S. Long
  G. Burger
  B. Rooney

1964-1972:

Dunsmuir High School didn't really have any teams. They played intramural.

1973:

The team played against other teams, but not in a league. The team consisted of:
  T. Flanagan
  R. Pon
  L. Strobe
  S. Aguilera
  D. Bogart
  M. Zanotto
  V. Hall
  J. Cosentino
  M. Zanotto

1974:

The coach: Bispala. It was a junior and senior team.
  T. Cascarina
  T. Connelly
  R. Knapp
  M. Zanotto
  K. Calzoni
  V. Hall
  R. Espinoza
Tigers became coeducational for the first time.

1975:

They had a league and real live uniforms. The squad worked hard and played many games. The team:
  V. Summers
  D. Rossi
  J. Ballard
  J. Hunter
  T. Jones
  H. Below
  M. Zanotto
  L. Levie
  E. Fraga
  S. Welborn

1976:

The team was:
  S. Welborn
  M. Zanotto
  D. Rossi
  V. Summers
  J. Ballard
  D. Kennedy
  J. Hunter
  T. Jones
  K. Meredith
The coach was Bispala. Their record: 11-1.

  Dunsmuir 57, Anderson 35
  Anderson tourney - 1st.
  Dunsmuir 30, Central Valley 28
  Dunsmuir 54, Enterprise 34
  Dunsmuir 41, Central Valley 18
  Dunsmuir 28, Shasta 27
  Dunsmuir 40, Trinity 36
  Dunsmuir 46, C.O.S. 29
  Dunsmuir 33, Shasta 34
  Dunsmuir 44, Trinity 54
  Corning tourny - 3rd.
  Dunsmuir 44, Enterprise 59
  Dunsmuir 54, C.O.S. 52
  Dunsmuir 47, Anderson 44
  Central Valley Tourney - 4th.
Jody Hunter was all tourney in Corning. J. Ballard was on the all tourney team.

This year they went to Poland over the summer. On July 21st the Tigerettes left for Poland. They were scheduled to play 6 games. Before their first game in Wroclaw, they stayed in Warsaw to do some touring. After 3 days, they went to Wroclaw and played their first game. At the half, the score was tied 22-22. In the second half they faded to lose at 55-33. The other 5 games went smoothly and the girls returned on Aug. 13.

1977:

Mrs. Marian Nichols was coaching this year. Her team didn't do too badly for an inexperienced team. They did have two victories. On the team were:
  L. Rossetto
  M. Zanotto
  D. Rossi
  H. Charles
  D. Kennedy
  J. Ballard
  J. Douglas
  K. Meredith
  K. Perry
  L. Hopkins

1978:

The coaches were Voruz and Morse. On the team was:
  M. Floyd
  L. Rossotto
  D. Rossi
  C. Spinks
  J. Douglas
  J. Harris
  M. Rossi
  K. Perry

1980:

The team was:
- M. McGuire
- M. Rossi
- P. Bryant
- T. Walker
- C. Spinks
- K. Kennedy
- F. Conley
- L. Hanson

They were a good team.

1981:

This team had a fairly good year. Their record was: 16-3.

Dunsmuir 24, Tulelake 34
Dunsmuir 47, Surprise Valley 16
Dunsmuir 53, Tulelake 41
Dunsmuir 40, Westwood 35
Dunsmuir 34, Butte Valley 23
Dunsmuir 52, McCloud 22
Dunsmuir 43, Fort Jones 47
Dunsmuir 42, McCloud 23
Dunsmuir 36, Alumni 29
Dunsmuir 24, Happy Camp 18
Dunsmuir 40, Fort Jones 35
Dunsmuir 45, Mt. Shasta 37
Dunsmuir 41, Etna 36
Dunsmuir 32, Happy Camp 23
Dunsmuir 43, Butte Valley 42 OT
Dunsmuir 35, Big Valley 49
Dunsmuir 27, Big Valley 29
Dunsmuir 38, Surprise Valley 32
Dunsmuir 30, Modoc 28

This team consisted of:
- A. McGuire
- F. Conley
- K. Pierce
- L. Young
- C. Spinks
- M. Mitchell
- W. Townsend
- L. Henson
- M. Rossi

1982:

The coach: Jim Rinne
On the team was:
- F. Hisey
- L. Young
- M. Meeks
- M. Smith
- W. Townsend
- A. McGuire
- K. Pierce
- D. Clemens

This team had fun, but their record wasn't so good.

Their record: 8-9

Dunsmuir 28, Modoc 16
Cunsmuir 28, Lassen 63
Dunsmuir 27, Tulelake 23
Dunsmuir 34, Butte Valley 36
Dunsmuir 24, Quincy 32
Dunsmuir 27, Las Plumas 49

Dunsmuir 60, Butte Valley 40
Dunsmuir 43, Fort Jones 38
Dunsmuir 28, Etna 36
Dunsmuir 49, Mt. Shasta 31
Dunsmuir 39, Happy Camp 37
Dunsmuir 31, Fort Jones 43
Dunsmuir 36, Mt. Shasta 45
Dunsmuir 35, Etna 37
Dunsmuir 50, Happy Camp 43
Dunsmuir 48, Fort Jones 40
Dunsmuir 46, Tulelake 47

1983-1984:

There was no varsity team; just a JV team in 1983.

Coach: Rinne
On the team was:
- C. Shields
- M. Williams
- R. Patrick
- C. Giacomelli
- C. Ballard
- S. Hall
- S. Rogers

VOLLEYBALL

Volleyball at Dunsmuir High School started in 1979. We were part of the Siskiyou County League, and the season ran through the winter. Doug Simpson coached both teams to co-championships with Weed.

In 1980 we played a winter season and again the following fall. In the winter both teams were league champs, and the Varsity won the Los Molinos Tournament in pre-season. In the fall, Linda Valenzuela became the JV coach and Dunsmuir joined the Evergreen League. The Varsity team was League champ. All-league players were: Nanette Christensen, Clayton Spinks, and Lisa Young. Nancy Orrell was the MVP. Dunsmuir was beaten at the TOC, but had the three girls named to the all CIF team.

In 1981, the Varsity lost to Tulelake in the league semi-finals. All-league players were Kristen Pierce and Lisa Young. The JV's were League Champs.

In 1982 there was no JV squad. Dunsmuir went undefeated in league. All-league players were Terri Pistorious and Bridget Mitchell, with Diana Clemens as MVP. Dunsmuir won the TOC and Diana Clemens was named to the all CIF squad, with Tammy Wilson as MVP. We advanced to the 3A-4A Tournament, where we were defeated.

In 1983, still we had no JV team and the Varsity placed 3rd in League. All-League players were Bridget Mitchell and Brenda Barnes.

In the five years the JV's played, they were league champs 3 times. The Varsity were Champions 3 times in 7 years, and they had won 1 out of 2 TOC championships.

TRACK
SINCE 1950

Track has been a fairly minor part of Dunsmuir's sports picture in most years. Weather problems and the lack of facilities have always been problems.

The better known coaches through the years since 1950 have been Lynn Elliot, Robert Shipley and an assortment of football and basketball coaches who took on track in the spring. Very often, no one was really interested in the sport. However, on May 18, 1976, Mike Kennedy set the meet and track record for shot put. Victor Padilla ran the 1½-mile in 8 minutes and 24 seconds.

BASEBALL
SINCE 1950

Baseball has always been one of the most popular sports at Dunsmuir; but, like Track, has often suffered because of our uncertain spring weather.

Coaches during these years have been Dave Blount, Walter Butcher, Dave Gobbato, Jim Bujol, Jim Harrington, and Ron Dolf.

Most years, Dunsmuir fielded a team, but the season was cancelled at least one time in the 60's because the field and fences were not in satisfactory condition and because of the weather.

In recent years, D.H.S. has had some outstanding baseball teams. Most notable was the 1981 season. We took the Evergreen League Championship and then went on to the North Section Play-offs, and captured the Small Schools Championship.

Over the years, the schedule has expanded. In the 50's and 60's, a normal season might include around eight games. It is now (1985) around twenty games.

TENNIS
SINCE 1950

Tennis is a fairly recent addition to interscholastic sports at Dunsmuir High School.

Though many students played tennis at school, there was no coach and no team as such before 1966, when Marian Nichols became coach at the request of players.

Mrs. Nichols continued coaching tennis until the mid-seventies, when Bill Birch took it over for a few years. Bert Norman coached one year, and James Rinne has been the coach since then.

Our tennis team has been quite successful, being league champions in the Boys, Girls or Team categories in most of the years since the late sixties.

The new tennis courts caved in to some extent in the late seventies, but the players still managed to do well, and that problem was finally solved.

CHEERLEADING

1950-1985

'50 — For 1950 the only information available is the name of a yell leader, SHIRLEY SMITH.

'51 — The cheerleaders in 1951 were MARY ELENA BACA, PHYLLIS BENDER and GRACE STANLEY.

'52 — DIONY ESTEP, MARIA BACA, and JOANNE FOURMET were the squad members in 1952.

'53 — The yell leaders in 1953 were DIANE BARBER and JOANN HALL.

'54 — The cheerleaders for 1954 were BETTY PALMER, JOAN IRVINE, AVERIEL GARRIOT, and JUDY SIRIANNI.

'55 — AVERIEL GARRIOT, VIRGINIA RODRIGUEZ, and DION SLADE were the cheerleaders in 1955, with DIANE BARBER as the head cheerleader. The songleaders were JOAN IRVINE and L. WHITLOCK.

'56 — In 1956 the yell leaders were KAY TUCKER and BETTY LOU AYOTTE, with head yell leader VIRGINIA RODRIGUEZ. The Mascots were LOUISE GIACOMELLI and RAYOLA HANLEN.

'57 — The head yell leader in 1957 was RAYOLA HANLEN. PAT McENEREY and WANDA WRIGHT were also yell leaders. Songleaders were JUDY PENMAN and ANN KILBORN.

'58 — The cheerleaders in 1958 were ANN KILBORN, NANCEE BURNS and PAT McENEREY was the head cheerleader.

'59 — The cheerleaders in 1959 were BONNIE BAUGHMAN, KAREN LEE, with NANCEE BURNS as head cheerleader. The songleaders were TERRI FAWCETT, SANDRA SMITH, and DONNA PARSONS.

'60 — The cheerleaders in 1960 were MARGARET WRIGHT, KAREN LEE, and MARY TOLIN. The songleaders were JOANNE ELMER, MARY LaBARRE, TERRI FAWCETT, and BECKY WOOD.

'61 — In 1961 the head cheerleader was BETH DEAN, with DARLENE WYLIE and SANDRA SMITH. The songleaders were LINDA LOCKHART, MARY LaBARRE, BECKY WOOD, and IRENE REA. The Mascots were DONNA PARSONS and NIKKI EDSON.

'62 — The songleaders for 1962 were DIANE LaBARRE, TERI INGERSOLL, PAM HARDIN, and IRENE REA. The yell leaders were JOANNE HANLEN and DIANA AYOTTE.

'63 — In 1963 the cheerleaders were PAT RODLEY, GLENDA PAGE and DIANA AYOTTE. The songleaders were SUE BARTON, PAM HARDIN, MARY LaBARRE, and LINDA LOCKHART.

'64 — In 1964 there were Varsity and Junior Varsity cheerleaders. The Varsity cheerleaders were CATHIE POE, TRUDI THOM, and CANDY EDSON. The JV's were MARIAN NAKAO, DIXIE INGERSOLL, and SARAH STAFFORD. The songleaders were CHRIS MURPHY, VICKI PETROVICS and SANDY ANDERSON.

'65 — The division of the squad in 1965 was similar to that in the previous year. The Varsity cheerleaders were SARAH STAFFORD, LINDA PADULA, and LORRAINE GRENVIK. The JV's were VIRGINIA DRAKE, DOLORES BRIENO, and JANICE WEEDON. The songleaders were DIXIE INGERSOLL, JANET EVANS, and SANDY ANDERSON. The three Mascots were JULIE LOWE, JAN SAUNDERS, and LOR ELLIS.

'66 — The Varsity cheerleaders in 1966 were MARIAN NAKAO, JANET EVANS, and DOLORES BRIENO. The JV's were VICKI FELKER, LINDA FULLER, and KATHY FISCHER, CHRISTINE RUSSELL, DONNA CROWE, and SUSIE COHEN were the songleaders. The Mascots were ANABELLE LAMM and GAIL BURGER. MRS. MARIAN NICHOLS became the cheerleader advisor and remained the advisor until 1983.

'67 — In 1967 the Varsity cheerleaders were CHRIS RUSSELL, JANICE WEEDON, and ROBERTA ANDERSON. The JV's were KATHY EVANS, CATHY KAY, and VIVIAN MASTERS. The songleaders were SUSAN COHEN and COLLEEN MEYER. The Mascots were CATHY HAYWARD and TERRY SNEAD.

'68 — The cheerleaders were ROBERTA ANDERSON, LINDA FULLER, KATHY EVANS, ANNE MURRAY, NANCY ELGIN, and PEGGY HOMER.

'69 — In 1969, the songleaders were ANNE KELBY, HELEN DIXON, and DEBBIE CLARK. The cheerleaders were PAM McGAUGH, KAY TALLERICO, and SALLY SPENCER for the JV's. The Varsity cheerleaders were PEGGY HOLMER, NANCY ELGIN, and ANNE MURRAY. The Mascots were JANICE HAMPTON and SHARON VAUGHN.

'70 — The members of the 1970 squad were VICKI SUMMERS, LORI LEVIE, FELICIA CHAPPELL, SHIRLEY MANFREDI, EVA FRAGA, JUDY HUNTER, and LORIE MADISON.

'71 — In 1971, the Varsity and JV cheerleaders and songleaders were JO FAUBER, SALLY SPENCER, LESLIE FULLER, ERIN SULLIVAN, LINDA STOKER, LINDA FEBRERO, CAMILLE CARLQUIST, DEBBIE CLARK, PAM McGAUGH, ELAINE PADULA, DARLENE MEYER, and CINDY CONNELLY. Mascots were MICHELLE LANCASTER and ESTHER SMITH.

'72 — The Varsity cheerleaders were MARGO ZANOTTO, LORIE STROBLE, and MARY SULLIVAN. The JV cheerleaders were LISA MELFY, DOROTHY BOGART, and MARGARET WILEY. The songleaders included MARGARET WILEY, MARCI PEREZ, DENISE YOUNG, and KAREN KLEAVER. The Mascots were EVELYN KENT and ESTHER SMITH.

'73 — The cheerleaders for 1973 were ROSIE PON, COLLEEN SANTANA, LORIE STROBLE, LISA MILLER, and MARCI PEREZ. The JV cheerleaders were VICKI SUMMERS, LORIE MADISON, and C. JACOBSON.

'74 — The members of the 1974 squad were VICKI SUMMERS, LORIE LEVIE, FELICIA CHAPPELL, SHARON MANFREDI, EVA FRAGA, LONNIE MOORE, LORIE MADISON, and JUDY HUNTER.

'75 — The members of the 1974 squad were VICKI SUMMERS, LORIE LEVIE, FELICIA CHAPPELL, SHARON MANFREDI, and DAWN CHAPPELL.

'76 — The cheerleaders in 1976 were EVA FRAGA, FELICIA CHAPPELL, SHARON MANFREDI, and LYNN ALAMEDA. The songleaders were TAMMY JONES, HEIDI BELOW, MARI ZANOTTO, and JUDY HUNTER.

'77 — The songleaders for 1977 were SUSAN DEWEY, COREY ROSSETTO, LUCILLE HOPKINS, and MARI ZANOTTO. The cheerleaders were DENISE CROWE, SUSAN DUNGAN, and CATHY SPENO.

'78 — The cheerleaders were DENISE CROWE, CAROLYN WRIGHT, LYNN ALAMEDA, and JEANNIE DOUGLAS. The songleaders were SUSAN DEWEY, COREY ROSSETTO, SUSAN DUNGAN, and HOLLY CHARLES.

'79 — The cheerleaders were KRISTI KLEAVER, DENISE CROWE, COREY ROSSETTO, COREY WAGNER, and JOLENE HARRIS.

'80 — The squad members in 1980 were NANETTE CHRISTENSEN, KRISTI KLEAVER, BRIGHT NICHOLS, COREY WAGNER, ANITA PADULA, and TAMIE WADE.

'82 — JILL HARRIS, STACIE DRAGMIRE. MARLA McDONALD, CAMI GIACOMELLI and head cheerleader BRIGHT NICHOLS were the squad for 1982.,

'83 — The cheerleaders in 1983 were JILL HARRIS, STACIE DRAGMIRE, MARLA McDONALD, CAMI GIACOMELLI, and DEBBIE SALMON.

'84 — In 1984 the Football cheerleaders were ADRIANNE ARATA, MARSHA MILLER, MICHELE MITCHELL, BECKY SMITH, BRENDA FLOYD, and RENEE GORSUCH. The Basketball cheerleaders were ADRIANNE ARATA, MARSHA MILLER, MICHELLE MILLER, BECKY SMITH, BRIDGET MITCHELL and LINDA LACUNZA. Their advisor was COREY LINARES.

'85 — The Football cheerleaders for 1985 were ADRIANNE ARATA, MARSHA MILLER, MICHELLE MITCHELL, KIRSTEN SKINNER, and KIM VAN HEEST. The Basketball cheerleaders were MICHELLE MITCHELL, KIM VAN HEEST, LESLIE WHITE, ADRIANE DAY, and SHELLIE KIRBY. Their advisor was COREY LINARES.

Front row (left to right): Debby Heiser, President of Class; Michelle Cox; Malena Sandoval, Representative to SIP; Mark Manfredi, Representative to Board of Trustees; Gus Martinez, Vice-President; Joe Hatten, Randy Belzer, John Data.

Second row: Heather Wood, Jackie Mitchell, Becky Smith; Marsha Miller, Secretary-Treasurer; Wendy Williams, Sheila Myers, Kim Sleezer, Michelle Mitchell, Shellie Kirby, Kristina Jones; Michele Rovai, Editor of 1986 Year Book; Martin Jimenez.

Third row: Nolberta Pizano, Roxanne Kay, Tony Miller, Craig Lohbeck, Jeff Pierce, Jerry Brown, David Routt, Bret Barnes; Don Crawford, Student Body President; David Wagner, Kim VanHeest, Ross Taylor, Mike Young, Brad Townsend.

NOT PICTURED: Kevin Connor, Jim Powell, Lorie Wade, Leslie White

ADVISORS (Not Pictured): Connie Crawford, Mark Reiner.

DHS CENTENNIAL GRADUATING CLASS — 1986

A SPORTING ANGLER'S DUNSMUIR

By Larry Green

Visiting anglers who look to the city of Dunsmuir as a sort of nucleus or base of operations for their annual summer fishing vacations might be very surprised to learn that a much broader, more encompassing range of diversified fishing actually exists within a relatively close proximity of this quaint little mountain community. From Dunsmuir itself, a visiting fisherman unfamiliar with the surrounding country might gaze at the canyons of the Sacramento River or the rugged, surrounding mountains with its unique rocky crags and surmise that this is strictly trout fishing country. Well, they would be only half right. Dunsmuir is the nucleus for some of the most spectacular trout fishing lakes and streams found anywhere in the western hemisphere. But it is also a lot more. There are other fisheries existing here besides trout.

Lying within some picture postcard pretty valleys and saddles of the slightly lower elevation ranges are lakes that support healthy populations of warm water game fish as well as trout. Game fish like largemouth and smallmouth black bass, crappie, sunfish and several species of catfish are in lakes that are but a short drive from Dunsmuir.

If you are an ardent black bass fisherman, you'll find it only a 30-minute drive south of Dunsmuir to the Antler's public launch ramp on the Sacramento River arm of Shasta Lake, where both largemouth as well as smallmouth bass provide almost year-round action for serious bass anglers. Lake Shasta is also noted for its fine catches of land-locked king salmon, Kamloop lake trout, rainbow and browns. But sharing the warm water bill with smallmouth and largemouth bass are the crappie, sunfish, catfish and even sturgeon.

North of Dunsmuir there are several close-in lakes that host warm water as well as cold water fisheries. Siskiyou Lake, just west of Mt. Shasta and merely a dozen miles from Dunsmuir, hosts both smallmouth and some lunker size largemouth bass, crappie, sunfish and catfish as well as brown, rainbow and brook trout. While the majority of the big bass come from the finger coves in the early fall, the catfish come from the north bank shallows, principally at night.

Siskiyou's lunker, brown, and rainbow trout generally come from the south end around Box Canyon Dam. Just seven miles north and east of the town of Weed, Dwenell Reservoir, more recently called Lake Shastina, started turning heads of serious bass fishermen, when by 1980 its populations of black bass reached noticeable numbers, enough to produce some eye-catching limits of husky black bass. Shastina is another of those close-in lakes with a greatly diverse fishery. Trout, catfish, bass or pan fish — it's all here at Lake Shastina,

which is open year-round for anglers.

One of the least known bass lakes close to Dunsmuir is a little, off-the-road lake called Hammond Lake, which is off of Old Stage Road, due west of Black Butte Mountain. There are so many largemouth bass in this little lake that they have actually stunted themselves, and thus the average largemouth is from six inches to ¾-pound. But a prettier bass lake you'll never see, as majestic Mt. Shasta rises out of the east to form a most perfect picture postcard setting over little Hammond Lake. Big catfish are known to be in Hammond Lake as well.

North of Weed, on the I-5 Highway, there are a couple of pothole lakes that also hold the promise of some good bass fishing, and these are only about a 30- to 40-minute drive north of Dunsmuir right off the I-5 north highway. If you're a winter steelhead or salmon fisherman, remember that it's just about an hour's drive to the Collier rest stop off the I-5 and the Klamath River, where each fall and winter season migratory salmon and steelhead come to the headwaters of this mighty steelhead stream.

But of all the diversified fishing that is within easy reach of the city of Dunsmuir, naturally it is the fishing of wild, native trout that is Dunsmuir's biggest drawing card for anglers, particularly the summer vacationing fishermen. The Upper Sacramento River, a stream many consider to be yet the finest 50 miles of fishable trout waters in all of California, flows within spitting distance of downtown Dunsmuir, and here in the canyons adjacent to the railroad tracks, a river rich with native rainbow and some brown trout provides great fishing during the regular summer trout season.

But it is not just the Upper Sacramento River that spawns Dunsmuir's fishing interests, it is dozens of little and large tributary feeder streams that fall from the mountain ranges of Shasta and Siskiyou Counties, which also host a variety of generally smaller size, but highly spirited and colorful trout. Feeder streams like Castle Creek, Little Castle Creek, Flume Creek, Dog Creek, Hazel Creek, Simms Creek, and many more fine, fishable trout waters can be found here.

If you could drop right over the mountain east of Dunsmuir, you would drop in on the Lower McCloud River below the McCloud Dam, and here lunker size trout abound, particularly for catch and release fly fishermen who work the Nature Conservancy section of the lower river. McCloud Reservoir is loaded with beautiful trout, as are some of its little known feeder streams.

Above McCloud Reservoir lies the Upper McCloud River with some fine native fish. East of Bartle yet, you'll come to Bear Creek, a stream worthy of your exploring, as is Antelope Creek north of highway #89

and northeast of McCloud. There are dozens of other interesting and highly productive trout streams and tiny creeks that flow in all four directions of the compass across lava rock, clover meadows, thick forests and open terrain, all of which offer a great challenge to summer stream trout fishermen who do not mind the short trip out a few miles from the town of Dunsmuir.

As to the fine trout lakes around Dunsmuir, they are almost too numerous to mention. Among the favorites outside of many of those already mentioned are some of the less conspicuous, better fishing lakes. Some like Castle Lake, a charmer of a crystal clear, high mountain lake lying in the rocky saddle behind majestic Castle Crags. Some of these lakes can be driven right up to on good roads, yet others like Toad Lake, Gumboot, and those further back in the Eddy range of mountains require either four-wheel drives or a jeep.

The color of some of the 14- to 20-inch eastern brookies within these waters will knock your eyes out. The further you venture westward into the Trinity and Marble mountain ranges, the more lakes you bump into, all of which are loaded with trout and regularly stocked by aircraft manned by California Department of Fish and Game crews.

The fingerling and fry trout, rainbows, browns, brookies, and Eagle Lake strain come from the famous Mt. Shasta State Fish Hatchery, which was the first and is still the oldest hatchery in California. The hatchery is a wonderful tourist attraction for visiting anglers, but it serves a much more important factor than tourism.

The beautiful trout, raised healthy and fat in Mt. Shasta's icy cold water ponds, are regularly planted in virtually all of the major trout waters accessible by truck in and about the Dunsmuir area as well as many far reaching areas. Lakes, streams, and rivers receive heavy plantings throughout the regular summer trout fishing season and provide a much needed host to the sometimes heavy fishing pressure that is placed upon trout waters within the Dunsmuir area.

These fat, sassy, catchable trout help supplement catch factors by anglers who fish other than for principally native trout. Naturally, the heaviest stockings occur in the heaviest summer use areas like parks, campgrounds, and town sites. As you may gather from this all too brief synopsis of Dunsmuir fishing potentials, it is a community that serves as a true nucleus from which ardent anglers of every means can strike out to all points of the compass and find wonderful, diverse fishing from as close as 150 feet, in the case of the Upper Sacramento River and downtown Dunsmuir, to the Upper Klamath River some 50 or so miles north of Dunsmuir on the I-5 highway.

Yes, Dunsmuir is in the heart of some of the finest trout fishing in all of the western hemisphere. But there's a lot more fishing around Dunsmuir, which includes warm water as well as cold water fisheries.

Time and space do not allow more, for in truth you could fill volumes of writing if you were to thoroughly cover all that is offered to anglers centering just around Dunsmuir. Hopefully, we have opened your eyes as to just a few of the great fishing potentials you may not otherwise ever have known existed in and around Dunsmuir.

A SPORTING HUNTER'S DUNSMUIR

By Larry Green

If you look on a map of northern California for the town of Dunsmuir, you would discover that Dunsmuir sits almost on the border, smack in the middle between Siskiyou and Shasta Counties, with Trinity County lying to the west and both Modoc and Lassen Counties lying to the east. Combined, these five counties comprise the greatest wealth of hunting lands, where numerous species of animals as well as game birds make their habitats. And Dunsmuir sits smack in the middle of it all, serviced by the major I-5 highway and Amtrak rail service.

Is it any wonder why so many avid sports hunters like myself choose Dunsmuir as a retirement area? Dunsmuir serves as a springboard for the diversified hunters who love all forms of sport hunting, be it big game, small game, predator, waterfowl or upland game birds. It is all hit within an easy striking distance of this quaint mountain community. The surrounding countryside abounds with deer, and many of this state's biggest bucks come from districts in zones that lie within a close drive of Dunsmuir.

The start of the hunting season around Dunsmuir begins late in the summer with the archery deer season, then into fall with the rifle season. Around Dunsmuir you get a mix of mule and blacktail deer, thick of horn and beautiful of hide. Often during the course of the season you will hear the echo of a rifle shot from town, meaning that close by perhaps, some lucky hunter bagged his buck.

As the madrone berries and choke cherries ripen in the fall, migratory flocks of bandtail pigeons often blacken the skies over Dunsmuir as they fly up the canyon between the high mountain ridges above the Upper Sacramento River. Migrating dove pass by these same narrow canyons and provide good shooting sport as well. One of the saddles in the mountains west of Castella and near the Crags is reputed to be one of the best bandtail pigeon hunting spots in all of northern California.

While both bandtails and dove are only seasonal, migratory visitors, Dunsmuir has many of its own resident game birds as well. The beautiful blue or mountain grouse are everywhere in the surrounding mountains, and even thicker yet are the quail. Around Dunsmuir, especially along the old logging roads, scads of quail can be seen each morning and evening, either filling their craw with gravel or dusting themselves in the red road dust on these logging trails. The two species that abound for hunters around Dunsmuir are the mountain quail, identified by their handsome, high quills atop their head; and the smaller valley quail, with their shorter but stockier topknotch that leans forward in a solid black curl.

Fast of wing and delicious in the pot, both the mountain quail and the valley quail provide top gunning sport for upland game bird shooters. There are pheasant, too, but you have to go north or south some 50 miles to get into good ringneck shooting, as is true with waterfowl.

Ducks and geese can rarely be seen moving directly over the town, but the principal waterfowl flyways are north towards Tule Lake and Klamath refuges and east towards the Pit River. In fact, the Fall River Valley, just a few miles east out on highway #89, has some of the best Canadian honker shooting of anyplace in the state. But if you know the pothole hangouts of puddle ducks, you can enjoy some wonderful jump shooting for mallard, sprig, teal and woodducks just minutes from Dunsmuir.

The most exciting and often the toughest hunting of all that occurs in two different seasons, one in the spring and another in the fall, is for wild turkeys. Once thought to range only as far north as Shasta Lake, more recently wild turkeys, with some help from the Department of Fish and Game planting crews, now range north and east of Dunsmuir and are, in fact, well spread in those mountains just east of town. Wild turkey — now there's a challenge for you.

If it's varmints or predators you seek, you only have to look north above Weed and Shasta Valley for an abundance of woodchucks, coyotes, some bobcat and cougar, though now protected by law. The Eddy mountain ranges just north and west of Dunsmuir, clear over to the Marble mountains and Trinity mountains, hold greater populations of bear than any other given acreage in the western United States for black bear. Bear hunting is big and highly successful for hunters who know how to track bear in these mountains.

As for smaller fur bearers like either brush bunnies or cottontails, you'll see plenty of those cross your path if you travel some of the off roads and logging trails around Dunsmuir in the early morning and late evening. If it's a crow shoot you're after, there are plenty of black crows, but try to outsmart them without a stuffed owl decoy if you can.

Ferral pigs, a cross between a true wild boar and a domesticated pig, are now ranging far north of their original flatlands ranges in the Upper Valley east of Red Bluff and Redding. Wild pigs have been signted as close as ten miles south of Dunsmuir, and numerous pigs along with wild turkeys are hunted at the northernmost end of Shasta Lake between the Sacramento, Squaw and Pit River arms of the lake. Dunsmuir is a community that is centered in the heart of country that abounds with wildlife, much of it to the flavor of seasonal sport hunters, but not all.

Much of Dunsmuir's wildlife is to be only admired by nature lovers and bird watchers. Rare birds, like the famed pileated woodpeckers and the more common osprey, eagles and ravens are everywhere along the Upper Sacramento River, as are the beautiful, if not destructive, hood mergensers, great blue herons, and egrets.

Colorful belted kingfishers and nervous little dippers are all along the river banks and tributary streams everywhere. Hawks and turkey vultures soar on updrafting currents high above the mountains, as do the ospreys along the river. Beaver, otters, minks, ferrets, weasels, raccoons, skunks, possums and martins also utilize the river and help broaden the spectrum of Dunsmuir's wildlife in action.

The highlight of road kills on the I-5 near Dunsmuir gives some clue to the abundance of wildlife around Dunsmuir. But to see this wildlife and to enjoy it in its natural habitat, you must venture out of town in any direction, and just keep your eyes and ears open, because the sights and sounds of wildlife abound around Dunsmuir. And it stirs the hearts of nature lovers as much or more than sporting hunters who come to test their skills during the legal seasons.

Be you hunter, photographer or just appreciator of wildlife in their natural habitats, Dunsmuir would be a fine nest from which you could venture out in a thousand directions to discover birds and animals so numerous that it bogs the imagination. No, you may never see that big buck come deer season, but I'll venture to say you'll see him often the remainder of the year. Dunsmuir is truly a sport hunter's paradise, if you are a hunter who pleasures most in diversity.

DUNSMUIR REMEMBERS THE LATE LEGENDARY TED FAY

By Larry Green

Dunsmuir's own Ted Fay
—Photo by Larry Green

Near the entrance to the picnic grounds of Dunsmuir's picturesque City Park, a large boulder stands erect within sight and sound of the Upper Sacramento River. Permanently embedded in this rock is a beautiful bronze plaque donated by the Siskiyou Fly Fishers and the Shasta Cascade Wonderland Association which pays a high tribute to a long-time Dunsmuir resident, whose dedication to fly fishing for trout on this river over many years earned this gentleman angler national recognition for his angling skills and conservation ethics: Dunsmuir's own Ted Fay. He is also paid tribute to in the National Fishing Hall of Fame.

Few people outside of Ted's close friends (of which there were many) fully realize how Ted Fay's fishing exploits locally so helped to put the Upper Sacramento River and the city of Dunsmuir on the map. Ted Fay was born in 1904 and died in Dunsmuir in January of 1983. Ted Fay came to Dunsmuir because of its exceptional trout fishing in the mid-1930's. In the early 1950's he, along with his wife, Lillian, and their children, Shirley F. Mazzei and Mike, opened and operated the Lookout Point Motel, once located at the north end of Dunsmuir Avenue.

During Fays' long reign as proprietors of that motel, Ted developed a unique and deadly effective method for catching the native trout out of the Upper Sacramento River by using two home-tied, weighted wet flies on a dropper leader. Ted's technique was to move upriver against the currents and then, using a fly rod, he'd make short casts, dropping the two wet flies into the pocket waters within this river, which is where most of the big fish lie.

Ted Fay's method of trout fishing was so effective that he began to receive national recognition for his angling skills, and thus over the years thousands of people who read accounts of Ted's angling skills on this river through newspaper, magazine, film and other national media coverage, flocked to Dunsmuir to fish with this trout fishing sensation named Ted Fay. After Ted and his wife, Lillian, lost their then famous Lookout Point Motel to the state for a freeway entrance (which was never built), Ted decided to open a fly shop adjacent to their new home further down the street, at 4154 Dunsmuir Avenue.

Before that, Ted had made it customary to take his motel guests fishing, acting as a guide. But by now his clientele had grown so that two close friends, Jim Murray of Mt. Shasta and long-time associate as well as friend, Joe Kimsey, of Dunsmuir, hired on as river guides to help Ted carry the load now put on his quaint little Ted Fay Fly Shop, which, incidentally, still serves angling customers, many of whom first learned to fish with Ted on the Upper Sacramento River.

Soon after moving into the home and fly shop, Lillian Fay, Ted's wife, became ill and passed away. She was a lovely lady with a big heart, and her passing emptied much of Ted's spirit until his own health began to go bad. Ted Fay, Dunsmuir's legendary fly fisherman, himself passed on in January of 1983. For awhile his close and trusted friends, Jim Murray and Joe Kimsey, kept his little fly shop open to serve Ted's faithful customers. This was until Ted's vacant home was finally sold. Everyone who had ever known Ted Fay mourned over the fate of the little, friendly fly shop that had by now earned national recognition.

But Joe Kimsey and Jim Murray vowed not to let Dunsmuir's summer trout anglers down, and thus in the summer of 1984 decided to open a brand new fly shop adjacent to the Garden Motel, just south of the old fly shop's location on Dunsmuir Avenue. And yes, the name, as a tribute to Ted's memory, still remains "The Ted Fay Fly Shop," where they still sell the same weighted wet flies used by Ted Fay. Joe Kimsey and Jim Murray continue to take big trout out of both the Upper Sacramento River and the Lower McCloud River with the same proficiency.

The guide service also remains the same, and thus the name Ted Fay and a long-standing tradition remains alive today in more than just memory. As a personal note to the legend of Ted Fay, I would like to add that as a close fishing friend of some 25 years, I remember best Ted's warmth, wit, and friendly manner in addition to this uncanny fishing skills. A skillful wader who knew every rock, riffle, and pool in this river, Ted's growing concerns for the conservation and preservation of the Upper Sacramento River and its fishery are something I, too, remember.

In his later years, Ted adopted and preached for the catch and release of these handsome, native Sacramento River rainbows. On numerous occasions while fishing together, Ted had expressed to me how his *only wish* was to remain close to the river he'd loved and respected for more than 50 years of his life. If you go to Dunsmuir's City Park, see and read the bronze plaque left in Ted Fay's memory. I think you'd agree with me that Ted Fay did indeed have his final wish fulfilled. It is a fitting tribute to a gentleman angler who contributed so much to the town of Dunsmuir.

CHAPTER XII

THE SAGA OF UPPER SODA AND CAVE SPRINGS

By
Louie Dewey

A SHORT HISTORY OF CAVE SPRINGS
1922 — 1985

Before all is said and done, one fact about CAVE SPRINGS stands out above all others. It was built on the backs of the women associated with it.

This should come as no surprise since the lodging industry from the biggest hotel chain down to the smallest bed and breakfast house traditionally, and to this day, exclusively relies on women to provide its most important products — a bed with clean, crisp sheets and a sanitized bathroom! In thirty-seven years of close association with motels and hotels, I have never seen a male maid. This could change as the culture changes, but until then, the female's traditional role of homemaker continues to provide the training and mental conditioning which make a top-quality maid.

When a good homemaker decides to go into a family-run motel business, she may not realize it, but she has just chosen a career as a professional maid. Cave Springs was no exception to this rule. This is not such a bad situation for a child of the depression and a war bride to boot . . . like my mom.

Being a professional maid with executive privileges right after World War II was a dubious honor. Most of the time was spent cleaning toilets and making beds and the fringe benefits were the abilities to watch four kids all day at the same time and be a desk clerk half the night. In fact, over 98% of the work was menial labor. When it came to the two percent of executive decision, Mom would consult with Dad, and they would make the decision together. Today, this sounds a little less than idyllic. However, at the time, it was a great way to make a living at what most other middle-class women were doing for free. Furthermore, when my mom and dad, Bob and Lois Dewey, got into the motel business with their partners, Johnny and Joalice Richards, they were going to make a small fortune in a few years and then sell out. The average length of ownership of a motel is right around five years. That was four decades ago, and the second generation is now running the same motel. The only difference is that this generation of women is college educated and very much aware of the traditional division of labor. That means, as you have probably guessed, that this man cleans toilets and makes beds!

But now I am way ahead of myself. Back when the history of this motel began, division of labor was a term used only by Henry Ford and the Marxists of the ghettos and coffee houses in central and eastern Europe. Automobiles were still a novelty and the steam engine was pressing into every frontier.

Cave Springs started out as Brown's Auto Camp, which was built by Clint and Ida May Brown. They were both early immigrants to Dunsmuir. In fact, Clint came to Dunsmuir when it was called Pusher and there was only one house in the town. His parents, Manley and Lucetta Brown, were frontier entrepreneurs who were born and raised in New York. Manley was 26 and Lucetta was 23 when they married, and shortly thereafter left to seek their fortunes across the Great Plains in California. This was around 1866, and Manley embarked for the Sandwich Islands for a time. It is not known if Lucetta went with him, but in the years after he returned, they settled in French Gulch and became miners, moved to Lewiston and operated a butcher business, and traveled up the Pit River to where it crossed the Oregon Trail to run the ferry there. Clint was born at that ferry crossing in 1875.

The family grew to five and left the Pit River to follow the railhead up from Redding to Pusher. They operated a store and saloon at the railhead, moving three times before arriving in town in 1885. One can only imagine how strong and resilient Lucetta must have been — raising three kids in conditions which can only be compared to camping today. Constantly migrating from home to home and living with a man whose reputation preceded him. In fact, before Manley arrived in Pusher, he seemed to be prone to carousing; and some said this was why he had not made his fortune already. Apparently, Clint and his brother had to fetch their dad from the bawdy houses of Redding more than once. Somewhere between Pit River and Pusher, Manley lost that reputation. It may have been a natural change in his life cycle or the fact that his family needed a place to grow up. It is highly likely that Lucetta told him that this was it, "No more moving!"

They settled for good in Pusher and soon after the town changed its name to Dunsmuir. Manley had a reputation in town of caring more for his family than anything else. He was upright and honorable and maintained a quiet disposition. His three children graduated from Dunsmuir Grammar School. They better have, because he built the school for the town at his own expense. He and a partner, Frank Marin-covich, also built the town's first hotel, The Dunsmuir. Before he died in 1901, he acquired or built several other houses and buildings. That he loved his family a great deal, cannot be in doubt. In the dedication page to the Brown family is a picture of him with his family. His daughter, Ella, has her baby girl on her lap and her son stands behind her. Both children are illegitimate and living in grandpa and grandma's house.

After Clint graduated from grammar school, he worked for the McCloud River Lumber Company. His standard policy was to quit work for deer season and head into the woods. He loved to fish, and especially if he could talk a pretty little girl named Ida May Beaton into going with him. Even after they were married, hunting and fishing remained his passions and often provided a supplement to their income. He became locally well-known for his abilities, and many stories were told of him and by him.

He loved to bet that he could catch his limit of fifty fish in an hour or two. Now days, that seems like a ridiculous feat. But at the turn of the century, it was not impossible. First-hand reports claim that the fish were, in general, much smaller then, but much more plentiful. One of Clint's "secret" techniques was to open one of the little cans of salmon eggs (salmon eggs were packed in small tin cans then instead of the glass jars used today). He would then scatter the eggs across a riffle in the river and sit on a rock and smoke his pipe. The length of time it took to smoke one pipe full of tobacco was just exactly how long it took the fish to work up to what Clint referred to as a "frenzy." He could then hook two or three fish with every cast. There can be little doubt about the effectiveness of that "secret" technique. It is called chumming and is very illegal now!

One time, when Clint was working at the store in Shasta Retreat, a fisherman came up to him, disgusted because the fish just weren't biting. Fishing was lousy. Clint tried to tell the gentleman that the fishing had never been better. When the man refused to be convinced, Clint offered to prove it — for a small wager. He came back an hour later with his limit and the disgruntled fisherman paid off the bet and packed up his bags and left.

Marrying Ida May seems to be the turning point in Clint's life. He certainly did not give up his sportsman's life, but he did curtail it by following his father's footsteps into business; or maybe they followed Ida

May's father's footsteps. Her father and mother, John and Lina Beaton, had also operated a hotel. In fact, her parents had many of the same experiences that Clint's parents did.

John Beaton was born and raised in Quebec, Canada. He just barely escaped from that country when he was forced to leave for what he claimed were "political reasons." He traveled down the east coast by boat, crossed the Isthmus of Panama by pack animal, sailed up the west coast, and stopped in California at a little town in Placer County, called Iowa Hill. If you think he became another gold miner, you are absolutely correct! He formed a partnership in a mine with his uncle and at age 23 courted and married Lina Frischgeselle. She was 16.

Lina was as strong a woman as Lucetta was. Being a miner's wife was no easy matter. Like Manley, John had a drinking problem. It is safe to say that a move toward domestication was just as much a reason as any other for John to sell out his interest in the mine and purchase the Iowa Hill Hotel. There, they raised six kids until a fire burned them out in the late 1890's. John and Lina packed up the kids and moved to Sacramento, where John got a job with the Southern Pacific. The S.P. relocated them in Dunsmuir at the turn of the century. Ida May worked in the public library and, in addition to being a real cutie, was the new girl in town. Clint never had a chance. It took them two years to make it official, and they were married in 1903.

Clint secured a loan from the Bank of Dunsmuir and lit off for San Francisco to business college. After two years, he returned to Dunsmuir and bought land from the Shasta Retreat Company. They built a store and several summer cottages for the fishermen, and they won the post office contract. This was pre-highway America and most of the travel was done by train. It could be a three- or four-day drive to Redding by wagon or horseless carriage. In the winter, the trip was just not possible. Only essential traffic moved by rail, and that was susceptible to killer snowstorms. All of the summer resorts along the tracks just boarded up the windows and closed down till the spring thaw, usually some time in April. So Clint and Ida May spent their winters in Sacramento, where Clint worked in a grocery store.

When the Shasta Retreat Company failed, Clint took over the balance of the property as receiver. They had two children, Ken and Aileen, and bought their first car, a Cross-Country Rambler. Clint did not learn how to drive it till the end of summer when they headed out for the winter. In the meantime, he let Charlie (Pete) Masson drive it all summer. Charlie ran the Upper Soda Springs Resort and used the car to take guests on tours of the area. At that time, the road was the old California-Oregon trail and express route. It ran right by Upper Soda Springs, which was in the flat land under the existing highway bridge, went uphill along what is now Old Stage Road, continued north over the hill and alongside what is now the tennis courts, and entered Cave Springs. It passed through Cave Springs down the existing road and out the present entrance. It is still possible to see some of the old road; but most of it has disappeared.

The Browns had a reputation for knock-down, drag-out arguments, but in 1914 they had a real dooser. It went on for days and weeks. Clint wanted to buy Castle Crags Resort. It had been the Crocker family mansion and was now being operated unsuccessfully as a resort. Clint thought he could make it a profitable business. Ida May didn't agree, but she didn't exactly win the argument either. Late that year, they leased the store and cabins to a newly revived Shasta Retreat Company and lived on the proceeds for a year. In 1916, they took over the management of Castle Crags Resort. Ida May had at least convinced Clint not to buy the place outright. This proved to be a small stroke of genius or some very good luck.

At that time, almost all resorts or hotels were along the railroad tracks or in towns. The rest were destination places like dude ranches. There were many little resorts in the Sacramento River canyon, and the train would stop at all of them. It would also stop at scenic spots like Mossbrae Falls, and there were water stops and fuel stops and stops in every little town for mail pick-up. It was common for fishermen to ride the train from Shasta Retreat up the river to Cantera Loop. It cost them a dime and they could fish all the way home. Everyone rode the train. And then came the AUTOMOBILE.

Clint was convinced that people were going to start traveling more by car and that they would need a place to stay where they could drive to easily and have plenty of room to park. Automobile travelers were camping for lack of a place to stay, and campgrounds that catered to them were springing up all around the county. Tent sites or tent platforms and single-walled cabins offered water, wood, and cots or beds. You had to bring your own linen and leave a deposit, which was returned if you left your place clean.

Charlie Masson's place at Upper Soda Springs reflected these changes as it was bypassed when the highway bridge was completed in 1916. In need of some money, he offered to sell Clint the half of a quarter of a quarter of a section of land where the old express route leveled out above the swampy meadow and joined the highway. It was actually Elda Masson's property.

Clint was in need of a change because his duties at Castle Crags had become too difficult for him to handle. While on the way out of the doctor's office, he slipped and fell down some stairs, breaking his arm near the shoulder. It was very painful and complications from the injury bothered him for the rest of his life. Another big fight dominated the Browns' domestic scene for awhile, and Ida May lost again.

They bought the property for around $2500 in 1922. It was already being used as an occasional campground by travelers. The only building on it was an old Indian shack that was located near what is now cabin #8. The Indians called the place Cave Springs because there was a soda water springs near the large mouth of a very short cave by the river. Clint's sister and her husband operated the property as a campground with showers and toilets until the Browns could move there three years later.

In 1925, the first six cabins and some tent platforms were built along the river. A store and a home were built next to the highway where the pool is now. The next year, the tent platforms were converted to double cabins and some small cabins without bathrooms were added at the top of the hill along the old road. The community bathroom, showers, and laundry were right next to the vista point and across the road was an old donkey boiler that had to be stoked with wood every morning to have any hot water.

The construction was pretty simple. The water main passed right in front of their property. Wood was readily available for heating and cooking, although they did put an oil-burning heater in the house. There were even some wood stoves in the camping area. All but the row of cabins that were built along the side of the highway where the Chevron service station is now, were of California Box-type construction. They have no studs and, therefore, no room for insulation. The outside boards are nailed to the floor plate and ceiling plate, and the ceiling joists keep the walls from falling outward. The walls were only one board thick with occasional glimpses of light through the cracks until the late thirties, when the inside plywood paneling was added. The foundations were even simpler — several large rocks and an occasional, conveniently-located tree stump. The roofs were cedar shake shingles. They have all been well-maintained and most of the original structures, including some of the original roofs are still in use today.

Natural soda water was much more popular than it is today. People drank it because they thought it cured a myriad number of ills. They drank it because it was unique or because they liked it or because they didn't like it. Clint felt that the steep path to the spring at the river was too far for people to have to go for a drink of water. He installed a pump at the river in 1926 to pump soda water at about a gallon a minute up the cliff to the front of his place. He tried several pumps before finding one that would do the job and be reliable. Since then, every kind of pump imaginable has been tried to replace that antique Montgomery Ward reciprocating pump. None of them have been up to the task and the original pump many times restored is still doing the job every summer.

In 1929, the Browns granted some land to the state to expand the highway in front of their place. They now had thirty units and a campground. It was called Brown's Auto Camp, later changed to Brown's Auto Park, and still later changed to Brown's

Modern Motor Lodge. Clint's hunting and fishing were curtailed because of his injured arm, but he still managed to bring home some trout. Ida May established a reputation around town as being always friendly. Brown's Auto Park struggled through the depression by becoming a campground again. Travelers could get a hot shower and wood for their fires for $.50 a night. This was much less than the prevailing price of $1.00 for a single cabin or $1.50 for a double cabin. In the thirties, natural gas came to Dunsmuir and the existing gas heaters and gas stoves were installed. And Clint gave up on life.

In 1936, this robust outdoorsman, his body racked with a constant pain from his arm and shoulder, rigged a shotgun in the fork of the tree where I built my first treehouse, and blew his brains out.

Ida May's sister, Maude Lina, came up from Sacramento to help run the lodge. They let a hired couple manage the place for awhile after Clint's death, but had to fire them because of loafing. They then ran the place by themselves, hiring only maids and night clerks. They would do all of the book-keeping and purchasing and daytime office work. Ida May's cheerful disposition was put to good use here. Weary travelers are often not in the best mood when they arrive at a motel. It is as important to be pleasant and accommodating as it is to provide them with a comfortable room. Most of the business at that time was overnight stays, but there were a growing number of regulars who stayed a week or more. Those are the people who became Ida May's and Maude's friends and who looked forward to their annual visit with the sisters as much as they anticipated their stay in the cool of the mountains. The cool of the mountains was the main reason for vacations and trips into this country. Fishing, scenery, soda water, good friends, mountain walks, etc., were each important to the magic of the area, but in an era without air conditioning, escaping the constant heat of the Sacramento Valley was the biggest attraction Dunsmuir had.

In 1942, 1943, and 1944, everyone decided to stay in the heat and fight the war. Gas rationing and the war effort caused the resort to stay closed. The sisters never returned to open the resort again. Ida May died of a stroke in 1944.

The Ida Brown estate sold the place to August and Irma Turner. They were farmers from Tulelake who needed a tax write-off, but neither of them were in good health. In one summer they tried to run the business; the most notable accomplishment was the installation of an oil-burning water heater which is still lying around here somewhere along with what is left of the original donkey boiler. Gas rationing was still in effect and the effort of running the motel proved too much for them. They sold out the next year.

Two young couples, fresh from fighting the war in Europe and on the home-front, saw an advertisement for the sale of Brown's Modern Motor Lodge. They left from their homes in Walnut Creek that night and got as far as Redding before they just had to rest. It was the end of the month, and like most young people, they were low on cash till the first, so they spent the night in the car and finished the trip the next morning. They spent two days in cabins #10 and #11, returned home to sell their houses, formed a partnership, and bought Brown's Modern Motor Lodge for $42,000. That was in April, 1946. The couples were my mom and dad, and "Aunt" Joalice and "Uncle" Johnny.

They had several years of small business background between them. Dad's mother had operated several restaurants, and he had owned a service station before the war when he was only 20. Mom's father ran a bakery in San Francisco, homesteaded in Oregon, and returned to the Bay area to open his last bakery in Walnut Creek. On one of his early trips to Oregon, he had even stayed in Brown's Auto Park. Joalice's father was a Columbia River fisherman, who drowned when she was seven. Her mother became a minister in the Unity Church and they moved to Walnut Creek, where Joalice and Mom became close friends in high school. Johnny's father was a naval officer and Johnny held several jobs after high school before he started work for the Bell phone company.

Like most people who have never operated a motel before, they did not realize how much work it would be. They actually arrived here in June and set right to work. There were repairs to make, and there were cabins for the girls to clean. But when that was done, there was lots of time to fish and swim and explore the country. It did not take long to figure out that all of the work wasn't getting done. Every year there was less fishing and more working. There was also less money than anticipated and more people to feed, as first Joalice and then Lois got pregnant. The two families decided to take turns between running the motel and working an outside job. Whoever ran the motel lived in the house and the other family lived in a cabin or in a rented house, wherever the work was. I remember one wonderful winter when my brother and I went to the beach every day because Dad was using the G.I. Bill to go to carpenter's school in Newport Beach.

The baby boom was on and both families were trying to have kids together. They came pretty close. The girls both got pregnant again within two years of their first ones, and now there were four little ones running around. Old-time customers still talk of how these young girls worked so hard cleaning cabins and pushing the wooden, bicycle-wheeled maid's cart around while they took care of their cute children. One of them was me, of course. Mom was only 24 years old then, and yes, the cart is still in use.

Dad and Johnny were no longer gone fishing. In 1950, they began changing the shape of Brown's Modern Motor Lodge to what it is today. They tore down the old showers and built the existing "modern" shower and laundry building. That was the same year that Lisa and Clark Green came to town to run the little restaurant across the driveway from our office. No one can tell me when the place was built, and few remember that the sign in front actually said "Koffie Kup." Everyone knew it as Ma Green's.

Ma Green was a legend in her own time. When people thought of Ma Green's, they may not have remembered Cave Springs, but it was impossible to think of Cave Springs without thinking of Ma Green's. It had six counter stools, two four-person booths, the soda water fountain in front, and two outside benches. They were very important because every summer night they were full of people waiting to get in. Hungry patrons would watch the bench till it emptied slightly and then they would fill it up. Her homemade pies, sour-dough pancakes, hamburgers, chicken-fried steak, and hospitality were famous from Canada to Mexico. She loved to get out in the mountains and her walls were covered with arrowheads she had collected. Some of them came from right here. When Mr. Green died, Ma Green lost the thrill of living. She tried to carry on by herself and running the restaurant was not a problem. She just did not enjoy living without her husband. She willed herself sick and then refused to eat until she died in 1965. She was one very fine lady, and in a sense, her legacy lives on. We still have pancakes every Saturday morning made from her sour-dough starter.

In 1952, the name was changed to Cave Springs after a loose translation of the Indian name for this location. In 1954, eleven trailer spaces replaced the old kitchenless "fisherman" cabins up on the hill, and the property next to Ma Green's was sold to build Mac's Market, now called Wiley's Market. The freeway was being built and it felt like everything was under construction. Half the town was in a state of transition as the state bought up and tore down houses to build the highway.

The cabins along the road were falling apart, and people no longer wanted to stay right on the highway. When those cabins were built, all freight moved by rail. By 1950, trucks were taking over what had been the railroad's exclusive domain, and trucks are not pleasant to sleep next to. The demand for trailer spaces was high because many of the freeway construction workers lived in trailers. The cabins were moved up the hill to be used as storage sheds and large trailer spaces were built next to the ball park to accommodate the latest development, the ten-foot-wide trailer. The name Mobile Home was not in use yet. Standard Oil built the existing service station and, in 1955, Uncle Johnny and Aunt Joalice decided to quit trying to do two jobs. Johnny was working for the phone company again, and was offered a big promotion; but they had to move to Redding, so they sold out to my folks. The rest of the Eisenhower years were spent catching up with all of the changes and getting kids through elementary school.

Every year, reservations for the summer grew and I would look forward to seeing old friends again. In spite of being sandwiched between the railroad and the highway, people love to be in Clint Brown's old cabins. Granted, they were right on the river, but a large part of why people keep coming back is because the cabins are well maintained and, above all, clean.

Clean was not an easy state to attain in the steam era. The romantic notion of giant noisy locomotives belching smoke under a full head of steam as they labored up the canyon has a few drawbacks in reality. When the new owners went to cut a Christmas tree from their very own property, they discovered it was black with soot! It took days to wash all the walls, ceilings, floors, chairs, furniture, windows, etc., every spring. This was one task that was shared. The men really got in and helped out the women. In fact, in fairness to my father, who is an extremely fair person, I must admit that he helped my mother clean every Sunday, before and after church, which we never missed; and, also, whenever everyone checked out all at once. However, the daily work was left to the women, and the throbbing O'Malley engines puffing by kept the ladies busy straightening out the mirrors and pictures on the walls.

It took ten years for the final phase of construction to begin. First, the RV spaces behind Mac's Market had to be leveled and hooked up to utilities. Then the culmination of a once in a lifetime dream was completed. Mom and Dad built themselves a new house! They also had to build ten new rooms to justify the expense, but there is no doubt in my mind that the real motivation for the expansion was to have a brand new custom home. The pool was considered essential by my father because of the changing expectations of the traveling public. Summer vacations mean swimming. Nothing could be simpler. With one exception, Cave Springs was now complete. It was 1967.

One outstanding feature of this place took several years to develop and is in a constant state of change. For the most part, God is the person in charge, but he had some wonderful help. Leo and Ethel Mellon decided to adopt the garden and landscape Bob and Lois's motel. This was strictly a labor of joy and love, and what a beautiful labor it turned out to be! Landscape architects with masters' degrees in horticulture and design marvel at the way the garden is planned. It blooms spring, summer, and fall, and has a different look for every season. What Leo and Ethel gave to our family cannot be quantified. It can only be sincerely appreciated.

Cave Springs feels complete now, and Mom and Dad are retired to pasture with the thousands of other retirees who ply the north forty of this continent in their recreational vehicles. Belinda and I are in charge now and striving just to keep up the high standards my parents set. We may even make some changes, but more than likely the changes will be forced on us by the changing nature of the business. Already, we have had to add cable TV, a movie channel, and remote controls to what started out as an industry standard black and white television. Mountain motels in the near future will be expected to have a jacuzzi and business motels will have computers in the rooms. Whoever thought disposable shower caps, razors, individual shampoos and shaving creams, deodorants, phones, and VCR's would be common features in a motel room? This is a far cry from bringing your own linen and cleaning your own room.

Just as Dunsmuir has gone through many changes in its short hundred-year life, so too has the motel industry. We are now in the midst of what amounts to a revolution in the business. Forgive the lapse into business jargon, but in the last couple of years the change in the motel industry is tantamount to the change in the railroad that occurred with the introduction of the diesel engine. The industry is centralizing and stratifying. In 1970 the economy sector alone contained some 10 chains, 250 properties, i.e., motels, and less than 20,000 rooms. Today, it encompasses over 60 chains, 2,400 properties and 240,000 rooms. This year, 12 major hotel companies changed hands, one giant folded, and several have the wolves at the door. The end result is enhanced competition and a new professionalism. Economies of scale and the best young talent in the business combine with a large equity base and increased cash flow to offer better appointed rooms for less money, expanding development, and elaborate marketing programs. Pictures of sailboats sell Holiday Inn and a standard cheap price sells Motel 6.

Small family-owned and operated motels will continue to exist, but most, if not all new construction, is already monopolized by corporations. In a sense, the changes that have occurred in Dunsmuir in the last thirty years are happening to the motels of Dunsmuir now. The well being of the motels in town is dependent on traffic passing by and has been independent of the town. Ironically, for the first time in our history, the futures of both will be interdependent on each other.

Railroading and logging are declining industries in our town. Relative real estate value has dropped to the point where it is increasingly feasible to survive on an income that is seasonal. Seasonal income is nothing new to the area. We have all been doing it for years now. The principal difference will be the source of the seasonal income — tourists. Tourism is not new, it is just more important than ever before, and for the first time there is widespread acceptance of this fact.

Dunsmuir has a big advantage over many newer tourist areas. After a hundred years, most of it is still here. In a land where most people live in suburbs and new shopping centers replace old buildings, Dunsmuir hasn't changed. Tourists travel for three reasons: scenery, history, and man-made attractions. We may not have Disneyland, but we sure do have scenery and history! A little maintenance and restoration is in order and already begun. There is already a demand for and a college class to train tour guides. Cottage industry is developing local products to trade to tourists. Most importantly, Dunsmuir is working with the other towns and communities in the area to promote tourism in the entire region.

The history of Cave Springs is just one story of many that could have been written about the people and buildings in our town. It is a nice thumbnail sketch of some of the early pioneers here. I feel fortunate to be able to write it because the research would never have been done otherwise. We would most certainly forget about Clint Brown, Ma Green, and even Lois Dewey if they weren't immortalized in a book. Most of all, I feel blessed because a short history of Cave Springs was fun to do!

Brown's Auto Park — About 1920

(L) K. Brown, (C) Small, (R) C. Brown at Brown's Auto Court

INTRODUCTION TO PART TWO
By
DICK MURDOCK

It is an honor and a pleasure to introduce the following pages of this centennial book — people who love the town for various reasons. They express themselves well, each in his own way, adding to the rich heritage that rightfully belongs to us and future generations. These dedications take their places in history now, so read them carefully and with appreciation. Study the pictures and captions and get to know the families.

Lest We Forget

When we consider people who have lived in Dunsmuir down through the years, their great diversity suggests a very special story. Few were notable for community service: some were simply characters, marching to their own drummer. Most were simply the good, quiet citizens who provide the backbone of any decent, small town. Of course, anyone trying to put all this together must remember that Thornton Wilder did it first!

To attempt to list all the people we remember would be very nearly impossible. It would read like a telephone directory; and even so, chances are it still would not be complete. Let each reader make his own list.

By Horace Porter

CO-EDITORS, PART TWO

Patricia Girard

Flora Wintering

148

PART II:
A CENTURY OF FAMILIES AND FRIENDS

"This is not a letter!

"If every other two pages have been put together with all the TLC reminiscences, smiles, yes, tears that my two pages have generated, the Centennial Book will be a completely miraculous accomplishment!

"Congratulations."

—*Bonita Cornish*

Co-Editors of Part Two
Patricia Girard
Flora Wintering

Alexander Dunsmuir

Alexander Dunsmuir
Provincial Archives
Victoria, B.C.

Alexander Dunsmuir, the young Canadian from Victoria, B.C., gave his name to the bustling, little railroad town called Pusher. In 1886, en route to San Francisco to make business arrangements for his father, Robert Dunsmuir, a mighty Vancouver Island coal baron, Alexander stopped in the lively, picturesque town and fell in love with it. Forthwith, he made a proposal to the town fathers of Pusher: "Name your city after me and I will send you a handsome fountain." His offer was accepted. In time the fountain arrived, as Dunsmuir had promised, but the young Canadian never returned. The fountain was installed at the S.P. depot and there it was an attraction for many years. During changes in the railroad, it was dismantled. Sometime later it was again installed at the City Park. Since we bear the name of Alexander's family, we feel very close to the beautiful Canadian city and, in truth, feel like a sister city.

TAU-HIN-DAULI
FAMILY

Father
Bill Tauhindauli

Wife
Lillie Hunt
Pit River Indian

Mother
Jenny Stump
Anchomawi Tribe
of
Pit River Indians

Groomed by his father to become headman of the Wintu Indians, he never assumed that position for by the time he was old enough to be headman, the Wintus were so dispersed that tribal unity was lost.

He was the last of his people, to our knowledge, to remain true to the teachings of his ancestors and carried on the customs and rituals of the ancient Wintu.

Grant, at the close of his wife's funeral, conducted in orthodox modern day manner, took from a paper bag many, many strings of beads which he placed in Lillie's hands. This he did in accordance with an ancestral Indian custom.*

Source book: Bag of Bones by Marcelle Masson

3

DR. JOSEPH WILLIAM REYNOLDS

Dr. J. W. Reynolds is a local boy who "made good," attending Dunsmuir schools until graduation, then leaving to enter college, medical school, and after having served his time with the military during World War II, returned to his home town to begin his practice of medicine. He delivered his first baby on January 14, 1948, at the old Weed Hospital; and during a career which spanned from 1947 to his retirement in 1981, it is estimated that he delivered about 1500 babies! He not only helped these children into the world, but went on from there to treat them for numerous cuts, bruises, scrapes, broken bones and other delightful conditions such as measles, mumps, chicken pox, and tonsillitis.

SOME OF "DR. BILL'S" BABIES

This is a tribute from some of those babies.

CINDY CONNELLY BARAJAS
TERRY CONNELLY MATHWIG
NICHOLAS CONNELLY
BRIAN CONNELLY
RICHARD J. PADULA
GARY L. PADULA
MIKE CASCARINA
THOMAS ANTHONY IMHOFF
PHILIP JAMES IMHOFF
MARK JOSEPH IMHOFF
JAMES PATRICK IMHOFF
NORMAN JOHN IMHOFF
TIMOTHY ALBERT IMHOFF
PATRICK WILLIAM IMHOFF
TONIA MARIE IMHOFF
THOMAS PADILLA
DANIEL A. PADILLA
DAVID A. PADILLA
ANTHONY J. PADILLA
VICTOR J. PADILLA
JOHN F. PADILLA
ANITA A. PADILLA
LESLIE LE MERE
LORI WAMSLEY PADILLA
BRIAN ANTHONY WAMSLEY
SCOTT HARRIS
CARL EACHUS
BECKY AGUILERA SCHOFIELD
SUSAN ANN AGUILERA
ANDREW JOHN AGUILERA
MARGO K. ZANOTTO
MARCIE A. ZANOTTO PADOVAN

MARI T. ZANOTTO ZIEOUR
MARK J. ZANOTTO
EDWARD DOMINGUEZ
CURTIS DOMINGUEZ
TONY CONGI
VIC CONGI
DEE OLSEN
KIM OLSEN WRIGHT
SUE OLSEN GRIFFIN
JIL OLSEN VANDEMARK
ZOE ANN OLSEN ROBINSON
JAN OLSEN COTTINI
LOUIS COSENTINO
MICHAEL PADILLA
PAUL VINCENT PADILLA
SHARON MARIE NEALON RHINESMITH
WILLIAM ANTHONY NEALON (BILLY)
ROBERT L. HUBBARD
KERRY L. ELLIS
ROBERT LAWRENCE KENOYER
KIMBERLY EVE VAN HEEST
ROBERT ARCHER VAN HEEST
VONETTE SUMMERS DAVIS
ROURY SUMMERS
ROBIN SUMMERS
RICHIE SUMMERS
CRAIG MEEKS
MISHELLE MEEKS (MISSIE)
MARK NYSTROM
SCOTT NYSTROM
DINA VALENZUELA
TRACEY LYNN BAILEY

TO "HAP"

This page is dedicated to V. L. "Hap" Richardson, our scout master and friend. He gave freely of his time and skills during our scouting years. We all believe it influenced our attitudes and our moral values in later life. For that we will always be appreciative and in his debt.

SCOUT LEADER
V. L. Richardson

HANNA,
City Engineer of Alameda, CA (Ret.)
Vice Mayor of Alameda

REYNOLDS, M. D. (Ret.)
Dunsmuir, CA

TUCKER,
Locomotive Engineer, S.P. Co. (Ret.)
Dunsmuir, CA

KELBY,
Civil Engineer Dept. S.P. Co. (Ret.)
Dunsmuir, CA

PETERSON,
Ichthyologist, Corp. Ex.,
Seattle, WA

BROWN, D.V.M.
Cupertino, CA

EAGLE SCOUTS
Back: John G. Peterson, Mark J. Hanna,
Ivan Tucker
Front: Joseph W. Reynolds, Joseph Kelby
Bottom: Joseph F. Brown

A WRITER'S LOVE AFFAIR WITH DUNSMUIR

By
Larry Green

My personal love affair with the town of Dunsmuir spans nearly 40 years. As a young lad, I was actually raised in the San Francisco Bay Area, but my parents had always been active outdoor people who whisked me off to the mountains for fishing, hunting, or camping at every opportunity that arose.

In 1947, one of my uncles and his family moved to Dunsmuir to take a job in a sawmill, then located near Crag View Drive. Thus, it was the following summer of 1948, when I was then at the tender age of 11 years, that my folks brought me north for my first look at the town of Dunsmuir to visit my uncle. I remember vividly that it was love at first sight. There was a lot here to impress a young, outdoor-minded lad of 11 with those rugged, rocky crags to the west, beautiful Mt. Shasta to the north, and east of the millhouse, where we stayed with my uncle's family, the Upper Sacramento River, which was then chuck full of native rainbow trout.

Also, there were the trains, and for a boy whose father had fired steam locomotives during the war years, I was held spellbound by those massive malleys called Cab-Forwards that grunted and groaned under the strain of pushing and pulling great tonnage over well polished rail in the canyons above Dunsmuir. How I then loved and now miss those wonderful old steam locomotives!

In the following years, I'd returned to Dunsmuir summer after summer with my parents long after the mill had burnt down and my aunt and uncle had moved back to the Bay Area. But for myself, at least, a seed had been planted. After marriage and while raising two children, my wife, Mary, and I continued to share our love of Dunsmuir with our children through annual summer vacations, some 20 in a row.

In 1960, I became an active outdoor sports writer and have since enjoyed the opportunity of traveling in search of the best fishing and hunting opportunities across 11 western states, Canada, and Mexico. But my heart remained in Dunsmuir, and thus it was in 1983 in planning for an early retirement that we had our life-long dream of a river front summer home come true. We chose Dunsmuir. Because in all honesty, of the thousands of miles I've hunted and fished all over the western United States, these fabulous Siskiyou mountains and the quaint, friendly little town of Dunsmuir appealed to us more than any place we've yet traveled. Here I can write with unending inspiration because the scenery, the people, the water, the town, the fishing, the hunting, the pure pine-scented air, and, yes, still the trains captivated our souls completely. And it is here in Dunsmuir that I expect I'll eventually expire, hopefully long after I retire. Because to our family, there's just no place on God's green earth quite like Dunsmuir.

—Larry R. Green
(Outdoors Writer)

Author-writer Larry Green shares an evening of dry fly fishing with his 11-year-old son, Scott, on the author's favorite fly pool in the upper Sacramento River at Dunsmuir. (Photo taken August, 1973.)

In Appreciation of
GEORGE RENTSCHELER

Editor of the Dunsmuir News
1979-1983

George was actively and vigorously interested in our little mountain town and left an indelible print in our community.

"The kind of care and concern shown by the people will be what I remember about the little town located in the beautiful mountains — those beautiful mountains, where I camped during the summer and skied during winter. The beauty and the kindness shown to me by the people will be the things I will always remember. They are the forces that will draw me back for visits with my good friends in the historic railroad town." by Rentscheler, from his last column in the *News*.

It was George, who set in motion the wheels of action to achieve a memorable centennial celebration. He saw that Reva Coon's dream could become a reality.

THANK YOU, GEORGE. YOU WILL ALWAYS BE A PART OF DUNSMUIR.

DIRECTORS OF RAILROAD DAYS CELEBRATION
JUNE 15-16-17, 1951

H. H. SCHROEDER
President
Chief Clerk S. P. Co.

R. E. FRYE
Vice-President, Treasurer
Manager Bank of America

D. A. SIRIANNI
Secretary
Real Estate-Insurance

E. H. PATTON
Distributor
Beer—Wine—Fuel

RICHARD COOL
5 yr. old Soloist
Grandson of R. R. Days Founder

N. M. GREEN
Founder of Railroad Days
S. P. Conductor

FRANK BASCOM
Retired

J. E. HANRATTY
S. P. Engineer

HOW RAILROAD DAYS WAS STARTED

Monday evening, February 19, 1940, an assembly of some 40 men representing the railroaders and businessmen, met in the Weed Hotel to plan Dunsmuir's first RAILROAD DAYS celebration . .

Jesse Fidler was the first speaker of the evening and stated that if the businessmen and the railroaders cooperated, the town wouldn't be able to count the people that would come. (This prediction came true.)

E. J. Cone said that the businessmen would liberally support the proposed celebration. Others who voiced their opinion were Dr. J. R. U. Campbell, Walter Minor, Roy Weaver, R. G. Renoud, S. M. Harrington, Alex O. Smith, "Beany" King, and Gus Schumacher . . .

Officers chosen to proceed with the program were Norman Green, president; Dr. J. R. U. Campbell, first vice-president; Alex O. Smith, second vice president; Stanley H. Sherwood, treasurer; and Elmer I. Jenks, secretary. Norman Green presided over the auspicious meeting.

(Excerpt from 1951 Railroad Days Souvenir Program.)

THE ADAMS FAMILY

Jack Adams

Howard "Jack" Adams, born in 1886 in Brentwood, California, married Hazel Hilda Ahlstrom, who was born in Ashland, Oregon, in 1886. They lived in Ashland where their daughter, Louise, was born in 1910. Later they lived in Dunsmuir where their son, George Howard "Red," was born in 1915. The family lived in Ashland again for a time; then Brea, California, until the lure of Dunsmuir and the Southern Pacific Railroad called them back in 1924.

Hazel Adams

When Jack and Hazel bought the two-story house on the corner of Wood Street and Dunsmuir Avenue, they joined the company of the Ahlstroms, Kelbys, and Fischers who were old Ashland friends; and together with the Branstetters and Hollands, they became known as "The Wood Street Gang." They and their children spent many happy times picnicking and celebrating in the many Parks in and around the railroad capitol of Dunsmuir. Hazel's brothers, North J. Ahlstrom and Tingner Ahlstrom — both Railroad Engineers for the Southern Pacific — also lived in Dunsmuir with their wives, Signe and Beatrice. The son of Jack's sister, a retired Southern Pacific man, Alfred Smyth, is still living in Dunsmuir with his wife, Pat.

Jack and Hazel's children went to Dunsmuir schools, where Louise was fortunate to have the young and lovely Reva Patrick (later becoming Reva Coon) as her high school teacher. Louise went on to attend Southern Oregon Normal School in Ashland, where she earned a teaching credential and then taught two years in Fossil, Oregon. By going to Chico State Summer session extensions in Mt. Shasta and a year on the campus in Chico, she earned a California State Teaching Credential, enabling her to

teach in Dunsmuir during the late 30's.

William (Bill) Dick came to Dunsmuir to work in the law office of Roy Weaver after hearing about the opening through his former roommate while attending UC Berkeley, Horace Porter. Bill and Louise were married in 1940, then made their home in Oakland for a time, where she gave birth to two sons, before moving to Stockton, California, where her husband established a law practice and she taught in the Stockton schools and attended the University of Pacific where she received her MA in Education in 1963.

Her brother, "Red," traveled in Australia, then served in India during WW II before returning to Dunsmuir to work for the Southern Pacific; he later established a successful Real Estate business in Mt. Shasta. Red married Argyll Millen, a nurse, and they had three children: George Howard "Rusty" Adams, who served as a Marine in the Vietnam War, then went on to earn his PhD at the University of San Francisco. He is now living in Mt. Shasta and working in Redding part time. Red's first daughter, Susan, is married to Lanny Wyatt and is living in Redding with sons Steven and Troy. Louise "Weegee," Red's last child, is now living in Reno. Red had owned a cabin overlooking the Sacramento

River in Sweetbriar, where his children and Louise's from Stockton, Howard and Bill Jr., often spent the summers together. Howard, the older of the two, later graduated from UC Berkeley and now makes his home in Fair Oaks, where he is married to Fern Weber and has three daughters: Lori, Corinne, and SalliAnne. Bill Jr. graduated from the University of the Pacific and earned an MA at San Francisco State University.

In 1952, Jack Adams died from a heart attack. From 1952 to 1980, Hazel lived alone in the large, gray house on the corner of Dunsmuir Avenue and Wood Street, and became the last of the Wood Street Gang still living on the Street. She was visited daily by Signe Ahlstrom, and frequently by her son, Red, who in 1978 lost his life in a plane crash with his second wife, Dawn. Whereupon her grandson, Rusty, then became her frequent visitor. In April of 1980, Hazel, Signe and Argyll passed away. During the last few years of her life, Hazel enjoyed the kind of help of the monks from Shasta Abbey who gave her loving care until she was taken to Stockton with her daughter to spend the last two months of her life, just four months short of her 92nd birthday.

In Memory of
EUGENE VIVIAN ANDERSON, M.D.
Born November 11, 1907 — Died April 9, 1976

Dr. Anderson was born in Mount Vernon, Washington, where he grew up. He was graduated from Stanford School of Medicine and received his Doctor of Medicine in 1934. He served his internship at San Francisco County Hospital, followed by a year as House officer in Medicine; and one in Surgery. In 1935, he married Nadine Nopel of Oakland.

Dr. Anderson and his wife came to Dunsmuir on January 10, 1938. Here they made their home and reared their two sons: Sigurd Peder and Richard Nopel, both of whom graduated from Dunsmuir High School. Peder and Richard went on to college and became teachers. They are now the proud parents of two boys each.

Dr. Anderson practiced medicine in Dunsmuir for 25 years as a family physician and as Southern Pacific District Surgeon. Over the years, he delivered more than 900 babies. He was active in the Siskiyou County Medical Society, youth activities, and civic affairs. His wife Nadine was also active in civic groups and the P.T.A. She has the distinction of being the first woman to serve on the Dunsmuir High School Board of Trustees.

After 25 years, the doctor left Dunsmuir and became a member of the Permanente Group in Hayward, where he practiced until his death.

Dr. Anderson was a fine and dedicated doctor; a loving husband, father, and grandfather; and an ardent sportsman.

THE "TAIL" OF TWO FAMILES:
AILES and ENGLE

Many buildings serving useful, productive purposes in present-day Dunsmuir pay tribute to the skills and capabilities of Joseph Ailes.

Joseph H. Ailes was born in Campbellsville, Kentucky, in 1900, into a construction family, and spent most of his childhood as one of ten children in Bellfountaine, Ohio. He joined the fledgling U.S. Air Corps, the predecessor of the U.S. Air Force, during World War I. While stationed in France, Joe flew in the same Corps with the likes of famous W.W. I fighter pilot Eddie Rickenbacker.

After the war in 1919, Joe traveled across the country and settled in the bustling community of Dunsmuir. There, he carried on the tradition of his father by entering the building construction trade. At the peak of his career, he ran one of the largest construction teams in the area from his office on Sacramento Avenue, designing and building structures throughout Northern California. During this time, Joe constructed numerous buildings in Dunsmuir, including the post office and many private residences.

Joseph was active in various civic activities such as serving as the police commissioner and as mayor for 2 terms in the 1950's. He established charters of the Veterans of Foreign Wars in Northern California, served as the Commander of the VFW, and was a member of the American Legion.

Joseph had two children by an early marriage; Marie Ailes Felgenhauer, now living in Sacramento, and Joseph W. Ailes, who was killed in an automobile accident while serving in the Marine Corps.

THE AILES and THE ENGLES

Having migrated to California from Indiana, Pennsylvania, before Joseph arrived, Ira P. and Hattie Pearl Engle had established a thriving family enterprise consisting of a hotel, general store, livery stable, and restaurant in Ydalpom (Copper City), Shasta County (now located beneath Shasta Lake).

In 1925 they moved to Castella with their son Ira A. and his daughter Marjorie. There they constructed the popular Engle Inn resort on the banks of the Sacramento River. Many notable guests, including ex-President Herbert Hoover and the then-renowned health advocate Bernard McFadden, stayed at Engle Inn to marvel at its breath-taking view of Castle Crags.

Ira A. Engle continued to operate the resort with his mother after his father's death until he moved to Redding to work for the State of California. He later married Charlotte Hammans, a Castella and Redding school teacher. The Inn still stands today as a private residence.

The paths of these two families converged into one when Marjorie Engle married Joseph Ailes. They raised two daughters in Dunsmuir: Kelsey and Kimberly. Joseph remained active in the construction business until his retirement in the early 1970's. He died in 1979. Marjorie still lives in Dunsmuir. Ira died in 1978; Charlotte is retired and living in Redding. Kelsey Ailes Bambino works in San Francisco and Kim Ailes Vardanega lives and works in Dunsmuir.

Although the names Ailes and Engle have come to the end of the line in this branch of the families, the many buildings in Dunsmuir and Engle Inn in Castella will continue as evidence of some of the contributions these two "pioneering" families made to the area.

IN HONOR OF AURORA AND JUAN BACA FAMILY

50th WEDDING ANNIVERSARY, JUNE 22, 1971

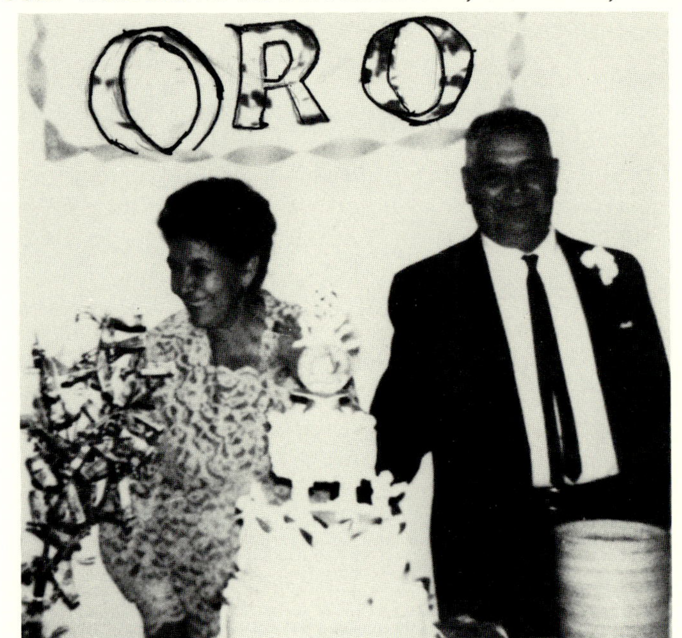

AURORA DELGADO and JUAN BACA
Married June 22, 1921

Aurora

Arturo

Leonor

Concha

Elvira

Lupe

Marie Elena

Alicia

14

AURORA BACA RECEIVED A VERY RARE HONOR

It is indeed a rare thing when a person receives a special blessing from the world leader of the Catholic Church.

But Aurora Baca of Dunsmuir is a rare person and Pope John Paul II thinks she's special. Mrs. Baca and her husband Juan, were honored December 12, 1982, when Bishop Alphonse Gallegos of Sacramento conferred a special blessing on Mrs. Baca from the Pope himself.

The honor was in recognition for the 50 years that Mrs. Baca has organized the Lady of Guadalupe Ceremony, which she started at St. John's Catholic Church on December 12, 1952.

The ceremony celebrates the meeting of an Indian peasant, Juan Diego, and the Blessed Virgin Mary on December 9, 1531. Our Lady of Guadalupe appeared before Diego and instructed him to tell the Bishop of Mexico that she wanted a temple built on the spot where she appeared.

After two trips to the bishop, Diego was told to bring back proof and Our Lady of Guadalupe instructed him to go to a frozen hill where, to his surprise, roses were growing. On instruction of Our Lady of Guadalupe, Diego brought the roses back to the bishop. When Diego unfolded his tilma, the bishop knelt to pray because on the tilma was the image of Our Lady of Guadalupe . . .

. . . In Dunsmuir, Mrs. Baca's efforts — which she says have been aided by the help of many members of the church — started the annual celebration and kept it going.

The first celebration was in 1952 and included a procession in the church with four junior high school students carrying a statue of the Madonna and young children carrying flowers which are placed at the statue's feet.

Thanks to her hard work, the celebration has become famous all over Northern California, and

Photo by George Rentschler
Courtesy of Dunsmuir News

Catholics flock to Dunsmuir to join in.

The number of people who have witnessed the ceremony and enjoyed the dinner has grown over the years, but she has always had more than enough food.

Mrs. Baca's contributions to the ceremony have been, among other things, ten dozen red and white gladiolas (red and white were the color of the roses that Juan Diego picked). She also supplied the groceries for the dinner which includes tamales, Spanish rice and beans, combination salad, punch and coffee.

She also makes 150 candy baskets for the children out of milk cartons which she covers with red, white, and green tissue paper. "Each is a work of art," said a church member.

Father Vincent Lyons of St. John's was so moved by Mrs. Baca's devotion that he felt her years of work should be recognized. He contacted Bishop Gallegos to see if he could officiate at this year's celebration, and Bishop Gallegos contacted Pope John Paul II to procure a special blessing . . .

. . . "Perhaps her greatest contribution is her spirit of devotion witnessed by all the people in the parish and Southern Siskiyou County."

—*Dunsmuir News* (December 22, 1982)

15

THE GIOVANNI BALDO FAMILY

To the great-grandchildren of Giovanni Baldo they are known as Tessie's Rocks. To others they are called the Castle Crags. The Rocks can be viewed from the kitchen window of the house Giovanni built over 60 years ago. The house stands on a small parcel of land carved from the sloping eastern side of the canyon that surrounds Dunsmuir. The terrain is not unlike the village of Cavaso, Italy, which lies in the mountains north of Venice — the birthplace of Giovanni in 1881. The house is stuck to the earth with a foundation that suggests tenacity, strength, and permanence. It has withstood the worst of Dunsmuir winters and spring runoffs for these many years.

Giovanni came to northern California in 1906 in search of a better place to live. Like so many other southern Europeans who immigrated to America during the 1900's, he found the dream elusive. Short on money, skills, and education, he struggled and endured until his death at the age of 59, in 1940. He is buried next to his wife, Brigida, in the Dunsmuir cemetery.

Brigida Baratto, also from Cavaso, Italy, was engaged to marry Giovanni's roommate when she left for America. While on the Atlantic passage, her fiance died. After spending a short time in Oakland, she married Giovanni in 1913. Giovanni had found work as a machinist for the Southern Pacific in Dunsmuir's legendary round-house.

They had four children, all born in the house on the side of the hill — first Gino, followed by Tersilla, Joe, and Peter.

Life was difficult for the growing family but they were together and thriving. However, the world economy and disease were to drastically change the family structure.

The Great Depression of the 1930's resulted in sporadic work for Giovanni and severely affected the family's ability to make ends meet. In 1927, pneumonia claimed Brigida's life at the age of 39. Unable to cope with raising four children, Giovanni arranged for their placement in the homes of friends and relatives. Approximately one year later the family was reunited. It was decided the task of running the home would fall to daughter, Tersilla. To cook, keep house, and care for her brothers, Tersilla was forced to leave high school in her sophomore year. After a three-year hiatus she returned, and received her diploma from Dunsmuir High School.

As the children grew older, they took separate paths but were unified in the belief their children would have a better life and that education was the key to the American Dream.

The eldest, Gino, moved to Weed, California, where he worked until his retirement for Long Bell Lumber Company and International Paper. He still resides in Weed with his wife, Ever. His son Peter holds a Master's Degree and currently is a school teacher in Hayward, California. Peter has a 13-year-old daughter, Majken.

Tersilla married Dino Bastiani in 1938. For the past 43 years they have lived in the house Giovanni built. Their son Richard, 41, is a graduate of Dunsmuir High School and received his PhD in chemistry from Michigan State University. Richard currently is a vice-president for Syva Corporation in Palo Alto, California. He resides in Los Gatos, California, with his wife, Janice, and son, John.

Brother Joe tried several jobs after his graduation from Dunsmuir High School before he purchased a small grocery store located on Sacramento Avenue, in Dunsmuir. He married Susie Mazzei, from McCloud in 1937. Using the initials of their first names the S&J Market opened for business in 1944.

In the true sense of the word, the S&J Market was a family operation. Joe formed a partnership with Susie's brother, Sam Mazzei. Known to its many loyal customers for its fine meat, fresh vegetables, and good service, the store employed Tersilla as a checker and her husband Dino Bastiani as a meat-cutter. The S&J also became a source of part-time employment for the family offspring, mainly during school vacations. The S&J Market was sold to a new owner in 1973.

Joe and Susie's first son Jerry was born in 1942; Bob, in 1945. A graduate of Dunsmuir High School, Jerry received his Master's Degree in history from California State University, Sacramento. He currently is an elementary school teacher in Sacramento. Jerry has three children from his first marriage: Jeffery, Matthew, and Jennifer. He is the step-father to his wife Sally's three sons: Greg, Steve and John Vivaldi.

Joe and Susie's second son, Bob, also went to California State University, Sacramento where he received his Master's Degree in Government. For the past 8 years he has been the Executive Director of Far Northern Regional Center, a human service agency serving persons with developmental disabilities. Bob currently resides in Redding with his wife, Jeanie, and two children, Bobby and Gina.

Joe & Susie still reside in Dunsmuir and have been known to frequent the local golf links.

Giovanni Baldo's youngest son, Peter, became a World War II Veteran and settled in Auburn, California. Known to Dunsmuir people as Rebelle, Peter became a highly successful life insurance agent and community leader until his untimely death at the age of 47 in 1967. He and his wife, Elaine, had one son, Russell who is an attorney in Auburn, California. Russell and his wife Susan have two children, Brittany and Peter.

Giovanni Baldo did not live long enough to see his dreams fulfilled. However, like the house he built, the family foundation he and Brigida created endured so the following generations of Baldos could realize the promise of America.

THE BARNES FAMILY
FOUR GENERATIONS IN DUNSMUIR

Posing for their sixtieth wedding anniversary picture, LeRoy and Letha Barnes stand before a picture of themselves taken many years before.

LE ROY	LETHA
Born Nov. 19, 1894	Born Nov. 27, 1897

Married Jan. 31, 1920

Children

Marjorie	Bernard	Donald

Grandchildren

Douglas Powers	Burt	Ross	Joan	Steven

Great-Grandchildren

Brenda	Michelle
Bret	Jennifer

BARNETTS

Barnett's was Dunsmuir's oldest business under one ownership in downtown Dunsmuir when Dearl and Dorothy Barnett closed it and retired in July of 1983. It had opened on a stormy March day in 1954.

Dearl came from Southwest Missouri in 1937 to work in logging. He and Dorothy met while she was in high school, and they married in 1943. After having served in the 310th Engr. Bn., 85th-Division through Africa and Italy during World War II, Dearl came home to work in Dunsmuir, first as Assistant Manager of Diamond Match Lumber Company and then as a carpenter for Contractor Joseph Ailes and for others.

Dearl commuted to his work from Mt. Shasta. In Mt. Shasta he and Dorothy lived in a house built across the front lawn from where Dorothy had spent her childhood. Dorothy's family had settled here in 1905.

The idea for their business was born when they bought a carpet for their living room and had to step over it rolled up for a year before they could find someone to install it. They decided that there was a need for that service in the area; so Dearl went to the Bay Area for school and training in floor coverings. They chose Dunsmuir for their business, because Dearl had liked his years working there. It was a good business community with a railroad payroll.

Before "Home Decorating Centers" were thought about, they came up with such an idea. In building their house, they had gone here and there matching floors, drapes, wallpaper, paint, etc., so they decided that at their store they would have all these things under one roof. Gradually they expanded into the office and the shoe shop on each side of them. They stocked furniture, carpeting, linoleum, window coverings, wallpaper, paint, and many sundries.

Dearl and Dorothy commuted the nine miles from Mt. Shasta daily, seeing the freeway replace the

"Closing the Store" picture of Dearl and Dorothy Barnett with Sam-the-store-Cat

old Highway 99 through Dunsmuir. They saw the railroad grow smaller when the shops and offices moved from Dunsmuir. When television first came to Dunsmuir, Barnett's store had the first one. They kept it running all the time for people to come in to watch. Dearl did his own installation work until back surgery forced him to sub-contract it. Their son, Bill, who is 37 (1984), grew up helping in the business until time for him to attend college. He is now an insurance agent in Southern California.

In 1982, after twenty-nine years of six-day weeks and long hours, Dearl and Dorothy decided to close the business and to retire in 1983. This was done with mixed feelings, because they had made many friends among their customers and members of the business community. Two generations had been coming to "5864 Dunsmuir Avenue," shopping for home decorating materials.

Sam-the-store-Cat, a big black mouser, had been born nine years before in the store basement. He had his very own carpet uphol-stered desk drawer. He happily gave this up and, also, retired with Dearl and Dorothy to Mt. Shasta. There he enjoys his new home with its lawns and its trees to climb.

18

MARIAN MALLORY BASS

(A NATIVE OF SHASTA SPRINGS)

Marian was born at Shasta Springs, California, May 23, 1895, the daughter of Fred L. and Mary Viola (Weston) Mallory. Her father was a superintendent of construction and operations at Shasta Water Bottling Works and Shasta Springs Resort. In the summer months the resort was a busy place for a little girl to live, because there were a lot of playmates to be found among the guests. Then in 1902, Mr. Mallory built the family a home that was considered "out in the woods north of town," according to Marian. Today the address of their house would be on Florence Loop in the central part of Dunsmuir.

Marian remembers that she and her mother had their picture taken riding in the first automobile that came to Dunsmuir, a 1904 Oldsmobile.

At first Marian went to the grammar school in Dunsmuir. In 1905 she attended the summer classes held here by the Sisters of Mercy from the convent school in Red Bluff, California; and in January of the following year, Marian went away to continue her education at the Red Bluff convent. One of the experiences she remembers from the years spent there was the dedication of St. Elizabeth's Hospital in Red Bluff. She was dressed in white and was wearing white high-button shoes as she stood at the door greeting visitors who entered. After she finished her education, she worked for Judge Jesse W. Carter of Shasta County.

In March of 1918, Marian became the bride of James Bass, who had been born at the old fish hatchery station on the McCloud River. The young couple's first home was at the Iron Mountain Mine in Shasta County. Later they went to live at Saldura, Utah, where Mr. Bass worked for the salt and potash company on Bonneville Flats, where, for months on end, they were surrounded by salt water. They stayed there until the potash part of the business was closed out

*Marian was about ten years old
when her mother took this picture.*

following World War I, when Germany was once again able to export potash to the United States.

From Saldura, James and Marion Bass went to San Francisco. While living there, Marian worked for the Associated Oil Company in the New Montgomery Street office. When it was decided that Marian's health would be better in another climate, she and James moved to Susanville, California, to work in Marian's Aunt Susan and Uncle Ben Lyle's Golden Rule Store. About 1924, the Basses returned to live in Dunsmuir and to help manage the auto court owned by Marian, her mother, and her stepfather, Jesse Fisher. Marian, also, worked for twelve years for Mr. and Mrs. Frank Bascom in the grocery store.

In 1935 Marian's mother, Viola Fisher, died, and Jesse Fisher died in 1938. Mr. and Mrs. Bass became sole owners of the Fisher Auto Court, which the couple continued to manage. In 1955 James Bass died, but Marian ran the auto court

for another year before she sold the business, retired, and moved to her present home on Shasta Avenue in Dunsmuir.

Since her retirement, Marian has had many active years. She has taken at least seventeen California Grange Tours. She has made many trips to Reno. She is a member of the California Grange and is an associate member of the Mount Shasta Hospital Auxiliary. For many years she was a member of the Dunsmuir Eagles Lodge and of the Dunsmuir Federated Women's Club. She is very proud of the sticker on her Bank of America courtesy card, for it tells that she has been doing business with the Dunsmuir bank for seventy-three years, first with the Dunsmuir State Bank and then with the Bank of Italy before it became the Bank of America.

Probably no one in Dunsmuir is more supportive of church and benefit meals than Marian. It is like a hobby with her. She enjoys eating out with her friends.

FAMILY HISTORY
OF
WILLIAM & FLORENCE ROBERTS

The history of the Roberts family in California had its beginning in 1849 when Great Great Grandfather Philander Lee, Great Grandfather Edwin Tallman Lee and other members of the "Hallelujah Wagon Train" of 1847 decided to leave Oregon and join the Gold Rush of '49.

Success at "OLD SHASTA" and at "HORSE CREEK" enabled them to return to their families in Oregon in 1850. Great Grandfather Edwin T. Lee married Kathleen Killen and Grandmother Mary Elizabeth Lee was born on July 3, 1853 at Elliot's Prairie, Oregon.

Following her father Edwin to California in 1869, Grandmother Mary E. Lee met and married the man who was destined to become our Grandfather. William Butler Roberts was born in the "Boone Tract" in Missouri in 1835, leaving there in 1853 to make the long ride to California.

Mary Elizabeth Lee and William Butler Roberts were married in Red Bluff, California in 1871, settling on a ranch just North of Red Bluff where our father William Lee Roberts was born in 1878. Dad left the ranch and went to work for the S.P. Co., coming to Dunsmuir as a "Fireman" in 1904 or 1905.

Once in Dunsmuir it wasn't long before he met and married Florence Emma Dorrell — Australian born daughter of English immigrants, James Edward and Emma Elizabeth Dorrell, who came to Dunsmuir in 1900. Married in Sacramento on October 5, 1908, they returned to Dunsmuir and purchased the home on Oak Street where Lois (Roberts) Bectel makes her home to this day.

ROBERTS FAMILY

W. E. "EDDIE" ROBERTS FAMILY
Back Row: Lewis Bazemore, Eddie Roberts
Front Row: Barbara Roberts Bazemore, Jodie Bazemore,
Clara Roberts, Beverlee Roberts

RUTH WHITE ROBERTS and G. W. "BUD" ROBERTS
Their two daughters' families are below.

LOIS ROBERTS BECTEL FAMILY
Back Row: Mohan Isaac, Shirley Bectel Isaac,
Lois Roberts Bectel, Tammy Bectel Cutting
Middle & Front Row: Susheila Isaac, Patricia Cutting,
Ramesh Isaac, Rebecca Cutting, Steve Cutting

DEWEY HOWELL FAMILY
Back Row: Sharon Roberts Howell, Dewey Howell
Front Row: Dana Howell and Steve Howell

AUSTIN ROBERTS FAMILY
Back Row: Brian Roberts, Janice Roberts, Austin Roberts, Alberta Roberts, Susan
Roberts McIntyre, Charles McIntyre, Ellen Roberts Johnson, Bruce Roberts
Front Row: Scot Roberts, Steve McIntyre, Craig Roberts, Caroline Roberts, Laura
Roberts, Katy McIntyre, Kathy Roberts, Ian Roberts, Chris Roberts,
Billy Roberts, Jennifer Johnson

ROBERT FOX FAMILY
Robert Fox, Trudy Roberts Fox,
Susan Fox and Bobby Fox

THE BECTEL FAMILY

Hattie Hubsch Bectel (1891-1922)

Erwin A. Bectel (1888-1949)

Robert Earl Bectel
Lois (Roberts) Bectel

Dorothy (Bectel) Adams

The Isaac Family

Back: Mohan Isaac
Front: Susheila,
Ramesh Craig,
Shirley (Bectel) Isaac

The Cutting Family

Back: Stephen Cutting
Middle: Tamara Lee
(Bectel), Patricia Lee
Front: Rebecca Ann

In Loving Memory

GLEN VORD BELNAP (1903-1947)
AND
LYDIA BELNAP (1904-1969)

Glen Belnap was born and raised in Ogden, Utah. Married Lydia Jeweldine Clevenger in 1922. He died October 9, 1969.

Children: son, Col. Glen Dean Belnap, killed in Vietnam 1967; daughters, Mary Lou Dietrick, Faith Coulter.

The Belnap family came to Dunsmuir, first in 1932, moved to Gerber 1935, back to Dunsmuir 1945. Glen worked for the Southern Pacific as a storekeeper. Glen and Lydia were both Eastern Star members. Glen was a member of Dunsmuir Masonic Lodge #297, F&AM, a Sciot, a deputy for the Dunsmuir Police, and a member of the Dunsmuir Volunteer Fire Department.

On November 29, 1947, his life was taken while helping fight fire. Twelve years later, in 1961, a fountain was dedicated, the "Belnap Fountain," as a memorial to Glen. The Belnap Fountain project was promoted by police officer Cliff Schwegerl and Fire Chief Jim Lambert. In 1977 the sign with the Belnap name was hung on the fountain by Bob Stover and Jim Davis, who worked for the city of Dunsmuir. The Belnap Fountain is a landmark in Dunsmuir in memory of a great man and a very loving father. Both father and mother are missed dearly.

A reality at last

The Belnap fountain, a landmark in Dunsmuir for many years, looks much the same today as it did when it was dedicated some 17 years ago. The only difference is that today it is adorned with a new sign, something it has never had. The fountain was a memorial to a Dunsmuir fireman, Glen D. Belnap, who was killed while fighting a fire in downtown Dunsmuir in 1947. The project took 12 years to complete, mainly due to the efforts of police officer Cliff Schwegerl. Belnap's wife, Mrs. Lydia Belnap, and his daughter, Mrs. Faith Coulter, who now live on Needham Ave. in Dunsmuir, and her children Rod and Diana were on hand for the 1947 dedication. The fountain was destined to have a sign but somehow it was never put up. Not until two weeks ago, that is. Bob Stover and Jim Davis undertook the project and hung the signs. A little late but a welcome addition.

—Taken from Dunsmuir News - 1977

23

A BRIEF HISTORY OF THE BILLINGTON FAMILY

Sidney Maurice Billington was born in Ballinger, Texas, February 22, 1900. Laura Vera Wallis was born in Roswell, New Mexico, April 8, 1907. They met and married on July 16, 1925. On the same day, they moved to Globe, Arizona. They had three children: Wallis Dee, b. September 15, 1930; Victor Z., b. January 26, 1934; Leota Joan, b. October 4, 1938.

In 1939, they moved to Chilliquin, Oregon, and lived there until Pineridge burned. They moved to Sprague River, where Sid went to work as a brakeman at Klamath Falls, Oregon.

In September, 1941, they moved to Dunsmuir and lived at Shasta Retreat. In 1965, Sid retired from the railroad as conductor. He was a member of the Dunsmuir Masonic Lodge #297 and Scottish Rite. On July 16, 1975, they celebrated their fiftieth wedding anniversary. Sid died June 5, 1979.

Laura worked with Ma Green for fourteen years. She was very active and served the community in many ways. She is Past Matron of the Fidelity Chapter 131, Past Noble Grand of the Oriole Rebekah's Lodge, and Past President of the W.B.A. They have ten grandchildren and three great grandchildren.

Wallis Dee, Leota Joan, Victor Z
Sidney and Laura Billington

IN LOVING MEMORY OF MEL AND CAROL BOYER

Carol and Mel on the Sacramento River

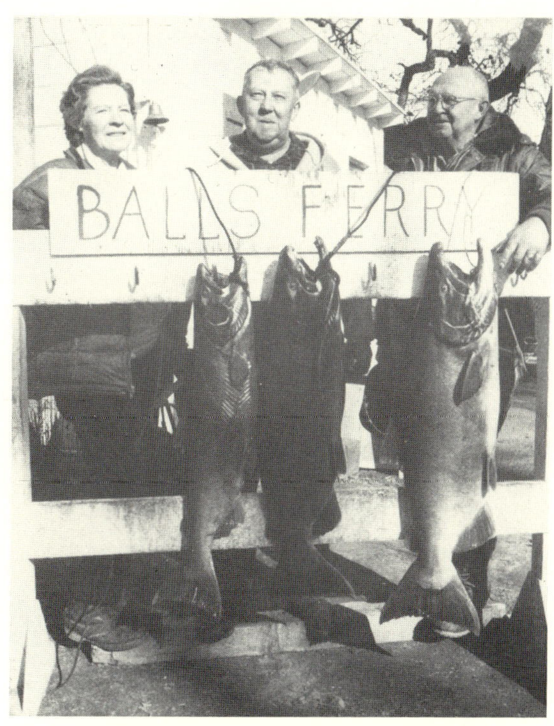

Elliott, Mel, and Harley Stoffel
Elliott caught the 35 "pounder"

Congratulations, Dunsmuir, on your Centennial! Little did we know in 1947, when we first started vacationing in this area, that one of us would be here to celebrate.

My husband Mel and my daughter Carol and I left our parents' home in Oregon, July, 1947, to visit Crater Lake. However, the weather was stormy so we continued South until we reached Sims, where we stopped for the night. There was still daylight so Mel went fishing despite the drizzling rain. Before dark he returned with a beautiful limit of trout. Irene and Earl Sabin, who owned the motel, "Best in the West," were wonderful hosts and made us feel at home. After this experience, we continued to stay there until they sold in the late '50's, and the Eggers owned it. At this time we were living in San Francisco, where Mel worked as "Walking Boss" (Supervisor) on the San Francisco Waterfront. There were times when we would arrive in the middle of the night without reservations, and we would camp down by the river at Sims long before it was a State campground. We also stayed at Ted Fay's Lookout Motel, Cave Springs, and the S.S. Motel at Dunsmuir. Thus we became acquainted with this unique town. We enjoyed many fine dinners at Motto's Cafe cooked by Bing.

Mel and I learned to love the mountains, trees, and shrubs, but most of all we were in love with the river. We thought what a privilege it would be if we could fish from the opening of fishing season to the closing. We both loved the sport and were very good at it. We decided that when Mel retired, we would wish to spend our remaining years at Dunsmuir for we had grown to love it.

In 1971 we bought the house on Shasta Ave. next to the Girard's. Some of its previous owners were the Staffords, Drakes, Bujols, and Jones'. How we loved and enjoyed the friendly people! A day did not pass that we were not fishing.

Regardless of the weather, there were few days when we did not get the limit.

There was much happiness for us, but as in all lives there is tragedy. Our daughter Carol, who had been in Jerusalem on the Israeli Police Force for thirteen years, had a heart problem and on February 19, 1980 had a fatal heart attack. She was an accomplished musician and taught all the wind instruments. She was a member of many orchestras and played in many concerts. Mel, full of grief, traveled to Israel for her funeral. On September 11, 1980, six months after Carol's death, Mel had a heart attack and drowned while fishing. Thus his last moments were spent on the river that he loved so much.

I still spend much of my time on the river and reminisce as I fish in many of our old favorite haunts.

Lovingly submitted,

Elliott Boyer

25

Susan Ann Branstetter

William J. Branstetter

IN LOVING MEMORY OF
MY GRANDPARENTS

By Elena Pinson

William Jackson Branstetter was born in New Harmony, Pike County, Missouri, on the 28th of October, 1835. At the age of nine years he started to school in a one-room log cabin with one book, a reader, from which to study.

In 1854, he left Missouri in a covered wagon for California and settled in Placerville. In 1864, in company with other pioneers, he passed through the present site of Dunsmuir and went as far north as Victoria, British Columbia, afterward returning to Roseville, where he became a merchant.

He was a charter member of Roseville Lodge of Odd Fellows, which was instituted on June 26th, 1872. He later withdrew from this Lodge to become a charter member of the Dunsmuir Lodge.

He first settled in Dunsmuir in 1886 and opened its first general merchandise store. He became one of the largest property owners in Dunsmuir, owning several business houses, residence properties, and Branstetter Lodge Hall which was known as the "Opera House." He donated land to the Odd Fellows to be used for Dunsmuir's Cemetery.

Mr. Branstetter took a keen interest in social and political affairs of the community, state, and nation. He was a lifelong Democrat. Through his long business career in Dunsmuir, he became acquainted with nearly everyone in Siskiyou County and was affectionately known as "Uncle Billy." He served the town of Dunsmuir in civic activities. He was a member of the city council, a school trustee, justice of the peace, and a member of the first fire department.

In one of the disastrous fires that swept Dunsmuir in early days, he lost his mercantile establishment, but he promptly rebuilt and reopened his business. So high was his standing in commercial life that the wholesalers in San Francisco asked no better recommendation for a customer's credit than that "Uncle Billy Branstetter" had sent them. As he would say, "The customer is always right."

He brought his family to Dunsmuir the year after he came to Dunsmuir as his children were settled in school at Roseville. He had married Susan Ann Williams in Roseville, March 6th, 1872. They had three sons and two daughters, and an adopted niece of Mr. Branstetter's, Lucy Barrett Campbell, whom they raised as their own. Mr. and Mrs. Branstetter's own children were: William, Jr.; Florence Maude, Claude, Grover, and Burnice. Florence Avenue, now Dunsmuir Avenue, was named for his oldest daughter. The younger daughter died in infancy.

Mr. Branstetter died July 26th, 1926, and he was mourned by many. The hall was crowded with sorrowing friends and grieving family members, and outside, the street was thronged with townspeople, who had known the aged pioneer for many years. The pallbearers were: Lou Gerkey, J. R. Eherenman, S. D. Root, Sam Kelby, Abe Huff, and Al Akers. Interment took place in the Dunsmuir Cemetery.

26

Honoring the Memory
of
FERDINAND BROWN

FERDINAND BROWN, for 60 years a resident of Dunsmuir, was born in Philadelphia, Pennsylvania. In 1917, he came to San Francisco to take employment with the Southern Pacific Company. Very shortly after having begun work there, he was sent to Dunsmuir for what was to have been a temporary job. However, Ferdinand fell in love with this beautiful country and settled down to spend the rest of his life in Dunsmuir. He retired in 1957.

Ferdinand was civic minded, deeply religious, and one of the most delightful raconteurs ever to entertain friends. For many years, he served as clerk for the Dunsmuir High School Board of Trustees; he was an active member of the Masonic Lodge #297, F. and A.M.; a lifetime member of the Episcopal Church, he acted for many a year as vestryman at St. Barnabas Church.

Ferdinand was beloved and respected by a host of friends and associates.

THE MANLEY M. BROWN FAMILY

By Ken Brown

Back (L-R): Frank, Clint, Lew
Front: Ella, Cora, Lucetta, Manley

MANLEY M. BROWN

Manley Brown was born in Cortland County, New York on February 22, 1838. At the age of twenty he married Lucetta Russell and moved to California. Before coming to Dunsmuir, he operated the Pitt River Ferry, where my father, Clint Brown, was born, May 15, 1875. His birthplace is now under the waters of the Shasta Dam.

In 1886 the Brown family moved to Dunsmuir. According to the Dunsmuir News, there was only one house there when they arrived.

Manley was always active in community affairs. He built Dunsmuir's first hotel and at his own expense, constructed Dunsmuir's first school house. He died July 24, 1901. His wife lived until June 8, 1914.

CLINT and MAE BROWN

DeWITT CLINTON BROWN

Clint Brown was eleven when he got to Dunsmuir. With many moves the family had had a pretty rough time, but now they were permanently settled in a good home. Clint worked at times for the McCloud River Lumber Company, but when deer season opened, he always quit his job and went hunting. Also, he was well known as an excellent trout fisherman.

At the age of twenty-eight, he married the girl next door, Ida Mae Beaton. For the next twenty-five years they were engaged in the summer resort business, first at Shasta Retreat and later at Castle Crags. He died April 30, 1933, followed by Mae Brown on April 24, 1944. They had two children: Ken Brown, born November 9, 1904; and Aileen Brown, born July 18, 1906.

KEN BROWN
and
AILEEN BROWN SMALL

KEN AND AILEEN BROWN

Ken and Aileen both were graduated from Stanford in 1928. Aileen married Francis M. Small. They have three children: Francis, Jr., Jone and Richard. The Smalls are retired and are now living in Carmel, California.

Ken, a World War II bomber pilot, fathered one son, Charles, a resident of San Jose, California. Ken is retired and living in Stockton, California.

KEN'S COMMENTS

Rarely is the black sheep called upon to write the family history, but I was given the job. The first step was to clean out the family closet. In the four generations of this history, there were three alcoholics, one bastard, and one gay. That is about average. I am one of the alcoholics, but I am not going to name any of the others. You have just finished reading the *good* part.

IN MEMORIAM
KENNETH BURNS
1919-1972

Kenneth and Marcene Burns

In memory of Kenneth Raymond Burns, who was born in Dayton, Montana, on March 1, 1919. At the age of thirteen, he moved to Ashland, Oregon, graduated from the high school there, and attended Southern Oregon College.

In 1938 he married the former Marcene Hastings, and two years later they moved to Dunsmuir, where he was employed by the Southern Pacific Company as a conductor.

He was a member of the Dunsmuir United Methodist Church; President of the Dunsmuir Railroad Days Committee; a charter member of the Elks Lodge #2333 in Mount Shasta; a past master of the Dunsmuir Masonic Lodge, F. & A.M.; President of the United Transportation Union in Dunsmuir; State Chairman of the Transportation Union in Sacramento; and Legislative Representative for the State of California during the last four years of his life.

Survivors included his wife, Marcene Burns, and two married daughters: Gloria (Whitmer) Flack of Mount Shasta, and Nancee Girard of Walnut Creek, California; a brother, Lee Burns of Sacramento and two sisters: Betty Jo Krug of Ashland, Oregon; and Dorothy Ford of Dunsmuir. He also left three grandchildren: Kevin Todd Whitmer, Susan Elaine Girard, and David Christopher Girard.

This page is dedicated in love by his wife, Marcene, and his daughters, Gloria and Nancee.

Nancee Girard and Gloria Flack

David Girard

Susan Girard

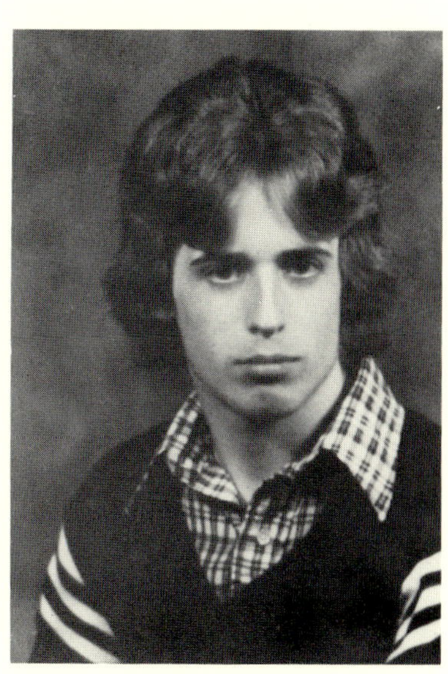

Kevin Whitmer

IN LOVE AND HONOR OF
MY FAMILY

Luigi Capovilla
Born in Cresparo, Italy
1892

Wedding
January 1, 1920

Geralama Capovilla
Born in Cresparo, Italy
1891

My father, Luigi Capovilla, railroad machinist, retired from Southern Pacific General Shops in Dunsmuir, in 1954, after 35 years of service. He died in 1960. My mother, Geralama Capovilla, died in 1947. They had spent their entire married life in Dunsmuir. My brother, Remo, graduated from the Dunsmuir schools. He served in the U.S. Navy during World War II, after which he became a rancher. He died in 1974.

Remo Capovilla

Sons of
Luigi
and
Geralama
Capovilla

Romolo Capovilla

This page is dedicated by Romolo M. Capovilla, a graduate of the Dunsmuir schools; he served in the U.S. Air Force during World War II. He retired after 27 years service as a brakeman-conductor for the Southern Pacific - Shasta Division. He now resides in Montague-Yreka area with his wife, Ruby K. Capovilla.

IN HONOR OF MY PARENTS
JOSEPH F. and KATE CHAMPION

The CHAMPION FAMILY, JOSIAH and BETHULIA, my grandparents, were among the first settlers in the Dunsmuir area. They had three children: JOHN, LENA (WHITFORD), and JOSEPH F.

JOE came to Dunsmuir in 1912 with his wife and two children: JOSEPH FRANCIS, JR., and KATHERINE BETHULIA. Joe and Kate settled in the section of Dunsmuir that was to bear his name: Champion Park. They did much for their community south of Dunsmuir.

Josiah Champion died in 1932. Joe was born in 1873 and died in 1951. Joe, Jr. was born in 1907 and died in 1977. He was married in 1926 and had two daughters: MAXINE (STRINGER) and SHIRLEY (ALLEY).

I am dedicating this page to JOE and KATE, because they were very special to me. They gave me LOVE and very precious memories.

Presented by their only surviving child,

KATHERINE B. JOHNSON

HONORING THE
VERNON AND IRENE CLARK
FAMILY

Norman Ansel (Red) Clark and his wife, Edna Adella (Della) Clark brought their family from Kennett to Dunsmuir in 1917. Norman had hired out in June, 1917, as a fireman for the Southern Pacific Railroad. He worked for several years in Dunsmuir before being transferred by the company; first, to Hornbrook; then, to Klamath Falls, and later, to Ashland. In September, 1926, he was promoted to engineer from which position he later retired. In 1936 the family returned to Dunsmuir. Della was an active member of the Methodist Church, "Lady Engineers" (GIA to BLE), and Eastern Star. She died in 1961 and Norman in 1964.

Norman and Della had five children: Carol married Leo Ulam; Vernon married Irene Freeman; Norman Ralph (deceased) married Mae Alexander; Elenor married Scott Howland; Catherine (deceased) married Lyle Turpin.

Ralph J. (Shorty) and Pearl Freeman came to Dunsmuir from Oroville, California, in 1937. Ralph was a car inspector for the Southern Pacific Railroad. A member of the Brotherhood of Railway Carmen of America, he served as a delegate to the national convention of the union. He was active in the town baseball team, Railroad Days Committee, and the Castle Grange. He died in June, 1971. Pearl Freeman still lives in Dunsmuir. She has been active in the Methodist Church, and is a member of the Castle Grange, Wonderland and Dunsmuir Senior Citizens, and the Women's Benefit Association.

Ralph and Pearl's children are: Lillie married John McDonald; Ralph Edward married Ethel Johnston; Irene married Vernon Clark; John married Beth Clark.

Vernon Ansel Clark came back to Dunsmuir in 1939. A second generation employee of the Southern Pacific Railroad, his seniority dates back to January, 1941, when he became a brakeman. He was promoted to conductor in 1949 but is now retired. He is a member of the Brotherhood of Railway Trainmen and of the Elks Lodge. His wife, Irene, still works in a dental office and is active in the Methodist Church and in the Eastern Star. She is a past president of the Dunsmuir Federated Women's Club and of "Lady Trainmen" (L.A. to B.R.T.)

Vernon and Irene have three children: Vernon Ross married Aurelia Avila. They live in Redding with their children: Christine, born January 22, 1964; Naomi, born October 12, 1965; Michele, born September 19, 1967.

Stephen married Kristen Nelson. They live in Eugene, Oregon, and have three children: Kimberly, born July, 1967; Chad Nelson, born April, 1978; Courtney, born May, 1980.

Deborah, who lives in Durham, California, is married to Paul Montgomery and has a daughter, Laura, born March, 1973.

All the Clark children love to "come home to Dunsmuir!"

J. G. COLLINS and JUNE COLLINS and FAMILY
The Moving "Tale of Two Cities"

Jerry - June and sons Michael & Lael — 1942

Lael - Michael - June - Jerry Collins — 1960

For more than forty years, the Collins Family has been a part of the social and business life of both Dunsmuir and Yreka; in fact, their story might well be called "The Tale of Two Cities." Married in Reno, Nevada, on July 1, 1940, Jerry and June moved into a little house on Blake Street in Yreka, owned by Tommy and Anna Cordoza; Jerry had helped finish the place. Upon being transferred to Dunsmuir Littrell Store, he moved his wife and son Michael to the railroad town and proceeded to buy a lot in Champion Park on 2nd Street. After installing all of the utilities, Jerry and June drove to Sacramento to buy a trailer home. They purchased a Sherwood, which had a front and back door "much luxury for those days." At that time a home on wheels was frowned upon because it represented, to many people, nomadic tendencies and irresponsibilities; finding a place to park one in those days was a real challenge. How different it is today! It was then not a popular thing to even associate with the residents of a trailer.

On June 26, 1942, Lael Gareld was born in the Cornish Hospital, located on the hill above the roundhouse in Dunsmuir.

When the Yreka Littrell Store burned in 1942 (being the war years), the Dunsmuir stock was moved to Yreka. Since Jerry was the only salesman left in Siskiyou County, the family returned to Yreka. There they put their trailer next to the tree-lined property where A & W stands today. In the spring, upon receiving word that the cottage where they had honeymooned was available, they immediately moved again. Jerry and June lived there until 1944, at which time they bought a house located between Yreka and Hawkinsville. This was home for three years. Again the Collinses transferred back to Dunsmuir, where the children attended school. Construction of the freeway took the place where they were living and forced another move.

Their new dwelling was the former home of Attorney Weaver, on Florence Avenue; this house afforded much living space. During the deep snow of 1950, the snow, roaring as it slid off the roof, piled up to nearly ten feet. Their old dog, Deek, perched on top of the snow, could watch the family going-ons inside the second-story windows. In 1955, the Collinses again went back to Yreka in order to manage the business there. For nine years, they lived on Oregon Street. In 1964, Jerry and June bought the Herman Ramp Old Ranch House, in back of the Fairgrounds and lived there seventeen years before deciding to remodel. It was a mammoth task, done by Roy and Bill Hetherington; upon pealing back the hide of the structure, walls were found to be insulated with burlap and old copies of the *Sacramento Bee* and the Portland *Oregonian*, many of which were salvaged. Added helpers on the project were R. Appadoca and Greg Collins; iron work by Jerry Collins and Steve Hetherington of Said; wallpaper by Toots Hetherington, June Collins, and Jack Spiva. Completion of the project is expected in the fall of 1984.

Jerry Collins spent most of his school days in Grants Pass, worked during the depression in the CCC, and afterwards worked as a mechanic and a salesman throughout southern Oregon and northern California. In 1940, Jerry married his school days sweetheart, June Blevins, of Prineville and Grants Pass, Oregon.

Mike Collins, after attending Merritt Davis Business College, was assistant office manager of Collins Enterprises for some time, which includes the Littrell Parts & Welding Supply Stores. Mike, now retired, lives in Hilt area with wife Judy and younger children, Shaun, Harold, and Ralph. Michele, the older daughter, is enrolled at COS.

Lael transferred from Happy Camp as manager to the Yreka store as manager on his 30th birthday. In 1981 Lael and Carolyn purchased the three Littrell Parts Stores. They reside near Montague with younger children Jeff, Darrel and Sarah. Chet is going to college in Salem, Oregon, and Greg, wife Betty and daughter Tracy live in Yreka.

THERE YOU HAVE THE MOVING TALE OF TWO CITIES.

JOE CHIMENT FAMILY

From a peaceful mountain valley at the base of Mount Grappa in the Venetian Alps, Giovanni Chiment left his family and migrated to California about 1910. Establishing a small truck farm in IGO (near Redding), he called for his three oldest sons, Umberto (Bert), Antonio (Tony), and Giuseppe (Joe), to join him.

Although Giovanni returned to his native Italy after a few years, his sons remained. During World War I, Bert served with the U.S. Army in France, while Tony and Joe worked in the mines in Kennett (now under the waters of Shasta Lake).

Following the war, Joe corresponded with Angelina Dal Bon from his native mountain village, and convinced her to join him in Caiifornia. She arrived in Redding in January, 1921, and they were immediately married. They made their first home in Dunsmuir, where Joe had found work as a pipefitter in the Southern Pacific shops. Here they built their home in Nutglade on the southern edge of town. It was here that their first child, John, was born. Their home was purchased by the Southern Pacific, and a second house was built on South Francis Street. It was here that Ray and Teresa were born.

Joe and Angelina lived the remainder of their lives in their South Francis home. John left Dunsmuir in 1939 to attend school, and now lives in Poway, California. He married Fides Pedroncelli, also of Dunsmuir, and they have six children. Ray, who married Helen Lamb, remained in the area and is now the owner-operator of the Pepsi Cola Bottling Company of Mount Shasta. They have three children, two of which — David and Jean — live in Mt. Shasta.

Teresa married Wayne Stafford and they moved from Dunsmuir to Victorville, California, in 1979. They have two children, of whom son John still lives in Dunsmuir.

Joe   *John*   *Teresa*   *Ray*   *Angelina*

THE RAY CHIMENT FAMILY

Ray Chiment and Helen Lamb were both born in Dunsmuir. Helen lived on Elinore Avenue while Ray lived in Nutglade. After attending the local schools, Ray was drafted into the U.S. Army, where he served several years during World War II in European theatre in the infantry, spending numerous months in combat. After returning home, he attended Chico State College for a short time. Helen, after graduating, continued her music training in Portland.

Ray and Helen were married on April 23, 1949, in Redding, CA, and lived in Dunsmuir at 102 Branstetter Street until 1961, when they moved to Mt. Shasta, where they own and operate the Pepsi Cola Bottling Co. They have three children: David, Jean Ferl, and Lynn; and three grandchildren: Mark, Heather, and Robert. David and Jean live in Mt. Shasta, where both of them work in the business as well as does our son-in-law Gary Ferl. Lynn lives in Monterey, CA, where she is an account executive in a Financial Group in Carmel Valley.

THE CHARLES B. LAMB FAMILY

Charlie and Matilda Lamb were married October 18, 1923, in Jacksonville, OR, Matilda, having been married before to Charlie's older brother, Archer Lamb. Archer and Matilda had two sons, Richard and Norman, who were very young when Archer was killed in a train wreck in Montana. Matilda, the boys, her mother and father and sister moved to Oregon, as did Charlie and his mother.

After their marriage in 1923, Charlie and Matilda moved to Red Bluff, then up to Dunsmuir, where a son, Eugene, was born in 1927; and a daughter, Helen, was born in 1929. They made their home there until Charlie, a retired railroad engineer, died in March of 1975. Matilda has been a patient in Weed Convalescent Hospital since very shortly after her husband's death.

Two of the children are still here. Gene, who lives in Atlanta, GA, with his wife and family of four daughters (two of them married), is soon to be retired as a Chaplain in the U.S. Army. Norman, retired manager of the Army Signal Depot Credit Union in Sacramento, and wife, Verna, have a daughter and son both married with families. Richard, who is a retired railroad engineer, resides in our parents' home here in Dunsmuir. Helen, who married Ray Chiment, resides in Mt. Shasta, where they own and operate the Pepsi-Cola Bottling Co.

Charles and Matilda's
Golden Anniversary
October 18, 1973

THE "FATHER" OF THE DUNSMUIR LIONS CLUB

DR. E. J. CORNISH

Among the pioneers of the City was Dr. E. J. Cornish, who came from Lamoine in the early 1900's.

After he had established a practice, he announced that he would build a hospital. This he did, and in so doing, provided facilities for many of the doctors of Southern Siskiyou County.

"Doc" was a compassionate man. No one came to him for treatment that did not receive it. Often he treated patients in his office or in his hospital and received no compensation for his services.

He was a leader in his community. He was the first president of the Dunsmuir Lions Club and served in that capacity for five productive years. He headed the governing body of his city and probably was instrumental in the paving of the city's streets and construction of cement sidewalks.

The Lions Club of Dunsmuir remembers you, "Doc," and they want all of the citizens of the town to be aware of your contribution to it.

DR. E. J. CORNISH

In loving memory of:

Edwin Joseph Cornish
1874-1948

Sue Pascoe Cornish
1884-1950

Edwin Robert Cornish
1912-1970

Ruth Muriel Cornish Waller
1921-1946

Robert married Bonita Clark, a Dunsmuir High School teacher from Live Oak, CA. They made their home in Fresno and had two children, Bill and Susan.

Ruth became a WAC, married Ted Waller of NYC, went to Russia in 1946 on a United Nations mission.

THE CORNISH FAMILY

Dunsmuir Hospital and Cornish Residence

The Dunsmuir Hospital was built in 1909 on Mountain Avenue by Dr. Edwin J. Cornish and his wife, Sue. Dr. Cornish was born in Minnesota, graduated from the University of Minnesota in 1899, studied in Germany and became a lumber company doctor in Lamoine. There he met and married Sue Pascoe, a teacher who had been raised in Scotia, CA, a daughter of a pioneer California Family.

The sixteen-bed hospital was closed in 1947 after both Dr. and Mrs. Cornish became ill. The vacant hospital building was demolished in 1958, but the residence section remains and is now owned and occupied by Mr. and Mrs. Robert von Hein.

The Cornish family was active politically and socially in Dunsmuir. The doctor was Dunsmuir's mayor during the early 1920's and a delegate to the Democratic National Convention in 1924. In the 1930's he suffered partial paralysis but continued a limited office practice while spending much of his time in his flower and vegetable gardens on the grounds that surrounded the hospital. Some of his flowers and fruit trees are still in evidence.

Dr. and Mrs. Cornish had three sons and one daughter who were born and raised in Dunsmuir: Richard, Robert, Ruth, and Peter.

Richard Pascoe Cornish of Monmouth, Oregon, married DeEtta Sangathe of Springfield, OR. They have one son, Rick.

William Peter Cornish, Redwood City, CA, married Betty Brodehl. They have one daughter, Eva.

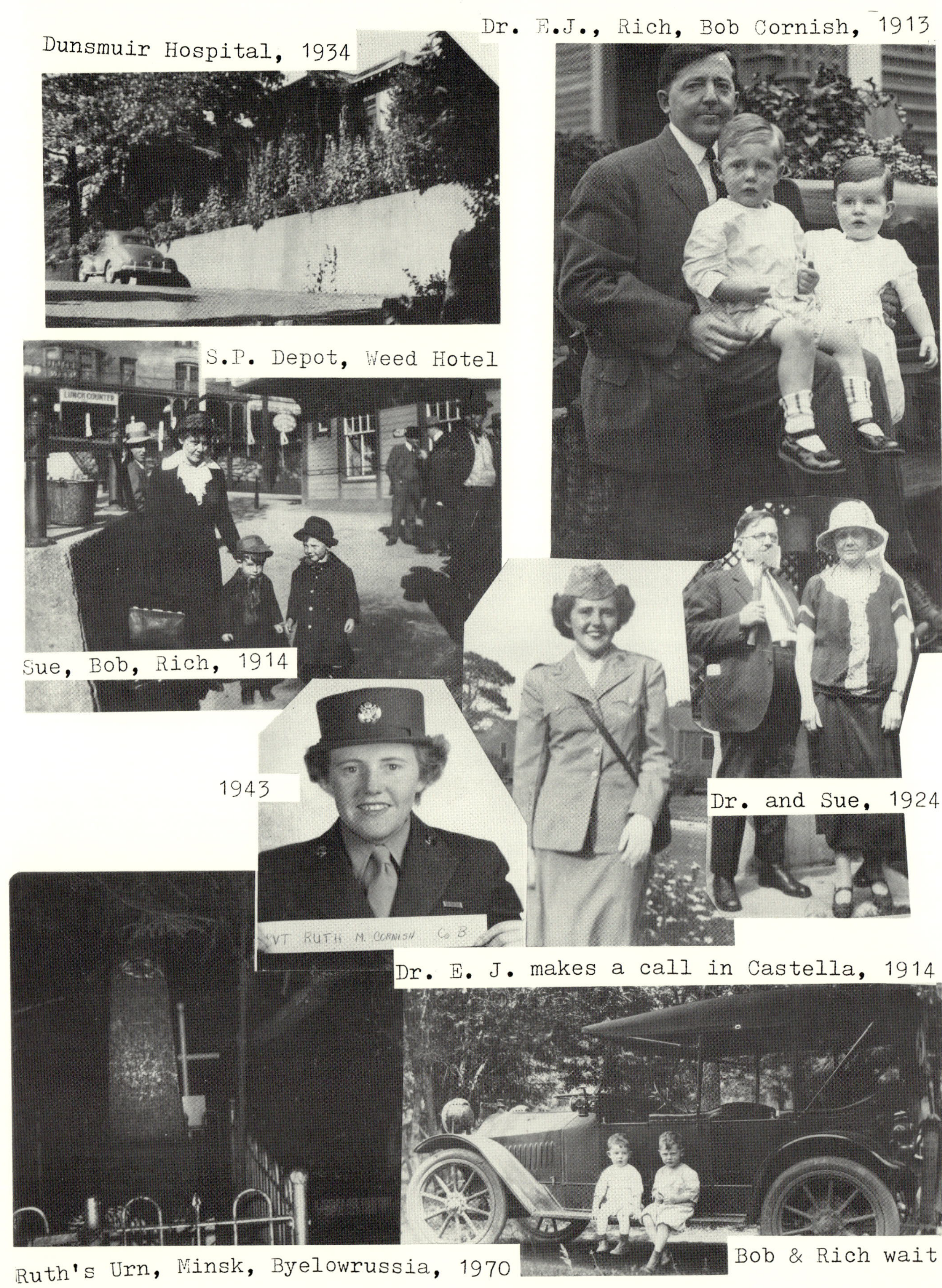

Dunsmuir Hospital, 1934

Dr. E.J., Rich, Bob Cornish, 1913

S.P. Depot, Weed Hotel

Sue, Bob, Rich, 1914

1943

PVT RUTH M. CORNISH Co B

Dr. and Sue, 1924

Dr. E. J. makes a call in Castella, 1914

Ruth's Urn, Minsk, Byelowrussia, 1970

Bob & Rich wait

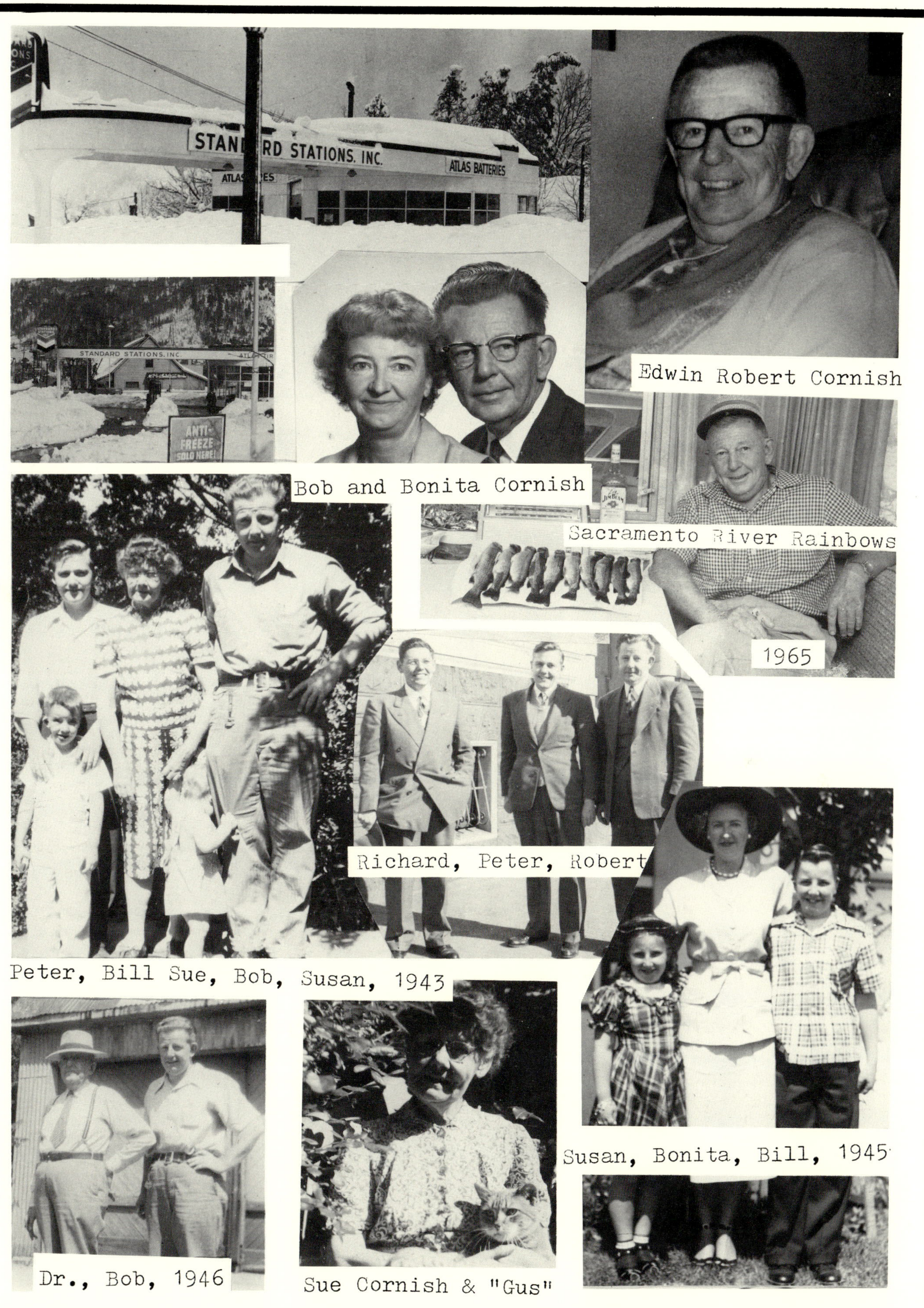

Edwin Robert Cornish

Bob and Bonita Cornish

Sacramento River Rainbows

1965

Richard, Peter, Robert

Peter, Bill Sue, Bob, Susan, 1943

Dr., Bob, 1946

Sue Cornish & "Gus"

Susan, Bonita, Bill, 1945

THE CONNELLY CLAN

Francis Connelly
Jan. 13, 1901
Mar. 22, 1980

Clara Wood
Apr. 23, 1900

Married
Apr. 28, 1925
Yreka, CA

Francis Richard Connelly
July 18, 1928
Married
July 10, 1951
Janet Norine Vollmers
Jan. 26, 1932

Cynthia Diane
Oct. 18, 1952
Married
Sept. 21, 1974
Rudolpho Barajas
July 12, 1950

Terri Lee
April 28, 1956
Married
Nov. 19, 1977
James Robert Mathwig
Nov. 16, 1956

Francis Nickolas
Oct. 1, 1959
Married
June 22, 1980
Deborah Johnson
Jan. 30, 1962

J. Brian
Aug. 11, 1963

Camay Renee
Oct. 6, 1977
Travis Vicente
May 22, 1979

Shanae Rose
Aug. 2, 1981
Jared James
Feb. 8, 1984

Nicole Nannette
Oct. 26, 1980

In Loving Memory
of
Dad and Mom

Fred A. Anderson
and
Bessie (Jordan) Anderson

They came to Dunsmuir in 1917.
He died in 1941, and she, in 1964.

Dedicated by their daughter,
Ethel May Anderson Cox
Chico, California

IN MEMORY OF OUR PARENTS:

John and Alice Covert — Fortunato and Onorina Diridoni

John and Alice (Middleton) Covert

THE DIRIDONIS

Fortunato Diridoni came from Italy to California and was the first shoemaker in San Bruno. There he met and married Onorina Giacomelli, who had come from Italy, also. While living in the San Francisco area, they had two children, Claude and Maria. In 1921 the Diridoni family decided to return to Italy to live. There Fortunato and Onorina had another child, their youngest daughter, Palmina.

Fortunato died in 1937 and Onorina died in 1983.

THE COVERTS

John R. Covert was born July 2, 1886 and died June 5, 1981. Alice E. (Middleton) Covert was born May 14, 1888, and died Christmas Day, 1967.

John R. Covert was a superintendent on Class A construction on some of the tall buildings in Los Angeles. In the Depression he brought his family to Willow Creek, Trinity County, to mine. From there he was called to build the bridge over the McCloud River at the Hearst Ranch, and he later worked on the Norman Village there. In 1934 he came to Dunsmuir with his wife and three children. He was a contractor and built or helped to build many houses here. He retired in 1950, and lived a reasonably healthy life until he was almost ninety-five years old.

Fortunato and Onorina (Giacomelli) Diridoni's wedding picture.

THE COVERT CHILDREN

1. Rhoda Alice, born February 25, 1913, married Claude Diridon. (Their family appears on following page.)

2. John R. M., born February 17, 1918, married Debra Carland. Their children are John R. M., Jr. and Kathy. John Covert is a retired Colonel in the United States Army. After Debra died, he married Tommie Masone.

3. Barbara C., born June 27, 1922, married Charles Taylor. (Details of their family appear on the page dedicated to the Wendell Family.)

Claude and Rhoda (Covert) Diridon

The Rodney Diridon Family:
Mary Ann (Fudge), Rodney,
Mary Margaret, Rodney, Jr.

The Richard Wagner Family: Corinna, Claudia (Diridon), David, Richard

The Thomas Diridons:
Thomas and Eda (Sciandri) with
Eda's daughters, Valerie Kent
and Laurie Phillips

IN HONOR OF THE COVERT-DIRIDON FAMILY

After having been born in Oakland, California, and taken to Italy by his parents, Fortunato and Onorina Diridoni, Claude Diridon returned to his native California in 1931. In 1934 he came to Sims Camp near Dunsmuir. He became a brakeman for the Southern Pacific Company from which position he retired many years later.

Claude met Rhoda Alice Covert in 1936, and in 1937 they were married at the Stone Church (St. Barnabas' Episcopal) in Dunsmuir. For a number of years, Rhoda taught piano and accompanied the school choruses as well as playing the organ in her church and other local churches.

Claude and Rhoda have three children. Their eldest son, Rodney, was born February 8, 1937. He is now a Supervisor of Santa Clara County, California. Rodney married Mary Ann Fudge; they have two children: Rodney, Junior, and Mary Margaret.

The Diridons' daughter, Claudia Dianne, was born September 20, 1942. She married Richard L. Wagner, and their children are Corinna Alice and David Earl. Richard Wagner is a conductor for the Southern Pacific.

The Diridons' youngest son, Thomas Harley, was born March 4, 1944. He is a Real Estate Broker in Belmont, California. He married Eda Sciandri, and he has two step-daughters: Valerie Kent and Laurie Phillips.

Rhoda and the Diridon children attended the Dunsmuir schools, as did the Wagners. All of them participated in sports and music activities.

IN MEMORY OF MY GRANDPARENTS

WILLIAM AUGUST
and
ANNA CLARA CLAUSNITZER

*William and Anna on their
Golden Wedding Day in 1925*

*Hiram and Hilda (Clausnitzer) Derby
and their daughter Adele about 1920*

William and Anna Clausnitzer were married in Germany on June 13, 1875, where their children Otto, Edwin, and Richard, and twins Peter and Molly were born. The twins died in infancy.

After coming to America around 1880, they settled briefly in Pennsylvania and Ohio, where two more children arrived, Mamie and George. Grandpa then decided to visit relatives in Bakersfield, California, in search of work and just the right place to settle down. He journeyed north, and when he came to a beautiful spot called, at that time, Pusher and saw Mount Shasta looming up to the north, he knew exactly where he wanted to spend the rest of his life and to make a home for his family. This happened in the early 1880's.

The railroad was coming north at the time, up the Sacramento River Canyon, and Grandpa went to work for the company that was to become the Southern Pacific. He stayed with them until he retired in 1926.

Together the family cultivated seven acres on the "west side hill." They had an orchard, a garden, chickens, a milk cow, and a horse, of course. By this time two more children had arrived: Howard and Hilda. Hilda grew up to become an excellent pianist and to become my mother. She died June 21, 1984. 21, 1984.

Grandpa died on January 7, 1927, and Grandma, on March 17, 1932.

In 1909 Elkanah and Louise Derby and their children Hiram, John, Albert, and tiny Arawanna, who died when she was ten, left Redding, California, to settle in Dunsmuir. An older daughter Helene, who had married, stayed in Redding.

About four years after the family came to Dunsmuir, Hiram Derby and Hilda Clausnitzer were married, and eventually I was born. I married Jack Brinegar, who also worked for the Southern Pacific Company, thus, making me a third generation "railroader." I have two sons, John and William of Monmouth and Salem, Oregon, and three grandchildren.

My grandparents' home and the home where I was born are now under the I-5 Freeway, as are many, many more of the old Dunsmuir homes.

This page is dedicated by Adele Derby Brinegar.

REMEMBERING
CAROL'S BEAUTY SALON

Al and Carol Coffman

For more than forty years Carol Feichko Coffman served the public as a beauty operator. When she came to Dunsmuir in 1937, she worked for Ina McCauley. Lillian Black McEnerney was the other operator.

In 1946 Carol opened her own shop in her home on Gleaves Avenue. Later she moved her shop to the mezzanine floor at Collet's Department Store (now Dunsmuir Hardware). In 1962 she moved to Pine Street and continued in business until she retired. Kathleen Graves, Sally Nealon, and Jimmy LeMere were some of her operators. Sally worked for Carol until she opened her own shop on Main Street which she is still operating. Kathleen worked for Carol until they both retired.

Carol's clientele was very large, and in order to accommodate everyone, she worked long hours six days a week. Through the years, she made many lasting friends. She still recalls losing three of them in a tragic accident which claimed the lives of Mr. and Mrs. Errol Beaughan, Mr. and Mrs. Morris Plymate, and Mr. and Mrs. Leonard Smith.

It happened on Mother's Day in 1966. They were on their way home from Yreka after dinner when the accident occurred. Mr. and Mrs. Souther Ward were on their way to Yreka. At Gazelle the Ward car hit the Smith car head-on. All six were killed instantly. Mrs. Ward was the only survivor, but she was left an invalid. The people of Dunsmuir suffered a great loss as the group were very prominent and influential.

In 1977 Carol retired for a well-earned rest. Shortly after her retirement, she suffered a severe stroke. But with the encouragement of her husband, Al Coffman, her loyal friends, and her great determination, she is able to get around with a brace and a cane. She does most of her housework. Al and Carol reside at their home on Shasta View.

GEORGE and ALICE COON

George and Alice Coon arrived in Dunsmuir from Ohio in 1903 with their three children, Doris, Burress, and Burton. They built their home at what is now 4334 Branstetter Street. Two more children were born to them: Phyllis and George ("Boose"). At first George worked as a switchman for the S.P. Later he served as Postmaster and after that as City Marshal. In later years, he went to work in the woods for the McCloud River Railroad Company. Before her marriage to George, Alice had been a telegrapher in Red Bluff. Alice was a wonderful homemaker. Her bountiful table often hosted other family members and family friends. The same round, golden oak table that served as dining table doubled as a card table. Many happy hours were spent at that table, which is now owned by a granddaughter, Barbara C. Murphy.

Oh, what stories that table could tell!

**The Coon Family and the City of Dunsmuir
have lives that are closely entwined.**

The Family Tree of

Burton "Bones" and Reva (Patrick) Coon
1900-1973   **1904-**

Dunsmuir's "Mr. Baseball"   *D.H.S. Teacher of English*
47 years S.P. Employee   *Director of Music and Drama*

THEIR CHILDREN

Alice-Jane	Robert Burton	Barbara Anne
married	married	married
Robert J. Eachus	Nancy Duarte	Leonard W. Murphy

Thomas J.	Carl John	Sean Patrick	Andy Burton	Susan Elizabeth	Cynthia Ann

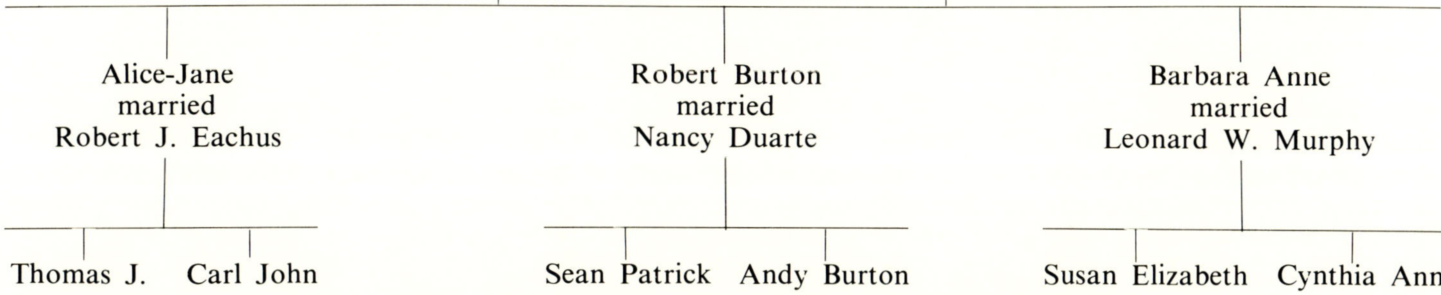

ARTHUR (RED) CROWE FAMILY

Crowe Bros. Logging
1964
Red, Don, and Mitchell
Crowe and Jimmy Garrigus

Crowe Brothers

BOX 133, CASTELLA, CALIF. 96017

PHONE 235-2770

Arthur (Red) Crowe married Frances Queiro in Cle Elum, Washington, on October 8, 1938. They settled in the Castella area with "Red's" cousin, Don Crowe, and his wife Katy Crowe in 1940.

"Red" and Don worked in the logging and construction industry for a few years before starting their own business, Crowe Brothers Logging, which they operated for 30 years.

"Red" and Frances had two sons and a daughter: Mitchell Dean Crowe, born July 21, 1939; Murray Don Crowe, born Sept. 1, 1942; and Janice M. Crowe, born Nov. 12, 1947.

On July 27, 1958, Mitchell married Betty Hale from Redding, California. They had three children: Arthur Dean Crowe, born July 21, 1959; Denise Rae Crowe, born March 7, 1961; and Darla Lorraine, born Nov. 24, 1962. Murray Don Crowe married Judy Harper from Medford, Oregon, on Nov. 26, 1965. They have three children: Brent, born Dec. 14, 1967; Kellie Ann, born Mar. 2, 1970; and Brenda, born Dec. 24, 1973.

"Red" and Frances were very involved in community affairs throughout the years. "Red" served as Master of Dunsmuir Masonic Lodge #297, F. & A.M., and was on the Castella Elementary School Board and the Dunsmuir High School Board for many years. "Red" passed away on Nov. 19, 1971. Frances still lives in Castella. Mitchell, Betty, and children have since moved to the Redding area. Murray and Judy have settled in Medford, Oregon.

Red and Frances Crowe

*"Red," Murray, Betty, Mitchell,
Frances and Janice*

*1966
Arthur Dean
Denise and
Darla Crowe*

*Frances,
Mitchell
Murray
Janice*

*Mitchell
and Dean
to left*

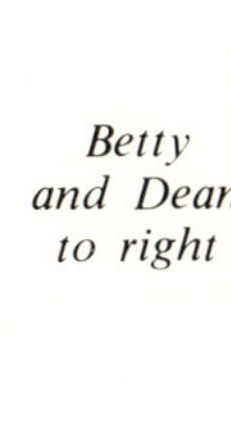

*Betty
and Dean
to right*

IN LOVING MEMORY OF OUR PARENTS

LUIGI and GIUSEPPINA CONSENTINO

Luigi Consentino was born February 17, 1883. Giuseppina Cosentino was born December 13, 1898. Although they were both born at Casino, Italy, Province of Calabria, they did not meet until they came to America. In 1901 Luigi came to the United States and settled in Mc-Cloud. He became a citizen in 1915. Giuseppina came to America in 1920. She lived with her sister at Weed. In 1921 she met Luigi. On June 4, 1921 they were married. They had three children: James Joseph, born April 9, 1922; Louisa Mary, January 27, 1924; and John Louis, February 17, 1928.

Luigi was a general contractor and had his shop at South Dunsmuir. His two sons, James and John, were in business with him. For sixty-five years the Consentinos have served the public. Luigi died on December 17, 1962, and Giuseppina died on February 23, 1983.

Luigi was an industrious and benevolent person. He contributed his labor and material to many projects in Dunsmuir. He was honored and respected by all who knew him.

In love and appreciation by:
James J. Consentino
Louisa M. Consentino Melo
John L. Consentino

IN HONOR OF THE JAMES J. CONSENTINO FAMILY

Rebecca, Deborah, James, Gloria.

James Joseph Consentino was born April 9, 1922. His parents were Luigi and Giuseppina Consentino. He has one brother, John, and one sister, Louise. They all reside here at Dunsmuir. After graduation from Dunsmuir High, Jim joined his father in the contracting and lumber business. In 1944, he joined the medical corps of the Army. He was made corporal and served until 1946. He returned to Dunsmuir and rejoined his father in business. In 1948 he met Gloria Georgis.

Gloria Georgis was born December 6, 1921 at Hilt, California. She attended grade school at Hilt and went to Redwood City to live with her sister. She was graduated from Sequoia High School. Later she returned to Mt. Shasta. It was at this time that she met Jim. They were married September 9, 1950. They made their home next to the shop. On September 20, 1951, twin daughters were born to them: Deborah Ann and Rebecca Louise.

On June 13, 1979, after a long illness, Gloria died.

For sixty-five years the Consentinos have served the public. Jim and John were in the business for forty-five years. This year (1984) the brothers are closing the business. They will be missed by all who know them. They were always generous and donated freely of their time and materials to all activities and events.

IN HONOR OF THE
JOHN COSENTINO FAMILY

The Cosentino Family on the occasion of John and Joyce's Silver Anniversary, May 15, 1979. Back row: Doug, Julie, Ellin, Joyce, John. Front row: Josie and Louis.

John, born at Dunsmuir on February 17, 1928, attended the local schools. After graduation from Dunsmuir High School in 1945, he joined the family business of L. Cosentino and Sons. He is a veteran of the Korean War. He rejoined his father, Luigi, and his brother, Jim, in business. He was ever interested and concerned with the growth and development of Dunsmuir. He served on the City Council from 1966 to 1970 and was mayor from 1969 to 1970. He was a volunteer for the Dunsmuir Fire Department from 1956 to 1984. He is currently a member of the Elks Lodge and Senior Vice-Commander of the Veterans of Foreign War, Lodge 4718.

In May of 1954 he married Joyce Young of McCloud. They have three children: Julie, Josie, and Louis.

Julie married Doug Caley of Mount Shasta, and they live at Anderson with their two children, Ellin and Blair.

Josie married Ken Dow of San Francisco, and they make their home at Redding, California.

Louis, currently attending O.I.T. in Klamath Falls, Oregon, plans on pursuing a career in diesel technology.

This Page is Dedicated To Our Mother's Mother,

ANNA BLEDSOE WELCH

She Was A Very Devoted and Kind Person.

We Loved Her Very Much.

Betty Cummings
and
Ronald Durling

Anna came from a pioneer California family. Her ancestors settled in Siskiyou and Modoc counties. On his ranch at Adin, her grandfather fed Captain Jack during the Indian War in the middle 1800's. She was a descendant of Daniel Boone of Kentucky and was related to the Bidwells of Chico.

Anna was born in Chico and came to Dunsmuir in 1892, when she was sixteen years old. She worked in a cafe on Sacramento Avenue and cooked in the old rooming house that stood where the Travelers Hotel is today. She told us stories about the early days in Dunsmuir, and how the wild animals would come into town at night.

Anna married our grandfather, Alfred Welch, who was a forest ranger in McCloud, where they lived. She worked as a cook in a logging camp; later, she became a dedicated practical nurse for Dr. Runkle. (She helped bring Joe Kimsey into the world.)

In 1938 Anna returned to Dunsmuir, where she lived until her death in 1950.

IN HONOR OF THE DABOVICH FAMILY

OUR GRANDPARENTS

Eleanor Helen Dabovich
Born February 10, 1898, Oakland
Died December 9, 1979, Redding

Cyril Hartwick Dabovich
Born January 20, 1897, San Francisco
Died June 12, 1962, Sacramento

AND OUR FATHER

Cyril Harron Dabovich
Born May 30, 1927, Oakland
Died August 13, 1981, Mt. Shasta

Dunsmuir was "home" for many years.

Ann Denise Dabovich, Austin, Texas
Cyril Stephen Dabovich, Redding, CA

Dedicated to:

NANCY and HAROLD FAWCETT'S FAMILY

Nancy Ring Fawcett
Born December 2, 1923
Died August 31, 1978

Harold Wentel Fawcett
Born August 26, 1923
Died February 8, 1971

CHILDREN:

Theresa Joy Juarceys of San Jose, CA
Michael Harold Fawcett, of Anchorage, AK
Pamela Yeteve Fawcett, of Mt. Shasta, CA

GRANDCHILDREN:

Gina Michelle Juarceys, of San Jose, CA
Brian Keith Fawcett, of Mt. Shasta, CA

"They would be so proud of all of you."

Aunt Rosemary
(Rosemary Johnson, Redding, CA)

A BRIEF HISTORY OF THE DALLA LASTA FAMILY

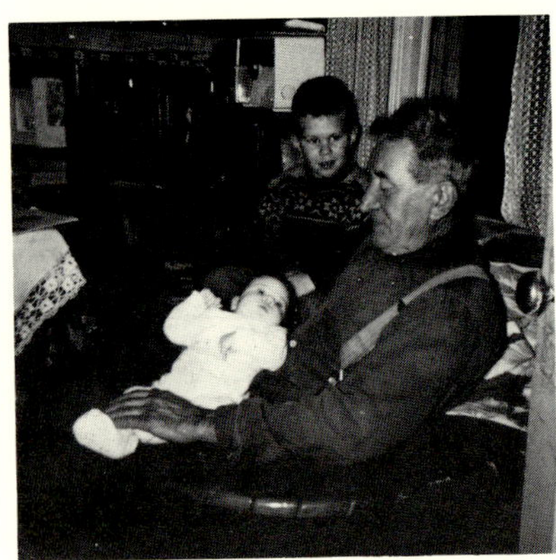

Sebastiano, Mary Roberts,
Adrian Roberts

Francis killed
at Okinawa, WW II

Maria Dalla Lasta
Mary Roberts

Sebastiano Dalla Lasta was born at Paderno Del Grappa, province of Treviso Italia, on June 29, 1884. When Sebastiano was about 10 years old, his father died and he had to help support his mother and sisters. Thus he was deprived of a formal education. In 1905 he came to Dunsmuir to work for the Southern Pacific. Lacking an education, he did hard manual labor. After a few years, he returned to Italy and married Maria Peruzzi, a childhood friend. His mother was ill, so Mary remained in Italy to care for her until her death five years later. Maria and Giovanna, four years old, came to the United States. Speaking only Italian, it was a long hard trip across the ocean to Ellis Island and then across the nation by railroad to Dunsmuir. Lugia (Lois) was born in 1916; Francis, 1920; Marie, 1922; Johnnie, 1924; and Dario (David), 1927.

Mr. Dalla Lasta (Bosco) worked for forty years for the Southern Pacific Railroad, first as a machinist, then as section gang worker. At the age of 73, he suffered a stroke, was paralyzed, and died ten years later in a rest home, December, 1965.

Maria, born June 22, 1889 at Paderno del Grappa, Italy, had a stroke when she was 59. She overcame her difficulties somewhat until she was 80. She suffered very poor health during her later years. She lived with Lois, who cared for her until she was taken to a rest home. She died August 8, 1969.

As for their children — Giovanna (Jennie) died in 1934 from childbirth complications. She had married Kenneth Dal Busco of Weed. She left a child, Kennie, who lived with his grandparents. He attended Dunsmuir schools, went into the Air Force, attended colleges at Tokyo, Hawaii, San Francisco State. He is an appraiser for the State at Milpitas. He is married and has two teenagers, Kennie and Jennie.

Johnnie died at age 15 in 1938 from a damaged heart caused by rheumatic fever. Francis was killed in action at Okinawa in 1945, four years after going into the Army (W.W. II). Three months before the end of the war with Japan, he was killed.

Lois attended Mills College, taught school for several years, and retired from her position of general supervisor of the San Leandro school system in 1978, after forty-two years in school work. Marie attended the University of California, Berkeley received a teaching credential, and taught at several high schools. She married Adrian Roberts of Cedarville, CA in 1946. They have been self-employed in the plumbing business for the past 26 years. They have four children: Adrian, Mary, William, and Kathleen. Adrian, Jr., 34, is in school work and lives at Chico; Mary, 30, married Dave Jeffers and works for Citizens Utilities at Susanville, where they live. They have one son, Jimmy, 6. William (Billy) is single and lives at Alturas. He works in the plumbing business. Kathleen, 17, recently graduated from high school and is attending junior college at Visalia.

David attended U.C. Berkeley, and after working for the State, he went to work at McClellan Air Force Base at Sacramento, where he makes his home. He retired in 1984. He and his wife, Marion, have two children: Dario, 20; and Diane, 24. Dario attends Pepperdine University. Diane graduated from Whitworth College, Walla Walla, Washington. She is now employed at a Savings and Loan Co. at Beverly Hills.

Thus, the dream of Sebastiano and Maria came true. They knew the worth and value of an education. They worked hard and sacrificed much so that their children could have a good education and so have a better and easier life than they had had. The family feels honored and proud to have had such courageous and loving parents.

Lovingly submitted by:

Mary Roberts
Lois Dalla Lasta
David Dalla Lasta

Marie, David, Maria, Ken Bal Busco, Lois

Adrian, Sr., Kathleen, Marie,
Adrian, Jr., Billy

DANIELS

Rhyll (Vet) Daniels was born in Independence, Idaho, in 1903 to Susan Bailar Daniels and Sylvester Daniels. His family moved to Gridley, CA, in 1914 and then to Sacramento in 1920.

Esther Jones Daniels was born in 1906 in Amity, Oregon, to Una Hodge Jones and Jesse Burr Jones. The family moved to Sacramento in 1920. Both Rhyll and Esther graduated from Healds Business College in Sacramento. They were married in Sparks, Nevada, in 1928, and made their home in Sacramento.

Rhyll worked as an accountant for a lumber company and then for a large construction company. Esther worked for several years as a secretary for an insurance company. Their only child, Gene, was born in 1938 in Sacramento.

In 1940 they purchased the Palisades Motel in Dunsmuir and moved up there. Running a motel and service station was a new experience to both of them, but they have never regretted moving to Dunsmuir.

During World War II, Rhyll went to work for the S.P.R.R. as a fireman while Esther and her mother ran the business with Rhyll's help on his off hours. When the war was over, he decided to stay with the railroad a little longer. He became an engineer and eventually retired in January 1969.

Rhyll and Esther Daniels

They sold the motel in 1945. Esther worked part-time for the then Department of Employment and also retired in 1969. They celebrated their 50th Anniversary in 1978. They belong to the United Methodist Church, are Charter members of the Retired Railroad Club, of which Rhyll is a Past President, the Senior Citizens Club, and the Eagles — and Esther of the W.B.A.

They have always enjoyed traveling and have done even more since they have retired. The highlight of their travels to date was a trip around the world in 1973.

Gene went from kindergarten through high school in the Dunsmuir schools. He went to Boy's State as a junior and was president of the Student Body in his senior year. He graduated from Stanford with a degree in engineering and as an Ensign in the U.S. Navy in 1960. He left immediately for Pensacola to start his training for a career as a Navy pilot.

He met and married Linda Arms in Albuquerque in 1966. They have two children, Terri and Scott. Gene decided to retire from the Navy when he had 20 years service and that time came while he was stationed in Bremerton as flight commander on the Carrier Enterprise. They all liked that area so well they are making it their permanent home.

Gene, Linda, Terri, Scott Daniels

THE
BOB & LOIS DEWEY
FAMILY

Arrived in Dunsmuir 1946

Even though they had been going to the same church together for several years, someone had to point out to Bob that Lois was growing up! Since she had older girlfriends, Bob assumed she was also older. He worked up enough nerve to ask her for a date, and here we see them at the 1939 World's Fair on one of their first dates. Lois is 14.

On her "sweet-16-and-never-been-kissed" birthday, Bob pops the question and Lois gets kissed and engaged all on the same day.

One year later Bob is a wiser man. He knows Lois is only 15, and he has the good sense to let her help choose his new suit. They are back at the World's Fair on Treasure Island in San Francisco for the closing ceremonies. By now they are hopelessly in love.

On August 16, 1941, they were married at the Claremont Hotel in Oakland; spent their wedding night at the Mark Hopkins in San Francisco, and honeymooned down the coast to Catalina Island. They return to Bob's service station and their new home (in Walnut Creek). Four months later, Lois is on her way to becoming a war bride as W.W. II breaks out.

The war just over, Bob returns to Walnut Creek; and together with their best friends, Joalice and Johnny Richards, they sell their houses to make a down payment on Brown's Motor Lodge in 1946. A year later they had their first son, Louis; and 19 months later they had their second son, Steven. The motel's name was changed to CAVE SPRINGS, and their third son, David, was born in 1953.

In 1962 this photo was taken in front of the new Methodist Church, which the family helped build. There is a new member of the family a little over a year old. After 13 years of trying, Bob and Lois finally got a girl, Susan. During this time, Bob became mayor, built a home and a swimming pool, and added 10 units to the motel.

The family on the left is Arwen (6) and Nancy in back of Steve with Amy (3) on his lap. The bearded one is Louie with Cabus (4) by his head; D'Arcy (1½) in his lap. Next to him is his wife, Belinda, holding their other twin, Shannamar (1½). "Suzy" is next to Belinda. Behind her is "Big Grandpa" and tiny Grandma. Next to them are David and Linda.

Twenty years later, the family has grown with the addition of spouses and grandchildren. Grandpa and Grandma still live in town, but have joined the Senior R.V. set; and son, Louie, and his wife, Belinda, run CAVE SPRINGS.

McGEE — DELGADO

JOSEPHINE AND ARTHUR McGEE

Arthur came to Dunsmuir in 1919. He hired out as a call-boy. He became a brakeman and later a conductor. Josephine worked at Bascom's Grocery and Gooch's Drug Store. She worked as a crew dispatcher for the S.P. during the war years. She was head of the Siskiyou County Cancer Society for 32 years.

VENTURA AND TEODOSIO DELGADO

Teodosio came to Dunsmuir from Mexico in 1919. He sent for his family the following year. He worked on the section gang and later on as a gardener. Many of the men thought his name was too hard to pronounce so they changed it for him — to John.

DOROTHY AND MICHAEL DELGADO

Dorothy (McGee) Delgado became a school teacher and taught for almost 30 years. They were married on May 29 which turned out to be the birthdate of both fathers.

Michael graduated from the local school, then worked about 9 years in McCloud in the woods and at the mill. During the war years he was an Aerial Gunner. On his return to Dunsmuir he worked as warehouseman for the power company for 27 years.

THE FAMILY TODAY

Michael Arthur is teaching in Redding and his wife, Joyce, works for the Jhirmack Co.

John is continuing the railroad tradition of the family — he is an engineer. Shown here with his wife, Gayleen, and their two children, Stephanie and John Jr.

Patricia works for the Forest Service in Redding and David is still attending school.

TO THE MEMORY OF
OUR LOVING PARENTS

HAZEL BATES DUNCAN AND JOHN ALBERT DUNCAN

God made a wonderful mother and father,
A mother and father who never grow old;
He made their smile of the sunshine,
And He molded their heart of pure gold;
In their eyes He placed bright shining stars,
In their cheeks, fair roses you see;
God made a wonderful mother and father,
And He gave the dear mother and father to me.

From your children, with love,

"Bethe" Bertha Elizabeth Duncan Obland
Laura Hazel Duncan Reames
John Albert Duncan, Jr.
Edward Franklin Duncan
"Conne" Constance Norma Duncan Gauthier
"Pat" Floy Patricia Duncan
William Bryan Duncan
Lyle Lester Duncan

IN HONOR OF A LOVELY LADY —

MOTHER, GRANDMOTHER, GREAT-GRANDMOTHER —
ALSO "NONIE"

MARTHA RAMONA FERRARI

You always knew how to brighten our day
With things that you did in your kind, loving way.
You knew how to see things from our point of view,
And be understanding and helpful, too.
You always knew how to give and to share,
To bring special joy and to lighten a care,
You knew how to add so much beauty to living,
For you knew the true art of loving and giving,
Each time we needed someone you were there to see us
    through,
Beautiful the earth around you
Peaceful the sky above
Harmony and joy surrounded you
Gentle was your love.

From your children, with love,

Mike   Mae Ferrari McGovern
  Peter   Antonieta "Toni" Ferrari Barber
    Steve

Your grandchildren, with love,

Wanda Marie McGovern Hackler
  Darlene Louise Barber Duncan
    Diane Martha Barber Agostini

Your great-grandchildren, with love,

Byran William Duncan	Eddie Raymond Hackler	Lance Steven Agostini
Bruce Anthony Duncan	Earlyn Marie Hackler Conn	Dino Anthony Agostini
		Mikeleen Louise Agostini

IN HONOR OF OUR LOVING PARENTS

TONEY ALFRED BARBER and ANTONIETA "TONI" FERRARI BARBER

God made a wonderful father
A father who never grew old;
He made his smile of the sunshine,
And he molded his heart of pure gold;
In his eyes he placed bright shining stars,
In his cheeks, fair roses you see;
God made a wonderful father,
And he gave that dear father to me.

> Mother, you always know how to give and to share,
> To bring special joy and to lighten a care,
> You know how to add so much beauty to living,
> For you know the true art of loving and giving,
> Each time we needed someone you were there to see us
> through,
> There are memories of your kindness,
> Of your warm and tender touch,
> Your sweet and gentle nature
> That we love so very much.

From your daughters, with love,

Darlene Louise Barber Duncan

Diane Martha Barber Agostini

IN HONOR OF THE DOMINGUEZ FAMILY

Guilermina, Jose, Eva, Raymond, Adela, Soladad,
Ruben, Maria, Ernesto, Delia, Elodia, Jose, Herbert, Olga, Marcelino

Jose Guillermo Dominguez was born June 25, 1900, at Hacienda la Gomera Chihuahua, Mexico. In 1918 he went to El Paso, Texas, to work at the American Melting Refining Co. Here he met Elodia Gutierrez. She was born August 28, 1902, in Hidalgo del Parrol Chihuahua, Mexico. Her parents were Francisco Gutierrez and Rosario Galindo Gutierrez. In 1920 Jose and Elodia were married. Herbert and Jose were born here. In 1922 they moved to L.A. for one year and in 1924 they came to Dunsmuir. He worked on the section and then worked as boilermaker and power plant operator for thirty-eight years. Elodia lived at Parrol in 1910 during the Revolution. When Pancho Villa and his soldiers came through the town, Elodia's mother would hide the girls in the cellar.

The Dominguezes have thirteen children. All of them attended the local schools.

Herbert Joseph, Nov. 25, 1920; Joseph Francisco, April 23, 1922; Soladad Rosealia, Dec. 21, 1927; Eva, Nov. 18, 1928; Guillermina, June 25, 1930; Adela, Sept. 4, 1931; Raymond Antonio, Aug. 2, 1935; Ruben Edwardo, Feb. 2, 1937; Maria Viola, Feb. 23, 1939; Olga Pauline, Aug. 30, 19___; Delia Amelia, Aug. 16, 19___; Eugene Marcelino, Jan. 1, 1944; Ernesto Elfonzo, Oct. 5, 1946. Marcelino died in 1979.

Lft. Elodia's Father,
Francisco Gutierrez

Rt. Jose Dominguez
at work

RUBEN AND DARLENE'S MARKET

(S and J Market)

Pictured above are Ruben and Darlene Dominguez, proudly displaying the silver dollar presented to them with best wishes by Dom Sirianni on March 19, 1973, the day they became proprietors of the S and J Market on Sacramento Avenue. There with Dom to wish them luck was Red Trimble, who gave them a horseshoe which hangs above the entrance to the store. For fifteen years prior to buying the business, Ruben was employed at the market working for owners, Sam Mazzei and Joe Baldo.

Ruben was born in Norden, California, February 2, 1937; and Darlene, in Weed, California, February 21, 1938. They were married June 23, 1956. They have two sons. Edward Dominguez was born in McCloud, California, April 14, 1958; and Curtis Dominguez who was born in Mt. Shasta, California, February 9, 1964.

In appreciation, we wish to thank all of our devoted customers who have been so faithful to Ruben and Darlene's Market for the past eleven years.

!FELIZ CUMPLEANOS, DUNSMUIR!

Harold Barr

*Franklin Barr
Two years old*

Nina Barr

Harold Barr

*Kora Barr
Harold's father*

Sabilla Bess Langdon

Mary Langdon Barr

Franklin and Linda Barr

Harold, Cheryl, Nina

*Harold's grandparents . . . Franklin P. and Ida Louise
Barr . . . his father, Kora . . . his uncle, Otho, in the
back*

*Cheryl   JoAnne
Easter 1969
Seventeen consecutive
weeks with snow*

Harold Barr's paternal grandfather, Franklin P. Barr, was born in Fairfield, Ohio. He made the Cherokee Strip Rush. He was married to Ida Louise Miller. They had two sons, Otho and Kora. Franklin died in Woodward, Okla., on Dec. 20, 1940. His wife preceded him on July of 1927 in Sharon, Okla.

Kora Barr, Harold's father, was **born in Wayne, Ohio, on June 28, 1882.** His wife, Mary Langdon, was **born in Turon, Kansas, on Nov. 13, 1888.** Harold was their first child, **born in Hackberry, Okla., on Sept. 8, 1909.** He had four sisters and five brothers (one lived only four months and the other nearly thirteen years.

Ross was born in Sharon, Okla., on Nov. 7, 1911.

Mildred Barr Graves was born in Sharon, Oklahoma, on June 13, 1913.

Willard (deceased) was born in Sharon, Okla., on Sept. 28, 1916.

Charles (deceased) was born in Sharon, Okla., on May 12, 1918.

Wilbur (Russell) was born in Sharon, Okla., on Sept. 10, 1920.

Ida (Ruth) Barr Wyatt **was born in Felt, Okla.,** on Dec. 24, 1921.

Opal Barr Hanson was **born in Waukomis, Okla.,** on Aug. 9, 1923.

Fae Barr Miller was **born in Felt, Okla., on** Aug. 10, 1925.

Burton Barr was born in Felt, Okla., March 16, 1927.

Opal and Fae have lived in Weed, Calif. since 1946. Ross lives in Reedley, Calif. Mildred and Burton live in Valliant, Okla. Russell lives in Paris, Texas. Ruth lives in White City, Ore.

Kora Barr died in Hugo, Okla., on Feb. 14, 1967. His wife preceded him on June 13, 1944 in Valliant, Okla.

Harold Barr's maternal grandmother, Sabilla Bess Langdon, was born in Indiana on April 13, 1827. She married Samuel Langdon, who was born on August 11, 1827. Samuel was a teamster in the Mexican War. He was a participant in the Cherokee Strip Rush. They had a daughter, Mary, who later became Mrs. Kora Barr. Sabilla died in Enid, Okla., on April 13, 1955. Samuel died on Aug. 8, 1913.

Harold Barr went to Reedley to live with his cousin and wife, Willie and Marie Barr. They lived near Nina's parents, who were friends of Willie and Marie. Harold and Nina met and married about nine months later. They were married by the Mennonite Brethren minister in his home in Reedley, Calif. on Aug. 19, 1937. After the reception at the home of Nina's parents, they spent the night with Nina's Aunt Martha Voth. The following day they drove **to Los Angeles, Calif., where they** lived for about seven months. They moved to Reedley, Calif. On Dec. 17, 1938, their only child was born in Fresno, Calif. He was named after his great-grandfather, Franklin P. Barr. Franklin was the first grandson or great-grandson on both sides of the family. After

Franklin P. received a large picture of Franklin, he requested that it be placed so that he could see it in each room in which he sat or rested in bed. After his death, when Franklin was about two years old, Willie, **Marie, Harold, Nina, and Franklin** drove to the funeral in Valliant, Okla.

When Franklin was four years old, Harold and Nina moved to San Diego, Calif. Nina was a draftsman **for Consolidated Aircraft Co., and** Harold was a machinest. In 1944, Nina was tranferred to Fort Worth, Texas. They had their first and last long train ride.

In 1945, Harold, Nina, and Franklin moved to Valliant, Okla. The following year, Nina began her two years of teaching in a one-room school. It was a very exciting experience. While there, Nina continued her college education at the State Teacher's College at Durant, Okla. Her first year's salary was $96.00 per month. The second year she had a raise of $30.00 per month. The first year, she had eighteen students of all grade levels; the second, thirty-eight, including eight in the first grade. To write of the wonderful experiences there, would be too long for these pages. Some of you may remember Carl Tidmore, of Weed, Calif. He was a barber there, had a country-western band which played in the area, gave concerts at the College of the Siskiyous in Weed, Calif. Carl was in her seventh and eighth grade at the Peaceful Home School. Carl and three of his brothers visited the Barrs in Dunsmuir.

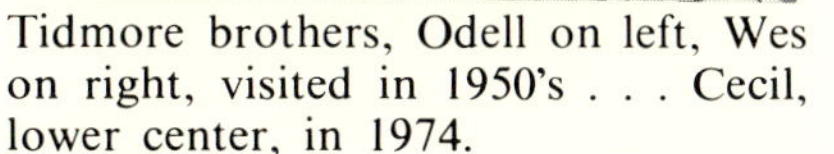

Tidmore brothers, Odell on left, Wes on right, visited in 1950's . . . Cecil, lower center, in 1974.

Mrs. Barr's first school . . . Peaceful Home School near Valliant, OK. Carl Tidmore is standing above others in center. Franklin is wearing the shirt with stripes.

Mrs. Barr's first class in Dunsmuir . . . second grade.

Boy's Chorus . . . 1953-1958

Jim Stanley Mrs. Barr's nephew

Double Quartette of Boy's Chorus . . . 1954

In 1948, the Barrs moved back to Reedley. Nina continued her education at Fresno State College and received her Bachelor of Education Degree. During this time, Harold did various jobs on farms.

The Barrs moved to Dunsmuir in 1951, after Mr. Hartsel Gray, the Dunsmuir Elementary School superintendent said that he needed a second grade teacher. That was the beginning of Nina's twenty-six years of teaching the Dunsmuir children of the elementary school. She taught the first grade for more than twenty years; the second grade for one year; the third grade for two; the Educationally Handicapped Class for three; Miller Unruh Reading for one; Boys Chorus for five; with the kindergarten class, she finished her teaching career in 1979. Nina taught under the supervision of Mr. Roger Ellis, Mr. Al Kempton, and Mr. Eugene Evans.

Harold worked for the railroad company for the Water Service until his health forced him to retire on March 29, 1968. He continued to fish (from boat instead of the river bank), to work in his flower and vegetable garden, and to learn new hobbies. He enjoyed making knives and giving them to relatives and friends. He was always ready to help a neighbor or friend in need.

Railroad Days 1955-1956

On June 5, 1979, Harold died at home during the last week of school. He was buried in Mount Shasta, with all of his brothers and sisters and a large group of friends and family attending the funeral. Franklin, with the help of Harold's brothers and sisters, moved his mother to a mobile home which she and her late husband had purchased in Benicia just a few months before his death.

Franklin attended the Dunsmuir Schools from the seventh grade through high school. His extra-curricular activities were singing (chorus and solo), band, football and shop. He attended Chico State College and the College of the Siskiyous after finishing high school.

After attending college, he worked for the Southern Pacific Railroad in Dunsmuir and Oakland.

On Sept. 30, 1961, Franklin married Linda Howell of Dunsmuir in the home of Franklin's parents. They had two daughters, Cheryl Anne and Jo Anne. Cheryl was born in Oakland on Jan. 23, 1963; Jo Anne, in Mount Shasta on May 3, 1966.

Cheryl married Robert Clymens in Pittsburg, Calif., on April 5, 1981. They live near Antioch, Calif. where they are employed in a convalescent hospital.

Jo Anne lives in Rocklin, Calif., with her mother. She graduated from high school in 1984 and is continuing her education at a college in Rocklin.

Franklin and his wife, Tresa Hutchinson Barr, live in Benicia. She works for Pacific Bell. Franklin is an engineer for the Union Pacific Railroad.

Harold Barr, left lower corner, with Water Service Department . . . 1959

Cheryl and Robert Clymens

Jo Anne Barr

Franklin and Tresa Barr

Nina's mother and her sister, Martha, in double wedding . . . second row. Left to right: Martha and Henry Voth; Lydia and Martha's parents, Abraham A. and Anna Neufeld; Fred's parents, John J. and Rose Nord; Lydia and Fred Nord . . . first row, left to right: Abraham D. Neufeld's father, Abraham A. Neufeld and stepmother; Anna Neufeld's parents, Anna and George Knaak.

Abraham A. and son, Abraham D. Neufeld . . . about 1877.

At right: Nina and Frances, daughters of Fred and Lydia Nord.

Nina and her mother at age seventeen.

Nina Barr's ancestors were born in Germany. During the years 1525-1550, they were among those who were severely persecuted for their religious beliefs. They took refuge in Holland. Here a priest, Menno Simons, left the Catholic Church to become their leader. It was at that time that the group received the name, "Mennonites." They lived in Holland for nearly one hundred years. Finally, persecution became so great, that they accepted the invitation of rulers to live in a Polish area, which later became Prussia. Here they lived until about 1789, when their religious beliefs were denied them. Shortly after that, the Russian Empress, Katherine II invited the Mennonites to settle the north area of the Black Sea, which is called the Ukraine. They were granted a one-hundred-year "Charter of Privileges." Before the expiration of the one hundred years, many unacceptable demands were made. This induced them to send a delegation to America to investigate opportunities there. These men were cordially invited personally by President Grant to settle in the new lands along the lines of the Santa Fe Railroad.

Beginning in 1874, a large number of the Mennonites from the Ukraine in Russia emigrated to areas near Newton and Peabody, Kansas, and other mid-west states. All of Nina's ancestors settled near Peabody, Kansas.

Nina Barr's ancestors were of the Mennonite faith. She attended the Mennonite Church in Reedley until she married Harold.

Nina's maternal great grandparents, George and Anna Klabau Knaak, were born in Germany. As a young couple, they walked to Prussia. Later, they went to Russia, where her grandmother, Anna Knaak was born Dec. 18, 1870. She was four years old when she and her parents emigrated to Peabody, Kansas. (Anna died near Reedley, CA on Feb. 18, 1931.)

Nina's paternal great grandparents, Abraham A. Neufeld and Agatha Friesen Neufeld, were born in southern Russia (Ukraine) near the Kuban River. Her grandfather, Abraham D. Neufeld, was born there on Jan. 18, 1867. He was nine years old when he and his parents emigrated to Kansas near Peabody at the same time as the Neufelds. (Abraham died near Reedley, California, on Jan. 8, 1958.)

On Oct. 29, 1890, Nina's grandfather, Abraham D. Neufeld married Anna Knaak. In 1894, they moved to Fairview, Okla. Her mother, Lydia, was born there on Sept. 25, 1895. In 1911, when Lydia was sixteen years old, she with her parents, sister, and four brothers moved to Reedley, California, by train.

Nina's paternal grandparents, John J. Nord and Rose Ritiskofski (partly Russian) were born in the southern part of Russia (probably in Ukraine). John J. and Anna, their first two children were born there. Nina's father, Fred J. Nord, their fifth child, was born in **Marion County, Kansas, on Sept. 6, 1892, after emigrating to Kansas** near Peabody or Newton.

At about the same time that the Neufelds moved to Fairview, Okla., the Nord family moved, too (1894). Later, when the Neufelds moved to Reedley, Calif., the Nords moved to Bakersfield, Calif. with about one hundred other families.

Sometime between 1911 and 1916, Fred met Lydia Neufeld, who had found work in Bakersfield. They were married at a double wedding with Lydia's sister, Martha, and Henry P. Voth in Reedley, Calif. on Feb. 23, 1916.

Fred and Lydia were divorced when Nina was very young. Lydia married Peter B. Regier from Enid, Okla. They were married for more than fifty years. (Lydia died in Palm Springs, Calif. on Sept. 11, 1976.) Peter died in Fresno on March 17, 1979.

Fred and Lydia had two daughters: Nina, born in Reedley on Jan. 28, 1917; and Frances, born in Reedley on July 28, 1918.

Lydia and Peter had one son, Roy, born near Reedley, California, on March 21, 1924.

Fred and Ermal (his last wife) had a son, Harry, born in Seattle, Wash., on Aug. 24, 1933, and a daughter, Ermal, born in Sacramento, Calif., on June 9, 1935.

Ermal Nord Patrick Stockel

Harry Nord

*Picture on right: The Regier Family
Second row, left to right: Nina, Roy, Frances
First row: Peter, Roy Lydia*

Fred

Harold and Nina Barr, 1937

Fred and Lydia Nord

Nina Nord . . . six months

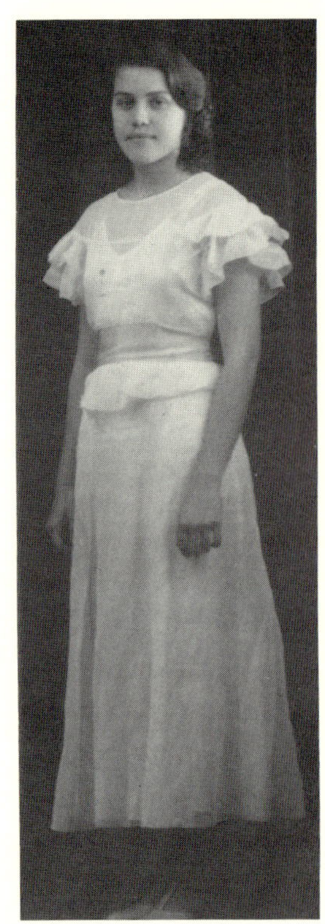

Nina . . . nineteen

Fred's parents . . . John J. Nord and Rose Ritiskofski Nord

On Oct. 10, 1981, Nina married Jesse Dryer in Vallejo, Calif. They enjoy traveling, visiting Dunsmuir annually to see friends and her former students and visiting their families. They have a busy and happy retirement.

Jesse has three daughters. Dorothy Turk lives with her husband, Curtis, in Lakeport, Calif. Genieve lives with her husband, James, in Olympia, Wash. Elizabeth lives with her husband, Charles, in Stockton, Calif.

Franklin, Nina, Jesse, Genieve, Dorothy, Beth

A BRIEF HISTORY OF
THE RUSSELL ELGIN FAMILY

Russell Charles Elgin was born April 28, 1935, at New Brighton, PA to Kenneth Charles and Lillian Gruber Elgin. In 1948 the family moved to Compton, CA. The Elgin family were musically inclined and always sang in church choirs. It was here that Russell met Molly Lee Pentarelli. Molly was born November 10, 1938, at Pasadena, CA to John Charles and Josie A. Howard Pintarelli.

On June 7, 1958, Russell and Molly married at the St. Elizabeth Church at Altadena, CA. They moved to Chicago, Illinois, where Russell attended the Loyola University, where he received his degree in dentistry in 1960. Their first son, Kenneth Charles, was born at St. Luke Presbyterian Hospital, Chicago, Illinois, on May 5, 1959. In 1960 they moved back to California where they were stationed with the U.S. Navy at Camp Pendleton for two years. Here Steven Joseph was born, September 2, 1960.

After this, the Elgins had to decide where they would set up practice. For two years they canvassed small towns in Northern California, and finally in 1962 they decided that Dunsmuir would be the ideal place. Kathleen Margaret was born September 13, 1962, and James Michael, December 13, 1963, at the Mt. Shasta Hospital.

Molly and Russell have been very active in church activities. For several years they worked with the young people of the parish and held the meetings every Sunday evening at their home. Molly still teaches junior high C.C.D. students. In addition to this Molly is assisting Russell in his practice. He claims she is his right hand.

They reside on Panorama Drive in their lovely A-frame home. They generously share their lovely pool with all their family and friends.

They now have two grandchildren.

IN LOVING MEMORY OF
KEN AND NANCY ELGIN

Ken and Lillian

Kenneth Russell Elgin was born June 21, 1912, at Kittaning, PA to Edward Sloan and Margaret Southworth. In 1928 the family moved to Beaver Valley. In 1931 he met Lillian Margaret Gruber at New Brighten, PA. She was born August 12, 1913, at Beaver Falls, PA to Joseph Andrew Gruber and Margaret Dolores Kramer. On October 12, 1933, Ken and Lillian were married. In 1948 they moved to Lynwood, California. They have five children: Russell Charles, born April 28, 1935; Patricia Ann, born April 14, 1937; Dorothy Margaret, born March 24, 1939, Susan Jean, born January 18, 1948; and Nancy Evelyn, born March 16, 1952.

Nancy attended Dunsmuir High School until her senior year. She was very popular and was liked by everyone. On June 8, 1970, tragedy struck and Nancy was killed in an automobile accident. Her family and her classmates mourned her loss.

The Elgins lived in Southern California for eighteen years. Their one great desire was to get out of the area. They spent vacations looking for property in northern California. They wanted a place where they could retire in a smog-free environment. They drove through Dunsmuir before the freeway was constructed and Lillian couldn't understand why and how people could live in such a hilly area. Though they looked at many places, they could not find one that suited them exactly. But fate intervened. Russell, now a dentist, came to practice at Dunsmuir. Through his efforts he found the property where they now live. The Elgins were delighted.

Although Ken was retired, there was a great demand for a man in his profession . . . tool maker. There were few problems that he could not solve. Everyone who knew him sang his praises. He was active in community and church affairs. He loved music and singing. He was a member of the community choir and a barber shop quartet. In 1978 tragedy again struck the family. Ken was stricken with an aneurism which left him a paraplegic. On April 11, 1981, he died.

There are eleven grandchildren and two great-grandchildren.

Lillian spends much of her time helping others. She is active in church functions and is a member of the hospital auxiliary.

In love and appreciation by:
The Elgin Family

In Memoriam

JACOB and LOUISE EHERENMAN

J. R. Eherenman, a pioneer businessman, came to Dunsmuir in 1908. With partners, Frank Teatreau, John Harmon, E. W. Elfendahl, and H. M. Brazilton, a corporation was formed which they named the Tetreau-Eherenman Mercantile Co. They purchased the grocery and hardware departments of the A. Levy Store on Sacramento Avenue. Fortune smiled on the enterprise and it prospered. In 1913, partners Eherenman and Harmon bought out the others and the corporate name was changed to J. R. Eherenman Co., which soon became one of the major suppliers for the citizens of the city. At the peak of their operation, they employed thirteen clerks, a warehouseman, two delivery drivers, and two solicitors. It is interesting to note that, through the years, many of the railroad workers found temporary employment at the store during slow business times on the railroad.

The corporation acquired and operated a plumbing shop for a time, and opened a "cash" grocery store in the Hutaff building (Traveler's Hotel) that was modeled after the Piggly Wiggly stores that were then popular in the San Francisco area. In 1927 Mr. Eherenman concluded that the grocery business was for younger men. All parts of the business except the hardware store were sold. He operated the hardware store — Dunsmuir's oldest mercantile establishment — until his retirement in 1942.

The greatest tragedy of Mr Eherenman's life was the loss of his wife, Louise, during the flu epidemic of 1918, shortly after giving birth to a daughter. Her passing was also a great loss to the community as she had been a valued nurse at Dr. Cornish's hospital and a guiding force in the Red Cross. Years later her daughter, Martha, followed in her footsteps as a nurse.

The other side of the coin was the humanity and empathy of this man. He made a home for his widowed sister-in-law and he became a father to her two young sons and raised them as his own. His daughter, Martha, was the joy of his life. Her every wish was his command — almost, but he knew when to say "no" and when to chastise.

Mr. H. Musket King — a sort of Mr. Everybody of the town — told of the Christmases when "Jake" came to him with $100. "Find someone who needs it," he told Mr. King, "and give them a Merry Christmas."

Such were the contributions of one of Dunsmuir's pioneer businessmen as remembered by one of his "sons," Jim Lockart.

This page is presented by Martha and William Van Horn and their children and grandchildren: Claude and Bernadette Van Horn and Laurie, Lisa and Christena; Lynn and René Beleveau and Jake.

In Loving Memory
MINNIE LOCKART

Minnie Steuber Lockart was born in Illinois to German emigrant parents. She was educated in German-American and American schools.

American farming was not the same as it had been in Germany. The family soon found themselves in financial difficulty. Then, quite suddenly, occurred the first great tragedy of Minnie's young life — her mother died, leaving the father with a poor farming operation and seven children to raise. Minnie's strong sense of responsibility rose to meet the crisis. She, being the oldest child, became the mother. It was through her efforts that all of the Steuber children turned into people of substance.

She married Monte G. Lockart, but tragedy struck twice again. In rapid succession she lost her first-born to polio and then her husband succumbed after an extended illness. She was left with two sons to raise: Charles, a baby of less than a year, and James, three years old.

At about the same time, her sister in Dunsmuir died shortly after giving birth to a daughter. A few months later, at the invitation of her brother-in-law, Minnie and her boys arrived in Dunsmuir to make their home with him and his motherless daughter, Martha.

It wasn't easy — coming into a strange home in a strange town — to mother three children of ages from six months to three years — but she was possessed of an unshakable sense of duty and an unfailing faith in God. She put both of them to work. The house became a home, the children became brothers and sisters, and they all became a family.

Mother's devotion to her church was typical of her support of those things in which she believed. In just a few years she became a pillar of strength to which others turned for help. During the depression years she was one of the ladies who kept the church alive. They served turkey dinners every year and sold tickets to everyone in town. They worked together — those ladies of the church — until their church was solvent, but they did not quit there. Mother worked until she was no longer able to perform the tasks — and then complained because she could not.

We miss you, Mom — you and Uncle Jake — who together made a home for three kids. Our only lament is that not all of your grandchildren were privileged to know you.

Minnie Lockart and granddaughters Mary and Linda

Jim and Mildred Lockart

Mary and Bob Ness,
Lori and Courtney

Linda and Richard Ridgeway,
Shawna and Jimmy

Carol and Jim May and Joel

Joan and Jim Rhodda and Brad

Charles and Leah Lockart

James, Esther and Charles

Cherie and Joe Coles

Nannette and Gary Samuelson
and Amy

Martha and Bill Van Horn

Claude and Bernadette Van Horn
and Laurie, Lisa and Christena

Lynn and René Beleveau and Jake

THE EACHUS FAMILY

Clarence and Helen Eachus on their wedding, June 25, 1918

When Helen Edgerton asked Clarence Eachus to a Leap Year Dance, it was the start of a long courthip and their marriage in Red Bluff. Helen worked for the Bank of Tehama County; Clarence was a fireman for Southern Pacific. After their move to Dunsmuir, Clarence was promoted to engineer, in which capacity he served the S.P. for 46½ years before retiring in Dec., 1955.

Clarence and Helen were active members of the Methodist Church. For many years, Clarence used his basso profundo voice in the church choir and served on the Board of Trustees.

Their four children — Marie, Mildred, Jim and Bob — graduated from both the Dunsmuir Elementary School and Dunsmuir High School. Bob and his wife (Alice-Jane Coon) taught in the elementary school from 1955 to 1957. In 1978, Helen passed away at the age of 89.

THEIR FOUR CHILDREN

Marie **Mildred** **Jim** **Bob**

 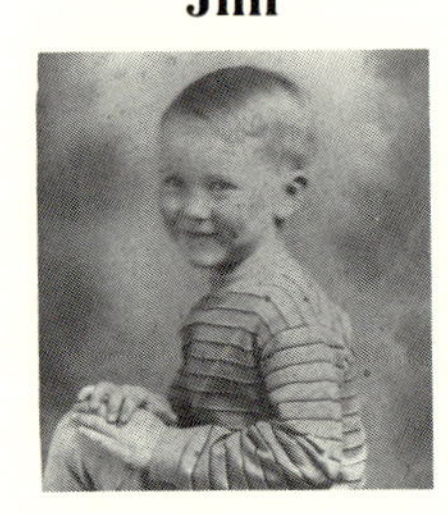 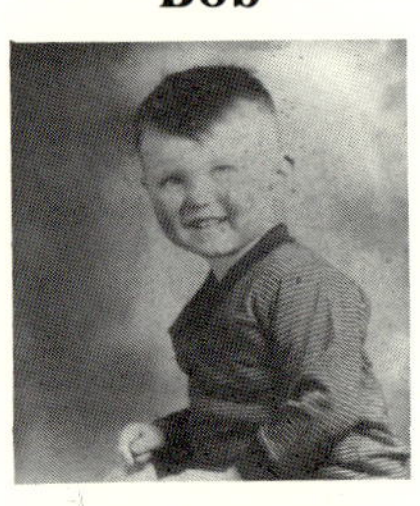

THE FIDLER FAMILY

JESSE G. FIDLER and ANNIE ROBERTS were married in Red Bluff, California, on Feb. 27, 1902. They came to Dunsmuir in the spring of 1906 and resided on Butterfly Avenue until the spring of 1912, at which time they moved to 419 Castle Avenue, where they lived the rest of Annie's life.

ANNIE was a member of Fidelity Chapter No. 131, O.E.S. and also a member of the Ladies Auxiliary to the Brotherhood of Locomotive Engineers. She was locally famous for her cooking, especially her "Boston Baked Beans and Brown Bread."

JESSE was a member of the Dunsmuir Masonic Lodge and also a member of the Brotherhood of Locomotive Engineers. He was well known for his singing, remarkable memory, and his interest in politics. They had five children; Annie died Nov. 4, 1949; Jesse died Dec. 7, 1961.

Roberta "Fid" Belland and her husband Dick Belland opened the first exclusive women's and children's shoe store in Dunsmuir in 1940. "Fid" joined Fidelity Chapter No. 131, O.E.S. in 1921 and is the 1946 Past Matron.

Gladys Fidler Martin was a registered nurse for fifty years. She was the 1947 Past Matron of Mission Chapter No. 155, San Francisco. She is the mother of two: Jon and Janna.

Jesse "Dinger" Fidler, Southern Pacific conductor, was the father of four: Jesse ("Skip"), Robert, Tressa and Merrie Ann. "Dinger" died Sept. 21, 1971.

David Fidler, Southern Pacific engineer, member of Dunsmuir Lodge F. & A.M., and the Brotherhood of Locomotive Engineers, is the father of three: David, Lane, and Thais Ann.

Alta Fidler Podva, podiatrist, is the mother of three: Cherie, Monty, and Diane.

All five of the Fidler children graduated from Dunsmuir Elementary School and Dunsmuir High School. Roberta "Fid" was a member of the first Dunsmuir High School graduating class.

THE FISCHER FAMILY

This Page is Dedicated to the Memory Of
HERMAN AND CORAH FISCHER

Herman and Corah moved to Dunsmuir about 1908 and lived here for the rest of their lives. Herman passed away in 1963.

Corah had preceded him in death.

This picture, taken in 1946, shows Herman and Corah with their two sons, Harvey and Sidney, and their daughter, Helen, and their families.

TOP ROW: Harvey (U.S. Army General, Ret.); Howard Woodside (Athletic Director, Sierra College, Ret.); Helen (Fischer) Woodside; and Sidney (Locomotive Engineer, Ret.).

MIDDLE ROW: Dort (Mrs. Harvey Fischer); Herman; Corah (holding Sid and Ellen's son, Edward); Ellen (Mrs. Sidney Fischer); and David (Sid and Ellen's oldest son).

BOTTOM ROW: Mike and Helen Jean Woodside; Sue and Ann Fischer (daughters of Harvey and Dort).

Since the above picture was taken, three more girls arrived in the family: Carla Woodside, Tina (daughter of Harvey and Dort) and Kathy (Sid and Ellen's daughter).

To Mom and Pops Fischer,
Your Family Will Always Remember

Gayle and Gordon
Railroad Days, 1953

Mary - Gayle - Gordon
and Gary
Easter, 1957

Gary (1960)

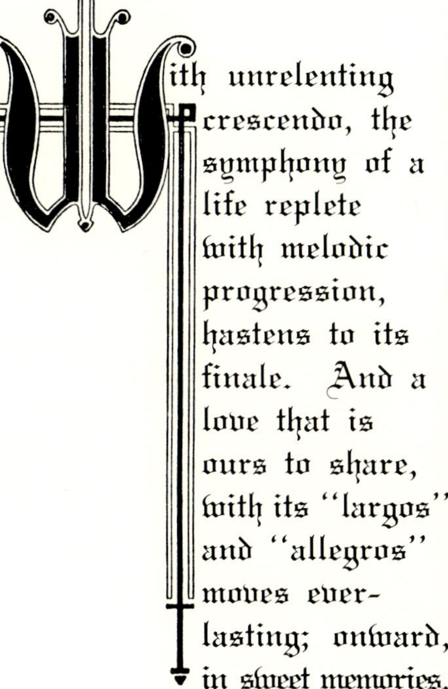

The Family
of
Gordon D. Frunz
Eugene, Oregon

IN HONOR OF THE
GADDY FAMILY

*Claud Gaddy pictured about 1953 on an engine
on the Modoc Line at Secret, California*

Claud and Martha (Lippencott) Gaddy, with their daughter, June, came to Klamath Falls, Oregon, in 1948 from Kansas City, Kansas. Claud had worked as a switchman for the Kansas City Southern Railroad. In Klamath Falls he hired out as a Southern Pacific fireman on December 3, 1948. On January 7, 1957, while working out of Dunsmuir, he was promoted to engineer. After thirty-six years of railroading, Claud retired March 8, 1982. He and Martha continue to make their home in Dunsmuir.

The Gaddys' daughter, June, has three daughters: Leslie, Kelly, and Shelly. Kelly has a son, Aaron.

IN MEMORY OF MY PARENTS
WILLIAM J. and CYNTHIA MOONEY
and MY SISTER
VIOLETTE MOONEY

By Alzade Mooney Gash

William, Violette, Cynthia Mooney shortly before Mr. Mooney's death.

My father moved to Dunsmuir in 1911 to work with Mr. Milburn at the California-Oregon Power Company's (Copco) Dunsmuir office. Because my sister and I were enrolled in school in Ashland, Oregon, my mother did not bring us to Dunsmuir until 1912. We started to school in the old Dunsmuir grade school. Mr. N. T. J. Beaughan was the principal. I was in the fourth grade, and my teacher was Annetta Girard.

At first we lived in one of the Miller houses in North Dunsmuir. From North Dunsmuir we moved to a house on Florence Avenue. Highway #99 still had not come through Dunsmuir. The wooden sidewalk was even with our yards, but after the highway was constructed through town, you had to walk up or down a number of steps to get to the sidewalk depending on which side of the street you lived.

My folks played an important part to make our growing up a happy one. While Mother was a homemaker, she and Father did much good. Holidays we had a full house of folks who had no families. During the recession food and coffee were always available for those going through town and needing food, especially those families with small children. Our church was the Methodist, and our doctors were Cornish and Thompson.

Over the years we watched the town grow and build up. Many changes came to it and to the railroad. My sister and I attended high school and business college in the Bay Area. World War I was with us. We came home and went to work for the Southern Pacific Company. Progress was everywhere. The Travelers Hotel and other businesses and buildings had come. Florence Avenue was now the highway and had become the main street for business. The new bank building and the Post Office were now up there.

Then came wedding bells for me! In 1924 I married George Gash, a locomotive engineer, who had returned from four years of U.S. Army duty in France. A son, William Wiley Gash, was born to us in 1928. Eight months later George died. Ten years later, up near Mossbrae Falls, my father died very suddenly of a heart attack. In the meantime I had moved to San Francisco to be with my sister. Mother later joined us.

In 1940 my son and I moved to Salem, Oregon, the home place of my husband. My mother and sister then joined us in Salem. Violette died in 1953, and my mother died in 1969. I am now a grandmother of two girls and a great-grandmother of three children.

I treasure the memories I have of my dear and wonderful family, and the memories of those many fine friends with whom I grew up in Dunsmuir. My home in Dunsmuir will always be first in my heart because of those memories. Being a "Railroad Buff," I like to remember the sounds of the steam engines, the train whistles, the clang of the bells, and the roundhouse with its steam and many metallic and mysterious noises. All of this was a part of growing up in Dunsmuir!

Alzade Mooney Gash

TO THE PEOPLE OF DUNSMUIR

We dedicate this page to the people who make Dunsmuir a community and a home. Being at home here and sharing in the spirit of this place have contributed enormously to our lives, and we want to acknowledge what we gained during the years our husband and father, Durward Gass, was ill with kidney disease. By a kind of magic that we call community spirit, Durward and his kidney machine became a focus for an outpouring of love and caring that sustains itself even now.

The many gifts and kindnesses we received are what small towns are about. Anyone can understand the importance of this kind of sharing. Much more difficult to express, but at least as important to everyone in the long run, is that this community was so willing to receive what Durward could contribute in return. Sharing with so many people his experience of living with approaching death and sharing their experiences was a source of great joy and peacefulness. The fundamental experience of community transformed the last years of Durward's life from a demoralizing struggle with death into an uplifting opportunity to grow and to contribute. We want you to know that this opportunity has made a great difference to us, and we want you to know that we are grateful for it.

Forest Gass
Lee Gass
Gerald Gass

IN LOVING MEMORY OF OUR PARENTS, JULIANNA AND ANDREW FEICHKO

Top: Mary, Carol, Pat
Bottom: Harry, Julianna, Andrew, Ervin, Gladys, Joe

Andrew (Fijacko) Feichko was born Oct. 12, 1883, to Jacob and Barbara Salkovic Fijacko at Krapina Semlica, (Croatia) Jugoslavia. He suffered many hardships and worked at many jobs to fulfill his one dream and ambition . . . to come to America. He went to work in a coal mine at Vrdnik near the Hungarian border. Here he met Julianna Papp who was born April 1, 1888, to Stephen and Veronika Mago Papp at Bac Topolya, Hungary. They were married Feb. 21, 1909. Mary was born at Vrdnik, Jugoslavia. In April, 1911, Andrew left for America and went to Clear Creek, Utah. In Oct. 1911, he sent for Julianna and Mary. Julianna was pregnant with Carol. They had four sons and four daughters. One son, Henry Columbus, born Dec. 12, 1918, died October 10, 1927.

In 1925, they bought a small farm near Price, Utah, and moved there. Although they owned a larger farm at Miller Creek, Julianna refused to live there as she had experienced two and a half years of extreme hardship and misery there. Four of the children still reside in the vicinity of Price. Carol, Pat and Gladys are now residing at Dunsmuir.

Frank Harry, Feb. 25, 1919; Gladys Jenny, Jan. 20, 1924; Andrew Ervin, Feb. 20, 1921, Patricia Olga, Dec. 30, 1916; Joseph, July 14, 1914; Carol, Dec. 25, 1911; Mary, Jan. 7, 1910.

In love and appreciation.

Mary Skerl

IN LOVING MEMORY OF OUR FATHER, EDDIE GIRARD

EDWARD WALLACE GIRARD

Our dad was a great outdoors man. He loved to fish and hunt and was one of the best fly-fisherman in this area. He spent many days at the Girard Ridge cabin with his father and his cousins. He was born at Castella in 1896, and grew up in this area. He would tell us how good fishing and hunting were in "those good old days." "A person could get a sack full of fish from the bridge to the roundhouse." This was before anything was limited. In those days the family depended upon game and fish to exist. He loved the surrounding area and only felt at home when he was in the shadow of Mt. Shasta.

Lovingly submitted by:

Wally, Jim and Mary Girard

A limit of ducks.

His biggest buck.

Left, Eddie at Girard Ridge Cabin

Eddie and his "Chevie"

THE PAT AND EDDIE GIRARD FAMILY

Patricia Olga Feichko Girard
b. Dec. 30, 1916
Clear Creek, Utah
m. Jan. 3, 1938
Reno, Nevada

Edward Wallace Girard
b. Mar. 5, 1896
Castella, CA
He retired after fifty years as S.P. engineer. He was charter member of the Mt. Shasta Order of Elks. Before he died he received his fifty-year pin.
d. Dec. 11, 1970

Mary Louise, b. May 18, 1947
Dunsmuir, Calif.

Wallace Edward Girard
b. June 7, 1940
Dunsmuir, California

Nancee Dee Burns Girard
b. May 4, 1942
Ashland, Oregon
m. Sept. 1, 1963
St. John's Church
Dunsmuir, California

Susan Elaine Girard
b. June 6, 1968
Mt. Shasta, California

David Christopher Girard
b. August 10, 1969
Jacksonville, Florida

James Joseph Girard
b. Sept. 3, 1944
Dunsmuir, CA

Mary Lynn Long Girard
b. Nov. 3, 1946
McCloud, CA
m. August 24, 1969
St. Joseph's Church
McCloud, CA

Steven James Girard
b. August 7, 1971

Gregory Neil Girard
b. August 31, 1973
Mt. Shasta, CA

(Below)

(Below)

IN LOVING MEMORY OF
BERNARD and DORA GIRARD

Bernard LaFayette and Dora Boyes Girard

Bernard L. Girard, one of Castella's oldest pioneer residents, was born at Trinity Center, January 25, 1889. He was the son of the late Louis and Charlotte Girard. His family moved to Castella in 1892.

In 1915, he was the first forest ranger with USFS at Bray, CA, and patrolled the area on horseback. He also broke horses for Frank Louie on the Louie Ranch at Big Springs.

On June 17, 1917, he married Dora M. Boyes, of Little Shasta, CA. After their marriage they lived in Castella for awhile, then moved to Dunsmuir, where their first daughter, Charlotte, was born in 1918. She passed away in 1924. They then moved to Tennant, CA, where their second daughter, Carol, was born in 1925. Bernard was employed with Long Bell Lumber Co. as an engineer until 1928, when they moved back to Castella. Bernard passed away in 1960. In 1954 Carol married Harold J. Carrington, Jr. They make their home in Dunsmuir, and are both employed by the Southern Pacific Co.

Dora Maria Boyes was born October 20, 1886, at Butte Creek, CA, to Charles Babcock Boyes, who was born in Pennsylvania, and Margaret Jane Coombs, who was born in Hawkinsville, CA.

They settled in Butte Creek, CA, on a cattle ranch approximately two miles south of Mt. Hebron, CA. In the winter of 1890 Charles Boyes died at the age of forty-five, after contracting pneumonia while moving cattle over Ball Mountain. He left his wife (Margaret) with seven older children, and the eighth child was born two months after his death. Margaret Boyes moved her family a couple of years later to Little Shasta, CA, where she raised her family.

Dora Girard moved to Yreka in 1963, and passed away in 1979. Francis Boyes Pope is the only surviving daughter. She now lives in Red Bluff, CA, and will be 101 on her next birthday, in Oct. 1984.

In love and appreciation by:

Carol and Harold Carrington

THE FAMILY OF
ANNA AND HAROLD J. CARRINGTON, SR.

Harold and Anna

Harold J. Carrington, Sr., was born in Wisconsin on June 27, 1901. He was the eldest of five children born to Christine and James Carrington, who with their children migrated west to Los Molinos, CA.

Harold J. Carrington, Sr., married Anna Lois Luman in Ashland, OR, on September 26, 1926. After their marriage they moved to Dunsmuir, CA. Harold was employed with the Southern Pacific Company as a clerk, and retired as Car Distributor in Dunsmuir in 1966, after forty-nine years service. In 1957, Anna and Harold moved to Castella, CA, where Anna still resides. Harold passed away November 23, 1967.

Anna Lois Luman was born in Centralia, Wash., on July 13, 1905. She was the youngest of eight children born to Ellen and Preston Luman. Preston was a rancher and later owned a meat market in Centralia. He passed away in 1908. After his death, Ellen Luman moved her family to Ashland, OR, where she passed away in 1929.

Anna and Harold had two sons. Harold, Jr. was born in Medford, OR, in 1928, and Raymond was born in Dunsmuir, CA in 1930.

Raymond resides in Fairfield, CA, and has been a math teacher in Vacaville High School since 1958. He does metal sculpturing, and also takes news pictures for several different TV stations.

Harold, Jr. hired out with the Southern Pacific Company in the Store Department in 1946, at Dunsmuir. In 1957 he transferred to the Southern Pacific Land Company at Mt. Shasta, CA, where he is now Operation Manager. In 1954 he married Carol Girard. They make their home in Dunsmuir, CA.

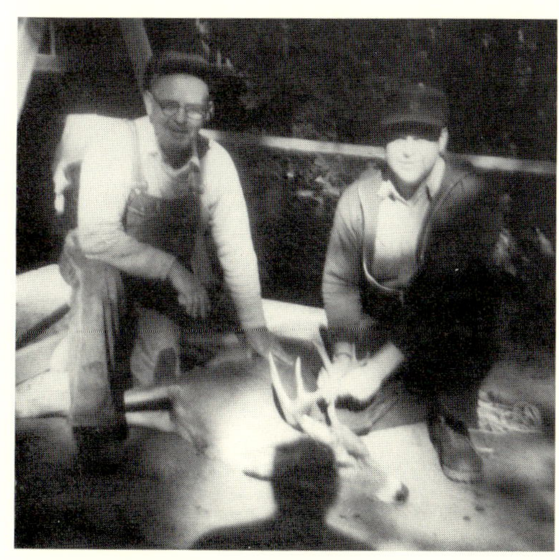

Harold, Sr. and Harold, Jr.

Harold, Sr. with his prize

IN HONOR OF THE
NEHER-GILL FAMILY
In Memory Of
LAWRENCE D. "DOC" GILL

By his wife, Edythe Gill

Above: Benjamin M. Gill, M.D.

*Above: Mary Louise (Mertes) Neher
and Simon P. Neher*

Dr. Benjamin M. Gill was graduated from Lawrence Medical School, Lawrence, Kansas. After his internship, he was hired to work as a company doctor for a lumber company at Mott, Siskiyou County, California, a few miles north of Dunsmuir. In 1886 the railroad had been completed through Dunsmuir, and shortly after that the Southern Pacific Company hired Dr. Gill to be the company's first doctor. He then moved his family to Dunsmuir.

Dr. Gill had married Nancy Devendorf, and they had two children: Waldo Devendorf and Myrtle. Waldo married Mertes Elgie Neher of Dunsmuir, and Myrtle married Charlie Johnson of Yreka, who later became District Attorney of Siskiyou County.

Dr. Gill appears to have been an enterprising young man. He had various business interests, one of which was a spa that he built on the Sacramento River near Shasta Springs. An avenue in Dunsmuir bears his name.

Simon P. Neher and his wife Mary Louise (Mertes) Neher came from Roseville, California, with their daughter Mertes Elgie about the time the railroad arrived in Dunsmuir. They started the Reception Bar on Front Street, which is now Sacramento Avenue. Mrs. Neher, her mother Margaret Schmidt Mertes, and her sister Augusta Mertes Sheafor (Mrs. J. J. Sheafor) had a rooming house where the Travelers Hotel is now. Mrs. Sheafor was Dunsmuir's first kindergarten teacher having started the classes by private subscription.

Mr. and Mrs. Simon Neher had a son, Dunsmuir Simon Neher, who was said to have been the first white boy born in Dunsmuir. When Dunsmuir Neher became a young man, he used the name of Don rather than Dunsmuir.

Waldo Gill and Mertes Neher were married on February 18, 1900. People said, "It will never last! A doctor's son and a saloon keeper's daughter!" But last it did. Waldo and Mertes had three children and sixty-seven years together. Their children were:

Desmond, born June 3, 1901
Lawrence, born May 15, 1913
Nancy, born January 1, 1915

Lawrence "Doc" Gill had two children:
Richard, born May 27, 1941
Caryl, born December 15, 1943

IN LOVING APPRECIATION
OF OUR PARENTS

LOUIS GIRIMONTE and CAROLINA GIRIMONTE

In 1924 Louis A. Girimonte and his brother opened a Men's Clothing Store in Dunsmuir. A few years later, Louis bought his brother's share and continued to operate the business as "Girimonte's."

The first store was located at 815 Sacramento Avenue. Later the store was moved next door to the Reception Bar and Cafe, which was across the street from the train depot.

Nick Girimonte joined his father, Louis, in 1946. In the year of 1948, the business was moved to a new and modern store on Florence Avenue, next door to the Flamingo Club. In 1950, Nick and his brother, Joe, purchased all of their father's interest in the business. A second location was opened in October, 1954, when Nick and Joe bought George Burke's store in Redding. Girimonte's of Dunsmuir remained open until 1957 when the entire operation was moved to Redding.

Giramonte's have clothed several generations of Northern California families for the past 60 years.

IN HONOR OF OUR
BELOVED MOTHER AND FATHER
William Ira Humphreys and Hannah M. Humphreys

William I. Humphreys was born in Foster, Oregon, June 8, 1892, and Hannah M. Humphreys in Pasco, Washington, November 18, 1892.

William I. Humphreys joined the United States Army in 1911, was discharged in 1914, as a Master Sergeant, and was held in the United States Army Reserve until 1919.

Bill went to Medford, Oregon, in 1914, where he met Hannah M. Winn. They were married on September 8, 1914, in Medford, Oregon, at the home of her parents, George and Louisa Winn.

Bill and Hannah lived in Medford, Oregon, until their first child was born; they then moved to Roseburg, Oregon, where he worked for the Portland Division, on the railroad as a brakeman. They had five children, two boys and three girls. Due to illness they lost their oldest son, Gordon Humphreys. They then moved to Brookings, Oregon, where Bill worked on a logging train. They then moved to Sacramento, Calif., to work on the Sacramento Division, as a switchman; later they moved to Gerber, Calif., and then to Dunsmuir, Calif., in 1926, where he worked on the Shasta Division on the railroad, as a brakeman and switchman until the depression, which left most all men without jobs. He then took the Civil Service Examination and went to work for the United States Postal Department in Dunsmuir, CA, until his retirement from the United States Post Office in Dunsmuir. Due to more illness, they lost their youngest son, Donald Humphreys. Their three daughters, Louise, Kathleen and Winnifred, attended the Dunsmuir schools, graduated, and were married.

Bill Humphreys was very active in the community. He was active in the Fish and Game from 1935 to 1955. He wrote many articles for the Fish & Game, which was printed weekly in the Dunsmuir News, for many years. He was an appointed deputy for the Fish & Game. During his life in Dunsmuir, he was active and very interested in local sports and very active in baseball, promoting the town team by drafting ball players to Dunsmuir to play baseball. He scored and took interest in the Little Leagues. He was a member of the Dunsmuir Lions Club, a Past Master and Secretary of the Dunsmuir Masonic Lodge #297, Free & Accepted Masons of California. He worked and served the Fraternal Order of Eagles, Lodge #1147, as Secretary for 25 years.

In 1940 during World War Two, he served the National Guard as Captain, and was an instigator in promoting the National Guard Armory in Mt. Shasta City, CA. He was an officer in the R.O.T.C. at the Dunsmuir High School and instructed classes. Bill also was an active member of the California Grange Lodge, and served as the President. He loved to fish the Sacramento River and hunt all game animals. His wife, Hannah, worked as a housewife raising their children. Hannah is a member of the Ladies Auxiliary of the Fraternal Order of Eagles Lodge Arie #1147 of Dunsmuir. She is a Past President and served as secretary for many years. She also served the Altar Society for St. John's Catholic Church. She also served the California Grange Lodge. Bill and Hannah had many friends and loved this little town of Dunsmuir. Their oldest daughter, Louise M. Humphreys, married Morris Estep, and had three children: Diony, David, and Lillian. Kathleen E. Humphreys married Elmer Graves, and they had two children, Christine and Frances. Winnifred married Nobel Day, and they had four children: Charlene, Connie, Bill, and JoAnna. Bill and Hannah had nine grandchildren, 29 great-grandchildren, and 2 great-great-grandsons. Bill passed away November 3, 1977, but his wife of 63 years still lives at the age of 91, and is still enjoying life. She now is living with each daughter, sometimes in Sacramento, Project City, and in Dunsmuir, Calif.

ELMER GRAVES AND FAMILY

Elmer graves, born in Red Bluff, California, September 18, 1916, moved to Gerber, Calif., and then to Dunsmuir, Calif., in 1916, with his mother and father, Josephine and Lloyd Graves. Here his father worked on the Shasta Division as a switchman and later transferred to being a brakeman on the railroad.

Elmer attended the Dunsmuir and Castella schools, graduated from high school in 1935, went to Chico State University until 1937. At that time, he came home from school, went to work for the McCloud River Railroad, at Mc-Cloud, Calif. In 1940 he transferred from the McCloud Railroad to work for the Southern Pacific on the Shasta Division, as an experienced brakeman. On June 23, 1940, he married Kathleen Humphreys, born in Roseburg, Oregon, in 1920 on February 29th. His wife, who came to Dunsmuir from Oregon in 1926, is a graduate of the Dunsmuir schools and a graduate of Staton's Beautician School of Chico, Calif.

Kathleen was working as a beauty operator for Mrs. Olive Kemp, at the time she married. Elmer and his wife have two daughters, born in Dunsmuir in 1943 and 1944 at the Dunsmuir Hospital. Their daughters are Christine and Frances.

Elmer was a member of the Brotherhood of Railroad Trainmen. Later the Union consolidated and the men joined the United Transportation Union. Elmer is a member of the Dunsmuir Masonic Lodge #297, Free and Accepted Masons of California; a past Patron of Fidelity Chapter #131 Order of the Eastern Star; a past president of the Fraternal Order of Eagles Lodge #1147, of Dunsmuir. His wife is active in the community. She is a past president of the Ladies Auxiliary to the Brotherhood of Railroad Trainman; a past president of the Dunsmuir Federated Women's Club, a past president of the Dunsmuir P.T.A.; and served as secretary for the District P.T.A. of California; a member of the Dunsmuir Elementary School Board for 10 years; a Past Worthy Matron, of Fidelity Chapter #131 Order of the Eastern Star; a past president of the Ladies Auxiliary of the Fraternal Order of Eagles Lodge #1147 of Dunsmuir. Kathleen worked at Carol's Beauty Salon in Dunsmuir for 25 years.Elmer and Kathleen are still active and working in different projects. They have helped to build several of the floats for Railroad Days. Elmer loves to fish and hunt game animals. He retired from the Southern Pacific as a conductor September 18, 1978. Elmer and Kathleen have one grandson, Eric Frank, who lives in Mt. Shasta City with his mother Frances. Eric attends the Sisson Mt. Shasta School, where he is very active in sports. He is also an active member of 4-H.

JOHN PETER

and

HENRIETTA NEASHAM

This is to honor the memory of John and Henrietta Neasham, who came to Dunsmuir on October 24, 1919. After living for a short time on Castle Avenue, they moved to what became their family home at 35 Hill Street. They are pictured here shortly after their wedding at Alturas, California, in 1879. Nine children came to bless the Neashams. At the time they came to Dunsmuir, five of them were living at home: Jasper, who worked for the California Oregon Power Company; Myrt, who became a pipefitter at the Railroad Shops; Albert, who followed in his father's footsteps and served as custodian at the high school; Frank, who worked at the Southern Pacific Shops and later became an engineer on the McCloud Railroad, and

their only surviving daughter, Eva Laura, who finished high school at Dunsmuir in 1925.

John and Henrietta began their married life at Fort Bidwell; they later lived at Igerna, Lyonsville, Red Bluff, and McCloud. John was a sawmill man, and he followed the lumber business. In Dunsmuir, thanks to his millwright skills, he became custodian at the high school and remodeled the house at 35 Hill Street. He retired after leaving the high school job, but, during the depression, he came out of retirement and worked as an expert saw filer with the Civilian Conservation Corps.

Eight of the Neasham grandchildren were born in Dunsmuir. These included: Ernest and Robert, the sons of Carl and Sarah Lena

(Stevenson) Neasham; Vernon Albert, the son of Albert and Barbara (Koller) Neasham; Elizabeth, James and Donald, the children of Arthur and Eva (Neasham) Johnson; and Theodore and Nancy, children of Frank and Loretta (Daw) Neasham. Born near Dunsmuir and living there for a time were the children of John and Ethal (Allen) Neasham: Pearl, Doyal, and Edith.

John and Henrietta grew a garden each year and were famous for their raspberries and blackberries. They were known for their hospitality and generosity.

Both John and Henrietta died in Dunsmuir, he on April 29, 1939; she on August 4, 1952. They are buried in the family plot in Red Bluff.

A BRIEF HISTORY OF
THE GRAY FAMILY

Esther Hough Gray

Hartsel Curtis Gray

Hartsel Curtis Gray was born in Langdon Township, Reno County, Kansas, on August 21, 1895, and moved to southern California with his family in 1903. After his graduation from Huntington Beach High School, his family moved to Union Mattole, Humboldt County, California, where he met Esther Hough, who was the teacher at Union Mattole School. Esther Hough, born May 16, 1896, at Upper Mattole, graduated from Ferndale High School and Humboldt State Normal School. She also taught in Coos County, Oregon, for two years before her marriage to Mr. Gray in Arcata on June 18, 1920.

Shortly after their marriage, Mr. Gray began the two-year teaching course at Humboldt State Normal School, while Mrs. Gray taught in the local schools until her husband received his credential. Later, Mr. Gray received a B.A. degree from Chico State Teachers College.

In 1932, the Grays moved to Siskiyou County, Mr. Gray first teaching in Etna, then working as Rural Supervisor in the office of the County Superintendent of Schools in Yreka. In 1939, he became District Superintendent of the Dunsmuir Elementary School, a position he held until 1955, when he returned to work as a consultant in the county office until his retirement in 1963.

During their years in Dunsmuir, Mr. and Mrs. Gray were active in many community, school, and church groups. Both Mr. and Mrs. Gray were honored with life memberships in the Parent-Teachers Association. Mr. Gray received the Silver Beaver Award for his many years of volunteer work with the Boy Scouts. He was a member of the Lions Club and the Masonic Lodge. Mrs. Gray did home and hospital teaching and managed the elementary school cafeteria for several years. During World War II, she organized the Red Cross home nursing classes and both she and Mr. Gray were members of the Eastern Star. The family participated in many activities of the Methodist Church.

Mr. and Mrs. Gray's daughters, who all graduated from Dunsmuir High School, are: Marjorie Holden, Mountain View; Evelyn Brooks, Albuquerque, New Mexico; and Dorothy Yale, San Jose. There were eight grandchildren: John Holden, Kenneth Holden (deceased), Thomas Harper, Janet Yale, Michael Yale, David Yale, Linda Yale Harris and Stephen Yale. There are four great-grandchildren: Tracy Harper, David and Carla Holden, and Micah Martin.

Mr. Gray died December 31, 1968. Mrs. Gray lives in Yreka, where she continues to be an active member of her community.

By Marjorie Gray Holden, 1984

IN LOVING MEMORY OF OUR PARENTS, SADIE AND NORMAN GREEN

Sadie and Norman's Golden Wedding Anniversary
December 30, 1966

Norman Mitchell Green was born September 20, 1895, at Red Bluff, California.

On December 30, 1916, Norman married Sadie Eola Myers at Grants Pass, Oregon. Sadie was born in Red Bluff, California, October 1, 1895.

In 1920 they moved to Dunsmuir, where Norman worked for the Southern Pacific. After forty years of faithful service, Norman retired as conductor.

Norman was a big man with a heart to match his frame. He was forever interested in politics and the growth and development of Dunsmuir. He loved parades and any activity that promoted Dunsmuir.

Before 1940, Dunsmuir celebrated "Dunsmuir Days" and Norman felt that Dunsmuir was a railroad town and the celebration should be "Railroad Days." Norman had dreams of having a three-day celebration with a program and a parade loaded with floats and bands galore. The dream became a reality. The story is on another page in this book.

After Norman retired in 1960, they moved to Sacramento, where Norman worked at the State Capitol as Sergeant-At-Arms for six years.

They have two daughters, Norma Reubens and Eola Cool; six grandchildren, and nine great-grandchildren.

Norman died August, 1971, and Sadie died November, 1981. Both are buried at Chico, California.

Lovingly submitted by:
Eola Cool and Norma Reubens

THE NORMAN GREEN'S FAMILY IN 1960

Back: Richie Cool, Jack Reubens, Leonard and Larry Reubens
Standing: Dick and Eola Cool, Juanita, Norma and Jackie Reubens, Cookie Cool, Susan Reubens
Seated: Judy Reubens and baby Clifford; Norman and Sadie Green, Julie Reubens
Floor: Mitch, Chris, and H. D. Reis

E. E. Hale and Nettie Hale

THE E. E. HALE
FAMILY

E. E. Hale came to Dunsmuir in August 1917 to work as a brakeman for the Southern Pacific Railroad. His wife, Nettie, followed a couple of months later with their four children. Two more children arrived in 1919 and 1926. He worked as a brakeman for four years and then was laid off. He then did carpenter work and house moving until 1926. He then took over the garbage business with his brother-in-law, Joe Tuttle, until 1934. In the following years, he went to work for the Southern Pacific in the Roundhouse. Later he transferred to Los Angeles remaining in the same position; he retired on disability from there.

After the Hales had moved to Dunsmuir, Nettie's sister's family followed. They were George, Lester, Abner, and Leonard Gilchrist; all four went to work as brakemen for the railroad. Nettie's brother, Rollen Woolley, came to Dunsmuir, where he and Mr. Hale did carpenter work and moved most of the houses that were moved in the 20's. Hale's brother, Oren, came to Dunsmuir to work in the shops for the S.P. Mrs. Hale's niece, Eva Pennington and husband Lester, came from North Dakota; he hired out as a brakeman for the S.P.

The E. E. Hale Family — 1936

When the family would get together after church, there would be 30 to 32 relatives present. They have all gone except for the Marvin Hale Family. Marvin is the third child out of six born to the E. E. Hale family.

The Marvin Hale Family — 1944

With love, appreciation and memory of our parents and our rare good fortune to have been born and raised in Dunsmuir, we present a thumbnail sketch of the J. S. Hanna Family that resided in Dunsmuir between 1908 and 1954.

James Stewart ("Jim") Hanna and his brother, Frank, came to Dunsmuir in 1908 at the behest of the Southern Pacific Railroad Co. which needed employees to work at the division point. "Jim" married **Clara Jane Parsons** June 24, 1909 and brought her to Dunsmuir, where they built a home and raised two children, **Margaret and Mark.** The first house was built at the northeast corner of Florence Ave. (Dunsmuir Ave.) and Grover St. but it burned to the ground just as it was being completed. Fortunately the house was completely insured and another house was constructed on the identical site in 1914. In 1928 the family home was moved 50 feet easterly to the site now known as 125 Grover St. and a service station was built where the family home had previously rested.

"Jim" Hanna, born in Pennsylvania, was a fireman and locomotive engineer for 50 years spread over five different railroads. He started work with the S.P. Co. on August 31, 1899 on the Sacramento Division, but the last 23 years were spent as an engineer on a passenger run between Dunsmuir and Ashland, Ore., which was the main line at that time. He was a member of the Elks Lodge in Ashland, retired in 1931 and passed away in 1942. Uncle Frank was also a fireman and engineer until 1952 when he passed away.

Clara Hanna was born near Woodbridge in San Joaquin County, where she was raised and taught school for many years. She was not only a loving mother and wife, but was dedicated to the betterment of Dunsmuir. She served as secretary to the Rebekahs and was elected as Clerk of the High School Board of Trustees until April of 1929. Then, in 1929, when the Depression had started and there was no money for a salary for the Dunsmuir Branch of the County Library, she undertook to serve it as librarian and continued to serve for nearly 25 years until late in 1953. At that time she became ill and passed away February 17, 1954. "Mom," as we called her, was also a member of the Auxiliary to the Brotherhood of Locomotive Engineers.

"Jim" and Clara never owned an automobile. The first car in the family was a 1932 Cheverolet purchased by Margaret, who was teaching 5th grade in the Dunsmuir Elementary School. In March of 1934 Margaret and Harold Yount of Chico were married, and on March 24, 1984 they celebrated their golden wedding aniversary.

Son Mark was born in 1915 and attended the Dunsmuir schools, was a member of the Civilian Conservation Corps in 1934 and 35, went to Junior College in Sacramento, where he met his future wife, Lois Russell, and in 1942 obtained a civil engineering degree from U.C. Berkeley. He worked for the U.S. Navy mine sweeping forces as a civilian physicist during World War II. In 1945 he was employed by the City of Alameda as a Junior Civil Engineer and was promoted to City Engineer in 1953 where he remained until retirement in January of 1981. In April of 1983 he was elected to a seat on the Alameda City Council and became the Vice Mayor. Wife Lois is also active in Alameda civic affairs and was elected to the Board of Education of the Alameda Unified School District for the years 1977 to 1981.

Daughter Margaret obtained teaching credentials from Southern Oregon Normal School in Ashland, Ore., and Chico State College and spent 35 years teaching in elementary schools in Dunsmuir, Stirling City, Graeagle, Beckwourth, Sloat, Delleker and Portola. She retired in 1973 in Portola, Calif., where she and husband Harold have lived for many years. Harold also retired after many years as a brakeman and conductor of the Western Pacific R.R. Co.

James Stewart Hanna in retirement.

Clara J. Hanna on her way to the library.

Frank Hanna in his engineer's attire.

It is with great affection for Dunsmuir and our friends and acquaintances that we offer this bit of information on our family which enjoyed, benefited from and, we hope, contributed to the Dunsmuir community.

— Margaret Hanna Yount and Mark J. Hanna

ROBERT CREIGHTON HARRIS
1916 — 1975
IN LOVING MEMORY

A third-generation Californian, born and raised in Sacramento, son of Marion Alva Harris and Nettie Ireland Harris. Came to Dunsmuir, first in 1937, then to stay in 1939. Worked for Southern Pacific as a trainman and conductor until his death. Married Grace Virginia Maddern in 1942. Children: Michael Maddern Harris, Kathleen Faye Harris, and Scott Eldon-Kirk Harris. Was Worshipful Master of Dunsmuir Lodge #297, F & AM in 1959, 1962, and 1970; Toparch of Pyramid #22 AEOS in 1972; served on Siskiyou County Grand Jury in 1972; awarded Grand Cross of Colors by Order of Rainbow for Girls; played on the Dunsmuir Merchants Baseball Team, member of the McCloud Golf Club and Dunsmuir Rod and Gun Club; worked toward the establishment of the secondary special education program in southern Siskiyou and helped found the Siskiyou Opportunity Center.

A very special husband and father; a "gentle-man" in the fullest sense of the word.

"Soft and safe, my brother, be thy resting place . . .
Bright and glorious be thy rising from it."

THE HERRIN
~ and ~
HAINES FAMILIES

Robert, Jessie, and Patsy

ROBERT W. HERRIN was the grandson of pioneer JOHN HERRIN, who came across the plains to settle in Ashland, Oregon, in 1853. Robert's uncle, WM. F. HERRIN, was Chief Council for the Southern Pacific. The large Herrin family were, for years, owners of Shasta Springs. ROBERT, born on Christmas Day in Ashland, Oregon, made his home in Dunsmuir from 1925 until his death in 1966 except for a few years when he was furloughed from the railroad. During this time, he resided in Fargo, North Dakota, and was employed by the Pioneer Life Insurance Co. as an accountant. It was at this time that he met and fell in love with JESSIE HAINES, his secretary. They were married July 3, 1937, and moved to Dunsmuir the next day. He was employed by the Southern Pacific as a locomotive engineer for 42 years. He served as Financial Secretary and Local Chairman for the Brotherhood of Locomotive Firemen and Engineers. He was a member of the Dunsmuir Lodge No. 297, F. and A.M.; Fidelity Chapter No. 131, O.E.S.; Brotherhood of Locomotive Engineers; and the B.P.O.E., Fargo, for 33 years.

JESSIE HAINES HERRIN, born Feb. 1, 1910, in Fargo, was reared in N.D. until coming to Dunsmuir. Here she lived for 34 years and served the community she grew to love. She is a member of Fidelity Chapter O.E.S. and served faithfully as their organist from 1952 to 1983. She also played for the Masonic Lodge, Rainbow Girls, and the churches when called upon. Many years she worked for her neighbor, George McLaughlin (McLaughlin's Grocery Store). When her husband passed away, she went to work for Rodley's Motors and continued working for Don Hilton Ford. She also served as city treasurer during this time. She and Robert were the proud parents of their only child, PATSY.

ISABELLA HAINES, mother of Jessie, was born in Loch Lomond, Scotland, on April 8, 1887, and came to the United States in 1895 and settled in Carrington, N.D. She moved to Dunsmuir in 1937, and resided there until her death in 1970. You may have known her as Isabella, but to her many friends and relatives, she was affectionately called "NaNa." It was a common scene to see "NaNa" with her granddaughter and later great-grandchildren hanging on to one hand and a dog on a leash going for long walks, greeting and cheering every one along the way. She was a member of the Methodist Church, a lifetime member of W.S.C.S., Past Noble Grand of Rebecca Lodge, and member of Women's Benefit Association. To have known Isabella and Jessie was to love them.

PATSY HERRIN NELSON, born Sept. 9, 1944, was reared in Dunsmuir and graduated from Dunsmuir schools. She was Worthy Advisor of the Rainbow Girls and a member of the Methodist Church. Her three children - HEIDI, ROBERT and RONALD, were all born in Mt. Shasta. Patsy, Robert, Ronald, and husband, Dennis, now reside in Yuba City, California. Heidi attended Yuba City schools, attended Biola University in Los Angeles, where she met and later married Breck Krager. She graduated from Apollo Dental School and is now employed as a dental assistant. Her husband, Breck, is a Youth Minister in Phoenix, where they reside.

Dunsmuir is a special place to this family. It touched the lives of many other members of the HERRIN-HAINES family throughout the years and will always be considered by those of us living, "God's country."

IN HONOR OF THE
NORMAN JOSEPH IMHOFF
FAMILY

30th Wedding Anniversary

Norm and Lupe

Norman Joseph Imhoff was born August 24, 1919, at Cedron, Missouri, to Phillip William and Mary Strickfadden. He has four sisters and three brothers. After high school, Norman went to work at the bank at Tipton, Missouri. When he was 19, the Bank of America recruited him and he came to the San Joaquin Valley. In 1949 he transferred to Dunsmuir because he loved to hunt and fish. Norman immediately fell in love with the area and knew he would like to spend the rest of his life here. He was doubly sure when he became better acquainted with Lupe Padilla, his secretary.

Lupe was born at Dunsmuir on May 18, 1932, to Francisco and Maria Delgado Padilla. She was graduated from the local schools.

On September 12, 1953, with Msgr. James Casey officiating, Norm and Lupe were married. They have eight children: Thomas Anthony, born October 1, 1954; Philip James, September 24, 1955; Mark Joseph, October 31, 1958; James Patrick, December 19, 1960; Norman John, January 10, 1964; Timothy Albert, November 18, 1965; Patrick William, April 9, 1969; and Tonia Marie, June 25, 1970.

Norm and Lupe are still very active in church and civic functions. Norm plans to retire on September 1, 1984, from his duties as bank manager of the Mt. Shasta and McCloud Branches of the Bank of America. Although Norm had other opportunities for advancement, he refused. He wanted his children to grow up in the land he loved so much. Norm and Lupe plan to spend his retirement traveling and enjoying their family and friends.

Mark, Jim, Norman, Tonia, Philip, Tim, Pat, and Tom

DEDICATED TO THE MEMORY OF MY PARENTS AND MY BROTHER

By Maxine Johnson Kildoo

My father, Adolph L. Johnson

My mother, Sylvia Johnson

The Johnson family, Adolph L. and Sylvia, and their two children, William Richard (Billy Dick) and Maxine Elizabeth, moved to Dunsmuir from Niland and El Centro, California, in 1916. Adolph was a Dispatcher with the Southern Pacific Railroad Company until his death in 1954.

Bill and Maxine graduated from Dunsmuir Grammar School and Dunsmuir Joint Union High School in 1928 and in 1929 respectively. Bill went on to graduate from Wentworth Military Academy, Lexington, Missouri; and Maxine, to graduate from Armstrong College of Business Administration, Berkeley, California.

Their lives went separate ways away from Dunsmuir after the death of Sylvia in 1931. Adolph moved to Sacramento, and Bill and his wife, Doris, and their three children lived in several areas in Southern California. Maxine lived in the Hawaiian Islands, the San Francisco Bay Area, and then settled down in the southern part of California.

Bill Johnson passed away in 1969 and Maxine and her husband, Robert W. Kildoo, retired to Arizona in 1979.

Adolph and Sylvia Johnson had five grandchildren and seven great-grandchildren.

THE HOWARD JONES FAMILY

The Joneses first came to Dunsmuir in September, 1957, when Howard decided to take over the practice of the late Gerald Shannon. At that time they knew nothing about the town or its people. Their initial reception showed them how warm-hearted the people were. The Joneses arrived in a U-Haul truck in the rain, knowing hardly a soul. However, when they pulled up to the house they had rented, four men, strangers then, were waiting to unload the truck; and Lucy Colthart, their landlady, had put a bouquet of flowers on the mantel to welcome them. This friendliness and attitude of caring by the people of Dunsmuir is one of the things that has kept them in Dunsmuir for the last 25-plus years.

"We have had an enjoyable and busy life here."

Howard practiced law here until January, 1977, when he became judge of the local justice court. He was part-time city attorney for 19 years. He served on the Board of Trustees of the Chamber of Commerce, the Board of Trustees of the Methodist Church, the Board of Trustees of the Dunsmuir High School (for 13 years), and the Board of the Friends of the Library. Howard also taught night classes at College of the Siskiyous for 21 years.

Ruth spent her time until 1966 rearing their three children, Cheri, Vicki, and Emmet. She was also involved in Girl Scouts, Cub Scouts, P.T.A., and teaching square dancing to children of the Methodist Church. Howard and Ruth taught square and round dancing from 1957 to 1981. In 1966, Ruth went back to college and received her B.A., M.A., general secondary credential, and school psychologist's credential. Since 1973, she has worked for the county schools as a psychologist.

The Jones children all graduated from Dunsmuir schools. Cheri and Vicki are now teachers; Emmet is a system analyst and program designer for a computer firm in Oregon.

"We fell in love with Dunsmuir as soon as we arrived, and this feeling has continued to grow stronger as the years go by. We have no intention of ever moving."

Judge Jones

IN REMEMBRANCE

Roscoe and I moved to Dunsmuir in 1935 where my husband was the Union Oil Company's agent. He replaced John "Bud" Lachenmyer, who was sent to Weed. Later Bud and his wife Charlotte returned to Dunsmuir where they operated "The Toggery," owned by Charlotte's father, Mr. Searce. We loved everything about Dunsmuir, the twenty-two years we lived there: the snow, hills, trees, shrubs and flowers; the river; the picnic areas, including the McCloud River area, where we often camped. But we especially loved the friendly people.

Many of our friends were like us with husbands at work, wives at home rearing two or three children. There were clubs, organizations, and parties galore.

I was an accompanist, and there was seldom a week when I wasn't playing for some group or individual. I played nine years for the Lutheran Church Choir made up of lovely young high school girls and young matrons. June Ames, Ruth Rupp, and Ruth Holcomb were the directors. Rev. Rische was pastor. His Easter Sunday services, held at the California Theater, were always packed.

I played for the Dunsmuir Male Chorus, the Dunsmuir Mothersingers, a dance class, where Betty Palmer shone, and a local but short-lived orchestra. Many groups met in our home. What a joy!

After busy four years at Chico, we returned to Dunsmuir, where we operated the Commercial Garage as Chrysler-Plymouth dealers. Some of our faithful employers were "Brownie" and his son Richi,

Robert Pitt, William Carlson, "Red" McGaugh, Richard Cornish, and "Dino" Bastiani. We hauled about eight cars into our garage the tragic day the runaway truck went through Dunsmuir. Two men were killed.

Roscoe was a member of the Elementary School Board under Principal Hartzel Gray, a member of the volunteer fire department, Lion's Club president and zone chairman. He helped with the cooking at Boy Scout Jamborees, played on the Dunsmuir baseball team, and officiated at the high school football games. He and I were Worthy Matron and Patron of the Dunsmuir Chapter, Order of Eastern Star, for two years.

I was a P.T.A. president, and was a Den Mother for several years, and helped out with the Girl Scouts for several years when we camped out at "September Morn" Campground on Soda Creek, courtesy of the Dunsmuir Lions Club. We enjoyed the "Merrymakers," a dance group. When we returned to Dunsmuir, we joined the Methodist Church. I was assistant organist and sang in the choir under the direction of Reva Coon. I had charge of the organ and building fund.

Our two children were very active. Judith was head of the Rainbow Girls and was a violinist and band and orchestra member. Kenneth was active in sports, band, and was senior class president.

We have ever been thankful for the years we lived in Dunsmuir and for the privilege of rearing our children in such a lovely area.

Mina and Roscoe Kimble

IN HONOR OF
NELLIE AND BEANY KING

Frank Thomas "Beany" King, who spent all his life in the state, was born at Franklin, Sacramento County, California, November 11, 1889. He worked in the engineering department of the Southern Pacific at Sacramento in 1908. On the completion of the Sacramento-Southern R.R., he went to Oregon where he was piling and concrete inspector on the Coos Bay Bridge and on bridges across other lakes in that area during the construction of the Willamette-Railway Engineers. On June 5th, 1917, he enlisted in Company F, 18, Railway Engineers. He received his honorable discharge on May 14, 1919. He came to Dunsmuir and was employed by the Southern Pacific until 1926, when he went into business at the Mossbrae Pharmacy with Herbert Marsh. In 1927 he bought the business; and in 1936 he became a registered pharmacist. He played semi-pro baseball for the Dunsmuir team, and in the 1920's he was on the board of directors of the Nor-Cal Baseball League. He was a charter member of the American Legion, and a member of the Dunsmuir Lodge, F & A.M.

He was active in all functions that promoted the growth and development of Dunsmuir. For thirty-seven years he and his wife, Nellie, served the public with love and devotion. Everyone who knew "Beany" loved and respected him. On January 21, 1971, Beany died at his home on Dunsmuir Avenue.

Nellie Bertha Wehinger was born August 18, 1899, at Miles City, Montana. In 1920 she came to Dunsmuir. On August 8, 1936, she married "Beany" King. Together, Nellie and "Beany" served the public. Nellie was famous for her lunches, homemade pies and cakes which she served behind the fountain at the drug store. When the drug store closed, it ended an era of the drugstore fountain. One of her great loves was selling the poppy for the American Legion. She started fifty years ago, and today you will still find Nellie selling poppies in May.

In 1960 the Business and Professional Women awarded her "Woman of the Year." Nellie continues to serve the public with her concern and thoughtfulness. If you see Nellie, she will have a basket tucked under her arm filled with "goodies" for some "shut-in" or for some friend. She is loved and respected by all.

IN HONOR OF
THE KOHLBAKER FAMILY

(They came to Dunsmuir in 1902)

*Myrtle Kohlbaker and Florin (Buzz) Kohlbaker with their mother,
Lula (Kohlbaker) Kendricks. Picture was taken about 1920.*

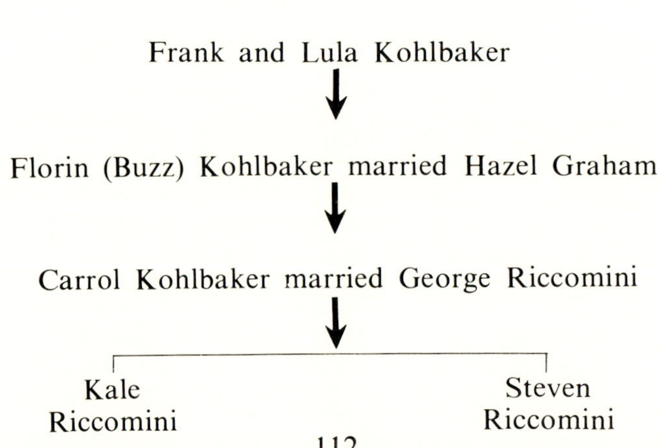

Frank and Lula Kohlbaker

Florin (Buzz) Kohlbaker married Hazel Graham

Carrol Kohlbaker married George Riccomini

Kale
Riccomini

Steven
Riccomini

Andrew Martin Leach
1840-1908

Cora Alice Leach (nee Cobb)
1870-1961

Cora Leach

In the early 1890's, both of my parents came to Dunsmuir, where I was born in 1897. Half of my life was spent in Dunsmuir, where I attended elementary and high school. I was a member of the 1917 graduating class.

CONGRATULATIONS TO DUNSMUIR
ON ITS
ONE HUNDREDTH BIRTHDAY!

Submitted by Andrew Leach
Pacific Grove

IN MEMORY
OF
"FRENCHY" and BOBBIE LE MERE

Olive Brooke Lewis, "Bobbie," and Francis "Frenchy" LeMere were married July 3, 1925, and lived their married life in Dunsmuir, where they raised two children, Mary and "Sonny." Bobbie worked for the Golden Rule Store for many years. When "Frenchy" retired, he was Assistant Postmaster at Dunsmuir.

This page is lovingly presented by their family:

Mary Parker Estes
Brooke and Byron Hatcher
Sonny and "Jimmy" LeMere
Leslee LeMere
Steve, Teri, and Erika LeMere

IN LOVING MEMORY OF
PAUL F. LIVINGSTON

 **Dedicated by his wife, Grace** 

*Paul and Grace Livingston celebrating
their fiftieth wedding anniversary.*

Paul F. Livingston was born March 23, 1900, in Hope, Arkansas. He and Grace Ramage were married February 10, 1918, at Nashville, Arkansas. He went to work as a fireman for the Southern Pacific Railroad in 1929 and had a loco-motive engineer's date of December 1941. On November 1, 1939, Paul moved his family to Dunsmuir. He retired on March 31, 1965, and he passed away February 24, 1976.

Paul R. Livingston, their son, works for the Southern Pacific Company as a locomotive engineer, also. He and his wife, Carole, live in Alturas, California, and have a daughter and a son, Peri and Kelly. Peri has a little daughter, Dca Ann.

Charley Loftus   *Verna Loftus*

MY ROOTS ARE HERE
TIM LOFTUS

My father, Jim Loftus, son of the Thomas and Ellen Loftus family and original owners of Sweetbrier Camp, met and married Olive Flugger, a young nurse in Dr. Cornish's hospital here about the year 1915. They later moved to Stockton, where he opened a garage repairing mostly Model "T" Fords. My sister Gertrude was born in 1916, and later I came along in 1918. Helping care for the many ill during the flue epidemic that year, she contracted it herself and died five months after I was born.

Though they already had three children, Nelda, Eva, and Tom Loftus, I was taken by Charley and Verna, the oldest of the eight Loftus children to raise as their own along with their children who were all in their teens. They became like a mother and father to me.

At that time they lived in the home that was torn down to build the Thriftway Market in Dunsmuir. Uncle Charley was a partner of Frank and Anna Talmadge in ownership of the old Palm Hotel across from the railway, roundhouse, and shops during the boom and busy railroad days. Many big poker games took place in their bar and card room including some of the famous historical gamblers. Needless to say, some ended up with gunfire.

Frank Talmadge also owned a large parcel of land north of the recently re-built bridge where he and Anna lived and where he had built many rentals for summer vacationers to the area, as well as a large beautiful dance hall and restaurant, where some of the "Big Name Bands" came to play for the

dances; and later the big swimming pool, still in use today, where my sister, my cousins, and I used to participate in swimming contests on the Fourth of July during celebrations held there.

Uncle Charley was also in partnership with Billy and Edna Lee in ownership of the old post office building with apartments above where Billy and Edna lived. It was located in the block just north of the theater about where Cornet Store now stands.

My cousin Eva, Uncle Charley's daughter, was a nurse at the Dr. Cornish Hospital at the same time as our recently deceased friend, Mrs. William ("Jo") Welsh. My cousin Tom and his wife later owned the Palm and built the Flamingo Club, just recently reopened.

Family friends, whom I remember so well, included Myrtle and Dick Moore (her famous big chicken tamales, a sinfully delicious gourmet's delight, and Jack and Hallie Wyatt, who owned the Commercial Garage, now torn down and the land used as a parking lot. He sold my first car to me on my 21st birthday. A 1929 Model A Ford!

I still had it when my wife, Hazel, and I were married in June the following year. Other friends of the family included Winnie and Henry Long, Brooks Bell and his wife, and many others.

I was baptized by Father Carr, Priest in Saint John's Catholic Church in Dunsmuir in about 1919. My wife and I are active members there today.

Hazel and Tim Loftus

FATHER VINCENT LYONS
Pastor of St. John's

I rejoice with all in our community in celebrating the centenary of our historic town. May this be the occasion of rededicating ourselves to the noble traditions of the past and face the challenge of our age as we walk into the future with renewed trust and confidence.

For this I pray:

O Lord, I pray for this the city of our love and pride. Help us to make our city the common workshop of our people, where everyone will find their place and task: — in daily achievement, building up their lives, and reaching out to others, especially those in need. Bind our citizens not by the bond of money or profit alone, but by the glow of neighborly good will, the thrill of common joys, and the pride of common goals. Grant us a vision of our city, fair as she might be — a city of freedom and justice, a city where virtue and equality prosper, a place of sharing and caring, where success shall be founded on service, with esteem and respect for all. May our community be blessed with peace, where order shall rest not on force, but on the love of all for each other. Hear, O Lord, this silent prayer of our hearts, as we pledge our time, our strength, and thought, to speed the day of her coming beauty.

Amen.

MAY THIS CHERISHED EVENT
LIFT OUR HOPES AND BRIGHTEN OUR LIVES.

Father Lyons

THE ROSSETTI and MANFREDI FAMILIES

Early view of the South Highway Grocery — Opened in 1927

Pietro Rosetti
  (b. Oct. 12, 1879; d. June 21, 1956)

Francesca (Gubetta) Rossetti
  b. Feb. 22, 1884; d. June, 2, 1967

Adolfo Manfredi
  (b. Jan. 14, 1883; d. May 18, 1971)

Corina A. Manfredi
  (b. Jan. 25, 1885; d. Oct. 17, 1954)

118

THE MANFREDI FAMILY

Aldo Manfredi (b. Aug. 28, '06)
Took over store in 1944

Mary A. Manfredi (b. 2/1/'08)

★ ★ ★ ★ ★

Ronald A. Manfredi (b. 11/1/'37)
Took over store in 1973

Dorothy L. (Hale) Manfredi
(b. Apr. 12, 1937)

L. Reeves Hale
(b. Feb. 28, 1908
d. Oct. 30, 1963)

Alice M. (Ince) Hale
(b. Aug. 10, 1911
d. July 21, 1978)

Sharon M. Manfredi
(b. Aug. 19, 1958)

Shirley M. Manfredi
(b. Sept. 9, 1959)

Michael A. Manfredi
(b. Feb. 23, 1962)

Mark A. Manfredi
(b. July 5, 1968)

✡ CONGRATULATIONS TO DUNSMUIR ✡
ON ITS CENTENNIAL!

LOOKING FORWARD TO
DUNSMUIR'S BICENTENNIAL.

IN FOND MEMORY OF THE
MANFREDI AND CHRISTOPHER FAMILIES

Recollected by Elisa Manfredi Kennedy

The first bakery and upstairs apartment where the Christofaros lived (next to the Mt. Shasta Hotel). The fountain Cosmo took so much pride in keeping beautiful.

It all began before the turn of the century when Cosmo Cristofaro migrated from Italy and settled in Dunsmuir. He was employed by the S.P. Company as caretaker of the grounds surrounding the homes of officials and offices of the company. His greatest pride was taking care of the fountain filled with fish that was located at the S.P. station. After Cosmo had earned enough money in 1907, he sent for his wife, Angelica, (1885-1923), and three small children, Josephine (Jan. 1894-1959), Domenic (1896-1974), Frank (1899-1928). They were the first Italian family to reside in Dunsmuir.

In 1923, a young man by the name of Sam Manfredi (1884-1981), 17 years old, arrived upon the scene. He worked at various lumber mills in the vicinity and met Josephine. They married in January, 1912, and had their first son, John, in November, 1912, at the Cornish Hospital. Shortly after, the family left Dunsmuir for San Francisco, where Sam worked for the Immigration Department at Angel Island for two years. During this sojourn in San Francisco, Dominic

was born, July, 1914 (d. 1977).

After returning to Dunsmuir, the family established the bakery and Italian goods store on Sacramento Avenue and lived in an apartment above the store. A few years later a daughter named Elisa was born, February, 1916. About this time, the Cristofaro family moved to Seattle, Washington, where the two boys, Domenic and Frank, went into the carpentry business and at the same time anglicized the name of Christofaro to Christopher. Thereafter, the Christophers would spend half a year with the Manfredi family, where the retired Cosmo built roads to the stone house built by Domenic Christopher on River Avenue, and where the Manfredi family had moved. This was in the early 1920's. Then the "big fire" struck, destroying their first store. The second store was a wooden building on the corner of Florence (now Dunsmuir Avenue) and Pine Streets. The city condemned that building, and a new one was built next to the Masonic temple, making a third bakery. A new building was later built on the corner of Florence and Pine, first being

occupied by Jones' Pharmacy.

This building extended to the rear (now the Dunsmuir News Office), where the 4th bakery was established, as the Sprouse Reitz Co. wanted the space next to the Masonic temple. Finally, in 1933, during the Depression, and after Domenic and Elisa finished high school, the Manfredi family moved to San Francisco. In the late 1930's, a building was erected on the corner of Pine and Shasta to house the Post Office. There are three separate buildings located in that area, having double firewalls throughout. Domenic Christopher helped build all three buildings, still owned by members of the Manfredi family. Cosmo, Angelica, and Frank Christopher are buried in the Dunsmuir Cemetery; Sam, Josephine, and Domenic Manfredi and Domenic Christopher are buried in Holy Cross Cemetery in San Francisco. John Manfredi resides in Vallejo in retirement; and Elisa Manfredi Kennedy resides in San Francisco. The siblings of the Christopher family reside in various parts of California.

[The fountain referred to is the famous Dunsmuir Fountain.]

THE SIGURD AND CLARA BJORGUM FAMILY

By Clara

Left:
Sigurd, Clara,
Leroy, Rob, Don

Right:
Leroy, Rob, Don

Matilda Simons (1873-1947) was my mother, and my father was Andrew Orvedahl (1865-1960), both of Norwegian descent and of the Lutheran religion. They had seven boys and five girls. Our family made their home in mid-western South Dakota near Faith, where I was born on May 9, 1916. The family lived there from 1912 until I graduated from high school in 1936. I received my teaching credential from Black Hills Teacher's College and taught for four years around the Black Hills. My parents left the farm to join three of my brothers who were living at Los Angeles.

In 1941, I married Sigurd Bjorgum, who was born February 13, 1906, at Eau Clair, Wisconsin, to Sigrid Arnstad (1873-1942) and Sigurd Bjorgum (1872-1946). They came to America in 1903 from Norway with three of their nine children and lived near Eau Claire, Wisconsin, where the other six children were born. When Sig was twelve, his family moved to South Dakota, where they had a farm. At seventeen, he began his career as a timber faller, interrupted temporarily by a cave-in which left him with a crooked leg.

In June, 1941, my two sisters, Louise Bjorgum and Annette Stedman, and I joined the boys who had come to California before us. We were disappointed with Alturas after the great build-up about California.

Sig and I were married July 12, 1941, and lived at McArthur until he went to work for the McCloud River Lumber Co. We moved to Ponderosa. Our boys were born while we lived there. Leroy, born October 1, 1942; Robert, January 23, 1944; Donald, June 16, 1945.

In 1946, we bought the Bartle station, a small gas and grocery store. My dad thoroughly enjoyed working there. In 1948, we bought our business at South Dunsmuir. We soon made a cafe out of the grocery store. We bought Mrs. Tripps property, which consisted of eight lots which we later sold.

Our boys enjoyed their life in Dunsmuir, especially the hunting, fishing, and gold panning expeditions with their dad. They were active in Scouts and in sports, particularly football at high school.

Leroy and Rob volunteered for the service. Rob was in the Para-troopers, stationed in Kentucky, and Leroy in the Signal Corps in Germany.

Rob married Susan Borem, August, 1967. They have two children: Brian, 14, and Carissa, 16. He has his own business — Doado Tree Service.

Leroy married Corinne Riche in 1971. They have two children: Aaron, 7, and Jennifer, 12. They live in a lovely home at New Castle.

We sold our home in Dunsmuir after losing our boy Donald by drowning in Shasta Lake, while he was home on leave from the service. We will always remember the love and support from our and his wonderful friends at that most difficult time in our lives.

We bought a home in Sacramento, where I worked at the school for the disadvantaged for twelve years. Sig disliked the city so that after he retired, we moved near Placerville. We planned to do many things, but Sig had a heart attack which altered our plans.

All of us remember our eighteen years in Dunsmuir as a very pleasant part of our lives full of happy memories of good friends.

IN LOVING MEMORY OF LOUIS AND CHARLOTTE GIRARD FAMILY

Cabin on Girard Ridge

Steve, Louis, Joseph, Estella, Annetta Girard

Charlotte Anastasia King Girard

Louis Napolean Girard was born at Quebec, Canada, October 12, 1849. He came to Northern California with his brother, Antoine and his sister-in-law. He was a man of many interests and pursued many avenues. Gold was paramount in his mind, and he was ever searching for the "Mother Lode." To mention a few of his diversities, he was a stagecoach driver from Redding to Yreka and lived at Old Shasta. His name, along with those of other stagecoach drivers, was on a rock monument beside the highway north of Redding and north of Yreka. There seems to be no evidence of them now that the freeway changed the course of the highway. While he lived at Old Shasta, he hauled brick into the growing town of Redding to build the first courthouse. He was superintendent of the Altoona Mine at Trinity Center, where he met and married Charlotte Anastasia King in 1882. Later he was mail carrier for Scott Valley and during the winter months went over Scott Mountain on skis.

In the early 1890's, the family moved to Castella, where he was town constable. While he was constable, a woman and her child were fatally stabbed by her husband. The wife dragged herself to the Girards' home where she died on the steps. Louis jailed the man. When the news spread to the newly growing Dunsmuir, a lynch mob was formed and they came to Castella on a handcar. They tied Constable Girard, took the prisoner, and hanged him on a tree in front of the school house.

In 1912, the family moved to Dunsmuir. Louis had a cabin on the then unnamed ridge. The Forest Service made him the first look-out. When they mapped the area, they automatically named it the Girard Ridge.

Louis Girard died on June 6, 1919.

Charlotte Anastasia King was born near Mission San Jose, California, November 7, 1861. The family moved to Yreka, where Charlotte attended school. In 1882, she went to Trinity Center, where she worked at a boarding house. Here she met and married Louis N. Girard. Louis Altoona was born April 21, 1884, and died of diptheria October 25, 1888. Annetta Emily was born January 25, 1889 at Yreka; and Bernard Lafayette Paul, January 25, 1889 at Trinity Center. Charolotte Estella, born November 24, 1892; Edward Wallace, March 5, 1896; Mary Illeen, July 24, 1898 at Castella.

"Mother" Girard, as she became known, worked as mid-wife and helped deliver and cared for many babies. During the World War I influenza epidemic, she nursed many of the afflicted. She had an Irish wit and sense of humor that left everyone smiling and with food for thought. Reva Coon remembers when she was downtown with her three children, and she met Mother Girard who said to her, "You can't run a wagon on three wheels."

In 1939 the Eagles Lodge named her "Mother of the Year." She died May 3, 1939 before she received the honor.

"Mrs. Girard was a lovable character and enjoyed the highest respect of all who knew her." *(Dunsmuir News.)*

Illeen (1898-1972), Edward (1896-1970), Estella (1892-1976), Bernard (1889-1960), Annetta (1886-1975)

122

IN HONOR OF THE
J. E. HANRATTY FAMILY

Pat, Agnes, Illeen, Jim

(Photo at left)
The day that Jim shook the hand of Harry S. Truman on his campaign train at Dunsmuir, October 1952.

Jim and Illeen

James Edward Hanratty was born May 29, 1893, at Missoula, Montana, to John Owen and Theresa Hanratty, and came to Siskiyou County as a youth with his family. His father worked in the lumbering industry. Jim was employed by the Southern Pacific Company as a "call boy" at Weed. He later hired out as fireman and was promoted to engineer at Dunsmuir. In November, 1978, he retired after working forty-eight accident-free years for the Southern Pacific.

On October 14, 1920, Jim married Mary Illeen Girard, born July 24, 1898, at Castella, California. They lived all their married lives at 1020 Shasta Avenue except 2½ years (1929-32) when he was working out of Klamath Falls, Oregon.

Both were very active in the community. Jim was one of the first members of the Railroad Days Committee from its inception in 1940. He remained active in that work and also helped acquire the engine for the enjoyment of future generations at the city park. He was a member of the Democratic Central Committee for many years, and a member of the Brotherhood of Locomotive Firemen and Enginemen. Illeen was an active member of the B. of L. F. & E. Auxiliary and the Women's Benefit Association. Both were active members of the Catholic Church. Jim died May 27, 1959. Illeen died April 8, 1972.

Their children are: Agnes Estella Hanratty, born March 21, 1923; and James Patrick, May 15, 1925. Agnes married Leo Stroble in 1950. Their children are: Karen Gaub, Loree Norgaard, David Stroble and Tricia Prentiss. The Strobles have seven grandchildren.

Pat married Sophia Wood in 1963. Their children are Gloria Alves, Carl Wood, Judy Corson and Renee Wallace.

Patricia, Karen, Lorrie, Agnes
David, and Leo Stroble

IN LOVING MEMORY OF
THE RICHARD HENRY BRUNJES, SR. FAMILY

Dave Michael Davis, Gladys and
Richard Henry Brunjes, Jr., Julianne Davis

Richard Henry Brunjes, Sr.

Richard Henry Brunjes was born at Los Angeles, July 16, 1882. His father, John Brunjes, erected the Brunjes Hotel in Azusa, California, in 1885. Richard spent his boyhood in Azusa. He met and married Ethel Schalahaas in 1916 at Oakland. He was employed by Standard Oil Company. He retired as asphalt plant superintendent at Richfield, California. After retirement, the Brunjes family came to Dunsmuir in 1944. He purchased 25 acres from Mrs. Bailey. Here he operated an old-fashioned service station with two hand pumps while he was building cottages which he called the Brunjes Motel until 1968. He was recognized for his integrity, honesty, and his readiness to lend a helping hand. Mr. Brunjes died January 15, 1966.

The Brunjes had one son, Richard Henry Brunjes, born July 26, 1918, at Richmond, California. He attended the local schools and was graduated from the University of California, Berkeley. He served in the United States Navy as chief petty officer from 1942 until 1945. He returned to Dunsmuir where he taught school for a time. He was very active in the Explorers and took many groups of boys on overnight trips. On June 8, 1959, he married Gladys Feichko Davis. She has two children: Julianna, born September 8, 1948; and Dave Michael Davis, February 27, 1950. Julianne married Joe Pugh on February 7, 1971. They have two daughters: Laura Jean, born August 12, 1971; and Janice Marie, February 22, 1976. Dave Michael married Rosalyn Madsen May 14, 1974. They have three children: Danielle Michele, born August 3, 1979; Eric Mathew, September 22, 1981; Andrea Candice, born July 30, 1984.

The Brunjes still reside at the same place. They converted the motel area into a mobile home park.

IN LOVING MEMORY OF

JAMES BENJAMIN AND CALLIE LAMM

James Benjamin (J.B.) Lamm
b. February 6, 1877; d. January 31, 1958

Callie Marie Howell Lamm
b. May 23, 1893; d. June 13, 1981

Callie and J. B. were married August 6, 1922, at Pendleton, Oregon. In 1923 they moved to Dunsmuir, where J. B. worked for the Southern Pacific as yard foreman for thirty-five years.

Callie was active in the W.B.A. and managed a small rooming house. J. B. and Callie had one son, Richard R. Lamm, born at home in 1924. Richard attended the Dunsmuir schools and as almost all the young male graduates did, he joined the Army Air Corps in 1943. Upon honorable discharge from the service in 1946, he returned to Dunsmuir to marry a Dunsmuir girl, Avanelle Joy Packwood, in 1947. They had four children: Annabelle, James, Richard, and Edward, all of whom attended and graduated from the Dunsmuir schools. Richard remarried in October 1956. His second wife is Maxine E. Galland. He recently retired from McClellan AFB, California. They are now residing in Sacramento, California.

THOMAS WARD LOFTUS

Thomas Ward Loftus was born at San Francisco, California, to Charles Thomas Loftus and Pearl Chase. His mother died when he was three years old and his father married Verna Bingham. In 1910 the Loftuses came to Dunsmuir. Tom attended the Dunsmuir Elementary School. T. J. Beaughan was principal. Tom's father and Frank Talmadge owned the Palm until the Volstead Act. The family moved to Redding so the children could attend high school. About this time the family bought the strawberry ranch at Lakeshore and made their home there.

Tom was a venturesome person and loved the night life. This led him to own at one time six taverns and bars. He was a personable person and was very well liked by all who knew him.

In 1923 Tom married Sadie Lloyd from Pollock. They had one son, Charles Richard Loftus, born August 8, 1926, at Dunsmuir. Tom has another daughter, Gloria Maurine Loftus Brush, who has a teaching job at Columbus, Ohio.

In 1940 Tom married Elinore Penhall at Reno, Nevada. In 1941 he bought the Palm from Frank Talmadge and ran it until 1956. In 1956, he sold the Palm and moved to Redding, where he bought the Roosevelt Club and the Golden Nugget.

His pride and joy was the Flamingo Club, which he built. It was one of the most fashionable night clubs in the county. He also owned the Round-Up at Summit. In 1963, he retired when the mall took his business. He is still living at Redding, California. A complete history of his illustrious family can be found in the Castle Crags booklet.

IN HONOR OF SAM AND CLARA MAZZEI FAMILY

Golden Wedding Anniversary, February 17, 1984

Sam Mazzei was born April 4, 1912, at McCloud, California. His parents, John and Teresa Scalise Mazzei were from Cassino, Italy.

Before Sam was graduated from the McCloud High School, he had organized the "Hot-Ten-Tots." (Story on another page.) On February 17, 1934, he married Clara Alberta Powers. They had two sons: John Albion, born May 15, 1936; and William Joseph, born November 30, 1943, at McCloud.

In 1947 they moved to Dunsmuir and Sam went into partnership with Joe Baldo at the S. & J. Market on Sacramento Avenue. He retired March 17, 1973. Although Sam had a full-time job at the store, his evenings were spent practicing and playing for dances throughout the county. At the present time, his "Hottentots" are still playing for dances.

Clara Alberta Powers was born September 5, 1915 at Tuolumne, California. Her parents Albion and Lillian Powers came to Dunsmuir in 1919.

John and Shirley Fay Mazzei have two sons and one daughter: John, Robert and Lorrie. William and Edith Scumeir Mazzei have one girl, Cynthia Jenine.

Bill, Edith, Sam, Clara, John, Shirley

Left to right: Ruben Dominguez, Bill and Sam Mazzei, Dr. "Bill" Reynolds, Herb Bell

IN LOVING MEMORY OF
ROBERT AND JOHN MARIN

*John Marin
World War I*

"Suzie," Robert, John, and Raymond

*"Suzie" worked
as boilermaker
helper during
World War II*

John Marin was born December 13, 1895 in Italy. He came to America in 1914. Louis Reginato helped him get work on the railroad. He was a World War I veteran. After the war, he worked as boilermaker for the S.P. until 1948 when he was retired on disability. John died August 26, 1983.

Suzanne Helen Mannebarth was born August 15, 1902 at Reims, France. During World War I at Verdun, France, she met John Marin and was engaged to be married. On June 20, 1920, she came to Dunsmuir. On June 23, 1920, they were married at the Sacred Heart Church.

George John was born June 6, 1921 and died June 6, 1925. Robert Paul was born September 9, 1923. Raymond John was born August 28, 1930. Both boys attended local schools.

Robert Paul worked as machinist's apprentice until World War II, when he enlisted in the Army Air Force. Sergeant Robert Marin served in the European theatre of operations until the end of the war. He had met Wanda Chiaroni in Rome and had planned to marry her and bring her home after the war.

The war ended and the Marins were overjoyed. Robert was safe and was coming home with his bride. The Marins were waiting for definite word of his arrival date. Robert had told them he had one more flight. "Suzie" was at work when a telegram was delivered to her. She was sure the message would tell her the exact date to expect Robert and his bride. "Suzie's" world came crashing down upon her. Robert had been killed on his last flight. On December 14, 1945, the plane crashed on take-off.

President Harry Truman sent the following tribute. "In grateful memory of Sergeant Robert Paul Marin who died in the service of his country . . . He stands in the unbroken line of patriots who have dared to die that freedom might live . . . Freedom lives and through it, he lives."

Raymond John married Kathlyn Push, January 23, 1953. They have two sons: Dennis Raymond born April 13, 1954; and Steven Paul, born January 14, 1955. Dennis married Suzanne. Raymond and Kathlyn make their home at Mt. Shasta. "Suzie" still resides at Dunsmuir.

IN HONOR OF THE ANTONIO REGINATO FAMILY

Antonio Reginato
b. June 8, 1895

Mary Rosseto
b. May 20, 1901

m. March 10, 1917

Florence Anunsiatta
b. May 19, 1920

Paul Natale
b. Sept. 23, 1918

Mary Rosseto and her family came from Italy and went to Portland, Oregon, in 1913. In 1916 they moved to Dunsmuir, where she met and married Antonio Reginato.

Paul Natale and Florence Anunsiatta were born here. In 1922 because of poor health, Mary and the two children returned to Italy. While there, Florence was stricken with the croup and died in 1924.

In 1926 Mary and Paul returned to America. Paul attended the local school and won a scholarship from St. Mary's, where he was graduated. In 1942 he enlisted in the U.S. Marines and was promoted to Major. He served and retired from the Reserve as Lt. Colonel. He married Barbara Macy in 1942. They have three girls.

Antonio retired from the railroad. He died April 26, 1966.

Natale Rossetto
b. Dec. 25, 1860
d. Jan. 26, 1945

Angela Sartor
b. Oct. 19, 1862
d. Jan. 24, 1954

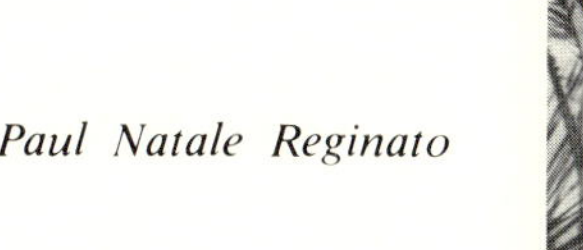

Paul Natale Reginato

PROFILE: LOUIS MAZLUM AMERICA'S ADOPTED SON

(Courtesy Dawn L. Kolograph, *Siskiyou Senior News*)

Louis S. Mazlum
President Siskiyou County Shrine Club

Alda Soeth Mazlum

"When I first stepped on American soil, I knelt down and kissed it; thanking Almighty God." The speaker is eighty-eight year old Louis Mazlum, a Servian native of Yugoslavia, who along with three male cousins, entered New York Harbor in May, 1909, thirty-six days after their departure by ship from the ancient city of Dubrovnik, Yugoslavia.

"I came to the United States to see the free world, the new country," Mr. Mazlum exclaims. "When we landed in New York, our agent greeted us through an interpreter and then took us to the Immigration office, where we were examined by three very strict doctors to determine if we were in good health . . . After passing our examinations and being dismissed, we boarded a New York Central train for Chicago, where our guardian and other relatives awaited us."

Once in Chicago, Louis Mazlum found work almost immediately as a track repairman for the Chicago streetcar system. Although trained as chef in Yugoslavia, he had a major obstacle to overcome before he could attain a similar position in this country. As he put it in his still very pronounced, yet beautiful accent, "I was a typical green horn. I spoke not a word of English." So at the end of a twelve-hour workday, for which he earned one dollar and eighty-five cents, Louis Mazlum walked to the local night school where he spent two hours every evening learning to read, write, and speak the language of his adopted country.

Four years later, having gained a proficient use of the English language, Louis left Chicago for Minneapolis, Minnesota, where he secured a position as a second chef in one of Minneapolis' better hotels. His sense of adventure (which was still very strong) and his desire "to see the rest of this great country," prompted the young man to spend the next fifteen years traveling and working in fine restaurants and clubs from coast-to-coast.

In 1931 he settled in Dunsmuir, where he operated the Travelers' Hotel for the next thirty years. At that time, the Travelers' consisted of a coffee shop, an elegant dining room, and a first-rate hotel. "The Travelers' was a first-class hotel, one of the nicest in northern California," Mr. Mazlum pronounces proudly. Its reputation was widespread, and the Travelers' Hotel, under the proprietorship of Louis Mazlum boasted such famous guests as Herbert Hoover, the 30th President of the United States, who stayed at the hotel in 1932 following his defeat, at the hands of Franklin Roosevelt, in his struggle

(Continued)

LOUIS MAZLUM: AN ADOPTED SON

(Continued)

The Travelers' Hotel as it looked in the early 1950's.

for a second term in office . . .

. . . Other celebrities who wined and dined at the Travelers' were Clark Gable, Esther Williams, Jack Dempsey, Ginger Rogers, and four California governors.

In contrast to the wealthy and renowned who patronized Dunsmuir's leading hotel, the town hosted another group of visitors in the 1930's. Mr. Mazlum describes depression days in Dunsmuir. "During the great depression, there were soup lines from coast-to-coast. The city of Dunsmuir provided a free meal each day from 4 to 6 p.m. in Branstetter Hall on Sacramento Avenue to feed the hobos who were coming into Dunsmuir on the trains from every direction. The meal was usually a mulligan stew, but, on Christmas, the city gave a free turkey dinner with all the trimmings for the hungry people. I used to give people a sack of beans (100 lbs.) for five dollars during the depression. The grocery stores and butcher shops in Dunsmuir gave away left-over vegetables and meats."

Louis Mazlum has been a civic, as well as a business leader in Dunsmuir. In 1951, as president of the Siskiyou County Shrine Club, he organized the annual railroad days celebration, which featured a four-hour parade down Dunsmuir Avenue. Other organizations in which Mr. Mazlum was active include: The Dunsmuir Chamber of Commerce, the Booster Club, the Eagles, the Hotel Greeters' Association, the Eastern Star, the Free Intercepted Masons No. 297. He remains a charter member of the Shasta Cascade Wonderland Association. In his own words, "When I was younger, I belonged to every organization that benefited our community."

Since his retirement from business and community affairs, Louis Mazlum spends his days watching baseball, tending to the flowers in his well-manicured yard, and preparing gourmet meals for himself and his lovely wife, Alda. Occasionally, as on October 16, when they celebrated their thirty-fifth wedding anniversary, the Mazlums dine out in style. Says Mr. Mazlum of his lifestyle, "I like to appear very prosperous. I love nice clothes and good food. I enjoy going out in the evening with my wife to dine at the finest restaurants."

The Mazlums have one daughter, Norma Harter of Bakersfield, five grandchildren, and six great-grandchildren.

Life in the new country has been good to Louis Mazlum, one of America's adopted sons. And Mr. Mazlum has been good to America.

IN MEMORIAM
DR. GEORGE E. MALONE

George E. Malone was born February 22, 1880, in Lincoln, Placer County, California, the son of John James and Mary Scott Malone. The family moved to Mott when George was nine years old. He later became a long-time resident of Dunsmuir.

Dr. Malone graduated from the College of Physicians and Surgeons, School of Dentistry, in 1903 and thereafter was in active practice of his profession in Dunsmuir for forty-three years. He retired in 1946.

In 1902 he married Charlotte Gould, who was born in Roseville, California, in 1881, and they lived at 422 Florence Avenue after their marriage. Their three sons were born in Dunsmuir: Cyril George "Doc," February 25, 1906; John Edward "Jack," October 27, 1910, and Robert Gould, October 8, 1914. The Malone boys attended and graduated from the Dunsmuir schools.

Blanche Petty, the only sister of Dr. Malone, and her husband, Union Petty, lived in Dunsmuir many years. Union died in 1922, and Blanche, in 1927. John Petty was their only son and Dr. Malone's only nephew.

Dr. Malone was elected Assemblyman in 1911 from this district to serve in the State Legislature. He served as a councilman and as mayor of the City of Dunsmuir in the days when the city governing body was known as "the board of trustees." He served as mayor from April 15, 1914, to April 19, 1916, and councilman from April 15, 1912, to February 6, 1924. He participated in many of the projects that promoted the development of Dunsmuir and Siskiyou County during the first half of this century.

Dr. Malone was a past president and fifty-year member of the Lions Club of Dunsmuir and a fifty-year member of the Dunsmuir Lodge No. 297, F. and A.M.

In 1932 his wife, Charlotte, died. He married Estelle Fuller in 1940, and they had a home on Beverley Way in Dunsmuir until Mrs. Malone's death in 1958.

In 1954 Dr. Malone's son, Cyril "Doc," died. Cyril's widow Juanita is now (1984) living in Houston, Texas.

Dr. George E. Malone died January 30, 1960, in Sacramento. The last rites were conducted at the Dunsmuir Masonic Temple with the Dunsmuir Lodge officiating. Interment was in the Dunsmuir Cemetery.

His son, John E. "Jack," died in 1973, and his widow Barbara lives in Sacramento.

His youngest son, Robert G., is a retired dentist who lives with his wife, Celeste, in Sacramento, also.

Dr. Malone's grandchildren are George E. Malone, Robert W. Malone, Paul R. Malone, Kathleen C. Flynn, Charlotte C. Remenih, Jeri Anne Laughlin, Margaret "Peggy" Hartup, and John W. Malone.

His great-grandchildren are Gregory Malone, Patrick Malone, Michael Malone, Kevin Malone, Kerri Paden, Scott Flynn, Mechelle Laughlin, Jeffery Harup, Jason Hartup, Jana Hartup, John D. Malone, Jennifer Malone, Christopher Malone, and Sean Malone.

Submitted by Barbara J. Malone, widow of John E. Malone and daughter-in-law of Dr. George E. Malone.

THE DAVID H. McCLINTOCK FAMILY

David Heath McClintock was born in Nevada on Sept. 3, 1920. At age 9, he moved to San Jose, attending schools there. During high school, he worked for Western Union as a lineman; another part-time job was projectionist at a neighborhood theater. In 1940 he hired out with Southern Pacific as a telegrapher-operator in Oakland. Later, while working the Shasta Division in Gerber (1942) he met and married Anna Bayles of Red Bluff. In Sept. of the same year, he made his date as a dispatcher in Tucson, Arizona. He also worked the Salt Lake Division in both Ogden and Reno; and the Sacramento Division in Roseville, where he also was Assistant Chief. In 1971 he was promoted to the Personnel Department in the main office as a Rules and Training Officer, the job he held until his death in 1982. Dave was well-known for his involvement with the railroad, his Masonic Lodge work, and public service as City Councilman. As Mayor, he greeted then Senator John F. Kennedy, who inaugurated his successful presidential campaign in Dunsmuir in September, 1960.

Anna Bayles McClintock was born and reared in Red Bluff, California. Her experience as office secretary and cashier at the theater in Red Bluff helped to qualify her as a theater manager — the position she held for 11 years. Anna was well-known primarily through her work as theater manager. Dave and Anna had two children.

John Herbert was born in Tucson, Arizona, on Dec. 18, 1943. He attended Dunsmuir Elementary and High School and was very popular. Athletically, he was active in Little League and later excelled in high school basketball. John was the unfortunate victim of Hodgkins disease. He died in 1959 in his junior year in high school.

Robert Bayles McClintock was born April 3, 1946 in Reno, Nevada. He attended both grade and high school in Dunsmuir but graduated from Red Bluff High in 1964. He worked as a trainman for the S.P. from 1965 to 1983. He is a composer of classical, jazz, pop and commercial works, having composed a concert requiem mass, large jazz ensemble pieces, pop songs, TV promotional music, and documentary film scores. He is also listed in several "WHO'S WHOS."

HENRY and MARY CATHERINE McGUINESS

On Sept. 22, 1853, Michael (born 1812 in Ireland), and his wife, Anne Madden (born 1813 in Ireland), with their children (Henry, Michael, Elizabeth, and Catherine) sailed from North Hampton, England, for Melbourne, Australia, where they arrived Jan. 6, 1854. Henry (2) was born at Tovlamba Goldburn Valley, Australia, Oct. 4, 1875. Mary Catherine, his wife, was born in Pleasant Valley, California, Sept. 29, 1877. Henry McGuiness's father was born at Dundalk, County Lough, Ireland, April 1, 1843. He, the first Henry, and his wife, Charlotte, had seven children: Henry, Thomas, James, Emma, Annie, Mary, and Frank. Henry McGuiness and Mary Catherine were married in Red Bluff, California, Nov. 13, 1901. Their children were Mary Ethel Drotar (deceased), Henry (deceased), Margaret Esther Hickey, and Kathleen Rose Farley. The McGuiness Family came to Siskiyou County, where he was associated with Victor Warren in the hotel business at Sisson (now Mt. Shasta). While working in the hotel, Henry studied Law and passed the California Bar in 1908. He practiced law in Sisson until 1918, when he moved to Dunsmuir. He was City Attorney of Dunsmuir from that time until his death, Feb. 22, 1936. He was also Justice of the Peace of Mott Township for two terms. In 1928, Henry was elected to the California Assembly, where he served two terms; in 1934, he was elected to the Senate of California.

**HONORING THE McGUINESS FAMILY
WITH LOVING MEMORIES.**

Submitted by KATHLEEN ROSE FARLEY

THE PETERSONS

Hazel Josephine Lee married John Emil Peterson in 1914. They had two children: Hazel Denise, born in 1915, and John Gordon. Hazel Denise married Eugene Nixon. Their one child, Jean Lee, born in 1939, married Thomas DeLaMare in 1957. They had four children.

John Gordon Peterson married Hazel Belle Paynter in 1940. They had two children: Isobel Lynne, born in 1942; and John Frank, born in 1944.

Isobel Lynne married George P. Carnes. They have four children: Cheryl Lynne, Leanne Elizabeth, Jonathon George, and John Frank.

Wilhelm Kistler married Adeline Kistler. Both were natives of Switzerland. They had two daughters, Josephine and Adeline.

Josephine married William R. Lee in 1882. This union produced five children. Winifred Rose, born in 1883 (died in 1977) married Henry T. Long. There was no issue from this marriage. William R., born in 1884 (died in 1948), married Edna Lee Nodman; they had two children. Myrtle Emma, born in 1889 (died in 1954), married Richard G. Moore, born in 1882 (died in 1940). They had two children: Audrey, born in 1910, who married John C. McLeod (died in 1979); Richard A., born in 1911.

Nona M. married Henie Hansen. They had two children: Wayne and Vyone. Vyone married Alan Hodgson and had two children. Hazel Josephine, born 1895 (died in 1979), married John Emil Peterson. Two children were born to them: Denise and Gordon.

THEIR STORY

William and Josephine Lee left Iowa, arriving at Mott in 1884, where he built a sawmill and acted as postmaster. In 1886, he left his business in Grandma's care and came to the foot of the Hill to Pusher, soon to be named Dunsmuir. Once there he bought all the property on Florence Avenue from the old Courts home through to Shasta Avenue and down to the corner of Pine Street. He built two houses, one of which still stands (just north of Cornet); the other, the family home, stood where Cornet is today. There was a livery stable where the Lee-Loftus Building is now. Two shops were at the corner of Pine and Florence. The post office was where the bank is now. The house next to the Lutheran Parsonage was where I was born. There was another home in back of what is the Burger Barn. Most of the places are still intact. When Grandpa finished the homestead, he moved his family from Mott. When he died in 1901 or '02, Grandma turned the stable over to the hired man to handle and prepared to raise her family. She owned an old recipe for Spanish tamales. Mrs. Bidwell of Chico had given the recipe to her. With this, she started a business of making tamales in her home. It became a very profitable enterprise. Does anyone remember our Grandma's tamales? There are no Lees left to carry on the name, but I hope those of us who carry her gene have a share of the strength and fortitude she manifested.

She was a very special lady.

Submitted by
Audrey Moore McLeod

THE MOORES

Bill Lee (1904) on Florence Ave. in front of where Cornet is now.

Richard A. Moore married Annie Holmes. Their son Richard married Martha Miller and they had three sons: Richard, Ernest, and Frank. Richard married Myrtle Lee in 1908. In 1910 their daughter Audrey was born; in 1911, their son Richard.

Great-grandmother Annie, Richard, Martha, and the boys left because of the turmoil following the Civil War. They left Virginia, lived for awhile in Kentucky and then in Missouri, where the father died. Soon after, Annie bundled up Martha, young Dick, Frank, and Ernest and moved to Sacramento, California. Later she bought an orange grove outside Oroville. Some of the happiest days of my life were spent there. The orange grove is gone now, but not the memories!

Myrtle & Dick Moore

Myrtle Moore, Grandma, Denise and Audrey Stutz

MASSON FAMILY

Father:
John Masson
Born in Scotland, March 9, 1858
Died February 28, 1911, Upper
Soda Springs

Mother:
Elda Alene McCloud Masson
Born December 28, 1860, Yreka
Died January 12, 1944, Dunsmuir

Children:
(Left) James Ross Masson
Born February 25, 1888, San
Francisco
Died August 3, 1975, Palo Alto

(Right) Richard George Masson
Born September 25, 1889, San
Francisco
Died February 10, 1931, Dunsmuir

(Lower Right) Charles Edson
Mason
Born April 26, 1891, Upper Soda
Springs
Died October 16, 1960, Dunsmuir

Family group photograph

*Children of James and Harriet
Masson*

*John Harbison Masson
Born November 16, 1918
Marysville*

*James Ross Masson, Jr.
Born June 28, 1921
Benicia*

*Charles McCloud Masson
Born February 14, 1924
Benicia*

*Eleanor Louise Masson Buehler
Born October 18, 1927
Vallejo*

*Harriet Josephine Harbison Masson
Born October 4, 1888, Vacaville
Died July 22, 1977, Sacramento*

James Ross Masson

Nellie Barbara Hunt Masson
Born February 21, 1892, Millsville
Died January, 1985

Richard George Masson

Charles Edson ("Pete") Masson

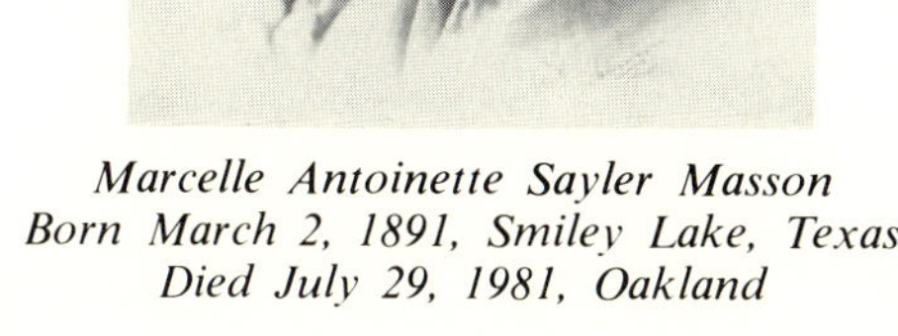

Marcelle Antoinette Sayler Masson
Born March 2, 1891, Smiley Lake, Texas
Died July 29, 1981, Oakland

Children of

Charles and Marcelle Masson

Peter Hotchkiss Masson
Born March 17, 1921, Dunsmuir

Lewis Sayler Masson
Born August 20, 1926, Dunsmuir

Valerie Ellen Masson Gomez
Born April 15, 1925, Dunsmuir

Charles Edson Masson, Jr.
Born November 27, 1927, Dunsmuir

IN MEMORY OF
REX WILLIS and CAROL (PETTY) McMILLAN

Carol and Rex McMillan were long-time residents of Dunsmuir, living in the same location at 4107 Walnut (formerly designated as 127 Francis Street). They were introduced to each other in Klamath Falls, Oregon, where Carol worked for the California-Oregon Power Company as a billing clerk. They were married November 30, 1936 in Medford, Oregon.

Rex had worked for the Southern Pacific Railroad, but from 1930 to 1936, he had been an employee of the Klamath County Sheriff's Office as a deputy sheriff. He then went back to work on the railroad and was promoted to locomotive engineer in 1939. He worked fifty years on the railroad, and when he retired in 1968, he was the oldest engineer in seniority on the Southern Pacific.

Rex had few hobbies, but hunting with his dog was probably one of his favorites. He was a meticulous and an innovative person about maintaining their house and car. Their house today reflects many of those innovations. Rex was a 50-year and life member of the Klamath Falls Lodge No. 1247, B.P.O.E.

As a wife of a railroad engineer, Carol was alone much of the time. Because of this she became active in lodge rituals, church activities, hospital auxiliary volunteer work, and bridge playing. She had served as officers in several of the organizations to which she belonged and was a member of the Past President Club of "Lady Engineers" (G.I.A. to the B. of L.E.). She was active in TOPS and COPS and had many friends in those groups, also.

Carol and Rex had a great fondness for Dunsmuir and will be remembered, not as civic activists, but as two people who loved their environment and their friends.

**THIS PAGE IS DEDICATED TO THEM
BY THE PETTY FAMILY**

THE HARRY MARSH FAMILY

Ethel and Harry Marsh

Ethel and Harry Marsh first came to Dunsmuir in 1912. Harry was employed by the S.P.R.R. as an engineer, but lay-offs forced him to move his family out of the area periodically. The family always managed to return and eventually made the community their permanent home.

The original Marsh residence was on Castle Avenue. The household was very active with four children: Isabel, Eloise, Harry A., and John, and eventually seven grandchildren.

Harry and Ethel were forced to sell their home when construction of Interstate 5 forced the removal of homes in the area.

Harry and Ethel were active in many local organizations. Harry was a member of the Masonic Lodge and R.R. Engineers. Ethel was busy in Eastern Star, Rebekahs and Lady Engineers. She also taught Sunday School for many years at the United Methodist Church and was active in Christian Women's Society.

Harry retired from the railroad in 1943, and many of his family continued to work for S.P. Eloise's husband, Ted Crocker, worked for the company as a conductor until retirement in the early 1970's. He passed away in 1978.

Both Harry A. and John Marsh worked for the company after returning from tours in the military during W.W. II. Harry was a lineman/engineer and later an official for Amtrak until his retirement. He and his wife, Mary, reside in Rocklin, California.

John worked as a brakeman, but left the company to finish his education. He is now a teacher; and he and his wife, Shirley, live in Morgan Hills, California.

Isabel Eiler Johnson now lives in Yreka. Her son, Robert, Jr., and his wife, Anne, and children reside at Fort Jones.

Harry and Ethel continued to live in Dunsmuir upon his retirement and enjoyed spending their days in the company of their growing family (which now includes 13 great-grandchildren) and their many friends. Harry took part with other "Old Timers" in annual R.R. Days celebrations until his death in 1967, at the age of 88.

Ethel sold the family home and moved into the Traveler's Hotel after losing her husband. She remained active in both lodges and church and became a member of the Dunsmuir Senior Citizens. She was a member of their "Kitchen Band."

Illness forced Ethel to leave Dunsmuir in 1982. She now resides in Yreka at Beverly Manor Convalescent Hospital near her daughter, Isabel. On September 26, 1984, she will celebrate her 95th birthday.

THE THOMAS MEIENBERG FAMILY

Tom "The Hummer" Meienberg as he posed with Southern Pacific steam engine 4449 when it stopped in Dunsmuir on its way from Portland to the New Orleans World Fair in 1984. He was one of the Shasta Division "pilots" for it as it made its trip south and back to Oregon.

The Meienberg family came to Dunsmuir from Beaverton, Oregon, in May of 1973. Tom Meienberg is the son of Dr. Leo J. and the late Frances Meienberg of Portland, Oregon. Tom's step-mother is the former Minnie Hughes of Portland. He was born November 8, 1938. He celebrated his twenty-fifth anniversary with the Southern Pacific Transportation Company on August 11, 1982. During those years he worked as a switchman, a fireman, and, finally, achieving his lifetime dream, a locomotive engineer. He is a member of the Transportation Problem Solving Committee for the Southern Pacific and a member of Division #425 of the Brotherhood of Locomotive Engineers.

Sandra Ann Meienberg is the daughter of the late Mary and Edwin Kurth of Portland. She was born January 18, 1939. She is a registered nurse who did ten years of pediatric nursing before coming to Dunsmuir. During the years in Dunsmuir, she has done volunteer work as a member of the Mount Shasta Community Hospital Auxiliary and in the local Hospice program. At Dunsmuir Elementary School she has helped in the Early Childhood Education program and has served as an officer for the P.T.A.

Mary Frances Meienberg was born June 8, 1970, in Portland, Oregon. She began school in Dunsmuir and graduated from Dunsmuir Elementary School in 1984. She has been active in swim team, soccer, Little League, softball, basketball, and bowling. She played the trombone in the school band.

Barbara Ann Meienberg was born in Portland on February 29, 1972, and is an honor roll student at Dunsmuir Elementary School. She participates in many sports. She, too, was active in the swim team and is in the bowling league. She plays the clarinet and is proud to be a member of Dunsmuir's outstanding marching band which is under the direction of Mr. Michael Wright. Barbara is planning to graduate in Dunsmuir Elementary School's Class of 1986.

The Meienberg family have been active members of St. John's Church (Catholic) in Dunsmuir. Mary and Barbie were among the first girls allowed to be acolytes, and Mary is presently a lector. Sandy has been a C.C.D. teacher and a president of St. John's Altar Society. She was named "1981 Siskiyou County Catholic Woman of the Year."

Mary Frances, Sandra, and Barbara Ann Meienberg in June of 1984

A BRIEF HISTORY OF THE NICK AND LOUISE MELO FAMILY

Louise and Nick

The Melo family is a well established and greatly respected family in this area. Antonio and Caterina Foglia Melo were born in Italy and came to this area to make their home. They had ten children, one of whom was Nicola "Nick" Melo.

Nick was born at Mt. Shasta, California, on April 19, 1919. Until World War II, he worked at odd jobs. He served five years in the armed forces in the South Pacific. After the war in 1945, he bought Little Castle Dairy. While delivering milk, he met Louise Cosentino, the daughter of Luigi and Guiseppina Consentino, well-known respected citizens.

Louise Cosentino was born January 27, 1924, at Dunsmuir. After graduation, she was bookkeeper for her father, Luigi Cosentino.

Nick and Louise were married October 19, 1946. They have one daughter, Judith Karen, born December 17, 1948.

In 1956, Nick bought the Richfield business. When the freeway opened in 1962, Nick bought La Barr's interest in the L and L Hardware Store (LaBarr and Lockhart).

Nick served the public and gave of his time generously. For forty years he was a member of the Dunsmuir Fire Department and retired as firechief. His current interest is in the Veterans of Foreign Wars.

Louise is manager of the Dunsmuir Water Corporation. Nick and Louise have always been active and have supported all local functions. Nick, "jack of all trades," is ever ready to give a helping hand wherever it is needed.

Their daughter, Judy, married James Robert Sakshaug April 28, 1973. On December 9, 1979, Erik Jameson was born to them.

The Melos live in the remodeled Cosentino home on Shasta Avenue.

Judy, Jim, and baby Erik

IN HONOR OF
THE HERSCHEL MEREDITH
FAMILY

Kelly, Herschel, Sr., Curtis, Herschel, Jr.

Dr. Meredith was involved in many aspects of Dunsmuir life and had a special interest in education. He served on the College of the Siskiyous' Board from its inception in 1957 to 1981, and was board president for 15 years.

Meredith was also a long-time trustee on the Dunsmuir Elementary School Board. He was a member and president of the Rotary and Lions Clubs. He was a member of the advisory board of the Heart Federal Savings and Loan and served on the Dunsmuir Airport Commission.

From his own experience, Herschel was very concerned with the visual problems of pre-school children and advocated early professional eye examinations. Few people realize the number of glasses he provided free of charge for those who needed them.

In 1947 Herschel met Maxcine Hubbard, who was born at Colone, South Dakota on May 14, 1924. The family moved to Pasadena, California in 1943 so that Maxcine could attend college.

On November 21, 1947, Herschel and Maxcine were married. After Herschel received his doctorate, they moved to Dunsmuir on October 16, 1950. Herschel set up his optometry practice and worked at it until he retired in September, 1983. The Merediths had many plans for the future, but it was short-lived as Herschel Allison died December 28, 1983.

There are three children: Herschel Allison, Jr., born May 14, 1951; Curtis Wesley, born April 11, 1955; Kelly Anne, born November 16, 1959.

HERSCHEL ALLISON MEREDITH

I, Herschel Allison Meredith, was born in a dug-out on February 23, 1920. The nearest town was Bellview, New Mexico. My parents, Marion and Annie Meredith, moved there about 1916 and filed a claim on a farm. According to the tales I heard as a child, those were very rough times. Their well dried up and most of the time they hauled their water in a wagon.

My father seemed to have the wanderlust, and we lived a few months here and a few months there — all in eastern New Mexico, the Texas panhandle, and a brief time at Oklahoma.

My earliest recollections of school were at Portales, New Mexico. I was in the second grade; and after two years there, we moved to Clovis, N.M. for about a year or so. Then we moved to Ruidoso, New Mexico, for a summer and on to Artesia for the fall months, where we all picked cotton. From Artesia, we moved to Roswell, New Mexico. I attended the elementary and high school and graduated in June, 1939. While in grade school, I sold papers on the street and later had a paper route for two or three years. I won a trip to the Texas Centennial for selling the most subscriptions to the *El Paso Herald*.

When I was twelve years old, I began to have blurry vision. I went to an optometrist; and when he began to place lenses before my eyes, a new world was opened that had been hidden from me for quite some time. This made a lasting impression on me, and I said to myself, "When I grow up, that is what I want to do."

While attending high school at Roswell, I started to work at the Sally Ann Bakery. My job was to wrap the bread, 800 to 1700 loaves daily, clean the sweet dough pans and mix 300 pounds of flour for the sponges for the next day's bread. It was a tough job for a kid going through high school, but I stuck it out for over three years. Mom and Dad moved to a farm north of Clovis in 1937 so I lived with my sister and brother-in-law, Paul and Dollie Baker.

In the fall of 1939, I enrolled at Bethany College as an education major, although optometry was still in my mind. My brother, Archel, was attending college as a theology student. In order to meet my expenses, I again resorted to a paper route, delivering papers twice daily on a twenty-five-mile route in an old Model A Ford roadster, and going to school in between.

During the next two years, the war in Europe kept getting hotter and more and more men were being drafted in the U.S. Army. In September 1941, I felt it was time for me to become involved before the draft forced me. I joined the ground forces of the U.S. Air Corps (later changed to U.S. Air Force).

My first ten months were spent at Sheppard Field, Wichita Falls, Texas. After basic training I had many duties but most of them related to the Headquarters Unit. In July 1942 I was sent to Atlantic City, N.J., and there I became base personnel Sergeant Major. This was followed by short assignments at Salt Lake City, Utah, and Tucson, Arizona. From Tucson, I went to Salina, Kansas, as First Sergeant of a new group learning to fly the new B-29. After a few months training, we picked up new planes and headed across the Atlantic for Africa. From Africa to Cairo, Egypt and on to India, where we were based about 70 miles southwest of Calcutta. After five months in India, I was sent to China where our forward Unit was based. From this base, we were the first Americans except the Doolittle raid to bomb Japan. The next April we returned to India and prepared to go to the South Pacific. We went to Guam first and later to Okinawa. All this time we were regularly bombing Japan. As a unit we received six battle stars and the Distinguished Unit Citation. Our squadron had about 60% dead casualties.

It was while I was at India that Mother was killed by a car in March, 1945.

I returned to the West Coast, where I was discharged on November 11, 1945. I had saved most of my money while overseas. My dream of going through optometry school began to look like a reality. With the money I had saved and the G.I. Bill, I could finally go to school and not work for support.

January 1946, I attended University of Pacific, Stockton, for three semesters. I was admitted to Pacific University School of Optometry, September 1947. After three years and two summer sessions, I received my Doctorate in Optometry June 1950.

During the summer of 1947, I met Maxcine, and we were married the following November. She was secretary to the vice-president of the college, and I did what odd jobs time would permit.

Following graduation and qualification by the State Board, we opened an Optometric office at Dunsmuir, California, and have been in practice for the past thirty-three years. It has been a most rewarding experience.

In 1957, I became involved in doing a survey to determine whether or not there was a need and sufficient justification for a Community College in Siskiyou County. In 1958, the people voted to form the college and I was appointed as one of five trustees to administer the district. We determined early that we build slowly on a pay-as-you-go basis. By 1975 we had built a college capable of handling eleven hundred students, and it was debt free. I served as Chairman of the Board from 1962 until I went off the board in 1981. I feel very proud of this achievement. Not many men have such an opportunity and have the joy of building a college where there was none.

As I write this in June, 1983, Maxcine and I are looking forward to retirement in September. We plan to travel some and sit back and relax a lot. Life has been hard at times, but good in many ways. We anticipate tomorrow's sunrise, and we are glad to be alive. We have reared three wonderful children and have seen them started on their adult lives and careers. We love God and feel His presence in our lives daily. We are proud of our Meredith heritage — for the Merediths are made of great stuff!

Note: At this time the College of the Siskiyous Board of Trustees have authorized President Eugene Schumacher to develop a plan for the naming of the Football Athletic Facility after Dr. H. A. Meredith.

HERBERT GEORGE MORGAN
HATCHETT and MARCUS FAMILIES

*Mr. & Mrs.
Herb Morgan
1969*

Herbert George Morgan was born on October 26, 1900, in Keswick, CA. He was the third child of John Henry Morgan, b. 1856 in Michican, and Lillian Josephine Frick. Lillian was born in Virginia City, Nevada, on May 8, 1875. She was the daughter of O. J. Frick. The children of John and Lillian Morgan were Ella Vaughn, b. Dec. 1895; Florence Kelly, b. Nov. 7, 1898 and d. May 11, 1935, in Yreka; Herbert George, b. 1900; and John Pierpont Morgan, b. 1902 - d. July 29, 1963, in Marysville. John H. Morgan died in the early 1900's in the Redding area. Later Lillian married Richard Jordan of Dunsmuir. She died Nov. 8, 1962, in Yreka, CA. Ella Vaughn lives in Rockland, CA.

Herbert Morgan began working for the Southern Pacific in the freight office about 1920. Soon afterwards he became a fireman. During the early 1930's, he was an engine watchman while working for the California State Highway Department at Macdoel, CA. He returned to Dunsmuir in 1936 as a fireman. In 1941 Herbert was promoted to engineer. He saw his service on the S.P.'s Oregon Division, formerly the Shasta Division. In 1965 Herbert retired after 42 years of engine service. He was presented with S.P.'s Award for 40 years of perfect safety.

Herbert belonged to the Masons, Scottish Rite, Ben Ali Shrine, and Eastern Star. In 1974 he served as Worshipful Master of Dunsmuir Lodge #197, F. & A.M.

It was while living in Macdoel, CA, that Herbert met the recently widowed Opal Icy Hatchett, who became his wife on Jan. 7, 1933, at Klamath Falls, Oregon.

Opal Icy Gunter was born on March 21, 1904, in the Oklahoma Indian Territory. She was the daughter of Dan Gunter, b. May 7, 1864, in Jacksboro, Texas, d. April 2, 1940, Foss, OK; and Elizabeth Simmons, b. Feb. 16, 1873, Triplett, N.C. and d. Aug. 30, 1918, Foss, OK. Opal married James Harold Hatchett in Sept. 1925, in Foss, OK. They had two children: Treva Jo Hatchett, b. July 9, 1926; and Harold Gene Hatchett, b. Jan. 28, 1929, both born in Foss, OK. James Harold Hatchett died suddenly due to an accident in 1931. Opal and the two children came to Macdoel, California, to visit her sister, Mrs. Esta Stanton.

Opal was one of eight children: Esta McCully Holland, b. Dec. 24, 1891 - d. Feb. 15, 1973, Medford, OR; Arthur "Jake," b. Jan. 20, 1893 - d. March 14, 1967, Prescott, Oregon; Carl, b. Jan. 5, 1896 - d. Jan. 12, 1902, Indian Territory, OK. These three children were born in Endee, N.M. The other children after Opal were born in Foss, Washita County, OK. They are Claude Lee, b. Aug. 13, 1909, now living in Medford, Oregon; Fern Nita, b. Dec. 28, 1912 - d. July 3, 1931, Clinton, OK; Mildred Reid West, b. July 12, 1925; and Dorena June Springer Price, b. Sept. 16, 1927.

Opal is a past president of G.I.A. Division 163, and a Past Matron and 50-Year Member of Fidelity Chapter #131, O.E.S. of Dunsmuir, CA. She is a member of the United Methodist Church of Dunsmuir as was Herbert when he lived. Herbert died on March 11, 1975. He is buried at Mt. Shasta Memorial Park.

The children of Opal Morgan attended and graduated from the local schools. Treva Jo attended the University of California at Berkeley before joining the Cadet Nurses Corps. She became an R.N. after graduating from St. Luke's Hospital in San Francisco, CA. In 1948 she married Donald Clarence Marcus, a teacher-counselor of San Francisco, CA. In 1964, she graduated from S.F. State University and became a Reading Specialist in the San Francisco schools. Children of Treva Jo and Donald Marcus are Gerrie, b. Feb. 1, 1954, Heidelberg, Germany; and Donald James Marcus, b. July 17, 1956, San Francisco, CA. Gerrie is a student at S.F. State University. Donald J. is an officer in the Merchant Marine. He married Gwen Foy on the island of Grenada on Nov. 8, 1979. Gwen Marcus is an M.D. They are living in Baltimore, Maryland.

Harold Gene Hatchett and his wife, Rose Hargrave Cambron, live in Redding. They were married Dec. 30, 1967, Reno, Nevada. Rose was born in Boise, Idaho, on Feb. 28, 1928. Harold graduated from Chico State University in 1950. He then spent four years in the U.S. Air Force, two of which were in Japan. The mother of his three children is June Ann Lockerman Lee. The children are Lynda Shawn Fertig, b. July 4, 1952, in Chico, CA; Valorie Gail, b. April 17, 1954, in Albuquerque, N.M. and married to Bob Spidel of Redding; and Dennis Carl Hatchett, b. April 22, 1959, in Chico, CA. Grandchildren of Harold Hatchett are David Shawn Fertig, b. Aug. 13, 1975, in Chico, CA; and Jesse Gene Hatchett, b. Aug. 21, 1982, in Sacramento, CA. Harold Hatchett works for Farmers Insurance in Redding, CA. Lynda Fertig lives in Chico, CA. Valorie Spidel works for Triple A Insurance in Redding, Ca. Dennis Hatchett works and lives in Sacramento, CA.

Opal I. Morgan just celebrated her 80th birthday. She is well and lives in Dunsmuir.

Above: Herbert and Opal Morgan, 1955; Above right: Herbert, Opal, and children, 1933; Left: Treva Jo Marcus, 1950; Right: Harold Gene Hatchett, 1950; Lower left: Herbert G. Morgan, Aug. 5, 1965, Recipient of S.P. Safety Award, 40 years of safety; Lower right: Grandchildren of Opal and Herbert Morgan, Dec. 1964 — Left to right: Donald James Marcus, Dennis Carl Hatchett, Valorie Gail Hatchett, Gerrie Marcus, and Lynda Shawn Hatchett.

IN HONOR OF OUR PARENTS

∽∽∽

GEORGE and CONSTANCE MILLARD

Our father, George Ellis Millard, was born in Illinois on January 22, 1872, and he was raised in Eldon, Iowa, from 1872 until 1890. He first came to Dunsmuir in 1902. He passed away June 27, 1944, in Weed. California.

Our mother, Constance Rainsberry Millard, was born at Petrolia, Ontario, Canada, on June 20, 1878. In 1899 she graduated from the Elmira (New York) School of Nursing as a registered nurse. She passed away April 7, 1955.

Our father hired out as a locomotive engineer at Rocklin, California, September 9, 1902. He had a home in Rocklin and would "work over the Hill" to Wadsworth, Nevada, or north to Dunsmuir. When the Shasta Division was established on the Southern Pacific in 1906, he transferred to Dunsmuir and purchased a house on the west side of Florence (Dunsmuir) Avenue.

In August of 1910, our father married our mother. Our sister, Helen, was born in Dunsmuir and died there August 18, 1911. We two, William and Richard, were born in Dunsmuir, also. William

The Millard Family in 1915:
William, George, Constance, and baby Richard

was born June 5, 1912, and Richard was born October 2, 1914. Our brother Joseph, who was born April 11, 1922, was killed in an accident in 1941.

We children were received "into the congregation of Christ's flock" at St. Barnabas Episcopal Church in Dunsmuir.

★ ★ ★ ★

This page is dedicated by Mr. and Mrs. Millard's sons:

WILLIAM
(A locomotive engineer for Southern Pacific, retired)

RICHARD
(The Right Reverend Millard, retired, Assisting Bishop, Diocese of California: Episcopal)

The Millard Family in 1923:
Richard, George, William, Joseph, and Constance

From 1954 to his demise in 1983, Peter Motto was owner and operator of Motto's Club on Sacramento Avenue.

After Papa (Secondo Motto) had established a home in Oakland, California, he was able to send for Mama (Geranima) and their three children, John, Olympia, and Peter. It was 1906 when they left Montemagna, Italy, and sailed across the Atlantic. By the time they boarded the train heading west, Mama was out of money. It was through donations given to Pete when he played his concertina that Mama was able to buy her bambinos food.

Pete, like so many foreign-born Americans, was ambitious and tried many kinds of work. At the time of his marriage in 1919 to Katherine Perman, he was manager of the Blue and Gold Market in Berkeley, California. After a few years, he left retail produce for the challenge of the wholesale market. He bought a prominent corner in the commission produce area just south of downtown Oakland. Pete was a gifted businessman; he could predict the yield from fields of produce. He also understood the produce commodity market; he knew when to buy and/or sell. He was well-established as a successful produce man when he abruptly left

that field and found a new challenge in the On and Off Liquor Sales. Shortly before World War II, he started purchasing olive acreage in Corning, California, eventually owning the most acreage under a single ownership. Not satisfied with just growing olives, he purchase a cannery. Later, with the assistance of an elderly Italian, he built an olive pressing plant. Overseeing the olive groves, cannery, and pressing plant was very time-consuming and involved a lot of hard work. In 1953, Pete started selling his various olive interests and bought the property on Sacramento Avenue, which he operated as a bar, a cafe, and a hotel for almost 30 years.

Pete was an avid golfer with a twelve handicap. Every morning, weather permitting, you could find him on his favorite golf course taking aim at that little white ball.

Peter Motto was a proud man, a kind man, a man who loved life and always met a challenge head-on. He was survived by his only child, Lillian Nibblett, two grandchildren, James Peter and Sandra Colacula; and two great-grandchildren, Domon and Shelley Colacula.

Submitted by Lillian Nibblett

THANK YOU, DUNSMUIR

DICK, JAYNE & WAXEY MURDOCK

● ● ● FOR THE YEARS 1951 through 1955 when - surrounded by your unsurpassed beauty - I worked in engine service for Southern Pacific and wrote columns and features for the Dunsmuir News, an unforgettable time of transition which moulded my future. In appreciation of those years, I have written SMOKE IN THE CANYON, a tribute to all you were and are.

● ● ● FOR BEING THE SPOT where I garnered experience in mountain railroading which became the basis for my winning entry in a 1981 San Francisco radio station contest: Why My Likeness Should be Cast in Wax.
    "Because, " I wrote in part, "I'm of a vanishing breed, the steam locomotive engineer." That won and Waxey stood for over a year at the Wax Museum on Fisherman's Wharf and is being considered for a berth at the California State Railroad Museum in Sacramento, all because I spent five remarkable rewarding,years here.

YES, THANK YOU, DUNSMUIR!

DICK MURDOCK

DEDICATED TO
FRED J. HOLLIS
Grandfather of William T. Murphy

Fred J. Hollis, with Dunsmuir pennant, leading 4th of July parade down Sacramento Avenue about 1906

Later, Hollis owned and operated the Reception Bar and Restaurant across Sacramento Avenue from the Southern Pacific Depot. It was a popular refreshment stop for passengers detraining in Dunsmuir.

Fred and Ella's daughter, Jennie Agnes, became the wife of Timothy Murphy. In 1902, when he was fifteen years old Tim had moved to Dunsmuir from Cheyenne, Wyoming. He began his career with the Southern Pacific as a young boy painting box cars until he was old enough to hire out as a brakeman in 1907. He was promoted to conductor in 1913 and retired after fifty years of service.

Tim and Jennie were the parents of Marjorie Jane, who married L. Almont Gibson; and William Timothy, who married Delberta Luttrell. Both couples make their homes in Dunsmuir.

Fred J. Hollis came from Maine to California in the early 1880's riding shotgun on the top of the train to ward off wild animals and Indians. He hired out on the Southern Pacific Railroad at Rocklin, California. He married Ella Abagale Johnson of Red Bluff. As a locomotive engineer, Fred Hollis transferred to Dunsmuir in 1897, bringing with him his wife and little Jennie Agnes who had been born at Red Bluff in 1886. The Hollises had two other daughters, Mildred and Marcia, both of whom were born in Dunsmuir.

Fred Hollis bought a block of land on Oak Street from the Southern Pacific and built a home on one part of it for his family. At the time, the SAN FRANCISCO CHRONICLE reported that Fred Hollis of Dunsmuir had purchased property and built a house in the "wilderness." As his daughters married, each was given a piece of the land for a home site.

Timothy and Jennie (Hollis) Murphy on their Wedding Day, September 2, 1907

THE WILLIAM T. MURPHY FAMILY

Tim, Bill, Del, and Chris Murphy about 1956

Bill and Del Murphy in the Club Car,
Railroad Park Resort, Dunsmuir, CA

William Timothy "Bill" Murphy, born in Dunsmuir on March 23, 1925, is the son of Timothy and Jennie (Hollis) Murphy and the grandson of Fred J. and Ella (Johnson) Hollis, who came to Dunsmuir in 1897.

Delberta (Luttrell) Murphy, born July 20, 1927, is the daughter of Delbert and Dorothy (Copeland) Luttrell, who moved to Dunsmuir in 1923.

Bill and Delberta were married in December of 1945 and are the parents of Gale Christine Murphy, who was born September 3, 1947, and now lives in Vancouver, Washington; and Timothy Hollis Murphy, who was born September 12, 1950, and is living in Castella, California, at the present time (1984). Both children attended the same Dunsmuir schools their parents attended and even had some of the same teachers. Later, they went to College of the Siskiyous at Weed, California. Chris graduated from Chico.

In 1955 Bill resigned his position as District Manager of California Pacific Utilities, and he and Delberta entered into private business. They opened and operated Siskiyou Plumbing and Appliance in Dunsmuir until 1964, at which time they sold the business and built and operated the Travelodge Motel, the only in-town motel in Dunsmuir.

In April of 1968, Bill and Delberta started a new project. With the help of their children, they have developed Railroad Park Resort, which has become a museum to rail buffs as well as a fine restaurant, lounge, motel, and R.V. park for the general public. The Resort has on display and/or in use a Willamette Shay engine, an 1887 Wells Fargo car, a water tank, a railroad station, and many more cars that are made into restaurant and motel units.

Railroad Park Resort is located a mile and a half south of Dunsmuir near Interstate 5 and on Little Castle Creek with the granite spires of Castle Crags in the background.

In Memory of Our Son
GALE LUTTRELL

Born May 20, 1925. Graduated from D.H.S. in 1942. Enlisted in the Air Force as a cadet in 1943. He was killed in a S.P. train wreck on the Great Salt Lake causeway, December 31, 1944.

Below is a picture of the family. Left to right: Gale, Dorothy, Delbert (Curly), and Delberta. Dorothy Copeland and Delbert Luttrell were married April 7, 1923, at Taklequah, Oklahoma. They came to Dunsmuir, November 1923. Curly owned and operated a barber shop in Dunsmuir for many years and retired in 1962. Delberta married Bill Murphy in 1945. They have two children, Christine and Tim.

LUTTRELL FAMILY

A. B. MURRAY FAMILY

Archibald Benjamin Murray I was born March 7, 1848, and married Rachel Downs, who was born July 9, 1853. He was a conductor on the Northwestern Pacific and lived in Ross, Marin County. He was also Judge of the Traffic Court in San Rafael.

A. B. Murray II was born in Los Angeles on October 10, 1876. He married Gladys E. Wood on Dec. 15, 1892. They lived in Weed where he worked for the Southern Pacific Railroad as Yard Master. Later he moved to Dunsmuir in 1914 where he worked as a brakeman and conductor. He also served as councilman and was Mayor of Dunsmuir. Anna L. Moran was Gladys Wood's mother, and she came to Dunsmuir in 1904.

Anna Moran's mother was Mrs. Guadalupe Roche, daughter of Don Jose Maria Sanchez, who was awarded a 40,000-acre land grant near present-day Hollister by the Spanish government. Don Jose married Encarnacion Ortega, a direct descendant of one of the leaders of the Portola expedition from Spain. It is said that Don Jose buried $60,000 in gold "somewhere on the rancho" for fear of cattle rustlers, but the gold has never been found.

A. B. Murray III was born in Weed on August 14, 1913, and, when the family moved to Dunsmuir, he attended school here. Later he attended junior college in Sacramento. He worked for Cal-Ore Power Company in Dunsmuir from 1936 until he later worked for the Southern Pacific. He retired as an Engineer after 33½ years of service.

A. B. (Ben) Murray III married Mildred C. Bell on March 27, 1937. She was working as a surgical nurse in Dunsmuir for the Cornish hospital. She was born July 18, 1910, in Red Lodge, Montana.

Ben and Mildred raised three children. Benton M., born March 14, 1940, married Sandra Bauer, Jan. 29, 1963. They have one child, Gregory, born Aug. 19, 1967, and all live in Livermore, CA. Douglas W., born Dec. 15, 1944, single, lives in Dunsmuir and works for the Southern Pacific. Anne E., born Aug. 16, 1952, married Michael Fay on October 30, 1981, and they live in Livermore, CA.

Left: Benton, Douglas, and Anne Fall '54

Right: Mildred and Ben

A. B. Murray I and Rachel

Gladys Murray and her mother, Anna Moran (Left)

A. B. Murray II and wife, Gladys Wood

A. B. Murray II and his grandchildren

THE HISTORY OF THE ANTONIO (TONY) BRUN FAMILY

Antonio "Tony" Brun was born in Cavaso, Italy, in 1881. He came from a large family of 11 brothers and sisters. They were millers. His father died when they were all very young; and as the boys grew older, they helped support the family. Tony came to the United States in 1910 and settled in Dunsmuir; he was one of the early settlers in Dunsmuir. He started to work for the Southern Pacific Company as a blacksmith. He retired from the S. P. Co. in 1946 and died in Dunsmuir in 1958.

Tony married his wife, Mary, in Dunsmuir in 1913. They had four children: a son, Guido, who attended the schools in Dunsmuir. He enlisted in the service during World War II, where he distinguished himself. He was a Captain and was in the North African Campaign. He received a citation from the Italian Government for bravery. After his discharge from the Army, he returned to Dunsmuir and went to work for the Southern Pacific Co. He married Cora Calvert, and they had two children: a girl and a boy. Guy is now retired and living in El Paso, Tex. Their son, Michael, lives in Tucson, Arizona, and works for the S.P. The three Brun sisters (as they were known) all attended Dunsmuir schools. Louise worked in the school cafeterias from the 4th grade through high school. On graduation she moved to Santa Barbara in 1936 and was married to John Golin in 1939. They have three children, a son and two girls. The twins, Norma and Emma, attended the Dunsmuir schools. Norma was the athlete in the family. She excelled in all sports, and received many trophies. Her trophies are still in the trophy case at the high school. She was also the cheer leader during her high school days. She moved to Santa Barbara, where she later married Marcus Peters. They have one son, who lives in Portland, Oregon, with his family.

(Continued)

THE BRUN FAMILY

(Continued)

Emma was in several activities in Dunsmuir High School: the Drama Club, the school office force, the A Capella Choir, and the Glee Club. She moved to Santa Barbara, where she married John H. Riffero. They have two children, a son and a daughter.

Tony Brun was very well-known and loved by all in Dunsmuir. He was a "Father Image" to all who knew and loved him. He was active in the Catholic Church, serving as a Deacon of the church for many years; in the Knights of Columbus; the Foresters of America; and the Italian Catholic Federation. He was also very active in many community affairs.

Tony sent for his two brothers, Valentino and Giuseppe from Italy, and they also settled in Dunsmuir. They, too, worked for the Southern Pacific Company. Valentino remained in the United States, married, and had three children: Renaldo, Aida Brun Hillway, and Edward Brun. Giuseppe stayed in the United States for only four years and then returned to his native Italy with his family.

Tony's sister, Pasqua Brun Guadagini and her husband, Batista, came to Dunsmuir. He also went to work for the Southern Pacific Company. They had three children: Maria Cahill, Angelo, and Anna Avery. (Maria and Angelo work for the S.P. now.)

Through the years, Tony brought over from Italy, three nephews and a niece. They all settled in Dunsmuir and worked for the S.P. Co. Antonia and Maria had three children: a son, who died at birth; and two daughters: Selvina Nealon, who lives in Dunsmuir and owns Sally's Beauty Shop; and Enes Leonard, who now lives in Po-

mona. Enes worked for many years for the S.P. Co., as did her husband who has just recently retired. Maria and Tony owned and operated the Bocce Ball Court and Italian Restaurant in Dunsmuir. People came from all over the county to enjoy Maria's good Italian food. After they closed the Bocce Ball Court, Maria continued with her cooking. She is now retired and lives in Dunsmuir.

Ettore and Andrew both married and lived in Dunsmuir. Ettore had one son. Andrew had two daughters and one son; he and his wife later were transferred to San Francisco where he still worked for the Southern Pacific Company.

Tony and Mary Brun lived in Dunsmuir for over 45 years. After Tony's death in 1958, Mary moved to Santa Barbara to live by her three daughters. She died in 1968.

Tony and Mary had four children (as named above), eight grandchildren, 16 great-grandchildren and twin great-great-grandchildren.

Tony and Mary on their 40th Wedding Anniversary

IN LOVING MEMORY OF
THE CHARLES ALLAN PACKWOOD FAMILY

Gertrude, baby Pauline, Alice, Pete, Charlie, Sherald Allan (child)

Charles Packwood's father, James Knox Packwood, and mother, Anna Wilson Packwood (third cousin to Woodrow Wilson), came across the plains from Iowa in 1874, when Charlie was two years old. Charlie was born May 11, 1872. The family settled in Bieber, Lassen C., Charlie grew up there and married Pauline Gertrude Null in 1898. She was born May 16, 1879. They had five children before moving to Dunsmuir in 1918: Alice, April 30, 1899; Nolan Charles "Pete," September 13, 1900; Sherald Allan "Buster," April 27, 1906; Pauline Evelyn, July 13, 1908.

Charlie went to work for the Southern Pacific Railroad and "Gertie" opened a boarding house on Butterfly Avenue to help rear the family. This was a popular home for the single railroad men. Many "hobos" were fed at Gertie's. She always made them work for their "hand-out." When they closed the boarding house, they moved to South Dunsmuir, where they had a large truck garden. Many families would drive down for the fresh vegetables. During the Depression they fed many needy families. They were noted for their generosity.

Gertie died in 1937. Charlie retired from the railroad in 1939. He died in 1943. Both are buried in the family plot in the Dunsmuir Cemetery.

Their youngest child, Hilda, died when the family home burned in 1912 at McArthur. Sherald (Buster) died in 1948. The three surviving children are living here. Alice retired from the Air Force as a Tech. Sergeant after twenty-two years service. She returned to Dunsmuir with her husband, retired Sergeant Major Robert Walker. "Pete" remained at Dunsmuir and worked for Charlie Carlquist. Pauline worked for the State of California for twenty-two years. She retired and moved back to Dunsmuir with her husband, Melvin Thorn (deceased) in 1972.

IN HONOR OF

MARY AND "PETE" PACKWOOD FAMILY

Golden Wedding Anniversary, December 16, 1976

Charles "Pete" Packwood was born September 13, 1900, at Beiber, Lassen County, California. He came to Dunsmuir in 1920 and worked at the round house and the Anderson Lumber Company. For six years he worked at Ralston's Grocery until the depression. In 1932, he went to work for Charlie Carlquist. There he continued until he retired in 1965.

Mary Schafer was born at Odessa, Washington, on March 7, 1897. She came to Dunsmuir in 1923 with her husband, Herbert Kendrick, who was killed in a motorcycle accident. Mary did confinement work for Dr. Cornish and Dr. Horner. She met and married Pete Packwood on December 16, 1926.

Mardell Willie was born Sept. 22, 1927. Joan was born April 27, 1929. Mardell married Harold Bowman June 27, 1948. Their children: Forest Whitney, b. Oct. 23, 1952; Brook Courtney, b. Nov. 10, 1954; Fawn Meredith, b. Jan. 30, 1958.

Joan married James Oliver Youngblood June 12, 1949. Their children: James Nolan, b. July 18, 1950; Jonathan Richard, b. Feb. 4, 1953; Jeffry Stephen, b. January 30, 1957.

Pete and Mary have nine great-grandchildren, five boys and four girls.

The Packwoods are still living on Butterfly Avenue, where they have lived since 1932. They served the community for many years and are highly respected and loved by all who know them.

IN LOVING MEMORY OF OUR PARENTS

FRANCISCO AND MARIA DELGADO PADILLA

Francisco, Vincent, Maria, Consuela, Salvador

Francisco Padilla was born on December 16, 1895 at Somberete, Zacatecas, Mexico, to Pedro Padilla and Atilana Yanez. Atilana was widowed at an early age, and Francisco and his brother worked to support the family. He met and married Maria Delgado on July 14, 1917. She was born on October 2, 1895 to Teodosio Delgado and Alejantra Hernandez.

Francisco's dream was to come to America. He had three children, and he wanted them to have a better life. With the help of his father-in-law, Teodosio Delgado, on May 5, 1923 (Cinco de Mayo),

Francisco, with his wife, mother and three children came to Dunsmuir. He went to work as store attendant for the Southern Pacific. He had taken a correspondence course to learn to read, write, and speak English. He received his diploma with honors. This was no easy task, but Francisco had the ability and perseverance which he has passed on to his children and grandchildren.

Because Francisco had only one brother and Maria was an only child, they wanted a large family. They had ten children: Consuelo, born May 23, 1918; Salvador, born

June 5, 1920, died November 26, 1970; Carmen, born June 16, 1922; Vincent, born July 19, 1924; Augustine, born May 28, 1926, died March 27, 1981; Lucy, born April 9, 1928; Tonia, born June 25, 1930; Lupe, born May 18, 1932; Peter, born June 2, 1934; and Filberto "Beto," born August 29, 1936. They had thirty-eight grandchildren and twenty-three great-grandchildren.

The Padillas were a very close and united family. They worked, played, and prayed together. Maria and Francisco had great faith and passed this love on to their children.

In love and appreciation by:

The Padilla Family

Maria and Vincent

Atilana, Augustine (Baby), Salvador

IN LOVING APPRECIATION OF OUR PARENTS
AUGUSTINE (TEENY) and CECILIA PADILLA

Augustine was born in Dunsmuir on May 28th, 1926 to Francisco and Maria Padilla. They immigrated to Dunsmuir from Mexico in May of 1923. Francisco was employed by the Southern Pacific Railroad Company for 38 years as a storekeeper. They had ten children.

Augustine attended Dunsmuir Elementary and graduated from Dunsmuir High in 1945. He was a veteran of World War II, serving from 1944 to 1947. He married Cecilia Vidaure, June 13, 1953. Cecilia was born November 22, 1929, at Sims, to Antolin and Maria Vidaure. She attended schools in Red Bluff.

Augustine was employed for 35 years by the Southern Pacific Company as a clerk. He and Cecilia raised six boys and one girl. They are Tom, Dan, Davy, Tony, Victor, John, and Anita. All attended and graduated from Dunsmuir schools. At this time, Tom, Dan, Davy, and Tony are married. Their wives are as follows: Tom's, Noreen Billman; Dan's, Lori Wamsley; Davy's, Marie McGuire; and Tony's Kim Wiley.

Augustine and Cecilia currently have five grandchildren: Eric, Gregory, Jennifer, Ryan, and Stephanie.

Cecilia died on November 11, 1978. Augustine died on March 27, 1981.

The children would like to say, "Thank you, Mom and Dad, for being the BEST parents anyone could ever ask for; and thank you for raising us in Dunsmuir.

NELSON FAMILY

Karl H. and Bernadine B. Nelson have lived in Dunsmuir for nearly forty years. They came here in 1947. Karl was an Investigator in the Police Department for the Southern Pacific R.R. Co., and was transferred to Dunsmuir from Klamath Falls, Oregon. He became Special Agent for the Southern Pacific R.R. Co., and worked for thirty years. He retired in 1972. Bernadine joined the staff at the Dunsmuir Elementary School; and after teaching for twenty years, she retired in 1972.

They have two children. Katherine Noel was born Jan. 17, 1941, in Red Bluff, California. James Russell was born Apr. 10, 1945 in Klamath Falls, Oregon. Both children went through the Dunsmuir schools and the University of California at Chico.

Katherine is now Mrs. Kenneth Gates and lives in Los Gatos, California. James is Safety Officer for Southern Pacific R.R. Co. with headquarters in Eugene, Oregon.

Left:
1960 — Karl Nelson in foreground, Presidential Candidate John F. Kennedy on rear end of train. Taken at Gerber, CA, by camera man on train.

Lower Left:
Katherine and Jimmy, 1948

Below:
Katherine, 11, Jimmy, 7, and Bernadine standing by fountain at S. P. Depot, 1952. Note railroad walkway over the tracks.

A BRIEF HISTORY OF THE "NICK" PADULA FAMILY

Linda, Nick, Chelsea, Irma, Treb, Cathie, Nick

Nicholas "Nick" Padula was born on June 5, 1915. His parents were born in Italy and came to America at the turn of the century with so many other immigrants who had dreams of a better life. His father, Antonio Padula, was born December, 1888. His mother, Mary Padula, was born August 16, 1891. Antonio worked as carman for the Southern Pacific at Dunsmuir to provide for his large family. On April 17, 1925, he was accidentally killed while underneath a Pullman car repairing it.

Nick attended the local schools and during the depression he joined the Civilian Conservation Corps. After this he hired out as blacksmith for the S.P. During World War II, he was repeatedly deferred because his job was vital to the war effort. He was able to join the State Guard. On May 25, 1941, he married Irma C. Zancanaro, who was born February 23, 1922. Her father, Noe Zancanaro, was born in 1884. Her mother, Maria DeRoss, was born Mar. 25, 1883, at Paderno Del Grappa, Italy, to Luigi DeRoss and Madalina Andreazza. Irma's parents were married at Redding, California, in 1921.

Nick and Irma have two children, Nicholas Allen and Linda Mary. Nick Allen was born February 24, 1942. On December 28, 1968, he married Catherine M. Booth, who was born July 31, 1948, at Ottawa, Canada. They have two children, Christopher Treb, born January 2, 1974, and Chelsea Lyn, born October 25, 1976.

Linda was born November 10, 1946. On May 5, 1973, she married Michael Kostiz, who was born November 24, 1948.

Nick retired as foreman of the powder gang after fifty years. He and Irma spend their time in their garden and helping others.

Marie, Noe, Irma

Nick, Nickie, Irma, Linda

PALETTA FAMILY

March 11, 1984

Dear Centennial,

Let me extend my hand in friendship to all my Centennial friends and pay respect to our little town that has been so good to our family. Give a cheer for my mom who is still doing "just great at 98" (this date), and give loving thoughts to the others who are no longer with us.

Thanks, Dunsmuir, for the myriad of experiences you gave. I remember playing ball on our hard dirt field. Turf? Are you kidding? It was the only turfless field in California — we loved it.

It was a gala affair when a spirited student body would turn out to pick up rocks prior to game time. Just simple things like that.

Thanks for the memories, Dunsmuir, and a happy 100th to you.

Sincerely,

Pace J. Paletta

DUNSMUIR, CALIFORNIA
1914 - 1970

BENJAMIN H. and ELECTA M. PERRY

Mr. Perry was a resident of Dunsmuir for 56 years. Ben, as he was known, was born in Sams Valley, Oregon, in 1878 and, during his younger days, worked in gold mines, logging camps and, at one time, worked in a box factory in Upton, just north of Sisson, which is now Mt. Shasta City.

Ben married Electa Marsh, of Grants Pass, Oregon, in 1898, and they settled in Sams Valley on a ranch where they had four children: Margaret, George, Ruben, and Doris.

Ben left his family in Gold Hill, Oregon, when he came to Dunsmuir in late 1914. He was employed by Southern Pacific Railroad Company as a carman and relief outfit engineer. The family followed him to Dunsmuir in February, 1915. The children graduated from Dunsmuir School.

Dunsmuir, at that time, had wooden sidewalks and unpaved streets. The railroad was the only industry, and most all residents worked for the railroad. Sacramento Avenue was the main street, and had mostly businesses. Florence Avenue was residential, except for Montgomery's Garage and Crowley's Grocery.

Ben was registered for the 1918 draft for World War I. He retired at the age of 65. He was a member of the Railroad Retirement Board. Ben was active in sport fishing and hunting, going salmon fishing at the age of 90. Ben and Electa were interested in gardening at their home, located at 102 South 2nd Street, and celebrated 62 years of married life.

Margaret, known as Maggie, married Vernon Conley, and had 3 children: Thelma, Ray, and Melvin. George married Wyvetta Conley, and had two children: George, Jr., and Jean. Ruben married Maloa Ackerman, and had two children: Edgar and Dale. Doris married Kenneth McGee, and they had one daughter, Dolores.

Maggie and Vernon lived in Ashland, Oregon, where he retired from the railroad, and Maggie retired from the Ashland School District. George worked for the SP Company in Dunsmuir in 1922, and transferred to Sacramento in 1935, where he later died from an auto accident. Ruben worked for the SP Company in Dunsmuir in 1925, in the Stores Department, and the Superintendent's Office, moving to Sacramento in 1936, and retiring in Roseville in 1970. Doris and Kenneth live in Dunsmuir, where he was employed by the SP Company as a brakeman in 1926, and was promoted to conductor in 1938. He retired in 1974. Doris had a grocery store in Champion Park for many years.

At the time of his death, Ben was Dunsmuir's oldest citizen, and an honorary member of the Eagles Lodge. Electa passed away in 1960 at the age of 82. Ben passed away in 1970 at the age of 92 years and 9 months.

Ben and Electa Perry are survived by 3 children, 8 grandchildren, 24 great-grandchildren, and 12 great-great-grandchildren.

WE REMEMBER DAD, BOB PEDRONCELLI,
AND
DUNSMUIR

**Marianna Pedroncelli
Gina George and Family
Anita Mei and Family
Fides Chiment and Family
Gloria Walker and Family
Robert B. Pedroncelli and Family**

*Battista and Marianna Peroncelli
on their wedding day
April 27, 1924, San Rafael, CA*

Battista "Bob" Pedroncelli was born at the Lake Como region of Italy. He came to America in 1920.

Marianna Cantoia was born at a small village near Milan, Italy, and came to America in 1921.

Marianna and Bob met at San Rafael while attending night school to learn the language. They were married at San Rafael on April 27, 1924. In May they came to Dunsmuir to make their living and home. Bob was a contractor and was awarded the contract to build the Episcopal Church (now First Baptist) on Dunsmuir Avenue. (Pictured on another page.) In his "spare time" he built the first family home located at 202 S. Highway and established a neighborhood grocery store. Marianna operated the store, and Bob worked as licensed contractor and mason.

In 1945 Mr. and Mrs. Pedroncelli bought a vineyard at Healdsburg, and established the B. Pedroncelli Winery.

Marianna Pedroncelli continues to make her home at 77 W. Grant, Healdsburg, California.

*Back row: Gina, Anita
Center: Fides, Bob, Gloria
Seated: Marianna holding Robert*

IN HONOR OF THE FABIAN PEREZ FAMILY

FIVE GENERATIONS
Fabian, grandfather; Lisa, mother; Victoria, great-great-grandmother; Juanita, great-grandmother; Jennifer, baby.

Fabian, Juanita, Marcella, Isabell

Fabian Perez was born at Zacatecas, Mexico, on March 4, 1902. In 1929 he came to America and went to work for the Southern Pacific. He met and married Juanita Castro on November 24, 1934, at Medford, Oregon.

Juanita Castro Perez was born on June 24, 1918, at Zacatecas, Mexico to Cirilo Castro and Victoria Matallanes Castro. In 1929 the Castro family moved to Dunsmuir. They had three boys and four girls.

Fabian and Juanita lived at Ashland, Oregon, where Fabian Anthony was born on September 11, 1935. Four years later they moved to Yreka where Alvino Michael was born on December 30, 1941. Two years later they moved to Montague so Fabian could go to school.

In 1944 the Perezes moved to Dunsmuir. Two girls were added to the family. Isabell Margarita, born November 13, 1946; and Marcella Annet, born September 29, 1955. All the children were graduated from the local schools. Alvino is the only one who still lives in Dunsmuir.

Fabian was maintenance man for the Southern Pacific and retired in 1978. Enjoying his retirement for a very short time, Fabian died on April 25, 1983.

The Perezes have three grandsons, two granddaughters, and two great-granddaughters.

Juanita has spent her entire life on South Francis Street. Her mother, Victoria Castro, lives across the street from her. Victoria is ninety-seven years old (1984) and is still taking care of herself. Nut Glade Street holds many memories for Juanita. South Francis Street was once so named.

Fabian, Marcella, Isabell, Alvino

DUNSMUIR PHARMACY

Where we started, 1945

Building before remodeling job, 1958

THANK YOU, DUNSMUIR; YOU HELPED US DO IT.

Dunsmuir Pharmacy had its start on Sacramento Avenue. The *Dunsmuir News* has an article dated 1904 about Gus Hutaff, a druggist. The store was moved to the Traveler's Hotel building on Florence Avenue (now Dunsmuir Ave.). E. J. Cone purchased the store and operated it for 18 years.

I purchased the Dunsmuir Pharmacy in October, 1945, from Mr. Cone and operated the pharmacy and fountain until 1959 when we bought from Hal Montgomery the building across the street. The building was formerly occupied by Everett Holecek of Mt. Shasta and was a surplus store. He closed it out that year. In the same building was California Pacific Gas Co., a Union office, and Clark's Cleaners in the basement of the building.

The building was completely remodeled and redesigned to bring another modern new look to Dunsmuir's main street downtown.

I had a keen interest in the Dunsmuir community and served as President of the Chamber of Commerce, President of the Siskiyou Crippled Children Association, City Councilman, Mayor of Dunsmuir, and a Lions Club Officer.

In 1970, I was presented a plaque from the Dunsmuir Booster Club for interest and support of the athletic program and named "Booster of the Year," for the Dunsmuir High School.

My wife, Maggie, and I have three daughters: Vicky, Stephany, and Lisa. Vicky attended College of the Siskiyous and was a student at Chapman College. She spent two years in the Campus Afloat program of the school, traveling over the world in her studies. Vicky received her B.A. Degree, plus standard Secondary and Elementary credentials, and at present is teaching at the Mt. Shasta Elementary School.

Stephany attended College of the Siskiyous in the Nursing Program and received her degree as a L.V.N. At present she is working in Fremont, CA.

Lisa attended Patricia Stevens Career School in Honolulu, Hawaii. She won the Beauty Pageant held in Honolulu and competed in Australia for "Queen of the Pacific." She also was a flight attendant for T.W.A. She now owns and operates STEPPIN' OUT in Mt. Shasta.

Maggie and I decided to retire after 34 years as owners of the Dunsmuir Pharmacy and had the distinction of being the longest continuous operators of a business in Dunsmuir in terms of years. Upon retiring, I received an "Honorary Life Membership" plaque from the Dunsmuir Chamber of Commerce.

In September, 1979, we sold the Dunsmuir Pharmacy to Jim Alspach of Yuma, Arizona.

It is our sincere wish that he may achieve the success and happiness that we derived from this business.

Petrovics Dunsmuir Pharmacy, 1959

IN ACKNOWLEDGMENT TO THE PHARMACISTS WHO WORKED FOR US FROM 1945 TO 1979

Our thanks,

Vic and Maggie Petrovics

E. J. Cone, 1946
James Quigley, 1946
Cethil Jones, 1950
Irma Coffeen, 1955
Milton Kiversham, 1962
LaVar Hill, 1963
Hal Huscher, 1965
Kay Rudesill, 1967
Ken Weinberg, 1973
Charles Olson, 1976

DUNSMUIR PHARMACY FOUNTAIN

YEARS OF OWNERSHIP, 1945-1959

The Dunsmuir Pharmacy fountain was built in 1924. The back bar was made of Philippine mahogany with marble columns and colored lights inside, surrounded by mirrors. The counter was made from polished aggregate rock that came from Inyo County. The counter section is now in the Canyon Bakery.

The fountain was a gathering place during the "hey day's" of the Southern Pacific railroad, and, especially when three shifts were working at the round house.

Many movie stars had visited the fountain. During the filming of "The Red Stallion" in Dunsmuir, the movie stars and extras of this film lunched at the fountain.

One of our most shocking experiences was in 1946. We had a 6- by 7-foot wooden oak ice box with 4 compartments. When we opened the store one morning, we found no ice box. Upon investigation, we found that the floor was rotted and the ice box had fallen through and was sitting in the basement. It was quickly replaced by a new and modern refrigerator.

Although two of our daughters, Stephany and Lisa, were too young to work at the fountain, they did help and work at the Dunsmuir Pharmacy's new store.

Several employees that started to work at the fountain also continued on at the new store.

To all our wonderful and loyal customers and tourists who visited our fountain, we will always remember, "HOW SWEET IT WAS."

In acknowledgment to our faithful employees who worked at the Dunsmuir Pharmacy fountain from 1945 to 1959.

In gratitude,
Vic and Maggie Petrovics

Norma Kahl, 1945
Joann Holcomb, 1945
Dan Phillips, 1945
Mary Helen Daw, 1946
Margaret Bolton, 1946
Charles Harris, 1946
Marybelle McBride, 1946
Dorothy Smishek, 1946
Rhoda Clausnitzer, 1946
Carolyn Reginato
Alice Jane Coon, 1947
Jean Griswold, 1947
Nellie Tracy, 1947
Virginia Wheeler, 1947
Ruby Rowell, 1947
Lucille Kivett, 1947
Peggy Dillard, 1948
Marge Olsen, 1949
Marlene Thompson, 1949
Lillie Winter, 1950
Betty Fox, 1950
Robert Carey, 1950
Marvel Garriot, 1951
Rita Giacomelli, 1952
Phillip Carey, 1953
Mary Rodriquez, 1953
Sue Murdock, 1954
Rayola Hanlen, 1956
Mae "Sis" Linebarger, 1957
Karen Lee, 1958
Terry Fawcett, 1959
Vicky Petrovics, 1959
Joan McGowan
Royce Dal Zell

Vic & Maggie, 1946

DUNSMUIR PHARMACY
TODAY

From Yuma, Arizona, Jim and Sherryl Alspach with sons, J. W. and Bobby Alspach, moved to beautiful Dunsmuir in September, 1979. They purchased the Dunsmuir Rexall Pharmacy from Vic and Maggie Petrovics. The store is located at 5826 Dunsmuir Avenue in the Rochford Building, which was built in 1925. In February, 1984, they spread out into the whole building with an expanded gift line.

Employees who are working or who have worked for them are:

Lillie Winters (now Mrs. Jack McDonald)
Kay Carlson (Chet the barber's wife)
Oralee Floria (owner of the Travelodge
in Dunsmuir)
Laura Hopkins
Lorraine Masters

HAPPY BIRTHDAY, DUNSMUIR!

PETTY

Union S. Petty, born March, 1868, in Igo, California, married Blanche Malone, daughter of John J. and Mary Jane Malone and sister of Dr. George E. Malone. Petty was bridge and building foreman for Southern Pacific from 1894 to 1904. A big project was the wooden trestle at Big Canyon.

He also operated a tire vulcanizing shop with Ed Flakus at 905 Florence Avenue in a two-story wood frame building later to be torn down and replaced by a new structure built in 1927. It stands there today.

One sister, "Kate" (Katherine, I suppose), married Tom Long, an airplane painter. They lived in Red Bluff. One brother, Jim (James?), was a prospector and had a productive claim south of Castella. He would often come to town and show his nuggets in his tobacco tins.

Union loved to shoot ducks in the then-sizeable pond before it was drained to become the ball park. He died January 21, 1922. His wife, Blanche, died October 19, 1927.

John U. Petty was born February 23, 1919. He worked for twenty-three years as volunteer fireman, five years as Deputy Chief of Police and fifteen years as Superintendent of Public Works. He served four years in the 11th Signal Service Corps World War II. He married Helen E. Kiskila (Simon) in 1950. They moved to the Bay Area in 1965 to work for the City of Mountain View. Retired in 1981, they both presently reside at Milpitas, California.

~~~PICKTHORN FAMILY~~~

ARTHUR JAMES PICKTHORN

ALICE E. ANDERSON

Married July 14, 1901, in Lake Jennis, Minn.
and returned to Dunsmuir.

Deceased:
Alice E. Pickthorn, 12-25-1955
Arthur J. Pickthorn, 1-3-1956

CHILDREN (All born in Dunsmuir):
Herbert B. - Deceased Sept. 1979
Arthur B. - Deceased July 1971
Lily M. - Deceased Jan. 1977
William E.
Albert E.
(two sons died in infancy)

Arthur B. Pickthorn - Grace A. Vrieling
Married: March 15, 1932

Lily M. - Joseph F. Lorkowski
Married: May 26, 1945
(both were serving in the Armed Forces
with rank of Lieutenant)

William E. - Mary Evelyn Hastings
Married: August 29, 1940

Albert E. - Frances Arnold
Married: November 4, 1934

Arthur James Pickthorn, a native of London, England, came to this country in 1890 and secured employment with the Southern Pacific Company, May 17, 1890, and continued in this employment until May 31, 1940. He worked as a telegrapher 6 months at Gravel Pit near Canby, Oregon; telegrapher, asst. agent, and agent in Roseburg, Oregon. It was while there he met Alice E. Anderson, an officer in the Salvation Army. He came to Dunsmuir on February 26, 1901, as agent, a position he held until his retirement.

Their marriage was blessed with seven children, ten grandchildren, and six great-grandchildren.

Their children attended schools in Dunsmuir. Herbert was a band instructor at the Dunsmuir High School for terms '26-'27 and '27-'28. Arthur joined the Dunsmuir Fire Department at age 18, or in 1923, and remained with the department until 1937 when he went railroading. He continued with the railroad until his death. His wife, Grace, also worked for the railroad as a steno-clerk until her retirement in 1968, and then she went to work full-time in 1969 in the Flower and Gift Shop. Arthur served as Dunsmuir Fire Chief from 1931-1937. He also served in the Armed Forces, 1942 to Dec. 1945, both in the United States and overseas.

William and Albert left Dunsmuir to enter the ministry. At present William is semi-retired, teaching one day per week at St. James College, San Bruno. Albert is presently working as a real estate appraiser.

Lily entered the field of nursing and served in this capacity during World War II with the rank of Lieutenant.

THE DELWIN POE FAMILY

Del Poe and his wife, Mayme, their son, Bill, 15, and daughter Cathie, 6, moved to Dunsmuir from Mount Shasta in the fall of 1952, when Del became Superintendent-Principal of Dunsmuir High School.

Del, a native son of California, was born in the Mother Lode town of San Andreas, Calaveras County, but moved to Sutter Creek, Amador County, a short time later.

Mayme was born in Canton, Ohio, but moved to Amador City, Amador County, at the age of nine. Both grew up in Amador County and both attended Sutter Creek High School, as it was known at that time, and which is now the Oro Madre High School.

Del entered U.C., Berkeley, after high school, but Mayme and her parents moved first to Arizona for two years, then to Riverside, California. When Mayme transferred to U.C.B., she and Del met again and marriage was in the offing. There was the little matter of educations to complete, so they were married three years later, at which time Del signed his first teaching contract with their old home high school.

While they lived in Sutter Creek, Bill was born. They moved to Galt for two years, then to Lassen County, where Cathie was born. Del was Director of the Extension Division of Lassen Junior College at Susanville for one year.

Then the family moved to Mount Shasta, where Del was principal of that high school for five years. At the resignation of John Glaese, the Poes moved to Dunsmuir in 1952, when Del became Superintendent-Principal of Dunsmuir High School.

They settled in — school and community-wise, to the extent that twenty years later, when it came time to retire, they had put down roots, becoming Dunsmuirites in every sense of the word.

The senior Poes still remain here, in the same home on Beverley Way which they have occupied for twenty-five years — a long time for otherwise nomadic school people.

After graduation from college, Bill found his niche in life working as a right-of-way agent for Caltrans (California Department of Transportation) out of the Redding headquarters — near enough to his former home, yet not obliged to shovel snow.

Cathie is the wanderer of the Poe family. After spending a year in Paris in line with her major of French at U.C. Davis, she returned to Davis for a teaching credential and a master's degree. In order to teach French, she went to Australia; then she returned home bringing an Aussie boyfriend, Wally Goodrope. A few months later, they married and returned to Australia to make their home in Kilmore, a suburb of Melbourne. They have a daughter, Olivia, and a son, Matthew.

Siskiyou County, and Dunsmuir in particular, have been good to the Poes. They are happy to call it home.

THE PONTIER FAMILY

The Pontier family is grateful and happy to celebrate the DUNSMUIR CENTENNIAL.

Sam, Sr., and Michelena Pontier arrived in Dunsmuir about 1905 and settled on River Avenue. Dunsmuir, being headquarters of the Southern Pacific Shasta Division, flourished. Sam worked for the S.P. as a plumber, under Mr. Frazier.

At about 1921 Louie Cosentino built a building for Sam at 905 Sacramento Avenue. Sam Pontier & Sons was the grocery store he operated until about 1931. Also, he ran the Dunsmuir Hotel, which was over the grocery store, and later a restaurant, The Bohemian Club, which was next door to the grocery store. Both were operated by him. The restaurant was replaced by a clothing store, the P & F Emporium.

The family moved to San Francisco about 1931.

Mr. and Mrs. Pontier had five children: Dr. Joe, who now lives in Richmond; Sam, Jr., who lives in El Cerrito; Mary (Griffiths), who lives in San Francisco; Dr. Lou, who is a returnee to Dunsmuir; and Lena, who lives in Saratoga.

Mr. and Mrs. Pontier are both deceased, and their children celebrate this Centennial in their honor.

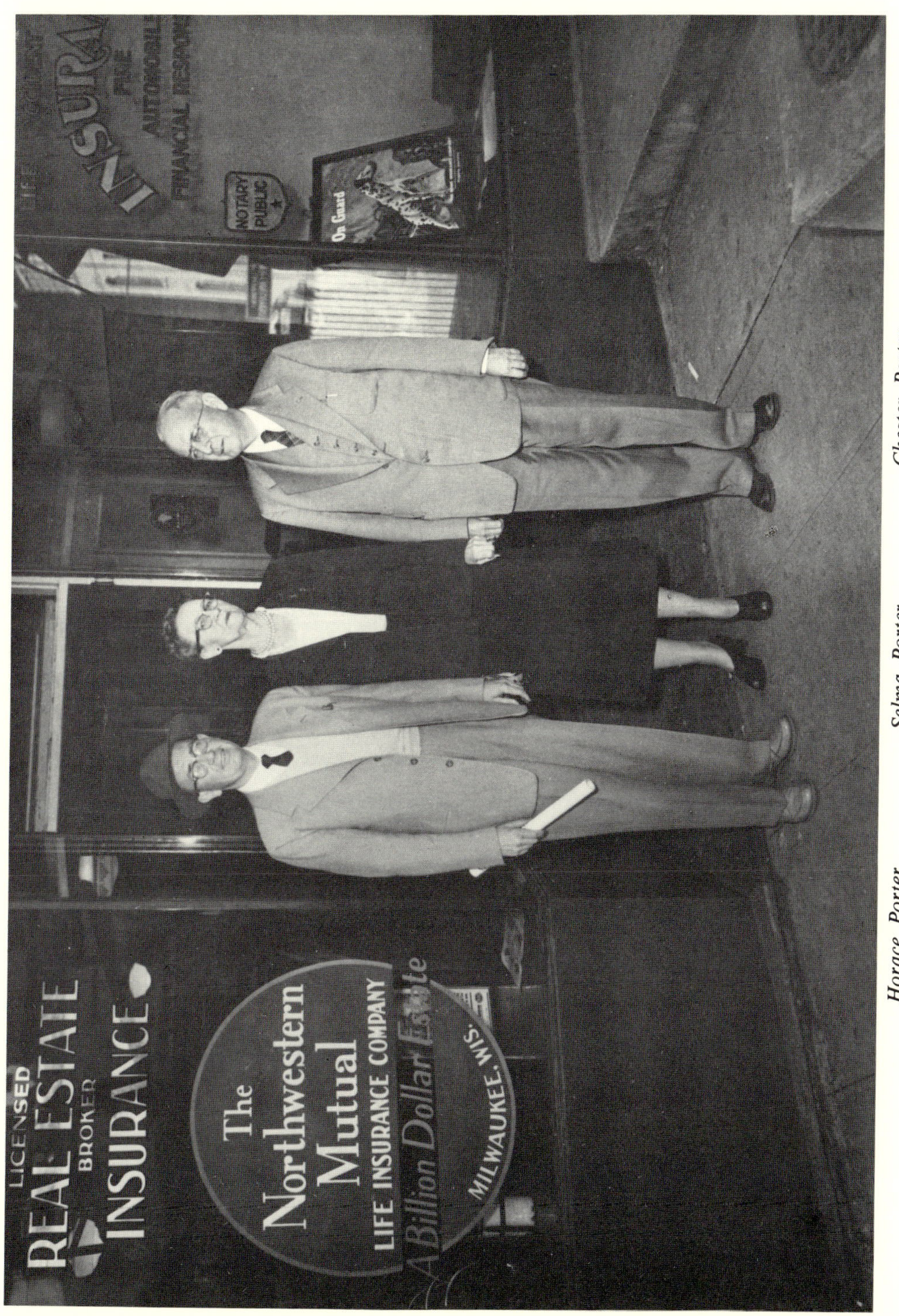

Horace Porter   Selma Porter   Chester Porter

In joyous memory of our parents and grandparents
CHESTER O. PORTER and SELMA PORTER
we wish to express their love, and ours,
for Dunsmuir

Horace O. Porter, Ithaca, N.Y.
Catherine Porter Lewis, Brooktondale, N.Y.
Dwight Gill Porter, Madrid, Spain

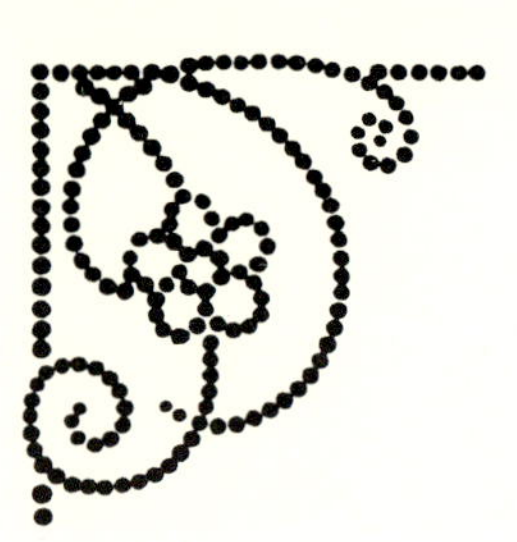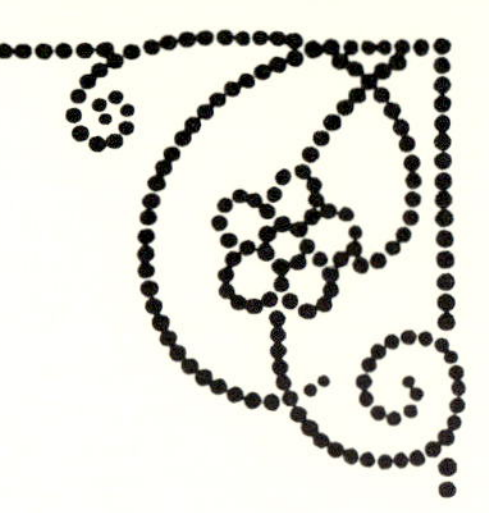

THE RENOUD FAMILY

Richard G. Renoud   Rita Wolff
Married: Medford, Oregon - Jan. 10, 1912

Richard G. Renoud, deceased Sept. 25, 1963

CHILDREN:
Harry R. — Erna Gerdes
Married Aug. 6, 1937
Children: Carl, Barbara, Paul, Robert

Gleason L. — Leila Buick
Married December 15, 1940
Child: Jere

Richard G. Renoud came to Dunsmuir in 1909; Rita Wolff, in 1910.

Richard, or Dick as he was affectionately called, was employed by the Southern Pacific Company in the locomotive shops, specializing in air brakes. He retired September 1, 1955, after 46 years of service. Besides his employment with the Southern Pacific Company, he was active in community affairs being on the Dunsmuir City Council, May 1932 until April 21, 1942, during which time he served as Mayor, April 16, 1940, to April 21, 1942. He was then again on the City Council, April 1952 to April 16, 1956. Rita gave her full support to his community service attending all City Council meetings with him.

Their marriage was blessed with two sons, five grandchildren, and seven great-grandchildren.

Both sons were interested in community affairs. Harry entered the field of teaching, retiring from Reedley Community College, January, 1973. While in Reedley, he was a member of the Volunteer Fire Dept., 1951-1961; and on the City Council 1966-1970. Coming home to Dunsmuir after his retirement, he served on the Dunsmuir City Council 1974-1982, including one year as Mayor. He married Grace A. Pickthorn October 20, 1972.

Gleason chose the field of civil engineering and worked for the Bureau of Reclamation as a civil engineer until his retirement.

Dick and Rita made their home on Branstetter Street, Dunsmuir. The following poem, written by Rita and included in the account of his retirement, describes their home.

"A Cozy little cottage with a great big lawn
Where the song birds start singing with the dawn
And a flower embroidered garden, where for healing
*   we can roam*
And a little love to sweeten it,
That's Home Sweet Home."

"Dunsmuir has been good to us."

OUR MOM AND DAD

**IN LOVING MEMORY OF OUR PARENTS
WHO REARED US TO CARE FOR OUR
FELLOW MAN TO BECOME GOOD CITIZENS**

Albion Thompson Powers was born in Sacramento, November 9, 1889. He met Lillian Mae McMahon in La Grange (Stanislous Co.), where she was born Dec. 23, 1897. They were married in Modesto on November 30, 1914. Their first two children, Clara and Bill, were born in Tuolumne. Jim was born in Jamestown. They moved to Dunsmuir in 1920, where Dad was hired as an S.P. fireman on November 15, 1920. Ethel, John, and Jerry were born here.

They were both active in lodge, Mason, Sciots, Eastern Star, and Rebekahs. Dad was Deputy Pharaoh for District #1 of the Sciots at the time of his death, December 15, 1951.

Mom spent several years living in LaGrange and Sacramento, where she passed away on July 22, 1978. She left five surviving children: Clara, Ethel, John, Jerry, and Jim (who has since passed away); ten grandchildren, twenty-two great-grandchildren and one great-great-grandchild.

With love and gratitude,

THE POWERS GANG

THE RADTKE FAMILY

Orin Leonard and Mary Jacobs Brown - 1921

Iyone Brown Radtke was born on October 14, 1898 in Motley, Minnesota. She was the youngest girl of six children: Daniel David, Lucy Ann Brown Rypka, William Leonard, Laura Olive Brown Joyce, and Winifred Rudolph Brown. Her parents, Orin Leonard Brown and Mary Jacobs Brown, made their home in Motley, Minnesota, where her father worked as a blacksmith and logger.

Iyone married Ernst Frederick Radtke on November 19, 1918 in Malta, Montana. In seven years the couple had four children. Erney Orrin was born on November 17, 1919 in Bowdoin, Montana. Ernst and Iyone moved to Dunsmuir when young Erney was 1½ years old. On September 21, 1921, Iyone gave birth to a daughter, Ione Genevieve; followed by Alfred Robert, born September 8, 1923; and Janice Arlene on May 3, 1925, all born in Dunsmuir. Mr. and Mrs. Radtke lived in Dunsmuir until 1946, when they moved to Alturas for two years. In 1948 they came back to Dunsmuir, where they lived until his death in 1966. In December, 1984, at well over 80 years, Iyone passed away in Dunsmuir, her home for so many years.

served four years in the Army, then returned to Dunsmuir to work for the railroad until he retired in 1975. On November 19, 1942, he married Emma Lou Dishman. They adopted one child, Robin Linnea, who now lives in Mt. Shasta with her two children, Katheryn and Steven.

Ione married William Alexander Hughes and made her home with him in Dunsmuir. Three children, Ione III, Thomas, and Rosemary were born in due time. Tom passed away in 1970; and Rosemary, twelve years later in 1982. Ione III lives in Sacramento with her husband, Don, and four children: David, Mike, Robbie, and Beth.

From Bob's marriage to Nadine Steelman in 1935, two girls, Roberta and Susan, were born. Roberta was born on January 6, 1956. She now has 5 children of her own. Susan, born 10 months later on November 16, 1956, has 3 children.

Bob was the wanderer of the family. He joined the Merchant Marines during World War II and has since lived in several cities in California. Today he lives in a converted school bus with his wife, Mardell. Together they spend most winters in Mexico, and most summers in Washington or Canada, spending their time in between traveling all over the United States.

Arlene married Henry Mehciz in June of 1942, and began using her first name, Janice. By 1951 she had had four children: Janice Marie, born June 1, 1944; Jean Ruth, born July 3, 1945; Henry Charles, born June 4, 1947; and William Lee, June 4, 1950. During that time, Jan lived in Mt. Shasta for six years and spent one winter in Alturas before returning to Dunsmuir.

In 1951 she was divorced. Two years later on June 19, 1953, she married James Craig McDonald in Reno, Nevada. Jim was a navy man and their first home was made in Albany, California, from September of 1953 to September of 1955. During that time, on November 4, 1954, a daughter, Joyce Alice, was born. The next move was to San Pedro, California, until 1957. In October of 1957, the family moved to Honolulu, Hawaii, where they lived until October of 1961. When they returned to the states, they lived in Dunsmuir until May 1962, when they moved to San Diego, California. After nearly two years, three months were spent in Pleasanton, California, before the move to Waterton, Wisconsin, in early September of 1964. Following Wisconsin, the family moved to Newport, Rhode Island, for six months and returned to Dunsmuir in July of 1965. In November of 1965, overseas duty called again, and Jim took his family back to Hawaii, this time to live in Pearl City until 1967. By this time there were only two children left at home. After leaving Pearl City, a return to Dunsmuir for one year was followed by a move to Salinas, California, when Jim retired in 1968. 1969 saw a return to Dunsmuir, where Jim passed away in 1976.

Of Jan's children, four are still living.

THE RADTKES

Erney and Iyone Radtke

Erney - Robert - Ione - Janice

THREE GENERATIONS

FOUR GENERATIONS

Jeffery Maroon

Danelle & Vearl
LeRoy Scarbrough & Joyce

Charles Mehciz
Burton Jacob Mehciz

Jim McDonald

179

THE RADTKES

Janice Marie married Larry James Heston in 1961. Three children, Larry James, Jr., Michael Dean, and Tyna Maree were born of this union. Divorced in 1972, Janice met and married James Cass Garrigus, Jr., in 1973. A daughter, Heidi Lyn, was born in December of 1974, followed by a son, James Cass III, in April of 1978.

Jean Ruth married Eugene Leland Maroon in 1964, which was followed by the birth of a son, Jeffrey Leland on September 21, 1965. Today Jean, a divorcee, makes her home in Wisconsin, while her son, himself married in 1984, makes his home in Florida.

The third child, Henry Charles, also known as "Chuck" passed away in 1961.

William Lee married Janet Schantz in 1977. Making their home in Castro Valley, Bill and Janet have two boys: William Charles, born on March 9, 1982; and Burton Jacob, born on May 13, 1983.

Joyce Alice married Vearline LeRoy Scarbrough in September of 1972. An Army man, LeRoy was stationed at Ft. Lewis, Washington, where their daughter, Danelle, was born on June 25, 1974. Following a year's tour in Korea, LeRoy was discharged from the Army and the family returned to Dunsmuir, where LeRoy went back to work for the railroad. On May 30, 1977, a son, Vearl, was born.

As of May 1984, Iyone, Sr., at age 85 and two of her children, Erney and Jan, as well as two of Jan's daughters, Janice and Joyce, still live in Dunsmuir. Must like the ol' town!

Bill Mehciz

Chuck Mehciz

PIETRO and ANTONIA REGINATO

The Venetians

Pietro and Antonia on their Wedding Day

One time a well-known children's writer told me that there arc many successful people, but they are not known to the world. Mama and Papa were a couple of those people.

Pietro Reginato left Venice when he was 15. His mother had heard that there was gold in the streets of California and that was the year 1908. Pietro arrived in Dunsmuir and did find gold in a way. He found the Southern Pacific Railroad, where he worked for 47 years.

In 1914 Antonia Bernardi arrived from Venice. She was a childhood friend of Pietro, and they were married. She was 18 and he was 22. They were married 60 years.

Antonio and Pietro had seven children, and he was very active in the Foresters of America, the Eagles, and railroad activities. Pietro had the opportunity to greet and help all the new immigrants as he worked right at the railroad station.

Later, after retirement, Pietro went to work for three years for the City of Dunsmuir and earned his Social Security along with his retirement from the railroad. The couple built and owned their own home on Butterfly Avenue, and lived there for 60 years. The house was just one block from the Southern Pacific Depot.

In 1970 when Mother became ill, a doctor here in the Bay Area asked if they had many callers. I told him, "Many people whom Mama and Papa had helped in the early years came from all over Siskiyou County to see her." They remember the old days when Antonia and Pietro greeted them at the railroad station and shared their home with the new immigrants from Venice.

In 1974 Pietro passed on. He was 83 years old, and 30 days later Antonia followed.

They are buried in Mt. Shasta under the shadow of the mountain — and the plaque says, "TO-GETHER FOREVER."

IN HONOR OF THE
HARVEY REID FAMILY

Harvey L. Reid was born in Napa, California, in 1893, where his father, George Reid, a native of Nova Scotia, ran a large livery stable. Due to health reasons, he moved his family to Azalea, where Mr. MacKenzie, a cousin, worked in the mill. Addie Reid, his wife, worked in the boarding house there, as did her cousin, Lucy Huff (grandmother to Almont Gibson). At that time there were one bank, three saloons, and one schoolhouse in Mott. George Reid and Mr. MacKenzie built the first sawmill in McCloud in the year 1897. Later, he returned to Dunsmuir to work in the mill. George and Addie had five children: William, Harvey, and Laura, all born in Napa; and Eva and Archibald, born in Dunsmuir.

Still living are Harvey, Dunsmuir; Laura and Eva, Sacramento.

Harvey attended the Dunsmuir grade school. In 1908, he went to work for the Southern Pacific Co. as an apprentice machinist, earning 10¢ an hour, but due to the strike of 1912, took a job on the donkey engine at Cantara. Later he was to work for his dad, who had started the Reid Dairy in Dunsmuir. When he was 22 years old, he was hired by the telephone company as a lineman. His work took him to the communities of Chico, Redding, and Hornbrook. It was during this time that he met a young telephone operator from Redding, Pearl V. Song. They were married in 1915. After a few years with the phone company, Harvey returned to work for the Southern Pacific Co. as a brakeman (1917), and in 1920 was promoted to a conductor. After 41 years on the road, he retired in 1958.

Harvey and Pearl had five children: Alois, Harvey W. (Bill), George (Heine), Robert, and Donald (deceased). All were born in Dunsmuir except Alois. Also, they had 7 grandchildren and 13 great-grandchildren. They had celebrated their 68th wedding anniversary in Nov. 1983. Mrs. Reid passed away early in 1984.

Harvey, 91, lives in the family home on Dunsmuir Ave., where he enjoys working in his garden. A devoted fisherman all his life, he still fishes whenever possible.

50th WEDDING ANNIVERSARY, 1965
Bill, Harvey, Pearl, Heine, Alois, Robert

THE REINEKINGS

Betty Kathleen Reineking
Born June 20, 1919
Retired Teacher

Willard Henry Reineking
Born Dec. 27, 1914
Retired from Convair
at San Diego

We came to Dunsmuir on a hot day in July, the 13th to be exact. We had been to Dunsmuir many times on our way to somewhere else. We finally stayed here for five days at the Garden Motel and fell in love with the beauty of the little railroad town.

Both of us come from the big city. Will came from San Diego and I came from Burbank, California. Will and I married in 1967 and lived in Burbank until we moved to Dunsmuir upon retiring. I joined clubs and organizations the first two months we were here, later to become vice-president and then president of the Dunsmuir Federated Women's Club, and later getting involved in the Beta Sigma Phi Sorority, the Kappa Phi Chapter. My community life has been a busy one, being a charter member of the Senior Citizens organization, and both Will and I helped to get a museum in Dunsmuir, a dream which we saw come true. Will and I were host and hostess at the opening of the museum.

Will has been very active in the community, helping to paint signs for our town celebrations, and taking pictures of the events such as the crowning of our first queen of the Centennial at her 100th birthday celebration. We both belong to the Centennial Committee and are helping in many ways to make Reva Coon's dream come true. Will has been Artist-of-the-Month in one of our stores in downtown Dunsmuir. We both were in the window for the Old-fashioned Family Christmas with our two adopted grandchildren. Will did the lettering on the Centennial Caboose, and I had the honor of singing in it with a group of friends during our Railroad Days in 1984.

We have found that Dunsmuir has helped us to grow in love and interest in our fellow beings. We have grown to love the town, and it hurts us when we see our little town losing business, but I truly believe that if we all make a big effort to give our town the best we have in us, we can't help but get back on our feet again.

Will and I feel very grateful that we have such a wonderful place in which to live and have developed such good and beautiful friendships. We hope we are fortunate enough to stay here the rest of our days.

—Betty Reineking

Dedicated to the Memory of
LLOYD C. and MARY HAZEL REYNOLDS

Lloyd and Hazel on their 50th Anniversary

Lloyd Reynolds was born in Park City, Utah, one of five children. His mother came from Tasmania; his father, from England. When he was five years of age, the family moved to Alaska during the Gold Rush of 1898. There he spent his childhood living in Juneau and Ketchikan. His father was killed in a mining accident; after that the family moved to Ashland, Oregon. At age 16, Lloyd dropped out of school and obtained a job as call boy and later as a fireman with the Southern Pacific Co. It was while working in Red Bluff that he met his wife, Hazel. They were married in August, 1916.

Mary Hazel Reynolds was born in Willows, California, April 30, 1894. Her mother died following childbirth, and she was adopted by Joseph and Mary Kernohan, a family living near Red Bluff. She attended elementary and high school there, graduating in 1912. After graduation, she did clerical and secretarial work in Red Bluff. It was there she met and married Lloyd.

After marriage, they moved to Dunsmuir, where they lived for the rest of their lives. Lloyd was promoted to the position of locomotive engineer; he retired after 49 years of service. During the Depression, he worked in the wholesale and retail oil business with Charles Lamb and Harry Stone. Retirement included trips to Canada, Mexico, Hawaii, and Cuba. He died following a third coronary in 1966.

Hazel became a housewife and mother; however, during the Depression, she worked as a comptometer operator for the S.P. She enjoyed her home, yard, and travel. After the demise of her husband, she traveled to Europe and North Africa. Until age 83, she lived alone and continued to drive and care for her house and garden.

The Reynolds Family descendants consist of one son, Dr. J. W. "Bill" Reynolds; three grandchildren: Sandra Williams, San Luis Obispo; Dr. Bruce Reynolds, Agana, Guam; Richard Reynolds, Kailua, Hawaii; two great-grandchildren: Nicole, age 7; Leslie, age 5 (1984); both children of Bruce Reynolds.

Dedicated by
Bill and Bobbie Reynolds

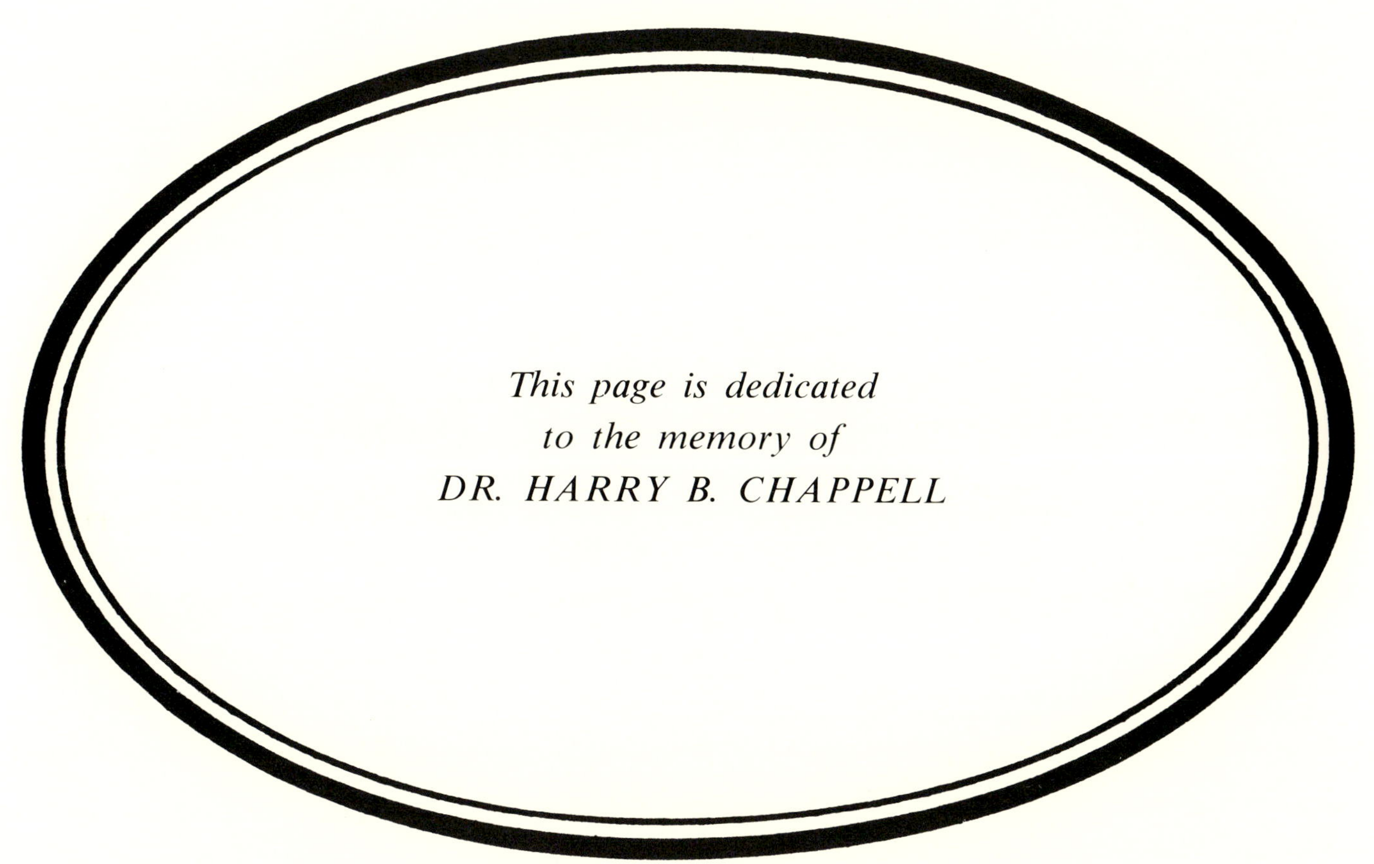

This page is dedicated
to the memory of
DR. HARRY B. CHAPPELL

Dedicated to the Memory of
W. L. (BILL) RIDGEWAY

Bill and Gladys Ridgeway

Bill and Gladys Ridgeway came to Dunsmuir in 1939 from Gerber, California. In 1936, Bill had started working for the Southern Pacific Railroad as a clerk at Klamath Falls, Oregon. At the time of his death on January 9, 1971, at the age of fifty-three, he was Chief Crew Dispatcher in Dunsmuir and a representative for the Railroad Clerks Union.

The Ridgeways had two sons. Richard was born March 17, 1941. He married Linda Lockart of Dunsmuir in 1962. They live in Stockton, California, and have two children: Shauna Lee, who was born in 1965; and Jimmy Lloyd, born in 1970.

Robert was born September 10, 1948. In 1974 he married Chris Smith of Chico, California; they live in Overgaard, Arizona. Their children are Ryan E., born in 1979, and Megan Marie, born in 1980.

Both Richard and Robert attended the Dunsmuir schools and College of the Siskiyous at Weed, California.

The Ridgeway family lived on Hill Street in Dunsmuir for many years before buying the present home on South First Street in 1949.

Gladys Ridgeway married L. M. (Mike) Brashear in 1976. Mike was a locomotive engineer for the Southern Pacific. He retired in 1982. He and Gladys continue to make their home at 678 South First Street in Dunsmuir.

In Memory of our Father and Mother,

HENRY RILEY and LUCY POORE RILEY

**who lived in Dunsmuir
from 1924 to 1958**

and with fond recollections of
growing up in Dunsmuir with
our late brother, Philip.

James R. Riley
(Redding)

Dorothy Riley Engelbert
(Chico)

Patricia Riley Woods
(Redding)

Marjorie A. Riley
(New York City)

THE LORENZO

ROSSETTO FAMILY

It was in the very early 1900's when a young Italian man with a gleam in his eyes and adventure in his heart broke the news to his parents, "I am going to America." Though the parents were sorrowful at the news of their son going so far away at such an early age, they were also happy because they knew that America was the land of opportunity and promise. So it was that at the age of seventeen, Lorenzo Rossetto boarded the ship in Italy for his newly adopted land, America.

It took a great deal of courage for a young man, unable to speak English, unfamiliar with the American ways, with limited finances, and hardly knowing anyone in this new country, to take such a giant step.

After docking in New York, Lorenzo, later known as Larry to his Dunsmuir friends, worked his way West and decided to settle in Dunsmuir. He worked at many jobs before settling with the Southern Pacific Company for 42 years of dedicated service and being very proud of becoming a top-notch machinist.

Several years later he went back to Italy and was married and brought back his wife, Ottavina. With lots of perseverance, determination, and hard work, Larry and Ottavina built a new life and home of which anyone could be

proud. They raised two children, Deiro and Eva, who are extremely proud of the accomplishments of their parents. Eva, in 1944, married Robert Kenoyer, and they both are upstanding residents of the great little town of Dunsmuir. Deiro married Mary DalleMolle of Mt. Shasta and settled in San Jose.

In the sixty some odd years that Larry and Ottavina lived in Dunsmuir, they made many friends and were active in the community. They loved their town of Dunsmuir and never considered leaving it.

One of their proudest moments was when they became United States Citizens. They have given their children a proud heritage for which we are very grateful.

IN MEMORY OF
HERMAN and LENA ROSTEL

Mr. and Mrs. Herman Rostel

Frederick Herman Rostel was born in Filehne, Germany, February 19, 1860, the son of Karl Gottlieb and Augustine (Puhl) Rostel. At the urging of an older half-brother who had come to Jacksonville, Oregon, Herman came to join him early in the 1880's. Shortly after arriving, Mr. Rostel left Jacksonville to make his home in Siskiyou County. He lived in Yreka for a few years. In Germany he had studied to be a barber, and in Yreka he put his training to use.

In 1886 Mr. Rostel went to Germany to visit his relatives. When he returned to California, he brought with him his bride-to-be, Adeline Schoeuck. Adeline, or Lena, had been born in Prussia on July 1, 1864. She and Herman were married in Yreka on June 24, 1886.

After their marriage, the young couple settled in Sisson (Mount Shasta), where Herman became owner of a barber shop and, by 1892, a general merchandise store. Both Mr. and Mrs. Rostel were very active in civic and fraternal affairs in Sisson until their deaths. Mr. Rostel died in a San Francisco hospital on May 29, 1909; and Mrs. Rostel died in Dunsmuir on October 21, 1937.

THE ROSTEL BUILDING

In 1892 Mr. Rostel had George W. Cooper of Yreka design a building to be built as an investment for him. Holt and Gregg of Redding was awarded the contract, and the structure was erected on Front Street (Sacramento Avenue) in Dunsmuir. This Rostel building was gutted by the fire that swept along Dunsmuir's main thoroughfare on April 5, 1903. Immediately, Mr. Rostel had the building replaced by a two-story, brick structure of the same design and by the same contractors. This building, although in disrepair, still stands in Dunsmuir's Historic Commercial District.

The Rostel Building is unique for Dunsmuir in that it is adorned with sheet metal and cast iron. On the base of the pilasters on the ground floor is the foundry mark of Mesker Brothers of St. Louis. It is said that of all the iron companies that shipped decorative metal elements to the West, probably Ben and Frank Mesker had the most flourishing of the businesses. Their work can be found all over the West, but the Rostel Building is the only example left in Siskiyou County.

The Rostel Building,
5743 Sacramento Avenue

THIS PAGE IS DEDICATED BY MR. ROSTEL'S GRANDNEPHEW, FRANK WINTERING, AND HIS WIFE, FLORA, OF DUNSMUIR.

IN RECOGNITION OF TWO SPECIAL PEOPLE
IN DUNSMUIR
"FRENCHY" and GWEN RUBIDOUX

Pictured above are "Frenchy" and Gwen Rubidoux with one of the first, if not *the first*, ambulances Dunsmuir had. They both gave many hours to the City of Dunsmuir and the County of Siskiyou. They served the community hours on end at times and still kept going. Often many members of the family pitched in to cover the taxis and ambulances. For 22 years, they kept going in service to others. Because of this, we want to recognize these two very special people. Without them, it is entirely possible that some of Dunamuir's citizens might not be here to celebrate the centennial.

Grandpa and Grandma, thank you for everything you've done for the city and for your family. Be proud of a job well done.

Dedicated by
John and Charlotte Fink

★ ★ ★ ★ ★

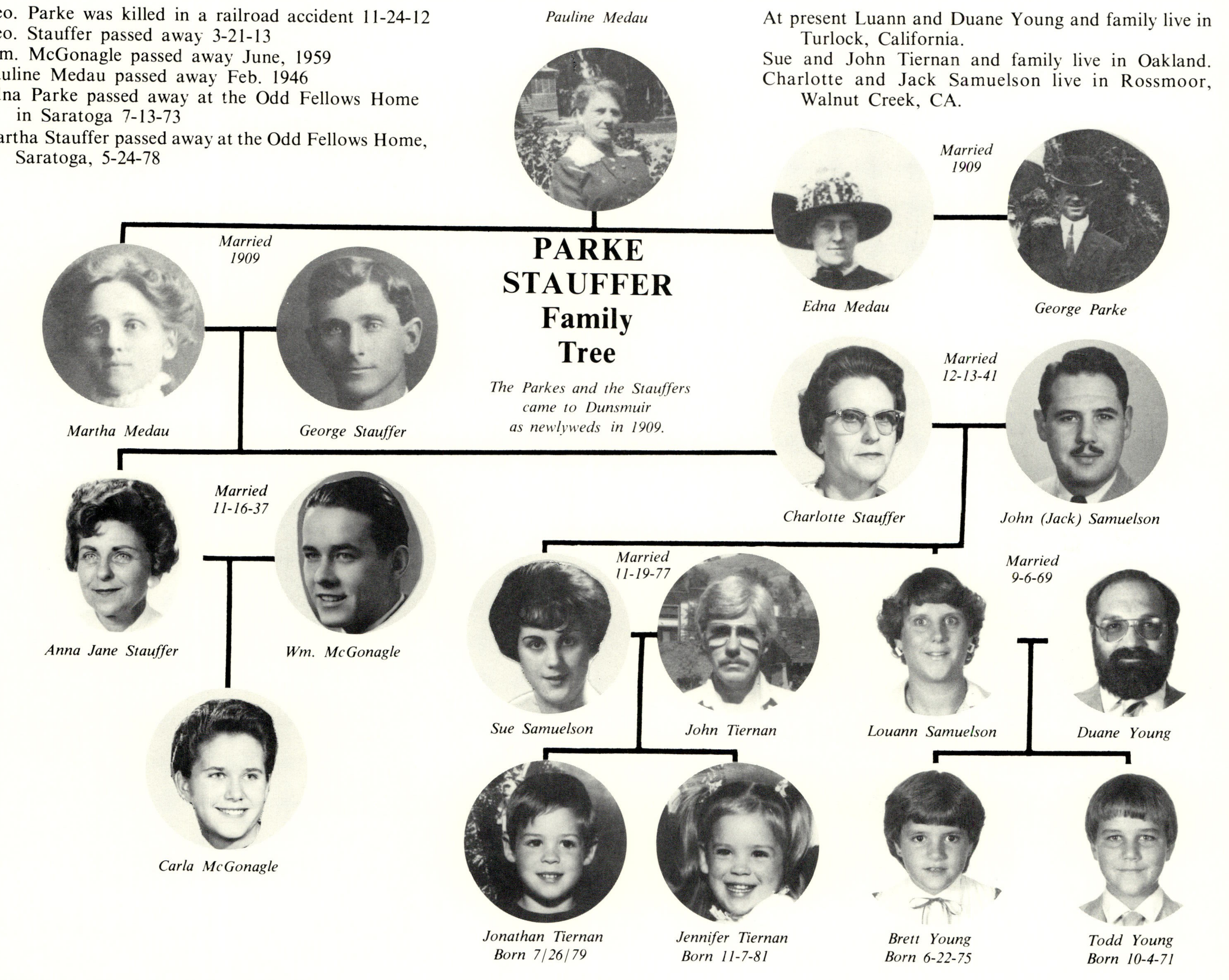

Geo. Parke was killed in a railroad accident 11-24-12
Geo. Stauffer passed away 3-21-13
Wm. McGonagle passed away June, 1959
Pauline Medau passed away Feb. 1946
Edna Parke passed away at the Odd Fellows Home in Saratoga 7-13-73
Martha Stauffer passed away at the Odd Fellows Home, Saratoga, 5-24-78

At present Luann and Duane Young and family live in Turlock, California.
Sue and John Tiernan and family live in Oakland.
Charlotte and Jack Samuelson live in Rossmoor, Walnut Creek, CA.

PARKE STAUFFER Family Tree

The Parkes and the Stauffers came to Dunsmuir as newlyweds in 1909.

191

THE W. E. SANFORD FAMILY

The Sanford Family in 1917
W. E. "Bud," W. E. "Elmer," Ivy and Helen
(The auto is a Velie)

W. E. "Elmer" Sanford arrived in Dunsmuir in 1905, after his marriage to Ivy Grigsby earlier in the year. Elmer was a recently promoted engineer for the Southern Pacific Company, having hired out as a fireman in Rocklin, California, in 1902. While firing "over the hill" between Rocklin and Sparks, Nevada, Elmer met Ivy, then a telegrapher at Champion station near Truckee, California. This was an unusual job for a woman in those days. Romance blossomed, and Elmer and Ivy were married in June of 1905.

The young couple had three children: Helen, Everett (who died at the age of four), and William "Bud." They resided in Dunsmuir except for a period from 1917 to 1927 when they lived in Ashland, Oregon.

Elmer worked as an engineer for the Company until he retired in 1944. He was an ardent fisherman and hunter and was active in the community. After his death in 1949, Ivy moved to Santa Cruz where she lived with her daughter until her death in 1972.

Elmer's son, W. E. "Bud" Sanford followed him into engine service with the Southern Pacific Company. He began firing in 1936 and was promoted to an engineer in 1942. Married to Kathleen Engelbert, the couple had three children and lived in Dunsmuir until Bud's appointment to Road Foreman of Engines. He served in five divisions until his retirement as Chief Mechanical Officer in 1970. After his retirement in Dunsmuir, "Bud" became a special deputy for the Siskiyou County Sheriff's Department. He was a sportsman and a trapshooter and belonged to the Dunsmuir Rod and Gun Club and the Mount Shasta Longrifles.

"Bud" and Kay's eldest son, W. E. "Bill" Sanford, Jr., is married to Mary Nicholson of Primghar, Iowa, and is now living in South Lake Tahoe, where he is a partner in a commercial insurance brokerage firm. His wife, Mary, teaches Spanish in the local schools.

Son Robert Lawrence Sanford, who is now deceased, was a professor at Delta College, Stockton, California. In 1964 he married Darlene Grisham of San Luis Obispo, California. The couple's two children are Michelle Marie, now 15 (1985); and William Lawrence, 13. He is called "Buddy" after his grandfather, and he will be the only one to carry on the Sanford name.

Daughter Kathleen "Kathy" is married to James Garing, a consulting engineer. They live in Arroya Grande, California, where Kathy is a dental hygienist and an associate realtor for Century 21.

"Bud" Sanford passed away January 9, 1984, but his family continues to love Dunsmuir, where his wife, Kay, still lives.

W. E. "Elmer" Sanford on his last run
as he retired in 1944 in Dunsmuir

IN HONOR OF OUR PARENTS

WILLIAM and KATHERINE
SELLMAN

We dedicate this page in Dunsmuir's history to our parents, William and Katherine Sellman. They came to Dunsmuir in 1907 to make their home. Here he was employed as a fireman for the Southern Pacific. In 1915, he was promoted to engineer. They both were active in church and community organizations. William was Mayor of Dunsmuir from 1932 until his death, the result of a railroad accident, December, 1939. Katherine lived in Dunsmuir until her death in 1980.

With loving thoughts and happy memories
this page is presented by their children:

Helen Carter, Marion Chichester,
Dr. William Sellman, Ruth Nichols (deceased)

IN MEMORY OF
DOMINIC A. SIRIANNI
Born in Dunsmuir April 9, 1904
Died March 10, 1976

David   Judy   Oliva   Dominic   Marilyn

Dominic A. Sirianni leaves his wife, Oliva, of Dunsmuir; two daughters, Marilyn Motta, of Freemont; Judy Wamsley of Redding; a son, David Sirianni of Chico; a brother, Amerigo Sirianni; and a sister, Ida Foti of San Anselmo; seven grandchildren and three great-grandchildren.

Dominic Sirianni was a well-known business and political figure in southern Siskiyou County. He demonstrated a special life-long commitment to the growth and improvement of Dunsmuir.

Dominic believed strongly in the idea that it was most important that people give to the community rather than just take from it. In the same spirit as President John F. Kennedy, Sirianni believed that it was important that people ask not what the community can do for them, but what they could do for the community.

He was a successful insurance salesman for a number of years and also ran a successful real estate business from 1944 to 1974. He was an active Rotarian and member of Dunsmuir Chamber of Commerce for 35 years. In addition, he was actively involved with Knights of Columbus and Sons of Italy.

A member of Siskiyou County Planning Commission for 15 years and member of the Siskiyou County Board of Supervisors for 4 years, he will be remembered by many as a man who could not say "No" to a civic responsibility. He will also be remembered by others for his sensitivity and response to others' needs, especially to his fellow Italian-Americans needing help in translating their business as well as personal matters from Italian to English.

His loss was deeply felt by many members of the community of Dunsmuir.

CONGRATULATIONS, DUNSMUIR!

*Although we moved from Dunsmuir
in 1952, we still have many
happy memories of friendly people
in a friendly town.*

*Helen and Vince Spanier
and Family*

IN HONOR OF
ED AND MAE STANLEY

The story of Ed and Mae Stanley is a true love story that spanned nearly sixty years. They met in Dunsmuir, fell in love, were wed, and lived happily ever after in Dunsmuir, where they spent their entire married life.

It was Fate that brought them together. Fate, in this case, was the San Francisco earthquake of April 18, 1906.

Ed was born in Ashland, Oregon, in 1887, was raised there, and attended the local schools. He worked different places and at odd jobs in Ashland until he went to Portland Business School. While going to school in Portland, he had a part-time job with the Southern Pacific Company. Upon finishing business school, he was accepted for a job in a bank in San Francisco. The job was to start on April 23, 1906, and he was staying in Oakland when the disastrous quake took place. With his job plans canceled, he came to Dunsmuir in the hopes of getting work with the Southern Pacific Company again. He was hired, and his first job was copying train sheets in the Chief Dispatcher's office. Through the years Ed held a variety of jobs for the Southern Pacific, including baggage man at Dorris when Dorris was the end of the line. His final job, until his retirement in 1954, was Chief Clerk for the Master Mechanic.

Mae Bess Stanley was born in Boonville, Iowa, in 1897 and moved west with her family in the early 1900's. Her father, Frank Bess, came to Dunsmuir to work for the railroad as a machinist. Later the family moved to Ashland, but, by this time, Ed and Mae were engaged, and they were married in Ashland in 1917.

Ed and Mae were active in the Methodist Church in Dunsmuir and sang in the choir for many years. Ed was an active member of the Oddfellows Lodge. Bookkeeping held a special interest for Ed, and at various times, he kept books for Crowley's People's Cash Store, Tom Wheeler's Reception, Hal Montgomery's Chevrolet Garage, Mac's Market, and Dr. Malone, to name a few.

Ed and Mae had four children, and all of them now live far away from their beloved "roots." Bob lives in Eugene, Oregon; Jack lives in San Antonio, Texas; Don lives in Decatur, Indiana; and Margaret (Pierce) lives in Monrovia, California.

Mae died in April, 1971, and Ed died in October, 1977. They are buried at the Mount Shasta Cemetery, together still.

The Stanley Family photograph taken in 1940.
Standing: Jack, Ed, Mae, Don, and Margaret - Seated: Bob

CONGRATULATIONS TO DUNSMUIR ON ITS CENTENNIAL

Dorothy Mogan and Art Stiegler were married in June 1940. Art worked as a B&B carpenter for Southern Pacific in Sacramento. On June 26, 1940, Art changed occupations to become clerk for Southern Pacific and bid on a job in Dunsmuir, July 15, 1941. We moved to Dunsmuir in August, 1941, lived in Shirley Auto Court (it was behind the swimming pool) for a few months, then moved to 5420 Shasta Ave. Our first daughter, Patricia, who is now Sister Teresa Marie, was born in the Dunsmuir Hospital on New Year's Eve in 1942. She now works for the Bishop of the Diocese of Monterey, and lives in Seaside, California.

1942: We bought a summer home in Shasta Retreat, and after renovation we moved there in 1943.

1945: April, our son Michael was born in Dunsmuir Hospital. Mike is now working for TWA and has a son, Michael, and a daughter, Christina. He lives in San Mateo.

1948: June, on our anniversary, our daughter, Marie, was born in the hospital at Weed. Marie is working for National Federation of Independent Businesses in San Mateo.

1952: Dorothy was born in Mount Shasta Hospital. She lives in Yreka and has a daughter, Carrie and a son, Daniel.

1953: Due to an appointment as Traveling Auditor, we moved to Sacramento, where our daughter, Carol, was born in 1954. Carol is Assistant Manager of Security for Macy's in Serramonte, Daly City.

1956: Another move, to San Mateo, and for 19 years Art commuted to work in San Francisco by train.

1975: After 39½ years with Southern Pacific, retirement came and we moved back to Dunsmuir, into the house in Shasta Retreat.

We felt we were a part of Dunsmuir even when we lived elsewhere. Dorothy had been a member of the Eagles and Women's Benefit Association drill teams. Art has been secretary for the Clerks Union, secretary of Dunsmuir Baseball Club, and held offices in the Knights of Columbus and Eagles. We were both active in Railroad Days, summer picnics, and Christmas programs.

Presently, we are involved in St. John's Parish, in the National Association of Retired and Veteran Railway Employees, in Dunsmuir Senior Citizens, and both of us hold offices in the Eagles Lodge.

We returned to live here because it's the most beautiful area we've seen. We enjoy four seasons, love gardening, fishing, and most of all the friends we have here.

Dorothy and Art Stiegler

Dorothy and Art in 1955

Dorothy with Pat, Mike, Marie, Dorothy and Carol - 1955

In Loving Memory of
LAWRENCE STEWART
DEDICATED BY HIS WIFE, BARBARA

*Lawrence and Barbara Stewart pictured
in a hotel in Paris in 1968*

Lawrence Stewart was born on October 22, 1895, at Fulda, Klickitat County, Washington, the son of Robert and Nellie (Cheyne) Stewart. By the time Lawrence was eleven years of age, both of his parents had died, so he moved to Klamath Falls, Oregon, to live with his aunt and uncle. While living there, he enlisted in the army during World War I and served in France in a machine gun unit. He was in Luxembourg when the Armistice was signed.

Lawrence came to Dunsmuir in 1926 and worked in the Brick Garage for Hal Montgomery and, later, for Jack Wyatt in the Commercial Garage. In 1936 he opened his own business, the Dunsmuir Garage, which he operated for thirty years. First, he had the Ford Agency, and then the Dodge and Plymouth agencies. He sold his business in 1966 and retired.

He was a sixty-year member of the Masonic Lodge, having joined in Klamath Falls before coming to Dunsmuir, where he affiliated with the Dunsmuir Lodge #297 of F. & A.M. He also belonged to Fidelity Chapter #131 of O.E.S. He was a member of the American Legion for sixty-four years and a charter member of the Dunsmuir Senior Citizen Club.

Lawrence passed away May 9, 1984.

In July of 1937, Lawrence and Barbara Parker were married in Dunsmuir at the home of Barbara's sister and her husband, Betty and Charles Wendell. The daughter of Robert and Cora (Walker) Parker, Barbara was born in Plowmans Valley, Siskiyou County, California, on August 4, 1904.

She attended the University of California at Berkeley and graduated from Chico State College in 1927. She taught first at Gazelle, California, and then in 1928 she came to Dunsmuir to teach for twenty-two years at the elementary school.

Barbara is a fifty-year member of Fidelity Chapter #131 of Dunsmuir. She belongs to California Retired Teachers Association and is a member of the Dunsmuir Senior Citizen Club.

Lawrence and Barbara enjoyed their retirement years together. Lawrence liked to garden. His specialty was raising miniature roses and begonias. He enjoyed planning in detail the many trips they took around the United States and in other countries. Barbara continues to live in their home in Dunsmuir.

IN HONOR OF OUR PARENTS
MR. AND MRS. ROY THORPE

A Reunion of the Thorpe Family in November 1983
Front: Andi Addison, April Noble, Debbie Austin,
Carrie Addison, Jake Bailey
Middle: Lois Austin, Roy and Rose Thorpe,
George Austin
Back: Grant Noble, Greg and Deana Bailey, Judy and
Phillip Addison, Dan Austin
Not pictured: Paul Austin

Rob Roy and Rosaline (Nies) Thorpe are both natives of Shasta County, California. They were married November 30, 1920, in Redding. Their first home was at the Hornet Mine, and later they lived in the Redding area.

Four children were born to Mr. and Mrs. Thorpe:

1. MAXINE was born in 1921 and died in 1978;

2. EDITH was born in 1923 and died in 1924;

3. BILL was born in 1924 and died in Korea in 1951;

4. LOIS was born in 1937 and lives with her family in Modesto, California.

Mr. Thorpe is a veteran of World War I, having served with the 347th, M.G.B. He worked for the State of California for thirty-two years before retiring in 1960, at which time he and Mrs. Thorpe moved to Dunsmuir. To be near their daughter, Lois Austin, they moved to Modesto in 1980, where they live in a retirement village.

STONE

Family History

1849 - 1985

Willard Perriman Stone

Lury Eddy Stone

The Stone Family has been identified with the history and growth of Northern California since 1849. The brothers Norton (1825-1891) and Willard Perriman Stone (1825-1894) were '49ers from western New York state. In 1854 they married the sisters Mary Alma Eddy (1833-1912) and Lury Cadelia Eddy (1835-1923) in New Lebanon, Illinois and started their third journey to California. Willard was wagonmaster for their six-month oxtrain trek to Shasta Valley. Their parents, Elias Stone (1802-1875) and Aurilia Hawley Stone (1807-1867) followed them a few years later. The family was primarily engaged in raising stock and ranching in the Edgewood and Yreka areas.

In 1860, as Stone and Company, they secured the franchise for the Soda Springs and Pit River Turnpike. They built the wagon road down the Sacramento River Canyon to Pit River Ferry, north of Redding. The toll road was in operation only a few months before the severe winter storms of 1863-64 rendered the road unusable. Old Highway 99 and the Southern Pacific Railway followed the old Stone and Company right-of-way through the Canyon. In 1870 Norton Stone and his family began ranching in the Adin and Big Valley areas of Modoc and Lassen Counties. The Siskiyou County Museum has a display of the pioneer Stone Family's trek and furnishings.

Castle Rock Ranch House, 2.5 miles south of Dunsmuir on the old stage road and was the C.H. Stone family home from 1904-1920. The ranch house was buildt in the 1870s as the Dollarhide Stage Station and survived until 1940 when it was destroyed by fire. The Joaquin Miller Cabin, built in the early 1850s, was located across the road. Miller, who gained world-renown in the 1870s as the "Poet of the Sierra" started his literary career in Siskiyou County.

Charles Henry Stone

Margaret Middleton Stone

STONE

Family History

1849 - 1985

Charles Henry Stone (1854-1917) was born near Gazelle to Willard and Lury Stone, the first of their seven children, and was a rancher and blacksmith before his 1896 marriage to Margaret Elizabeth Middleton (1868-1945). In 1904 they established the Castle Rock Ranch (old Dollarhide Stage Station) just south of present-day Railroad Park. Their children, Willard Huff (1898-1983), Harry Adelbert, and Ramona Margurite (1904-1973), graduated from Dunsmuir schools.

Harry enjoyed the outdoor life and became an avid fly-fisherman and hunter. In 1923 he and Yvette Agnes Baker (1899-1963) were married and they became involved in Dunsmuir social, church and Masonic activities. Harry retired in 1965 as a locomotive engineer after 46 years service. Yvette taught at Dunsmuir Elementary during the 1920s, and from 1945-1963. Their children, Harry Jr., Robert David, and the twins, Bernard Charles and Barbara Jean, all attended local schools and graduated from Dunsmuir High School during the 1940s.

Yvette Baker Stone and Harry A. Stone, Sr., in 1960.

June 1943 Dunsmuir Graduation scene: Robert, Barbara, Bernard and Harry Jr.

Harry Stone, Sr., received his 50-year Masonic award in 1973 and the Hiram Award in 1981. Left to right: Robert (Los Angeles), Harry Jr. (Chico), Harry Sr., Barbara (El Cerrito) and Bernard (San Jose).

The Stone Family home on Hill Street in Dunsmuir.

THE REV. AND MRS. IVER J. TORGERSON

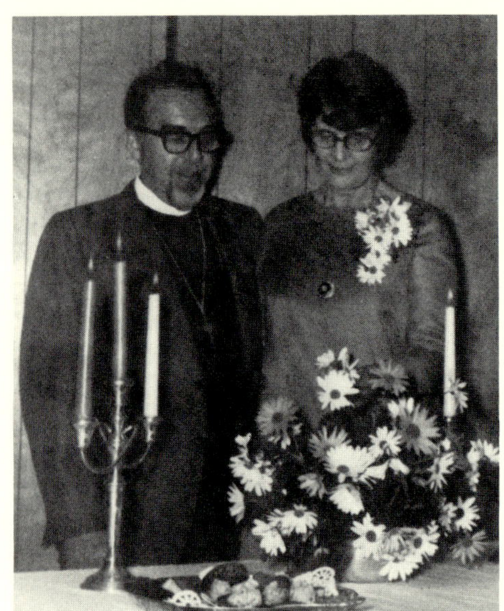

Father Torgerson and Dora at a reception honoring their arrival in Dunsmuir in 1974

The Rev. and Mrs. Torgerson came to Dunsmuir in 1974 to minister to the Episcopal congregations of Southern Siskiyou County. Father Bud, as he is affectionately known by the people of Dunsmuir, served as vicar of St. Barnabas' Church until his retirement in 1981.

Iver Torgerson was born December 16, 1916, in Parshall, North Dakota, the son of Salvation Army officers. He was attending Riverside (California) Junior College and was activity director at the Salvation Army Youth Center in Redondo Beach when he met Dora there. She was born in LaGrande, Oregon, November 16, 1918, the child of Salvation Army officers, also. She and Iver were married in 1941 and have two children. Their son, Donald, was born in 1942 and lives in Arlington, Virginia, with his wife, Jean, and their children, Kristin, Aaron, and Peter. Their daughter, Doreen, who was born in 1946, lives in Placerville, California, with her husband, Dennis Youngdahl, and their sons, Scott and John.

Both Iver and Dora Torgerson attended a Salvation Army training school. Upon finishing their training, their first appointment was in Idaho Falls, Idaho. While living there, Captain Iver Torgerson was drafted into World War II and assigned as a medical corpsman in the naval hospital at Corvallis, Oregon. During the war years Captain Dora Torgerson continued her ministry in Idaho Falls.

After Iver's discharge from the Navy in 1946, the family moved to Los Angeles, where they were in Salvation Army youth work among the ethnic groups of East Los Angeles. In 1949 the young couple was sent to Hawaii. While serving there, Iver and Dora decided that they wanted to do something different. They gave up Salvation Army work, and Iver became administrator of a home run by Buddhist businessmen for old and disabled plantation workers.

The Episcopal faith seemed to offer the change in religious form that Iver and Dora were seeking, and in 1956 Iver enrolled in the Virginia Theological Seminary and was ordained as an Episcopal priest in 1959. "Back to Hawaii" it was for the now "Father Torgerson" and his family, where he was to serve parishes on Oahu and Maui. 1968 found the Torgerson family stateside again. Father Torgerson was associate vicar at St. Andrew's in Arlington, Virginia. A move to California came in 1970 when Father Torgerson became Chaplain at Fresno State University and, later, a vicar at St. John's, Stockton.

St. Barnabas' Church called Father Torgerson to Dunsmuir in January of 1974. He was an active vicar until a heart attack forced him to retire in December of 1981. Since that time he has recovered sufficiently to have spent five months of 1984 setting up a pilot chaplaincy program for St. John's Cathedral's retirement home in Jacksonville, Florida.

Both Father Torgerson and Dora have been active in several organizations in Dunsmuir. Dora became involved in city government and was a member of the City Council from 1977 to 1980, and she took her turn as Mayor of Dunsmuir.

Since Father Torgerson's health has improved, he and Dora have enjoyed traveling, substituting for parish priests, and spending the winter months away from Dunsmuir. However, they continue to make Dunsmuir their home.

Father Torgerson's first Confirmation Class at St. Barnabas Church
FRONT: Charles Englebert, Kenneth Gilek, Kevin Englebert
BACK ROWS: Margaret Levie, Chris Stromsness, Connie Englebert, Sharon Stromsness, The Right Reverend Clarence Haden, Jr.; Ruth Spencer, Cherie Lambert, William Charles, Mary Day, and Father Torgerson

HERBERT WALLACE TRAPNELL

I am hesitant to write this page, but I have been encouraged to do so by some of those referred to at its conclusion.

Although I am in no way a pioneer of Dunsmuir or Siskiyou County, nor was my family, we definitely do qualify as pioneers in California.

One of my great-grandfathers on my mother's side, James Moffitt, walked from Galveston, Texas, to California in 1849. He mined gold in Georgetown and Mokelumne Hill in the Mother Lode region before going to San Francisco in 1855, where he started the family business which became Blake, Moffitt & Towne, a wholesale paper house which spread throughout California and into Nevada, Oregon, and Washington as well. He later started the First National Bank, which became, in association with Charles Crocker, one of the "Big Four" and a cousin by marriage, the Crocker First National Bank, and now the Crocker Bank.

My other great-grandfather on my mother's side, William Jolliffe, was Port Commodore of San Francisco in the 1850's and 1860's.

The offspring of both of these forbearers either did very well in their own right or married very well. The ladies tended to stay home and raise children, but the men most certainly did not.

My grandfather became Dean of the University of California Medical School and one of the best known diagnosticians on the West Coast. He was likely the first member of the family to come to Dunsmuir, which he did soon after 1900. He became friends with Dr. Robert T. Legge in McCloud in those years, and talked him into leaving McCloud to come to Berkeley to head the University Hospital there, an act which did not sit too well in McCloud at the time!

Assorted uncles headed the Kennecott Copper Corp. and the Nevada Northern Railroad, Blake, Moffitt & Towne, the Crocker First National Bank, Ingersoll-Rand, and various other enterprises over the years.

On my father's side of the family are found mostly Episcopalian ministers and career military officers. They were Easterners; my father was an Annapolis graduate and career Navy man. He rose to be an Admiral, and was a test pilot (he flew the first American jet), and for a number of years commanded the Mediterranean (6th) Fleet, among other assignments.

I elected to come to Dunsmuir in 1960, and have looked upon it as my home since that time. While I have no actual family in Dunsmuir, I do have a "family" of extremely fine and close friends here, who are in fact as real a family to me as any blood relations could be.

It will be in their and their children's hands to see that Dunsmuir's second hundred years are happy and productive ones.

THE TUCKERS

William Rice Tucker was born in Kansas, Feb. 15, 1872. As a young man, because of ill health, he came to California and chose Dunsmuir because he had a friend living there. Helen A. Tucker, born in Minnesota, May 11, 1874, moved with her family to the State of Washington when she was a young girl. When she came to Dunsmir to visit her sister, Alice Pickthorn, she met Wm. Rice Tucker, whom she married Oct. 5, 1904. A year later they built their home at 311 Wood St. At that time their neighborhood was considered out-of-town, and a trail was the only way of reaching the home from downtown. He was employed as a machinist by the S.P. Co. for 45 years.

William and Alice had five children, all of whom were born in the home on Wood Street: Hazel, born March 20, 1906; Lloyd, December 14, 1907; Alice, June 15, 1910; Gladys, November 25, 1912; and Ivan, December 4, 1916.

Hazel married Verne "Happy" Richardson, Oct. 13, 1926. They had three children: Laverne, Edmond Leroy, and Phyllis.

Alice married Wayne Palmer, Feb. 1, 1936. Their marriage brought three children: Robert, Betty, and Roger.

Gladys married Wm. Butler, June 15, 1933. They had two children, William and George. Wm. Butler died Dec. 30, 1945. Later Gladys married James Somers, Oct. 14, 1946; he died Apr. 28, 1954. On Mar. 2, 1957, Gladys married Edward Helmann.

Ivan married Ardella Williams, Dec. 10, 1939. Their two children

Taken in 1904

Alice Anderson Tucker

William Rice Tucker

are Kaye and Thomas.

Lloyd died Oct. 15, 1942; Esther Tucker, Sept. 8, 1944. Mother Tucker continued to live at 311 Wood Street until her death, May 15, 1957. At that time the house was sold to Mrs. Tucker's nephew and wife, Arthur and Grace Pickthorn. Grace still makes her home there. Alice Palmer died May 30, 1980.

The three surviving Tucker children are Hazel Richardson, who lives at Mott; Gladys Helmann and Ivan in Dunsmuir. There are ten grandchildren, twenty great-grandchildren, and four great-great-grandchildren.

All are proud of their heritage from their hard-working and loving parents.

Front row: Gladys, Ivan, Alice
Back row: Hazel, Lloyd

HONORING THE UPTONS

John Henry (Jack) and Effie Upton were life-long residents of Siskiyou County. Jack attended school at Mott and Effie attended at Sisson. He was one of the last blacksmiths to work for the Southern Pacific.

Effie and Jack
with granddaughter Jackie

Their only child, Marvin, attended the schools, graduating from high school in 1924. He was called "Miggs" because he was a marbles champ. He married Mae in 1932 and worked as a clerk in several grocery stores. They operated the Cash Market at 427 Florence Avenue for two years, then bought the South End grocery from Milners in 1936. It was relocated a few doors south and sold in 1941 as Marvin went to work for the SP. They lived in Alturas from 1950 to 1970, and when he retired, operated a small mobile home court in Junction City, Oregon, where Mae had lived as a young girl.

Mae's brother, Geo. Dewey Myhre, and his wife, Beulah, moved to Dunsmuir in 1947 and operated Myhre's Dress Shop for about five years. It was located in the Bank of America building.

In Loving Memory of My Parents
RALPH T. WATTENBURGER
and
ESTHER (STARK) WATTENBURGER

In 1927, Ralph T. Wattenburger, with his wife, Esther, came to Dunsmuir to begin his first teaching job and to coach basketball at the high school. After three successful years, he left to become the principal of Ione High School. Sorely missed by his friends and colleagues in Dunsmuir, he returned to D.H.S. as principal in 1933. Once again he coached the Tiger basketball teams and lead many to championships. He was a life member of the Lions Club; an active member of the Masonic Lodge #297, of which he was Worshipful Master; a valued member of the town basketball team, playing with the team that went to

Wattenburger as Principal of D.H.S.

San Francisco to compete as Northern California champions. In 1946, Ralph accepted the position of Livermore High School principal. Here he continued coaching C and D basketball for several years. He helped organize the Livermore Aquacowboys, an organization of swimmers highly competitive and respected, and with which Ralph and Esther's daughter, Carolyn, competed for seven years.

Ralph made the May 1st issue of NEWSWEEK, because he had started a course, DEMOCRACY vs. COMMUNISM, in his high school; this controversial course later was adopted by many other California high schools. He was also the subject of one of Herb Caen's columns in the S.F. CHRONICLE, because he refused to have a new school named after him. Caen quoted R.T.W.'s remark: "With a name like Wattenburger, the cheer leaders would have a terrible time!"

Livermore Eagles named him "Man of the Year." In 1982, Liver-

more Area Recreation and Park Department dedicated the "Ralph T. Wattenburger Park" in the northern section of the city, a park to be developed over the next ten years.

Esther was a member Fidelity Chapter #131 of O.E.S. and served as Worthy Matron. She taught at Dunsmuir High School. A talented pianist, she played for many affairs. After their move to Livermore, she taught high school subjects to the TB patients of the Arroyo Sanitarium. Later she taught 3rd grade and then 5th and 6th grades. She retired in 1967, one year after Ralph's retirement. She was a lifetime member of A.A.U.W. She especially enjoyed playing the piano and traveling; her favorite trip was the Alaskan cruise.

Their daughter, Carolyn, presently lives in Pleasanton and is married to a firefighter, Ray Thornton.

Ralph and Esther's two grandsons, John and Rick, made their lives very special.

Esther and Ralph - 1927

In Honor of Our Parents
FRANK & AGNES WEAMER

In 1908, as newlyweds, Frank and Agnes Weamer came to Dunsmuir where he worked for the Southern Pacific Railroad for forty years. Civic activities, combined with bringing up three children and keeping up a large garden and orchard, made their lives full and rewarding. They were always proud of Dunsmuir and of their Dunsmuir friends.

Frank was a city councilman, president of the elementary school board, on the selective service board, a Worshipful Master of the Masonic Lodge, then secretary for 32 years; secretary of the Dunsmuir Masonic Temple Association for 25 years, and active in Railroad Days activities. As Toparch of the local Pyramid of Sciots, he brought "big bands" such as Anson Weeks, Guy Lombardo, and Harry James to Dunsmuir as Sciot money-raising projects.

Agnes Weamer served as Dunsmuir Elementary PTA president, Matron of Fidelity Chapter, Order of the Eastern Star; Deputy Matron for Siskiyou County, a state office of the O.E.S., and for many years secretary of Fidelity Chapter. Throughout her fifty years in Dunsmuir she was a devoted member of the Methodist Church.

This page is presented by the three children: Viola Naron, Long Beach, CA; Myrtle Steck, Pittsburgh, PA; George Weamer, Walnut Creek, CA.

In Honor of My Parents
EDWIN J. WEBB and ANNA BOYLE WEBB

Edwin "Ed" Webb was born September 7, 1890, in Yreka, California. Anna "Ann" Boyle was born July 13, 1892, also in Yreka. They both grew up and attended school there. (The Webb and the Boyle families were pioneers in the Yreka and the Shasta Valley areas of Siskiyou County.)

Ed and Ann were married in Yreka in December of 1915. After their marriage they moved to Mc-Cloud, where Ed was to work for the McCloud River Lumber Company for forty years. He held various jobs, but he will be remembered as superintendent of the White Horse and Pondosa logging camps. Ann was a housewife, and she taught in the McCloud Grammar School for seventeen years.

When Ed retired in 1956, he and Ann moved to Dunsmuir to make their home. Ann died on December 1, 1956, at the age of sixty-four. Ed continued living in Dunsmuir for many years. He was a great walker, and he enjoyed gardening. One of his favorite activities was going on camping and fishing trips with his grandson, Bob. Ed died on March 8, 1979, at the age of eighty-eight years.

This page is dedicated by their daughter,
ELEANOR WEBB VAUGHN
and her son and his family,
ROBERT EDWIN VAUGHN,
GILDEE AMBERCROMBIE VAUGHN,
ROBBY and KELLY

In Memory of
JANICE WEEDON

1949 - 1977

Her helping hand was always first to render aid. What we would give if we could say, "Hi, Jan," in the same old way. To hear your voice, to see your smile, to sit with you and talk awhile. It broke our hearts to lose you; but, you did not go alone, for part of us went with you. More and more each day we miss you, though our thoughts are not revealed. Little do others know the sorrow within our hearts concealed. We pray for guidance and strength from above. Overwhelming is our loss. Great is our love. Our Janice sadly missed, but never forgotten.

From her Loving Parents
"Stub" and Irene Weedon
and brother, Steve

In Memory of
JO and BILL WELSH
With Love From Their Friends

*William Welsh
(1896-1977)*

*Josephine Welsh
(1904-1984)*

*Bill and Jo pictured as they celebrated their
Fiftieth Wedding Anniversary on June 28, 1974.
They were married in San Francisco.*

William Welsh was born in Redding on November 21, 1896. During World War I, he served in an Army Tank Corps and was stationed in France for eighteen months.

In 1920 Bill Welsh came to Dunsmuir, where he managed the Dunsmuir baseball club. He owned the IXL Men's Store for several years and then sold cars for the Brick Garage in Dunsmuir.

Bill was appointed postmaster at Dunsmuir in 1933 from which position he retired in 1965. He served as State President of the National Association of Postmasters.

Among his many other activities, he was past-president of the Dunsmuir Lions Club and a past commander of American Signal Post 129. He was a drum major for the Dunsmuir Bugle Corps and a fifty-year member of both the Elks Lodge in Redding and the Knights of Columbus.

Bill Welsh died February 21, 1977.

Josephine (Volonte) Welsh was born in McCloud, California, January 16, 1904 and died in Redding February 24, 1984. She was a lifetime resident of Siskiyou County.

Jo was a registered nurse. She did private care and, also, worked as a supervisor in the Cornish Hospital in Dunsmuir. Many hours of her time were given to volunteer Red Cross work during the years of World War II.

In later years, as a homemaker, Jo was a member of the Mount Shasta Community Hospital Auxiliary, the Children's Home Society, the National Association of Retired and Veteran Railroad Workers, Dunsmuir Senior Citizens Club, and the Salvation Army.

Jo was a member of St. John's Church of Dunsmuir and was a very active member of the Altar Society. In 1979 she was named the Siskiyou County Catholic Woman of the Year. Jo truly dedicated her life to God and to helping others.

Jo and Bill Welsh left the town of Dunsmuir a gift of inspiration given by them through their many years of love and service to this community.

In Loving Memory of
ELIZABETH (BETTY) WHEELER
May 30, 1908 - May 24, 1974

Betty was graduated from the Dunsmuir High School
in 1927. She was one-time owner of the Big Liquor
Store.

●

Sister of:
Edward Knowles - Wentachee, Washington

●

Mother of:

Avanelle Joy Behnke	Anabelle May Packwood
January 9, 1928	January 9, 1928

●

Grandmother of:
Annabelle Hillebert - Nov. 15, 1948
James Lamm - July 3, 1948
Richard Lamm - Dec. 10, 1951
Edward Lamm - Feb. 15, 1954

●

Great-Grandmother of:
Brian Hillebert - June 22, 1970
Rebecca Hillebert - March 20, 1974
Roberta Hillebert - April 19, 1982
Jennifer Lamm - Sept. 6, 1973
Rachel Lamm - Oct. 27, 1975
Alicia Lamm - Nov. 13, 1979

WITH LOVE AND APPRECIATION
WE GRATEFULLY REMEMBER OUR PARENTS

**THESE PAGES ARE DEDICATED BY
GEORGE AND ALICE WHITE**

James M. White (1861-1902)

Julia S. Reichert (1863-1962)

James M. White was born in Grass Valley, California. In 1886 he came to Dunsmuir as a locomotive engineer for the Southern Pacific Company. Julia S. Reichert was born in Sacramento. She and James were married there in 1887 and spent their honeymoon at Upper Soda Springs while their home in Dunsmuir was being built. In 1902 James was killed in a railroad accident at the switch at Girvan Siding south of Redding, California. Following his death Julia devoted her life to raising their four sons, Clarence, Joseph, George and Ellsworth. Their son, Elmer, had died shortly before his father died.

Julia appears to have been a good business woman. Left alone to support her family, she did so, in part, by investing in property. At one time she had five rentals in Dunsmuir. She did well enough financially renting and selling houses, that later she was able to buy property in Oakland.

James' and Julia's son, George, went to work for the Southern Pacific Company in 1915 as a machinist apprentice. In 1920 he became a fireman and later was promoted to engineer. He married Thelma Swanson, who died in 1945. They had two daughters. In 1947 he and Alice (Humphrey) Noyer were married, and they still live in Dunsmuir.

George White, born in 1898

GEORGE WHITE

VERA WHITE married Joseph Brown
1. Ann
2. Ruth Ailes
   Erin
   Andy
   Danny
3. Mark

RUTH WHITE married George Roberts
1. Sharon Howell
   Steven
   Dana
2. Trudy Fox
   Boby
   Susan

Jesse Humphrey was born in Gridley, California, and came to Dunsmuir as a machinist for the Southern Pacific Company. Phoebe Ward was born in 1887 in Beswick, Siskiyou County, California. The Ward family farm is now under the waters of Copco Lake.

On April 10, 1907, Jesse and Phoebe were married in Yreka, California. They had two children. Alice was born in Weed, California, in 1908, and Chester was born in Dunsmuir in 1909 and died in 1943. Jesse Humphrey died February 14, 1974, and Phoebe, November 4, 1961.

Alice married Robert Noyer, and they had two sons. In 1947 she married George White.

ALICE

GENE NOYER
1. Terri Adcock
   Timothy
   Colleen
2. Nancy Beechler
   Brian

BILLY NOYER
1. Linda
2. Larry
3. Kevin

213

This Page is Dedicated in Honor
of the
WENDELL FAMILY
by
Elizabeth Wendell and Charles and Barbara Taylor

Pictured together in Dunsmuir about 1912 is the Wendell Family:
Charles Claude, John Eggert, Leta Fay, Carrie, George Eggert,
and Ruby Henrietta

In 1899 John and Carrie Wendell came to Dunsmuir from Vacaville, California. With them were four children: Leta and Ruby Michell, Carrie's girls by a former marriage, and Charley and George, sons of John and Carrie's marriage.

John Wendell, a butcher by trade, established a meat market on Sacramento Avenue just north of the Weed Hotel. He ran this business until 1904 when the family moved to Lakeview, Oregon. In 1907 the family returned to Dunsmuir, because Charley wanted to go to work for the railroad. Upon returning to Dunsmuir, John and Carrie purchased property on the corner of Sacramento Avenue and Grover Street for their home.

John Wendell started another market on Sacramento Avenue just north of the Branstetter building. This store was a combined meat and vegetable store called City Market. Mr. Wendell would travel to the Shasta Valley to purchase the cattle for his meat. A trip to Montague would take him all day. The cattle were shipped to Dunsmuir by train and were slaughtered south of town at Nut Glade whenever the meat was needed. Mr. Wendell operated the City Market until he sold it in 1924.

Carrie Wendell was born June 30, 1860, and died January 5, 1924. John Wendell was born September 27, 1854, and died October 8, 1925. They both are buried in the Dunsmuir Cemetery.

John and Carrie's son, Charley, went to work for the Southern Pacific Company as a locomotive fireman in 1907. By the time the United States entered World War I, his brother George, and both of his sisters' husbands had followed his example and become firemen, also.

All of the four children of the Wendell family married. Leta had two daughters by a previous marriage when she married Loyal Taylor in 1913. They were Reta and Fay Handley. Leta and Loyal had two children. Their son, Charles, was born in 1916, and their daughter, Fern, in 1917. Ruby Wendell married Frank Brown. George married Marjorie Nicholls in 1920, and their son George was born in 1922. His widow, Irene "CiCi" Wendell, lives in Virginia. Charley Wendell married Elizabeth "Betty" Parker in 1936. She still lives in the Wendell home on Sacramento and Grover.

Leta and Loyal Taylor's son, Charles, married Barbara Covert, and they have two sons, Loyal and Fred. Loyal married Carolyn Clark, and they have Cathlene (Mrs. James Harris) and Loyal Frank. Fred Taylor married Mary Burr, and their sons are Ross and Allen.

• In Honor of My Parents •
RAY FRANKLIN (PEE WEE) WILSON
and
ADA MAY WHEELER WILSON

Ray F. was born at Red Bluff on August 1, 1892. Ada was born at Lowrey, Tehama County, on September 24, 1898. They were married at Redding on September 24, 1919. On December 1919, Ray was promoted to engineer after working nine years as fireman.

Ray Junior was born November 15, 1920, at Red Bluff. He grew up in Dunsmuir and joined his parents in their love of hunting and fishing.

Ray F. passed away March 26, 1961. Ada was appointed librarian of the Dunsmuir branch in 1962. She loved her work and enjoyed helping people, especially the children. She retired in 1973 and passed away December 17, 1978.

They are sadly missed by their family.

•

Ray J.
Ethel (daughter-in-law)
Carol Anne (granddaughter)
Jim and Aaron (great-grandsons)
Amanda (gr.-gr.-granddaughter)

THE E. F. YOUNG FAMILY

E. F. "Ted" Young
1871-1924

Clara H. Young
1869-1959

E. F. "Ted" Young came to Dunsmuir in August 1920 for the purpose of buying the Furniture and Funeral business of A. A. Ward. His wife, Clara, and two daughters, Marjorie and Aliceruth, joined him on December 31, 1920.

The furniture business was conducted in the south side of the old Branstetter building on Sacramento Ave. until 1927 when it was moved to the Petty building at 909 (Florence) Dunsmuir Ave. In 1954 the business was moved to the store space presently occupied by the Dunsmuir Hardware and was carried on there until it was sold in 1958.

After "Ted" Young's death in 1924, Clara continued the business with the help of managers. In 1930 she was joined by her daughter, Marjorie, and in 1938 her son-in-law, Ronald Wood, joined the organization. Aliceruth worked in the local hospitals. She took time off to raise a daughter. Then in 1961 she resumed her nursing until she retired.

To right:
The family home was built by Stille Brothers in 1923. The funeral business was conducted in the space on the ground floor. That part of the business was sold in 1945 and moved to Mt. Shasta.

HAPPY BIRTHDAY, DUNSMUIR
from the
Mt. Shasta Area Audubon Society

Mt. Shasta Area Audubon was formed in 1971, and has worked to protect resources in and near Dunsmuir ever since then. Early in its existence, the Chapter worked to help save Hedge Creek Falls in north Dunsmuir. From 1972 through 1984 the Chapter also worked hard with the U. S. Forest Service and Congress to assure designation of important wilderness areas on Mt. Shasta and Castle Crags. Other Chapter activities have included hosting a West Coast Wilderness Workshop, helping arrange National Wildlife Federation purchase of the Lava Lakes Nature Center near Grenada, and helping arrange Forest Service purchase of the Three Sisters Bald Eagle Roost near Mt. Hebron.

Dunsmuir citizens prominent in Audubon during its first fifteen years include Lew and Michelle Arno, H. W. Trapnell, Bob and Ginny Von Hein, Bill Caraway, and Chris and Sharon Stromsness.

Mt. Shasta Area Audubon will continue to seek to protect the wildlife and other resources which surround Dunsmuir, and it will continue to welcome the participation of environmentalists from Dunsmuir and enrivons (call 235-4881 or 235-2066).

Castle Crags

Photograph courtesy of F. F. Kohlbaker

THE DUNSMUIR CHAPTERS
OF BETA SIGMA PHI

IN MEMORY OF THOSE WHO WALKED PART OF THE WAY WITH US

Dunsmuir's Kappa Phi Chapter pictured November 30, 1954
First Row: Isobel Brunel (Jones), Harriet Spatafora (Alto), Betty
Cornish, Esther Whalen, Jo Felde, ?, ?, Argyle Adams
Second Row: Jean Schoenfelter, Rosemary Dabovich, Camille
McCormick, Roberta Reynolds, Veronica Kelby, Margaret Pereira,
Billie Mathes, Maxine Lee, Margaret Petrovics, Delia Swesey,
Marcella Williams, Charlotte Samuelson
Back Row: Reva Coon, Marie-Therese Bruneau, Ellen Fischer,
Elaine Loney, Jane Doyle, Betty Kelby, Forest Gass

There are three chapters of Beta Sigma Phi International in Dunsmuir dedicated to the "cultural and finer things of life."

1. Kappa Phi (Ritual of Jewels chapter) was organized August 23, 1951. The members initiated during the first year were Helen Bell (Marske), Jane Doyle, Ellen Fischer, Forest Gass, Jane Hardisty, Helen Herring, Beth Jones, Betty Kelby, Jacquie Larsen, Onnalee O'Brien, Marie Reid, Roberta Reynolds, Charlotte Samuelson, Huldah Seed, and Marcella Williams.

2. Xi Zeta Zeta (Exemplar chapter) received its charter October 29, 1956. The Charter Members were Helen Bell (Marske), Marie-Therese Bruneau, Ellen Fischer, Forest Gass, Betty Kelby, Veronica Kelby, Billie Mathes, Roberta Reynolds, Charlotte Samuelson, Jean Schoenfelter, Huldah Seed, Harriet Spatafora (Alto), and Delia Swesey.

3. Epsilon Lambda (Preceptor chapter) was started with the initiation of the following members in May, 1973: Marcene Burns, Viola Dorst, Rose Ellis, Ellen Fischer, Jessie Flanagan, Betty Kelby, Billie Mathes, Ruth Osborne, Margaret Pereira, Roberta Reynolds, Betty Spencer, Romona Summers, and Flora Wintering.

December 8, 1981, the Preceptor Laureate degree was conferred on the following members of Epsilon Lambda chapter: Viola Dorst, Rose Ellis, Ellen Fischer, Billie Mathes, Ruth Osborne, Betty Spencer, and Flora Wintering.

CASTLE CRAGS
INTERPRETIVE ASSOCIATION

Castella, California

Photo courtesy of Buzz Kohlbaker

Dominated by soaring spires of ancient granite, Castle Crags State Park is located in the forested Klamath Mountains north of Redding and the Sacramento valley. Six miles south of Dunsmuir, the park is surrounded by primitive backcountry, and includes two miles of the cool, quick-running waters of the upper Sacramento River. The pioneer California-Oregon Toll Road passed through the park west of the present freeway in the general vicinity of the park road. For many years travelers on the toll road, including the horse-drawn stages of the California-Oregon Stage Company, struggled up and over Kettlebelly Hill before descending back down into the canyon.

The Castle Crags Interpretive Association is a non-profit educational organization dedicated toward promoting a greater appreciation of human and natural history of Castle Crags State Park.

DUNSMUIR CHURCH OF CHRIST

4101 HOPE LANE
Phone 235-4810

We the members of the Church of Christ do not claim to be the only Christians, but we do claim to be Christians only. We have no rule for our lives except what is found in the Bible. We have no creed to confess to, except our faith in Jesus Christ as the Son of God. We find Jesus to be a real blessing to our lives and we want to honor Him for what He has done for us.

We have found Him to be a God who answers prayer.

We have found He helps us in overcoming sin.

We have found Him to be a forgiving God.

We have found He gives hope for the hereafter.

We have found He gives guidance for each day.

We know He cares about each one of us.

Come worship with us at the Church in the wildwood; we think you will feel welcome and be blessed.

THE TOWN OF DUNSMUIR
Incorporated
August 7, 1909

BOARD OF TRUSTEES
A. Levy, President
A. J. Knight
Henry Wentz
J. M. Campbell
C. U. Huff

EMPLOYEES
A. E. Parker, Clerk
D. I. McDonald, Clerk
F. M. Albaugh, Clerk
B. O. Tupper, Treasurer
S. H. Fiske, Marshal

Jere L. Wilson, Recorder
W. R. Garrett, Attorney
Abe Huff, Fire Chief
Clyde Hamilton, Nightwatch

BOARD OF HEALTH
Dr. Cross, Health Officer   E. W. Englebright
H. Woodward   B. F. Dunn
B. G. Vermillion

THE CITY OF DUNSMUIR
Elected Officials & Employees
as of 5/30/84

Billiejean Blank, Councilwoman
Dolf, Ron - Councilman
Hill, Emmett - Mayor
Seely, Joe - Councilman
Thunborg, Margaret - Councilwoman

Stromsness, Chris - City Attorney
Ritchie, Elizabeth - City Clerk
Young, Ivan - City Treasurer

Hurlburt, Jack - City Manager
Arata, Jim - Finance Coordinator
Ritchie, Elizabeth - Finance/Personnel
Newman, Patricia - Customer Service
Thompson, Phoebe - Computer Operator

Rowland, John - Chief of Police
Johnston, Robin - Police Sgt.
Wederbrook, Vernon - Patrolman
Salanti, Dennis - Patrolman
Nelson, Dianne - Dispatcher

Kenoyer, Bob - Fire Chief
Nystrom, Sid - Asst. Fire Chief
Van Heest, Dave - Fire Marshal
Newman, Gary - Captain - EMT
Valenzuela, Ish - Captain

Lawson, Charles, WWTP Chief
Johnson, Ron - WWTP Operator

Larrabee, Dan - Public Works Supervisor/Building Insp.
Kay, Steve - Assistant Working Foreman
Morzenti, Carl - Sr. Maintenance Worker
Calzoni, Brian - Seasonal Maintenance Worker

THE CHRISTIAN LIFE CENTER

(Pentecostal Church)

There has been a Pentecostal Church in Dunsmuir holding services and preaching the good news of the Gospel of Jesus Christ for over seventy years, making us the second oldest established church of our denomination in California. We enjoy our rich heritage and count it a great privilege to share a little of our history with you in the anniversary of the City of Dunsmuir's Centennial.

The Reverend and Mrs. Wayne A. Edwards and the Congregation

HISTORICAL SKETCH OF
FIRST CHURCH OF CHRIST, SCIENTIST, DUNSMUIR

In 1912, students of Christian Science held their first meeting in a room in the Hotel Weed in Dunsmuir; afterwards they meet in different houses and then in Branstetter Hall. The Dunsmuir Christian Science Society was organized and recognized by The Mother Church in 1914. It was re-organized on June 22, 1921, and incorporated July 15, 1923, as the First Church of Christ, Scientist, Dunsmuir.

The Church property was purchased on September 29, 1920, and the Church edifice was erected in the winter of 1923 and '24. It was dedicated July 10, 1932.

```
SUNDAY SERVICE ................ 11:00 A.M.
SUNDAY SCHOOL ................  9:30 A.M.
WEDNESDAY MEETING ............  8:00 P.M.
READING ROOM ....... 11:00 A.M. to 2:00 P.M.
            on Saturday Afternoon
```

One may purchase or borrow all authorized literature, including paperbacks of THE HOLY BIBLE, the King James Version, *Science & Health with Key to the Scrpitures* by Mary Baker Eddy, and *The Christian Science Monitor*, an International Daily Newspaper.

DUNSMUIR HIGH SCHOOL
CLASS OF 1986

Dunsmuir's Centennial Class, the Class of '86, decided two years ago to contribute a page to this Centennial Book. Four students, Mark Manfredi, Nolberto Pizano, Mike Young, and Brad Townsend, did a little research, a bit of talking, and a bit more writing during the summer of '84. This account begins with the Manfredi clan.

Among the Dunsmuir families who have had several generations in attendance at Dunsmuir High School is the Manfredi family. Mark Manfredi, his parents, and his grandmother, discussed some of the similarities and some of the differences of the school from the Class of '27 to the Class of '86. This is Mark's report.

"My grandmother, Mary A. Rossetti Manfredi, attended high school when it was located across from the current Payless Gas Station. Enrollment at that time was approximately 100. My parents, Ronald and Dorothy Hale Manfredi, attended high school when it was located up the hill on Oak Street at High School Way. Enrollment then was approximately 200. My classmates and I attend D.H.S. at a site right next to the one my parents' school occupied. The present school building was constructed in 1974 and now, ten years later, has an enrollment of 160.

"One area where there have been a few changes is the athletic program. Over fifty years ago, the major sports were football, baseball, and basketball, all with A, B, C, and D teams. In addition to these sports, the school had a track and field team that attended one meet in Yreka each year. Some thirty years later, during my parents' high school years, football was divided into varsity and junior varsity; baseball and basketball retained the A, B, C, and D teams; track and field no longer existed; and girls' volleyball was added. Today, our high school has varsity and junior varsity football and basketball teams, girls' basketball, girls' volleyball, baseball, track, and tennis."

"Our school," adds Nolberto Pizano, "is known as the home of Scholars and Champions. Our class has definitely contributed to maintaining the championship tradition!! Our class has been very active in the different sports at D.H.S. for the past two years. Brad Townsend, Kevin Connors, Martin Jimenez, and Ross Taylor are the people who have played three sports every year for the last two years. Kevin Connors, Martin Jimenez, and David Wagner played on the varsity basketball team in their sophomore year. Kevin Connor also did very well in the track finals held at C.O.S. Brad Townsend, Martin Jimenez, Ross Taylor, Kevin Connors, Bret Barnes, David Wagner, and Gus Martinez have already earned their varsity letters. Our class has contributed much to D.H.S. athletics already, and we still have two more years to go. Our class is going to be one of the better athletic classes to come out of D.H.S. in a long while."

"Sports has played a big role over the years, with some changes for the better, but," says Mark, "so has our curriculum. No new classes were added to the curriculum during my grandmother's nor my parents' high school years, whereas the school has added French I, weight training, computer classes and arts appreciation (in the G.A.T.E. program), and drafting within the first two years of our high school career. The high school also offers work experience, a program that was non-existent during my grandmother's and parents' times. However, my grandmother's class had an opportunity to enroll in Latin, and girls' glee club, while my parents were offered Latin, mechanical drawing, senior problems, and glee club. These classes are no longer offered."

"Speaking of new classes," Mike Young adds, "one of the most interesting to me is computers. It is said that the eighties is the Age of Computers. A good thing to see is that our school, which is relatively small, has an extensive computer center. We have a computer in the office, and in an English class, plus a large computer class with twenty computers. For classes without computers, we have two mobile computers that teachers can check out for their classes. Right now we have a complete computer literacy class that teaches students how to operate computers and a computer programming class is in the works for the coming year. In addition, use of the computers is offered as an extracurricular opportunity one evening a week during the school year, and one day a week during the summers."

"Right," says Mark. "That's one example of extracurricular activities we enjoy today which, of course, were not offered to my grandmother. However, her generation could participate in girls' league, girls' glee club, honor art society, drawing, domestic art, student council, dramatics, and band. My parents had a choice of glee club, F.H.A., fire department, girls' league, pep club, drill team, cheerleaders, marching band, head majorette, Tigerettes, Precisionettes, mascot, Promerettes, Tiger Tracks, Y.M.C.A., academic decathalon, and drama.

"Other extracurricular items of interest are honor societies. Honor societies during my grandmother's time were honor art society and Block D. My parents' time offered Block D society for boys and girls, D.A.R., Boys' and Girls' State, C.S.F., Richardson Springs (a conference), football crowning with a queen and two princesses. The honors of today are C.S.F., N.H.S., Tiger Awards, Boys' and Girls' State, and a homecoming for both basketball (Carnival) and football (Homecoming) seasons that have a queen, two senior princesses, and one junior, sophomore, and freshman princess."

With the various offerings of the curriculum, extracurricular activities and honors, Dunsmuir High School is the home of scholars. As Brad Townsend adds, "In the field of academics, the Class of '86 looks very prosperous. Already, after two years of high school, our class has a large percentage of students who are going and want to go to college or trade schools now and after completing high school. The Class of '86 has also had 23% of the class nominated for and presented with awards in the field of academics — and this has only been in the first two years of high school. Good luck to the Class of '86 and their dreams!!"

The
Dunsmuir
News
has been reporting,
supporting and boosting
Dunsmuir since
1890
We look forward to an even
better 100 years for
Dunsmuir to
2086
L. JOHNSON & CO.

HAPPY 100th BIRTHDAY, DUNSMUIR

From
DUNSMUIR LODGE #297 F. & A.M.
Chartered October 10, 1889

★ ★ ★ ★ ★ ★ ★

Dunsmuir Lodge shares with the City ninety-seven of its years. Space does not permit the listing of every brother who has performed beyond the call of duty in his lodge. We list below all of the brothers who have served as Master:

MASTERS

*1889 Andrew W. Kreelman	*1913 J. C. Gardner	*1938 R. T. Wattenburger	*1963 Alex O. Smith
*1890 William B. Roberts	*1914 F. C. Nourse	*1939 C. C. Spencer	1964 James F. Lockart
*1891 George H. Ingham	*1915 B. F. Dunn	1940 Joe H. Conley	1965 Laurence E. Newton
*1892 R. S. Culverwell	*1916 F. L. Weamer	*1941 E. W. Carlton	*1966 Russell G. Hickerson
*1893 R. S. Culverwell	*1917 C. O. Porter	1942 C. E. Neal	*1967 Kenneth R. Burns
* George H. Ingham	*1918 C. O. Porter	1943 F. M. Stone	1968 Laurence E. Newton
*1894 John D. Cummings	*1919 B. R. Fauber	1944 C. E. Neal	1969 James F. Lockart
*1895 John D. Cummings	*1920 B. R. Fauber	*1945 J. Morgan Jones	*1970 Robert C. Harris
*1896 Harry L. Walther	*1921 F. L. Callisch	*1946 J. Morgan Jones	*1971 Carl Jones
*1897 Alexander Levy	*1922 C. R. Walker	1947 Joseph T. Seikel	1972 James F. Lockart
*1898 Alexander Levy	*1923 C. R. Walker	*1948 George E. Thornton	1973 Emmett F. Hill
*1889 Alexander Levy	*1924 A. R. Wilkins	*1949 Alfred A. Smith	*1974 Herbert G. Morgan
*1900 Alexander Levy	*1925 A. R. Wilkins	1950 W. R. Petty	1975 Forrest G. Tittle
*1901 George W. McCoy	*1926 A. R. Wilkins	1951 John L. Glaese	1976 William J. Hatfield
*1902 George W. McCoy	*1927 S. S. Kent	1952 Earl A. Whitson	1977 Alfred T. Coffman
*1903 J. W. Hawkins	*1928 J. W. Day	*1953 W. L. Humphreys	1978 Chester F. Conley
*1904 J. W. Hawkins	*1929 C. H. Weaver	*1954 Arthur Crowe	1979 N. Walter Spears
*1905 Alexander Levy	*1930 E. W. Hamilton	1955 Don C. Crowe	1980 Forrest G. Tittle
*1906 B. F. Dunn	*1931 E. W. Hamilton	1956 Regis F. Jones	1981 Fernando P. Felix
*1907 G. A. Hutaff	*1932 J. A. Martin	1957 T. M. McCormick	1982 Chester F. Conley
*1908 G. A. Hutaff	*1933 J. A. Martin	1958 Nicanor Manlapig, Jr.	1983 Alfred T. Coffman
*1909 J. W. Hawkins	*1934 A. D. Lininger	*1959 Robert C. Harris	1984 Sam Catalano
*1910 B. F. Dunn	1935 E. R. Deering	1960 William A. Hughes	1985 G. Kenneth Wilch
*1911 F. C. Nourse	*1936 C. C. Roberts	1961 Paul A. Radebaugh	1986 Fernando P. Felix
*1912 W. R. Lee	*1937 R. T. Wattenburger	*1962 Robert C. Harris	*Deceased

Two of the Past Masters served as secretary and their combined service in this office spanned a time of over fifty years — half the age of the Lodge. They are pictured here.

Brother
Frank
Weamer

Brother
A. A. (Shorty)
Smith

Brother Alexander Levy, the great old man of Dunsmuir Masonry, served the lodge as Master five times — four times filling in for one of the members who was unable to serve.

Brother J. Morgan Jones — in addition to filling the office of Master twice — served on the board of directors of the Dunsmuir Masonic Temple Association. At one time he leased the building for five years in order that he might make necessary repairs on the building at no expense to the lodge.

Brother Robert C. Harris served as Master three times. He, too, was active on the Masonic Temple Ass'n. board and for many years donated his time and his money in maintaining the building. James Lockart has also been Master three times.

Brother Chester O. Porter contributed in every way to the cause of Masonry in Dunsmuir. For many years he was the guiding light of the Order of DeMolay (for boys).

Many of the members served the lodge in many ways. Though they did not hold an elective office, they were the work horses of the craft. Some of those still serving are: Brothers George Belskey, Glenn Lamb, Harry Stone, and K. H. Strasburg.

Many Masons have served the City of Dunsmuir in various offices. We will continue for as long as there is a Dunsmuir.

GRAND MASTER OF
MASONS IN CALIFORNIA

**BROTHER G. A. "GUS" HUTAFF, A MASTER MASON.
A MEMBER OF DUNSMUIR LODGE NO. 297**

G. A. Hutaff came to Dunsmuir when both he and the city were young. For some years he operated a drugstore, and he was an energetic, ambitious man.

He was the first president of the Bank of Dunsmuir. Under his management the bank grew to prominence in both Siskiyou County and Northern California. The financial institution was purchased by the Bank of America and now stands on the corner of Dunsmuir Avenue and Pine Streets.

Gus was also a builder. He built and operated the Traveler's Hotel. He was a prime mover in the building of the Dunsmuir Masonic Temple and participated in the laying of its cornerstone by the Grand Lodge of California.

In his travels through masonry, Brother Hutaff became a Past Master, a District Inspector, and held several offices in the Grand Lodge of California before becoming Grand Master for the year 1929.

We, the members of Dunsmuir Lodge No. 297, are proud to have been associated with this fine man.

DUNSMUIR FEDERATED WOMEN'S CLUB

In April of 1952 twenty-five interested women met in Dunsmuir to form a Women's Club. At the second meeting of the group in May, the following officers were elected: Hazel Peterson, Marjorie Berryhill, Hazel Chipman, Rae Gill, and Jane Porter. Elinore Harrison, Ethel Paul, Bess Clay, Esther Gray, and Helen Herring were appointed to draw up the by-laws. In August of the same year, the Dunsmuir club received its Charter from the California Federated Women's Club.

The members who held the office of president following Hazel Peterson were Marjorie Berryhill, Dorothy Petty, Josephine McGee, Helen Dabovich, Ethel Clark, Evelyn Harper, Gwen Baymiller, Alice Chandler, Helen Terrell, Claudia Mather, Irene Clark, Edna Newton, Hilda Kessler, who was installed but died before serving; Kay Sanford, Kathleen Graves, Marcene Burns, Jo Manning, Jean Thom, Rhoda Diridon, Betty Reineking, Alvira Hatfield, who was installed but unable to serve; Flora Wintering, and Catherine Bennett.

*A GROUP OF WOMEN'S CLUB MEMBERS POSED FOR THIS
PICTURE IN MAY of 1984*
*Back Row: Grace Harris, Margaret Brown, Alvira Hatfield,
Betty Reineking, Meme Albright, Melba Arne, Eleanor Vaughn
Front Row: Lila Cox, Catherine Bennett, Flora Wintering,
Marcene Burns, Jean Thom*

FRATERNAL ORDER OF EAGLES

DUNSMUIR AERIE #1149

The Fraternal Order of Eagles was founded in Seattle, Washington, on February 6, 1989. Dunsmuir Aerie was chartered on August 10, 1905. Charter members included J. G. and W. J. Branstetter, Ben and George Oliver, I. M. and Frank LaDue, Ed Weed, U. S. Petty, F. M. Walker, W. A. Wilkins, Tim Murphy, O. Dixon, W. F. Vaughn, J. P. Clark, E. A. Wood and J. A. Davis. Many descendants are still living here.

Aerie means a home or nest for a predatory bird, so when the Eagles lodges were started, the home was called an Aerie and was distinguished by its number; thus, Dunsmuir Aerie #1149.

Dunsmuir Aerie held meetings in Branstetter Hall, then moved to the Masonic Temple. However, in 1965 they purchased a building at 5941 Sacramento Avenue; and after renovation, it became their home.

The Eagles Auxiliary at Dunsmuir was granted a charter in November 1936. Present members Farlin Cantrell and Marian Whitlow are charter members.

Dunsmuir Aerie had a men's drill team in the 1930's and 1940's which made trips to all parts of northern California for drill team competition and to participate in parades. The Ladies Auxiliary had a drill team for many years after its inception in 1936. The drill team worked at all meetings, for the installation of officers, and on other special occasions.

Eagles sponsored the Dunsmuir Baseball team for several years. The rock work on Belnap fountain was done by Eagle members.

Nationally, Eagles sponsored America's first widows and orphans pension act, America's first workmen's compensation act, America's first state old-age pension act, and co-sponsored the Social Security Act. Presently Aeries contribute to funds for cancer, heart, kidney, diabetes researches and have funds for children and senior assistance.

Eagles have homes in 13 foreign countries and have 30 Eagles-CARE trade schools overseas.

The American Bald Eagle is the symbol of the Eagles Lodges. This symbol is found on many American flags and on some of our coins. In 1982 all Aeries celebrated the Bicentennial of the choice of the American Bald Eagle by our nation as its national emblem.

Dunsmuir Aerie is proud to be a part of this Centennial Celebration.

ORDER OF THE EASTERN STAR
FIDELITY CHAPTER #131

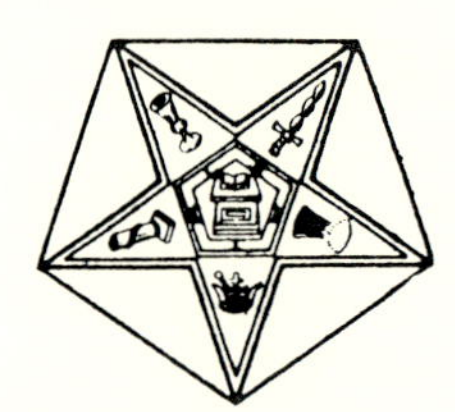

Fidelity Chapter #131, O.E.S., was instituted on August 31, 1894, and the charter was issued by Grand Chapter on October 18, 1894, signed by Allen Bosley Lemmon, Worthy Grand Patron; Emma Hapgood, Worthy Grand Matron; and Katr Josephine Willats, Grand Secretary.

Those installed were: Benjamin Marvin Gill, Worthy Patron; Mayme L. Cummings, Worthy Matron; and Martha Ada Culver, Associate Matron.

The original charter was destroyed by fire on April 25, 1924, and a duplicate charter was issued and signed by Maude Bigelow Sibley, Worthy Grand Matron; and Katr Willats, Grand Secretary.

McCloud Chapter #381 was issued their charter on October 19, 1921, signed by Roy Mussey, Worthy Grand Patron; Effie Easton, Worthy Grand Matron; and Katr Willats, Grand Secretary. McCloud Chapter #381 consolidated with Fidelity #131 on March 25, 1976, with Worthy Grand Matron Donna M. Smith and Gladys M. Johnson, Grand Secretary, signing the consolidation.

Dunsmuir Chapter #536 was instituted on September 8, 1934, and granted a charter on October 21, 1934. It turned in its charter on November 1, 1959. Many members chose to affiliate with Fidelity Chapter.

There were 19 original charter members of Fidelity Chapter. None are now living.

FIFTY-YEAR MEMBERS
as of June 1984

Mildred Snipes	Hilda Derby
Laura Jones	Evelyn Gordon
Roberta Belland	Gertrude Graham
Josephine Beckman	Helen Stanley
Ethel Marsh	Florence Willock
Virginia McAnaw	Ruth Newman
Harry Stone	Allie Tryer
Ione Seavey	Cleo Lambert
Alzade Gash	Wilma Hale
Vera Cattani	Thelma Lamb
Myrtle Palmer	Opal Morgan
Jean Seikel	Harriet Sloan
Lucille Spengler	Mary McDermott
Elizabeth Wendell	Barbara Stewart
Frances Deering	Eloise Crocker, 1985

AFFILIATED PAST MATRONS
AND PAST PATRONS

Ione Seavey	Dorothy Purdy
Myrtle Palmer	Betty Sloan
Evelyn Gordon	Mina Kimble
Florence Willock	Elizabeth Wendell
Evelyn Holmquist	Barbara Stewart
Edith Parentice	Thelma Lamb
Julia Oloveson	Nancy Trimble
Betty Maxine McIntosh	Betty Jo Hurlburt
Elsa (Wetzel) Perry	Robert McIntosh
Harriet Sloan	St. Elmo Bewley
Ada Tannehill	Ralph Howarth
Velma Maxwell	Roscoe Kimble
Agnes Howarth	

PAST MATRONS

Mayme L. Cummings
Mary J. Robinson
Tillie E. VanFossen
Jennie H. Whited
Cherrie J. Walthers
Florence A. Gill
Ida Hobart McCoy
Harriet E. Joesink
Sarah S. Hestwood
Hattie May Hobart
Bina Eubanks
Rose Miller Thompson
Vera May Mason
Sylvia Emerson
Ethel C. Knight
Bessie Gongwer
Anna Micander
Avoric E. Woodward
Jennie Fisk Ward
Anna Herron
Georgia A. Milnew
Agnes R. Weamer
Jennie V. Dickson
Sylvia L. Johnson
Orie Micander
Martha A. Eagles
Mary Reubena Sears
Norma Kintgen
Ora Hornor
Nellie Coleman
Kate Berry
Florence Johnson
Ethyl L. Milner
Josephine (Weeks) Beckman
Ethel Beckman
Olga Orr
Gertrude Graham
Grace Bascom
Helen B. Cochenour
Goldie A. Wood
Erma L. (Cooper) Harrell
Josephine A. McGee

Emily Crenshaw
Roberta Belland
Margaret Olsen
Frances Binnion
Ethel Burt
Cleo Duggan
Vivian Williams
Ellen Smith
Mildred Davis
Edna R. (Reed) Gould
Opal I. Morgan
Alice Langdon
Gwendolyn Baymiller
Josephine McNely
Genevieve Tillotson
Laura Billington
Mildred Tillotson
Althea Belsky
Ruth Walter
Vera Van Diver
Kathleen Graves
Jeanne Gray
Dorothy (Welch) Lowe
Ruth Asher
Ione Hughes
Dorothy Delgado
Grace Harris
Alberta Stoffel/Grace Harris
Rose Ellis
Dorothy (Welch) Lowe
Carolyn Miller
Rose Tittle
Francis Homer
Donna Linebarger
Rotha (Stewart) Taylor;
Phyllis Ingersoll
Rose Tittle
Reba Smith
Lois Wilch
Dorothy Lowe
Carolyn Miller*
Betty Jo Hurlburt*

*Expected to serve in 1985, 1986

PAST PATRONS

Dr. Benjamin M. Gill
George H. Ingham
Harry L. Walther
Jerry H. Whited
Alexander Levy
George E. Shearer
Dr. Charles E. Thompson
Dr. Charles A. Curl
Jeffrey W. Hawkins
Dr. George E. Malone
Alexander Culver
Gustave A. Hutaff
Henry S. Herron
George C. Barton
Samuel H. Hill
Alfred E. Parks
Fred E. Slater
Thomas A. Roseberry
Jesse C. Brown
Henry McGuinness
Clyde H. Weaver
Hugh C. Corwin
Harry O. Brown
Arthur L. Shoupe
Arthur E. McGee
James A. McDonough
Albert McCann
James R. Prather
J. Morgan Jones
Kenneth Goode
William Petty
Charles Banish
Arthur Crowe
Jay M. Smith
Cloyd Haney
Glenn Hull
Fred O. Lloyd
Charles Langdon
Paul Collins
Ernest Swift
Elmer Graves
Herman Gray
Cecil Welch
Robert C. Harris
Harley Stoffel
William Hatfield
Forrest Tittle
Walter Spears
Charles Ingersoll
Kenneth Strasburg
Chester Conley
Roger Ellis*
Jack Hurlburt*

FIRST BAPTIST CHURCH

5962 Dunsmuir Avenue
Dunsmuir, California 96025

Pastor, Steve Rogers
(916) 235-2618

Church Phone
(916) 235-2527

First Baptist Church of Dunsmuir started as a mission of the First Baptist Church in Mt. Shasta on August 18, 1962. After a very difficult year the mission organized into a church on November 3, 1963, with 24 charter members.

In 1969 the struggling Baptist congregation began negotiating to purchase the Episcopal Church at 5962 Dunsmuir Avenue. The beautiful rock church built in 1925, was purchased at a price which included their church building in North Dunsmuir as a down payment. On December 3, 1969, the Baptist Church met in its new building for the first time. Over the years much work has been done to build classrooms, and refurbish the building. The stone architecture, stained glass windows, and church bell give the church a unique appearance and warmth. In 1981 the house on the south side of the church was purchased and converted to office and classroom use. The new building was named "Faith House" which reflected the faith and vision that led to its purchase.

First Baptist Church is affiliated with the Southern Baptist Convention which includes over 36,000 churches nationally and over 1000 in California. It supports cooperatively with its sister churches over 6000 full-time missionaries in every state in the Union and in over 100 foreign nations.

First Baptist Church is a fundamental Bible-believing church. Our primary mission is to share the Gospel of Christ with our community, and through our mission program, with the world. We seek to do this through a Bible-teaching program for all ages, a Bible-preaching ministry, mission organizations, prayer ministries, and other efforts to share our faith in Jesus Christ as our Lord and Savior. Our message is best summarized in the Gospel of John, "For God so loved the world, that he gave his only begotten son, that whosoever believeth in him should not perish, but have everlasting life." (John 3:16 KJV)

FLOYD'S PHARMACY

Floyd goes to work

Floyd's Prescription Pharmacy opened its doors in north Dunsmuir on May 26, 1967.

Floyd Glica was born in North Tonawanda, New York. After serving with the Navy, first on a landing craft in the Mediterranean and then on a mine sweeper in the East China Sea during World War II as a pharmacist's mate, he moved west and attended Oregon State College at Corvallis, where he graduated with a B.S. in pharmacy in 1953.

Prior to moving to Dunsmuir, Floyd owned the McCloud Pharmacy for 8 years.

His wife, Teresa, a native Californian, now spends her time helping Floyd at the pharmacy and as a homemaker. Floyd and Teresa have two sons: James S. and David F. and five grandchildren.

Floyd was president of the Dunsmuir Lions Club 1969-1970.

Floyd and Teresa take this opportunity to thank the friendly people of our town for their great support and friendship during their happy years here.

*Teresa and Floyd Glica
1967*

At right: David and Jim Glica, 1967

DUNSMUIR'S FIRST
WOMEN'S SOFTBALL TEAM
1947-1954
"THE MERCHANETTES" - 1947

First row: Jan Radke Mcdonald, Arlene Mehciz, Muriel Newman, Ione Hughes.
2nd row: Olivia Arnold, Lottie Ross, Beverly Todd, Marion Kreuger, Lorna Gray, Rita Giacomelli.
3rd row: Coach Ray Arnold, Esther Penman, Barbra Vose (absent, Lennie Dittner).

Baseball was one of the great pastimes of the Dunsmuirites. For over thirty years the town team had the full support of the people. Wherever the team played, the town followed. Women watched and itched to play. Why not have a women's team? Thus in 1947 Ramon Arnold organized the first women's softball team. Sponsored by the merchants, the team was named "The Merchanettes."

Women's softball became so popular in 1948 the "Hornets" team was organized by Al Marske and sponsored by other merchants. In 1949 the Corral picked up the sponsorship and the team was named the "Corral Mustangs." In 1950 Bob's Dairy sponsored the team which then became "The Bob's Dairy," still coached by Al Marske. By 1951 the original members retired and fewer girls went out for baseball so the teams merged with the "Merchanettes" coached by George Ince.

1948 - Dunsmuir Hornets - 1954

Back: Concha Baca, June Collins, "Dode" Brown, Donna Young, Mary Reams, Erma Welliver, Bobby Clark, Coach Al Marske.
Front: Alicia Baca, Beverly Gounce, Jerry Orton

234

"Corral Mustangs" 1949 and "Bob's Dairy Girls" 1950

Back: Concha Baca, June Collins, "Dode" Brown, Mary Reams,
Donna Young, Erma Welliver, Bobby Clark, Coach Al Marske.
Front: Alicia Baca, Beverly Gounce, Jerry Orton

LIGHTS FOR THE FIELD

Men's baseball team had priority of the field, thus making it difficult to get the field for practice or games. With the united effort of the teams and the Dunsmuir people, the lights were turned on in 1953.

All the teams displayed good sportsmanship. The leagues were comprised of many towns from Medford, Oregon, to San Francisco, California. They won many championships and play-offs and were awarded many trophies. They helped put Dunsmuir on the map.

The reorganized "Merchanettes" - 1954

Back: Muriel Newman, Rayola Hanlin, Angie Eddy, Donna Young
Valenzuela, Bobby Vose, Coach George Ince.
Front: Mildred Edie, Marge Welliver, June Collins, Ione Hughes,
Leah Radar.

"LADY ENGINEERS"

The 1957 Installation of Elizabeth Shoupe as President of G.I.A.
Front: Amelia Ahl, Grace Livingston, Althea Belskey, Mrs. Shoupe,
Elaine Dews, Frances Homer, Thais Fidler, Winnie Maxwell.
Back: Reta Langrehr, Signe Ahlstrom, Helen Eachus, Betty
Wendell, Thelma Boggs, Christine Allen, Opal Morgan,
Carol McMillan, Maude Silva

"Happiness is belonging to G.I.A.
and loving someone in the B. of L.E."

"Happiness" was the theme in 1971 for the seventy-fifth anniversary of Mrs. J. A. Filmore Division #163 of the Grand International Auxiliary to the Brotherhood of Locomotive Engineers. The Division received its Charter in November of 1896 and was named for the wife of Southern Pacific Company Superintendent Jerome A. Filmore. Through the years it served as a social and supportive organization for the "Brotherhood" and for the "Ladies" themselves. Then after eighty-three years of being united in sisterly love, the Division sadly gave up its charter and met for the last time in December of 1979.

PAST PRESIDENTS OF
G.I.A. TO THE B. OF L.E.

*Left: Minnie Pearl Wells, Grand President of G.I.A. on her
official visit in 1967 to Division #163.
Right: Reba Smith, President of Mrs. J. A. Filmore Division.*

*In 1969 a group of past presidents posed.
Back: Elizabeth Shoupe, Betty Wendell, Edna Frizell, Carol
McMillan, Elizabeth Cavin, Carole Livingston, Mildred Childes,
Francis Homer, Opal Morgan.
Front: Ethel Marsh, Grace Livingston*

The Mount Shasta Parlor #13 of the Past Presidents of "Lady Engineers" received its Charter in February of 1922 and celebrated its fiftieth anniversary in October of 1972. The Grand Lodge met in June of 1973 and decided, since only six Past President parlors were still active, they should be dissolved. Being one of the six, the Mount Shasta Parlor closed its books, but the members continued to meet informally until December of 1977.

*Honor and praise
  For the labor spent
Love and affection
  Is your just due
Accept our deep gratitude
  Know in our hearts
Dear, Past Presidents,
  WE LOVE YOU!*

Listed below are as many of the Past Presidents as could be identified: Florence Williams, Helen MacDowell, Irene Freel, Ella Hollis, Mabel Conger, H. Silsby, Jennie Dickson, Grace Winne, Georgia Milner, Anna Fidler, Nellie Taylor, Alice Clark, Margaret Marsh, Margaret Hickey, Corah Fischer, Eddie Cole, Lucy Campbell, Maude Silva, Laurette Smith, Bea Ahlstrom, Frankie DuBose, Julia Wagner, Margaret Moelk, Gladys Creason, Florence Roberts, Katherine Sellman, Hazel Stanley, Kathryn Harrington, Ethel Marsh, Dora Bispham, Signe Ahlstrom, Audrey Kelby, Grace Selby, Cornelia Trafton, Betty Wendell, Beth Jones, Edna Frizell, Emma Leslie, Ruth Van Dyke, Adella Clark, Carol McMillan, Ethel Cahow, Elizabeth Cavin, Grace Livingston, Ruth Bachand, Ada Wilson, LaVera Carlson, Elaine Dews, Elizabeth Shoupe, Francis Homer, Alleene Lovelle, Carole Livingston, Mildred Chiles, Phyllis Ingersoll, Opal Morgan, Mary Marsh, Reba Smith, Maleta Green, Flora Wintering, Althea Belskey, Juanita Harris, Dorothy Conwill, and Thelma Lamb, who is past president of Division #356, San Luis Obispo, California.

A REGIONAL NON PROFIT CORPORATION

PLANNING AND TECHNICAL
ASSISTANCE

HOUSING REHABILITATION

NEW HOUSING CONSTRUCTION

COMMUNITY FACILITIES

EXECUTIVE DIRECTORS

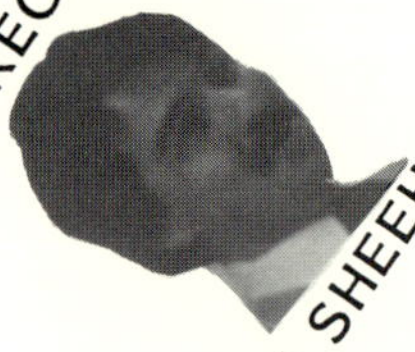

JOHN SHEEHAN
1981 -

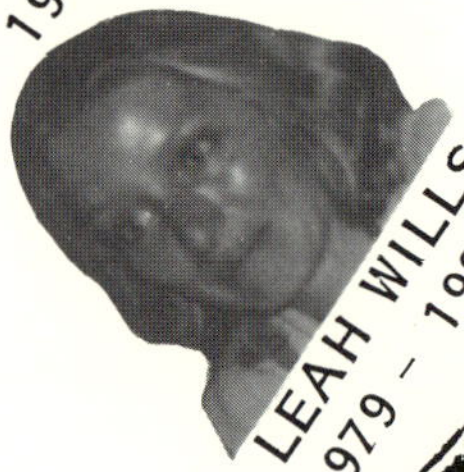

LEAH WILLS
1979 - 1981

COORDINATORS

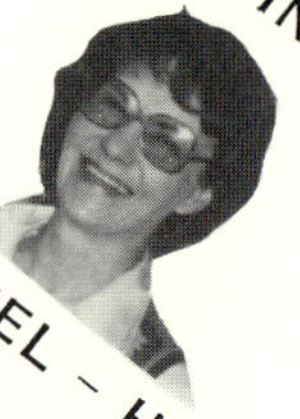

PEGGY HEISEL - HOUSING
1979 -

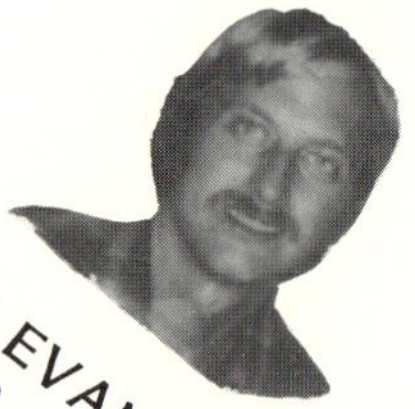

JIM EVANS - COMMUNITY FACILITIES
1979

GREAT NORTHERN CORPORATION

RENT ASSISTANCE

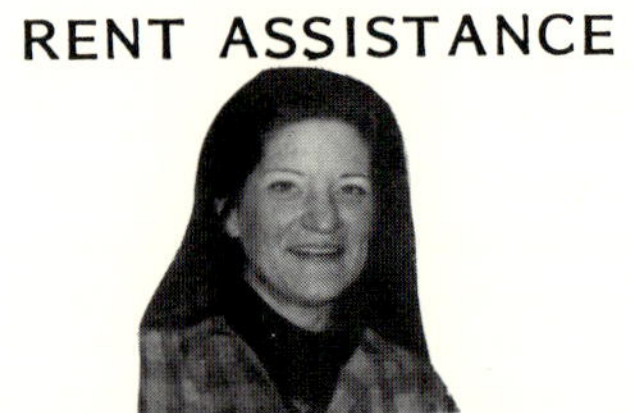

CHRIS BAILLIE
1983 -

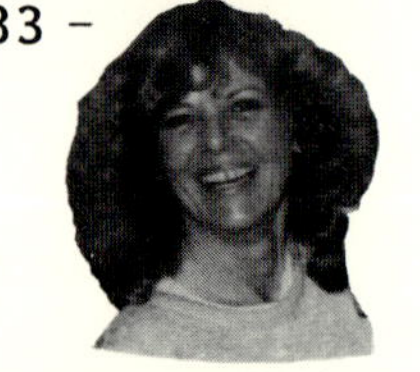

CAROL BUNNELL
1979 - 1983

GREEN THUMB

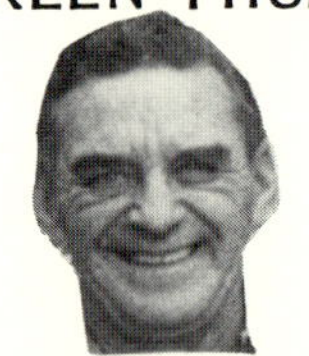

PAUL HURLEY
1980 -

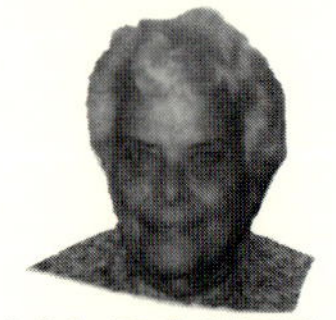

LU BAUER
1982

LOAN PACKAGERS

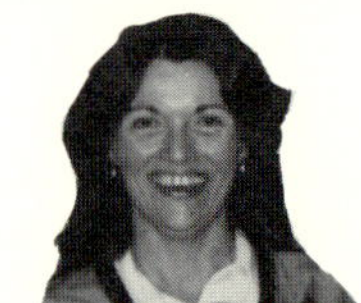

MARILYN BEHRENS
1981 -

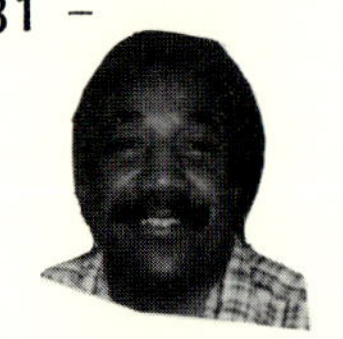

TED BROCK
1980 - 1982

SAM MAZZEI AND HIS "HOTTENTOTS"

THE ORIGINAL HOT-TEN-TOTS

Top: Russell "Bud" Thorpe, Dan Fenno, Carl Danielson,
Doug Dragoo, Dick Hyland, Lawrence Tolsano, Mgr.
Joe Mazzei, Edwin Cook, Melvin Martin, Sam Mazzei, Leader, 1930

Sam Mazzei was born with a deep love for music. In those early days at McCloud after paying the company house rent and the bill at the General Merc., there was little money left over for instruments or music lessons. Sam did get a mandolin and spent many hours playing it.

His tremendous love for music was stifled until his junior year when M. D. Stanley was hired for the music department. Sam was virtually the first to sign up. His dream was to learn to play all the instruments and become a band director. He did master the reed, wind, and percussion instruments along with the banjo. Fate had other plans for Sam.

As soon as they could play, Sam, with Mr. Stanley's help, formed the first orchestra. For two years they played at all school functions.

Before graduation in 1929, Druscilla Boss prevailed upon her father, care-taker at the Hearst Castle, to get an engagement there for the group. Mr. Boss was successful and the group was on their way. What anxiety, excitement, and apprehension they must have felt when they realized that they would be playing for William Randolph Hearst, Marion Davies, and world-famous celebrities. After their performance Hearst asked them what they would like. They needed uniforms desperately and made this request. Hearst furnished the entire band with satin lapel tuxedos and white flannel trousers with a black stripe down the leg. For fourteen years they played at the castle.

Thus, before graduation, the die was cast and the "Hot-Ten-Tots" were on their way. Sam realized that his dream of band master had to be delayed as few students could go on to college during the depression.

Their first big engagement was at the Hippodrome at Weed. Sam Mazzei and his "Hottentots" (newly named) sang and played along with the big name bands of that era. From one end of Siskiyou County to the other, and at Monko's Open Air Pavilion in Shasta County, the "Hottentots" were in great demand.

By 1962 the band had dwindled down to a few. "Rock and Roll" had taken over. The group retired. But a spark still burned in Sam's heart. In 1968 he revived the combo. With his two sons, Bill at the piano, John on the trumpet, Ruben Dominguez as vocalist, and others who sit in occasionally, the "Hottentots" made a comeback.

For over fifty years the band has entertained thousands. Those who know Sam Mazzei respect and love him. He is truly a dedicated man and a credit to his profession.

Old Hearst Castle - Built 1913, Burned 1930

IN REMEMBRANCE OF THE LADIES OF SHASTA DAISY LODGE #292 OF THE BROTHERHOOD OF LOCOMOTIVE FIREMEN AND ENGINEMEN

Mabel Hull   Mrs. Canoff   Grace Selby
Katherine Sellman   Carrie Ervine   Mamie Rogers

From 1910 until the "sixties" Shasta Daisy Lodge flourished and grew.

The members enjoyed many social gatherings of dancing and dining.

Conventions were held state-wide with many of the members attending. On August 24, 1946, Dunsmuir hosted a convention.

With the change in the railroad, many members moved away. The membership dwindled until it could no longer rent a hall. Meetings were held at private homes until 1974 when the lodge gave up the charter.

LITTRELL PARTS HISTORY
1922 - 1984

In 1922, Al and Earl Littrell formed a partnership in an auto parts store known as Littrell Parts, in Medford, Oregon. Later, branches were established in Grants Pass and Brookings and, in 1932, in Yreka. In 1935, Al became the sole owner of these stores. Al, following a fire in Erickson James Buick Agency & Parts House in Yreka, bought the store and the parts not damaged by the fire to add to the stock in his Yreka operations. Soon after the fire, Ermine "Battie" Batson became the outside salesman for Littrell Parts. On Nov. 26, 1939, he married Hattie Mason of Dunsmuir, daughter of George Mason and Sarah Brown Mason. George was employed for many years at the Reception, a popular pool and card room across the street from the Round House in Dunsmuir. Hattie and her two brothers, Jess and Edwin Brown, went through school in Dunsmuir. Jess and his wife live at Greenhorn near Yreka, as do Hattie and her husband. All are retired.

Back to the Littrell story. The store was located on Main Street across from what is now Rex Club. G. J. Collins started work at the Littrell Parts Store in Yreka, Mar. 15, 1940, in the capacity of shipping clerk. In 1941, Batson was transferred to the Dunsmuir store, and he and his wife moved into a house on Branstetter Street. The store was located south of Travelers Hotel on the same side of the street and was the second business north of the Associated Service Station. The Commercial Garage and the Associated Service Station (no longer in existence) were directly across the street from where Cedar Street meets Florence Avenue. During this time Harold Noyer, while still in high school, worked at Littrell Parts. While he was in a school play, he acted the part of "Pete," and the name stuck with him down through the years. Harold is remembered as one of the "Bob's Dairy Boys." He is retired and lives in Yreka.

In the fall, 1942, Littrell Store in Yreka burned. Because of the crunch of the war years which created a great shortage of manpower, Jerry Collins, being the only salesman left for Siskiyou County, went back to Yreka along with the stock of the Dunsmuir store which was closed. Batson was sent to Grants Pass as manager. 1946 saw Jerry Collins and Batson buy in as partners with Al Littrell. In 1947, the store was returned to Dunsmuir and was situated across the street from the California Theater. The Rainbow Club was on the north; Mannee's Drug Store on the south. Collins was manager. 1946 was the year that Littrell Parts, Incorporated, opened a branch in Redding and later in Red Bluff and Susanville. In 1952, Batson and Collins bought out Al Littrell's interests in the California stores. The Yreka store was to move from the corner of Main and Miner to the old Fledderman Building where Aubrey's Western Store is today.

In 1961, the store was moved to Mt. Shasta with Bill Andreatta of Mt. Shasta as its manager. 1964 saw Littrell Parts open a branch in Happy Camp, to be relocated in 1971 in a new building; new supplies included cable and logging equipment.

1965, upon Batson's retirement, Jerry Collins bought out his interest.

A new store was opened in Medford in 1970 under the name of Littrell Welding Supply of Oregon. Don Cauble of the Redding store was sent to Medford as manager. He still holds that position. There are branches of this store in Grants Pass, Roseburg, and Klamath Falls. For a number of years Mike Collins was office manager in Yreka.

1973: Collins Enterprises purchased from Jack and Fred Meamber the "Old Coca-Cola Bottling Plant." They placed the bookkeeping offices next to Littrell's and turned the old structure (with the expert help of Roy and Bill Hetherington) into the today's small shop, air-conditioned "Old Bottling Works Mall."

1981: Lael and his wife, Carolyn, purchased the three Littrell Parts stores from his parents. He has also taken over the management of the seven welding supply stores.

Editor's Note: This is really a capsulated account of the history of the Littrell Parts business as told by June Collins.

FIRST LUTHERAN CHURCH

The first services were held in the kindergarten room of the Dunsmuir Elementary School, March 3, 1930. Rev. Henry Rische was called and took up work in late 1930. A machine shop was purchased and transformed into the Rustic Chapel. The dedication was held on May 22, 1938. A replica of the chapel was erected and installed in the World's Fair on Treasure Island, where thousands visited it in 1940. A choir from Dunsmuir performed there. In the belfry hangs an old abbey bell obtained in Exeter, England, and sent to Dunsmuir in 1945. It rang for the first time on V E Day in 1945; it will ring again in 1986 for the Centennial.

Rev. John Rische
1948-1953

Rev. John Cramer
1968-1971

Rev. M. Schabacker
1953-1965

Rev. Ehard Rupp
1971-1979

Rev. Wm. Woollen
1979-

Rev. Henry Rische

THE MOTHERSINGERS
1953 - 1963

First appearance in concert - 1954

*"When you're smiling, when you're smiling,
the whole world smiles with you."*

Director . . . . Reva P. Coon
Pianists . . . . Mina Kimble
Ruby Slade

Last appearance - a surprise
on the occasion of Reva Coon's retirement - 1966

UNIT NO. 68

The NARVRE chapter of Dunsmuir was chartered in June, 1957, with 80 charter members. The club became nationally associated in September, 1957. The names of the charter members appear below:

C. L. Carter	Edward Kelly	Carl McCune	R. Burleigh	Marie P. Brun
Albert McCann	Irene McCann	Charles F. Powers	Delcia Burleigh	Elia Zanotto
Joseph M. Seitz	N. E. Beaughan	Cora W. Powers	Alma L. Forrester	Mary T. Zanotto
Ruth E. Seitz	Sidona Beaughan	Fred H. Goode	Th. A. Smith	Millie Aldridge
C. N. Bryan	George E. Carey	Mrs. Fred Goode	Mrs. A. Smith	Mrs. C. F. Odegard
Henry T. Long	Signe Ahlstrom	Orney B. Weedon	Wm. D. Smith	Glen H. Lamb
Wm. Aldrich	Hazel Adams	James E. Cantrall	A. F. Hollingsworth	Winifred Maxwell
C. F. Odegard	C. A. Cornelius	Velma M. Cantrall	Jesse D. Humphrey	Edward J. Lovelle
Russell McMullen	Albert R. Opdyke	Norman Green	Mrs. Jesse Humphrey	Alleene J. Lovelle
F. Z. Smith	George O. McLaughlin	Sadie Green	Shilo Smith	Martha C. Stauffer
Ch. C. Wendell	Gladys Creason	Nellie Cunningham	Lauretta R. Smith	Ch. H. Jones
J. L. Holland	Amanda Cook	Katherine Sellman	Henry Waldron	Mrs. J. L. Holland
W. E. McDaniels	Floyd Creason	Florence Taylor Gaines	Mary F. Waldron	R. S. Daniels
Edna Mae McMullen	T. T. Ahlstrom	Bert Bachand	Winnie Long	Esther Daniels
North J. Ahlstrom	Asa D. Ash	Ruth Bachand	Anthony Brun	

1984 OFFICERS

O. S. Weedon, president and charter member
George Nakao, 1st vice-president
N. Walter Spears, 2nd vice-president
Paul Collins, secretary
Letha Barnes, chaplain

The main interest of the National Association of Retired and Veteran Railroad Employees is to support and fight for the rights of retired railroad employees. The organization meets monthly on the first Tuesday and enjoys a potluck meal, which is followed by the business meeting.

GREETINGS TO DUNSMUIR
ON ITS CENTENNIAL!

HAPPY BIRTHDAY, DUNSMUIR!

DUNSMUIR ROTARY CLUB
Chartered September 30, 1950
7600th Charter Club Into Rotary International

CHARTER MEMBERS

H. H. Miller, Jr. (Bank of America); W. F. Kennedy (Dunsmuir Hotel), Jack L. Dempsey (Dunsmuir Lumber Co.), Jay M. Smith (Smith's Appliances & Service), Dan Rygel (Rygel Fir Manufacturing Co.); D. R. Heath, Jr. (Dunsmuir News); Wilbur W. Carlson (Bill's Drive-Inn), Victor J. Andreatta (West Coast Life Insurance), A. R. Hiland (Hiland Music Co.), L. A. Gibson (Gibson's Union Service), Ben L. Slimmer (Slimmer's Furniture Store), Dr. Tom B. Clay (Chiropractor), Reginald K. Thom (M. & M. Chevrolet Co.), Leon Rygel (Rygel Fir Manufacturing Co.), D. E. Warner (California-Oregon Power Co.); Richard Brunjes, Jr. (Brunjes Auto Court); Francis E. LeMere (Dunsmuir Post Office), Charles Huff (City Clerk), Dr. J. W. Reynolds (Physician), Fred Potter (Potter's Sporting Goods Store), and C. O. Porter (C. O. Porter Insurance).

HISTORY OF THE DUNSMUIR ROTARY CLUB

An organizational meeting was held July 12th, 1950, in the Dunsmuir Hotel, to form a new service organization in Dunsmuir. On September 30th of that year, the Dunsmuir Rotary Club was granted its charter from Rotary International. A formal dinner ceremony was held at Shasta Springs Lodge. The District Governor, Arch B. Davidson, presided at the presentation of the club's charter, and on hand were members of the Rotary Club of Chico, which sponsored the Dunsmuir Club. The officers for the newly established club were H. H. Miller, Jr., President; Ben Slimmer, Vice President; Jack L. Dempsey, Treasurer; J. M. Smith, Sergeant-At-Arms; Donald L. Heath, Jr., Secretary.

Eighteen Rotary Clubs from throughout Northern California had delegations present for the presentation. The charter was numbered 7600 in Rotary International.

The Dunsmuir Rotary Club is small in numbers, but always is big in spirit, much like the City of Dunsmuir. Dunsmuir's Rotarians expect big things from both the Club and the City during Dunsmuir's second century.

*The Chancel at St. Barnabas' Church
prepared for Holy Eucharist on Christmas Eve.*

*This page is dedicated to the Glory of God
by the Reverend Howard M. Park and the
Episcopal Congregation
of*
*ST. BARNABAS' CHURCH
in
Dunsmuir, California*

ST. JOHN THE EVANGELIST'S CATHOLIC CHURCH

Special effort was made to copy the Sacred Heart Church, which was demolished by fire in 1932. Luigi Cosentino, with much volunteer help of the parishoners, constructed this building. In 1933 Father Michael O'Connel dedicated the church.

After Vatican II, the interior was changed and new altars were built by Luigi's son, James Cosentino.

No record can be found when the Sacred Heart Church was completed and dedicated. However, a parish was established in 1899, with the Rev. Daniel Meagher as the first resident priest.

The First United Methodist Church
SERVING GOD and OUR FELLOW MAN

The Original Church

UNCONQUERED BY
THE BIG FIRE
April 25, 1924

Castle Avenue Church of the Electric Cross

Dedicated Oct. 27, 1929

INVINCIBLE
though
CRUSHED BY SNOW
January 4, 1966

The Present Sanctuary

Dedicated
December 27, 1959

UNDEFEATED
by
ECONOMIC
DEPRESSIONS

THE GATES OF THE TEMPLE ARE OPEN

VETERANS of FOREIGN WARS
Dunsmuir Post #4718

As the City of Dunsmuir celebrates its one-hundredth anniversary, the local V.F.W. Post will be having their forty-first. Dunsmuir V.F.W. Post #4718 was instituted November 17, 1945; the parent organization, Veterans of Foreign Wars of the United States, will have been in existence eight-seven years.

The fall of 1899 marked the founding of the Veterans of Foreign Wars of the United States. There were no pensions, compensations, or hospitalization awaiting those veterans who returned home from the War with Spain, the Philippine Insurrection, and the China Relief Expedition. These men banded together for the purpose of helping their disabled, needy, and less fortunate comrages. Three groups in widely separated sections of the country organized almost simultaneously, each without the knowledge of the other. Located in Columbus, Ohio; Denver, Colorado; and Altoona, Pennsylvania, they merged in 1913 to form what is known today as the Veterans of Foreign Wars of the United States.

Because of their small number, the voice of the veteran was unheard and unheeded. Few veterans benefits were written into the statute books prior to World War I. The lessons that V.F.W. members learned between 1899 and 1917 in their effort to help their less fortunate comrades created the pattern for the numerous veterans benefits that exist today. This period also established the vital importance of the organization in the promotion of good citizenship, adequate Armed Forces and a greater appreciation of America's patriotic traditions.

The same patriotic objectives of the farseeing founders of over eighty years ago are the objectives of the Veterans of Foreign Wars today. The things we are doing today and developing for the future depict pretty accurately the long-established character of the Veterans of Foreign Wars of the United States. The fundamental purpose agreed upon and handed down to us by the founders is as applicable today as it was more than eighty years ago. Briefly those purposes are comradeship, perpetuation of the memory of our departed comrades and assistance to their widows and orphans, loyalty to our country in peace or war, to foster true patriotism and to extend the institutions of American freedom.

The V.F.W. has always been a service organization. The word "service" in our vocabulary means action. It means things accomplished for the benefit of our members and their dependents. It means service to the communities in which we live, and to the welfare of the nation at large.

On Memorial Day, 1922, the Veterans of Foreign Wars sold the first replicas of the Flanders Field poppies on a national scale. The memorial flower proved popular. In 1923 the National Encampment decreed that the poppies sold by the Veterans of Foreign Wars must be made by disabled veterans. In 1924 disabled veterans in Pittsburgh made V.F.W. flowers for that year's sale. These men coined the phrase "Buddy Poppy" and in 1924 our National Headquarters copyrighted the trade name. Since the first Buddy Poppy sale, the objective has been "to honor the dead by helping the living." Funds from the annual sale of Buddy Poppies are devoted exclusively to veteran rehabilitation and welfare work, and to help maintain the V.F.W. National Home.

IN REMEMBRANCE OF THE
WOMAN'S BENEFIT ASSOCIATION REVIEW 25

ROW 1: Edna Gilcrist, Farlin Cantrall, Gladys Creason, Barbara Neasham, Doris Geiger. ROW 2: Grace Stanley, Helen Keeler, Anita Barnum, Harryette Howel, Sadie Green, ________ Carey. ROW 3: Norma Mickel, Callie Lamm, Naoma Redman, Josephine McGee, Bessie Beale.

On January 17, 1930, the Woman's Benefit Association received its charter. The membership was comprised of insured and social members. From 1930 until 1970 Review 25 enjoyed many social gatherings and attended conventions. The Review featured a drill team that was invited to perform at many places including the Cow Palace at San Francisco. On June 21, 1967, the name was changed to North American Benefit Association. The membership has dwindled to a few who meet occasionally at private homes.

ROW 1: ________ ________ , Ethel Bert, Donna Harris, Ellen Smith, Leora Gonzales, Laura Billington, Norma Myers, Anna McClintock, Delcia Burleigh, Sweezy. ROW 2: ________ ________ , Isabella Haines, ________ . ROW 3: Esther Daniels, Ruth Bachand, Bessie Anderson, Wanda Spowart, Hazel Wagner, Farlin Cantrell, ROW 4: Reta Langrner, Teresa Weedon, Gladys Creason, Carol McMillan, ________ ________ , Agnes Hayden, Helen Grochel.

RUSSELL and ELOISE ERICKSON

Managers of
Sears Roebuck Catalog Sales

Congratulate Dunsmuir

on its

CENTENNIAL

THE MILES RICHMONDS

extend greetings

and congratulations

to Dunsmuir

on its

CENTENNIAL

MRS. MARY REGINATO
and
the PAUL REGINATOs

congratulate

Dunsmuir

on its

HUNDREDTH BIRTHDAY

The
CHESTER and ALICE
HAMPTON Family

offer Congratulations to

Dunsmuir

on its

One Hundredth Birthday

and

extend best wishes

for the

SECOND CENTURY OF LIVING

PART III
ONE HUNDRED YEARS OF
MEMORIES

Circa 1910

For a hundred years
Men in striped overalls and caps
Have hastened down the hills
To man the daily trains
That raced beside the river,
Then bringing cargo back,
They whistled their return;
And wives and mothers hearing,
Would open forth the doors.

—From "Memories of Dunsmuir"
by Mina Kimble

MEMORIES OF AN OLD
HOME AND ITS FAMILY

by
Austin Roberts

Our home, originally the Jeff Hawkins home, was moved to its present site prior to the time that Mother & Dad were married in 1908. However, they purchased the home shortly after the wedding because I remember Dad telling me that the yard was completely covered with "mountain apples" (huge rocks) and that he had to have forty-seven large wagon loads of rocks hauled away before the yard could be used. Many rocks were in evidence about the place when I was a wee lad; we used many of them to build the old rock wall that enclosed the front yard, tearing it down many years later because rattlesnakes had moved into the cracks left by the weather and frost. When moved, the house was placed directly over the many enormous boulders, reaching to a spot just under the floor joists. Dad, with help from brother Ed and myself, excavated the complete basement as you know it today. When it was time to remove one of the large rocks, I would hike over the mountain behind the Cornish Hospital, over the two ridges beyond and then up Soda Creek until I found the old miner — Jim Barnett. Jim would show up later in the week and spend a day or more drilling holes in the boulders. When the shot holes were drilled, Jim would cover the rocks with old mattresses and then set off the dynamite. Jim was such an expert powder man that he never harmed the floors above or any of Mother's dishes or glassware. All of the rocks removed from the yard were hauled down to Sacramento Avenue and used to make the foundation of the old Weed Hotel.

The Roberts Home on Oak Street

Photo by Joe Kelby

2

Their first home in Dunsmuir was on Florence Avenue, near the intersection of Florence and the street that came down from Fidler's place. They lived next door to Mother's best friend, Ida Nealey.

The old Holis home and our house were the only residences on the even side of Oak Street when they first moved to that area. Later Mr. and Mrs. Friel built the home that we knew as the Burgess house. Apparently Mrs. Friel was my favorite neighbor, because Mother told of the times that I would end up sleeping under her piano.

Oak Street was ankle deep in red dust in the summer and nearly impassable in the winter because of the mud. Horse-drawn sleds were used when the snows arrived, the first cars being unable to navigate under winter conditions. Frank Van Fossen and Doctor Mason owned the first motor vehicles that I can recall. Later, U. S. Davis, Fred Burgess, and Fred Stanley became proud owners. Fred Burgess, who owned the "Toggery" near Chambers Pool Hall on Sacramento Avenue, bought the fanciest automobile to grace the streets of Dunsmuir for many years. To be exact, it was called "The Apperson Jackrabbit Eight," a yellow roadster with a big insignia on the radiator depicting a rabbit jumping through a figure eight.

Wooden sidewalks were the norm for the whole town; often only one side of a street would be blessed with the up-and-coming convenience. The one on Oak Street graced the north side of the street, leaving our side the option of the middle of the dirt road or a narrow meandering path. I remember that the plentiful dust on Oak Street was just right for making of lucious "mud-pies," or to pass the time on a hot summer day the calling of "doodle bugs" from their hideouts in the deepest of dust.

Oak Street was, in retrospect, the finest winter coasting area in the vicinity. From Van Fossen's mill to the bluff at the top of the railroad embankment at the bottom of Oak Street was the fastest course in town. "Bones" Coon always took the honors with his extremely heavy, home-made racer. Our little store-bought "Flyer's" were poor competition for the "champ." The speed of the hill was helped by the chain gang of kids who would spend the cold winter afternoons carrying buckets of water to "ice" the track.

Fall, with its myriad of oak leaves, provided everyone with the opportunity to rake the fallen beauties into huge piles, set them on fire, and then add bushels of raw Irish potatoes. When the coals had cooled, the baked spuds would be snaked out completely cooked. What a delightful morsel they would make when covered with butter!

The armistice for World War I had been declared, and I remember we were burning leaves when Edgar Shoupe appeared in his uniform, walking up Oak Street on his way to the Hollis home. Mildred Hollis was out "leafing" with the rest of us, and she nearly blew apart — Edgar was her boy friend.

Our dad first went to work for the Southern Pacific Co. as a member of the bridge building crew, later going to Rocklin, California, to accept employment as a road fireman. Rocklin was the division point for that area. The engines at that time were powered by wood-burning boxes that heated the boilers to produce the steam needed to set the wheels in motion. Thus the connotation of "firebox" and "steam engine." His first run began in Rocklin and took him over the mighty Sierras to Sparks, Nevada — the worst stretch of track on the system, becoming famous as "The Firemen's Hell" because of the back-breaking labor needed to feed the hungry man of the firebox on the trip over the hill. What a break for the overworked fireman when fuel oil replaced the large stacks of cordwood in the tenders! Dad managed to get away from the run to Sparks after a couple of years, trading for a job on the neophyte Shasta Division. I thought that I had recorded the different dates, but I have been unable to find them in my family history file.

Our grandparents, Jamie and Emma Dorrell, lived in a little unpainted house that was located across the street (Florence Avenue) from Jack Wyatt's Traveler's Garage. All of the houses on that side of Florence Avenue — from the site of the present City Hall to the alley way that led down to Aunt Frankie's home — the property was owned by a man by the name of Leland. The Lelands, both Mr. and Mrs., were perfect examples of grimness: they could have been the subjects for Grant Wood's painting of the Kansas farm couple — unsmiling, with an austereness of countenance that I haven't forgotten since childhood. Needless to say, when anything was in need of repair at the Dorrell residence, our dad was the repairman, for Leland did not believe in pampering his renters. The building between our grandparents' home and the present City Hall was occupied by a Mrs. Chapman, a French lady who ran the town's only millinery shop. Unfortunately, Mrs. Chapman was deaf and used an ear trumpet that was nearly equal to her own size. She knew very little English, chattering away in French to anyone who would listen.

When running errands for our patient grandmother, I would leave her back porch and take a path down the hillside that led to Sacramento Avenue, the area occupied by the majority of the town's business establishments. Halfway down the short-cut stood a little red building with no windows and with access only through a heavy door that was graced with a huge padlock, chain and a small window laced with iron bars. The town jail — large enough for not more than two prisoners at a time and equipped with nothing more than a rough cot for sleeping. No lights, no bathroom facilities and no heat. My morbid curiosity often led me, although nearly shaking with fear or excitement, to venture a hasty peek through the barred window. When I was permitted to catch sight of some unfortunate occupant, my retreat down "Jail House Hill" must have set a record for downhill running.

My attendance record throughout my formative years of grades one through eight at the local grammar school was not one of which our long-suffering mother would be apt to be proud. The lure of the beauty of our mountains seemed to be much more enticing than the three "R's" or for that matter, the known consequences of the visit to Mr. Kleaver's office, and the trot around in a circle while he attempted to reach my posterior with his ever-present rubber hose. Fortunately for me, that portion of my anatomy and the garden hose were not compatible.

I remember a paper route that I enjoyed for a time. Ernie and Tom Wheeler had taken over the dealership for the *"Bee," "Chronicle,"* and *"Examiner."* I don't remember the names of the two other delivery boys, but each of us drove a two-wheeled cart with a large box anchored between the wheels. The horse that I drove was a non-descript bay pony who would fall asleep every time I stopped for a delivery, waking only when it was time to return to the stable.

Later, and not yet in high school, I worked for Charlie and Dick Masson at their dairy that was located just beyond the old highway bridge in north Dunsmuir. I would arise at three o'clock in the morning, have breakfast, and walk through the dark streets of the town until I reached the dairy. Once there, we would take off in an old truck and drive to Edgewood. Picking up the raw milk at the big cooperative, we would then make the return trip to the dairy in Dunsmuir, run the milk through the pasteurizer, sterilize and fill the bottles, and load them into milk crates in preparation for the morning delivery. Reverting back to the "old days," we would load the crated milk and cream into a light wagon, hitch up the big black stallion, "Jerry," and proceed to wake the good people of Dunsmuir to the tune of clanking bottles. "Jerry" was a great horse, big and strong and easy going — until — the last delivery was accomplished. His stable was located on the far side of the river at the bottom of Wilkins Hill, the road dropping down from the bluff near Selby's Blacksmith Shop in a steep curve that ended with the crossing of the bridge spanning the river. "Jerry," bless his ornery soul, would charge down that hill like the "Charge of the Light Brigade," bottles banging, wooden brake shoes smoking, wagon and driver bouncing from side to side, not stopping until he reached the spot where we parked the wagon and unharnessed the black beast.

This could go on forever it seems, so I had better detour from memory lane.

—*Austin Roberts*

I REMEMBER WILDWOOD

by
Dolores Richmond Scalise

I hesitated to write at length about my home, as I didn't know if it were suitable subject matter. I was five years old when I moved to Wildwood. It was built in 1903 to serve as a summer retreat for the William F. Herrin family of San Francisco and attracted guests like John Muir, the naturalist, and Alice Eastwood, the botanist. Mr. Herrin was chief counsel for the Southern Pacific Railroad and gave the water rights to the town of Dunsmuir.

Mr. Herrin's son, William V. Herrin, married my grandmother. She planted the many flower beds and planned the Japanese tea garden with the three ponds.

The sharply delineated seasons of spring, summer, autumn, and winter dominate my memories of Dunsmuir. I became aware of seasonal changes at an early age.

This was the result of living in a remote wooded area during my childhood and growing-up years. My home was an elongated, two-story structure with a steep roof, balconies, and wide verandas. Trees with massive trunks loomed high above the house and shaded the spacious lawns, flower beds, and a formal Japanese garden with three ponds. My playground was acres of forest land filled with evergreen and deciduous trees, fresh water springs, a creek with a waterfall, and wild flowers of every variety. The place was called "Wildwood."

After the snow disappeared and the ground thawed, I learned to listen for the signs of spring. I remember the distant humming of the Sacramento River, rushing with the run-off from melting snow banks. My mother always said, "Listen to the river sing. Spring is here."

There were the shrill night noises; the nocturnal sounds from frogs and crickets near the ponds. Occasionally, high-pitched cicadas clamored and an owl called out. I heard their voices when I opened the balcony door in my bedroom.

The air was soft; the sunshine warm. I exchanged heavy winter clothing for starched cotton dresses and white shoes. The flannel sheets on the beds were replaced with cotton ones. Ear muffs, scarves, sweaters, and knit caps were stored with moth balls or placed in cedar chests.

Spring weather brought hop-scotch, marbles, jacks, and jump ropes. Chalk-drawn circles and squares appeared on the sidewalks. Girls carried their metal jacks and small rubber balls in draw-string bags. There were jump rope chants like "Spanish dancer, do the splits. Spanish dancer, give a high kick" and "Down by the river, down by the sea, Johnny broke a bottle and

4

he blamed it on me." And shouts of "Red hot pepper!", meant the rope was turned as fast as possible with only the agile jumping without tripping.

I noticed bright new growth on the tips of the fir trees and the fuzzy gray pussy willows along the creek. The barren branches of the dogwood sprouted green leaves and showy white flowers. The earliest wild flower was the prickly, low-growing squaw carpet. Then, the tiny bell-shaped manzanita appeared, followed by stubby Indian warriors, miniature white iris, fragile salt-and-pepper bells, and delicate kitten ears. I didn't know the botanical names for the flowers and used the common ones.

Recess at school brought games like London Bridge's Falling Down, Crack the Whip, In-and-Out the Windows, Dodge Ball, and boys chase the girls. Teachers disapproved of "boys chase the girls." They interpreted the game as "boys discover girls," but it was only a harmless rowdy version of tag. Crack the Whip, however, wasn't harmless and involved vicious yanking of arms. I didn't like being part of the "whip" and often skinned my knees from falls on the asphalt.

After the confinement of winter, it was agonizing to be cooped up in a classroom and look out the windows at bright sunshine. The captivity encouraged restless, unruly, feisty behavior. In elementary school, boys tended to push, shove, and taunt each other until the scuffles provoked challenges to a fist fight behind the Safeway store adjacent the school yard. Cries of "Back of the Safeway after school!" sent excited spectators to the scene of the fight.

It was the season for hikes to Oxone Springs, Hedge Creek Falls, Cave Springs, and for skipping stones across the pool beneath Mossbrae Falls. Skipping stones was difficult. If the stone selected were the wrong size or shape, it sank without skipping. But thin, flat stones skimmed the water successfully if thrown underhand from a low, crouching position. I was in awe of those who sailed the stone until it skipped, not one, but two or three times across the water.

Summer began when school was dismissed in June, and I was free to enjoy the long, leisurely days. For me, summer meant hammocks, and I anxiously waited for my father to take them out of storage. There were several that he slung between porch posts or attached to tree trunks. I liked to hide in hammocks, swinging and reading books from the living room shelves. I swung through an assortment of authors like John Muir, Jack London, and Rudyard Kipling.

Or my little brother and I invented hammock games. Most of them involved ways of dumping each other out of the hammocks. I remember twisting and turning my brother round and round while he lay tightly wrapped in the hammock like a cocoon. Then, I released the hammock and it spun over and over until he fell out. Or my brother swung me until the hammock soared to such heights that it flipped over, and I slipped out on the ground.

And there was the airplane game. Suspending reality, we transformed a hammock into an airplane. I was the pilot and my brother the passenger. He sat in the center of the hammock while I straddled the ropes on one end and pumped with my feet. Swinging and cruising at a sensible speed, we flew over mythical countries and traveled through foreign lands. I stuck my feet on the ground to brake the hammock and land the plane.

Games associated with summer were kick the can, softball, and run sheep run. The evenings stayed light a long time. It was possible to play tag, toss a ball, or ride a bicycle until nine o'clock. Hide-and-seek was adventurous in the twilight hours when darkness provided safe but scary hiding places. There were yells of, "Ollie, Ollie Oxen Free!", whenever a player was home free.

In summer, Hedge Creek was a sluggish stream. Tangles of dry, dusty blackberry vines grew like a barrier of brambles along the bank. They were as hazardous as a barbed wire fence, and I wormed my way through the thorny vines. I came here to search for wild tiger lilies that huddled in the shady spots near the water. One afternoon I witnessed a moment of rare beauty. While sitting quietly on the creek bank, I saw a Monarch butterfly settle on a tiger lily. The reddish-orange petals swayed under the gentle touch of the black and orange butterfly. Their vivid colors harmonized. Slowly and seductively, the butterfly fanned its wings. Back and forth, they moved with a languid rhythm. I sat very still, not wanting to startle the butterfly. But the interlude was brief. Abruptly and without warning, the Monarch drifted off to seek a new diversion.

The tough, wild rhubarb plants flourished along the creek where they grew big and wide. On warm days, I snapped a glossy oversized leaf from a rhubarb plant and put it on top of my head like a pixie hat. I pretended to be an elf under the floppy hat with the stubby stem sticking up in the air. By dipping the leaf in water and replacing it on my head, I stayed comfortably cool.

Sometimes, my little brother and I hiked down the very steep trail behind our house. It led to the natural springs that overflowed into Mossbrae Falls. These were the springs that furnished the water supply for the town of Dunsmuir. Five finger ferns fringed the water that poured out of the hillsides. We heard the roar of the falls. The path along the springs was damp and muddy from the constant spray. Fragile bleeding hearts and columbine grew in rocky crevices overhanging the water. Stinging nettles guarded the trail.

As a child, I never came here alone. The cascading water coming from unseen sources within the hillsides, the dank smell of marshy vegetation, and the disturbing shadows from the tall trees made me uneasy. I felt as if I were in a strange and secret place.

Summer hours passed quickly while I looked for Indian arrowheads and four-leaf clovers, hunted the elusive pine orchids, and tracked my father into the woods where he sawed the dead trees that had fallen during the winter. He was easy to find. I followed the whine of the chain saw. The huge rounds from the tree trunks smelled of pitch and were sticky. My father neatly axed them into quarter-size chunks that fit in the fireplace or stove. By the time winter arrived, they were dry and ready to burn.

When school began in September, the morning air was brisk and the daylight hours shorter. Autumn brought an end to the garden flowers. When my mother sensed that the first heavy frosts were coming, she cut and picked the chrysanthemums, asters, and French marigolds that remained in the garden. These last bouquets were the prettiest. There wouldn't be any more flowers until spring.

The foliage mellowed and aged. There was a bite in the autumn air. I watched the squirrels sneak acorns and pilfer pine nuts. Bitter tasting choke cherries decorated the bushes and wild grapes tempted the birds. Poison oak turned a flamboyant red. Doves fed on the mullein and vanished before the frost. Bees, grasshoppers, and beetles disappeared from the garden. Teasels, Queen Anne's lace, milk weed pods, cattails, goldenrod appeared in the ditches and along the roadsides.

In the fall, my father raked and burned the brittle, dried leaves and pine needles. They had an acrid, clean odor. I liked to stick potatoes under the hot pine needles to roast in the ashes. After removing the blackened skins, the potatoes were flaky with a smoky flavor. Or it was fun to find forked sticks to skewer marshmallows to toast over the fire. The heat melted them into gooey globs under blistered brown crusts.

In our yard, the viney maples and Virginia creeper were the first leaves to color and drop. On the lawn, the mountain ash trees turned a glorious gold with clusters of orange berries that remained until the snow brought birds to eat them. The dogwood trees became russet red with gnarled seed pods. The oaks were slow to lose their foliage. The antique gold leaves gradually deepened to a burnished bronze before the November weather banished them from the branches.

After Thanksgiving, the landscape looked bleak. Withered brown stalks lay broken and bent on the ground. Plant life was dormant. The birds had gone. The sunshine was thin, lacking any real warmth. The woods were silent and empty.

As I remember, the winter season in Dunsmuir was beautiful but inconvenient. Deep snow created problems of mobility. Schools closed and social activities ceased during severe storms. Electrical power failed and water pipes froze. Snowplows and car chains were the noises of winter.

But winter was fun for a child. Long icicles became dueling swords when carefully detached from their mooring. These tapering spikes of ice were used for fencing until broken to bits by a slashing opponent. Snowmen, snowballs, and sleds were favorite pastimes. Or my friends and I liked to fall backward with arms outstretched into untouched snow banks and leave an impression of our bodies. We called this game, "playing angel."

Then, there were aimless winter activities like shattering the crust of ice covering puddles and ponds or knocking the snow off the flattened bushes and watching them bounce back. I sucked on icicles and poured pineapple juice over balls of compact, clean snow to make snow ice cream.

During winter months, cloak rooms in the elementary school smelled of damp wool mittens and wet knit caps. Black galoshes lay in heaps along the floor. These waterproof overshoes were identical in style, and boys as well as girls wore them. Trying to locate the matching pair that belonged to me was a chore, and tugging them over sturdy oxfords was a struggle.

When the weather was too stormy to be outdoors, recess meant playing hang man on the blackboards, having spelling bees or talent shows, and listening to the teacher read aloud from books like *The Secret Garden, Call of the Wild*, and the Nancy Drew mysteries. Or the teacher played the old upright piano while we sang "Yankee Doodle Dancy," "Pop Goes the Weasel," "Annie Laurie," and rounds of "Three Blind Mice."

After a storm, many kinds of birds and animals came to forage for food in our yard. The birds left funny fork-shaped marks on the surface of the snow. Raccoons sought shelter on the porch and scrawny deer nibbled on any available foliage.

Snow concealed the ugliness in a landscape. Even an ancient, splintered fence was transformed into an object of beauty by a thick layer of snow. Tree stumps became white pillars. Shrubs had strange, surreal shapes. Feathery snowflakes coated the telephone wires and covered the street signs. Bushes bent low until they blended into the snow banks. I remember the soft silent sound of falling snow, and the "plop, plop" noise it made when clumps dropped from the branches onto the ground.

Winter meant flannel sheets and hot water bottles. My second floor bedroom was unheated. In extremely cold weather, a hot water bottle that fell out of bed during the night became a lump of ice in the morning. I wore mittens to keep my hands warm while reading in bed and slept under layers of wool blankets that weighted me down.

When trickles of water began to run from under the snow banks and the drifts shrunk smaller and smaller, I knew winter was retreating. The dormant season was ending. Temperatures were warmer and daylight hours longer. I listened for the wild geese, honking and calling as they flew in formation on a northward journey. The snow banks melted in the high mountain regions, swelling the water in the Sacramento River until it hummed and sang a song of spring.

I no longer live in Dunsmuir or in the mountains. There are no woods or creeks or waterfalls to explore in my backyard. The place called "Wildwood" is gone. But the shift in seasons stirs childhood memories and wistful recollections come with the gentle spring breezes and crisp autumn air. I remember and am a child again, eager to hunt the wild flowers and kick the piles of fallen leaves.

THE VAN FOSSEN — MASON — HARRISON — WILSON FAMILY:

A Pioneer Family in the Growth and Development of Dunsmuir

by
Jack Wilson

The Van Fossen family arrived in Dunsmuir in the spring of 1888, when the town was just two years old. The members of the family at that time were Levi, his wife Matilda ("Tillie"), their son Frank Bradley (aged 12), and their daughter Vera Mae (aged 7). Vera later recalled the extraordinary beauty of the canyon that particular spring, with quantities of azalea and dogwood in bloom. She remembered her childhood impression that this spot must indeed be Heaven.

Levi, whose ancestors had arrived in America from Holland in 1700, was a member of a pioneer California family. His father, who was also named Levi, had sailed in 1849 on the ship *Prometheus* to Panama and from there around the Horn to San Francisco on the *Brother Jonathan*. The senior Levi returned east to bring his family to California in 1853. This time they all crossed the Panama Isthmus and thence to California, making their first home in Hangtown (later changed to Placerville).

The younger Levi returned to Ohio eight years later to enter Oberlin College; and when the Civil War began, he and a number of collegemates formed Company K of the 150th Ohio. Following this military service, he enrolled in Northwestern University in Evanston, Illinois, graduating with a Ph.B. [sic] in 1870. Levi was appointed Professor of Natural Sciences the very next year at the University of Tennessee at Knoxville. While a professor there, he met, courted, and married on June 30, 1873, Matilda Elizabeth ("Tillie") Post, the daughter of Stephen Titus Post, a manufacturer of carriages and president of the Blount County Bank.

Levi began his return west with a brief stop in Humbolt, Kansas, where he spent two years as principal of the public schools. It was in

Levi Van Fossen about time of
arrival in Dunsmuir

Matilda Van Fossen

Humbolt in 1875 that Frank Bradley was born to Levi and Tillie. From Kansas the Van Fossen family next moved to Red Bluff, California, where Levi served two years as superintendent of the Red Bluff Public Schools (1877-1879). It was in Red Bluff that their daughter Ruby Yree passed away at the age of one-and-one-half years. Leaving Red Bluff and professional life, Levi became identified with business, owning a drug and bookstore in Biggs, California. Biggs was the birthplace of their third child, a daughter, Vera Mae, who was born in 1880.

Vera Mae

Frank Bradley

Deciding to leave Biggs in 1888, Levi and Tillie chose between Berkeley (Tillie's choice, based upon its greater cultural opportunities and its proximity to the University of California, which she hoped her children would attend) and Dunsmuir (Levi's choice, based upon the beauty of its locale and the business opportunities he foresaw). Levi prevailed, and it did not take long for Tillie to share his love for Dunsmuir. Together they became one of the leading families of the growing community.

Levi lived in Dunsmuir until his death on February 27, 1905, and his obituary at the time noted that "he had accumulated considerable property — owning more houses, lots and valuable business blocks than any other citizen here." He was president and principal owner of the Mossbrae Falls Water and Power Company, which, according to his letterhead, "supplied water and electric lights at Dunsmuir." He was the owner of Mossbrae Falls, from which he brought the water supply to Dunsmuir. He owned property to the west of Dunsmuir on which there remains the water system established to serve the residents of the Van Fossen Addition. Streets in the addition are named after the grandchildren of Levi and Tillie: Beverley Way for Beverley Mason, Elinore Avenue for Elinore Vesta Van Fossen, and Richard Road for Richard Mason (Richard Road would disappear when Interstate 5 was constructed). Levi was the Dunsmuir Postmaster after the post office was moved from Upper Soda Springs and located in the corner of the Van Fossen drugstore.

Life in Dunsmuir was not all business, however. The Van Fossen family was active in the civic and social life of Dunsmuir for many years. They were instrumental in establishing the Fidelity Chapter of the Order of the Eastern Star. In the Chapter's First Quarterly Social program, May 21, 1895, Tillie chaired the reception committee, Levi served on the refreshments committee, and daughter Vera presented a song and tableau. The "social" was actually a ball, which opened with a Grand March and included waltzes, polkas, quadrilles, schottesches, waltz quadrilles, Lancers Quadrilles, and medley. Both Tillie and Vera served as Worthy Matrons of Fidelity Chapter. Vera became District Deputy and traveled over primitive mountain roads to visit chapters in her district. The stagecoach in which she traveled to Weaverville is now in a museum in the town of Old Shasta outside of Redding.

Mrs. Van Fossen was an organizer of the Azelea Club, said to be the oldest club in Dunsmuir. At first the meetings alternated be-

Original flume

tween whist and embroidery, with the club ultimately becoming exclusively devoted to the latter. The Azelea Club disbanded only recently.

In 1916, Mrs. Van Fossen moved to a new home on Beverley Way, in which she lived until she passed away on April 18, 1933.

★ ★ ★ ★ ★ ★

Richard & Beverley Mason by Grandmother Van Fossen's home

Frank Bradley Van Fossen, son of Levi and Tillie, born June 13, 1875, in Humbolt, Kansas, arrived in Dunsmuir in 1888 with his parents. He returned to the East for college preparation at an academy, living with his grandparents in Maryville, Tennessee, after which he again came west to attend Stanford University. While there he formed an acquaintance with Herbert and Theodore Hoover and remained a loyal friend and admirer of the President. Frank studied electrical, mining, civil and hydraulic engineering at Stanford, graduating in 1898, after which he took a year of postgraduate work at the University of California, Berkeley. He then returned to Dunsmuir where he took a prominent part with his father in carrying on the Mossbrae Power and Light Company, which was ultimately sold to the California Oregon Power Company.

Frank Van Fossen home and the mill

*Last big log off the hill for the mill
Last man left, Frank Van Fossen*

Frank Van Fossen

On April 22, 1903, in Oakland, California, Frank married May Sarah Dunsmore, daughter of William and Mary Dunsmore of Oakland.

Their daughter Elinore Vesta Van Fossen was born the following year.

Frank and May lived in Dunsmuir all their married lives, with Frank passing away in 1938 and May in 1942. The obituary which followed Frank's death detailed a few of their social and community contributions:

The Van Fossen estate, of which Mr. Frank Van Fossen was the manager, together with his own

May Van Fossen

property combined to form one of the largest, if not the largest property holdings in Dunsmuir. Besides these interests, Mr. Van Fossen was engaged in the insurance and also the ice business, and maintained a water distribution system to serve residents in the Van Fossen addition . . .

He never shirked the responsibility of civic advancement, but chose to work quietly and without great public notice. However, when his leadership was needed, he never failed his community, in which he was a real pioneer . . .

Mr. Van Fossen was a leader in the campaign to establish Castle Crags State Park. It was largely through his tireless efforts, together with the cooperation of M. E. Dittmar of Redding, that the state park is a reality . . .

He was prominent in the activities of the Chamber of Commerce, Lions Club and local fire department. Fraternally, he was a member of the Dunsmuir Masonic Lodge and local pyramid of Sciots and was a Shriner . . .

Mr. Van Fossen loved his home and his spacious house on the hill was widely known for its hospitality. His thoughtfulness for others, honesty, unfailing willingness to go out of his way to accom-

modate a friend and his complete reliability were only a few of the fine qualities that gave him command of the esteem of all who knew him . . .

He was well and favorably known throughout the county and this section of the state. One of his friends said of him: "Dunsmuir has lost one of its best citizens; his family a loving husband and father."

Frank Van Fossen

Elinore in woods near home

May Van Fossen was a very public-spirited person. When her daughter Elinore was beginning elementary school in Dunsmuir, May determined that the city should have a high school. With the assistance of Mrs. Herman Woodward and Mrs. Rose Thompson, she started a petition to present to the county superintendent of schools asking that a high school be established in Dunsmuir. After many setbacks they were successful, and Dunsmuir High School became a reality in 1913. She was very active in the American Red Cross during World War I and continued her interest in all types of relief after the war ended. She was a long-time correspondent for the *"Sacramento Bee"* and occasionally was "substitute editor" for the *"Dunsmuir News"* when the owners were on vacation. She enjoyed entertaining and many young people had very happy times at "Frank and May's."

Elinore during college days

Frank and May Von Fossen's daughter Elinore attended public schools in Dunsmuir and then attended Stanford University, where she was a member of Alpha Omicron Pi sorority. Leaving college, she spent a year in New York and Europe as a traveling companion. She returned to Dunsmuir and was an "extra" clerk at the Golden Rule store. Following the death of her father, Elinore undertook the management of the Van Fossen family business interests. During the war, she spent some months working in Washington, D.C. On February 9, 1946, she married George Harrison, son of William and Beatrix Harrison of Santa Clara, California.

Elinore and George Harrison

Elinore is a longtime member of the local Dunsmuir Business and Professional Women's Club, a member of Fidelity Chapter, Order of Eastern Star, a member of the Dunsmuir Women's Club, and social advisor to the Kappa Phi Chapter of Beta Sigma Phi.

George Harrison graduated from San Jose State Teachers College in 1935 with a B.A. in commerce-accounting. He served in the U.S. Army and while doing an audit of the Shasta Daisy Ice Plant for the State Compensation Insurance Fund, he met Elinore Van Fossen on October 9, 1945. He proposed at Christmas, and they were married the following February. When George first arrived in Dunsmuir after leaving his job with the Fund, he first worked for Dan Regal at Dunsmuir Lumber. George and Elinore built the locker plant on Oak Street in 1947, and sold it in 1951, after which he worked for a San Francisco auditing firm, traveling throughout northern California until the early 1970's. He is a longtime member and past president of the Dunsmuir Lions Club, a member of the Dunsmuir Masonic Lodge, and the Elks Lodge.

Elinore and George continue to live in the Van Fossen family home, having moved it to its present position above the freeway when Interstate 5 was constructed. They manage their property as well as the remaining Van Fossen estate. They have continued the tradition of gracious hospitality and community involvement established by Frank and May Van Fossen and their home continues to reflect the warmth and affection with which the residents of Dunsmuir continue to greet each new day.

★ ★ ★ ★ ★ ★

Vera Mae Van Fossen, born in Biggs, California, came to Dunsmuir at the age of seven with her parents in 1888. She attended the public schools in Dunsmuir. She had a beautiful singing voice and was sent by her parents at the age of eighteen to San Francisco for training in voice and piano. There, she received a fine musical education and sang professionally. She had an opportunity to sing in opera, but her mother Tillie felt that such a life was inappropriate for a "proper" young woman, and Vera returned to her family in Dunsmuir. An undated, unidentified newspaper clipping which is now a family keepsake offered the following review of one of Vera's performances:

The soprano solo, "Flower Song," by Miss Vera Van Fossen, requires special mention. The "Flower Song," which is taken from that famous opera "Faust," is the most difficult and yet the most beautiful thing ever penned by the great, inspired German composer Goethe. Miss Van Fossen has a sweet voice, a pleasing voice and a voice of great range; she has a graceful and unassuming stage presence, and her interpretation of this most beautiful song was true to nature. One could plainly see that she had caught and did portray the soul and spirit that the great composer had woven into the song. We dare say that there are many opera singers of no mean order who cannot do nearly so well as did Miss Van Fossen in the rendering of the "Flower Song." For an encore she sang "The Sweetest Story Ever Told," the rendering of which further proved that the young lady truly is a vocal artist.

On October 27, 1904, in the Van Fossen family home in Dunsmuir, Vera married Dr. William Beverley Mason. Dr. Mason, who was born October 27, 1875, in Downey, California, was the son of the late Reverend William Herbert Mason and Priscilla Louise Arthur Mason, who arrived in California in 1868 from Maryland, coming by way of the Isthmus of Panama. Rev. Mason preached in the Methodist Church South in Santa Rosa and in Stockton. At the time of Dr. Mason's birth, Rev. Mason was President of Wilson College, a Methodist Church South College in Wilmington, California.

Vera Mason

Dr. William "Doc" Mason

11

Dr. Mason had graduated from the school of dentistry at the University of Southern California in 1902, begun the practice in Los Angeles, and had come to Dunsmuir on vacation in 1903. However, he fell in love with Dunsmuir and with Vera, and cancelled the lease on his new office in Los Angeles, opening an office in Dunsmuir instead where he practiced until his retirement. Following his retirement, Dr. Mason devoted his time to property and business interests.

The Masons' home with 60' long veranda

Richard Mason

Vera and "Doc" were the parents of two sons: Beverley Francis and Richard Herbert, both of whom were raised in Dunsmuir. The Masons had a home built on Beverley Way in the Van Fossen Addition, a spacious home among the pines and oaks overlooking the town. With its sixty-two-foot-long front porch, it was an ideal home for a growing family. Cousin Elinore Van Fossen Harrison can remember the sounds of youthful roller skates echoing from the wooden porch throughout the town below.

"Doc" and Vera moved to a smaller home which they had purchased and remodeled extensively on Dunsmuir Avenue in 1945. They celebrated their Golden Wedding Anniversary in 1954, just months before Doc's death on March 17, 1955. The obituary in

The Masons on their 50th Wedding Anniversary

the *Dunsmuir News* noted that "Dr. Mason was one of Dunsmuir's best known and most beloved citizens." He was active in community affairs, having served as President of the Chamber of Commerce and was a member of the Lions Club. His fraternal affiliations included the Dunsmuir Masonic Lodge, Sciots, the Shriners, and Scottish Rite.

Vera continued an active life in Dunsmuir for nearly twenty years after "Doc" passed away. She managed her own business interests and the Van Fossen estate for many years following the death of her brother Frank. Youthful in appearance and still with that beautifully sweet singing voice, she lived to an age of 95 years, 8 months.

Of the two sons of Vera and "Doc," Richard Herbert ("Dick") was a very popular young man in Dunsmuir, an avid skier, and graduate of Dunsmuir High School. He died at the age of 19 years.

Beverley Francis attended Stanford University, graduated from Chico State College with a B.A. in education, received his M.A. from Oregon State University in Corvallis, and did graduate work at the University of California, Berkeley, where he received his General Administration credential. He was a member of the Phi Delta Kappa Education Honor Society, the Kappa Delta Pi Education Honor Society, and the Epsilon Pi Tau Industrial Arts Honor Society.

On November 3, 1934, in Orland, California, Beverley married Katharine Louise Chaney, daughter of Avalin French Chaney and the late William Chaney, who had been in business in Orland for many years. Beverley and Katharine met while attending Chico State College. Beverley later worked in the Hicks and Chaney family business, a hardware and implement business, as a farm machinery salesman. After their marriage, they moved to Dunsmuir, where they lived for five years in the Mason family home on Beverley Way. The pre-World War II years in Dunsmuir were very happy years, with many dances, dinners, and other parties in which to participate. During this period, Beverley taught at Dunsmuir High

School. They then moved to Oakland, California, where Beverley taught in the Oakland Public School system for two different time periods, 1943-1952 and 1959-1969. Between 1952 and 1955, Beverley was principal of Orland Joint Union High School. In 1954-55 he served as Secretary of the California Association of Secondary School Administrators, District 9, and was a member of the statewide CASSA Curriculum Committee. Between 1955 and 1959, after the death of his father, Beverley and Katharine and their family moved back to Dunsmuir, where Beverley busied himself managing and maintaining the family property, Katharine taught for four years in the Dunsmuir Elementary School.

Beverley and Katharine Mason

Beverley was a member of the Kamloops Club on Lake Shasta, as well as the Siskiyou Outboard Club. He and his family spent many happy days on Lake Shasta. He was a past president of the Dunsmuir Lions Club. A life-long enthusiast of Scouting, Beverley served on the Board of Directors of the Oakland Area Council of Boy Scouts, and also worked with the Piedmont Sea Scout Ship Committee. He was a scoutmaster, first in Dunsmuir and, in 1934-36, in Orland. He was a member of the Orinda Masonic Lodge and Scottish Rite. Beverley Mason passed away in Oakland on October 1, 1969.

Katharine Chaney Mason attended Chico State College, where she earned her B.A. degree in

Education. She was a member of Omicron Theta Epsilon science honor society and Delta Phi Upsilon kindergarten-primary honor society. She taught at Dunsmuir Elementary School between 1956 and 1960. When her husband became ill, while they were living in Oakland, she took over his classes and became a long-term substitute. After his death she taught intermittently in the Oakland Public Schools, becoming certified as an instructor in special education. She continued teaching until 1978. In 1980, she sold her home in Oakland and moved to Dunsmuir, where she resides in the Mason home on Dunsmuir Avenue. Katharine is a member of the Dunsmuir Women's Club, the Business and Professional Women's Club, and the Siskiyou Historical Society. She retained her membership in Oakland in the Women's Athletic Club, Ebell Society, and King's Daughters. Katharine also belongs to the Colonial Dames of America, Chapter 5, and The Willows Chapter of the D.A.R. She has traveled to Europe on three occasions, on one of which she obtained her official "reindeer driver's license" after participating in a reindeer safari in Lapland.

Beverley and Katharine Mason had three children: David William, born in Dunsmuir August 5, 1942; Richard Chaney, born in San Francisco May 26, 1947; and Marianne Louise, born in San Francisco March 3, 1950.

David William attended public

schools in Dunsmuir and graduated from Dunsmuir High School in 1959. He attended College of the Siskiyous in Weed during the first year of its operation — his student body card was number 10. He worked at the Ski Bowl during its first year of operation as well. He was active in Scouting in Dunsmuir, and attended the National Boy Scout Jamboree in Valley Forge, Pennsylvania. He also spent ten days hiking on the ten-thousand-acre Philmont Scout ranch in New Mexico. After the family moved to Oakland, Dave attended Hayward State College and the University of California, Berkeley after receiving his A.A. degree from the Peralta Colleges. He served with the U.S. Marines in Vietnam and later became a commissioned officer and pilot in the Army National Guard. He completed 20 years of service with the rank of Captain. He currently resides in Sacramento, where in addition to working as a real estate agent, he continues to serve in the California National Guard.

Richard and Virginia Mason

Captain David W. Mason
Medical Evacuation Pilot
California National Guard

Richard Chaney attended public schools in Dunsmuir, and was active in cub scouts. He graduated from high school while the family was living in Oakland, and attended Oakland City College. He married Virginia Maude Russell, the daughter of Charles and Virginia Russell of Lebanon, Kentucky, on November 25, 1972.

Richard served eleven and one-half years in the U.S. Army, during which he and Virginia spent two tours of duty in Germany. Richard and Virginia are currently living in Dunsmuir, which allowed them to attend the College of the Siskiyous, from which Virginia has just received her A.A. degree. She had been a student at Eastern Kentucky University when she and Richard were married.

Marianne Louise attended the public elementary school in Dunsmuir, and belonged to the Brownies. Like her brother Richard, she graduated from high school while the family was residing in Oakland. Marianne was presented as a Daughters of the American Revolution Debutante at the Sheraton Palace Hotel in San Francisco in 1967. She attended the College of the Holy Names in Oakland prior to and during the first year of her marriage to John William Wilson II ("Jack"), the son of John William Wilson and the late Eleanor Bonner Wilson of San Bernardino, California.

Marianne's many activities include the following: in Sacramento, for the Crocker Art Gallery, vice-chairman of the Docent Program; in charge for the advanced training for all docents; on the Research Committee, she researched early California artists represented in the Crocker Collection and lectured on the results of the research; as a member of the Kingsley Art Club, she served on the board of directors and chaired two Crocker-Kingsley juried art shows; a member of the Cerebral Palsy, she did graphics for the POPPYCOC-TIONS II cookbook and served on the recipe committee; the Children's Home Guild claimed her as a member and here she was on the Guild Creations Committee and on Promotions and created for the La Casita Gift Shop a lifesize soft sculpture for a Hallowe'en promotion. In Roseville she organized the Young Women's Craft Circle, a support group for young women with small children. In Citrus Heights, she conducted children's art classes in her studio. Personally, Marianne has won awards in competitive art shows and has sold art to collectors.

Jack graduated from the University of California, Berkeley, in 1967, from the Coro Foundation (San Francisco) in 1968, and McGeorge School of Law (Sacramento) in 1983. He worked for the California State Legislature for nearly ten years, after which he served for six years as principal legislative advocate for the California School Boards Association. Marianne, an artist, and Jack, now an attorney in private practice in Sacramento, live in Roseville, California, with their two children, Elizabeth-Anne Louise ("Betsy") and John William Wilson III.

Betsy, who was born May 10, 1980, and John, who was born August 4, 1982, are the great-great-grandchildren of Levi and Tillie Van Fossen. Betsy took her first swimming lessons in the summer 1983 at the Dunsmuir municipal pool, and participated in the Playtime Partners program sponsored by the Dunsmuir Recreation Department. Both children have hunted Easter eggs in Dunsmuir park as part of the community activities. As the fifth generation of a pioneer family, they know that Vera Van Fossen Mason was correct when she remembered her first impression of Dunsmuir in 1888 as "Heaven."

Marianne Wilson

"Jack" Wilson

Castle Lake — Elinore V. F. Harrison (R.), granddaughter of one of Dunsmuir's founding fathers, Levi Van Fossen

LEVI
VAN FOSSEN
b. October 25, 1841
d. February 27, 1905

married
June 30, 1873

MATILDA
ELIZABETH
POST
b. August 24, 1850
d. April 18, 1933

FRANK BRADLEY
VAN FOSSEN
b. June 13, 1875
d. February 23, 1938

married
April 22, 1903

MAY SARAH
DUNSMORE
b. October 23, 1878
d. December 21, 1942

RUBY YREE
VAN FOSSEN
b. October, 1877
d. May 13, 1879

VERA MAE
VAN FOSSEN
b. July 29, 1880
d. April 3, 1976

married
October 27, 1904

ELINORE
VESTA
VAN FOSSEN
b. June 20, 1904

married
February 9, 1946

GEORGE
HARRISON
b. April 21, 1909

BEVERLEY
FRANCIS
MASON
b. February 5, 1906
d. October 1, 1969

married
November 3, 1934

KATHARINE
LOUISE
CHANEY
b. January 31, 1911

RICHARD
HERBERT
MASON
b. April 15, 1913
d. May 31, 1932

DAVID
WILLIAM
MASON
b. August 5, 1941

RICHARD
CHANEY
MASON
b. May 26, 1947

married
November 25, 1972

VIRGINIA
MAUDE
RUSSELL
b. June 15, 1953

MARIANNE
LOUISE
MASON
b. March 3, 1950

married
July 25, 1970

JOHN WILLIAM
WILSON II
b. April 3, 1945

ELIZABETH-ANNE
LOUISE
WILSON
b. May 10, 1980

JOHN WILLIAM
WILSON III
b. August 4, 1982

FOND MEMORIES

by
Alzade Mooney Gash

When I first came to Dunsmuir in 1912, there were no high bridges to cross the Sacramento River as there are now. Parts of the old Stage Road bridge were across the river, but the bridge was not usable. We used the road by Selby's Blacksmith Shop. At the foot of that hill there was a bridge that crossed the river to Wilkins' Mill. On Sundays many folks went down the hill to the railroad tracks and up them to Upper Soda Springs (Massons), Shasta Retreat, or on to Shasta Springs. All these were summer resorts. People usually came by train and stayed for a time. Summertime was always exciting with the tourists. I worked for two summers at Shasta Springs for the Watsons. I was their secretary. What fun! As I remember, the waters from the springs made delicious lemonade. One sad memory I have of Shasta Springs is that in 1923 one of our small orchestras left to go to Japan for the opening of a new hotel. It was the year of Japan's terrible earthquake, and no one ever heard from any of them again.

Haines Laundry was located in our neighborhood. They had replaced the washing cylinder. The old wooden one had been discarded on the side hill. I well remember that day when the neighborhood kids took a down-hill ride in it. It was rough (no paved roads), and we were tumbled around and badly bruised. The cylinder rolled to a stop landing with the door, our only out, on the bottom. Our screams drew our parents' attention. Needless to say, we didn't try that again.

When we first came to Dunsmuir, the main street and shopping area was Sacramento Avenue. Florence Avenue consisted entirely of homes. The highway had not yet gone through our city. There were Parks' Grocery, Hutaff's Jewelry Store (later Carlquist's), Wendell's Meat Market, Burgess Men's Store (later the Toggery), White House,

Levy's, Crawford's Drug Store, Tetreau-Eherenman Mercantile Company, an Italian Bakery, and Talmage's Restaurant. There was the Post Office and the Bank, and also several saloons, and, I'm sure, other places that I no longer remember. Our movies (silent) were shown in Branstetter Hall. It was managed by the Gardners. (Mrs. Gardner was Carl Summers' mother.) We had the Weed Hotel and the Weed Annex. The tiny jail was on what we called Jail Hill, a fine hill to go sledding on.

Dunsmuir had a Chinese Laundry. The Chinese picked up and delivered all the laundry in baskets, carried on their heads. (One of the children was in school when I was.) At Christmas we would receive gifts from the Chinese: silk hankies, Chinese lilies, lichee nuts, and coconut candy.

Brown's Dairy delivered milk. I remember that Mrs. Ward walked and delivered milk, also. We used to picnic at Brown's Meadow across the river. There were lots of tiny black garter snakes. Ugh!

Many families, including ours, spent vacations up on Soda Creek. In summer we swam in the Sacramento River. Oh, so cold! One favorite place was down near Crag View. Later we went further south to the deep holes.

I remember Sam Hill who ran the *Dunsmuir News.*

I remember the Fourth of July celebrations with carnivals and many city activities. One Fourth, Senator Abner Weed spoke. Mrs. Wheeler sang the "Star Spangled Banner," and what a lovely voice she had! I remember that one Fourth, Horace Selby was married at a public wedding. I think that was in 1927. Such a time!

In winter, what snow we used to have! We had snowshoes and skis. The skis were such long, heavy wooden ones. A truck with chain drive used to take a group of us up near Shasta Springs. From there we would come down on bobsleds.

That tells you how little highway traffic there was at that time.

Once a month Father had to go to Castella to take care of the electric work and collect for Copco. My sister and I went with him in the horse and buggy. He always left us with the Valentis while he was busy. What great fun we had there!

I remember when the Travelers Hotel was built, burned, rebuilt.

My father named many of the streets in Dunsmuir in order to identify the locations of water mains and electric poles which were to be shown on the Copco maps. This was part of Dunsmuir's growth. All the Old Timers will remember the horse (Old Jim) and buggy that my father drove for Copco in the early days. Practically every young person had a ride or a picture taken on the horse. Father's first truck for the company was a chain-driven Dodge.

When we lived in North Dunsmuir and had heavy snows in the winter, my father would break a trail to town for the children. When we lived there, our neighbors with children were the Mitchells, Mackeys, Jordons, Bonesteeles, and Carpenters, whose daughter Alyce was my very close girl friend.

When we lived on Florence Avenue, our close neighbors were the Hutaffs (later the Carlquists), J. Thorntons, Sanfords, Moores, DuBoses, Bartons, Bennetts, Weamers, Van Horns, Liningers, Bartletts, McGuinnesses, Hawkins, Hargroves, and Olivers.

Tragedy struck the town when the D'Autremont brothers blew up the train in Tunnel 13 south of Ashland, Oregon, and we lost well-known friends. I was working in the Civil Engineering Department for the company at the time, and we had much office work in connection with this tragedy. I worked with Jay Givens, George Taylor, Jim Weeks, and many others.

And I remember and remember . . . .

DUNSMUIR: A SURVIVOR

by
Reva P. Coon

Many times Disaster has struck fierce blows to Dunsmuir. Every time Dunsmuir has bounced back better and stronger than ever. So many times has this occurred that the town might well have been called Phoenix. Why? The Phoenix was the legendary bird that, having been consumed by fire, rose from its ashes more beautiful than before.

Just after the turn of the century, Dunsmuir suffered its first disaster. February 9, 1902, a huge avalanche roared down Alder Creek Canyon sweeping everything in its wake and dropping giant boulders as a token of its ferocity all the way down to the river.

Anyone walking up or down Oak Street today will see several of these monstrous reminders of the destructiveness of Nature on the rampage. The *Dunsmuir News* of February 15, 1902, carried the following article about the avalanche:

HOW WATER COMES DOWN AT DUNSMUIR.

One of the Most Appalling Freaks of the Elements.

Narrow Escapes From Death and Serious Damage to Personal Property. Heroic Actions of Citizens.

The people of Dunsmuir were startled from their revery at 5:50 Sunday evening by a blast of whistle signals apprising them of immediate danger. Everyone looked about supposing a fire had started, except those citizens who had heard a most portentous sound and who were in position to apprehend disaster. Those who heard the noise, and there were many in the southwestern portion of town, began to bestir themselves. However, it was but a moment before a catastrophe presented itself; for on looking up the gulch toward Mount Bradley a scene that beggars description presented itself.

A torrent of water apparently 20 feet high

Sacramento Avenue after the avalanche

and spreading many feet came rushing down carrying with it mighty monarchs of the forest, root and branch, and great boulders which had lain undisturbed for years, as if they were mere trash. The avalanche was coming and threatened dire disaster to life and property. Those in the most immediate danger hardly had time to escape with their lives.

The first residence struck by the flood was that of F. H. Simmons one block west of Florence avenue. The wood shed being near the channel caught the force of the stream and barred the logs and rubbish from ruining his house, turning the same on its course. The damage done was considerable, as the pressure of the flood moved his house a few inches.

Fifty yards below in its path was the home of T. J. Miller. Mrs. Miller saw the impending danger and with the children screaming she aided her husband to fight the common enemy attacking the premises. By constant hard work, and the solid foundation of the house, the damage sustained was slight except washing the yard into trenches.

The new building about half completed which belongs to A. M. Leach on the opposite side narrowly escaped destruction. The foundation was racked and piles of lumber moved and scattered around. The frame was shoved forward several feet, which will necessitate the outlay of many dollars to right.

On rushed the torrent striking a newly completed house belonging to J. W. Hawkins which came near being demolished as immense quantities of debris piled

up against the front and much damage was sustained. Mr. Hawkins thinks $75 will cover the loss.

But on rushed the flood to Sacramento avenue where greatest damage was done. The immense volume of water, mud and rubbish became fiercer as it reached the declivity of the main street of the town. Probably the Magoffins suffered the most of any one family. They occupied a small frame building owned by L. Van Fossen. Mr. Magoffin was down town and his wife was at E. A. Bissel's, but apprehending evil went to her home just in the nick of time, for seeing the danger, as the water struck the house, gathered her little boy and ran for safety. It was but a few minutes until the home was invaded and everything the family had was washed out or destroyed by water and mud. One side of the house was forced away, and the building left in a most dilapidated condition.

The next house north owned by a Mr. Baker was occupied by W. L. Maxey, but he and wife were down south visiting a son at school. Mrs. Charles Harper who had the premises in charge worked heroically to save the belongings. Much damage was done but not so serious as others received, the house being more on the upper incline.

The home of S. H. Depew, night foreman of the Southern Pacific round house—was a close victim. The family had just set the table and were about to sit down to supper, Mrs. Depew being in the pantry, when the fierce elements rushed in, following the dreadful uproar just heard. In less time than it takes to tell there were two feet of water and mud on the first floor deluging the *occupants and almost imprisoning Mrs. Depew before she could escape from the room. Their little child to escape from the water jumped and hung to the door knob, while Mr. and Mrs. Depew were trying to collect their thoughts to know what to do. They could save nothing but themselves leaving the contents to the fury of the flood. Besides destroying carpets and crushing large chairs a $600 piano was only saved by raising it above the slush. Mr. Depew would not estimate his loss which is considerable. The house was a new one just finished this winter and belonged to L. Van Fossen.*

Then the laundry of Sam Sing, a China-man, suffered a total loss as to contents. Sam had just received $200 worth of imported goods, and with a whole weeks laundry lost all by the waters carrying away or soiling everything almost beyond redemption. Mr. Sing said his loss was $500—all he had in the world. A reporter for the News found Sam in his shanty Tuesday with tears rolling down his cheeks bemoaning his fate. The mud was several inches deep in each room. Sam was busy Wednesday shoveling up and washing out the mud and hunting for valuables—all same as placer mining. This house is owned by L. Van Fossen.

The little cottage occupied by A. S. Griffith and wife one would suppose was above high water mark but not so, but most of the damage was done in the basement. Mrs. Griffith in trying to save some of her possessions, the house threatening to leave its foundations, seriously injured her right hand and before escaping the water had almost enveloped her. She said she was very thankful to save her life and what few things she could. A. S. Griffith is one of the dispatchers in the Southern Pacific Train-master's office here. They are temporarily domiciled in the Furlong house on Spruce street.

Then Mrs. A. D. Kilborn's large residence did not escape a visit from the overflow but with the exception of a lot of mud swept around her premises the damage was slight. This lady owns the whole block up to the Chinese laundry, and the damage to her property was about $50.

The reporter has followed just one of the three streams of water brought down from the mountains they having diverged a few hundred yards west of Florence avenue.

Just west and north of B. H. Joesink's residence the middle gulch came down with a vengeance clearing everything in its course. Logs three feet in diameter and forty feet long came rolling down like so many twigs. But fortunately there were no homes in its direct pathway. The residence of ___________, though near where the waters divided was saved by having a slight raise. There was much rubbish deposited on the premises but no actual damage.

The elegant new residence of Fred J. Hollis on which he has spent so much time and money was in great danger from logs and boulders; and but for a number of scrub trees, on a lot owned by Mrs. J.

Green, which stopped their progress, nothing could have saved total destruction. As it was mud and debris piled in the rear and banked up two feet, the mud holding the water out of the kitchen. Mrs. Hollis who was sick in bed upstairs called to her mother and nurse to come to her; that if the first floor was submerged they might be safer there.

The Joesinks and Shearers and others went to the rescue of the Hollises and worked manfully to protect the property and lives of the ladies, Mr. Hollis being below seeking health. Mrs. Hollis bore up under the strain and excitement with much fortitude, though unable to leave her bed. Geo. E. Shearer's residence, half a block east of the Hollis home, did not escape visitation of mud and debris. But his woodshed caught most of it and saved his living quarters. Many feet of wire fencing and one large apple tree were destroyed, and the yard left in a damaged condition. From here the overflow turned into the south or third channel which was the largest of all and acres of ground mostly unoccupied were washed and trenched strewing underbrush and immense stones all over. Mr. Fox's new residence was on the edge of the current but escaped any damage. Not so with the George Williams place, a new house about finished. It withstood the storm but was somewhat damaged by large logs wedging underneath. The basement

not being boarded in probably saved the whole building from tumbling. Mr. Williams estimated his loss at upwards of $75.

Frank Talmage, of the Home Bakery restaurant, was the greatest sufferer in this section. He owned a nice little home where he has been cozily situated with his family. Before the storm the street was in good condition and sand and grass held sway. Now it looks like a deserted mining camp which had been hydraulicked for a whole season, gulleys and rocks large and small are all over the ground. One large boulder came tumbling down and was seen by Mrs. Talmage apparently coming against the house, but turned and

CONTINUED ON PAGE 3, COLUMN 5.

NOTE: The remaining part of this article not available.

Hardly had Dunsmuir recovered from this disaster when another, even worse, hit the town. On April 3 or 4, 1903, a big fire consumed practically all of the business district as well as several homes. One of these homes was that of Levi Van Fossen. The picture below shows Mrs. Van Fossen standing in the midst of the smoldering rubble that had once been her home.

Mrs. Van Fossen in ruins of home

18

L. Van Fossen home

A very personal account of the fire was written in a letter by Levi Van Fossen to his wife and daughter, Vera. The Frank, herein referred to, is his son, who was to have been married just a few days after the fire. His marriage to May Dunsmore took place as planned despite Frank's hands having been burned. It is with the permission of the Van Fossen Family that the letter appears here.

My Dear Wife and Daughter:

I let Frank write yesterday, as I could not see to write, my glasses are in the ashes. But as Frank saved two drawers out of the cases, to day when he brought the drawers to our new house, I found a pair in one of the drawers. Our over coats that hung in the hall Frank grabbed as the flames drove him out. And from the dining room he saved my drawer, and I think, a drawer from your dressing case, and some clothes of that hung behind the curtains in your room, and then as he ran out with these he grabbed the type writer. Every thing else was burned. I tried to stop the fire in the house next to ours, but the flames covered the whole place from the business building and wrapped around our house and the others north of it, and before I was forced to flee, five houses in front of ours were all in flames at once, so we were almost shut in and had to run. I tried to get into our house after I abandoned the hose, but the flames scorched my eye lash as I opened the door, so I tumbled backwards and we ran. My dear little camera is gone. The negatives of May were in some books on the table with all our acct. books, and all went together. My dear little Vera, I have found a few of your little cups and some other things. About ten minutes after the fire crossed the street from the hotel, the whole lower part of town was in flames. It did not burn one building after another, but the strong north wind carried the flames from Gongwer's building clear down to Gills lodging house and the flames of the Western clear over our house, so we were in the midst of an ocean of flames. Our store house and machine shop were burning before we abandoned the home. From the store house and shop, nothing was saved.

Frank has collected a dozen or so of the dishes he and May had in the store house. Forsythes did not save any thing. Some of our neighbors across the street saved a few things. Coles saved three beds and the clothes, but some body gathered in two lots of the bed clothes, and one of the odd mattresses they have loaned us, and now if some other kind neighbor will lend us some bed clothes, we need not walk sentinel to keep warm. Beds and eating places are at a premium, but we have been overwhelmed with kind invitations to some thing to eat and places to sleep. Last evening I had supper at Campbells. But as Malones offered us shelter and plenty to eat we will stay there to eat till the restaurant gets started, that will be tomorrow. Of course we will pay them. Silbys are with Campbells. Dougherty has the car shops for a dining room, Specht is building a shack on the site of the old restaurant and will give meals tomorrow. Three saloons were rebuilt and opened before the ashes were cold (15 hours after the flames hit them). Dougherty and Mc-Mann's will be opened to day. Before sundown Sunday we had our new home built, and lacking a cook stove, dishes, table, and something to cook, we were again at home. The cracks between the boards do for windows and the door can stand open for more light. King is here and I will order a stove and some cooking things, and you may get some dishes, a table (or we can make a temporary one), some chairs (I am sitting on a saw horse now), bed clothes, matresses, pillows and other things you may think of, and then it might be well to get some clothing for me as now I have on Ward's shoes, Malones shirt, O'Malley's socks and drawers and a stay hat, but my own pants. The night was very cold and I was perfectly drenched, and as we were at O'Malleys when we stopped the things we saved, they asked us in, so we left the things there and they offered us dry changes. And my shoes were so soaked that when I got them off they would not go on again, and Mr. Ward who now lives in the next house loaned me an old pair of his.

*We fought mid flame and smoke
To save the old home place
In fury the north wind broke
And the flames rolled over the
   place.*

*With flames on all sides
From a sea of fire we fled,
Blistered and bleeding
To the cold mountain side*

I wrote Frank and Annie today, so that they might not get a false impression from what might be said in the press dispatches about the fire. I don't want grandpa and grandma to worry over it.

Tonight is pretty cold so I will go to bed early. Four different parties contributed to make up my bed outfit. Mrs. Jeter loaned us two rocking chairs and the bed springs, the only things she saved. Mrs. C. Gill was just in to see me in my new home (Frank is out somewhere), poor boy, it is a hard blow on him. I want him to go ahead and get married and go ahead with the mill. He and May can do better together than he can alone. But I don't want to advise very much, as I make enough mistakes of my own.

Mrs. Gill said she wished she had as good a house as ours on her lot, and she would rather live in it than to board out.

Mr. King promised to see me again, but went away and did not call, so he may have been afraid to sell to us. So you had better select a stove. It will do till we get another range.

If you came home now it might seem odd as you would have to stop with some of your friends till we can fix a place, as there is no place we could rent, and it would seem hard to ask a tenant to move when there are no houses, so I thought it might be better to stop a few days at uncle's, as a visit there might do you good.

I will sleep in the new home tonight. Mrs. Reading let me have some bedding. I think Frank told you about the start and ending of the fire. Every business place was burned except the meat market. It took the business street from the market to Lelands - house next to plumbing shop, which is now the P.O. and all on our street from the stable to the next street south except Malones homes, 13 buildings. About twenty minutes decided all.

If we could get lumber, we would rebuild immediately, but it may be several weeks before we can get any building lumber, so I don't see that you can do a thing if you were here. So it may be better for you to stop a short time in the Valley, as by that time we may fix up a place where you can stay and not have to depend on going to the neighbors who would be very glad to give you a place. The new home is 12 x 16, but we can stand up a lean-to, or bedrooms. But we were in good luck to get the lumber for this. (We need towels and lots of soap.) My hands are African brown.

Frank's hands are better today and his mustache is improving after the scorch.

The Post Office is in the M. F. & P Co.'s plumbing shop. The telephone office is in the old jail, and across the street from the burnt block, on the RR land, are several tents all full of business, and four or more temporary sacks are being

built for business. Jerry Wilson, the jeweler, is building one, and says he has sent for a large plate glass window, and says, he is going to have a nice plate glass window, even if he has to stand and hold it without any house. I have given the barber permission to build on the line of the sidewalk in front of the old place, as all the new temporary buildings are on the sidewalk ground and in the street. It is a busy town now. Forty or more men are hammering and sawing.

How I wish I had my dear little camera. Last night was freezing cold and where the broken hydrants are there were many icy clusters.

*Love and kisses,
PaPa*

Almost immediately after the fire, Dunsmuir began rebuilding. Fine, wooden structures rose from the ashes.

On August 15, 1921, the News carried the account of another fire. This time it struck the Hutaff Building, which is now the Travelers Hotel. The hotel did not burn, but the auditorium next to it did. The conflagration roared south devouring the People's Cash Store and the new Frank Talmadge Building. If the Hutaff Building had not been fireproofed, many other businesses to the north would have gone up in smoke, too. The fire had started in the auditorium where men had been cleaning up and burning trash after a Sciots Ceremonial. The big, new apartment building (known as the Hollis Apartments) on the corner of Shasta Avenue and Pine Street was scorched but saved. Eight days after the fire, a movement was started to reorganize a volunteer fire department.

One of the West's most sensational robberies took place on October 11, 1923. A horribly bungled attempt to rob the S.P. train, "The Gold Special," was perpetrated near Tunnel 13 in the Siskiyou Mountains on the Siskiyou Line. This unsuccessful heist left three railroaders and one postal clerk dead. Killed in cold blood were Engineer Sidney Bates, Fireman Marvin Seng, and Brakeman

Charles O. Johnson. The mail clerk was burned to death in the mail car when it was dynamited. All Dunsmuir was grieved and shocked at the tragic loss of the railroaders.

The would-be robbers did not net a dime for their audacious crime. The hold-up men were three brothers: Hugh, Roy, and Ray D'Autremont. The search for them triggered the greatest manhunt ever conducted by the inspectors of the U.S. Postal Department. No fewer than 2,450,000 circulars were sent all over the civilized world in the search for the robbers. Even with this barrage of publicity, the D'Autremonts remained at large until 1927. It was a newspaper story that lead to the identification of the brothers.

A giant conflagration brought Dunsmuir to its knees in April, 1924. This fire destroyed twelve buildings. Completely incinerated were the Methodist Church and Parsonage (loss: $30,000 — only $13,000 insurance); the residences of Cora Leach and that of Dr. Horner; the Dunsmuir *News* Plant; the Riverview Rooming House; two Southern Pacific houses; Manfredi Bakery and Store; the Episcopal Church and its Parsonage; and the Knights of Pythias Hall. It was there that the fire had started. Earlier that evening the Eastern Star had had a banquet in the hall. Members of the Star had left the

A search party forms near the south entrance to tunnel No. 13 after the "Gold Special" had been blown open and four men killed in one of the west's most sensational train robberies

Sacramento Avenue the morning after the fire. Note the only remaining building: DES School

building about an hour before the fire broke out. By the time the fire was discovered, the hall was almost totally involved. It was thought that the fire had ignited from the flue. All of the buildings except the Methodist Church were wooden structures, and so the blaze spread like wildfire.

Fire crews of the Pacific Power Company, the City, and Sisson (now Mt. Shasta) and adequate water pressure prevented the fire from spreading further. What follows is an eye witness account of the 1924 fire as Audrey Moore Mcleod (then a young teenager) saw it from across the street in the second-story window of her Grandmother Lee's home.

I SAW THE 1924 FIRE

by
Audrey Moore McLeod

My Grandma Lee's home was situated on Florence Avenue (now Dunsmuir Avenue) just north of the California Theater on the lot where the Cornet Store stands today. I don't remember how it happened that I opted to stay that particular night with Grandma in the front bedroom. I woke up with a start — strange, eerie shadows were bouncing off the walls. Men were shouting in the street below, and most frightening of all, the Southern Pacific fire siren was shrieking like all the banshees this side of Ireland. That siren was really something! It made the chills run up and down my spine even if it sounded only for a dry run. I crawled to the window at the foot of the bed.

Flames were leaping high over the hill from Sacramento Avenue. The BIG FIRE was well on its way. The day was April 25th, 1924; the time, 12:20 A.M. Across the street from me I heard Mrs. Leach's prize canned fruit and vegetables exploding like giant firecrackers on Fourth of July. It was a terrifying experience for anyone but especially for a young teenager! I had to desert my vantage point; the flames were too hot. Good thing I did!

Seconds after I backed away the window panes shattered into a million pieces. The paint on Grandma's house blistered. All the foliage on the trees and the shrubs in the front yard were seared.

In all, twelve buildings burned that awful morning. It was thought the fire had started in the Knights of Pythias Hall, which stood just on the northeast corner of the lot where the old elementary school had stood. The conflagration consumed the River house, Moran Apartments, Manfredi's Grocery, the Southern Pacific homes of Superintendent H. A. Culp and Division Engineer J. A. Given. To the north between Florence Avenue and Sacramento Avenue, the Episcopal church and Parsonage went up in flames, as did the Methodist Church and Parsonage (on the spot where TEXACO is today). The fire continued devouring its way with the Leach home and the offices of the Dunsmuir *News* (at that time). Elmer Jenks was owner and publisher then.

Dunsmuir has suffered a number of destructive fires, but this one in 1924 would be hard to beat. It is remembered as the BIG FIRE.

Those of us who are left to remember will never forget!

Once again the indomitable spirit that had filled people in the past brought about newer and finer buildings than those which had been destroyed. The News reported 1925 as a year of much building activity.

On July 29, 1935, Dunsmuir was dealt another heavy blow when Police Chief Jack Daw was shot to death by a hold-up man. Daw had been called to apprehend two men who had robbed Mike's Place in Castella. Traffic officer "Doc" Malone was with him and was grazed by the bullet that hit Daw. In the search for the hold-up men, an abandoned car was found on the McCloud Cutoff. Two miles south of Dunsmuir, two men were seen walking along the highway. On being stopped, one man opened fire, killing Daw. He then fled. As soon as word of the killing reached town, a posse was immediately formed to search for the culprits. One was apprehended, a C. L. Johnson. He admitted to being implicated but denied the killing. After being taken into custody, he was brought to the Yreka jail.

On August 3, 1935, a vigilante party of approximately 50 men left Dunsmuir about midnight and

Dunsmuir Elementary School burned June 5, 1925

22

drove to Yreka. There, at the County Jail, they overpowered Deputy Sheriff Lange. Then they spirited Johnson out of Yreka to a spot about 300 feet down the Fort Jones road. There they strung him up to a gree and hanged him. No one ever knew who the vigilantes were, and no one ever admitted to being a part of the posse. In July 1936, the G-Men launched a search for the slayer of Chief Daw. Robert Miller Barr was captured in San Pedro on suspicion of burglary. He denied that he had fired the shot that had killed Daw. Barr told an amazing story. He had hidden in the hills three miles from Dunsmuir while being hunted. For six days, he claimed, he was without food. Later he worked two or three weeks for the highway crew near Weed. Amazingly, also, he had appeared in eight scenes in the movie, ROSE MARIE, which was filmed in the Lake Tahoe region.

In September, 1944, a fire roared into Dunsmuir again, this time striking the Weed Hotel. It was as though Demon Fire had jeered to himself, "So-o-o-o I didn't get you in 1924 when I stormed into town. Ho! He! He! I'll get you this time!" The Weed Hotel was completely gutted. This night fire lit up all Dunsmuir with the brilliance of noonday; this time the Demon claimed two lives: Jack Mays and Delbert Taylor. Jim Murdock and Harold Kramer distinguished themselves as heroes in saving Austin Badger, trapped on the fourth floor of the hotel. They also rescued Miss Blanche Fowler from the fourth floor. Clyde Jordan helped Murdock in bringing her to safety. (Full story in the chapter on the Dunsmuir Fire Department).

The building was completely ruined, leaving only the brick walls standing. From the ashes of the old structure, a new, exciting hotel was erected, a beautiful hotel which boasted northern California's first rooftop parking area and was acclaimed as perhaps the most attractive hostelry in the north state. In recent years, the building has been converted into apartments for senior citizens.

A blaze in a liquor store across the street from the "Best Water On Earth" fountain claimed the life of a Dunsmuir fireman, Belnap. This tragedy hit on November 29, 1947. Honoring the memory of Belnap, the fountain was built by firemen comrades and friends. Now it invites the thirsty traveler to stop and drink of the best water on earth. A fuller account of the fountain can be found on the page dedicated to Fireman Belnap by his family.

Flooding of the Sacramento River on several occasions has threatened Dunsmuir residents. The river has swept over its banks damaging and sometimes washing away homes, gardens, and prop-erty. One young woman who had lived in a home on the river remembers being carried from their home in the arms of her father during high water.

During the first half of the century about to end, winter snows were always deep and usually lasted until spring. Occasionally, in more recent years, the snow has been deep enough again to "write home about." The extremely heavy, wet snow of January, 1966, did a great deal of property damage. Among the spectacular victims of the storm was the Methodist Church building on Castle Avenue. It was being used at that time as the Sunday School Building. Under the heavy weight

Raging Sacramento engulfs home

Rescue on Butterfly Avenue

of the snow, the church crumpled
and fell into the basement, a pile of
rubble in which only one thing was
found: an upright piano which had
received no serious damage.

Dunsmuir had to be strong to
withstand the repeated attacks of
Disaster. Its strength comes from
the strong people who make it live
and from the strong mountains
which surround it and support it.
Marching down the years, Dunsmuir has been indomitable against
the assaults of avalanche, flood,
crime, and fire. May its strength
grow as it moves into its second
century of living and is transformed
from the lusty, little railroad town
of the last century to the heart of
one of the most beautiful recreation
areas in the entire country.

A home being swept away

The river twisted and tore out rails and ties

—Photos by David Van Fleest

*Dunsmuir Band
- Circa 1920*

THE PIONEERING MASSONS
By Marcelle Masson

Dunsmuir Pioneer Receives Interesting Early-Day Data

On Tuesday of this week, Mrs. Elda Masson of Upper Soda Springs was visited by a friend of her girlhood days, Mrs. Mae Helene Bacon Boggs of San Francisco. Mrs. Boggs, who is soon to publish a book called "My Playhouse was a Concord Coach," and which is a reminiscence of pioneer life in Shasta and Siskiyou Counties, left some excerpts from her manuscripts with Mrs. Masson.

Mrs. Masson has kindly consented to permit the News to publish the selections from Mrs. Boggs' book. They constitute a most interesting account of happenings that took place in Siskiyou and Shasta county during the years from 1855 to 1857. Lack of time in which to set the material in type for today's paper makes it necessary to postpone its publication until the next issue of the News. It will be well worth looking for in next week's issue of this paper.

—*Dunsmuir News*
October 4, 1940

Shasta Wonderland History Taken From Old Papers

The News is indebted to Mrs. Elda Masson, the oldest living pioneer resident of Dunsmuir, and to Mae Helena Bacon Boggs of San Francisco, author of "My Playhouse Was A Concord Coach," for a most interesting bit of history of the Sacramento river canyon.

As stated in the last issue of this paper, excerpts from the manuscript of Mrs. Boggs' work will be published in this issue. It will undoubtedly be of great interest to every resident of Dunsmuir and vicinity. The several excerpts, all of which are taken from various newspapers published in the fifties, and which were collated by Mrs. Boggs, are of such length that lack of space will not permit publishing all of them in this issue. Therefore, they will be published in two or more installments.

The "Ross McCloud" mentioned in the old newspaper clippings was the father of Mrs. Masson and the original owner of Upper Soda Springs, known before railroad days as "Soda Springs" until a resort at Castle Crags was called Lower Soda Springs.

Mrs. Masson says the trail spoken of in these articles crossed the Sacramento river about two hundred yards west of the present highway bridge and that she remembers it distinctly. The clippings were intensely interesting to Mrs. Masson since it all took place before she was born and she had no idea so much data on the "McCloud Trail" could be found.

Along with the historical interest of the following old clippings, one is amused at the amount of punctuation used in the writings of those days in

(Continued on page three.)

—*Dunsmuir News*
October 11, 1940

SACRAMENTO UNION, Thursday, September 24, 1857.

THE SODA SPRINGS OF SISKIYOU COUNTY. Mineral springs are not confined to any particular location of our state, and everywhere they are being converted to the pleasure and recreation of our citizens. The Yreka UNION of September 17th, ___?___ speaks of the springs in Siskiyou county. There are numerous soda springs in the county. Most or all of which, we believe, possess valuable medicinal properties; but the local spring which is generally understood as being referred to when we speak of "Soda Springs," and which we have now in mind, is situated about forty miles from Yreka, at the first crossing of the Sacramento river in the McCloud or Sacramento road. The place is fast becoming one of public resort, and bids fair, at no distant day, to equal in attraction any of the watering places in the country. During the present summer, especially the sick season, many of our townsmen, ourselves among the number, have tested the benefits of the water and the unrivaled mountain air, as it floats down, pure and uncontaminated, from the snowy summit of Mount Shasta which overlooks the spot. The water of the springs is strongly impregnated with soda, iron and sulphur; it is pleasant to the taste, and, by the addition of a little lemon or other syrup makes a delicious beverage. The active medicinal properties of the water combined with the pure mountain air, the excellent trout fishing in the Sacramento and the small streams putting into it in the neighborhood, and plenty of game in the mountains and hills, make the Soda Springs a very desirable resort during the summer season for invalids and persons of leisure who can afford time for a little healthful recreation. The property is owned by Ross McCloud, the pioneer of the Sacramento trail, who has spent the last six or seven years without profit or reward, in opening this route to the public, but who is now about to reap the fruits of his praiseworthy efforts. He is now erecting a spacious new house on the premises, which, when completed, will furnish accommodations to visitors and travelers. The house is kept by Mr. and Mrs. Stephens, formerly of the Yreka hotel.

—*Copies for Mrs. Elda McCloud Masson, by Mae Helene Bacon Boggs.*

(Conclusion)

Drinking fountain just south of S.P. Depot

SACRAMENTO BEE, Wednesday, July 23, 1930.

SUPERIOR CALIFORNIA NEWS
Old-Time Cookstove Good Enough For Her

Daughter Of Dunsmuir's First Settlers Recalls Days When Alexander Dunsmuir Gave Fountain To Town

---

Dunsmuir (Siskiyou Co.), July 23.—"My old cook stove," says Mrs. Elda Masson, the oldest settler in Dunsmuir, "suits me better than the finest electric range in the country." Mrs. Masson uses the stove, which has served her family more than a half a century.

The old stove, purchased in 1876 for a hotel, is older than Dunsmuir. The town came into existence in 1886, nearly thirty years after Mrs. Masson's parents settled near the Upper Soda Springs.

Settled By Shastans.

For nearly three-quarters of a century this pioneer ranch has been the home of Mrs. Masson. She lives there with her two sons, Charles and Richard, and their families. A third son of Mrs. Masson's, James, lives in San Leandro.

Mr. and Mrs. Ross McCloud, Mrs. Masson's parents, were the first and only persons in Dunsmuir for many years. Coming from what was old Shasta, to their new home on pack horses in 1855, the McClouds purchased their property from two brothers who were mining on the Sacramento River, which winds through the present Masson farm. For years the McClouds were the only settlers between the Castle Rock Station and Sisson.

Doctor 45 Miles Away.

Their only companions were travelers and the Indians, who came to the deep pools of the Sacramento River to spear salmon. The nearest doctor was forty-five miles distant.

Mrs. Masson recalls her father surveyed the first wagon road from old Shasta to Yreka. This road was finished in the early '60s, shortly after Mrs. Masson was born. What was then the only highway through this part of the country runs by the Masson home to-day, a dirt road.

Roadhouse Still Stands.

On the Masson ranch stands the oldest building in this section. Built in 1864 as a hotel, the building stands as a monument to the early pioneers of Dunsmuir. The old landmark was the only lodging house between Sisson and a roadhouse fifteen miles south of Dunsmuir. It served as a stopping place for the old stage coaches which tarried, as do the motorists of today, to allow the travelers to drink from the soda springs, which abound in this district.

Another hotel was opened ten years later, near the one built in 1864. It is still standing, too, Mrs. Masson's favorite half-century-old cookstove was purchased for the later hotel.

British Nobles Visit.

Many are the stories told by Mrs. Masson of the English sportsmen who made the McCloud-Masson hotels their headquarters while they fished and hunted in Siskiyou County.

"In the middle '70s," she says, "a Sir Rose Price, a Welshman, who later wrote a book about his experiences in California, made our place his headquarters. He was a great athlete and sportsman.

Towed By Salmon.

"One day he discovered a new pastime. While fishing in the upper Sacramento River he hooked an enormous salmon. Unable to draw in the fish, he jumped into the pool, line and all, and clung to the line while the fish furnished him a free and exertionless swim by pulling him about in the water. When the fish tired of being a locomotive Sir Rose Price landed his catch."

Dunsmuir's oldest living pioneer pictures early Dunsmuir as a tiny flat heavily wooded and without inhabitants until the '80s. In 1887 Dunsmuir sprang into existence with a boxcar as a depot and a cluster of log cabins housing about 200 persons.

Boxcar Was Depot.

"The boxcar, resting on a siding," declares Mrs. Masson, "served as a waiting room, ticket office, telegraph office and express station."

The place derived its name from Alexander Dunsmuir, a coal baron of British Columbia, who passed through the little hamlet in the early days. Alexander Dunsmuir agreed to donate a fountain for the depot plaza if the town were given his name. The townsfolk accepted the proposal, and the fountain still adorns the little park.

SAN FRANCISCO CHRONICLE
July 23, 1948

Siskiyou County Notebook — Part IV

By Robert O'Brien

The country around Dunsmuir, just south of Mt. Shasta and close to the southern border of Siskiyou county, is a country of river canyons and gorges, of tall pines and firs standing high on mountain ridges against the sky, of logging camps and loaded lumber trucks pounding down the highway, of tourist camps beside the road and clear, sharp, pine-scented air, of swift fishing streams and the hills that hunters love.

The background of the region is mainly the story of the trappers' trails, and the development of the California-Oregon Trail, which wound down past Shasta linking Oregon and the far northern mines with the Sacramento valley, and the dusty mountain stage roads that later skirted Shasta's base.

It would, perhaps, be an offensive omission to Dunsmuirians to neglect a mention of one of their proudest boasts: Their town, they believe, in addition to being the center of some of the greatest hunting and fishing country in the West, drinks "the best water on earth."

In fact, the mineral springs inspired its first name, Soda Springs, which later, in Uncle Dick Mannon's time in the sixties and seventies, was changed to Upper Soda Springs. In the past of the town, it is the names of the McClouds, the Frys, the Campbells, the Massons and Uncle Dick Mannon that stand out, for at one time or another they were all connected with the inn, built of sugar pine timber, that stood near the springs and beside the stagecoach road.

The McClouds, Ross and Mary, were the first to operate the inn, arriving there in 1855, three years after the discovery of gold 50 miles up the Shasta valley at what is now Yreka. One might assume that it was for this pioneer family that the McCloud river and lumber town of McCloud was named, but this was not the case. It seems the river (and later the town) was named for Alexander Roderick McLeod, a Hudson's Bay Company trapper and brigade leader who traveled through the region in the late 1820's. Early mapmakers misspelled his name, writing it "McCloud."

When the McCloud family finally settled there and became prominent in the area (Ross McCloud was the first county surveyor of Siskiyou), newcomers logically took it for granted that the "McCloud" river honored his industry and contributions to the development of the country. Many natives are still under this impression, and the name of Alexander Roderick McLeod has been forgotten by nearly all but students of local history.

Parenthetically, it was Elda, daughter of Ross and Mary McCloud, who named the Dolly Varden trout, for which the McCloud river is famous, and thus perpetuated, among fishermen at least, the fashionable dress style of the sixties. Elda, who later married into the Masson family, died only four years ago.

It was in the seventies, when Uncle Dick and George Campbell were operating the hotel at Upper Soda Springs, that the community became nationally known for an incident that is still a lively topic of conversation among old-timers of the region.

One day, Mrs. Campbell was standing on the hotel veranda watching her four-year-old son play on a low hillside above the springs. All at once, to her horror, she saw a panther spring from behind an oak tree, pounce upon the child and knock him to earth. Screaming, she ran up the hill to defend the child from the beast. Uncle Dick followed her with his rifle, pursued the panther into the woods near by and killed it. The animal, a brute half-grown and lean, had painfully but not mortally torn the boy's cheek and throat with its teeth and raked his back with its claws. The oak tree, still standing, is to this day called The Panther Oak.

Uncle Dick's favorite pastime in his last years was playing cribbage with Elda McCloud, and when he won he would look at her and chuckle, "It's all in the peggin', Elda." In 1886, he fell ill. One July day, he called Elda to his bedside, told her his money was hidden beneath the toolbox in the woodshed, said good-by, and died. That year a post office was established at Upper Soda Springs, and to honor Uncle Dick the name of the town was changed to Mannon.

Meanwhile, the Southern Pacific laid its tracks down through the Sacramento river canyon, and here put down the switching yards, the roundhouse and shops of a division point. You see the yards and the chuffing engines and the freight cars down below you on the canyon floor today as you drive into Dunsmuir from the south.

The year after Uncle Dick died, Alexander Dunsmuir, a British Columbia coal baron, stopped off at Upper Soda Springs to take the waters. Invigorated by their tang and effervescence and enchanted by the mountain town, he approached officials (the legend goes) and offered to erect a public fountain there at his expense if they would change the name of the town to Dunsmuir. They agreed, and thus it has been known ever since.

(To be continued)

OAKLAND TRIBUNE
Sunday, July 8, 1945

Upper Soda Springs

"The other day, on my way from Yreka to Oakland," says Alex Rosborough, "I turned off the highway, just before crossing the bridge over the Sacramento River at Dunsmuir and drove down to the little meadow near Upper Soda Springs, where I found the hotel built in 1874, being torn down. The Summer following the erection of this building and for several summers following, our family went from our home in Yreka to spend a vacation at this resort. The doors to the rooms in the new hotel had not been numbered, the first time we arrived there, which led to some confusion at times. I being something of a paint-brush youngster, Mr. Fry, the proprietor, designated me to put numbers on the outside of each door, which I did with black paint. On this last trip to the Springs I found the lumber salvaged from the old building carefully piled and the doors, bearing the numbers I put there 70 years ago, saved nearby. Back in those days of the great forests of sugar and yellow pine and fir were practically untouched and what lumber the small mills sawed for local consumption was clear. Of such material was the old tavern constructed, a fact which now makes such lumber in great demand and worth saving. The old stage road ran in front of the hotel and a quarter of a mile below cross the Sacramento River and a wooden bridge, almost under where the high concrete highway bridge now goes over the river. This was a 'toll bridge' and the franchise for operating same was held by 'Uncle Dick' (Richard Mannon) who lived at the hotel and the charge for crossing the bridge was paid to him there. One day in the Winter, there was snow on the ground, the stage driver when he stopped at the Springs, reported to Uncle Dick that not very far back and only a little way from the road he had seen a mountain lion, which looked lean and hungry. Some time after the stage had proceeded on its way, little Charley Campbell, the three-year-old son of George Campbell, who was then running the place, came along to show Uncle Dick, sitting on the hotel porch, the new little hatchet his father had given him and to let Uncle Dick see how he could use it. He toddled across the road to the hillside and proceeded to chop on a small oak tree. Suddenly Uncle Dick heard him scream and looking across to where the little fellow had been, saw a California lion dragging him into the brush. Yelling as he went, Dick charged across the road and after the panther, which saw the enraged

man rushing on him, dropped the child and made off up the hill. After handing the child to his mother, who, hearing the child's screams and Mannon's yells, had rushed to the scene, the old frontiersman ran to his room, grabbed his rifle, took up the big cat's tracks, followed up and killed it. The lion was the same animal seen by the driver of the stage. One of the lion's teeth went into the little fellow's mouth and another pierced just under his chin. 'Uncle Dick' then well along in years, was a very active man. He hewed out the big timbers for the toll bridge and I have heard him tell of having walked from Yreka to the Springs, 45 miles between sun-up and sun-down, carrying a rifle on his shoulder.

First Post Office

Old-Timer Says: When the new railroad camp or station was named "Dunsmuir" in 1886 the first post office in the vicinity was established at Upper Soda Springs the following year and was called "Mannon." The Yreka Journal, Wednesday, January 12, 1887 says:

"A new post office called Mannon, has been established at Soda Springs, named after Uncle Dick Mannon, the old pioneer and former proprietor of the Springs and hotel at that place. Miss Elda McCloud, daughter of the pioneer, Ross McCloud, deceased, who first located the property, is to be post mistress of the office."

The stages would pick up the mail from whatever railroad station happened to be at the end of the line as the work of building the track progressed up the canyon, and would carry it over the gap between that place and Ashland, by way of Yreka, stopping at all Inns or stage stations en route as they had done prior to the advent of the "Iron Horse."

The post office of Mannon served its purpose for nearly a year when the new town of Dunsmuir was ready for its own post office. After the railroad had progressed to

Sisson and beyond, in 1887, the new Shasta Division was to have its headquarters at Dunsmuir and a round house, machine shop and division superintendent headquarters were in the course of erection by October, 1887.

On November 28, 1887, George McCloud, brother of Elda McCloud, was appointed the first postmaster of Dunsmuir by the Postmaster General, Wm. F. Vilas.

Old Stage Road

"The old stage road," the story continues, "passed in front of the hotel and across the road was the big barn where the stage horses were kept. The early stages changed horses every 12 miles and 'Sims' was one of the stations. The stage passengers had a meal at the tavern while the horses were being replaced. Old Sims was a great host, with a glad hand for everybody — a joker a story-teller, who loved to spin yarns for the tourists. One day the stage was ready to start and as the driver gathered up his reins there was Sim Southern standing in front of the horses, in the middle of the road, with his back to the stage, his eyes shielded with one hand, talking to himself and looking intently at Mt. Shasta. There is a beautiful view of the snow-clad mountain from this place. The stage driver called out 'What's the matter Sims? Get out of the way. What are you looking at?' (Of course the driver knew from experience that something was coming from the old innkeeper.) Sims kept standing in the way, still looking at the steep snow-covered old peak and finally said: 'I wonder if I can make it?' 'Make what?' said the driver of the stage. 'Well, you see,' replied Southern, 'there is a big party of tourists going to ride to the top of Shasta today and I was just wondering whether I could haul a load of hay up to the top for their horses and get back home before dark'."

THE NEWS
Southern Siskiyou Section
THURSDAY, SEPT. 5, 1963

Sold After 108 Years In Masson Family; Lore of Upper Soda Springs Still Lingers

The Upper Soda Springs property, after 108 years in the Masson family and their forbears, and one of the historic places in Siskiyou County has been sold to Dr. and Mrs. Harry B. Chappell. The Chappells are quite pleased with the old property and its potentials for development.

Ross McCloud, a pioneer, bought squatters rights to the property in 1855 from two Lockhart brothers who settled there in 1852 and built a log cabin and corral for the use of travelers using the trail up the Sacramento River canyon.

McCloud and a partner, Isaac Fry, built a two-story wayside inn of shakes and in 1864 built a long, low building of planed lumber from a mill McCloud had built at Berryvale (now Mt. Shasta). This old building still stands near the residence built in 1898 which the Chappells now occupy.

In 1874, Mr. Fry, who married McCloud's widow after his death in 1867, built a long two-story building, southern style, with verandas the entire length of the building; Fry, a former Mississippi River steamboat captain, placed the floors of the upstairs bedrooms a foot above the level of the verandas, so, as with his steamboat, they would not become "awash."

The older residents of the area will recall this building across the road from the mineral springs which, legend has it, were used for medicinal purposes by the Indians and are still in use.

The late Chas. E. "Pete" Masson had this picturesque old building razed in 1945 since it was in bad state of repair and a fire hazard.

For many years the two old buildings formed the basis of a summer resort business conducted by the Masson family until 1920 when the new auto camp grounds made the resort business unprofitable. It was in 1887 that Elda McCloud, Ross McCloud's daughter, married John Masson, a bookkeeper for the masonry contractor on the new Central Pacific railroad then being built up the canyon and it was they who developed the property as a summer resort.

The original property sold to McCloud contained 160 acres much of which was sold as the community settled.

Across from the property, and directly west of the buildings there was a depot (flag stop), a suspension bridge across the Sacramento River both built by the new railroad to compensate for the first right of way granted them by the owners of the property, the bridge is long since gone, as is the depot, but a piece of the cable reportedly of the type used on San Francisco's cable cars, still lies on the hillside.

The actual railroad construction which inched up the Sacramento River canyon was mostly done by pick and shovel gangs of Chinese laborers, supervised by Irish bosses; Slavonian workmen built the stone bridge piers and their work is still to be seen at the rail crossings of the river between Redding and Mt. Shasta.

The elder Mrs. Masson's autobiography says, "Tons of giant powder were used in blasting through the rock cliffs for the railroad and occasionally an unfortunate Chinese was killed by the blasting. Our hotel, not far from the construction work, was peppered with small rocks and the cows in the meadow ran wildly at the sound of the blasts.

"On long summer days freight teams with their musical bells slowly traversed the dusty, rutted road which was the old Oregon trail along the Sacramento River and the main route between Oregon and California; all our groceries, sugar, green coffee in 100-pound bags, and which we had to roast in the oven and then grind in little hand mills, chests of tea, in fact, most of our staple groceries came by freight teams from Redding, the trip taking a week to ten days; we raised our potatoes and fresh vegetables, our flour was ground in Shasta Valley mills and some came from Ashland and Fall River."

So the sale of this property, rich in pioneer lore, ends an era in the history of Southern Siskiyou, to quote Mrs. Marcelle Masson, widow of the late Chas. E. Masson, and to whom, along with Mrs. Nellie Masson, widow of Richard Masson, I am indebted for the data appearing in this article, "Time has finally caught up with us Massons and the old home place, Upper Soda Springs, now passes, for the first time, out of the family and into other hands."

THE NEWS
DUNSMUIR, CALIFORNIA
THURSDAY, AUGUST 29, 1963

Historic Masson Property Sold To Harry Chappell

Upper Soda Springs, one of the oldest residences in the area, was recently sold by Nellie Masson to Dr. Harry Chappell and his wife Patricia Chappell.

The property was acquired by the pioneer, Ross McCloud, in 1855 and was developed as an inn for wayfarers in the early days. For a number of years it was managed by George and Edna McCloud, son and daughter of Ross and Mary McCloud.

In 1887 Elda McCloud married John Masson and they developed the place into a prosperous summer resort. After his death in 1910, Elda Masson and her three sons ran the resort until 1920.

Nellie Masson married the late George Richard Masson in 1923 and came to Upper Soda in 1924. When left a widow in 1930, she began teaching in the Dunsmuir Elementary School. She retired in 1957.

Elda Masson passed on in 1944 and in 1946 Nellie Masson purchased the Upper Soda Springs property from Charles and James

Masson. She maintained the rentals on the place and kept a beautiful garden a show place of the area. She now lives at 1831 Riviera Drive, Redding.

Nellie Masson has been active in Dunsmuir Business and Professional Women's activities, the Siskiyou County Artists Association and other civic affairs. She has been interested in the preservation of the history of the early days and the activities on the old property.

In order to assist in the Museum-Park development project here both Nellie Masson and her sister-in-law Marcelle Masson of Oakland have made contributions of manuscript and artifacts to be put on display at the Museum to tell some of the history of the Massons and the Upper Soda Inn. A booth has been set aside at the Museum and many display items are already there to set up the Masson booth.

The Masson property is located just west of the Sacramento highway bridge along the Sacramento River.

Some of the earliest happenings in this area took place at the old inn where the traveler was compelled to stop for rest and food in their journey north to reach Yreka where there was gold in those early days.

Stage depot, post office, and all the early day contacts with the outside world centered in the Upper Soda Inn. Its first owner, Ross McCloud, was the power behind the building of the road to Mount Shasta (Sisson) and on to Yreka in those days.

Joaquin Miller, the fabled poet, writer and Indian fighter who lived at what is now known as the Berry Estate (Old Soda Springs) stayed at the inn.

At one time a move was started in Dunsmuir about three years ago to get the city to acquire the property for a memorial and turn it into a city recreation area.

Old timers in the area are keen on telling of their early day experiences around this old inn and relate the many "rich people" of that day who came here and spent their summers in Dunsmuir, from all over the west coast.

THE SISKIYOU PIONEER
III:2 (1959)

Early-Day Inns of Southern Siskiyou . . .

AND SOME HISTORY OF THE AREA

By Charles and Marcelle Masson

With the same zeal that prompted him to leave his comfortable home in the East and face the uncertainty of the West, the pioneer innkeeper of the 1850's dared to venture into virgin territory and there set up his public house or inn. He followed in the wake of the miner, hoping to reap his fortune in that manner.

In northern California at that time there were no established routes other than the old trails of the Indians and the Hudson's Bay trappers upon which he could choose a suitable location for a stopping place. Just such a trail followed up the Sacramento River canyon where, by this time, the goldseekers were operating in every gulch and stream. So with much foresight and faith in the possibility of a good road becoming established along that route at some future time, some of the early settlers — the pioneer hosts to a traveling public — began to erect their crude inns beside this old trail.

Among the earliest of those hardy pioneers to put up a log cabin where the wayfarer could stop overnight and perhaps get a meal were the Lockhart brothers, Samuel and Harry. In 1852 they took up a squatters' right to about 160 acres at a place called Soda Springs, later to be known as Upper Soda Springs and now a part of the town of Dunsmuir. They built a cabin near the mineral spring and a split rail fence for a corral.

In that same year Mary McCloud left her home in Iowa to join her husband, Ross McCloud, in Shasta, California. Then, with the influx of miners on Dog Creek and Slate Creek, the McClouds went up to Portuguese Flat in the next year

or two and operated an inn there, Mrs. McCloud getting girls from an Indian settlement down on the Sacramento River below her place to help her with the work. Through the Indians Mr. McCloud learned of the soda springs farther up the canyon. Upon investigation, he recognized their value as a natural stopping place on what he deemed to be the shortest route to the northern mines; so he bought the squatters' rights to the property from the Lockhart men for about $100. This was in 1855. Two years later he built a two-story inn of shakes and logs near the log cabin that was already on the premises.

The few settlers along this route by now had become road conscious as had those to the east via McCumber's Mill and the Pit River, and likewise to the west through Trinity. Having widened the trail considerably from Shasta to Soda Springs by way of Sugar Loaf and Backbone Mountains the settlers now took steps to build a road over the trail by forming a company and soliciting for funds. The construction of this hazardous road and its eventual completion in the following years is a story in itself.

The McClouds by now had neighbors to the north and south although at a distance of a good many miles. Up in Berryvale, today the city of Mount Shasta, were Mr. and Mrs. Joseph S. Fellows. In 1866 this couple left Yreka and bought the squatters' rights to the Berryvale property from two men who had a cabin there (across the road from the present State fish hatchery). Mr. Fellows added a two-story log house to the cabin. This was known as the Mt. Shasta Hotel when Mr. Fellows and his wife operated it as a stage station. It had a colorful history during the years it served the needs of the public. Mr. and Mrs. Fellows were the great-grandparents of Mrs. Lucille Ream Morgan who lives on the property now. It was her father, Henry Ream, who built a frame house on to the log house in 1902. The name was changed to the Berryvale Inn and it became a well-known summer resort. This place was razed by fire in recent years. Nearby was the Berryvale post office which was established in 1866. This small one-room building which served as both store and post office is still standing.

Washington Bailey was the name of the man who was Mr. McCloud's neighbor on the south. In 1859 Mr. Bailey acquired his property on what is now the Berry estate on Soda Creek. Through a brother who was mining on Soda Creek in 1859 Wash Bailey, as he was called, heard of the mineral spring there and was told that the place was owned by one, Amisa Ball who had the squatters' rights. (It appears that all of the choice places along this route were in the hands of others before the potential inn-keeper got there and it leads one to wish he could follow up the story of the squatter. We know what happened to the Lockharts, and it is an interesting story; but what of the others — one with a name like "Amisa Ball," for instance?) At any rate, Mr. Bailey bought the land from Mr. Ball, put up a log cabin and called his place "Lower Soda Springs" to distinguish it from the McClouds' "Soda Springs"; they, in turn, decided to call their place "Upper Soda Springs."

By 1859 some of these homes or inns could have been made of sawed lumber for the sawmill was making its appearance. Ross Mc-Cloud at that time had constructed a sawmill at Strawberry Valley, near Berryvale. In a letter to her relatives in Marysville, California on January 23, 1859, Mrs. Mc-Cloud wrote in part, " . . . Contrary to my expectations, McCloud's Mill runs finely and saws first-rate. He built it after a plan of his own and nearly all prophesied it would not go at all . . . The stage takes only one meal here now and not often that. Their time is changed for this winter. Going down, they run from Yreka to King's ranch and stay all night, next to Dog Creek, next day to Shasta. Wm. Sullaway has bought King's place and King is driving stage. There is no travel at all. They will come back here in the spring. But Sullaway was at so much expense and making so little

that he took the station for this winter . . . We had a cook until they made the change the first of December. Since then I have done all the work so you need not say I have not much to do. We board Loag's hostler all the time; and then there's one driver every night for supper and breakfast and the stage driver for dinner. Loag pays for the hostler's board but the rest are free. It is an uphill business for us but seems the best we can do at present. I prepared dinner for the up-train for awhile but found it would not pay. Going up, the train don't average four a week. But the other Road is no better off, that is some comfort. But we have some way customers from the Soda Creek mines. Little, very little it is.

"We have an old chap here who gets me wood and water and makes himself generally useful. Ross stays at the Mill most of the time. He has got a fine lot of logs to saw this coming summer. Sometimes he talks of building a little house at the Mill for us and renting this place, and again, he says he will not rent another time on no terms. Mrs. Stevens is staying with Mrs. Eddy since leaving here. The old man and Marshall have been trying to mine on Soda Creek but do not think they will get rich there soon; Marsh has been here the last two days. It is storming badly and he don't like to go.

"Mrs. Eddy was down last week and made me a good visit. Stayed three days and was intending to stay a week longer but they thought at the ranch she must come home, and sent for her. I was almost mad. Oh, it is so lonely here sometimes. If it was not for little Louie I could not stand it now. She is so much company for me and will be more as she learns to talk . . ."

We have included most of Mrs. McCloud's letter in this article on early days because it is from just such an old letter that one can get a picture of the oftentimes hard life of a pioneer wife and mother accustomed to a more genteel way of living. And from her letter particularly, we are able to learn of the progress made on the building of the road. Apparently the stages

were now able to negotiate at least a part of it. On April 2, 1859 the Soda Springs Turnpike Road Company had been organized at a meeting held at Dog Creek. A franchise was secured, a survey made by Ross McCloud, and the contract for building the road let to "Elias Stone and sons, a pioneer family from Shasta Valley."

In 1860 Mr. McCloud sold a half interest in the Upper Soda Springs property with its buildings and toll bridge to Mr. Isaac Fry, a former mining partner of his. The Mc-Clouds moved to a ranch he was buying east of Gazelle and Mr. Fry ran the Resort, as it was sometimes now called. He continued to improve it and in 1864 he built a long, low building of sawed lumber, the first of its kind in the area that was to become the town of Duns-muir. That old building, minus its porches, still stands at Upper Soda Springs. One can see the hand-cut nails and the heavy hewn timbers used in this old hotel of another day. Water for domestic use came in a flume from the river. The furniture was all homemade.

Continuing the history of the progress of the inns, Mr. Fry, in 1874, found it necessary to tear down the old buildings of logs and shakes and to put up a more imposing edifice on the premises. Ross McCloud had died in 1868 and his widow became the wife of Mr. Fry. The hotel that he built was similar in style to many that were now being built for the traveler, and as stage stops. It was 100 feet by 25 feet exclusive of the porches that surrounded it both downstairs and upstairs. There were 16 bedrooms and a large office. Mr. Fry had been a captain on a Mississippi River boat at one time, so his new hotel was unique in the fact that he dropped the floor of the upstairs porches a foot below the level of the outside bedroom doors as they did the decks of those old steamboats so the rooms wouldn't "go awash."

During the next year, 1875, a Mr. Robert Hanlon built a large two-story house about four miles below Upper Soda Springs that was to accommodate stage drivers and passengers. It was known as the

Hanlon House at the time. Across the road from it was a log cabin called the Castle Rock station where Mr. Hanlon first lived with his wife, his son William and two stepchildren, Abaija and Etta Cahow. Mr. Hanlon collected toll for Mr. L. Autenrieth who, by this time, was the owner of the Sacramento and Soda Springs Turnpike Road. In 1877 a Mr. Alex McMillen was employed by Mr. Autenrieth to take charge of the station and Mr. Hanlon devoted his time to his hotel.

From Mr. Frank Mullen now a resident of Dunsmuir we learned some of the early-day history of the canyon that was below the Hanlons' and Baileys' Lower Soda Springs. In 1879 his parents took up government land on what is now the town of Castella. Between their land and Wash Bailey's and along Castle Creek, he said, was the Huffacre place. Andy Weiger's acreage was south of the Mullens' and what is known now as Sweet Brier.

The Mullens first lived in a log cabin across the Sacramento River. Then they built a boardinghouse that stood near the site of the present Mike Padula place. Mrs. Mullen served meals mostly to those running the pack trains to the Altoona and other mines. They called their home Castle Rock. Later on, with the advent of the railroad up the canyon in 1885, Mr. Mullen changed the name of their place to "Castella," a name he had formed from the word "Castle" and the name that the railroad company adopted for their station.

Added to the history of the locality we were told that a Mr. Wheeler then built and operated a sawmill on Castle Creek. This industry started the town of Castella and the Mullens began to sell lots to the home seekers. About the year 1891 Mrs. Mullen sold a parcel of land to Mr. H. O. Wicks who, in the years following, built up a well-known summer resort there called Crag View.

The manner of travel up the Sacramento River canyon from footpath, mule train, wagon, stage and now railroad train between those years of 1850 to 1885 brought corresponding changes to those places where the wayfarer or traveler could stopl the life of those first old inns was spent, and in their place came the town hotels and the summer resorts. The REDDING REPUBLICAN FREE PRESS under the date August 4, 1883 reported "Wash Bailey, who visited Redding Tuesday says he has about completed the sale of his place at Lower Springs to the railroad company. It is rumored that the price is $20,000, and that a large hotel will be erected." He sold his place to the Pacific Improvement Company, a holding of the railroad company. Mr. Bailey went to Sisson and built a summer resort hotel, buying the land from Mrs. Fellows. But before he had left the Springs he had bought a farm near the Sacramento River in the Castle Crags area where there was a mineral spring. Eventually, the place in Sisson burned down so he and his wife moved down to this farm, calling it Castle Rock. Mr. Bailey in writing of his life years later said that the spring on this place near the river was discovered by two miners who wing-dammed the ground for mining purposes and that they had taken out about $1,400 in gold there. The Baileys later sold this Castle Rock property to a syndicate in Sacramento headed by Mr. George Parkinson which soon sold out to the Traveling Men's Association. This group, it is reported, expended a great many thousands of dollars in improvement and the resort became very popular. There was a large two-story hotel beside the road with a separate long dining room and kitchen. These buildings stood across the road and were not far from the present State park buildings north of Castella. Across the railroad tracks was a bottling works, and nearby, a swinging bridge across the Sacramento River to the mineral spring that the aforementioned miners had uncovered at an earlier time.

This resort closed about the year 1919, we were told, and the buildings were either destroyed or burned. This area is now included in the State park at Castle Crags.

Dunsmuir made its appearance in 1886, decidedly a child of the railroad, for it was there that the company decided to establish a railroad terminal with shops, a roundhouse and offices. Soon, it was a thriving community with a hotel, rooming houses, churches and a school. The town received its name from the Dunsmuir family of Vancouver Island, British Columbia. They were very wealthy owners of coal mines in British Columbia. Alexander Dunsmuir, a son, took care of the family interests on the wharves in San Francisco where they shipped coal and it is said that he promised that their family would present the new settlement with a fountain if the railroad officials would call the place "Dunsmuir." The *Yreka Union* dated August 28, 1886 reported that "The railroad named for the new station at Cedar Flat is Dunsmuir." And the Mott newspaper, the *North Star*, on June 3, 1888 stated that the "Hon. R. Dunsmuir, the millionaire owner of coal mines in British Columbia, after whom the town is named, intimated while in Dunsmuir lately that he would present the town with a fountain to be placed in the open space in front of Bilicke's Mount Shasta Hotel, the fountain to be supplied from Mr. Bilicke's hydrant." This is the same fountain one sees on the small terraced lawn south of the railroad station in Dunsmuir. Mr. Bilicke's hotel was where the Weed Hotel was built in later years, and is now a part of the Dunsmuir Hotel.

The once-famous summer resort, Shasta Springs, about five miles north of Dunsmuir began its colorful life shortly after the new railroad made its way up the canyon. The spot also had its share of pioneer history prior to that. From Mrs. Annie Scott Fussler, a long-time resident of Dunsmuir, we learned its story: In 1886 the Scott family arrived in Dunsmuir from Roseville, California. The trip was made to Redding by train, to Sim's Station by work-train and then on to Upper Soda Springs in a spring wagon. The hotel at the Springs was crowded so the family went on to Galpin's place which was a stage stop with a store and rooms and was a mile up the road and opposite what is now the entrance to Shasta Retreat.

Mr. Scott together with three other men filed on four timber claims, some of them later to become Shasta Springs holdings. Each man built a one-room cabin on the adjoining corners of the sections making it a four-room dwelling, as well as abiding by the laws of the homesteader. The other men were bachelors so they turned over their interest in the cottage to the Scott family for the time being in order that they might have a more spacious home. Mr. Scott soon discovered mineral springs on his section of timbered land. He put a barrel over the spring, then a roof overhead and some benches around it. He built a sawmill on his property that became known as Scott's Mill. Thinking of the value of his mineral spring, he suggested to some men who had come up from the Bay area that a corporation be formed to bottle the water and market it. This was the beginning of the Shasta Water Company and then the Shasta Springs Resort. The mineral spring was conveniently close to the new railroad line where the water could be bottled and shipped. Cabins were built on the level ground above, and eventually more imposing buildings took their places and a tramway ran from there down to the railroad station and bottling works below.

A few more resorts and towns appeared now in conjunction with the progress of the railroad in southern Siskiyou. The town of Mott, for instance, north of Shasta Springs, became a thriving sawmill community supplying lumber for the new little towns as well as helping to provide fuel for those wood-burning engines on the railroad. Frank Mott was the name of the first roadmaster in Dunsmuir, hence the name. The Blohm Hotel in Mott must have been lavishly furnished judging from a few very handsome mid-Victorian pieces that we recently saw in a Dunsmuir home, the owner telling us they had come from this old hotel when the furnishings were sold and the town of Mott became only a memory.

The most pretentious summer resort in the southern Siskiyou area in 1892 was the Castle Crag Tavern built by the Pacific Improvement Company — a holding of the railroad company on Wash Bailey's former Lower Soda Springs property. He had sold this property to the railroad people, some of whom (the Crocker family) had built large summer homes there. A saddle trail of 15 miles was built east to Horseshoe Bend on the McCloud River where Mr. Sisson kept a lodge for anglers. A 10-mile trail was built on the west side to Castle Lake and a trail up Castle Crags for the hiker. As well as a hotel, there was a club house and a private dining room for children and their nurses. In a May 14, 1892 copy of *The Wave* magazine it was stated in an article about this very fine new tavern that "Comfortable accommodations will be made for 150 persons, and the charges will be moderate, averaging $14 per week. It is now expected that the Tavern will be ready for occupancy on June 1st, and remain open until the last of November." It was short-lived, however, being razed by fire about 1900. One of the Crocker cottages burned in later years but one still stands on the grounds and has been used in subsequent years as a summer resort hotel, the property having changed hands several times. Now it is in private ownership.

Another popular summer resort in its heydey was Shasta Retreat, northwest of Dunsmuir and on the Sacramento River. The land was first owned by some Methodist ministers who, in 1895, formed what they called the "Shasta Vicino Camp Association." They sold stock in the venture and laid out home sites and streets on both sides of the river, naming the streets after some of the ministers. The undertaking proved successful and the area became the property of others who sold lots for private summer homes. It supported a store, recreation hall, hotel and dining room in the summer season. A railroad station is still there but out of use and there are now many private homes, especially in the area between the river and the present-day highway. One can still see the remains of the fine swimming pool that was down by the river in those early 1900's.

With the coming of the automobile, the summer boarder who used to come up on the train with his trunk prepared to spend a vacation of two weeks or even a month at one of the summer resorts mentioned, now came by auto and merely stayed overnight, planning to cover as much territory as possible. A descendant of Mary and Ross McCloud who was operating the Upper Soda Springs Hotel — it having always remained in the hands of that family — finally decided in 1920 to close the resort. After a lifetime of catering to the public, this daughter of a pioneer family in her late years felt that it was time to let the old Inn go the way of all those others that once held sway along the old Sacramento trail. Hers was the first of the early-day inns to become established in the canyon and the last to go.

(Material for the above article was obtained from the newspaper excerpts in the book, "My Playhouse Was a Concord Coach" by Mae Helene Bacon Boggs; from old family records of Mr. Charles Masson's mother, Elda McCloud Masson; and from information gotten from friends.)

Permission of Masson family to use the foregoing articles has been granted.

---

*THE DUNSMUIR NEWS
FRIDAY, JUNE 8, 1948*

Oldest Building In This Vicinity Being Torn Down

(By Marcelle Masson)

The building familiarly known in this vicinity as the "old hotel" at Upper Soda Springs in north Dunsmuir and well remembered throughout the state by its many patrons of former years is being demolished. The work of tearing it down began two weeks ago.

It is one of the last of the pioneer inns of its type that were built in the 1870's and '80's along what was then known as the Sacramento trail, running from the old mining town of Shasta in Shasta County to Strawberry Valley, later called Sisson, and now Mount Shasta, and following closely the older trail of the Hudson Bay trappers between northern California and Oregon.

These old wayside inns sprang up along this route with the influx of the pioneers and the gold miners to this region in the 1850's.

Among the earlier ones was Southern's place at Sims, one at Portuguese Flat, Wash Bailey's in the Castle Crag area, one at the spot below town that was later known as the Stone place where an old cabin remained for many years; and one at Upper Soda known then as "Soda Springs"; also another on what is now the Ream property near Mount Shasta.

These first hostelries were crudely built of shakes and logs. Some of them had two stories. With the advent of the sawmills in 1860, many of the log buildings were replaced with structures of planed lumber.

About this time, the Sacramento Trail had been widened and made into a road and the ox teams and stagecoaches joined the pack trains going back and forth through the Sacramento river canyon. It was necessary to have still larger places in order to take care of the traveling public that was fast becoming a tourist trade. In fact, with the coming of the railroad in 1888, this area developed quickly into a vacation land, bringing more elaborate and more modern hotels, as well as many private summer homes.

But of all the pioneer establishments that were erected in this vicinity as stopping places for the travelers, only the "old hotel," and another smaller and older building at Upper Soda have remained standing through the years. Most were eventually razed by fire, such as the old Castle Crag Tavern, the "Hanlon Place" and Sisson Tavern, (razed by fire twice in its lifetime.)

Some of those that were torn down were Southern's place, the Castle Rock hotel and, among the more modern ones, the hotel at Shasta Retreat.

The old inns and hotels came and went, leaving the one at Upper Soda Springs the only relic of those past days.

It was built in 1874 by Isaac Fry, the step-father of its late owner, Elda McCloud Masson, who had made her home on the premises most of her life.

Isaac Fry, who had been a captain on a Mississippi river boat before coming to California in the early days, built the hotel on the lines of one of those boats, even to having the rooms of both floors a foot above the level of the porches that surrounded them.

Mention of the charming architecture of the old building is to be found in an old book of memoirs, "The Fantastic City," by Amelia Ransome Neville, and edited in later years by a relative of hers. In her notes, she writes of a trip up the Sacramento river route in 1880 to Sisson Tavern with a stop at Upper Soda Springs "where 'Uncle Dick' Campbell had built a hotel like a boat — long and narrow with double deck piazzas . . ."

The lady was somewhat confused in the names for the reason that both Mr. Fry and his wife had died by this time, and the hotel was being operated by George Campbell, an uncle of Mrs. Fry, and a partner, 'Uncle Dick' Mannon.

Also, at the time of its erection, the Yreka Journal, dated April 1, 1874, contained the following article:

"NEW HOTEL. Isaac Fry intends putting up a large hotel at Soda Springs, this spring, which will be 100 feet in length and 25 feet wide, with balconies in each side. The balconies will serve the double purpose of affording a delightful promenade and outdoor retreat, as well as entrance ways to the various rooms, the stairs to be built on the outside.

"E. Ramous of this city is now making the doors and sashes, and the building will be ready for visitors this summer."

There were sixteen bedrooms in the building and a larger room, with a fireplace, for an office. It was a solid structure and rested on heavy timbers, hand-hewn on the place. The lumber came from a sawmill near Sisson and was put together with cut iron nails. The bricks of the old chimney appear to have been mortised with a clay-like mud, with only the part above the roof having had a lime coating in later years to preserve it.

The late owner had recounted to her family that, after the floor was laid, a dance was held there and friends from all over the county attended, including the Southern girls, as she called them, from Sims. Dunsmuir, at that time, was only a wooded hillside and neighbors lived miles apart.

The site of this old building and that of the older one on the place is of interest due to the fact that it has always been a stopping place for travelers through this canyon. For those going south it was the first place that the Sacramento river had to be crossed, and the last crossing if they were headed north. Also, the mineral spring on the place caused many to pause there.

Two ancient salmon-roasting beds, made of flat rocks, still remaining on the bank of the river down on the "flat," testify to the fact the place weas used by the Indians before the advent of the white man.

With the coming of the Hudson Bay trappers as early as 1835, one reads in their annals of stopping at "Soda Springs."

Following them, after gold was discovered in the state, came prospectors with their pack trains to camp overnight here; and in an old history of the county one reads that two brothers, Harry and Samuel Lockhart, built a cabin on the place in 1852.

Ross McCloud, father of the late Elda McCloud Masson, while operating his small inn at Portuguese Flat, learned of the mineral spring through the Indians and in 1855, becoming enamoured of the beautiful spot and recognizing its possibilities he purchased the squatter's rights of the Lockhart men, building a cabin in 1857 and building a corral to further accommodate the ever-increasing pack trains passing through.

With the growth of the old trails into roads along the river, in the 1860's, he, with a partner, Isaac Fry, built the long, low building in 1864. It still remains on the place.

After his death, his widow married Mr. Fry.

By this time, better hotels were supplanting the original ones made of logs and shakes and Mr. Fry tore down the first log house, a two-story structure, and on its site built his "hotel that looked like a boat."

It had been operated as an inn during winter and summer, and later only as a summer resort, by some descendants of Ross McCloud's family, continuously until 1921. With the coming of the automobile, the late owner realized many improvements would be necessary to accommodate a changing tourist public. Rather than conform to the demands of a "motel" or "auto park" she merely decided that she and the old hotel had served their time and closed the buildings, leaving them to the ravages of time and the elements.

She continued to make her home with members of her family in a residence on the place, while the gray squirrels, coming for the nuts of a black walnut tree that overhangs the old hotel, have claimed the place as their own, and a porcupine has maintained a residence underneath the building nearly every summer.

Curious but interested folks, going to the near-by mineral spring for water during the years of the old resort's decline, have stood there, gazing at the lovely old building tucked in snugly and protectingly beneath the overhanging limbs of the walnut trees and the two immense poplars growing beside its porches and wondered what its history was.

Like a lady of long ago, peeking through the sticks of her fan at a crowded, gay assembly, the "old hotel" has peered through the protecting trunks of these old trees at the many hundreds of people who entered her front door in all the past years — coming first by foot, and by mule-back, then in freight teams, and by stage coach; later by train and automobile.

One old hotel register dated 1876 and another dated 1899 are now being preserved by the heirs as mute reminders of a long and interesting life for the "old hotel" at Upper Soda Springs, bowing out now to the exigencies of time.

DUNSMUIR NEWS
FRIDAY, MARCH 27, 1953

First White Settler Came Here 100 Years Ago; Dunsmuir History Unfolds

By Marcelle Masson

It was one hundred years ago, in 1852, that the first white settler took up land in the vicinity of what is now the town of Dunsmuir. Samuel and Harry Lockhart, twin brothers, acquired a squatter's right to all the land lying below what is now the highway bridge in North Dunsmuir, and the adjoining wooded hillsides, about one hundred sixty acres, known at that time as the Soda Springs.

In old accounts of the early-day history of the county, we learn that the Lockhart brothers, in 1851, were in the Scott River mining country. Then they operated a saloon in Yreka. And from there, in 1852, they went down to Soda Springs and built a log cabin and a corral for pack trains.

At that time there were two main routes west of the Sacramento River to the northern mines: From Reading Ranch and the mining town of Shasta, then in its golden heyday, one could take the trail through Trinity and the Scott River country to get to Yreka; or one could follow up the Sacramento River Canyon by way of the old Hudson's Bay Trapper Trail.

Following the discovery of gold on the Scott River by 1850, and on the Shasta plains, later called Yreka, in 1851, there was such an increase in population in the north that, on March 22, 1852, the California legislature created Siskiyou county with the county seat at Shasta Butte City, soon to be changed to the name Yreka.

The Soda Springs, situated on the old trail of the Hudson's Bay trappers, had been used as a stopping place for the old fur traders since 1882. The Indians before them had worn a footpath on the same route through the canyon. Now, in 1852, it was the miner and his mule heading for the gold diggings in the north who needed a place en route where he could lodge for the night. The Soda Springs, where one crossed the Sacramento River for the first time, if he were going south, and for the last time if he were headed north, afforded an excellent place to rest overnight. With its fine meadow and good mineral spring, the Lockhart men could well see it was an advantageous spot on which to build a cabin for the wayfarer, and a corral for his mules. These first two white men to settle in the vicinity of what later became known as the town of Dunsmuir, operated their crude inn until 1855, when they sold their squatters' rights to the pioneers, Ross and Mary McCloud, for about one hundred dollars.

From this time on other simple inns made their appearance along the old trail. In 1859 Washington Bailey bought the squatter's rights to property on Soda Creek from one Amisa Ball. A soda spring was on this property. He called his place Lower Soda Springs; so eventually Mr. McCloud's place became known as Upper Soda Spring. To the south of Mr. Bailey's place there was the Sweet Briar Ranch. Sim Sothern had an inn farther down and there was also an inn for travelers at Portuguese Flat. A place called Knapp's Ranch had been established at what was known later as the Stone Ranch and also Hanlon's, now the vicinity of the Dunsmuir Lumber Company. Leaving the canyon and going north, there was Sisson's Tavern and the Berryvale Inn. No towns or settlements as yet had been established, and the place we know as Dunsmuir was still a wooded hillside. By 1859 the old trail had been widened into a road to accommodate the pack trains, wagons and stagecoaches of the pioneers and early settlers. And sometime after 1855 Mr. McCloud had built a toll bridge over the Sacramento River just east of the present highway bridge. The first road, which he and the other interested settlers built, passed in front of his inn at the Soda Springs, went through the place now occupied by the Copco sub-station, then across the toll bridge and up the hill and along the road in front of the present site of Rodley's Garage. Then it went down the present Florence Avenue to Spring Street, as we know it now. In those days there was a spring where Sacramento Avenue and Florence now join and the area was swampy and impassable. All of that area in early days was first owned by Manley Brown, father of the late Clint and Lew Brown and a sister.

At that time due to this swamp a detour was made down the present Sacramento Avenue until one came to a spot in the vicinity of the present Purity Store. There the first old stage road continued down the present Florence Avenue until it reached what is now Pine Street. Pine Street, north of the present Bank, was a gully. The road turned south at the foot of the hill, following the present Sacramento Avenue down to where we now have Scherrer Avenue. It followed to the south end of Scherrer Avenue, then down along the bottom of the hillside where we now have the railroad tracks and through what is now Nutglade. This old stage road crossed Little Castle Creek at about the present highway crossing in South Dunsmuir.

Railroad surveys from the Mississippi to the Pacific coast had been going on since 1854 to "ascertain the most practicable and economical route." The opinion at that time was that the Sacramento River Canyon wasn't feasible. However, as we now know, it was routed up the canyon. By 1884 the railroad had reached Redding. Then shortly after that the canyon became wracked with the birth pains of progress, and stations along the route came into being, midwifed by the construction gangs, and christened with the names the stages or old-timers had used. The stage was on its way out, to be supplanted by wood-burning locomotives and railroad stations. And Dunsmuir, through various stages was born in 1886.

Construction crews were camped at Cedar Flat, now called Nutglade. A boxcar served as the station, telegraph office and general place of business. Another camp was established about a mile north and called Pusher. It was the site of our present railroad station.

In the Yreka Journal, dated August 28, 1886, we read: "The railroad name for the new station at Cedar Flat is 'Dunsmuir' and the stage company name is 'Castle Rock' . . ."

It must have been at this time that Alexander Dunsmuir, member of a wealthy family with coal holdings in British Columbia, made the suggestion that if the new station were called "Dunsmuir" his family would donate a fountain to the new settlement. Alexander Dunsmuir was in charge of the family's affairs in San Francisco, so he must have often passed through the canyon on the stages.

But Cedar Flat was not to become the main site for the new town, for in January, 1887, the boxcar railroad station called "Dunsmuir" was moved up to the station formerly called "Pusher"; and in that same month a new post office called "Mannon" was established at Soda Springs, named after Uncle Dick Mannon, who was the proprietor of the hotel there following the deaths of Ross and Mary McCloud and Isaac Fry, a partner of Mr. Mannon. Miss Elda McCloud was the postmistress. In November, 1887, her brother, George McCloud, was appointed postmaster in Dunsmuir.

In chronicles dated 1888 we learn that Dunsmuir had a population of three hundred fifty people. It was the location of the railroad company's car works. W. B. Lobner was the postmaster; H. Bugg, carpenter; H. P. Back, newsdealer; W. J. Branstette, general store; M. M. Brown, hotel; Crowder and Pegg, saloon; J. Delano, meat market; W. A. Dougles, hotel; T. C. Gaunt, shoemaker; Cal Griffen, constable; J. J. Scott & Co., lumber manufacturers; J. Sponogle, physician.

The new town of Mott, located in 1887, was a neighbor to the north. Their newspaper, the North Star, antedates those of Dunsmuir, and in a June 3, 1888, edition one reads the following: "Hon. R. Dunsmuir, the millionaire owner of coal mines in British Columbia, after whom the town is named, intimated while in Dunsmuir lately that he would present the town with a fountain to be placed in the open space in front of Bilicke's Mt. Shasta hotel, the fountain to be supplied from Mr. Bilicke's hydrant."

This is the fountain one sees on the terraced lawn south of the railroad station in Dunsmuir. The figure of a girl that formerly graced the tip of the fountain is now gone.

Mr. Bilicke's hotel was then on the site of the old Weed Hotel near the railroad station, now part of the Dunsmuir Hotel.

Another item from the same paper states: "Mr. Bilicke has opened a sanatarium at his urban villa, the old Galpin place, where he accommodates those who are of a quiet temperament, or suffering from debility, where they can avail themselves of the springs near the villa." This spot is what we of today know as the Harry Brown ranch, and the springs alluded to are those to be found at Shasta Retreat.

The newspaper, "Dunsmuir News," apparently made its debut sometime in 1890. The San Francisco Chronicle carried the following excerpt from the Dunsmuir News edition of June 28, 1890: "Dunsmuir is only about four years old, having been founded in 1886, upon the extension of the Oregon line through the Sacramento river canyon. This is the terminus of the Shasta division, and large shops and roundhouses are located here. Some 300 men live here who are in the employ of the railroad, and except a few sawmills and logging camps, the town depends entirely upon the railroad for its support. Nearby are some noted soda springs, which are much visited and are very popular, attracting many hundreds of visitors during the season. M. M. Brown is the pioneer settler of the place, and he was shortly followed by J. W. White, W. J. Branstetter and L. Boylon, all of whom engaged in business. L. Van Fossen is another early settler, and is the postmaster of the town. The town is provided with water works, has a good public school, two churches and other necessary public institutions. G. D. Cummins has recently commenced the publication of a weekly newspaper (the News), which bids fair to become a paying institution. The population is about 500 and is constantly increasing. A reading room and library are maintained by the railroad men and Dunsmuir deservingly ranks highly in the estimation of visitors as well as residents."

(Continued next week.)

---

*DUNSMUIR NEWS
FRIDAY, APRIL 3, 1953*

Early Day Editor of News Known as 'A Character'

(Continued from last week)

(Editor's Note: In the fifth paragraph of the first installment of this historical sketch, printed last week, the date from which Soda Springs was used by fur trappers should have read "1832" instead of "1882.")

★ ★ ★ ★

An old-timer of today remembers that this Mr. Cummins, the editor, was considered quite a character. He was called "McGinty" by his friends. His old-fashioned style of editing is a far cry from modern style, and as well as reading those old copies as a source of local history, one gets a lot of pleasure from them.

Another well-remembered editor of the News in Dunsmuir's past was Sam Hill. His style was equally as flowery. But some felt he had over-extended himself when one day they read his obituary for a local woman: "She has gone to another and far better land — we trust."

But to return to history, one notices in a July 12, 1890, edition of the North Star considerable activities in Dunsmuir real estate. Town lots were for sale and every inducement offered — easy terms, profitable investment, only one-fourth down on magnificent lots, etc. The Pacific Improvement Company, a holding of the railroad company, surveyed lots and put them up for sale in the first place, and marked out the streets.

In those days Sacramento Avenue was the main street (but often called the "front street"), and Florence Avenue, now the main street, was then called the "back street."

The street off Butterfly Avenue that goes up to the old Cornish Hospital was named "Woodin" Street from a Mr. Woodin, one of the first local engineers. Now one sees it usually spelled "Wooden," which is incorrect.

The old Rostel Building is said to be the oldest remaining one on Sacramento Avenue. It has an iron front, the same as found on some old buildings still standing in famed Virginia City. It stands on the northeast corner of the old Weed Hotel block. Long ago it was the grocery and drygoods store of A. Levy. North of it one sees the remains of an old rock wall in the back of a vacant lot. This wall is said to be the remains of a butcher shop operated in early days by John Wendell and then by Ralph Waldo Emerson, a relative of the noted poet of the past. Two doors north of the butcher shop was McGinty's print shop. North of that (where the stone residence stands today) was the K. P. Hall, where all the minstrel shows, etc., were held.

The Mt. Shasta Hotel, operated by Bilicke, was where the old Weed Hotel stands, on the corner of Pine and Sacramento.

Across the street, on the corner, was a restaurant. It had a big water wheel out on the sidewalk for water power to turn two great fans on the ceiling of the restaurant, mostly to keep off the summer flies.

Without extensive research it is hard to name and locate the businesses and their exact locations as early as 1886. But for the early 1900's one can get quite a bit of information by talking to the descendants of those early-day residents. They tell of the K. P. Hall up near where the present grammar school stands; of Aunty Hendrick's rooming house near by. It, later, was built into the Riverview Hotel following a fire that had burned most of the business section on the front street up to Emerson's butcher shop. This was probably the big fire of 1903, said to have started in the Mt. Shasta Hotel.

And the story goes that when it was realized that all the places of business on the front street were in the path of the fire and could not be saved, the owners of the saloons along the street told everyone to help themselves to all they could get out in the way of beverages. As a consequence, many of the town's alcoholics were noticeably tipsy for several days following the fire.

Lucy Neher's house, a three-story rooming house, was near Emerson's. It later became the home of Mrs. Annie Fussler, present-day descendant of the pioneer J. J. Scott family. W. D. Nunamaker had a jewelry shop combined with telephone, telegraph office and post office.

At one time the present site of the Loftus Building was Sam Gongwer's saloon with rooms above. Where the News office now stands (1953) Culver & Harris operated the California Hotel; and in the Si Neher Building (now the Reception) there was another saloon. Van Fossen had a drug store in this block. There was also a restaurant and Dixon's barber shop. And the Arlington Hotel, operated by J. J. Malone. Next came the Branstetter Building. In it was a jewelry store, W. J. Branstetter's general merchandise, a tailor shop, Monty Love's saloon and Boylan's drug store. For a time there were no sidewalks down this main thoroughfare. Then later on heavy wooden sidewalks, a foot or more from the ground were built.

White's residence, comprising roomers and millinery, and McEnerny's boarding house, brings us up to the vicinity of the present S. & J. Market on Sacramento Avenue. There was a Chinese washhouse in that neighborhood and a few residences.

In front of the many saloons on this street stood rows of beer kegs, for only draft beer was to be had there. A keg would be carried as needed into the saloon and placed in an icebox. A hole was bored into the door so the spigot in the keg could be easily accessible to the outside of the icebox. The ice came from the supply that the railroad company brought from Truckee for their icehouse.

One of the earliest settlers in Dunsmuir, the late W. J. Branstetter, father of Grove Branstetter and Mrs. Florence Maud Silva, bought 26 acres of land from the Pacific Improvement Company. It was situated between the present Branstetter Street and the cemetery in South Dunsmuir. He first planted an orchard on the land; then he subdivided it into lots. He named the streets in this subdivision for members of his family: Grover Street, Rose Avenue (for Rose Panabaker, the sister of his wife), Frances Street (for the daughter of Rose), and Florence Avenue (for his daughter, Mrs. Florence Maud Silva). Florence Avenue was a short street at the time, it is understood, and when the "back street" became a through street it continued as Florence Avenue. Up until about 1912 it went only as far south as the present site of the Commercial Garage, and one drove out of town via lower Sacramento Avenue and the old stage road.

On Back Street there was a livery stable owned and operated by the Lee family. Mrs. Winnie Long, Mrs. Myrtle Moore and Mrs. Jack Peterson are the daughters of those early settlers, the family having first lived in Mott. The livery stable was where the California Theatre now stands. Mr. Lee bought the livery stable from a former owner. He also had a house brought down intact from Mott and it is still standing at the corner of Branstetter and Sacramento Streets.

A jail stood south of the livery stable. In later years the late Billy Lee used it as a young men's athletic club, a more worthy cause.

Speaking of jails, Pat Furlong, as Irish a person as one could find, was one of the town's early-day peace officers. He had a pet eagle, an immense thing, that he kept chained up in his basement at night. One night a prowler saw it, mistook it for a turkey and grabbed it. The result was that the eagle grabbed the prowler — a hobo — and hung on until Mr. Furlong, hearing the commotion, went down and arrested the man.

From Charlie Wendell we learn that Pat bought the first phonograph in town. It played big cylindrical records. He bought it for his saloon, but while it was still a novelty he played it up at the K. P. Hall and charged admission.

Where one now sees the new Dunsmuir Hotel on Florence Avenue, in the 1890's one saw the Wing Sing Laundry. The Chinamen always wore faded blue jeans. They carried the laundry in baskets on their shoulders until the advent of the automobile, when they bought a Ford. On Chinese New Year they gave lily bulbs to their customers. They were an integral part of the community. There was Big Sam, Jim Ming, Little Lee and Chung Lung, to name some of them. Jim Ming was generally accepted by the big shots around town, and he was especially pleased to be the friend of Horace Weed — delighted when he could tell someone of the activities of "Me an' Ho's Weed."

The first Methodist Church was on this street, about where the Texaco Service Station now stands. A Presbyterian church stood in the vicinity of the present addition to the grammar school. Later it became an Episcopal church. A fire in the K. P. Hall in 1924 razed the hall, chhurch, two residences, and the building that housed the Dunsmuir News print shop on Florence Avenue.

The first Catholic church was built on the present site of the church, about 1887. It burned down in 1933.

The first school was in the Isgrigg house, now 319 Florence. Mr. Isgrigg was one of the first train dispatchers in town. School was next held in old Levy residence, now 615 Florence. From there it was moved to a newly-built two-story school building on the site of the present elementary school. The old bell used in that school is now in the cupola of the present Episcopal church.

The duplex residence at 982 Florence Avenue was originally the first high school in town and built for that purpose. Miss Minnie Hudson was the first principal.

Favorite old-time school teachers who held their positions for many years were Mrs. Scheaffor, who taught the first grade; and N. T. J. Beaughan, who was the principal and taught the seventh and eighth grades.

A delivery wagon, usually that of Mr. A. Levy, served the community in early days as a hearse. Painted on the side of this wagon were the words, "A. Levy, General Merchandise."

Later Mr. A. A. Ward came to town, presumably the first undertaker for the community. He had a more suitable small black wagon for a hearse.

The first blacksmith shop — Dewey's — was near the livery stable.

The first motion picture house was run by Gardner and Lee and stood about where the Reception pool hall now stands.

On the site of the old Mt. Shasta Hotel, Abner Weed, in 1904, erected the Weed Hotel for his sons, Horace and Ed. The first State Bank of Dunsmuir, owned by Levy, Gus Hutaff and other prominent men, was in the Weed Hotel on the Pine Street side. Jerry Wilson, jeweler and watch repairer, had a store in the building. He was a huge man and had very large feet. His footprints can still be seen in the cement sidewalk, outside his former doorway.

The first electric light plant was Herman Scherrer's, father of Miss

Clara Scherer. He first had a dam in the Sacramento River, back of the roundhouse. The water was carried in a flume from there to his plant on Scherrer Avenue.

The first telephone was built and operated by W. D. Nunamaker. It ran from Dunsmuir to Scott's Mill in the vicinity of what we now refer to as the old fox farm above Shasta Springs. A story concerning that telephone line says that one day George McCloud, who was then managing the Upper Soda Springs Resort, tried for the better part of a day to call Scott's Mill, but with no success. So finally he sent an Indian boy, Grant Towendolly, up there on foot to tell them to hang up their receiver so he could talk to them by phone. Also, on the hillside near the mineral spring at Upper Soda there is still one of those old telephone poles, albeit standing at an angle and looking rather decrepit from age.

(Concluded next week)

DUNSMUIR NEWS
FRIDAY, APRIL 10, 1953

Early Day Cafe Operators Beat Drums for Business

(Concluded from last week)

Branstetter and Bill Roberts had the first water system for the slowly growing town. They had a big tank up on the hill west of town where the Van Fossen Ice Plant is now situated. Mr. Van Fossen acquired considerable land there (it is thought that he bought it from Mr. Champion) and he bought the water system from Branstetter and Roberts. Van Fossen also had one of the early water systems east of town, bringing the water from Mossbrae Falls in a wooden flume. It came across the hillside one sees north and east of the present highway bridge and was piped across the Sacramento River at what is known as Wilkin's Bridge. Water mains were then laid along the streets. Old boards of that flume can still be found on the hillside embedded in the leaves.

The Van Fossens also had a light plant up on their property west of town, and later another down on the flat below and east of the highway bridge. The old wheels are still there under the brush and wild grapevines.

Water for the Southern Pacific Company in early days was piped along the track from Bear Creek in Shasta Retreat.

Speaking of the railroad company, the roundhouse in those days had brick archways and doors with glass windows for each stall. The turntable was operated by hand.

When trains arrived at the station in the 1890's the nearby restaurants and hotels competed with each other in seeing which could make the most din and thereby attract the most customers. Big brass Chinese gongs hung on ropes outside these establishments and were beaten upon, creating a deafening noise. The Mt. Shasta Hotel and a nearby restaurant placed long counters on the sidewalk outside their entrances, and under awnings. Just before the trains would arrive long rows of coffee cups were placed on the counters to be filled as each customer arrived. There were also pies and plates of doughnuts. Then, in their bid for service each sent runners down to the trains to direct the passengers to its counter. A Fred Everest, it was remembered by one old-timer, was one of those runners. There were no dining cars on the trains then.

Another well-remembered character who always met the trains long ago was "the candy man." It is said he was always dressed in immaculate white and wore white gloves. He was a solemn-faced man and had long, drooping mustaches. His delicious homemade candy, pink and white taffy, was carried on a tray hanging by a strap around his shoulders. He broke up the twists of confection by striking them with a little silver hammer.

As much a part of the town as the candy man was a large, black old dog who seemed to belong to nobody, but could always be found lying in the dust somewhere about town. He was noticeable in that he seemed to be afflicted with something akin to palsy, for when he was standing or walking he shook, but only up and down, like a water ousel, to the amazement of the young fry.

As well as its characters, every town has citizens who might be called picturesque. One such person in Dunsmuir long ago was an old gentleman, Mr. Mertes, who was the father of Mrs. Sheaffor, the first-grade school teacher. He always wore a derby hat and a "clawhammer" coat. Every fine day he was seen walking out to the mineral spring at Upper Soda to get his fill of the water.

Another likeable old fellow was W. G. Scripture, who had a small greenhouse near the livery stable. He also did photography there.

Some say that the first automobile was owned by Barney Dunn, the roundhouse foreman. When he was married he bought some household furniture, ordering it from Breuner's in Sacramento. On such purchases this store was giving away tickets on an automobile. Mr. Dunn was the lucky winner. He didn't want the automobile so he sold it to a saloon man named Leo Herman, whose saloon was called Fancy's Cale. Everyone called him Fancy. The car was a one-cylinder Oldsmobile. It had detachable back seats with the door in the back, and could be made into a roadster by lifting out the back seats and door.

Others say that Dr. Thompson had a black motor buggy before Fancy had his automobile.

Dr. Thompson and Mr. Gongwer built what was known as the Annex, adjoining Weed's Hotel on the north. Mr. Hutaff had a drug store in this place.

Most of the early-day buildings in Dunsmuir were made of the lumber from Scott's Mill above Hedge Creek. From Mrs. Annie Fussler, daughter of that pioneer family, we received many interesting details of local history dating from 1886. In that year the Scott family came up from their home in Roseville to Redding by train. From Redding to Sims they had to travel in a work train. The track wasn't completed any farther, so the parents and their three children, two girls and a boy, drove up to Upper Soda Springs in a spring wagon. The hotel at Upper Soda was crowded, Mrs. Fussler remembers, people even sleeping on the billiard tables, so the family was driven on up to Galpin's place, a sort of stage station, store and rooms for travelers. This place later was where Mr. Gilicke had his sanitarium, known in recent years as the Harry Brown place and now owned by Mr. and Mrs. Henry Dorner of Dunsmuir.

Mr. Scott, together with a Mr. Shattuck, Mr. Neher and Mr. Shaeffor (the same Shaeffor who later married the first-grade school teacher in Dunsmuir) had filed on four timber claims, the land beginning at about Hedge Creek and covering what we now call the Shasta Springs property and old fox farm. Scott, Neher and Shaeffor bought out Shattuck and each built a one-room cabin on the corner of the four adjoining sections of land to prove their claim and to connect the cabins for a dwelling. Neher and Shaeffor were not married as yet so the Scott family moved into the three-room house on July 11, 1886, after having been at the Galpin place in the meantime.

Mr. Scott discovered mineral springs on his section and over the main soda spring he placed a barrel so one could easily get the water to drink. Then he put a shed overhead later, and placed benches there. And he had machinery for his lumber mill brought up by freight teams.

Realizing the value of his soda spring, Mr. Scott suggested to some of the Bay Area wholesale grocers and hardware people with whom he dealt that a corporation be formed to market the mineral water. That was the birth of the Shasta Water Company at Shasta Springs. Mr. Scott had about 600 shares. The newly-formed company bottled the water and also built some cabins on the property. A Mr. Tomlyn was the first manager of the bottling works and of the summer resort cabins, the forerunner of famed Shasta Springs.

An item of interest to all who are familiar with Poison spring, east of Shasta Springs, was revealed by Mrs. Fussler. She stated that this spring, which was formerly on their property, was at one time four distinct and different kinds of springs — one on each corner of a perfect square. They called the spot the "Sylvan Spring," and built a cover over it. Some curious and investigating person probably thought it a cache for gold, she said, and dug up the spot, making quite a depression. Since then it has had the appearance of one spring, the carbonic acid gas in the water predominating and causing all small wild life which goes there to drink to become asphyxiated and die. Thus it became known as Poison Spring.

Hedge Creek received its name from a Mr. Hedge who, long ago, had a berry farm in the vicinity of where the new Shasta Springs Lodge is built.

Another item of historical interest to this locality one might include is that the Weirheim place about a mile north of town was formerly known as the Father Quinn place. An undated clipping from the Mott Star reported the following which we give in part:

"A NEW CATHOLIC SUMMER RESORT. — We have just been informed that a site for a large summer resort has been selected by the Rev. Fathers Quinn of Red Bluff, Reynolds of Willows and McGrath of Yreka, between this town and Dunsmuir on the Furlong tract, which lies between Upper Soda Springs and Hedge Creek Cave. Forty acres of this tract have already been purchased, the land surveyed . . . A large and commodious building will be erected . . . The entire charge and management of the whole will be held by the Sisters of Charity, and the resort is intended for the use of Catholic families throughout the state . . ."

Shasta Retreat was the first owned by some Methodist minister who, in 1895, formed what they called the "Shasta Vicino Camp Association." They sold stock in the venture but it never became successful. The place eventually was called "Shasta Retreat," and became a summer resort and colony of private summer homes, maintaining that status for many years.

The old swimming pool at one time east of the river at Shasta Retreat was built by Dr. Gill, one of Dunsmuir's early-day physicians. He had a four-wheel bicycle built that could run on the railroad track. In his spare time he could be seen pedaling up the track, his long coattails flapping in the breeze behind him, going up to see how his philanthropic project was getting along, for it was open to the public.

The old Gill home, one of the fancier residences of the town at that time, still stands as the doctor had it built. One can see it now at 513 Sacramento Avenue.

Some of the descendants of Dunsmuir's early-day settlers who are still living here, or frequently return for a visit, are the following: Mrs. Florence Maud Silva, Mrs. Annie Fussler, Mr. Grover Branstetter, Mrs. Winnie Long, Mrs. Hazel Peterson, Mrs. Myrtle Moore, Mrs. Eleanor Van Fossen Harrison, Mrs. Vera Mason, Dr. G. E. Malone, John Petty.

Mrs. Marion Mallory Bass, Harry Stone, Miss Clara Scherrer, Miss Helen Hutaff, Hugh Clarke, Hilda Derby Clausnitzer, Pauline Weed Heibner, Mrs. Fanny Scholes Walker, Mrs. Farlin Beam Cantrell.

Erroll Beaughan, Ben Oliver, Lucille Beaughan Evans, Charlie Wendell, George Wendell, Ruby Brown, Mrs. Leta Taylor and Charles Masson.

A number of Dunsmuir's permanent residents were newcomers to the town in the early 1900's. Among them are Mr. and Mrs. George Dickson, Dr. W. B. Mason and Mrs. L. E. Gibson. Mrs. Gibson's parents, the Lorenzo Huffs, lived in Mott when it was a thriving lumber town. He was a millwright. The family then moved to Dunsmuir and Clara Huff (Gibson) attended Mrs. Shaeffor's first grade.

Mrs. Jim Pendleton is also a pioneer Mott resident. Her parents, Mr. and Mrs. J. W. Davis, went to Mott in 1886. Mr. Davis, with two partners, Florin and Powers, had a lumber mill on the river between Mott and Small, called the Mott Manufacturing Company. Mr. Davis bought out his partners. But the heavy snow storms of 1890 wrecked the mill and the family moved away. In 1911 Mrs. Pendleton came with her husband to Dunsmuir.

All of these old-timers speak of the heavy growth of timber that once covered all the territory between Dunsmuir and the town known then as Sisson. The late Elda McCloud Masson once stated that when she was a young girl one could leave by stagecoach from her home at Upper Soda Springs and never be able to get a glimpse of Mt. Shasta until he had reached Sisson, because of the dense forest all the way. But the early-day lumber mills providing fuel for the new railroad, and lumber for the new homes that were being built, soon left the area denuded as we see it now.

A list of the names of some of those first railroad engineers should not be amiss in this collection of old memories: John Wagoner, C. O. Bissell, "Pop" Bissell, Charlie Silsby, Hi Gardner, Mr. Church, Jim Dickey, Denny Freel, Henry Wentz, Jim White, Henry Woodin, Joe Poor, Jack Campbell, George McDowell, Tom Herbig and George Shearer. As far as we could ascertain, Mr. Poor is the only one on the list who is still living.

Dunsmuir has always remained principally a railroad town. But its face has been occasionally changed or "lifted" with the advent of new highways or streets, causing business districts to shift or expand. With the building of the highway bridge about the year 1919, a new residential area, called North Dunsmuir, opened up as an addition to the town; and with the proposed new four-lane highway scheduled to be routed through the town in the near future, its citizens stand by to see what resulting changes it will cause.

(The End)

Marcelle and Jim Masson Families Give New Park Property to City of Dunsmuir

Tuesday night was a winner for Dunsmuir and for the boys and girls of this community.

A committee of Little League representatives headed by Don Cheney met with city manager William Hansen and Mrs. Marcelle Masson and Mr. and Mrs. Jim Masson to discuss the possibility of using the fill area west of the river for a Little League Ballpark.

Councilman Roger Ellis was the only councilman present.

Mrs. Marcelle Masson, acting as spokesman for the three said to the group, "Well, get prepared for what I am going to say." And then in the Marcelle Masson style, graciously said, "We have decided that we are going to give the property to the city as a Memorial."

Needless to say, the committee was speechless.

Mr. Masson went on to say that the property had extreme sentimental value and memories to the families and because it was such a favorite spot on the old Masson Homestead, that has dated back to the mid-1800's, and because mother Masson liked the spot so well, decided that they would like to have it dedicated as the "Elda A. Masson Memorial Park."

The Massons later told the News that they were aware that there would be problems of access approval to the land if it were privately owned, and that in order for the Little League group to have it they would have to give it to the city.

Mrs. Masson said that when she and Jim began to discuss the problem Dunsmuir was faced with, he suddenly suggested, "Why don't we just give it to the city in memory of Mother Masson." Marcelle quickly exclaimed, "that is just what I wanted to do, but didn't know how you would feel about it."

In this spirit of generosity and personal interest in Dunsmuir and its future, both Massons agreed that they wouldn't want it any other way.

In behalf of the city and the Little League organization, both Mr. Ellis and Mr. Cheney expressed their thanks for the most generous act that helped to solve one of Dunsmuir's immediate and most real problems.

Mr. Masson told the News that he could remember the days that he and other boys had to play ball on the unpaved street now Florence Avenue, along by the present Masonic hall, and that he and Marcelle both having raised several children felt they wanted to do something tangible for Dunsmuir children in making this gift to the city.

Mr. Ellis requested the Massons to return to Dunsmuir and be the honored guests of the City on the date of the Dedication of the "Elda A. Masson Memorial Park."

They accepted the invitation and declared that they would be honored to do so.

The only step now necessary for the Little League park development program is access to the site from the Southern Pacific Company along whose property the access will follow.

There will be about 10 acres that will be Deeded to the city for the Memorial, and will be designated as park property for the City of Dunsmuir to have and to hold forever.

Dunsmuir Gets Park as Gift

DUNSMUIR — Ten acres of land have been given to the city of Dunsmuir for a recreational park.

The land was donated by Marcelle Masson, James Masson and Harriet J. Masson, with the condition that the park be known as Elda A. Masson Memorial Park. (All three donors are children of Elda Masson, an early settler of Dunsmuir.)

City councilmen received the deed to the land at a meeting this week.

The Little League will have a baseball field on the site, west of the Sacramento River Bridge.

City councilmen also signed an agreement with Siskiyou County to purchase tax-deeded land along the Sacramento River for $150. The land extends from the Wilkins Bridge to the south city limits. Its length is about two miles, and does not exceed 20 feet in width at any location.

RECOLLECTIONS

by
William Millard

Next door to our house on Florence Avenue (now Dunsmuir Avenue) lived Engineer Ervin Bectel, his wife Hattie, Hattie's mother, and the two Bectel children, Robert and Dorothy.

In back of our house, facing Shasta Avenue, lived Engineer Sid Bates and his wife. In 1914 Evert Taylor and his wife and their two children lived there.

Next door on the north side lived Hiram and Mrs. Woodward and their son Carl.

In back of the Woodwards lived Dispatcher Johnson, his wife, and their two children, William (Billy Dick) and Maxine. The sidewalk in front of our house was a board walk made of 2 x 12 planks elevated about 18 inches above the dirt street.

The main road, forerunner of Highway 99, ran through town on Sacramento Avenue, crossing the river at the Shasta County line bridge. It continued up the east side of the river through Champion Park, across the Scherrer Avenue bridge and then over the S. P. tracks to Sacramento Avenue. Going north on this street, it went by Ward's Furniture Store and Funeral Parlor. Crossing the street at the corner to the left, one could look up Jail Hill as he continued to walk north past the Van Fossen Building, the Old Branstetter Hall, BuBose and Kilburn's Ice Cream Parlor, next "Jake" Eherenman's General Merchandise and Grocery, and the Waggoner Building. On the ground floor of this building was a

Carl on the back of the horse, 1912

saloon; upstairs was the old Strand movie house. The main road went on by Chamber's Reception Parlor, C. C. Wickes' saloon, the Weed Hotel, and a bakery that was in the Weed Hotel Building annex, then on by the Episcopal Church, the Catholic Sisters' Home (in back of the present post office), down the hill at Del Selby's Blacksmith Shop to the Wilkin's Mill Bridge. Here the road continued north on the east side of the river to Soda Springs old stage stop, then up the grade to Shasta Springs and Mott, Pioneer, and at last to Sisson (now Mt. Shasta).

The completion of the Highway Bridge at the north end of Dunsmuir Avenue (formerly Florence Avenue) across the Sacramento River brought about great changes in Dunsmuir, for the highway was routed directly through the heart of town on Dunsmuir Avenue. All traffic was diverted from Sacramento Avenue to the upper street. Celebrating the completion of the bridge, a dance was held on the bridge. Interspersed among the dances were lots of talks and speeches.

I would like to mention the Dunsmuir Light Company. They built a flume and ditch from above Wilkin's Mill on the east side of the river. The Turbine and Power House was situated between the Roundhouse and the Butterfly Bridge. I remember that everyone was on a flat rate: one dollar-fifty cents a month for five lights; fifty cents additional for a washing machine or a hotplate. We had electric lights most of the time, but it was necessary to have kerosene lamps in case of an emergency.

Sam Fiske was the constable and the man who could put you in jail if you weren't a good boy. Mary (Fiske) Ward was the babysitter for my brother and me when we were little.

I don't know if anyone has said anything about the trail over the hill to Soda Creek. The trail took off at the Dunsmuir Hospital, which was situated on the east hill above the roundhouse. From the hospital, the trail went up the hill through a saddle and down the other side coming in at Little Soda Creek at the Horse Trough. This trail was used by the miners on Soda Creek to reach Dunsmuir for supplies. The trail was used from the 1880's until most of the mining ended. I walked this trail in 1925.

An old miner, Jim Barrett, was working a mine up Little Soda Creek. The road up Soda Creek was the Old Toll Road from Soda Springs to McCloud. The Toll House was just past Little Soda by the Toy Factory. The toll road ended when it came into the Sisson-McCloud Road at Ponto Park. The toll road was the better road because of two facts: its maintenance was better and the grade was less than on the Sisson-McCloud road. Jim Barrett and Jim Murphy had a mine and stamp mill up Little Soda. This they operated from 1926 until about 1933. I walked over the trail several times to visit the Murphys, who were friends of mine when we lived in Weed. Jim Barrett told me that this Soda Creek Trail was used mostly by the Chinese, who mined this trail from 1880 until the turn of the century. The Chinese used this trail to get back and forth to and from Dunsmuir for supplies. The

last time I walked over the Hill to Soda Creek was the summer of 1973, when I worked into Dunsmuir on AMTRAK. I found the trail very overgrown with brush; it was very hard to see where it had been.

There were several railroad engineers that left the railroad to go into business in Dunsmuir. John Waggoner left in about 1904 and built the Waggoner Building. In 1906, Charlie Wickes constructed the Castle Crags Resort in Castella. Al Wilkins had the Wilkins Mill with his brother. Charlie Williams started a dray and fuel business in Dunsmuir.

I vividly remember Big Canyon. The Old Road to Sisson from Dunsmuir went UNDER the trestle at Big Canyon. Going north it went under the south end, made the loop of the canyon, and went back under the north end and on to Sisson.

CASTLE CRAGS WAS
POPULAR RESORT

By Marcelle Masson

(Editor's Note: Mrs. Masson, who was hunting for material for an article on the old summer resort at Castle Crags requested by a member of the Siskiyou County Historical Society, came upon the following article on the subject.)

In searching for material on the history of the old Castle Crags resort south of Dunsmuir we are very fortunate in having an account of it written by the old pioneer who first acquired the property in early days. He was Washington Bailey, known to his friends as "Wash." His story appeared in a Dunsmuir News supplement published Saturday, October 14, 1905, as follows:

"By request of the editor of the *Dunsmuir News*, I write a sketch or narrative of my life and struggles in the rural districts of California. I first saw the light of day in Franklin, Mo., in the year 1829. I was

raised on a farm and received a smattering of education from subscription schools, and by my own exertions. After attaining my majority in Missouri, I taught country schools by subscription for about two years. When I was 25 I married a Miss Cox in St. Clair Co., Mo. That same year (1854) we crossed the plains with our other relatives and landed in Oregon late in the fall. In crossing the plains I with six other emigrants had a desperate fight with a band of Snake Indians near Boise river. The Indians had just annihilated 25 persons, excepting two of the Ward boys. One of the boys was rescued by our party, and the other got into the brush and escaped with an arrow sticking in his back. We lost one of our party who was shot just behind where I stood.

"I went into the mines the same year we reached Oregon at Sterling-

ville, Jackson County. I mined with but poor success, and in the spring of 1855 I caught a violent cold and became an invalid for several years. What is known as the Rogue River War of 1855-6 broke out in all its fury, and I volunteered and served during the hostilities, coming out unscathed. I then emigrated to Siskiyou County.

"My first business in California was to teach a district school in the town of Hawkinsville, near Yreka. When my school was finished I with two brothers mined on Greenhorn. In the year 1859 I was very near to death's door, and Dr. Gatliff of Yreka said I would die inside of three months (but I didn't). I had a brother at that time mining on Soda Creek; he informed me that there was a beautiful bubbling mineral spring at what is called now Tavern of Castle Crag. I bought a squatter's right of Amisa Ball who owned the place. There was a wagon road at that time from Yreka to (as I named the place) Lower Soda Springs.

"The nearest neighbor we had was at Upper Soda Springs on the north and Sweet Brier ranch on the south. Next came a few years after S.F. Southern to what is known as Sims station. I rapidly gained my wonted health, and it had to be thus or I never could have endured the privations that a wild and desolate country brings. There were hundreds of wild and roving Indians that infested the upper Sacramento, who since the building of the railroad have vanished from their old haunts. A great many have died; others have gone to the little towns along the railroad line. I sold the Springs to the P.I. Co. (Pacific Improvement Company) who have expanded a quarter of a million dollars in building and maintaining the place.

"I then went to Sisson and built a nice summer resort which became very popular; but unfortunately the buildings and contents were all destroyed by fires. During our short run with the hotel we had for our guests some of the foremost people in the land; Leland Stanford and wife, Jesse Grant and family, Judge Houghton and many others of note.

"After losing the hotel at Sisson we went on to our farm at Castle Rock. That famous spring the waters of which are being so successfully bottled was the incentive for my buying the place before I left Castle Crag ranch. The spring was discovered by two miners who wing-dammed the ground for mining purposes. C. C. Huffacre and James Cramer were the discoverers. They took out about $1400 in gold. I sold the Castle Rock property to a syndicate in Sacramento headed by George Parkinson; the latter was the man who was afterward local manager, but since has sold to a Traveling Men's Association.

"The present management has expended a great many thousand dollars in improvements and there is no wonder that the resort is so popular. When we left Castle Rock we went to the town of Castella and bought a little cottage home where we are now living as peaceable and quiet a life as the surrounding circumstances will permit.

"Very respectfully,

"W.B."

It is probable that many of the old-timers living in Castella and vicinity still remember their former citizens, the "Wash" Baileys. It is related that after he bought the Castle Crag property he built a small Inn, put a bridge across the Sacramento river at his place, and catered to the needs of the early day prospectors and travelers. As he said in his article, he and his neighbors were miles apart along the river and along the old Oregon Trail that followed the river in many places. A later Inn was Hanlon's which was on property that is across the highway from the present Dunsmuir Lumber Company. A man by the name of Hibbs lived on the spot which is now across from the State Park residence in Castella, old-timers say. And a man by the name of Root lived where the Ammirati store now stands on the highway.

Then came Sweet Brier ranch and then Southern's hotel at what is now Hazelcreek. Wash Bailey lived to see many changes take place in the canyon. He saw the railroad built up the Sacramento river canyon in 1886 and it was then that he sold his Castle Crag property to the Pacific Improvement company which was a part of the Southern Pacific. The railroad company began buying hotels and resorts along their line, and improving them.

They built a hotel at Castle Crags which burned down in 1890 or thereabouts. A second hotel was then built in the center of the property on the site of the former one and an annex built. It was all very elaborate. A large fountain, a yellow-painted clubhouse on Soda Creek that is said to be still standing; bridal paths and a tree-lined walk to the mineral spring. The Crocker families, who owned stock in the railroad company, built summer homes on the place. The Henry Crockers built their place on Soda Creek, across from the hotel grounds. It was said the house was a copy of a small castle in Germany. Many residents in this vicinity have visited it after it had been abandoned in later years. It eventually burned down. The Charles Crockers built their home west of the hotel and near the Sacramento river. That residence is still there.

The Castle Crag hotel burned down in June, 1900, and was never rebuilt. Older residents of Castella and Dunsmuir remember that fire, and there are many who can show one of the different articles of furniture that they purchased from the resultant fire sale that was held — dining room chairs, old andirons that were made by bending a short length of rail; a buckboard, silver, pictures, etc.

From that time on the P.I. company leased the resort to many operators. The first is said to have been a San Francisco woman who had 18 or more log cabins built, which are still on the place. The name "Solinsky" is remembered by some as one of those who leased the place. In 1913 or '14 came the Pendleton brothers — P.H., Charlie, and Jim. They operated it for about two years. Then Clint Brown leased and successfully operated the resort until 1925 when C. C. Oswald took over, planning to add a golf course as an added attraction in the field near the mineral spring.

The Joe Crosby family from southern California were the next lessees and managers of the resort. Then came the time when the old resorts of the canyon were giving way to more new and modern ones that had begun to spring up closer to populated centers; and with the advent of the automobile the tourist trade changed to a more or less traveling public. People came no more by train, bringing heavy trunks and baggage for a month's stay as they formerly had. And Castle Crags, like many of the other old resorts in the vicinity, remained closed with only a caretaker.

In recent years the Castle Crag property was sold to the Berry family of San Francisco for a summer home and is now known as the Berry Estate. The old Charles Crocker cottage, as it was called, that had served as a hotel after the resort was leased each summer, has now become a residence again. And the Castle Rock spring that old Wash Bailey once owned is now the property of the state park.

The Castle Crag station where the trains were flagged for departing guests long ago, was torn down. But in the old barn still standing on the Castle Crag property is a relic of the past. The old station wagon still bearing the gaily printed sign — "Castle Crag Hotel."

THE CHAMPION CHRONICLE

By
Katherine B. Johnson

I came to Dunsmuir with my folks, Joseph F. and Kate Champion, in 1912 to settle on my grandparents' acreage, Josiah and Bethulir Champion. There were 365 acres at that time. My folks eventually bought this and my grandparents moved to Oakland, after a few years. At that time there were only two houses in Champion Park. My dad sub-divided the ground in several additions and started to build houses for rentals. He built a saw-mill and turned out most of his own lumber. He had a water right which was called Rose Creek. He used that to send the logs down the hillside and after a few years made it into a water system to furnish water to his rentals. I can remember of him building twenty-five houses. I was in grammar school then and had to walk all the way to town to school. In 1922 when my brother and I finished grammar school we moved to Sacramento for the school year. During this time it was in the planning of building a grammar school on the old ball diamond. My dad, Joe Champion, donated the ground for the school. I think about 1924 the school was built. There was a brick kiln there that Dad ran but I can't remember who built the school house in Champion Park. It was only open a few years. I think Mrs. Ralston was teaching in 1928 when our daughter was born but it had closed by the time she started to school. That would have been in 1934. I never will forget the 4th of July celebrations made in Champion Park at the ball diamond. There was also an open-air dance floor where Almont Wheeler's orchestra played for the dances.

I can remember the little store my dad opened and was run by my sister-in-law, Rita. That was in 1926.

I can remember when the Methodist Church burned and when the school was so crowded we had to go to school in the old K.P. Hall. I was in the 6th grade then in 1920.

That walk to grammar school in the winter time was awful. The snow used to get so deep.

After we returned from Sacramento my dad started selling the houses to the renters; and he moved to Ashland, where he bought some rentals.

The Diamond Match bought in the sub-division across the river from Champion Park and the land was sub-divided and lots sold there, too.

One sub-division was set up on the hill east of the ball diamond. He called that Black Berry Hill. There were over four sub-divisions in different sections south of Dunsmuir. The Well's Addition adjoined the City Limits and our property on the east side of the river and the Scherrer Addition on the west side of the river.

My granddad logged the hill and furnished ties for the first railroad into Dunsmuir from the south. Nutglade at that time was only one set of tracks. In my time the work crew stayed on our place to build the set of tracks that are in Nutglade now. That was in 1923-24.

When the highway was built, it took all the teams to make the big fill by the cemetery. In 1929 after my marriage, we built a home in the southern part of Champion Park. We built up the Johnson Dairy to 150 customers and then sold to Bob and Alice Noyer. We moved to Mount Shasta in 1933.

Katharine (Champion) Johnson

●

Highway North Dunsmuir, circa 1925

DUNSMUIR NEWS CLIPPINGS

STATE OF JEFFERSON

11/21/41: *"Yrekans advocate formation of 49th State — Siskiyou and Del Norte Counties and Curry County in Oregon brought together by the asserted neglect of Sacramento and Salem. The Sisk. Co. Brd. of Sup. set aside $100 to finance an investigation of new statehood possibilities and find a name for the proposed commonwealth. Del Norte Supervisors took similar action. Creation would have to be approved by the legislatures of Oregon and Calif., the voters of States and the 2 counties, Congress and the President."*

11/28/41: *"Move for new state is comedy Setting." No doubt the advocates of a 49th State feel they have reason — Siskiyou County hasn't had much consideration from the State in the matter of development of natural resources and in regard to highways. Probably real purpose of insurgent move is to impress State authorities in Calif. and Ore. that that needs here exist and have been ignored for years. The world has real problems to deal with now. Our little flare of comedy will have its day, then we will return to business with nerves perhaps relaxed a little and prepared to again "make the world safe for democracy."*

12/5/41: *"Jefferson State puts on show for news cameramen." Movie newsreelmen show up at Yreka and a public rally was arranged featuring whiskerinos and a torchlight procession. It seems the hoped for publicity has been accomplished.*

Clint Kintgen made a trip to Yreka thinking he might be considered a candidate for Governor but was offered only Lieutenant Governor. With the turning down of their favorite son, Dunsmuir citizens have decided "It's great to be a Californian" and have started a movement to secede from State of Jefferson and become Californians.

*Researched by
Mildred Lockart*

DUNSMUIR YOUTHS PUNCTURED YREKA'S CAPITOL DREAM

By Robert D. Stone, DHS Class of 1943

The history lessons on taxation and individual freedom were not lost on a handful of Dunsmuir High School students in the early 1940s when they participated (anonymously) in the "State of Jefferson" movement. Other than casual conversations about their activities, this is the first coherent account of the "Northern Counties Anti-Jefferson Committee" which has been cloaked in mystery all these years.

The State of Jefferson was a novel tax-protest movement started by politicians, businessmen and chambers of commerce in five northern California and seven southern Oregon counties to get a more equitable return on taxes for economic development. The prime goal was road and highway improvement so that agricultural and timber products could be brought to market. Other issues were involved but they all were tied to a greater return of taxes to local governments and incidentally, to the political aspirations of the founders.

The Jefferson movement had mounted a public relations effort to dramatize their story and so, on every Thursday the State of Jefferson would come into existence. Signs were erected on the highway "borders" warning travelers that auto insurance issued in other states was not valid and, further, that sales taxes would not be collected that day. Needless to say, these secessionistic tactics reaped newspaper and radio coverage throughout the country.

Jefferson support was high in Siskiyou County and Yreka was dubbed the provisional capital. Although the Dunsmuir students supported the basic goals, they concluded that the pompous secessionists in arch-rival Yreka warranted a counter-movement just for the fun of it.

The ring leaders of the "Anti-Jeff" committee were Pat Hanratty, Joe Norred, Leslie Carlson, Pete Cornish, Bob Stone, and Cal Hughes, who furnished the basement for meetings and space for Hanratty's small printing press.

During the hot summer and long autumn of 1941, the Anti-Jeff group ground out press releases and leaflets pointing out the errors and problems of the pro-Jefferson movement. Response to the press releases was immediate from the Siskiyou Daily News which reprinted the material along with editorial comment on the "short-sightedness" and the dark "sinister" nature of the Anti-Jeff group. The battle of press releases and leaflets was now joined.

The San Francisco Chronicle and the Portland Oregonian carried pro- and anti-Jeff articles. During all this time, no one was aware that Dunsmuir teenagers were the "dreaded" opposition to the "noble and high ideals" of the founders of the State of Jefferson.

The anti-Jeff press releases were mailed in Mt. Shasta City and on railroad post offices (RPOs) so that postal marks would not betray the secret headquarters of the mysterious anti-Jeff group. Several forays into "enemy territory" were undertaken to Yreka to post handbills during Secession Thursdays when Yreka became the provisional capital. Other more extensive sorties were planned but due to the fragile nature of pre-1940 automobiles, the price of gasoline (17 cents a gallon), nubile Dunsmuir girls, and homework, these mighty efforts never took place.

After Pearl Harbor, the Jeffersonian leaders bravely announced that the movement was to be shelved for the duration. The great states of California and Oregon heaved a collective sigh of relief and retained their errant counties. The anti-Jeff group, having grown tired of the game, agreed wholeheartedly, and in the hectic war years that followed, all served in the American armed forces.

As a postscript, the State of Jefferson was reincarnated (and died again) as the "State of Shasta" during the 1950s. This time, however, Pat Hanratty was on the pro-forces as the "provisional secretary of state" and spark-plugged the issue of water-rights as the prime reason for the embryonic State of Shasta.

Siskiyou County Almost Succeeded!

By Emilie A. Frank

It happened about a half-century ago, in 1935, when five counties (including Siskiyou) along the Southern Oregon and Northern California border planned a serious attempt to secede from the two states and establish a new state which would be named "Jefferson."

The state never materialized, but what a state it would have been! No other state would have equaled it in scenic beauty — Jefferson would have combined the beauty of Oregon's Curry County (77 miles of simply spectacular coastline) with Siskiyou County's forests and rivers. And shining over it all, Mt. Shasta.

Its founder and first governor, John L. Childs of Crescent City was "elected" to administer the affairs of the area. The fact that this territory "seceded" was never formally acknowledged by the United States government, nor the states of California and Oregon.

The new state was named in honor of the president who first envisioned the boundaries of the nation extending to the Pacific Coast, covering a territory where Spanish and English cultures met and mingled. (Actually, the state of Jefferson's roots were in a serious movement back in 1851 when there was agitation to form a state called Shasta, which covered much of the same territory. A bill to form the new state was introduced in the first California legislature in 1852, and died only because of the pressure of other business at that session.)

Since that day in 1935 when citizens of those "orphan" counties met in Crescent City in their mock-serious attempt to form a new state, most of the very real grievances of that time have been solved through the joint efforts of those very men, and also the great states to which they legally and spiritually belong. Today the citizens of that vast area which would have been the state of Jefferson have excellent highways, progressive programs to conserve the area's abundance of water and rapidly-developing diversified industry.

The descendants of those men who wished to form a new state are now quite happily Californians and Oregonians. But there are a few old-timers around who think about that wondrous almost-state of Jefferson (the attack on Pearl Harbor and the entrance of the United States into World War II put an end to the dream) and they still get a gleam in their eye when they think of a state which would have included the Rogue River, the Umpqua River, Crater Lake, Gold Beach and Brookings, Crescent City, the Alturas area and all of Siskiyou County.

Had it happened, we would have been Jeffersonians instead of Californians.

THE VENETIANS
By Mary Hudson

With air travel the way it is today, it has made it possible for us, the first generation of American Venetians, to visit the country that our parents were forced to leave to seek work, not necessarily a better life because Venice has all the culture and class and magic of a fairyland that exceeds an unknown life that most Americans could not realize unless they visited Venice — the city that is built on water.

Most Venetians are blond and very tall. We speak our own dialect, that is like a constant song of joy.

Living in a new community like Dunsmuir in 1908 the Venetians gathered together in the same neighborhoods to live and taught us, all the Venetian children, to speak our own dialect. As American Venetians we proved to be hard workers, honorable people, calm, and non-violent. We minded our own business and raised our children to be good Americans and serve this new country. All the young men served in World War Two and were all great athletes. They played basketball and football and were track stars.

My sister, Kathryn Reginato, is one of the finest athletes who has ever passed through Dunsmuir High School. Her name is engraved on several trophies. Her name is in gold and silver. No one has exceeded her record in 50 years. She was also an honor student.

There were many other Venetians from McCloud, Weed, Mt. Shasta and the outskirts of Siskiyou County.

The Venetians own their own homes, work hard, save their money, send their children to college.

The 1908 Venetians is a generation of people we will not see again; and we, the new American Venetians, hope to reflect their qualities and their stability so we, in turn, can say proudly, and our children's children can say, "It was our great-grandmother — the immigrant Venetians — who taught us to be good Americans."

THE DUNSMUIR LIGHT PLANT

By
William Harmon

The Dunsmuir Light Plant, the first electrical power plant in Dunsmuir, was built in 1893 by Herman Scherrer. This hydro-electric power plant was located on the west bank of the Sacramento River behind the family home at what is now 1226 Scherrer Avenue. Water to power the hydro-electric turbine was taken from the river by a wing dam located just northeast of where Scherrer Avenue crosses the Southern Pacific tracks. The diverted water was then flowed along an eight-foot-wide canal for about 200 yards south to where it was then dropped to spin the generating dynamo.

The primary purpose of the power plant was to furnish electricity for lights. These lights were 32 candle power Edison light globes with the old type carbon filaments. One of those light bulbs was purchased in 1902 by Frank Toleman, a railroad locomotive engineer, who kept it burning in his garage until 1934 when it was removed and placed on display at the Dunsmuir office of the California Oregon Power Company.

The cost of electricity at the turn of the century was high. In 1903 those dim 32 candle power globes cost 25¢ each, and the flat rate monthly electrical bill for six lights cost the customer $1.50. This may not seem that much today, but back then that was a full day's wages for many a working man. Several of the business customers paid for their electricity by barter; paying either by merchandise, groceries or by some kind of service. A Joe Thompson once paid part of his bill with horseradish.

Herman Scherrer came to Dunsmuir in 1888 to work as a machinist for the Southern Pacific Railroad while they were setting up the shops here. Herman had been born in Zurich, Switzerland, moving to the United States in 1866 at the age of 22 years. He married Mary Ann Floyd on January 1, 1872, at Terre Haute, Indiana. The couple moved west in 1879, living first in San Francisco, then in several towns in Washington and Oregon.

Mary Ann Scherrer — Herman Scherrer Photo taken in front of home, 1266 Scherrer Ave., about 1930.

When Herman decided to build the power plant, he purchased 100 acres of land where Scherrer Avenue is now for 60¢ an acre. This flat area, lying between the Southern Pacific railroad tracks and the Sacramento River had been used by the Native Americans as a seasonal hunting and fishing campground for many centuries. On this land by 1910 — besides the power plant — were five houses, a steam laundry (the first in Dunsmuir), a blacksmith and plumbing shop, stables, a small orchard and many other large and small buildings, these in addition to another power plant the Scherrers built on Castle Creek in 1908.

All of the seven children of Herman and Mary Ann Scherrer did chores around the power house at one time or another. Albert Scherrer, who went to work for his father at the power plant in 1900 when he was 16 years old, told of what he remembered about the electrical works in a 1954 article printed for the *Fresno Bee*:

"We wired the houses free and provided the first supply of light bulbs without charge in order to get the customers. Of course it was the simplest sort of wiring, just one drop cord with a single globe in each room.

"We just ran the plant at night, starting about dusk and shutting down an hour after midnight. If people wanted light after that they had to use their lamp or lanterns.

"People had not heard of toasters, vacuum cleaners, powered washing machines or electric ranges, they thought it pretty nice to have light at the flip of a button and not have to fill and clean and light coal oil lamps.

"There were plenty of duties. In one day [we] might set a pole or two . . . string some wire, place a fuse for a householder, read a few meters, collect some past-due accounts and catch up on the bookkeeping between times."

Albert, who married a Dunsmuir girl, Winifred O'Malley, worked until the plant was closed, then moved to Fresno, California.

The oldest son, Oscar, who lost an arm after he had been struck by a Southern Pacific rotary snowplow in 1898 just south of the Butterfly Avenue bridge, went to work at the plant operating the dynamo. He never married and died in 1936 of a heart attack after being chased by a reportedly deranged transient.

Another son, Emil, worked at the plant until he was old enough to work for the Southern Pacific as a brakeman. Less than two years later he was killed in an accident. The Redding *Morning Searchlight* of September 15, 1900 headlined his death:

"E. SHEARER [sic] IS KILLED

"Terribly mutilated and warm with its fresh blood, the body of Emil Shearer, a young brakeman, was found Friday Evening at 7 o'clock in the yard of Keswick Station a few minutes after the young man had been run over by the car he was assisting in switching . . . he was 23 years of age and unmarried."

(In a tragic afternote, another young man, J. W. Hale, was fatally injured as he attempted to show authorities how Emil had been killed.)

The youngest boy, Walter, worked as a machinist, carpenter and general handyman at the dynamo until it was sold, then he moved to Central California. He last worked at the Naval Yards at Mare Island.

Walter Scherrer
Photo taken before 1898,
location not known.

Of the girls, the oldest, Helena, married David McLellan and moved to Pullman, Washington. The second, Laura, married William J. Avery and lived in Richmond, California. The youngest daughter, Clara, kept house and looked after her parents until they died: Herman in 1936 and Mary Ann in 1937. Clara never married, lived in Dunsmuir almost all of her life, and was an avid and excellent fly-fisherman.

By 1905 there were almost 200 customers of the Dunsmuir Light Plant, about equally divided between residential and business customers. In that year the company was incorporated and its name changed to Scherrer Light and Power Company. It operated

Clara Scherrer with hand on boy's head.
Location Sacramento Ave.,
near S & J Market.

under this name for a number of years until it was sold to the California Oregon Power Company. COPCO ran the plant until the mid-1920's when they shut down the operation and removed the generating dynamo and the other electrical equipment. Most of the shop buildings were torn down in the 1960's. The dynamo shaft was not removed and a part of it can still be seen at the old power plant location.

Clara Scherrer. House on Sacramento Ave.

DLP CUSTOMERS: 1903-08

A. LEVY & SONS (Department Store)
ALPINE HOTEL
ANDERSON, WILLIAM
ARMSTRONG
BALDY'S EMPORIUM (News stand)
BAND BOYS
BAVIERY
BAYAN, W. W.
BECKER, JOHN G. (Shoe Store)
BEEM, JOHN
BELLMAN, C. B.
BILLIARD PARLOR
BIRMINGHAM HOTEL
BIRMINGHAM, MRS. A. B.
BISSELL & BISSELL
BODKINS, MRS.
BRANSTETTER, CLAUD
BRANSTETTER, W. J.
BROWN, LEW
BROWN, MRS.
BULIS & NEAHAM (Laundry)
BURK, D. B.
CANDY STORE
CAMPBELL & TALMADGE (Lights & Piano)
CARNEY, ED (Paid by Cash & Sewing)
CARPENTER, H.
CARR, MRS. A. B.
CASTLE ROCK HOTEL (J. C. Waggner)
CHACE, H. H.
CITY MEAT MARKET
CLARKE, JUDGE
CLAUSNITZER, WILLIAM
CONROY, B.
CLEMENTS
COLLIER, B. K. (Attorney)
COOLEY
COOPER
COURTZ (Successor to Frank Gongwer)
COY, J. A.
CROSS, DR. HUGH
CRUMLEY, S. B. (Mahattan Saloon)
CURRIN, WILLIAM
CULVER, ALEX E.
CUSICK, CHARLES
DEAN, E. F.
DE BOSE, MRS. EVAN
DE VORE, J. S.
DIXON, O. (Eagle Barbershop)
DOOLEY & WALTER COMPANY
DORREL, JAMES
DUNNIGAN, MISS
EAGLE LODGE
EMERSON, R. W. (People's Market)
EMERALD, MRS.
ENGIVICHT (ENGWICHT), GEORGE
ENGLEDORN, T. S.
EVERRETT, FRED (Weed Lunch Counter)
FIDLER, ROBERT
FISKE & BAKER
FISKE, SAM
FITSGERALS
FITSGERALD
FOLTZ, MRS.
FORRESTER, JOHN
FOULKES, MRS. TOM
FOURTH OF JULY COMMITTEE
FREASE (Manhattan Saloon)
FREEL, D.
FUSSLER, E.
GHERKY, FRED (Store)

GOODFELLOW
GONGWER & HERMAN (Saloon)
GONGWER, FRANK
GOUGH, ALBERT (Bakery)
GRAND RESTAURANT
GREGORY & OLVER BROTHERS
GROVE, D.
HAINES, HARRY H.
HALL
HALSEY, FRED
HANSCOM, R. H. (Baldy's Emporium)
HARTER
HARRISON, BEN
HEFFNER
HELLAWELL, G.
HERMAN & GONGWER
HERMAN, LEO M.
HICKMAN
H. HILLER & STACKPOLE
HINKLE, MRS.
HILL, SAM (Dunsmuir News)
HIRCHER, NELLIE
HODGKINSON, JOHN
HODGKINSON, WILLIAM
HOLDER, A.
HOLLIS & WRIGHT (The Reception)
HOLLIS, FRED J. (Dunsmuir Cigar
   Store)
HOME RESTAURANT
HUFF, ABE
HUFF, C.
HUFF, FRANK
HUGHES, J. S.
HURN, FRANK
HUTAFF, G. A.
JANAK, MRS.
JOHNSON & WILLIAMS
JOHNSON
JONES
JUDY, W. T.
KANEY, MRS.
KELLY
KELSO, MISS MARY
KESSLER
KILBORN, MRS. A. D.
KIRKENDALL (Dunsmuir Meat Market)
KNIGHT, AL
KNIGHT & LYLE
K OF P HALL
LA DUE, MILT
LADLOW, W.
LAMBERT, J.
LANDERS, JEFF
LARSON-TAYLOR
LEACH, M.
LEE, MRS. J.
LELAND, WILL
LEVY, ALEXANDER (Paid by Groceries)
LIVERY STABLE
LIEF, MRS.
LONG, H.
LYON'S MEAT MARKET
NEELEY, D. A.
NEELEY, JOHN
NEELEY, L.
NEELEY, S.
NEHER, S.
NOONAN, J. G. (Shooting Gallery)
NOONAN, M. J.
NORMAN, MRS.
NORRIS
NUEHE, WILLIAM
NUNAMAKER, W. D.

MALONE, DR. GEORGE E.
MANHATTAN SALOON "IDLE HOUR"
MANNING (Printer)
MARSH
MAUPIN, JESSE
MAXEY, MRS.
MAYNARD (Lunch Counter)
MEYERS, CHARLEY
MILLARD, G. E.
MILLER, DICK
MOELK
MOSS, M.E.
MT. SHASTA BARBER SHOP
MT. SHASTA SKATING RINK
MT. SHASTA STEAM LAUNDRY
MORAN, THOMAS
MOUNT, BERT
McCARRVILLE, J.
McDOWELL, AL
McMICHAEL, LYNN
McMICHAEL, LYNN (For C.Y.M.O.A.)
NORRIS
ODDFELLOWS
OLIVER, BEN
OLIVER'S BUTCHER SHOP
OLIVER BROTHERS' ICE HOUSE
OLMSTED, JIM
PALM LODGING HOUSE
PALM RESTAURANT (Campbell &
   Talbert)
PALM RESTAURANT (Larson & Taylor)
PALM SALOON
PEASE, C. A.
PENTZ, MRS. F.
PETTERSON, CHARLEY
PETTY UNION
PICTHORN, A. J.
PINKSTON, MRS. HARRY
POST, H.
POST OFFICE, U.S.
PULLIAM, C. E.
QUINN, MISS J. F. (Riverside)
RAY'S BLACKSMITH SHOP
REDDING
REGAN
RIVERVIEW
ROCHFORD, MRS.
ROBER, FRANK (Paid by Merchandise)
ROUSE
ROLLER SKATING RINK
SAM GONDIVER & COMPANY
SCHADT, AL
SCHERRER, ALBERT H.
SCHERRER, OSCAR
SCHOLES, GEORGE SR.
SCHULER & WOODEN
SCOTT, MRS. KATE
SHARP, MRS.
SHOE SHOP
SHOOTING GALLERY
SILSBY, CHARLEY
SIMPSON, MRS.
SKILLINGTON, TOM
SMALL, MR.
SNYDER, MISS
SPAETH, G. E. (Spaeth Drug Store)
SPENSER, FRANK
SPENSER, OLD MAN
STUCKEY, HARRY F.
TALMADGE, F. A. (Piano & Lights)
TERWILEGER, MRS.
TELEPHONE COMPANY
TETREAN-EHERMAN MERCANTILE

COMPANY
THOMPSON, DR. C. E.
THOMPSON, JOE (Plumber)
TONY
TRUDELL
TUCKER
TUCKWELL, MRS.
TURNER, M. R.
VAN DEVENDER
VAN DEVENDER & WILLIAMS
VAN FOSSEN, L.
VAN HORN, MRS.
VAN LANDINGHAM, ED.
VAN VACTOR
VAUGHN, G.
WAGONER, JOHN
WALKER, F. M.
WEED HOTEL
WELLS BROTHERS (Paid by Groceries)
WELLS, HENRY
WENDEL, JOHN
WESTERN UNION TELEGRAPH
WHITE & O'NEIL
WHITE, MRS. CHESLEY
WHITINGAN, TONY T.
WILLIAMS, HARRY
WILLIAMS, JOHN
WILSON, J. J.
WILSON, H.
WILSON LODGING HOUSE, MRS.
WINNE, C. J.
WOODARD, H.
WRIGHT (Manhatten)
YOUNG, MRS.

REFERENCES

Morning Searchlight, Redding, Shasta County, California, Vol. 6, No. 92, Sept. 15, 1900.

The Dunsmuir News, Dunsmuir, Siskiyou County, California, issues:
   Vol. 11, No. 21, Saturday, Sept. 22, 1900.
   Vol. 18, No. 51, Friday, April 3, 1908.
   Vol. 45, No. 28, Friday, Nov. 2, 1934.
   Vol. 46, No. 48, Friday, March 20, 1936.
   Vol. 47, No. 6, Friday, May 29, 1936.
   Vol. 48, No. 16, Friday, Aug. 6, 1937.
   Clipping, Nov. 18, 1954, in re: *Fresno Bee* article 1954.
   Books, Dunsmuir Light Plant/ Scherrer Light & Power Company, 1903-1911.
   Pacific Improvement Company receipt No. 4127, Feb. 27, 1895.
   Water Rights Records of Siskiyou County, Vol. 5, pg. 322, April 17, 1901.
   Incorporation Certificate No. 42201 State of California, Feb. 23, 1905.

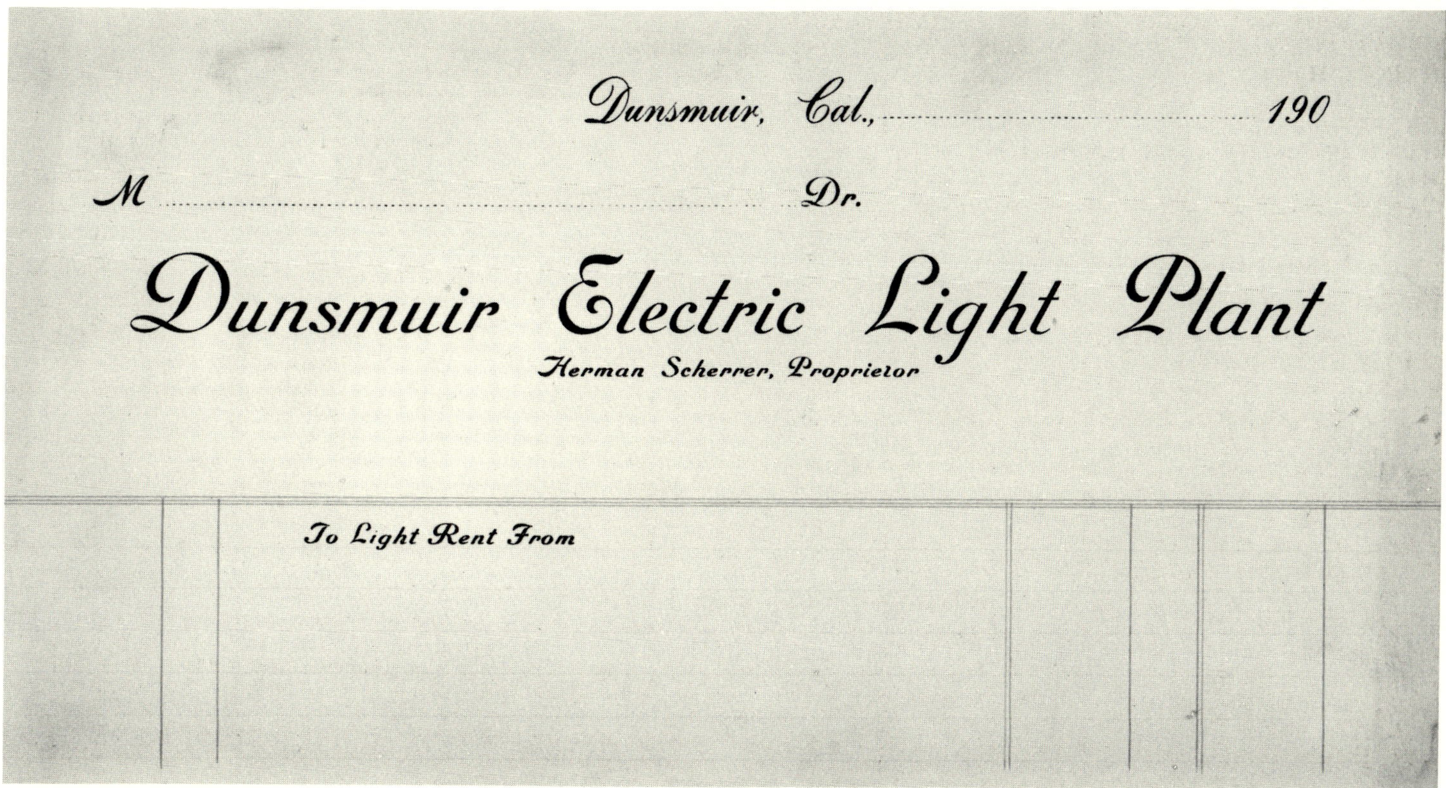

SISKIYOU MEMORY

I know a place where the ferns are deep
And the giant fir waves high
Where a dripping lodge hangs cool and steep
And a laughing brook leaps by.
It is there to be with a soul that's free
From the streets disconcert joy,
With a blanket spread on a cedar bed
And the wealth of the world afar.

★　★　★　★

I know a pool in a leafy dell
That weary trout love best
And a timid trail through a chaparral
Where red deer lie at rest.
A shadow falls and the night birds call
And a cougar's lonely cry,
A silence deep and a dreamless sleep
Under the open sky.

Author unknown
Presented by Mrs. Gilbert Lord

A CHILD LOOKS AT YESTERYEAR

By Dorothy Delgado

I have been reading many stories of the past as we approach our celebration of the Dunsmuir Centennial and it is very annoying that no one mentions the things that stand out as the most memorable to me.

Do you know how Butterfly Avenue got its name? Before the street was paved there were huge swarms of butterflies all summer, especially at the south end of the street.

The outstanding thing about the Hotel Weed was the revolving door — a marvelous contraption built as a perfect merry-go-round to delight a small child. I went around 'til I was dizzy or was dragged away by some irate adult.

Hunt's Candy Store was a dream world — I remember the ice cream parlor chairs with the curled wire backs. They even had a table and four chairs in child's size especially for me.

Farther down the street was a butcher shop. The meat hanging on the large hooks was not nearly as fascinating as the yellow sawdust that covered the entire floor.

Up the street north of the Hotel was a Chinese store with strange looking baskets and tins in the window. One of them said Leche Nuts, but the most important things were the firecrackers and rockets for the Fourth of July. The Strand Theater was special because it had a balcony.

A pungent memory to me was in Levy's clothing and shoe store. I always associated it with new shoes, but it was gone when they put tiles on the floor so I finally realized it was the oil that was put on the wooden floors — but what a delightful aroma!

The drinking fountain between the S.P. Men's Clubhouse and the Crew Dispatcher's with the famous legend "Best Water on Earth" which is now at Murphy's Railroad Park was built especially for children with extra steps and the famous Dunsmuir Fountain was perfect for a child to walk around. I noticed they put wires around the inside — somebody must have fallen sometime!

As a young child I remember being sent to The Reception to buy the Sunday Paper. It smelled of forbidden tobacco smoke, and once in awhile someone would go through the swinging doors so I could catch a glimpse of the smoke-filled back room of tables and chairs where men frequently went to play cards and part with their entire pay checks. Once I was able to see the famous vault which, over the years, had held many valuables and huge amounts of money.

I cannot leave the "Streets of Memories" without mentioning Branstetter Hall. I am sure I learned to dance there at the Old Time Dances on Saturday nights. The Squares, Reels, and Paul Jones when everyone changed partners. The Schottische, polka, and varsouvianne — everyone had a good time and some of those old gentlemen would really stomp during the squares. I remember Mr. Fisher — he didn't really dance, he walked in time to the music. He always went forward, never turned or whirled, so his partner always went backward. Of course, the best part was the delicious refreshments the ladies served during the Supper Hour. The stairs were on the north side in early years. Then there were steps on the south side in the late 40's. No matter where they were they always seemed rickety — it must have been from all that stomping.

I knew Talmadge built the swimming pool just for children. We could rent a swimming suit; and when we got out, there was a wringer to put the suit through to get out as much water as possible. I took Red Cross lessons and learned to swim there. He also built a wonderful miniature golf course at the back of the Ball Park. The outdoor dance floor wasn't as important at that time — at least not to me although I heard they had

big name bands. Joyland had special memories. I remember the Walkathon and the special Heel and Toe races they had on special nights, wrestling and boxing matches with some between very small boys five and six years old, a car show, a Halloween march with prizes for the best costumes — a darling little girl dressed as Mae West, many dances. One of the special ones I remember was for Leap Year. The boys were given ten small rings and instructed to give one to a girl when they asked her for a dance. Then, at the end of the evening, the girl who had collected the most rings would win a real diamond ring. My best memories of Joyland was when it became a Roller Skating Rink. At one point they raffled off an old jalopy and the winner was Francis (Mohawk) Dalla Lasta.

But, the most important place of all was the California Theater — my home away from home. The Saturday matinee wasn't just a serial and a picture. We had talent shows, costume contests, and all kinds of drawings. There were many live shows. I remember a minstrel show, a violin virtuoso, bands, and vaudeville acts. At some time in the early thirties a complete wedding was performed on stage. The little Micander boy was the ring bearer and the happy couple received bounteous gifts from the local merchants and everyone. Later on there were several local performances put on by Reverend Goode. One was an all-male cast, with doctors and teachers appearing as small boys and a wedding in the final scene with Don Basham as the bride. I heard they had a terrible time finding shoes to fit him. About this time, the late thirties, they even held Easter services for several years with Rev. Rische wishing us all a Merry Christmas since he knew he wouldn't see us 'til next Easter. There was a wheel that was spun on Tuesday nights. I won ten percent of the jackpot. It was only $9.00 but I thought it was a fortune.

One last memory. Did you know that Dunsmuir had a lemon? That is a place where they squeeze fresh lemonade and orange juice. It was located out north of the Ball Park first so they could use the soda water in the juice. Later it was moved downtown across from the California Theater. It served delicious ice-cold drinks. My mother ran it, and I was her best customer.

—Dorothy M. Delgado

THE TRAINS

Our lives were governed by the trains. Their huge, huffing bodies, hissing out steam as they lumbered through our mountain valley, were like angry Minotaurs who demanded our deference and tribute. In the dark of night their whistles cried out to us, reassuring us that our world, which depended so entirely on their movement, continued. The whistles called to us, telling us the time of day, the time to eat, the time for work. The rhythms of the trains were the rhythms of our lives.

Our fathers, brothers, uncles, nephews, all worked on the trains: those who shoveled coal, those who laid track, those who switched tracks. The conductors, the firemen, the engineers, the boilermakers who crawled into their enormous bellies searching for their heartbeats — all served their master, the train.

Its breath came into our homes. We washed black soot from our walls, our curtains, our windows, endlessly battling coal dust year in and year out. For those who labored in its belly, the blackness sunk into their very skin, under their nails, and into their psyche.

We rode the trains. We, who knew little of the world outside our canyon. We, with our free passes, passes to the world, traveled up and down the rails, visiting aunts, uncles, brothers, and sisters, those who were no longer part of our world of trains, those who had left to find a larger existence.

—Caroline Reginato Hamlin

Old-time train photos speak for themselves

Railroad buffs welcome steam engine #4449, Dunsmuir Depot

COMING HOME
By
Michael M. Harris

In the fall of 1962 I left Dunsmuir to go to college, and I never returned, except for vacations and, later, to visit my parents. But in another sense I've never stopped returning. The place has a hold on me, like the invisible force that binds the planets in their orbits. I seem to have been circling it all these years, a battered and wayward asteroid, like a chunk of Black Butte rock blown into space by some vast volcanic explosion, only to be tugged gently homeward at the apex of my flight, thousands of miles out . . . except there was no explosion. I just grew up. It was, as with most people, a gradual process, but I can remember with some precision when I first became aware of it. My father was a freight conductor for the Southern Pacific, and when I came home from the University of Oregon for Christmas I would ride the "milk train" from Eugene on his pass. Those rail journeys, in my freshman and sophomore years especially, shine in my memory out of all proportion to anything that actually happened on them. They have long since become part of my secret code, part of the symbolic history that, I'm convinced, each of us constructs of the events of his life to explain the kind of person he turned out to be.

The train left Eugene around 2 a.m. It had no Pullman cars, and I slept upright in my seat. The last thing I saw before I dozed off was the white neon cross atop Skinner's Butte, wavering and blurred by the mist on the windows — an apt commentary on the state of my religious faith. I had never gone to church much, never "believed"; so the pain I felt under the standard assaults of academia had come as a shock. I seemed to be discovering faith only in the act of losing it. Unlike many small-town boys who, in the vein of Thomas Wolfe, grow up hearing train whistles in the night and yearn for the golden cities of the plain, freedom and knowledge, I had gone off to college

reluctantly. I loved Dunsmuir; I wanted to stay there. Tender-minded even for my age, even for those times, I viewed the atmosphere of the campus as corrosive, gnawing relentlessly into those undefended — because never tested — values that I equated with the warmth, the humanity, the innocence of home. Looking back on myself then — a skinny figure in a quilted winter coat, hunched into a corner of the seat: short haircut, horn-rimmed glasses, dark, frightened eyes — I see someone who might easily have retreated into bitterness, rejecting the outside world. I might have joined the John Birch Society, for instance. That I didn't was, ironically, a product of weakness more than strength. I felt that I was an ignorant hillbilly, that I couldn't fight the Outside and thus had no choice but to try to match it in sophistication (those eyebrow-lifting professors and city-wise students, those books that flicked out their serpents' tongues) so that it wouldn't laugh at me anymore.

I couldn't imagine that a time would come when I would not only reconcile myself with the Outside but find campus life, with its liberalism and tolerance, more congenial to me than any other. I was desperately homesick. As the train groaned up the canyon of the Willamette River (so like the canyon of the Sacramento), I had unpleasant dreams. I may have opened my eyes once or twice, but at night a scattering of trees looks like a forest, and a real forest, Douglas firs laden with snow, hardly less gloomy than the tunnels we periodically roared through. Even the sky gave no relief. In Eugene, city lights and humidity had discouraged all but the strongest stars; here in the Cascades, clouds muffled everything. Only when we passed over the summit — mountain-bred, I could sense it, just as a coast-dweller senses the turning of the tide — did I sleep more

easily. The clouds ended. Waking again on the eastern slope, near Chemult, I beheld an eerie landscape of rain-starved trees, perfectly straight and densely clustered but thin as fence posts, as spears, against a wide expanse of moon-polished space. But it wasn't until dawn — just south of Chiloquin, north of Klamath Falls — that I really felt I had escaped.

The train was clicking along in the shadow of a bluff to the east, with Klamath Lake to the west. The water stretched bruise-colored, dark; but white birds circled up into the light, gulls and pelicans far from the sea. The coach itself rocked gently, as if on a swell. The few other passengers still slept. Already, in the early '60s, train travel had gone out of fashion, and these were mostly elderly, unpretentious people, local farm folk or dead-heading railroaders like my father. Since I didn't have to talk to them yet — which might have broken the spell — I could let affection creep over me as softly as the sunlight crept over the worn plush of the seat. I was going home, I thought. I would eat turkey and pumpkin pie, be with my parents, brother and sister; I would go to Christmas Eve services and perhaps see the girl I loved (who, to spare her embarrassment, I will not name). Then the light broke full over the bluff, setting the frosty sagebruch and scrub pines ablaze; it streamed pinkish-gold through the window so that every dust mote in the air seemed to vibrate with joy.

# # #

Here time slows down. The train seems to linger at the California border, as if the whole meaning of the trip were concentrated there. I remember staring out the window at the brightening land, wondering at this surge of emotion. Where did it come from? Hard to say. It wasn't just Dunsmuir or my family. Other students I knew who had come from small towns seemed less deeply marked by them; even others from Dunsmuir had left, apparently, without a qualm. It was, after all, an ordinary place. Its people were ordinary people. They hadn't had time to establish a regional culture before TV and the freeway pre-empted it: no dialect, no down-home music, no unusual amount of racial or religious prejudice. In fact, as a railroad town (the others in southern Siskiyou County were logging towns), it was relatively cosmopolitan. Its buildings and streets, set down on the Great Plains or the desert, would have seemed as humdrum as any. But that was the point, or part of it, anyway: Dunsmuir *wasn't* on the plains or the desert. As the train chugged toward Dorris, I could already see, 70 miles away, what had loomed over me all my childhood and made me gaze back up at it in awe, exactly as an Indian boy would have gazed 150 years ago: twin cones of purest white in winter, volcanic grey-brown in summer, violet and rose at sunset, and now, at dawn, an outline of gold etched on the sky as delicately as cloud-vapor: Mt. Shasta, mother mountain, pointing straight like a signpost to some of the most beautiful country in the world.

The English novelist John Fowles has described a tradition extending down through Western literature, beginning with Eden: that of the "sacred combe" or valley, "a place outside the normal world, intensely private and enclosed, intensely green and fertile, numinous, haunted and haunting." For me, that was Dunsmuir. Growing up there, I had two conflicting perceptions: that the beauty of the country was extraordinary, but also that it *was* normal, the way the world should be. Other places just failed to measure up. Sometimes I would sit on a rock on the bank of the Sacramento River, near George West's bridge, and stare so hard at the trees on the opposite bank that the whole mountainside seemed about to become as translucent as leaves under sunlight: the thinnest of film separating me from an even greater beauty, which, if I only held

my breath and looked closely enough, might suddenly be revealed to me. Houses, road cuts, logged-off areas — everything that man created — seemed a scar and a desecration. But it didn't matter too much, because here nature was vast and the works of man insignificant. I was one of the last Americans to grow up with a sense of the frontier. I could hike west toward the ocean or east toward Salt Lake City, up ridges and down, until I dropped; there was no end of empty space, of freedom. That Dunsmuir lay deep in a canyon didn't limit this freedom but enhanced it. I could stand in the middle of town (or daydream out the windows of school) and never lose contact with forested slopes and the unseen world behind them. In a place like this, I wondered, how could adults seem so unmoved? How could they just go about their jobs, no different from city-dwellers?

I sometimes think that this upbringing explains something in me: a certain passivity, a lack of overt ambition. All ordinary ambitions seemed trivial beside simply being in the country and contemplating it, letting my mind slow down enough to match its rhythm, surrendering to it until, in the blink of an eye, I might catch that moment when the forest opened. My wife teases me: "You were an aristocrat. You grew up in a national park — it might as well be one. No wonder you never were hungry, like a kid from the ghetto." But I was an American boy, reared in a culture that had little use for mysticism; and I think I realized, too, that the ultimate aim of contemplating nature is to merge with it — in other words, to die. I didn't want to die — not yet — and living meant doing something, even if it wasn't the same thing my father and his friends did.

George Orwell wrote: "No one who is really involved in the landscape ever sees the landscape." I could see it; therefore I must not be involved in the same way as the practical, hard-working people who had built the town and sustained it. My disdain for development meant accepting the economic stagnation that kept the area so unspoiled. I

had more in common with that gaggle of retirees, hippies, artisans, backpackers and Zen monks who would trickle into southern Siskiyou once the railroad started to pull out, undermining Dunsmuir's status as a self-sufficient community (which always was more illusion than fact, given the county's near-total ownership by SP, the federal government, power and lumber companies and absentee ranchers) and bringing closer the day when it might be only a suburb of Redding or Mt. Shasta City. In short, I thought like a tourist, even while I lived there. And that was the real reason for my emotion on the train: for the first time I was experiencing nostalgia and recognizing it for what it was. The very keenness of my love for Dunsmuir was proof that I no longer belonged there, and perhaps never had. The Outside was inside for me.

# # #

I was young; therefore, when I remember the Outside closing in on Dunsmuir, I may only be remembering my growing awareness of it. But the two developments seem to have coincided. My first real hint of how fragile was our isolation — how all this time men in government and corporate offices, with maps on their desks, had been looking down on our heads, so to speak, and deciding our destinies — came in October 1960, when John F. Kennedy arrived on the last of the great whistle-stop campaigns. I was 16, a junior in high school. Morning classes were canceled so that we could attend — though since Kennedy's train pulled in before 8 a.m. and stayed barely 15 minutes, we couldn't have missed much. It was already warm, promising to be hot. Many of us stood on the black-painted footbridge that arched over the tracks from the station to the engine shops and roundhouse (long gone now); we could look almost directly down on the platform of the rear car. (No bulletproof security bubbles then.) Kennedy stepped out. Next to the politicians who accompanied him — whose pudgy, mushroom-pale faces seemed to betray lives spent exclusively in the smoke-filled rooms of legend — he looked like an outdoorsman, lean and tanned, with bright eyes and that bushy, vigorous reddish hair. We have since grown accustomed to, and learned to distrust, the "media candidate," and Kennedy no doubt was the first of the breed. But the sight of him then undeniably thrilled me.

His speech, though, was disappointing. Partly it was the flat Massachusetts accent, so odd to Western ears. But partly it was what he said, or didn't say. I wanted to hear the words that sustained the thrill of his physical presence — flights of idealism such as he delivered in his inaugural address a few months later. This speech seemed so obviously tailored by his advance men, who knew Dunsmuir to be full of old-line labor Democrats like my father. His appeal was strictly partisan: stand by your party, get out the vote. That was all. It bothered me that Dunsmuir could be "scouted" like any other place, known better than it wanted to be; just as I disliked the civic boosterism that put signs in the center of town advertising the "Best Water on Earth." It *was* the best, I thought — rock-cool and mineral-rich, filling the mouth as city water never could; but why give away our secret? Aside from the unseemliness of boasting, we ran the risk of losing it: those thirsty Angelenos might pipe it all away. After the speech, Sandra Smith, a senior at Dunsmuir High and the reigning Miss Siskiyou (who had recently cut the ribbon on the section of Interstate 5 that had gutted a quarter of town and would route traffic around it, hastening its economic decline), presented Kennedy with a bouquet and a glass jug of Dunsmuir water. Her abundant sexuality (forgive me, Sandy) — a delight in school plays or in the not-so-secret daydreams of us boys — seemed somehow tawdry when officially recognized in beauty contests or, as now, put on display for middle-aged men in blue suits to leer at. It belonged to us, not to the Outside. I imagined then that she

shared my feelings, was embarrassed; though now, of course, I hope she felt only the thrill. Kennedy thanked her. Maybe he shook hands. The water, I suspect, came in handy as the train panted down the canyon into the inferno, to Redding; maybe he thought of us again, for a moment, as he drank it.

\# \# \#

Here time speeds up. After my vision of the morning, I remember very little of the middle of the trip, as the train passed through Dorris, traversed potato fields and ranchland and climbed toward the Mt. Hebron summit. The day lost its promise, became dull. The sky didn't exactly cloud over, but a whiteness spread across it just thick enough to hide the sun, and Shasta itself somehow disappeared in the complexities of the canyons. Maybe I dozed off again. I do remember smoke-colored brush and stands of Ponderosa pines, their grey-orange bark fissured into blazoned slabs like shields, opening south toward the old logging camp at Tennant. Grass Lake — even in December more grass than lake. And then, finally, Weed. Black Butte.

\# \# \#

Could this trip really have taken all of even a short winter day? It hardly seems possible. I must be confusing different trips, taken on different trains. Yet I seem to recall twilight setting in as early as Mt. Shasta City. I was impatient to arrive . . . yet the only arrival I remember at all clearly now was not by train at all, but by Greyhound bus, on Nov. 22, 1963, the day Kennedy was assassinated. I had written a play, a three-act comedy called *The Plaster Bandit*, which was to be performed that evening at Dunsmuir High. My former English teacher, Reva Coon, would direct it; my sister, Kathy, would act. It was a play that, in retrospect, I can only marvel at — written with what now seems supernatural speed (I had yet to lose my innocence about first drafts) and with that cold-blooded profession-

alism of which only the very young and the very experienced are capable. I can't even relate to the author; he seems a totally different person. I suspect that everyone, in growing up, must pass through a stage where he becomes a kind of monster, belonging neither to his home town nor to wherever he's going. Nourished by neither, he feeds only off his own ego. I had reached that stage. I was still insider enough to guess (successfully, as it turned out) what would please my audience. But I wrote from the viewpoint of the arrogant college sophomore I desperately wanted to be, treating the town with all the scorn and condescension I myself feared. Dunsmuir, I decided, wasn't up to "significance"; it would get an old English manor house, young love, ghosts. That darkening afternoon, as I watched the land flow past the windows of the bus, I had little doubt it would work.

But in Medford or Ashland — I forget which — I got off to go to the toilet, and walking through the station lobby I saw racks of newspapers with headlines saying PRESIDENT SHOT. I didn't even think of buying one. It seemed a tasteless joke, or maybe an hallucination. Such things couldn't happen, not in the world I knew. I was still half asleep, a sour taste in my mouth; and even when we resumed the trip, the sickly bluish-green tint of the bus windows made everything seem somehow artificial, not to be taken seriously. I wondered whether the news would affect that night's performance, but decided not. Even if Kennedy died (the papers said only that he had been wounded), why should that spoil my premiere? So I thought. But when I arrived home — it was cold, spitting snow — my parents told me that the play had, in fact, been postponed. (It was staged a couple of weeks later.) I still didn't realize that the Outside that mattered wasn't the phantom antagonist in my mind, but those forces that, in the next few years, would convulse the nation and hurl me into an Asian war. Dunsmuir, as usual, had more sense.

\# \# \#

And here time slows down again, almost stops. From Mt. Shasta City to Dunsmuir by car is only a few minutes, yet the train had to double back around Cantara Loop, an interminable detour, and in my memory it was already so dark that the lighted windows of the coaches on the other end gleamed yellow against the rock walls of Box Canyon (undammed then), that trout fisherman's paradise. Stars were beginning to appear — the stars of home, untold thousands of them. The mountain, when I glimpsed it, was faintly phosphorescent, as if in the afterglow of sunset. A ghost of light. I recalled a childhood illusion: that the summit of Shasta was in Heaven. I hadn't ever wanted to climb it, quite, because that meant finding out for sure that it wasn't.

And I remembered the story — did I read it in the *Dunsmuir News* or simply imagine it? — of an Italian mountaineer, a veteran of the Alps, who, in his 80s, had climbed it in winter and died, apparently by intent. It seemed an ideal death; and I felt more than my usual discomfort over the intrusions of the Outside when Hollywood, in 1972, filmed a grade-B movie — on Shasta itself! — that had much the same theme. It was called *Climb an Angry Mountain*. Joe Kapp starred as a fugitive from the law, an Indian, who, in accordance with half-forgotten tribal custom, climbs the "white mountain" to get in touch with his gods and put his life in order. It's winter; the folksey local sheriff (Fess Parker) tries to catch him before he falls into the hands of the hard-bitten city detective (David Janssen?) or freezes to death. I watched this movie with my family in a Motel 6 room in Las Vegas, near the Dunes. They had come to see me for Christmas — a far cry from those other Christmases. I was unhappy living there, unhappy with my job; for the past several months I had been prescribed drugs to ward off a near-suicidal depression that may or may not have followed me back from Vietnam. Watching, I squirmed with the agony of one whose inmost secrets have been

violated, which I tried to disguise with caustic comments about the film's technical errors. (Kapp was climbing the McCloud side of the mountain, his pursuers the Weed side; when he supposedly reaches the summit, to perish in a swirl of snow, he's only alongside the Ski Bowl Lodge, barely above timberline.)

But it doesn't matter anymore. If I'm not as special as I once liked to think — if my fantasies are accessible to the Outside, even to second-rate Tinseltown producers — it's no longer a threat. The bad years are over. I can look back at myself again in that train seat, tired and hungry, and see myself unconsciously accepting what my conscious mind would reject for a long time to come: that the faith I was "losing" was no faith at all — just the forms of institutional religion through which my real faith had been filtered, knowing no other outlet. That real faith, the message of Dunsmuir, persisted: that the world was beautiful and that it stood for something more. Beauty awaited me now. The Methodist church would smell of cedar, glow with candlelight; the carols would work their old magic; and the eyes of that girl, if I saw her — even if she ignored me — would be windows on that other world, just as the snow on frosty nights could reflect the stars, revealing a parallel universe, infinite space, beneath my feet. So it remains. My life is one long Cantara Loop. I circle, a speck of space dust, forever outside the town but connected to it, as surely as to my own death; and as the dark comes on, I think I see its lights a little nearer.

*ABOUT THE AUTHOR
MICHAEL M. HARRIS*

Education:
University of Oregon, Eugene, OR, Bachelor of Arts in English (honors).
Harvard University, Cambridge, MA, Master of Arts in Teaching.

University of Iowa, Iowa City, IA, Master of Fine Arts in Creative Writing.

Honors:
Phi Beta Kappa at University of Oregon; Harvard-Oregon Fellowship; Teaching-Writing Fellowship at University of Iowa Writers' Workshop.

Newspaper Experience:
1969-71, Reporter for the Redding Record-Searchlight (daily: circ. 22,500); covered city government, police, education and sports. Wrote movie, book and drama reviews and some editorial Columns; won first prize in the 1970 California-Nevada AP writing contest, state sports division.
1971-72, Reporter and columnist for the Voice of Bellevue, Wash. (weekly: circ. 35,000); covered county government and general assignments; wrote movie, drama and book reviews and a weekly column.
1972-73, reporter for the Las Vegas Review-Journal (daily: circ. 80,000); covered city and county government, the medical beat, police and general assignments; wrote movie, book and drama reviews and some editorials.
1973-75, book reviewer and occasional feature writer for the University of Iowa Daily Iowan; during this time, also sold six book reviews to the Washington Post and two to the Chicago Tribune.
1976-78, reporter for the San Luis Obispo Telegram-Tribune (daily: circ. 22,500); covered city government and worked on general assignment. Wrote weekly movie reviews and many features and op-ed columns; spent five months on the copy desk.
1979-present, copy editor for the Long Beach Press-Telegram (daily: circ. 100,000); for the past several months, wire editor for the morning edition; written book and movie reviews and occasional features for the Life/Style section.

Other Experience:
1967, ten weeks of student teaching at Newton South High School, Newton, Mass., as part of M.A.T. program at Harvard Graduate

School of Education.

1969, Autumn's work as forestry aide (surveying and brush-cutting) with the U.S. Forest Service, Mt. Shasta, Calif.

1974-75, Instructor in undergraduate fiction writing and core literature at the University of Iowa (TA).

1975-76, Lecturer in English composition at California State Polytechnic University, San Luis Obispo.

1978-79, Teacher of conversational English at Business English Center of Tokyo, Japan; students were mostly Japanese engineers who were going to work abroad.

Military Service:

1967-69, two years of active duty in the Army; honorably discharged with rank of first lieutenant; worked on the post newspaper at Fort Sill, Okla.; attended the Defense Information School at Fort Benjamin Harrison, Ind.; and served as an information officer with the 1st Air Cavalry Division in Vietnam, working on divisional publications.

Personal data:

Born Sept. 28, 1944; married (Takako); no children; excellent health; no physical disabilities; military status 4-A.

Michael Harris

Dunsmuir House, Oakland, California

TIL WE MEET

By

David Seed

In a time when time dissolves
And we can step beyond its bonds,
Let us meet again.
On some soft summer night
Let us walk hand in hand
Down by the river
To find a place to sit together
Where we can watch the moonlight
Drifting through the trees
And listen to the symphony
Of moving water as it swirls
and dances past our feet.
Then let us speak of love
And other pleasant things
And know that our thoughts
Will murmur to the music
Of the river forever.

EDITORIAL STAFF

Reva P. Coon................... Editor-in-Chief
Grace M. Harris .... Editor

Chapter Writers:

Ch. "Bud" Carlquist	Phyllis Bender Hubbard	Will Reineking
Eva Carlquist	James Lockart	Flora Wintering
Dorothy Delgado	Mildred Lockart	Frank Wintering
Larry Green	Carolyn Miller	Robert Wright
Marjorie Young	Richard Murdock	June Wright

Staff Photographers:
Joe Kelby, Dr. J. W. Reynolds, Will Reineking

Typists:
Sharon Hall, Mildred Lockart

THE CENTENNIAL COMMITTEE

Photo by Roy Haile

CENTENNIAL COMMITTEE

Back Row (L to R): Dr. J. W. Reynolds, Chris Stromsness, Louie Dewey, Jim Lockart, Brian Hembling, Frank Wintering, Betty Reineking, Michael Wecksler

Middle Row (L to R): Will Reineking, Chris Bailie, Lou Bauer, Eleanor Vaughn, Pat Girard, Mildred Lockart, Jan Garrigus, Forrest Gass, Peggy Heisel

Front Row (L to R): Lois Wilch, Rose Ellis, Ila Brown, Lois Bectel, Reva Coon, Marsha Hayden, Marjorie Young, Flora Wintering

Not pictured: Grace M. Harris, Delwin Poe, Mayme Poe, Sharon Hall, Marilyn Behrens, Dorothy Delgado, Joe Kelby, Carolyn Miller, Ruth Spencer, Carol Fraga

Reva P. Coon, Chairperson; Grace M. Harris, Treasurer; Mildred Lockart, Secretary; Peggy Heisel, Coordinator.

Chris Baillie, Lu Bauer, Lois Bectel, Marilyn Behrens, Ila Brown, Dorothy Delgado, Louie Dewey, Rose Ellis, Eloise Erickson, Carol Fraga, Jan Garrigus, Forrest Gass, Patricia Girard, Marie Glover, Sharon Hall, Marsha Hayden, Brian Hembling, James Lockart, Joe Kelby, Carolyn Miller, Beth Nelson, Green Thumber; Ken Palmore, Del Poe, Mayme Poe, Betty Reineking, Will Reineking, Dr. J. W. Reynolds, Ruth Spencer, Chris Stromsness, Eleanor Vaughn, Michael Wecksler, Lois Wilch, Flora Wintering, June Wright, Michael Wright, Robert Wright, Marjorie Young.

AFTERWORD

Dunsmuir's first exciting one hundred years have passed into history. This book has touched some of the highlights. To have told the complete story would have required another, huge volume.

All aboard, Dunsmuir! Train now leaving for the year 2086. Happy journey — Bon Voyage — Vaya Con Dios.

All aboard!